THE EFFECTIVENESS AND APPLICATION OF EU AND EEA LAW IN NATIONAL COURTS

THE EFFECTIVENESS AND APPLICATION OF EU AND EEA LAW IN NATIONAL COURTS

Principles of Consistent Interpretation

Edited by
Christian N.K. Franklin

intersentia
Cambridge – Antwerp – Chicago

Intersentia Ltd
Sheraton House | Castle Park
Cambridge | CB3 0AX | United Kingdom
Tel.: +44 1223 370 170 | Fax: +44 1223 370 169
Email: mail@intersentia.co.uk
www.intersentia.com | www.intersentia.co.uk

Distribution for the UK and Ireland:
NBN International
Airport Business Centre, 10 Thornbury Road
Plymouth, PL6 7PP
United Kingdom
Tel.: +44 1752 202 301 | Fax: +44 1752 202 331
Email: orders@nbninternational.com

Distribution for Europe and all other countries:
Intersentia Publishing nv
Groenstraat 31
2640 Mortsel
Belgium
Tel.: +32 3 680 15 50 | Fax: +32 3 658 71 21
Email: mail@intersentia.be

Distribution for the USA and Canada:
Independent Publishers Group
Order Department
814 North Franklin Street
Chicago, IL 60610
USA
Tel.: +1 800 888 4741 (toll free) | Fax: +1 312 337 5985
Email: orders@ipgbook.com

The Effectiveness and Application of EU and EEA Law in National Courts. Principles of Consistent Interpretation

ISBN 978-1-78068-655-4
D/2018/7849/78
NUR 828

British Library Cataloguing in Publication Data. A catalogue record for this book is available from the British Library.

PREFACE

This book is the result of a research project borne of a combination of coincidence, curiosity and cooperation. As an English lawyer, I have lived and worked as an academic at the University of Bergen in Norway for many years now. Turning my hand from teaching EU law to EEA law, I was fascinated to see just how differently courts in the UK and Norway seemed to approach conflicts between national and EU/EEA law – particularly through the application of the principle of consistent interpretation. Casting my net a little further, I was further surprised how little I could find (in a language that I could master) on how courts in other EU/EEA countries have dealt with such conflicts. As it turned out, thankfully there were many other like-minded academic souls out there, at relatively similar stages in their careers, who shared my interest. Approaching potential contributors was made all the more easier given the timing of this project, which seems particularly ripe – not only in light of the book's EEA dimensions in the context of Brexit, but also considering the broader discussions raised over the past few years concerning the very dialogue and cooperation between the EU and EFTA Courts and national courts in practice.

Unlike many anthologies, this book represents a truly collaborative and cooperative effort. Core members of the project group were invited to a preparatory "kick-off" seminar at the University of Bergen, where potential issues to be addressed by all of the participants were discussed, and a time-line for the project settled. Following the preparatory seminar, a comprehensive questionnaire was designed, setting out a multitude of potential research problems related to the reception of the principle of consistent interpretation. First draft contributions provided the basis for further discussion, reflection and debate at a fruitful, two-day workshop. The workshop in fact proved key to the entire process in the end, providing a tangible point of reference for developing our texts in a more cohesive and in-depth manner. As readers will note, the contributors were encouraged to write their contributions as academic articles rather than mere mechanical responses to the questions provided. The workshop also therefore helped to provide a stronger sense of direction and common purpose to our research.

That is not to say that we consider our work complete. To the contrary, as a first edition, we hope to have provided merely the start of a discussion. Our own contributions will no doubt benefit from feedback and further reflection, and further digging into national case law. We have set up a blog for this purpose, where we would kindly invite any feedback, comments, tips on cases, etc. related to any of the issues covered in this book. The blog can be accessed at http://consistentinterpretation.blogspot.com/. We have also only been able to provide a fragment of the entire picture in this first edition. The experiences of many countries are unfortunately notable in their absence. The reasons for this are partly due to financial limitations, and partly in an attempt to keep the project to manageable proportions in its infancy. Hopefully we will be able to add experiences from more countries in the next edition. If you might be interested in taking part in this project, please do not hesitate to get in touch (christian.franklin@uib.no).

There are many people that deserve special thanks in helping to see this project come to fruition. First and foremost are the contributors themselves, without which the plans for this book would have remained on the shelf, slowly gathering dust. It has been a joy working with and getting to know you all. My heartfelt thanks for all your time, patience and efforts. Our project has also been generously funded by various Research Groups at the University of Bergen's Faculty of Law, without which our seminar and workshop would not have been possible. I would also like to thank the staff of Intersentia, and particularly Ann-Christin Maak-Scherpe and Rebecca Moffat for their enthusiasm in taking this project on, and for giving us such excellent support at all stages of the publishing process.

Christian N.K. Franklin
Bergen, August 2018

QUESTIONNAIRE

Christian N.K. Franklin*

This questionnaire is intended to provide a framework for and to stimulate national reports on the application and effectiveness of the principle of consistent interpretation under EU and EEA law at national level. The national reports will in turn serve as the basis for a general report aimed at providing a comparative analysis of the main challenges facing both the national and EU/EEA legal orders in this regard. National reporters are therefore asked to respond to the issues and questions raised in the questionnaire from the perspective of how decisions of the ECJ and/or EFTA Court pertaining to the scope and content of the principle of consistent interpretation are applied in their jurisdiction.

It is important to stress that the questionnaire should be viewed as a source of inspiration, not of strict inquiry. Not all of the questions might be relevant to your country, or have been considered by your national courts. Equally, there may well be other issues or perspectives which are not addressed by the questionnaire which you feel deserving of mention – you should naturally feel free to do so.

Reporters should also not feel bound to considering only those decisions of national courts where a referral for a preliminary ruling or advisory opinion was made to the ECJ or EFTA Court. To the contrary, in light of the project's overall aims, it is probably even more important to try to uncover practice related to cases where national courts apply the principle without making referrals.

Regarding the format of the individual national reports, although the headings suggested have proven helpful in shaping the questionnaire itself, you should feel free to structure your report as you see fit. You are nevertheless encouraged to write your report more as an academic article than a strict mechanical response to each and every question and issue put forward below. The reports are to be written in English.

The national reports will form the backbone for the presentations and discussions to be held at the workshop. (…) You should view your report as

* Many thanks go to Joxerramon Bengoetxea, Sara Drake, Claes Granmar, Gunnar Thor Petursson and Grith Skovgaard Ølykke for their input and discussions on an early draft of this questionnaire, following a preparatory seminar held in Bergen at the start of the project.

a first (and not necessarily final) draft. Issues concerning common rules for formatting, annotations, citations etc. need therefore not concern us at this stage, but will naturally be addressed well before the deadline eventually set for final drafts for publishing.

BACKGROUND INFORMATION

One of the main aims of the project is to make accessible for a broader (European) public how national authorities apply EU/EEA principles in practice in their countries. In order to do so, it would be helpful for most readers to know more about the context in which EU/EEA law is applied at national level in your country. In addition to some general background information (e.g. population of your country; how long it has been a Member State of the EU/EEA, etc.), you may therefore consider providing some pointers on how your national court system is structured and how it functions in the context of your national constitutional order.

You should also aim to provide the reader with some basic, general guidance concerning the relationship between national law and international/EU/EEA law in your country – e.g. does your country take a monist or dualist view to the relationship between national and international law (or perhaps some hybrid of the two)? What are the defining constitutional (or equivalent legal) features regulating the relationship between your national legal system and the EU/EEA legal order?

It would also be helpful – both for readers and the general reporter – to know more about the empirical data forming the basis of your report, such as e.g.:

- What sources form the basis of your report (i.e. court decisions, administrative decisions, etc.)?
- How were the sources accessed and compiled – through databases available online, or manually?
- Have you focussed on a selection of data in your report? (E.g. limiting your enquiry to decisions of certain national courts; or to decisions addressed in academic literature of your home country and/or other countries?)
    - If so, how and why have you decided to delimit the decisions on which your analyses rely (e.g. to reduce the documentation to manageable proportions; due to accessibility problems; are all cases simply not reported)?
    - How (if at all) has your selection of data impacted on the overall picture presented in your report?
- How many decisions of national courts involve the application of the principle of consistent interpretation in your country? Indeed, is it possible at all (on the basis of the research tools available) to get such an overview?

- What policy areas do the cases you have looked at primarily concern – are there any patterns to be seen here?

Certain general observations concerning the relationship between national courts in your country and the EU/EEA (or EFTA) institutions may also provide helpful context, such as e.g.:

- Approximately how many cases (per year or as a whole) have been referred by national courts in your country to the ECJ or EFTA Court for a preliminary ruling or advisory opinion?
- In how many decisions of national courts in your country involving the application of the principle of consistent interpretation was a request made to the ECJ or EFTA Court for a preliminary ruling or advisory opinion?
- In cases where referrals were made to the ECJ/EFTA Court concerning the ambit and/or application of the principle, what were the final outcomes of those cases?
    - Did the reply from the ECJ/EFTA Court enable the national court to reach a final decision in the case?
    - Was the referring national court's decision appealed – and if so, what was the outcome?
    - Alternatively, have any cases been settled out of court following a reply from the ECJ/EFTA Court? If so, what is the culture for using settlement mechanisms in your country more generally – are settlements encouraged by national courts in your country, or subject solely to the wishes of the parties involved in the dispute?

THE CONCEPTUAL BASIS FOR THE OBLIGATION TO PERFORM CONSISTENT INTERPRETATIONS

Many different terms are used in the English language to describe the principle: Consistent interpretation, harmonious interpretation, conform interpretation, and indirect effect – to name but a few.

- How is the principle described in your country's language? Are various terms used, and what do they mean?

Most EU/EFTA states have long traditions in applying national principles of consistent interpretation to reconcile conflicting national and international rules. The ECJ for its part has repeatedly held that the obligation imposed on Member State authorities to interpret and apply national law in conformity with EU law is "inherent in the Treaty", and rests on several legal bases (i.e. the duty of cooperation and the binding nature of Art. 288 TFEU).

- Do national courts in your country apply the principle of consistent interpretation directly, as an EU/EEA obligation in its own right; or do they apply similar national principles of consistent interpretation instead?
- If the latter, what do national courts say (if anything) about the relationship between the two? Put in another way; do national courts in your country consider the EU/EEA principle of consistent interpretation to have influenced the scope and/or application of national principles of consistent interpretation in any way; and if so, how and to what extent?
- In what way (if any) have national methods of construction needed to be adapted or modified in light of the EU/EEA principle of consistent interpretation?

Many (and presumably most) cases involving the application of the principle of consistent interpretation are raised by individuals seeking to protect their rights under EU/EEA law – either against other individuals, or against the state. In some cases, however, Member State authorities may (somewhat contradictorily) seek to rely upon the principle in a case against an individual. In principle – and subject naturally to adherence to general principles of law (legal certainty, etc.) – there should arguably be nothing to prevent this from happening under EU/EEA law: Whilst the protection of individual rights is an obvious and important facet to the very existence of the principle, so too is securing the effectiveness of EU/EEA law. And EU/EEA measures may very well have been designed, both in word and in purpose, precisely so as to impose obligations on individuals.

- Are there any examples of your country's authorities seeking to rely on the principle of consistent interpretation to their benefit in cases brought against individuals; and if so, how were they resolved by your national courts?

Where national courts face issues concerning (potentially) diverging EU/EEA rules and national law, the effectiveness of the former might naturally be secured through the possible application of several different EU/EEA principles in practice. In certain cases (such as e.g. C-282/10, *Dominguez*, ECLI:EU:C:2012:33), the ECJ has indicated a clear order of sequence for national courts to follow when seeking to apply them: Consistent interpretation, followed by direct effect, and finally state liability. In other cases, however, it has not been so clear as to the methodology (if any) which national courts should adopt in this regard.

- How do national courts in your country approach such issues – do they follow an established methodology, i.e. following a set sequence in each case?

- In cases where the principle of consistent interpretation has been applied by courts in your country, did they also consider applying the principles of direct effect and/or state liability to resolve the issue? If so, did the national court indicate any priority or preference between the application of these three principles?

THE GENERAL SCOPE OF THE PRINCIPLE OF CONSISTENT INTERPRETATION UNDER EU/EEA LAW

The ECJ has long held that the principle of consistent interpretation applies equally in vertical (state vs. private party) and horizontal situations (private party vs. private party).

- Do the national courts of your country do the same when applying national or EU/EEA principles of consistent interpretation?
- Do national courts in your country view the principle as applicable to all EU/EEA law, or only directives?

Drawing further on the duty of loyal cooperation, the ECJ has held that prior to the expiry of the implementation deadline for directives, national courts must refrain as far as possible from interpreting national law in a manner which might seriously compromise attainment of the objective(s) pursued by the Directive in question (see e.g. C-212/04, *Adeneler*, ECLI:EU:C:2006:443, para. 123).

- Have there been any cases where national courts in your country have been called upon to interpret national law in light of a directive prior to expiry of the deadline for its implementation?
- If so, how have they tackled such a task?

Although most cases will usually involve the interpretation of national legislative measures of some kind, according to the ECJ, the obligation to perform consistent interpretations extends to "national law as a whole" (e.g. C-397–403/01, *Pfeiffer*, ECLI:EU:C:2004:584).

- Are there any examples of other national legal sources – e.g. case-law, general principles, practices, contracts etc. – which national courts in your country have applied (or have considered applying) the principle to?
- In cases where they seek to perform consistent interpretations of national law, do national courts in your country treat measures specifically introduced

in order to implement EU/EEA law, and measures which are not, differently (i.e. as subjected to different standards)?

The ECJ has held that the obligation to interpret national law so far as possible in the light of EU law applies "(...) notwithstanding any contrary interpretation which may arise from the *travaux préparatoires* for the national rule" (C-371/02, *Björnekulla*, ECLI:EU:C:2004:275, para. 13.).

- What status do preparatory legislative works enjoy in your country's legal system?
- Is the extension of the duty to perform consistent interpretations regardless of what might be stated in preparatory legislative works in any way problematic under your national law (according to views of national courts)?
- Have any such issues been raised (directly or indirectly) in cases proceeding before national courts in your country – if so, how were they resolved?

Concerning the approach to consistent (and purposive) interpretation more generally: Are there any indications of national courts in your country paying more attention to the purpose of national (implementing) law (i.e. the national legislature's intent) than the purpose of the EU/EEA law with which it is to be interpreted in conformity with?

LIMITS TO THE PRINCIPLE OF CONSISTENT INTERPRETATION

The ECJ has often stated in its case-law that it is for the national courts to interpret and apply national law in conformity with the requirements of EU law, the general limitation being that they will only be required to do so "as far as possible". Of course, who is to determine what is possible or not – the national court or the ECJ – remains a debated issue to this very day. In many cases, the ECJ will be content to leave the issue for the national courts to decide by themselves. In certain cases, however, it will be much more forceful in its guidance to the national courts – e.g. either requiring a particular interpretative outcome in the case, or dismissing potential interpretations of national law put forward by the parties to the case and/or the referring national court. This raises inevitable questions concerning the outer limits and reach of the principle itself. According to the ECJ, the principle does not extend so far as to require interpretations in breach of general principles of law. Consequently, and connected to the general principle of legal certainty, national courts are, for example, not (generally) required to provide interpretations that the national law in question simply cannot bear (so-called *contra legem*-interpretations). There are nevertheless numerous examples from the case-law which indicate that the ECJ will not always be sympathetic to such claims (see e.g. C-404/06, *Quelle*, ECLI:EU:C:2008:231; C-18/13, *Maks Pen*, ECLI:EU:C:2014:69; and C-306/12, *Spedition Welter*, ECLI:EU:C:2013:650). It is also difficult to know whether the "general principles" acting as limitations in this connection are those developed under EU/EEA law, or those existing under the national laws of the Member States, and what (if any) differing results their application might lead to in practice.

LIMITS TO NATIONAL METHODS OF INTERPRETATION AND OF THE JUDICIAL FUNCTION OF NATIONAL COURTS

- How far are national courts in your country willing to go to bring national law into line with EU/EEA law obligations?
- Have they given any indications (explicitly or implicitly; general or specific) as to how they read the "as far as possible"-limitation – e.g. as fashioned and tamed by national principles of construction and interpretation, or the role that national courts play in your legal system? Do they tend to focus on what may be possible in order to achieve consistent interpretations, or do they tend to focus on what is not possible (i.e. limitations to the principle)?
- Are there any examples of national courts neglecting to bring national law in line with EU/EEA obligations on grounds of lack of competence (i.e. because this was in some way beyond the limits of the judicial function of the courts under the national legal system)?
- Are there any examples of national courts neglecting to bring national law in line with EU/EEA obligations because the limits to national rules of interpretation were viewed as reached?
- Are there any examples of national courts performing consistent interpretations of national law in spite of any misgivings they may have had owing to fears of lack of competence and/or stretching the boundaries of national rules of construction/interpretation?
  - If so, are there any indications (explicit or implicit) as to whether they felt forced or (alternatively) empowered to do something they otherwise (normally) could not, under reference to their EU/EEA obligations?
- If any of the above, how open or transparent are national courts in your country in detailing the reasons underlying its decisions in such cases?

GENERALLY CONCERNING GENERAL PRINCIPLES AS LIMITATIONS

- Are there any examples from the case-law of your national courts where general principles of law (e.g. legal certainty, non-retroactivity, equity,

equality, *nulla poena sine culpa*, proportionality, etc.) were relied upon to limit application of the principle of consistent interpretation?
- If so, did the national court take national principles or equivalent EU/EEA law principles as their point of departure?
  - If the former, did the national court (explicitly or implicitly) further discern the scope and application of the national principles in light of their EU/EEA law equivalents?
  - If national general principles were applied, would/could the application of their EU/EEA equivalents have led to different results being reached?

SPECIFICALLY CONCERNING THE *CONTRA LEGEM*-LIMITATION AND LEGAL CERTAINTY

The term "*contra legem* interpretation" is used here to describe situations where national law is given "a meaning which clearly deviates from an initial (literal) reading of the provision concerned",[1] and interpretations "which cannot reasonably be supported by the relevant national texts".[2]

- Do national courts in your country use the same (or a similar) term, and if so, how do they define it in practice?
- Are *contra legem*-interpretations (as defined above) permitted more generally in your national legal order? If not, how are they prohibited (e.g. by express statute, constitutional provision or convention, precedent)?
- Are there any examples from the case-law of your national courts where strained/artificial interpretations of national law were carried out in order to avoid/resolve conflicts between two or more measures of *national law*?
- Are there any examples from the case-law of your national courts where the *contra legem*-limitation has been relied upon (explicitly or implicitly) to prevent the resolution of a conflict between two or more measures of *national law*?
- Are there any examples from the case-law of your national courts where strained/artificial interpretations of national law were carried out in order to achieve an interpretation consistent with EU/EEA law?
- Are there any examples from the case-law of your national courts where the *contra legem*-limitation has been relied upon (explicitly or implicitly) to rule out an interpretation of national law consistent with EU/EEA law?
- Are there any examples from national case-law in your country where specific interpretative results were required by the ECJ or EFTA Court

---

1 S. Prechal, *Directives in EC Law*, 2nd edition 2005, p. 207.

2 M. Dougan, "When worlds collide! Competing visions of the relationship between direct effect and supremacy", 44 (2007) *Common Market Law Review*, 931–963.

(such as e.g. in C-106/89, *Marleasing*, ECLI:EU:C:1990:395; and C-306/12, *Spedition Welter*, ECLI:EU:C:2013:650; where the national courts were precluded from interpreting national law in a way which did not comply with the directive)?

- Are there any examples from national case-law in your country where the ECJ or EFTA Court suggested that a consistent interpretation might be possible (such as e.g. in C-105/03, *Pupino*, ECLI:EU:C:2005:386; C-282/10, *Dominguez*, ECLI:EU:C:2012:33; and C-42/11, *Lopes Da Silva Jorge*, ECLI:EU:C:2012:517)?
  - If so, how was this dealt with by the national court in question when the case was returned for its final decision (i.e. what was the practical outcome of the case)?
- If any of the above, was it (theoretically and/or practically) possible to ensure the effectiveness of the EU/EEA rule in question by some other means in those cases (i.e. direct effect or state liability)?

CONTENTS

LIST OF CASES

EFTA COURT

EUROPEAN COURT OF JUSTICE

EUROPEAN COURT OF HUMAN RIGHTS

CYPRUS

DENMARK

FINLAND

FRANCE

GERMANY

ICELAND

ITALY

THE NETHERLANDS

NORWAY

POLAND

SLOVENIA

UNITED KINGDOM

LIST OF ABBREVIATIONS

CSDP	Common Security and Defence Policy
DDA	(UK) Disability Discrimination Act 1995
EAT	(UK) Employment Appeal Tribunal
EAW	European Arrest Warrant
EC	European Community
ECB	European Central Bank
ECHR	European Convention on Human Rights
ECJ/CJEU	European Court of Justice/Court of Justice of the European Union
ECSC	European Coal and Steel Treaty
ECtHR	European Court of Human Rights
EEA	European Economic Area
EEC	European Economic Community
EFTA	European Free Trade Association
EMU	Economic and Monetary Union
ESA	EFTA Surveillance Authority
ET	(UK) Employment Tribunal
EU	European Union
EUCFR	EU Charter of Fundamental Rights
EURATOM	Treaty Establishing the European Atomic Energy Community
FD	Framework Directive
FSAC	Finnish Supreme Administrative Court
FSC	Finnish Supreme Court
GFCC	German Federal Constitutional Court
IO	International Organisation
ItCC	Italian Constitutional Court
JHA	Justice and Home Affairs
OHIM	Office for Harmonisation in the Internal Market
OLW	Overleveringswet (Dutch Surrender Act)
SCA	Agreement between the EFTA States on the Establishment of a Surveillance Authority and a Court of Justice
TEC	Treaty Establishing the European Community
TRIPS	Agreement on Trade-Related Aspects of Intellectual Property Rights
TUPE	(UK) Transfer of Undertakings (Protection of Employment) Regulations 1981

LIST OF CONTRIBUTORS

Judit Altena-Davidsen
Assistant Professor at Leiden University, the Netherlands

Vincent Couronne
Lecturer at the University of Versailles and Sciences Po Saint-Germain, France

Małgorzata Cyndecka
Postdoctoral Research Fellow at the University of Bergen, Norway

Sara Drake
Senior Lecturer in Law at Cardiff University, Wales, United Kingdom

Mohor Fajdiga
University of Ljubljana, Slovenia

Christian N.K. Franklin
Professor at the University of Bergen, Norway

Nils Grosche
Postdoctoral Research Fellow at Johannes Gutenberg-Universität Mainz, Germany

Tatiana Guarnier
Senior Researcher at the University of Camerino, Italy

Katerina Kalaitzaki
PhD Candidate and Research Fellow at the University of Central Lancashire, Cyprus

Elisabetta Lamarque
Associate Professor at the University of Milan Bicocca; Clerk of the Vice-President of the Constitutional Court, Italy

Stéphanie Laulhé Shaelou
Professor at the University of Central Lancashire, Cyprus

Samuli Miettinen
Associate Professor at Tallinn University, Estonia; Lecturer and Adjunct Professor at the University of Helsinki, Finland

Grith Skovgaard Ølykke
Associate Professor at the Copenhagen Business School; Director at Kammeradvokaten, Denmark

Gunnar Thor Petursson
Professor at Reykjavik University, Iceland; Director of the Internal Market Affairs Directorate, EFTA Surveillance Authority

Omar Berg Runarsson
Legal Officer at the Immigration and Asylum Appeals Board, Iceland

Christina D. Tvarnø
Professor at the Copenhagen Business School, Denmark

Saša Zagorc
Associate Professor at the University of Ljubljana, Slovenia

SYNTHESIS

Drawing Some Lines on the Application of the Principle of Consistent Interpretation in National Courts

Christian N.K. FRANKLIN

1. INTRODUCTION

In the current decentralised system of European Union (EU) and European Economic Area (EEA) law enforcement, national courts play a pivotal role in securing the effectiveness and application of the law. A great deal of legal research has been expounded over the years concerning how and to what extent the Court of Justice of the European Union (ECJ) and the European Free Trade Association (EFTA) Court have sought to determine the more precise scope and content of one of the key mechanisms for doing so – namely the principle of consistent interpretation. Much less attention has been paid to how national courts charged with the duty of applying these principles in practice actually do so when faced with such issues in cases before them. This is in many ways surprising, since the remit and limits to this EU/EEA principle can only be fully appreciated and understood if one looks beyond the decisions of the ECJ and EFTA Court, and to the final outcome of the cases at national level. Yet for obvious reasons connected to our (lack of) linguistic abilities, attempting to delve into decisions of national courts of other countries, and academic literature which might broach such issues from a national perspective, will often prove a rather daunting – if not impossible – task. Language barriers therefore pose one of the key challenges to increased knowledge in this field. And, even if one is able to read such judgments in other languages, a lack of contextual understanding (legal, cultural, political, etc.) may pose further barriers to increased knowledge on such issues.

This book aims to take a step towards diminishing that knowledge gap, by asking how and to what extent domestic courts make use of the EU and EEA principles of consistent interpretation. Uniformity and homogeneity are keystones of the EU and EEA projects. Given the expectation that the principles are to have a uniform and homogenous understanding and application throughout the EEA, the practice of domestic courts is considerably more diverse. As we shall see, the findings set out in the individual contributions identify a considerable tension between the goals of uniform and homogenous application of the principle of consistent interpretation and a plurality of different approaches at national level.

The present contribution offers an attempt to synthesise some of the findings in the individual contributions from the very outset, cross-referencing to later chapters along the way. We shall start by looking at the main objectives of the project and the methodological approach adopted in seeking its completion (section 2). Along the same general lines as provided in the questionnaire upon which the individual contributions are based (see page vii in this book), we shall then proceed to focus on the reception and understanding of the very concept of consistent interpretation by national courts (section 3), and how the criteria for its application have been applied and understood at national level (section 4), before finally considering the perceived and/or actual limits to the EU/EEA principles in practice (section 5). Several important questions will be addressed directly or indirectly from a more overarching perspective – such as whether EU and EEA law require a uniform interpretative approach by domestic courts and whether this is desirable, whether a common methodological outlook can be found in national court practice, and also the potential reasons (constitutional, political, cultural and/or historic) which might serve to explain similar and/or divergent national practices in various EU/EEA Member States.

2. OBJECTIVES, METHODOLOGICAL APPROACH AND CONTEXT

Beyond the pre-requisite contextual references to relevant decisions of the ECJ and EFTA Court which have established and developed the principle itself, and which are dealt with in countless accounts of EU (and to a lesser extent EEA) law more generally, the primary focus of the analyses in the individual contributions rests on appraisals of *national* case-law and practice. Whilst certain attempts have been made to study the application of particular aspects of the principle in some of the EU/EEA States covered,[1] many of the contributors (e.g. Finland, Iceland, Italy, Slovenia, UK) note an almost complete silence in domestic doctrine regarding how the principle is applied by national authorities. Legal culture may also naturally have played a role here – for example, as pointed out by the French contributor, given the succinct nature and format of court decisions in France, and their status as legal sources under French law, it is perhaps not so usual to carry out case analyses in this way. Where academic commentaries do exist in certain countries, they would appear to be limited mainly to case notes of the most significant national decisions (typically those reached by constitutional or supreme courts), and in any event mainly written in the national languages of the countries in question.

The contributors to this book have therefore attempted to break new ground by digging further into national case-law in their research. Although

---

1 See e.g. (UK) A. Arnull, "The Law Lords and the European Union: swimming with the incoming tide" 35 (2010) 1 *European Law Review* 57–87; (Netherlands) G. Betlem and P.A. Nollkaemper, "Giving effect to public international law and European Community law before domestic courts. A comparative analysis of the practice of consistent interpretation" 14 (2003) *European Journal of International Law* 569–89; (Norway) C.N.K Franklin, "Om innholdet i og rekkevidden av det EØS-rettslige prinsippet om direktivkonform fortolkning" (The Content and Scope of the EEA Principle of Consistent Interpretation) (2012) 5 *Jussens venner* 269–317.

national reception and application of the principle was raised as one of several lines of enquiry under a more general topic at the XVIII FIDE Congress 1998 in Stockholm,[2] the collected volume containing the FIDE reports from that year have not been officially published, although there are some copies in second-hand circulation. The reports to the FIDE Congress did not reflect the EEA dimension fully, either – which may (or May not) – prove of increased interest in the future, particularly in the light of the UK's triggering of the procedure for withdrawal from the EU under Art. 50 of the Treaty on European Union (TEU) ("Brexit").[3] The principle has in any event developed significantly over the course of the past two decades, in the light of more recent ECJ decisions.[4]

A more recent attempt to map out national reception of various EU principles – including, but not limited to, consistent interpretation – has also been carried out in the particular field of environmental law.[5] The approach in the present account is nevertheless more general in terms of the policy areas covered, with the cases discussed touching on pretty much all areas of the law – criminal law, tax law, administrative/public law, employment law, tort law, insurance law, intellectual property and health and safety law, to name but a few. The approach adopted in this book is also more specific, as it focuses on the reception of the principle of consistent interpretation alone. That does not mean, however, that this principle will be viewed in isolation. To the contrary, the individual contributors have been encouraged to raise issues connected to the symbiotic relationship and application of other related mechanisms for ensuring the effectiveness of EU and EEA law in practice – i.e. direct

---

2 *Les Directives Communautaires: Effets, Efficacite, Justiciabilite – XVIII Congrès FIDE, Stockholm 3–6 Juin 1998* (internal FIDE publication). Similarly, see the various reports submitted as part of the 19th Colloquium of the Association of the Councils of State and Supreme Administrative Jurisdictions of the European Union from 2004, as summarised in L. Senden's *General Report*, pp. 68–70, available at <http://www.aca-europe.eu/index.php/en/colloques-top-en/241-19th-colloquium-in-the-hague-from-14-to-15-june-2004>.

3 Whilst the FIDE volume in question also contains a report from Norway, there was little (if any) practice of national courts to speak of at this point in time, as it was only a few years after the entry into force of the EEA Agreement itself. Indeed, even today, there is little to be found on the creation and development of the EEA principle by the EFTA Court beyond a few, cursory mentions in the standard, English language EEA texts, see e.g. C. Baudenbacher (ed.), *The Handbook of EEA Law* (Springer, 2016); The EFTA Court (ed.), *The EEA and the EFTA Court – Decentred Integration* (Hart, 2014); F. Arnesen, H.H. Fredriksen *et al.* (eds.), *Agreement on the European Economic Area – A Commentary* (Beck/Hart/Nomos/Universitetsforlaget, 2018).

4 e.g. Case C-456/98, *Centrosteel*, ECLI:EU:C:2000:402; Joined Cases C-397–403/01, *Pfeiffer*, ECLI:EU:C:2004:584; Case C-371/02, *Björnekulla*, ECLI:EU:C:2004:275; Case C-404/06, *Quelle*, ECLI:EU:C:2008:231; Case C-282/10, *Dominguez*, ECLI:EU:C:2012:33; Case C-441/14, *Ajos*, ECLI:EU:C:2016:278, etc.

5 J.H. Hans, R. Macrory and A.-M. Moreno Molina, *National Courts and EU Environmental Law* (Europa Law Publishing, 2013).

effect and state liability. The data compiled has allowed us to further analyse the symbiosis and interaction between these principles in a more holistic manner.

As mentioned in the preface, unlike many anthologies, this book represents a truly collaborative and cooperative research effort. The countries chosen to take part were selected to represent a wide range of legal cultures and traditions – ranging from the UK with its common law system, to several countries embracing the civil law tradition (e.g. France and Italy), and certain countries which may be said to have adopted more "hybrid" or mixed legal traditions (e.g. Cyprus and Norway). Uniquely, both the EU (10 contributions) and EEA (2 contributions) dimensions of the principle are also covered. Countries with both monist and more dualist traditions are, importantly, represented. The individual contributions also represent a good blend between both longstanding and (relatively) new EU Member States – readers will note here that the contributions have in fact been ordered in this book according to the year in which the country in question joined the EU or EEA, starting with experiences in some of the founding Member States (the Netherlands, Germany, France and Italy).

By focusing on case analyses, the methodological approach adopted in the individual contributions is primarily legal dogmatic, although some of the contributions also exhibit traces of both legal cultural and legal sociology methodologies. The main question addressed (i.e. how and to what extent domestic courts make use of the EU or EEA principles of consistent interpretation) is tested by analysing the decisions of national courts where the principle has been applied in the light of the case-law of the EU and EFTA Courts where the principles were created and developed in the first place. The contributors have been strongly encouraged to analyse not only cases where national courts have been engaged in a formal dialogue with the ECJ or EFTA Court concerning application of the principles, but also cases where national courts have chosen to do so of their own volition, without having requested any specific guidance.

It is important to emphasise that the present account is not – and does not intend or pretend to provide – a general exposé on how the EU and/or EEA principles of consistent interpretation have been created and developed by the ECJ and EFTA Court in their case-law. It is assumed that readers coming to this book will already possess a certain, basic knowledge as to the principles themselves.[6] For ease of reference, a few basic reminders will nevertheless be provided at appropriate points along the way. And, where

6 For those unfamiliar with these developments, there are several good options from which to start, as far as the EU principle is concerned – e.g. P. Craig and G. de Búrca, *EU Law – Text, Cases, and Materials* (6th ed., Oxford University Press, 2015), pp. 209–16; S. Prechal, *Directives in EC Law* (2nd ed., Oxford University Press 2005).

necessary, the peculiarities of the EEA legal system relevant to understanding the principle of consistent interpretation as matter of EEA law will also be explained in more detail.

Selection of data for the project was an issue which was much discussed in planning this book. On the one hand, it was integral to the aim of this book to ensure that the contributors conducted their research on the basis of as comprehensive a volume of national court and administrative decisions as possible. On the other hand, it was also important to ensure that they were not crushed under the weight of the number of decisions to be examined – such as might easily prove the case for contributors from some of the large(r) EU States. Attempting to provide a fully comprehensive picture was nevertheless made difficult by a number of other factors. Accessibility has sometimes proven an issue, with some of the contributors being held hostage to the vagaries of case-reporting in their countries. For example, whilst most countries' online databases list all senior court decisions, in some countries only a selection of decisions from lower courts are readily accessible (e.g. Finland, France, Norway). In certain countries (e.g. Finland), access to first instance decisions may in any event prove of little assistance, as only summaries of such decisions are published.

Where national databases do provide more comprehensive reporting on the decisions of national courts, searching for and finding cases may still prove difficult for other reasons. From a systemic point of view, national courts in certain countries may generally be less open to detailing the reasons underlying their decisions (e.g. France). Some of the contributors also note that their national courts do not tend to elaborate on the specific issue of consistent interpretation in much detail, seldom referring to the principle – or even the case-law of the European Courts from which it is derived – explicitly in their decisions (e.g. the Netherlands, Norway, Slovenia). This can make it difficult to see immediately where (but not necessarily always how) the principle is used by the courts in practice.

A certain degree of selectivity was therefore called for, with several of the contributions limiting themselves to appraisals of Supreme and/or higher court decisions (Cyprus, Denmark, France, Slovenia). Others have cast their nets wider. It is nevertheless submitted that the data relied upon in the individual contributions has proven sufficient for our aims. More detail concerning how the contributors have gone about selecting the materials forming the basis of their research can be found in the individual contributions.

Several of the contributions have also provided a great deal of contextual information. This was considered essential in trying to understand national courts' powers and place in the legal and judicial systems of their countries, and highly relevant to trying to understand how the principle of consistent interpretation has been received and applied by them. Further, this has also allowed the contributors to produce chapters which may be read as stand-alone narratives in their own right, whilst still forming parts of a collective whole. The contributors were therefore encouraged to view the questionnaire as a source of inspiration rather than a straitjacket, and to pursue other relevant and related lines of enquiry where appropriate. From a constitutional perspective, certain contributors therefore point out how the reception of EU law more generally has led to an empowerment of lower courts in practice. The Italian account, for example, explains how, after initial reluctance on the part of the Italian Constitutional Court, lower national courts have become increasingly constitutionally empowered (and instructed) to handle conflicts between EU and national law on their own, without direct involvement of the Constitutional Court itself. Whilst the full reception of supranational EU law may have led to an increased sense of solidarity between higher and lower courts in Italy, the contributors nevertheless also point out that judges of the ordinary courts appear to have embraced the concept of consistent interpretation in line with the Italian Constitution more fully than the corresponding principle under EU law. Although this might naturally be explained in institutional terms (i.e. that lower courts feel more readily empowered to do so where the norm conflict concerns the Constitution), the practical result is that lower Italian courts tend to opt for a more prudent approach to interpretations consistent with EU law. The constitutional context in Cyprus seems rather similar to Italy on this point. In spite of a specific constitutional provision which seemed to indicate the contrary, not only the Supreme Court but also lower courts enjoy jurisdiction to review the constitutionality of Cypriot laws in practice – a development which in turn has served to empower lower courts to deal with (and resolve) certain conflicts between national and EU law as well (barring family law and certain other executive matters), without having to refer such cases to the Supreme Court.

A rather different picture is revealed concerning the constitutional context in Iceland. The Icelandic contributors point out, for example, how the direct oversight carried out by the Icelandic Supreme Court of any question or issue that a lower court might want to refer to the EFTA Court for an Advisory Opinion might play a role in stifling application (and consequently development) of the principle of consistent interpretation in practice.[7] Similar sentiments are raised in the contribution on Norway, where the troubled relationship between the EFTA Court and particularly the Norwegian Supreme Court may have played a part in limiting development of the principle – and EEA law more generally – in practice.[8] The peculiarities of EEA law, and its impact on the constitutional paradigms of the EFTA States, are naturally important to bear in mind when reading the Icelandic and Norwegian contributions.

[7] Iceland, pp. 387–89.
[8] Norway, p. 321.

Indeed, a great deal of EEA context is therefore also provided in both. For the benefit of readers less familiar with the idiosyncrasies of EEA law, some of the most important points will be set out here as well.

Whilst the substantive provisions of the Main Part of the EEA Agreement should seem inherently familiar to EU legal practitioners, as mirroring the EC rules on the four freedoms and competition as they stood when the Agreement was signed in the early 1990s, the scope of its objectives are much more limited than those found under the EU Treaties.[9] Securing access to the EU internal market nevertheless came at a cost for the EFTA States, who have agreed to ensure that EEA developments keep up to speed with the underlying EU law upon which it is directly based. This has been largely ensured by insertion of the fundamental EEA principle of homogeneity, which requires the Contracting Parties (i.e. the EU and its institutions, the EU Member States and the EFTA States) to strive to ensure that identical rules under EU and EEA law – including unwritten principles such as consistent interpretation – are interpreted and applied in a uniform manner.[10]

Since taking part in the EEA was not to involve any transfer of legislative or judicial sovereignty for the EFTA States, the institutional set-up of the EEA is also markedly different from that of the EU. Whilst the EFTA States were unwilling (and arguably unable, constitutionally) to submit full authority and control of EEA matters to the EU institutions, the EU for its part could not accept a situation whereby the EFTA States would be free to monitor their own compliance with the provisions of the Agreement. The compromise reached saw the construction of a unique two-pillar structure for decision-making, monitoring and enforcement of EEA obligations under the Agreement – with the EU acting collectively under the one pillar, and the EFTA States acting collectively under the other.[11] Several common EEA institutions were further established to act as a bridge between the two pillars, yet notably with no common court or supervisory body.[12] The Agreement therefore presumed the establishment of a system for supervising and enforcing EEA obligations which would be indigenous under each pillar. Whilst the ECJ and the Commission are charged with doing so under the EU pillar, two EFTA institutions – the EFTA Court and the EFTA Surveillance Authority (ESA) – were established

9 Unlike the EU's objective of securing an "ever closer union between the peoples of Europe", the EEA was designed to be more limited to elements primarily connected to economic integration. As can be seen in several of the Preamble recitals, and also highlighted in Art. 1(1) EEA, the aim of the Agreement is to "promote a continuous and balanced strengthening of trade and economic relations between the Contracting Parties with equal conditions of competition, and the respect of the same rules".

10 Arts. 1 and 6 EEA, and e.g. recitals 4 and 5 of the EEA Agreement's Preamble.

11 For an overview, see e.g. the EFTA website <http://www.efta.int/eea/eea-institutions>.

12 Indeed, the idea of a common EEA court was ruled out altogether following the ECJ's *Opinion 1/91 (EEA Agreement)*, ECLI:EU:C:1991:490.

under the EFTA pillar to this end.[13] In order to keep up to speed with legislative developments in the EU internal market acquis, an EEA Joint Committee was established, charged with taking the necessary, consensus-based decisions to incorporate novel EEA-relevant EU secondary measures (primarily regulations and directives) into various Annexes to the EEA Agreement.[14]

Concerning the relationship between the two courts, the principle of homogeneity formally obliges the EFTA Court to interpret EEA provisions in conformity with relevant rulings of the ECJ.[15] This has been integral in establishing and developing certain legal principles – including the principle of consistent interpretation – as a matter of EEA law.[16] Homogeneity nevertheless has its limits: since EEA membership was not to entail any transfer of legislative sovereignty, there is no direct effect or primacy of EEA law – at least not as these principles are understood under EU law. Contrary to certain misguided statements made by the ECJ,[17] the EFTA Court has on many occasions confirmed that the EEA Agreement does not require direct effect of non-implemented EEA provisions.[18] And unlike EU law, where regulations are of direct applicability and only directives require transformation, all directives *and* regulations incorporated into the Annexes of the EEA Agreement require national implementation – at least in the dualist EFTA States of Norway and Iceland.[19]

---

13 Agreement between the EFTA States on the Establishment of a Surveillance Authority and a Court of Justice [1994] OJ L344/3 (SCA).

14 Art. 92 EEA. There are approximately 5,000 EU legal acts currently in force as part of EEA law. The Joint Committee's decisions encompass not only legislative acts (as defined in Art. 289 TFEU), but also many delegated/implementing acts, decisions and recommendations.

15 Art. 6 EEA provides that the EFTA Court must interpret EEA provisions in conformity with the relevant case-law of the ECJ rendered prior to the date of signature of the Agreement (i.e. 2 May 1992). Notwithstanding the potentially less burdensome formal duty under Art. 3(2) SCA, which merely requires the EFTA Court to take "due account" of the principles laid down in rulings of the ECJ after the EEA Agreement's date of signature, the EFTA Court's practice reveals that it has consistently taken into account relevant rulings of the ECJ also after this date. See e.g. Joined Cases E-9-10/07, *L'Oréal*, [2008] EFTA Ct. Rep. 258, para. 28. Although it is worth pointing out that the ECJ also routinely takes EFTA Court practice into account in its own case-law, there is little denying the formal and practical hierarchical relationship between the two.

16 The principle was first mentioned by the EFTA Court in Case E-04/01, *Karlsson* [2002] EFTA Ct. Rep. 240, para. 28.

17 See e.g. Case C-431/11, *UK v. Council*, ECLI:EU:C:2013:589, para. 54, where the ECJ stated that as regards an EU regulation, Art. 7(a) EEA "expressly provides that such an act is 'as such' to be made part of the internal legal order of the Contracting Parties, that is to say, without any implementing measures being required for that purpose" – thus clearly implying that EEA regulations are directly applicable. Further in Case C-83/13, *Fonnship*, ECLI:EU:C:2014:2053, para. 24, where the ECJ stated that the provisions of the regulation in question were "an integral part of the legal order of all of the States that are parties to the EEA Agreement by virtue of Art. 7(a) of the EEA Agreement and Annex XIII thereto".

18 See e.g. Case E-18/11, *Irish Bank* [2012] EFTA Ct. Rep. 592, para. 122.

19 Art. 7 EEA – the situation concerning implementation is naturally different in the monist EFTA state of Liechtenstein.

Protocol 35 to the Agreement goes on to provide that the national laws which implement EEA directives and regulations are to be afforded primacy over all other conflicting provisions of national law, thus establishing a sort of "quasi-primacy" between potentially conflicting measures of national law.[20]

One final point on the EEA context of crucial importance concerns the EFTA Court's jurisdiction to render Advisory Opinions under Art. 34 SCA, which have led to all of the EFTA Court's decisions concerning the EEA principle of consistent interpretation so far. Whilst the Advisory Opinion procedure was modelled on (and consequently looks rather similar to) the preliminary ruling procedure under Art. 267 TFEU, these are far from the same. Firstly, unlike decisions of the ECJ, the opinions of the EFTA Court are considered advisory, and not formally binding on the national courts of the EFTA States.[21] Secondly, national courts – even of last instance – have no duty to refer questions on the interpretation and/or application of EEA law to the EFTA Court.[22] The EFTA States are further allowed to limit the right to request Advisory Opinions to courts and tribunals against whose decisions there is no judicial remedy under national law.[23] Although this option has not been directly implemented in Iceland, it may also help to explain why the Icelandic Supreme Court, as mentioned above, has been allowed to vet applications by lower Icelandic courts to refer matters to the EFTA Court. The nature and complexion of the dialogue between national courts and the EFTA Court is therefore rather different to the more hierarchical set-up under the EU legal system. Whilst there are undoubtedly many similarities between the EU and EEA legal principles of consistent interpretation, it is important to bear in mind that they exist and are developed in rather different legal settings.

---

20 However, the effects of the Protocol – which is considered equally binding and of the same legal value as the Main Part of the Agreement – may potentially be rendered nugatory by national courts in certain cases: Serious conflicts between EEA rules and pre-existing national law will often arise as a result of incorrect implementation of the EEA rules in national law. (Quasi-)primacy arguments can potentially be avoided in cases where the EEA rules have been incorrectly implemented into national law.

21 Although the threat of infringement proceedings raised by the ESA (or one of the other EFTA States) will usually entail a high threshold before national courts would consider arriving at a different result in practice. See e.g. the Norwegian Supreme Court' s decisions in Rt-2000-1811, Rt-2004-904, Rt-2007-1003, and Rt-2013-258. For similar pronouncements made by the Icelandic Supreme Court, see e.g. H.1999 4429 and H.1999 4916.

22 The "refer or not to refer" debate has been much discussed in EEA legal academic literature. Compare e.g. the views of C. Baudenbacher, "The EFTA Court: Structure and Tasks" in C. Baudenbacher (ed.), *The Handbook of EEA Law* (Springer, 2016), pp. 139–78, at p. 157, with the more skeptical views of H.H. Fredriksen and C.N.K. Franklin, "Of pragmatism and principles: The EEA Agreement 20 years on" (2015) 52(3) *Common Market Law Review* 629, 672–73, and C.N.K. Franklin, "Article 3 EEA" in F. Arnesen, H.H. Fredriksen *et al.* (eds.), *Agreement on the European Economic Area: A Commentary* (C.H. Beck/Hart/Nomos/Universitetsforlaget, 2018), pp. 180–96, at p. 195.

23 Art. 34 SCA.

A further layer of contextual information is provided by some of the contributors who have attempted to draw on (and in certain cases compare) how national courts in their countries attack conformity issues between national and EU/EEA law on the one hand, and national law and obligations under international law and/or the European Convention on Human Rights (ECHR) on the other. Certain contributions (e.g. France, Germany, UK), for example, point to a process of cross-fertilisation within the national legal order on how such issues are approached. The UK narrative shows how the approach of national courts in the UK today (and for as long as it remains in the EU fold), is based on how the courts deal with similar issues regarding conformity between national law and the ECHR under the Human Rights Act 1998.[24] Other contributions nevertheless note how national courts in their countries generally seem prepared to do more, and to stretch themselves further, in order to achieve interpretations of national law consistent with their national constitutions and/or ECHR obligations, than in situations where national law conflicts EU law obligations. The Italian contributors, for example, draw attention to certain cases where lower national courts – perhaps uncharacteristically – went rather far in seeking to ensure EU-conforming interpretations of national law, yet argue that this only really occurs in cases where support for the same result might equally be drawn from either the Constitution and/or the ECHR.[25] They also compare the approach of the Italian Constitutional Court to interpretation in conformity with the Constitution (where it has performed exceptionally bold and creative interpretations of national law), with its approach to EU-consistent interpretations (where bold interpretations generally seem harder to come by) – apparently, whilst the letter of the national law may be worth sacrificing on the altar of the constitutional provision, less so on that of EU law. The Icelandic contribution similarly points out how national courts in Iceland generally appear to be more open towards seeking interpretations of national law in conformity with ECHR obligations than they are with regards to EEA law obligations.[26] As contended by the Icelandic contributors, bearing in mind that both the ECHR and the EEA Agreement are established to give certain rights to individuals – even fundamental human rights – the Icelandic Supreme Court's differentiated approach seems questionable. Much the same can be drawn from the narrative on Cyprus, according to which the use of EU law – and in particular the EU Charter – by the Supreme Court of Cyprus in interpreting national law, may be regarded as far less developed than the (much older) use of the ECHR.[27]

---

[24] UK, p. 229.

[25] Italy, p. 211.

[26] Iceland, p. 403. The same may also be seen in Norway.

[27] Cyprus, pp. 508–09.

3. RECEPTION AND UNDERSTANDING OF THE CONCEPT OF CONSISTENT INTERPRETATION

The EU principle of consistent interpretation – according to which national authorities must interpret the whole of national law, as far as possible, in line with EU obligations – was first established by the ECJ in the seminal *Von Colson* case in 1984,[28] with the EFTA Court making its first mention of the corresponding EEA principle in *Karlsson* almost 20 years later.[29] The principle is often touted as the least taxing or invasive mechanism for ensuring the effectiveness of EU and EEA law at national level,[30] as compared to the principles of direct effect and state liability, as ultimately it will involve an application (as opposed to the substitution or exclusion) of national law to resolve the issue. This view is also seemingly shared by some of the contributors (e.g. Finland, Italy). Whilst this might well be true more generally, especially in "soft cases" where national law seems more readily pliable to consistent interpretations, the principles have been subject to a considerably dynamic development over time – particularly by the ECJ. In "hard(er) cases", where national law does not appear as amenable to interpretations consistent with EU/EEA obligations, the ECJ has certainly appeared willing to push the limits of the principle very far in an attempt to secure effectiveness of the EU rights and duties in question.[31] It is not therefore altogether surprising to find the Slovenian contributor pointing out how loyal interpretation in some cases in fact presents national authorities with one of their most challenging tasks – having to interpret a national legal rule in a different way to before, on the basis of the purpose of an EU/EEA rule which may not have been taken into account by the national legislator when elaborating the national legal rule in the first place.[32] Many of the accounts nevertheless also reveal how reception of the principle by national courts, and the true extent of the duties it entails, has been a rather piecemeal, developmental process, in several stages – although the speed of the development seems to have varied from one state to another. There also seems to be resounding agreement in most of the contributions that the principle applies not only to national courts, but also to all public and administrative authorities in their countries. In Slovenia, for example, the Constitutional Court now requires administrative authorities to apply the principle, and for this to prevail over national legislation in cases of incompatibility.[33]

28 Case 14/83, *von Colson*, ECLI:EU:C:1984:153.

29 Case E-04/01, *Karlsson* [2002] EFTA Ct. Rep. 240, para. 28.

30 See e.g. S. Prechal (n. 6), p. 180.

31 See e.g. Case C-456/98, *Centrosteel*, ECLI:EU:C:2000:402; Case C-404/06, *Quelle*, ECLI:EU:C:2008:231; Case C-441/14, *Ajos*, ECLI:EU:C:2016:278.

32 Slovenia, p. 426.

33 Ibid.

3.1. DEFINITION AND DIRECT/INDIRECT APPLICATION OF THE CONCEPT

According to a well-known proverb in many European countries, beloved children have many names – which would certainly seem to be the case as far as the principle of consistent interpretation is concerned. The terms used by national courts and in legal doctrine are indeed many – ranging from indirect effect to pro-European or European friendly interpretation, directive-conforming interpretation, EU/EEA-conform interpretation (or EU/EEA-conforming interpretation), harmonious interpretation, interpretation reservations, the *Marleasing* principle, and many more. Of course, the fact that it is called many different things by different courts may not tell us much concerning its scope or content, although it has posed certain challenges from an editorial point of view in completing this book. We therefore spent some time discussing whether a common term could be agreed upon – for the benefit of the readers, more than anything – and, if so, which we would use. There was general consensus that "consistent interpretation" best reflected the various terms used by national courts in the majority of countries taking part. The individual contributions still attempt to make clear to the reader which terms are actually used by the relevant national courts in practice.

More importantly, it has been interesting to see how national courts may have adopted differing views as to what this principle actually is. Whilst many national courts would appear to view it as a legal principle in its own right, others seem to define it more specifically as a rule of conflict resolution (e.g. France), and others still as an indigenous method of statutory construction, additional to the standard national rules on statutory interpretation (e.g. UK). In Norway, where as we shall see a national equivalent has been applied in place of direct invocation of the EEA principle in certain cases, the concept has been viewed by some academic commentators as a more general consideration to be weighed against other legal sources, and at times by the Supreme Court as a mere exception to the general conflict-resolving rule flowing from the principle of dualism (i.e. that in cases of conflict between national and international/EEA law, the former will prevail).[34] How the very concept itself is construed is naturally important in more practical terms, since it in turn may potentially impact on the ways in which national courts seek to implement and apply it in practice.

Concerning the issue as to whether national courts apply the EU/EEA principles directly or in some "translated" form (i.e. applying similar/equivalent national principles), it would seem as though almost all national courts in the EU Member States covered in this account apply the principle directly as an EU obligation in its own right. In the Netherlands, national courts apply

[34] Norway, p. 329.

the EU principle directly as a consequence of the automatic primacy of EU over national law under the Dutch Constitution (i.e. monistic approach). Notwithstanding the general dualist approach to international law in Denmark, Danish courts similarly apply the principle directly as an EU obligation in its own right based upon EU law, without applying an equivalent Danish national legal method or principle. The situation appears to be the same in Finland: whilst academic literature notes how consistent interpretation involves a method similar to that traditionally endorsed by the Finnish courts in situations involving the giving of judicial effect to constitutional provisions or international treaties, no discernible attempts have been made by national courts to assimilate the EU principle to national principles of interpretation. Interestingly, however, earlier Finnish cases make no mention of the content or source of the principle actually applied, even though it seems apparent from the results and/or reasoning in the decisions themselves that an attempt was being made to interpret national law in line with the EU obligations in question – a similar lack of express reference to the EU/EEA principle in national case-law is in fact noted in many of the contributions (e.g. the Netherlands, Norway, Cyprus).

Several of the national narratives also reveal how direct reliance on the principle has been ensured through a process of internalising the very concept itself, tied largely to national courts' constitutional mandates in performing EU-consistent interpretations. In Poland, for example, the principle of consistent interpretation is viewed as being derived from both EU law (i.e. the Accession Treaty, and the principles of primacy and loyal/sincere cooperation), and national law (Arts. 9 and 91(1) of the Polish Constitution).[35] The principle was well-known even before Poland's accession to the EU, however, as Polish courts had applied a "Community-friendly" approach when seeking to interpret national law in light of the EC-Poland Association Agreement.

Application of the principle by Italian courts had initially rested on a purely internal foundation – a national presumption of conformity with EU/international law, as a species of the more general duty of interpretation in conformity with the Constitution.[36] Although the Italian Constitutional Court in the seminal *Granital* case eventually came to embrace the EU principle of consistent interpretation more directly, its application is still clearly linked to Art. 11 of the Constitution.[37] The tendency is therefore, in effect, for interpretation in conformity with EU law to be absorbed by interpretations in conformity with the Italian Constitution. A similar cross-fertilisation of approaches, based primarily on analogous duties of ensuring consistent interpretations of national legislation with constitutional rules, may also be spied in certain other countries (e.g. France).

35 Poland, pp. 479–80.
36 Italy, pp. 195–96.
37 ItCC, dec. no. 170 of 1984.

As a result of its approach, the Italian Constitutional Court also appears to have applied the principle of consistent interpretation as a mere supplementary argument in certain cases – i.e. the actual interpretative result flows from conformity with the Constitution, a result which is merely reinforced by application of the EU principle.[38] Slovenian courts had similarly tended to treat the principle as one of many (potentially competing) methods of interpretation, and a mere "additional argument" reinforcing the interpretative results otherwise flowing from application of more traditional (i.e. literal, historical and systemic) canons of interpretation.[39] The Slovenian Constitutional Court has subsequently moved to internalise the principle, however, by making it a constitutional principle in its own right. Following Art. 3a(3) of the Slovenian Constitution, the fundamental principles of EU law defining the relationship between internal law and EU law, including consistent interpretation, are at the same time internal and binding principles of constitutional law.

The EU principle has also been internalised in Germany and Cyprus. According to the German contribution, the mechanism enshrined in Art. 101 of the Basic Law concerning the guarantee of the lawful statutory judge is linked to the application and efficiency of EU law, as it allows for a subjective complaint with regards to the handling of EU law by national courts.[40] A national court's failure to comply with the principle of consistent interpretation may therefore amount to a violation of a constitutional right. And in Cyprus, anchored seemingly in primacy considerations, issues of EU law and the exercise of judicial control arising as a result of its application appear "*prima facie* to be encompassed within the fabric of the Constitution".[41] As a result, the tendency of the Cypriot courts is to concentrate merely on the protection of fundamental rights in accordance with express constitutional or ordinary legal provisions – ignoring EU law (and even the ECHR) on most occasions. Similarly to the Italian contribution, the Cypriot account also calls attention to a certain absorption of the EU principle by other (national) methods: Since the protection of constitutionally safeguarded fundamental rights have always been at the core of the case-law of the Cypriot courts, the protection of such rights may be seen as a "routine" exercise for them within the fabric of the Constitution, which in turn arguably may be seen to encompass the duty of harmonious interpretation under EU law under national tests of necessity and/or proportionality.

In the UK, the EU principle of consistent interpretation is applied as a duty imposed on all national courts by the ECJ by virtue of a joint reading of Sections 2(4) and 2(1) of the European Communities Act 1972, according to

---

38 Italy, pp. 203–04.
39 Slovenia, p. 425.
40 Germany, pp. 130–31.
41 Cyprus, p. 509.

which "[a]ny enactment passed or to be passed [by Parliament, subject to certain exceptions] shall be construed and have effect subject to the foregoing provisions of this section".[42] This provision thus contains the mandate for English courts to apply the principle directly when seeking to interpret domestic legislation in accordance with applicable EU law. The application of the EU principle has in more recent times nevertheless also been assimilated by the judiciary with the application of Section 3 of the Human Rights Act 1998, which provides for ECHR-conforming interpretations of national law.[43] Interestingly, this provision uses the same wording as the ECJ in *Marleasing* concerning the EU principle of consistent interpretation.[44] By assimilating the approaches in these two fields, we see a rather unique form of cross-fertilisation developing between different European legal regimes and UK methods of ensuring effectiveness by way of consistent interpretations. And in spite of the many differences in construction of the two interpretative obligations, the UK courts have so far appeared to refute all attempts by counsel to try and differentiate between them in terms of their scope.

Just because they can, however, does not necessarily mean that national courts in the UK always will apply the EU principle in order to ensure consistent interpretations of national law. Although application of the principle is not constrained by conventional rules of statutory construction, the UK contribution notes various examples of national courts using domestic techniques in order to achieve the same results that would have flowed from application of the EU principle.[45] There may also be good and understandable reasons for doing so in certain situations, for example where application of a national method could serve to avoid future litigation in the event that a dispute were to arise over the same part of the statute at issue, but in a "domestic only" case. Furthermore, the UK account also provides an example of a case where national canons of (contractual) interpretation were applied in order to ensure an outcome consistent with specific EU obligations, in a situation where the EU principle had arguably reached its limits.[46]

As regards reception of the EEA principle of consistent interpretation at national level, the contributions on Iceland and Norway reveal a slightly different picture. Unlike its EU counterpart, the EEA principle of consistent interpretation is rooted in distinct EEA/international authorities, and is deemed inherent in the objectives of the EEA Agreement itself.[47] Although the

---

42 UK, pp. 223–25.

43 *Ghaidan v. Godin-Mendoza* [2004] UKHL 30, [2004] 2 AC 557.

44 Case C-106/89, *Marleasing*, ECLI:EU:C:1990:395.

45 UK, p. 235.

46 *White v. White* [1999] 1 CMLR 1251.

47 See e.g. Case E-01/07, *Criminal proceedings against A* [2007] EFTA Ct. Rep. 246, para. 39; Case E-6/13 *Metacom* [2013] EFTA Ct. Rep. 856, para. 69; Case E-25/13, *Engilbertsson* [2014] EFTA Ct. Rep. 524, para. 159; Case E-28/13, *Merrill Lynch* [2014] EFTA Ct. Rep. 970, para. 42.

EEA principle in light of the demands of homogeneity has been developed along much the same general lines as provided by the ECJ, the EFTA Court has not elaborated on the scope and boundaries of the EEA principle to anywhere near the same extent as its EU counterpart. This is perhaps not surprising in light of the significantly lighter caseload of the EFTA Court as compared to the ECJ, and the relatively low number of referrals made to it by national courts of the EFTA States.[48] Yet given that the EFTA Court's Opinions are not formally binding in any event, the national courts of the EFTA States have arguably enjoyed a somewhat free(r) hand than national courts in the EU Member States in their reception and understanding of the EEA principle of consistent interpretation. Whilst the principle appears to be fully accepted (at least in theory) by national courts in both Iceland and Norway, it has been internalised in a slightly different way. The Icelandic contributors note how the Icelandic Supreme Court applies the principle in a rather independent manner, never citing the EEA principle of consistent interpretation or the case-law of the EFTA Court related thereto.[49] The duty is seen as incorporated into national law by virtue of Section 3 of the Icelandic EEA Act. In many cases the courts therefore refer to this provision when seeking (or ruling out) EEA-consistent interpretations of national law, although in some important cases it does not, even if the result clearly shows that the court interpreted national law consistently with EEA law. The contributors point out that whilst this may have the natural explanation that Section 3 has been a binding statutory norm since 1994, many years before the EFTA Court had established the EEA principle, that the principle as developed by the EFTA Court (largely along the lines of the ECJ's case-law) has the ability to be more far reaching than Section 3 of the EEA Act, even if the latter theoretically has all the potential to be compliant with the principle.

In Norway, the national courts similarly do not apply the EEA principle directly – at least not expressly. Where a specific principle is relied upon or mentioned at all, which is not always the case, the courts instead apply the national principle of presumption of compliance with international law in seeking (or ruling out) EEA-consistent interpretations of national law. Application of national principles as equivalents to the EEA principle may naturally seem unproblematic with a view to achieving effectiveness and homogeneity as to the interpretative outcome in a given case, as long as the same results in fact prove achievable under both. As shown in the contribution on Norway, however, this may not always be the case. Similarly to the Icelandic account, it is claimed that uncertainty exists as to whether the EEA principle and the national principle

[48] The total number of referrals from 1994–2015 (discounting referrals from former EFTA States Austria, Finland and Sweden prior to their joining the EU) is 94 – an average of less than five per year, from all three EFTA States combined.

[49] Iceland, p. 399.

of presumption really entail the same duties in practice, even though they might theoretically be capable of doing so, depending on the willingness of the courts in applying them.[50] Given that all unwritten EEA principles – including consistent interpretation – may be regarded as incorporated into Norwegian law by virtue of Section 1 of the Norwegian EEA Act, the application of national principles in their stead would in any event appear somewhat redundant. The continued use of a national equivalent in Norway in certain cases, and the experiences in Iceland, nevertheless go some way in underlining one of the main differences between the EU and EEA legal constructs: that membership of the EEA was not to entail a transfer of sovereign powers.

At a conceptual level, one might in any event also question whether national principles of presumption, as commonly found in most (if not all) dualist EU/EEA Member States, really are synonymous with the EU/EEA principles of consistent interpretation. Similarly to the contentions of the Icelandic and Norwegian contributors, several other contributions (e.g. UK, the Netherlands, Italy) also claim that the EU principle of consistent interpretation – in practice, if not also in theory – requires more of national courts than national principles of presumption or the like. Principles of presumption relate to parliamentary intent to transpose and uphold binding international obligations faithfully, and may at times prove rather easy for national courts to rebut in practice. Whilst there may be a general intent to transpose a particular EU/EEA rule, often traceable in national preparatory legislative works, it may subsequently prove (typically following clarification by the ECJ/EFTA Court) to have been based on a misguided notion of what the EU/EEA obligation entailed to begin with. In such cases, the intent to transpose may be seen as related to a different understanding of the norm, thereby providing potential – and in some cases actual – grounds for rebutting the presumption altogether. As pointed out in the Dutch account, parliamentary intent may in such situations in fact work against the interpretative result required under EU (and EEA) law, thus ruling out the possibility for consistent interpretation.[51] By comparison, the EU principle of consistent interpretation may not prove as easily rebuttable. As the ECJ for example has held in *Björnekulla*, the duty to perform consistent interpretations applies regardless of anything that might be gleaned from preparatory legislative works.[52] Certain academic commentators have contended that the ECJ's decision in this case may be seen to expose differences between EU and EEA law of such magnitude to warrant a different approach under EEA law (i.e. that the limits to homogeneity are reached).[53] Although the EFTA Court has never specifically addressed the ECJ's decision in *Björnekulla*,

50 Norway, pp. 327–30.
51 The Netherlands, p. 87.
52 Case C-371/02, *Björnekulla*, ECLI:EU:C:2004:275, para. 13.
53 H.H. Fredriksen and G. Mathisen, *EØS-rett* (Fagbokforlaget, 2018), p. 382.

it did state in *Merrill Lynch* that in cases where national courts of the EFTA States are dealing with disputes concerning the interpretation of domestic law provisions specifically enacted for the purpose of transposing EEA law, "the national court *must* presume that the EEA/EFTA State had the intention of fulfilling entirely the obligations from the EEA directive [or regulation] concerned".[54] It remains to be seen whether national courts in the dualist EFTA States would agree.

3.2. THE IMPACT OF THE EU/EEA PRINCIPLES – ADAPTATIONS OF NATIONAL LAW AND/OR RULES OF INTERPRETATION

Reception of the EU/EEA principles appears to have entailed varying degrees of modification of national methods of construction and interpretation – sometimes quite dramatically. Although this may not seem surprising in itself, the individual contributions nevertheless also reveal that national courts appear to hold different views as to whether the principles are to be seen as imposing an obligation of process (i.e. as impacting on the methods to be applied), or an obligation of result alone – or perhaps even both. Given that the "result and/or method" issue may also be seen as linked to the "as far possible" requirement, and hence to the very limits of the principle, we shall return to it in more detail later on (section 5.1 below). It is nevertheless also worth noting already here, as related to reception of the conceptual nature of the EU/EEA principles themselves.

Case-law of the ECJ clearly shows that the EU principle of consistent interpretation not only entails a duty of results, but may also impact on the national methods applied in order to reach them. As mentioned in the previous section, for example, following *Björnekulla* the duty of national courts to interpret national law as far as possible in the light of the wording and the purpose of a directive "applies notwithstanding any contrary interpretation which may arise from the *travaux préparatoires* for the national rule".[55] The ECJ also recently clarified in *Ajos* and *Ognyanov* that the duty entails the obligation for national courts to change their established case-law if it is based on an interpretation of national law that is incompatible with EU law.[56] As we have also just seen, the EFTA Court's guidance in *Merrill Lynch* was clearly directed towards the method to be applied by the national court in seeking an EEA-consistent interpretation (i.e. requirement of presumptive legislative intent), and not simply the result to be reached.

---

54 Emphasis added. Case E-28/13, *Merrill Lynch* [2014] EFTA Ct. Rep. 970, para. 41.

55 Case C-371/02, *Björnekulla*, ECLI:EU:C:2004:275, para. 13.

56 Case C-441/14, *Ajos*, ECLI:EU:C:2016:278, para. 33; with further ref. to Case C-456/98, *Centrosteel*, ECLI:EU:C:2000:402, para. 17; confirmed in Case C-554/14, *Ognyanov*, ECLI:EU:C:2016:835, para. 67.

The fact that national methods of construction and interpretation might therefore need to be adapted to fit the requirements under EU law also seems largely accepted by national courts of the EU Member States covered in this book.[57] Contrary to Slovenian legal tradition, as already mentioned above, the Slovenian Constitutional Court now for example requires administrative authorities to apply the EU principle of consistent interpretation, and for this to prevail over national legislation in cases of incompatibility. It also formally views the principle as a unique interpretative method in its own right, notwithstanding that it might also potentially be seen to fall within the teleological interpretative method under Slovenian law.[58]

In Poland, following the introduction of the EU principle of consistent interpretation, Polish courts may no longer limit themselves or give precedence to an outcome obtained by way of a literal interpretation alone, even if that result is unambiguous.[59] The courts are obliged to apply all principles of interpretation. As a consequence, the result obtained by performing functional or systemic interpretations in a situation where the result of the linguistic interpretation was unambiguous and clear-cut will no longer qualify as an interpretation *contra legem*. Further, amongst the results obtained by applying all so-called "first degree principles of interpretation", the court must choose the one which is most EU-conform.

In the Netherlands, the Dutch Supreme Court has held that as a result in part of its obligations under the EU principle of consistent interpretation, the wording of the Dutch law is not always decisive for its interpretation.[60] In practice, this means that the wording of a national provision may thereby be "trumped" by the (almost non-rebuttable) presumption of intent to transpose. And whilst it used to be that Dutch courts could rebut presumptions of conformity by reference to the legislative history of a given national provision, the presumption is now based on an understanding that the legislature should be deemed to have intended to transpose EU obligations correctly, unless it has explicitly stated otherwise.[61] There are also cases from recent times showing that certain Dutch courts and judges appear to view the duty to take all of national law into account as establishing a (flexible) hierarchy of national interpretative methods – if one method can lead to conformity, then this one takes precedence over all others (so-called "primacy of conformity with European law").[62]

---

57 The Finnish contributor notes more generally in this context how the influence of the ECJ's case-law may be described as in turn having developed the role and importance of case-law also in the national legal system.

58 Slovenia, p. 424.

59 Poland, p. 480.

60 The Netherlands, pp. 86–7, with further reference to Supreme Court 5 April 2013, ECLI:NL:HR:2013:BZ1780, *NJ* 2013/389 (*Albron*).

61 See e.g. Supreme Court 10 August 2007, ECLI:NL:HR:2007:AZ3758 *AB* 2007/291 (*Vierdaagse*).

62 The Netherlands, p. 96.

Intriguingly, the Dutch contribution also illustrates a fundamental change over time in the general methodological approach of its national courts in seeking out EU-consistent interpretations of national law – from viewing national law in isolation first (which will often bar consistent interpretation, as there is nothing left to interpret), to interpreting the EU obligation at issue first before viewing national law in the light thereof.[63] The practice of Norwegian national courts, although mixed, shows signs of potentially growing awareness on this point, too.[64] We shall return to this issue later on, when looking at the limits to the principle (section 5 below).

The EU principle of consistent interpretation has also led to significant adaptations of national law and method in the UK. Reception of the principle has led to a new (and much farther reaching) method of statutory interpretation being added to those already in existence, allowing courts to effectively add words to statutes which are not there in a bid to ensuring conformity with EU law – the only qualification being that such changes must be deemed consistent with the underlying aims of the national legislation in question.[65] Similarly to the Netherlands, some academic commentators also suggest that this new canon of construction would henceforth take precedence over other canons of interpretation, thus establishing a hierarchy of interpretative techniques.[66] French courts have in certain cases appeared to implicitly apply much the same method as adopted in the UK, of effectively rewriting national law to ensure conformity with EU law, with the proviso that any changes would be in line with the underlying objectives of the national law at issue.[67] The French contributor is nevertheless quick to point out that the courts will only seemingly be willing to go so far where conformity with EU Treaty rules (not secondary EU measures) are at stake.[68]

The German contribution points out how it is quite common for German courts to refer to the principle today. Certain parts of academic literature also even consider it an independent method of interpretation, as opposed to a mere addition to other interpretation methods, in the sense that it not merely results from implementing the classical canons of interpretation giving due consideration to the EU law background of the respective national law

63 The Netherlands, with reference to Supreme Court 10 August 2007, ECLI:NL:HR:2007:AZ3758 *AB* 2007/291 (*Vierdaagse*); Supreme Court 21 September 2012, ECLI:NL:HR:2012:BW5879 *NJ* 2012/532 *AB* 2012/367 (*Thuiskopie*); Supreme Court 5 April 2013, ECLI:NL:HR:2013:BZ1780, *NJ* 2013/389 (*Albron*).

64 Norway, pp. 357–58.

65 See e.g. *Vodafone 2 v. Revenue and Customs Commissioners* [2009] EWCA Civ 446; *EBR Attridge Law LLP v. Coleman* [2010] 1 CMLR 28; *Jessemey v. Rowstock Ltd* [2014] 3 CMLR 24.

66 UK, p. 228.

67 France, pp. 172–73, with further reference to *Bitouzet* [1998] Conseil d'État 158592; and *Dorries v. Ministère de la jeunesse, et l'éducation nationale et de la recherche* [2003] Conseil d'État 239085.

68 *Ambulances de France* [2013] Conseil d'État 346683.

in question.[69] According to the contributor, this view may also be attributed to the fact that the interpretative approach differs when consistent interpretation is in play: interpretation is matched to a known result (i.e. the meaning of the EU measure in question), and not only the pathway to an unknown meaning of the law. Further, *Rechtsfortbildung* seems to be taken quite far by some German courts, following the lead of the Federal Court of Justice:

> *Rechtsfortbildung* requires a gap in the texture of the statute, meaning a particular deficiency regarding its underlying purpose. In case of a national statute implementing a directive, such an underlying purpose can be reconstructed so as to serve the correct implementation of the respective directives. Therefore, whenever there are new insights on the basis of ECJ judgments with regard to the interpretation of a directive, it can be presumed that the legislator would not have issued such national legislation having known its inconformity with EU law. Thus, a gap contrary to purpose as a requirement for *Rechtsfortbildung* can almost always be supposed whenever legislation is (also) intended to implement a directive.[70]

Interestingly, the Cypriot contributors note how national courts in Cyprus generally appear to have adopted a rather narrow conception and application of the EU principle of consistent interpretation.[71] Whilst Cypriot courts have long recognised the principle of harmonious interpretation with international law – at least as far as human rights treaties are concerned – EU membership does not seem to have changed this vision enough. A similarly narrow conception may also be spied in the EFTA States of Iceland and Norway, where national courts seem to generally view the obligations imposed by the EEA principle of consistent interpretation as primarily related to the results to be reached, and not as impacting on the processes in reaching them. Of course, arguments in support for such a view can potentially be drawn from the peculiarities of the EEA legal system itself: since EEA membership was not to entail any transfer of sovereignty, national law is viewed as a matter for national courts to interpret following recognised canons of interpretation and techniques for conflict avoidance. Great emphasis seems to be implicitly placed on the EFTA Court's references to consistent interpretations being achieved by application of "interpretative methods recognised by national law", as if these might somehow thereby remain untouched by the requirements under the EEA principle.[72] Indeed, as pointed out in the account on Norway, the very application of a national principle of presumption in certain cases in seeking to resolve conflicts

69 Germany, p. 121.
70 Germany, p. 123.
71 Cyprus, p. 515.
72 See e.g. Case 14/83, *Von Colson*, ECLI:EU:C:1984:153, and Case C-106/89, *Marleasing*, ECLI:EU:C:1990:395; and Case E-01/07, *Criminal proceedings against A*, para. 39; Case E-6/13, *Metacom*, para. 69; Case E-28/13, *Merrill Lynch*, para. 42; Case E-25/13, *Engilbertsson*, para. 159.

between EEA and Norwegian law in itself indicates a clear predisposition for viewing the EEA obligation as merely related to the results to be achieved, and not the processes used in reaching it.[73] Norwegian courts have also appeared somewhat reluctant to apply the principle of consistent interpretation to all national law (particularly past case-law and preparatory legislative works), once again indicating that national methods are not to be meddled with. And in cases where national courts in Iceland and Norway have gone further in stretching national methods in order to achieve EEA-consistent results, the precise influence of the EEA duty will in any event often be hard to discern, as not mentioned at all in the decisions in question.

3.3. PRIMACY AS A (JOINT) BASIS OF THE DUTY TO PERFORM CONSISTENT INTERPRETATIONS UNDER EU/EEA LAW?

The individual contributions reveal diverging views on the relation between the principle of consistent interpretation and notions of primacy or supremacy under EU and EEA law. Confusion seems to exist as to whether primacy is to be understood as part of the legal basis of the principle of consistent interpretation itself – notwithstanding the fact that the ECJ has never said that this is the case – and what this might mean in terms of how far one must go in seeking to achieve consistent interpretations.[74] Whilst some contributors are keen to note how their national courts treat primacy as an issue separate to consistent interpretation (e.g. Finland), the contribution on Italy, for example, links application of the principle of consistent interpretation with primacy concerns. In Slovenia, the national courts have at times said that the principle stems from the duty of cooperation (i.e. Art. 4(3) TEU), whilst at other times claiming that it rests on the principle of supremacy. And in finding that the duty to perform consistent interpretations applies not only to courts but also to administrative bodies, the Slovenian Constitutional Court seemed to do so on the basis of a

73 Norway, p. 327.

74 The ECJ has set out (and developed) its view as to the bases of the EU principle many times, referring to Art. 289 TFEU, the principle of effectiveness and the principle of sincere cooperation (Art. 4 TEU) – see e.g. Joined Cases C-397–403/01, *Pfeiffer*, ECLI:EU:C:2004:584. The EFTA Court has similarly set out its views concerning the legal bases of the EEA principle in several cases, although on distinct legal authorities – including the EEA principle of sincere cooperation (Art. 3 EEA), the public international law principle of effectiveness, the objectives of the EEA Agreement, and the objectives sought by Art. 7 and Art. 104 EEA (i.e. the duty to implement EEA directives and regulations into national law). It is interesting to note, however, that the EFTA Court has in one case referred to Protocol 35 to the EEA Agreement (i.e. EEA quasi-primacy requirements) in the same breath, which may be indicative of a slightly different view as to the relation between consistent interpretation and (quasi-)primacy under EEA law (see Case E-18/11, *Irish Bank*, paras. 122–23). Both courts nevertheless seem to be largely content today to merely reiterate that the principles are inherent in the EU Treaties and EEA Agreement.

primacy argument.[75] The Cypriot contribution points out for its part how the mandate of national courts to perform consistent interpretations appears anchored in the principle of supremacy.[76] It is also suggested in the Norwegian contribution that cases such as *Ajos* may be seen to contribute to blurring the lines between primacy requirements and consistent interpretation as a matter of EU law.[77]

The reasons why confusion appears to exist on this point seems difficult to pinpoint, but may possibly be linked to certain decisions of the ECJ where it has gone quite far in instructing national courts as to the interpretative results to be achieved.[78] It is potentially more difficult to explain in an EEA context, however, since the EFTA Court to date – whilst not remiss in reminding national courts of the general duty to perform consistent interpretations – has generally refrained from requiring particular interpretative outcomes in cases referred to it by national courts under the Advisory Opinion procedure. Icelandic courts nevertheless appear to view consistent interpretation and quasi-primacy under EEA law as more intricately linked.[79] The reason for this seems largely connected to the way in which the EEA variant of primacy is said to have been incorporated into Icelandic law under Art. 3 of the EEA Act. Although the bare wording of the provision would only appear to set out a duty to perform consistent interpretations,[80] the explanatory notes to the Act state that it is also to be understood as providing a rule requiring priority of EEA rules based on *lex specialis*. The latter is strictly speaking not a rule of interpretation as such, but a rule to solve conflicts between norms. The somewhat confusing message in terms of it being a rule to secure primacy have landed Iceland in potentially hot water, with the ESA at the time of writing currently looking into possible action against Iceland for failure to adequately implement Protocol 35 under national law.[81]

3.4. SYMBIOSIS AND SUBSTITUTABILITY WITH DIRECT EFFECT AND STATE LIABILITY

The individual contributions show signs of an increasing (and welcome) awareness amongst national courts of the symbiotic relationship between the

75 Slovenia, p. 426.
76 Cyprus, p. 503.
77 Norway, p. 328.
78 See cases mentioned in nn. 228 and 229 below.
79 Iceland, p. 372.
80 "Statutes and regulations shall be interpreted, in so far as appropriate, in conformity with the EEA Agreement and the rules based thereon form."
81 See *Letter of formal notice to Iceland concerning Iceland's implementation of Protocol 35 to the EEA Agreement*, Brussels, 13 December 2017, Case No. 71655, Decision no.: 212/17/COL.

three mechanisms for ensuring the effectiveness of EU law – i.e. consistent interpretation, direct effect and state liability. As far as developments in the EFTA States are concerned, it is naturally important to recall that EEA law does not require direct effect – although the EFTA States remain free to apply such a principle of their own accord.[82] In practice this means that there are only two ways by which to enforce wrongly or unimplemented directives and regulations under EEA law – namely consistent interpretation and state liability. And as pointed out in the Norwegian and Icelandic contributions, given the lack of direct effect (and full primacy), and the inability of state liability to remedy a situation in the same way (i.e. beyond mere compensation), the principle of consistent interpretation may arguably be seen to play an even more integral role under EEA law than in EU law.

In spite of its relatively clear guidance on the issue, national courts do not always consider the three principles in the systemic order implied by more recent ECJ case-law: with consistent interpretation as the first port of call to be tested, followed by application of direct effect (coupled with primacy), and finally compensation by way of state liability.[83] The EFTA Court has mirrored the ECJ's approach, providing that consistent interpretation should be attempted first before venturing the issue of state liability.[84]

The explanation as to why consistent interpretation should be considered before direct effect/primacy seems linked to the general contention that the application of national law (as opposed to exclusion or substitution thereof) in order to give effect to EU law will always be the least invasive measure on the national legal orders of the Member States. Whilst this may well be the case in many situations, perhaps less so in cases where the ECJ imposes strong duties to achieve particular interpretative outcomes, in turn requiring the national referring court to perform strained or creative (if not to say potentially *contra legem*) interpretations of national law. The fact that state liability is considered as a last resort should come as less of a surprise, as only consistent interpretation and direct effect will ensure that breaches of EU/EEA law are remedied, by rendering the specific EU/EEA rights and duties at issue enforceable before national authorities in practice. See e.g. the *Ajos* case, where

---

82 See e.g. Case E-18/11, *Irish Bank* [2012] EFTA Ct. Rep. 592, para. 122.

83 It is certainly true that the ECJ in some cases has not followed a clear order itself. Indeed, this is not perhaps surprising. In certain cases, it may well prove that consistent interpretation seems more problematic than e.g. setting a provision aside and applying EU law in its stead (i.e. through the combined effects of direct effect and primacy), in which case it would seem to make more sense to revert to these principles directly. ECJ decisions of the past 20 years or so nevertheless reveal a much clearer emerging pattern as to the order to be followed – see e.g. Case C-222/84, *Johnston*, ECLI:EU:C:1986:206; Case C-327/00, *Santex*, ECLI:EU:C:2003:109; and Case C-441/14, *Ajos*, ECLI:EU:C:2016:278.

84 Case E-28/13, *Merrill Lynch*, paras. 40–45.

the Danish Supreme Court seemed to suggest in its referral for a preliminary ruling that it should be allowed to weigh the possibility of state liability as a factor in considering whether it might be possible to perform a consistent interpretation of national law – a contention ultimately refuted by the ECJ, thus indicating that state liability should not be viewed as a substitute for consistent interpretation, but as a mere third (and seemingly lesser) choice.[85]

Discernible patterns of the order followed by national courts are also starting to emerge in many countries. In *Gunnarsson*, the Icelandic Supreme Court for example appears to have implicitly adopted the EFTA Court's preferred sequence – looking at consistent interpretation before state liability (although both were ultimately ruled out in the end). Norwegian court practice also seems in line with the EFTA Court's understanding, at least as far as can be implied from the two *Finanger* cases: since consistent interpretation was not possible in the seminal *Finanger I* case, the Norwegian Supreme Court strongly hinted that a subsequent claim for compensation on the basis of state liability would be the way to go – a claim which was raised, and ultimately proved successful, in *Finanger II*.[86] Italian courts also appear to implicitly recognise that conforming interpretation is to be preferred where possible, with disapplication viewed as a secondary measure, and state liability "nothing more than a pale surrogate available to the few, which is incapable of guaranteeing the effectiveness and superiority of EU law".[87] Much the same may also be implied from the experience of French national courts, in that direct effect is attempted only where consistent interpretation proves impossible. Further in Poland, in *Magoora*, where the Supreme Administrative Court impliedly adopted the same approach, as indicated to it by the ECJ in a referral at an earlier stage in the proceedings.[88]

The preferred order of sequence seems more expressly embraced in Finland. In *KKO:2005:145*, referring to the ECJ's decisions in *Murphy* and *Engelbrecht*, the Finnish Supreme Court for example held that the question of direct effect should only be examined if it is not possible to interpret national law consistently with EU law.[89] Both legal doctrine and case-law further make clear that consistent interpretation is the primary way in which courts give effect to EU law in

---

85 Case C-441/14, *Ajos*, ECLI:EU:C:2016:278.

86 Rt-2000-1811 (*Finanger I*); Rt-2005-1365 (*Finanger II*).

87 Italy, pp. 201 and 205, with further reference to Council of State, V Division, 14.12.2011, no. 6543. The contributors further point out how it may be implied from case-law of the Italian Constitutional Court that the presumption of conformity is to be preferred to a declaration of unconstitutionality or to the non-application of the law only because it is a judicial measure less traumatic than the other two aimed to ensure the compliance with art. 11 Const.

88 I FSK 1471/09 of 18.3.2011; Case C-414/07, *Magoora sp. z o.o.v Dyrektor Izby Skarbowej w Krakowie*, ECLI:EU:C:2008:766.

89 Case 157/86, *Murphy*, ECLI:EU:C:1988:62; Case C-262/97, *Engelbrecht*, ECLI:EU:C:2000:492.

practice, and that such cases significantly outnumber those involving direct effect or primacy.

In Denmark, although there certainly appears to be a general awareness of the interplay between the various mechanisms – particularly when looking at the ECJ decisions and national responses in cases such as *Ajos* – no set sequence appears to be strictly followed by the national courts.[90] Likewise in Slovenia, where the national courts instead look to simply provide reasons why one particular principle has been used in the case at hand. Indications from the Slovenian Supreme Court nevertheless suggest that consistent interpretation should be considered before direct effect/primacy.[91] It is also commonly accepted (at least in legal doctrine) that state liability remains an *ultima ratio* measure for restituting breaches of EU law.

Experiences of the UK courts illustrate the adoption of different approaches: whilst for example the possibility of direct effect was ventured before consistent interpretation by the House of Lords in *White v. White*,[92] other cases seem to follow a pattern of assessing consistent interpretation, direct effect and state liability in this order.[93] According to the UK contributor, however, the general approach of the UK courts is to first consider whether the application of direct effect is possible before turning to the principle of consistent interpretation. In later cases, there tends to be no mention of the doctrine of direct effect if the dispute arises between two private parties.[94]

Beyond the issue of the order of sequence to be followed, there are nevertheless indications from national case-law that awareness of the symbiotic relationship could be even better. In Cyprus, for example, a majority of the Supreme Court in *Motilla* ruled out consistent interpretation, without apparently discussing alternative routes for ensuring effectiveness (i.e. direct effect/state liability).[95] Certain decisions of the Icelandic Supreme Court are also very interesting from the perspective of venturing alternative routes of ensuring effectiveness. In *Flugastraumur* and *Gunnarsson*, having first ruled out the possibility of consistent interpretation of the relevant Icelandic laws at issue on the basis of

---

90 Case C-441/14, *Ajos*, ECLI:EU:C:2016:278; and the final decision of the Danish Supreme Court, *UfR A 2017.824*. See also Case C-321/05, *Kofoed*, ECLI:EU:C:2007:408, following which the case was subsequently withdrawn by the Danish Ministry of Taxation before the Eastern High Court had the chance to reach a verdict.

91 Slovenia, pp. 429–30, with further reference to *Judgment X Ips 18/2013* of 19 September 2013 (*Pelati* case).

92 UK, p. 249, *White v. White* [1999] 1 CMLR 1251.

93 See e.g. the Court of Appeal in *Google Inc v. Judith Vidal-Hall* [2015] EWCA Civ 311.

94 See e.g. *EBR Attridge Law LLP v. Coleman* [2010] 1 CMLR 28, *Jessemey v. Rowstock Ltd* [2014] 3 CMLR 24, and *Google* (ibid).

95 Cyprus, p. 518, Supreme Court (full bench), Administrative Case No. 673/2006, *Cresencia Cabotaje Motilla v. the Republic* [2008] 3 CLR 29.

Art. 3 of the EEA Act, the Supreme Court touted two alternative avenues of redress: infringement proceedings raised by the ESA against Iceland on the basis of Art. 31 SCA, and state liability, respectively. As it proved, however, both of these alternatives have certain weaknesses. Firstly, infringement proceedings are the sole prerogative of the ESA, and there is no guarantee that it will raise a case against the EFTA State concerned. Furthermore, even if such proceedings were to be raised and the EFTA State found in breach of EEA law, in the event that the ESA's decision was to be challenged, the EFTA Court ultimately lacks the same effective enforcement powers of the ECJ. Secondly, as demonstrated in the *Gunnarsson* case itself, given the narrow construction of the conditions for state liability – and particularly the difficulties in fulfilling the "sufficiently serious"-criterion – the prospect of winning through with such claims will often prove more illusory than real in practice.[96]

The difficulties of winning through with state liability claims may naturally be offset in other ways in the EU Member States – such as illustrated in the UK Court of Appeal's decision in *Google v. Vidal-Hall.*[97] After ruling out the possibility of a consistent interpretation of the relevant provision of the Data Protection Act, although the Court hinted to the possibility of state liability as an alternative remedy, the offending national provision was ultimately struck down under reference to Art. 47 of the EU Charter instead.[98]

Finally, the fact that Danish courts have only set aside national legislation once in 160 years not only indicates potential preference for consistent interpretation as the main (and first) port of call – it may also be potentially indicative of an exceptionally high threshold for winning through with claims based on direct effect to begin with.[99]

---

96 As pointed out by the Icelandic contributors, only one-third of cases of this nature in the UK finally end up recognising state liability, and only one-quarter of cases in Germany (T. Lock, "Is private enforcement of EU law through State Liability a myth? An assessment 20 years after Francovich" (2012) 49 *Common Market Law Review* 1675–1702). In Iceland, over a period of more than 20 years, state liability has only been acknowledged once, in the case of *Sveinbjörnsdóttir*.

97 n. 93 above.

98 Yet the options may not always be so apparent to the national court dealing with the case, or perhaps not raised by the parties thereto. The Dutch contributor, for example, points to two decisions of national courts in the sphere of criminal law as "obvious examples of interpretations *contra legem*". Indeed, in one case, the national court added a condition to a criminal offence so as to avoid a prohibited restriction on the internal market, and in the other, the court interpreted "50 mg/kg" as "100 mg/kg" so as to avoid a violation of European law. Although the interpretations were understandable as clearly to the benefit of the defendants in the cases, the question remains whether it might not have been easier to simply disapply the national measures in question instead.

99 Although the tendency for many cases involving issues of direct effect and consistent interpretation referred to the ECJ by Danish courts to end up being settled out of court before the national referring court had a chance to arrive at a final decision may also provide a somewhat misleading picture.

4. RECEPTION AND UNDERSTANDING OF THE PRINCIPLE'S SCOPE AND CRITERIA FOR APPLICATION

The ECJ's constant and dynamic evolution of the principle through its case-law over the last 30 years has provided increasing amounts of guidance and clarity concerning the more precise ambit of the principle and its criteria for application. The case-law of the national courts nevertheless shows how such questions still arise relatively often in practice today. The individual contributions reveal that uncertainty still seems to exist with regards to several key issues, such as how far the duty to consider "national law as a whole" actually extends in practice (section 4.1); the principle's impact on the use of national preparatory legislative works as aids to interpretation (section 4.2); application of the principle to national legislative measures that pre-date the EU/EEA measure in question (section 4.3); whether the requirements for direct effect need to be satisfied for consistent interpretation to apply (section 4.4); whether national courts are required to apply the principle prior to the expiry of a directive's (or in the EFTA States, also a regulation's) transposition period (section 4.5); whether and to what extent national courts are under a duty to apply the principle of their own motion (i.e. *ex officio* – section 4.6); whether the principle applies with equal force in cases involving both vertical (individual vs. State) and horizontal (individual vs. individual) party constellations, and whether it may be applied to the benefit of the State (i.e. inverse vertical reliance – section 4.7). These issues will now be ventured in turn below.

4.1. ALL EU/EEA AND NATIONAL LAW

Although as rightly pointed out in the German contribution, the principle is usually applied in relation to directives, there seems to be little doubt amongst national judiciaries in the EU Member States covered in this book that national law is generally to be interpreted in the light of all EU/EEA law. As far as the two dualist EFTA States of Norway and Iceland are concerned, this of course also extends to EEA regulations, which are not directly applicable under EEA law and must be incorporated into national law according to Art. 7 EEA. The individual contributions therefore contain several examples of national courts performing interpretations of national law consistent with a wide range of EU and EEA law in practice – including the Treaties, the Main Part of the EEA Agreement, general principles, framework decisions, case-law of the ECJ, and even certain soft-law measures.

Unsurprisingly, the examples raised in the individual contributions also show how the majority of cases entertained by national courts will usually involve the interpretation of national legislative measures in the light of EU/EEA law.[100] According to both the ECJ and EFTA Court, however, national courts are clearly under a duty to consider "national law as a whole" in their efforts to secure interpretations consistent with EU/EEA law.[101] It seems clear from the various accounts that national courts have adopted somewhat different understandings as to how far the duty to consider all national law actually extends in practice.

We have, for example, already seen how the principle may potentially or actually have impacted on national methods of construction/interpretation, and how experiences have varied on that front.[102] Concerning the duty to interpret national constitutions in the light of EU/EEA law, practices also seem to vary from one country to another. In Germany, in a case concerning the application of substantive fundamental rights for foreign legal entities, the Federal Constitutional Court provided an interpretation in contrast to the wording of Art. 19.3 of the Basic Law.[103] Without explicitly referring to the principle of consistent interpretation, the First Senate based its argument on the drafters of the Basic Law's lack of desire "to permanently exclude legal entities from Member States of the European Union", since they could not have foreseen such a high level of integration. According to the German contributor, "[t]he result of this historical reflection is openness towards interpreting the constitution in a way which avoids conflicts between the obligations of Germany under European Union Law from arising". Similarly in France, the *Conseil d'État* exhibited willingness to interpret the French Constitution in the light of an EU directive on the conservation of wild birds.[104] And in a Slovenian case from 2015, the Constitutional Court seems to have read constitutional rights to family life very broadly, and in line with the Family Reunification Directive, thus leading the contributors to conclude that "the principle of consistent interpretation had a radiating effect on the Slovenian constitutional system beyond the scope

100 Interestingly, the French account also notes an abstract application of the principle by the French *Conseil Constitutionelle*, conducting *ex ante* appeals prior to promulgation of the law when called upon to assess the constitutionality of an Act that transposes an EU directive.

101 See e.g. Joined Cases C-397–403/01, *Pfeiffer*, ECLI:EU:C:2004:584, para. 115; Case C-239/09, *Seydaland Vereinigte Agrarbetriebe*, ECLI:EU:C:2010:778. The EFTA Court has put the duty in many different ways, varying from a reference to "national law" (Case E-4/01 *Karlsson*, para. 29; Case E-1/07, *Criminal proceedings against A*, para. 39; Case E-25/13, *Engilbertsson*, para. 159), to "domestic law" (Case E-18/11, *Irish Bank*, para. 123), "the whole body of rules of national law" (Case E-18/11, *Irish Bank*, para. 124) and "the whole body of domestic law" (Case E-25/13, *Engilbertsson*, para. 163; Case E-28/13, *Merrill Lynch*, para. 43).

102 Section 3.2 above.

103 Germany, p. 128, *Legal Entities Domiciled outside of Germany* [2011] DE:BVerfG:2011:rs20110719.1bvr191609, para. 75.

104 France, p. 164, *Association ornithologique et mammalogique de Saône-et Loire et rassemblement des opposants à la chasse* [1999] Conseil d'État 164789 and 165122.

required by EU law as such construction is an expression of autonomous and spontaneous deliberation of national authorities".[105]

That is not to say that willingness to apply the principle to national constitutional law may be traced in all of the countries covered. In Cyprus, for example, the Supreme Court in *Costas Costantinou* refused to accept primacy of EU law without amendments to the Constitution, even though it had been argued (and perhaps hoped) in several quarters that the Cypriot courts would enable such acceptance by construing the Cypriot Constitution harmoniously with the obligations arising from EU membership.[106] The Supreme Court instead upheld the supremacy of the Constitution, pointing to the need for formal constitutional amendment in order to change it stance.

The ECJ has further made clear following its decisions in *Ajos* and *Ognyanov*, that national courts cannot validly claim that it is impossible for them to interpret national provisions in a manner that is consistent with EU law by mere reason of the fact that they have consistently interpreted such provisions in a manner that is incompatible with EU law – in such cases, they are obliged to change their case-law in order to arrive at result consistent with their countries' EU law obligations.[107] Although the EFTA Court for its part has yet to say anything explicitly on this point, the fundamental EEA principle of homogeneity leads to a presumption that the same must apply under EEA law.[108] The case-law of national courts nevertheless reveals a less than uniform approach to this (admittedly at times rather controversial) issue at national level. In Slovenia, whilst the Supreme Court appeared reluctant at first in the *Vnuk* case to change prior case-law where it had interpreted national law in a particular (non-EU-conform) manner, the response of the ECJ in its preliminary ruling in the case seems to have led to a subsequent change of heart in its final decision.[109] In Finland, the Vantaa District Court in

---

105 Slovenia, p. 425, *Decision of the Constitutional Court U-I-309/13, Up-981/13* of 14 January 2015 (Uradni list RS, št. 6/2015); Council Directive 2003/86/EC of 22 September 2003 on the right to family reunification [2003] OJ L251/12.

106 Cyprus, p. 500.

107 Case C-441/14, *Ajos*, ECLI:EU:C:2016:278, para. 33; Case C-554/14, *Ognyanov*, ECLI:EU:C:2016:835, para. 67: "it must be made clear that the requirement to interpret national law in conformity with EU law includes the obligation, on national courts, including those ruling as courts of last instance, to alter, where necessary, settled case-law if that case-law is based on an interpretation of national law that is incompatible with the objectives of [the EU measure in question]"; and Case C-614/14, *Ognyanov*, ECLI:EU:C:2016:514, para. 35.

108 As pointed out in the Norwegian contribution (pp. 328–29), although it has been suggested by some that this particular development might perhaps have exposed differences of such magnitude as to warrant a different approach under EEA law (see H.H. Fredriksen and G. Mathisen, *EØS-rett* (n. 53), p. 382), the general signs from the EFTA Court do not appear to support such a conclusion.

109 Slovenia, p. 421. Similarly in the UK, see the House of Lords reaction following the preliminary ruling in *Webb* – although the House of Lords had initially claimed in its referral that a consistent interpretation would not be possible, following the ECJ's reply, it subsequently changed its mind on how it had interpreted certain provisions of national law in earlier case-law.

Liskojärvi v. Juntunen also, for example, changed an established interpretation under national law, through the performance of a new, conforming interpretation.[110] Further, in *KKO:2007:34*, the Finnish Supreme Court referred to the principle of consistent interpretation as grounds for nullifying a previous judgment, despite it being *res judicata*, thereby bringing its interpretation of the relevant national law in line with an EU directive.[111]

The willingness of the national courts in these cases to apply the principle to prior case-law should nevertheless be compared to the approach in other countries. In Denmark, in the *Ajos* case itself, the Supreme Court (in)famously refused to adopt a different interpretation of national law by changing its case-law, claiming that this would amount to an interpretation *contra legem* national law.[112] The Danish Supreme Court arrived at this decision notwithstanding the clear requirements imposed by the ECJ in its preliminary ruling in the case. The account on Norway further points out how the limited national case-law on the issue to date seems mixed at best.[113] Likewise in Iceland – as we have seen, in *Flugastraumur*, the Icelandic Supreme Court implicitly rejected a request to ask for an Advisory Opinion of the EFTA Court amongst other reasons because the dispute concerned how precedents of the Supreme Court should be interpreted.[114] This should nevertheless be compared with the decision in *Arnarsson*, where the Icelandic Supreme Court – although not explicitly referring to the EEA principle of consistent interpretation, or some national equivalent – overruled longstanding case-law so as to allow for an interpretation which in result was consistent with EEA obligations.[115]

Whilst some confusion appears to have existed concerning application of the principle to contracts, it may be implied from the ECJ's ruling in *Evans* that if a contract serves to transpose a directive, then it should also be made subject to consistent interpretations in line with EU obligations.[116] This is potentially controversial, especially in light of the oft vexed and largely unresolved issue of whether (and if so what) obligations may be imposed on individuals as a result of its application. The French reporter for example points out how the principle has been applied by national courts to collective bargaining agreements in a few cases.[117] In the UK, however, courts appear generally reluctant to

---

110 Finland, p. 298, *Liskojärvi v. Juntunen*, Vantaa District Court, case 95/9236, judgment of 17 June 1996.

111 Finland, p. 308.

112 Denmark, pp. 283–84.

113 Norway, pp. 337–41. Compare the findings of the Supreme Court in *Finanger I* (where it was not willing to change precedent) with its findings in *Lifebuoy* (where it was willing to do so).

114 Iceland, p. 381. Interestingly, whilst the District Court in the case had also initially ruled that a reference was not to be made, it did so even more expressly on this ground.

115 Supreme Court Case No. 129/2001 of 25 October 2001, *Arnarsson*.

116 Case C-63/01, *Evans*, ECLI:EU:C:2003:650.

117 France, p. 165.

impose new obligations on private parties to a contract by way of consistent interpretation.[118] Greater clarification by the ECJ and/or EFTA Court may therefore be warranted on this point.

Concerning the duty to interpret public administrative decisions in the light of EU/EEA law requirements, it would seem as though most countries generally view this as (at least theoretically) unproblematic. The French contribution nevertheless points to an exception concerning individual administrative decisions – i.e. decisions targeting single individuals, concerning for example appointment as a magistrate or teacher, subsidy grants etc. – which are not made subject to consistent interpretations by French courts. Following the landmark decision of the *Conseil d'État* in *Mme Perreux*, the only path to complying with EU law in cases involving individual administrative decisions is by way of direct effect.[119]

Finally, the French contributor also calls attention to an interesting point concerning the theoretical (albeit not altogether improbable) application of the EU principle of consistent interpretation to international treaties to which France is party. Recalling the predominantly monist relationship between French and international law, Art. 55 of the French Constitution provides that "[t]reaties or agreements duly ratified or approved shall, upon publication, prevail over Acts of Parliament". The contributor argues that given the *Conseil d'État*'s general acceptance of direct effect of international treaty provisions under French law,[120] in the event that a directly effective provision of an international treaty falling within the scope of EU law were to be invoked before a competent national court, there would be little to prevent that court from applying the principle and interpreting it in line with EU requirements.

4.2. NATIONAL PREPARATORY LEGISLATIVE ACTS (*TRAVAUX PRÉPARATOIRES*)

Connected with the requirement of interpreting the whole of national law as far as possible in the light of the wording and purpose of EU/EEA obligations, the ECJ ruled in *Björnekulla* that the duty further "applies notwithstanding any contrary interpretation which may arise from the *travaux préparatoires* for the national rule".[121] Notwithstanding the fact that it is the final statutory text

118 UK, pp. 249–50. See e.g. House of Lords in *White v. White* (n. 46), although an EU-conform result was in fact achieved by applying other national methods of contractual construction. Compare nevertheless with the High Court's findings in *UK Insurance Ltd v. Holden* [2016] EWHC 264.

119 *Mme Perreux* [2009] Conseil d'État 298348.

120 *GISTI* [1997] Conseil d'État 163043. The criteria for direct effect have been updated and approximated with those applicable under EU law, see e.g. *GISTI et FAPIL* [2012] Conseil d'État 322326.

121 Case C-371/02, *Björnekulla*, ECLI:EU:C:2004:275, para. 13.

and not the preparatory works which are directly communicated to the public, and on which they might therefore be expected to rely, the ECJ's decision is still controversial – the use of *travaux préparatoires* as aids to interpreting national legislative (and other) measures is considered second nature in many national legal cultures, and an extension of the text of the legal provisions to which they relate. Whilst preparatory legislative works are not to be used to rule out or bar consistent interpretations of national law, the individual contributions nevertheless provide several examples of national courts doing just so.

In Slovenia, "genetic interpretation" is considered as simply one of many competing national methods of interpretation to which no greater significance is supposed to be attached than any others. Notwithstanding the Constitutional Court's findings in *Up-2012/08*, where it implied that the principle of consistent interpretation must apply irrespective of the purpose of the national legislation as reflected in the *travaux préparatoires* thereto,[122] the Slovenian account also calls attention to certain decisions where the National Review Commission for Reviewing Public Procurement Award Procedures (NRC) relied on the *travaux préparatoires* of national rules at the expense of interpretations consistent with EU law. In one of its decisions, the NRC appears to have used the *travaux préparatoires* in order to interpret national provisions concerning the amendment of procurement bids broadly, contrary to the restrictive approach adopted under the EU Public Procurement rules as interpreted by the ECJ.[123]

The Danish contribution provides two specific examples of Supreme Court decisions – *Grøngaard and Bang* and the *Compensatory Vacation* case – where interpretations of national law consistent with EU obligations were ruled out *inter alia* under reference to preparatory acts of the national implementing legislation.[124] The result in *Grøngaard and Bang* seems all the more contentious in light of the ECJ's clear guidance as to the interpretative result to be achieved, which it had provided by way of preliminary ruling at an earlier stage in the proceedings.[125]

In Finland, although preparatory works are widely used by national courts in interpreting national law, the contributor suggests that they generally tend to be ignored where they contradict later EU measures.[126] In *Candolin*, the Finnish Supreme Court therefore appeared to interpret national law in line with an EU directive, even though the preparatory works to the national provision called for another solution.[127] And although the Finnish Supreme Court in

---

122 Slovenia, p. 435, *Decision Up-2012/08* of 5 March 2009 (Uradni list RS, št. 22/2009; OdlUS XVIII, 65).
123 Slovenia, p. 435–36, *Order no. 018-260/2014* of 18 December 2014.
124 Denmark, pp. 276 and 268, *U 2009.2142.H*; and *U 2014.914 H.*
125 Case C-384/02, *Grøngaard and Bang*, ECLI:EU:C:2005:708.
126 Finland, pp. 310–11.
127 *KKO 2005:145*, 30.12.2005.

KKO:2005:139 cited preparatory works in support of the literal meaning of a national statutory text as grounds for refusing to reach an interpretation consistent with the European Arrest Warrant Framework Decision,[128] the preparatory works did not appear decisive of the issue, and the final decision was in any event arguably in line with the ECJ's ruling in *Pupino.*[129]

In the Netherlands, national courts have in earlier case-law relied upon preparatory legislative acts in order to rule out consistent interpretations – such as, for example, in *Asseldonk/Ter Schure* (1995), where both the wording and parliamentary history of the national legislation were referred to by the Dutch Supreme Court in finding that a result in line with Directive could not be reached.[130] More recent case-law nevertheless appears to have reversed this trend. In *Vierdaagse* (2007), the Dutch Supreme Court – echoing the ECJ's decision in *Björnekulla*, yet not explicitly referring to it – held that as long as the wording of a national provision allows for a consistent interpretation, then its legislative history may not be invoked in order to refuse reaching a result in conformity with EU law.[131] As pointed out by the Dutch contributor, the only way in which legislative intent may therefore stand in the way of consistent interpretation is where the legislature explicitly states that it did not intend to faithfully transpose an EU measure – no other intent can be inferred from, for example, misunderstanding what the EU law obligation entailed to begin with.[132]

According to the German contributor, national *travaux préparatoires* are generally considered to be a supporting yet not decisive factor when interpreting the law, and there is no rule to give them special preference in the event of conflicting obligations. An example is provided of a case where national legislation allowing for price adjustments in consumer contracts for the supply of electricity and gas did not provide any requirements regarding the provision of adequate notice, thereby failing to meet the requirements of two EU directives. The Federal Civil Court held that a consistent interpretation was not possible due to the fact that the preparatory works had expressly conceived this issue to be addressed by way of decree.[133]

---

128 Council Framework Decision 2002/584/JHA of 13 June 2002 on the European arrest warrant and the surrender procedures between Member States [2002] OJ L190/1.

129 Case C-105/03, *Pupino*, ECLI:EU:C:2005:386.

130 Supreme Court 20 October 1995, ECLI:NL:HR:1995:ZC1846, *NJ* 1996/330 (*Asseldonk/Ter Schure*).

131 Supreme Court 10 August 2007, ECLI:NL:HR:2007:AZ3758, *AB* 2007/291. See also the *Thuiskopie* case, Supreme Court 21 September 2012, ECLI:NL:HR:2012:BW5879, *NJ* 2012/532 *AB* 2012/367.

132 The Netherlands, p. 87, with further reference to e.g. *Albron*, Supreme Court 5 April 2013, ECLI:NL:HR:2013:BZ1780, *NJ* 2013/389.

133 Astonishingly, the court did render the respective price adjustment clause itself inapplicable due to its incompatibility with the directives – without elaborating on the question on what grounds national legislation shall not apply (and even discussing the issue of direct

The situation under EEA law seems more complicated. According to certain academic views in Norway, the limits to homogeneity may arguably be seen to be reached in the *Björnekulla* case.[134] As much is echoed by the Icelandic contributors, who argue that since EEA membership was not to entail any transfer of legislative authority, the obligation does not apply under EEA law.[135] Whilst the EFTA Court has not explicitly reiterated the ECJ's findings in *Björnekulla* to date, it has stated that in cases where national courts are dealing with disputes concerning the interpretation of national law specifically enacted for the purpose of transposing EEA law, "the national court *must* presume that the EEA/EFTA State had the intention of fulfilling entirely the obligations from the EEA directive [or regulation] concerned".[136] National authorities in both Iceland and Norway nevertheless clearly assume that this presumption may be rebutted by a clear statement of the national legislator (e.g. in preparatory works to the national measures in question) that it had no intention of implementing the EEA obligation in question. Although the issue has remained more theoretical to date in Iceland, in its final decision in *Merrill Lynch*, the Supreme Court nevertheless clearly indicated that it would not be prepared go against a clear and unambiguous statement of the legislator to such effect.[137] The *travaux préparatoires* to the Norwegian EEA Act also make the same proviso, and have been emphasised by the Norwegian Supreme Court in certain cases. Certain decisions of the Norwegian Supreme Court also show how even less clear indications in preparatory works may be relied upon to rebut the presumption of parliamentary intent to legislate in line with EEA obligations, and as partial grounds in ruling out consistent interpretations.[138] There are nevertheless also examples of Norwegian courts seeking to exploit the equivocal

---

applicability of the Directive and negating it in the case at hand), Federal Civil Court: NJW 2016, 1718, 1721, 1724.

134 See H.H. Fredriksen and G. Mathisen, *EØS-rett* (n. 53), p. 382.

135 Iceland, p. 401.

136 Emphasis added. Case E-28/13, *Merrill Lynch*, para. 41.

137 Supreme Court Case No. 231/2015 of 17 April 2015, *LBI hf. v. Merrill Lynch International*. See also the Icelandic Supreme Court's decision in Case No. 181/2006 of 25 January 2007, *Criminal proceedings against Jóhannesson and Others*, where it appeared to indicate that a lot will be required of the preparatory works before an intention not to implement in line with EEA obligations may be drawn from them. Applying the method of interpretation which was the most favourable to the defendant (literal interpretation instead of a broad interpretation), the Supreme Court concluded that it would not be possible to interpret the then applicable Art. 43(1) of Act No. 144/1994 in conformity with Art. 43(1)(13) of the Fourth Council Directive 78/660/EEC of 25 July 1978 on the annual accounts of certain types of companies [1978] OJ L222/11, despite the fact the *travaux préparatoires* stated that the Act in question was supposed to be consistent with the said Directive. The reasoning of the Supreme Court nevertheless seems fully in line with ECJ and ETFA Court practice, since a consistent interpretation in this case would have established an additional criminal act which was not stipulated in Art. 43(1) of Act No. 144/1994.

138 Expressly in Rt-2000-1811 (*Finanger I*); implicitly in Rt-2006-1473 (*Lifebuoy*).

nature of preparatory legislative works in order to arrive at EEA-consistent interpretations of national law.[139]

4.3. ANTERIOR NATIONAL LEGISLATIVE MEASURES

Practice of the national courts in the EU Member States seems to indicate general adherence to the requirement of applying the principle of consistent interpretation to national legislative measures both pre- and post-dating the EU directive in question. The guidance provided by the ECJ in *Marleasing* seems to have had an important, clarifying effect for many national judiciaries in this regard. For example, in earlier (pre-*Marleasing*) times, the UK courts had clearly refused to interpret pre-existing national legislation to comply with EU law enacted at a later date, on grounds of a lack of parliamentary intent to transpose the EU directives in question.[140] This was so regardless of the fact that the national measures in question represented fulfilment of the UK's obligations under the directives at issue. Preliminary rulings were not requested in these cases, either. Following *Marleasing*, however, the attitude of the UK courts has clearly changed – today, both pre-existing and new transposition measures are rendered equally subject to consistent interpretations.[141]

The practice of national courts in other EU countries seems to reveal much the same picture. In Denmark, the EU principles of primacy and consistent interpretation are, for example, said to form a substantial part of Danish law, effective even in situations where the legislator has not implemented specific EU rules by statute or other binding legal sources.[142] Likewise in Finland, where the Supreme Administrative Court has held that even national law promulgated before the entry into force of an EU directive, or which does not seek to achieve the legal situation mandated by it, should where possible be interpreted in line with the wording and objectives of the directive.[143] The German contributor also points out how German courts are only obliged to choose an interpretation favourable to a directive as long as it appears justifiable according to the recognised methods (including *Rechtsfortbildung*), and that this general constitutional structure is decisive irrespective of whether or not the national law in question is intended to implement an EU directive.[144]

---

139 Rt-1997-1965 (*Stavanger Catering*), Rt-2013-1665 (*Aluminium – State Aid Recovery*), RG-2004-187 (*Tripp Trapp*).

140 UK, p. 227, see e.g. House of Lords in *Duke v. GEC Reliance* [1988] 1 All ER 626, and *Finnegan v. Clowney Youth Training Programme Ltd* [1990] 2 AC 407.

141 UK, p. 228.

142 Denmark, p. 264.

143 Finland, p. 303, with further reference to *18.12.2002/3339 KHO:2002:86*.

144 Germany, pp. 121–22.

Notwithstanding the general acceptance of applying the principle equally to measures adopted before and after a given EU measure, the Polish contribution raises some interesting examples from the case-law of the Constitutional Tribunal, in situations where national legislation is subjected to constitutional review.[145] Apparently, when verifying the constitutionality of an Act, the Constitutional Tribunal may only rely on the principle of consistent interpretation if the national law in question, where adopted before the accession to the EU, does not explicitly differ in its approach to the relevant issue from that provided for under EU law; and further, subject to the national law being open to more than one possible interpretation (i.e. allowing it to choose the interpretation being the most conform with EU law).

Fully in line with the ECJ's case-law, the EFTA Court also clarified in *Merrill Lynch* that the corresponding EEA principle of consistent interpretation applies to national law both pre- and post-dating the EEA directives or regulations concerned.[146] As pointed out in the Icelandic account, however, in light of the Icelandic Supreme Court's view on consistent interpretation in situations of posterior statutory norms conflicting with older EEA norms, it may have some issues in seeking to adhere to the view of the EFTA Court.[147] In its material ruling in *Merrill Lynch*, the Supreme Court held that it would only apply the Icelandic legislation that was finally amended (following intervention of the ESA) to comply with the Directive in line with the interpretation of the EFTA Court, to facts or law arising subsequently to that amendment.[148] Attention is nevertheless also called to the Icelandic Supreme Court's decision in *Akureyrarbær*, where it interpreted anterior national legislation on gender equality in compliance with a directive which came into force with the EEA Agreement in 1994.[149] As far as the practice of Norwegian courts is concerned, whilst the Supreme Court's decision in *Finanger I* seemed to hint rather strongly at EEA measures having to be specifically implemented in order to trigger application of the principle (or its Norwegian equivalent), the more recent decision of the Court of Appeal in the *Tippinga* case nevertheless points in a different direction.[150] With practice at best pointing both ways, it seems fair to contend that the EFTA Court's contention has proven somewhat difficult for the national courts of the EFTA States to fully

145 Poland, p. 492, *K 2/02; K 33/03.*

146 Case E-28/13, *Merrill Lynch*, para. 42: "Moreover, it is inherent in the objectives of the EEA Agreement, as well as in recital 15 in its preamble and Art. 1 and 3 EEA, that when a national court applies domestic law, whether adopted before or after the directive, it is bound to interpret national law within its competence in conformity with EEA law."

147 Iceland, p. 400.

148 Supreme Court Case No. 250/2015 of 21 April 2015, *Kaupþing hf. v. Merrill Lynch International.*

149 Supreme Court Case No. 11/2000 of 31 May 2000, *Akureyrarbær v. The Equal Right Complaints Committee.*

150 LB-2009-99914 (*Tippinga*).

embrace in practice – notwithstanding the clear homogeneity concerns this ultimately raises.

4.4. SUFFICIENT CLARITY/PRECISION OF THE EU/EEA MEASURES?

The ECJ has long held that the duty to perform consistent interpretations exists even for provisions of EU measures which do not satisfy the basic conditions for direct effect (i.e. sufficient clarity, precision and unconditionality).[151] Many national courts appear to adhere to this in practice, too. The contribution on Cyprus, for example, refers to the *Constantinos Oikonomou* case, where the judge referred to the duty of consistent interpretation applying irrespectively of whether or not direct effect could be triggered.[152] The Finnish contributor also refers to a decision where the Finnish Supreme Administrative Court expressly stated that national law with relevance to EU law is to be interpreted in the light of the wording and the purpose of the directive regardless of whether it has direct effect.[153]

The practice of national courts is not always consistent on this point, though – as can be seen, for example, in the Danish Eastern High Court's decision in *U 2003.233 Ø*, where it appeared to wrongly assume that EU-consistent interpretation required the provisions in EU directives to be precise and unconditional.[154] The Dutch account similarly points to examples where national courts have rendered application of the principle subject to the EU law measure in question being sufficiently precise.[155] Examples such as these are not altogether surprising, however – as pointed out by Prechal, a certain basic level of clarity must naturally be required of the EU/EEA measure in question.[156] The question in practice will then be how clear, precise and/or unconditional the EU/EEA measure must be, before a national court may refuse to apply the principle? Although there seems to be a lack of general guidance on this issue, if a national court were ever in doubt, it can naturally always ask the ECJ (or EFTA Court). In any event, one point seems very clear: the same clarity or precision conditioning direct effect will not be required in order to trigger a consistent interpretation. As much can be implied from ECJ case-law, which has constantly reminded national courts ever since *Von Colson* that the

151 See e.g. Case 14/83, *Von Colson*, ECLI:EU:C:1984:153; Case C-98/09, *Sorge*, ECLI:EU:C:2010:369, paras. 49–51.

152 Cyprus, p. 322.

153 Finland, p. 303, *18.12.2002/3339 KHO:2002:86*.

154 Denmark, p. 266.

155 The Netherlands, p. 92.

156 S. Prechal (n. 6), p. 185.

duty is not confined to the wording of the EU measure, but extends equally to its objective.[157]

The French contributor points out how in many decisions, the lack of unconditionality or sufficient precision was not seen as an obstacle to French courts applying the principle.[158] In certain cases where there is a margin of discretion, however, the *Cour de cassation* has appeared to require more than is even required for direct effect. This is interesting, as there does not appear to be any direct guidance provided by the ECJ (or the EFTA Court) on the point to date. The *Cour de cassation* has nevertheless held that consistent interpretation will not be possible "in proceedings between individuals" if the EU provision is not "binding" – i.e. "when an option is offered" by the directive to the Member State.[159] Where a right to waiver is offered to a Member State – such as, for example, under Art. 15(1) of Directive 85/374 concerning liability for defective products, which allows Member States to waive Art. 7(e)[160] – the absence of transposition means the provision is not binding. Consequently, in decisions involving Art. 7(e), the French courts have maintained that consistent interpretation of national law is impossible.[161] Similar outcomes may be seen in relation to Directive 2000/29 on protective measures against organisms harmful to plants.[162] This seems to go beyond even what is necessary in order for provisions to have direct effect. As stated by the ECJ in *Kügler* and confirmed in several cases since, once a directive's transposition period has passed, it cannot be argued that the Member State would have chosen to waiver the directive's provisions.[163]

According to the EFTA Court, whilst the priority afforded under the EEA principle of (quasi-)primacy requires the EEA implemented norm to be sufficiently clear and precise,[164] it has never required the same as far as application of the EEA principle of consistent interpretation is concerned. It is interesting to see how a clarity doctrine nevertheless still appears to be imposed more generally by Norwegian courts, and which has led to consistent interpretations

157 Case 14/83, *Von Colson*, ECLI:EU:C:1984:153.

158 France, p. 170, with further reference to e.g. *Motorola Mobility France v. Copie France* [2016] Cour de cassation, 1st civil chamber 15-10896.

159 *Ferring SAS* [2007] Cour de cassation, 1st civil chamber 05-10234.

160 Council Directive (EEC) 85/374 on the approximation of the laws, regulations and administrative provisions of the Member States concerning liability for defective products [1985] OJ L210.

161 *Les Laboratoires Servier* [2009] Cour de cassation, 1st civil chamber 08-12777; *Ferring SAS* [2007] Cour de cassation, 1st civil chamber 05-10234; *GAN v. Christophe X.* [1996] Cour de cassation, 1st civil chamber 93-19160.

162 *Société de conception de presse et d'édition v. société 1633* [2009] Cour de cassation, 1st civil chamber 07-21063.

163 Case C-141/00, *Kügler*, ECLI:EU:C:2002:473, paras. 59–60; Joined Cases C-453/02 and C-462/02, *Linneweber and Akritidis*, ECLI:EU:C:2005:92, para. 35; Case C-226/07, *Flughafen Köln/Bonn GmbH*, ECLI:EU:C:2008:429, para. 32.

164 Case E-1/94, *Restamark* [1994–1995] EFTA Ct. Rep. 15.

being ruled out in certain cases, although academic commentators tend to frown upon the practice.[165]

4.5. APPLICATION PRIOR TO EXPIRY OF TRANSPOSITION DEADLINE?

The individual contributions reveal that uncertainty continues to persist on the issue as to whether or not national courts are required to apply the principle of consistent interpretation prior to the expiry of a directive's transposition period.[166] Some national courts do, whilst others categorically refuse to do so. It would seem as though divergent practices on this point are directly connected to different readings of the ECJ's decisions in *Inter-Environnement Wallonie* and *Adeneler*, where it held that national courts are to refrain as far as possible, in the period between entry into force and the transposition deadline, from interpreting domestic law in a manner which might seriously compromise attainment of the objective pursued by an EU directive.[167] The question as to whether or not this duty, which flows from the principle of sincere cooperation under Art. 4(3) TEU, is synonymous with the principle of consistent interpretation, seems to continue to cause national judiciaries a great deal of confusion.

The contribution on Slovenia calls attention to several examples of the principle of consistent interpretation being applied prior to the transposition deadline, at all levels of the judiciary.[168] In *Decision Up-2012/08*, the Constitutional Court declared that administrative authorities and courts must apply the principle "from the moment of the Directive's entry into force, irrespective of whether the time-limit for implementation has expired or not".[169] The contributors also provide a rather striking example from the Administrative Court (upheld by both the Supreme and Constitutional Courts), in *Judgment U 713/2007*, where an interpretation of the Slovenian Asylum Act consistent with a directive was performed, even though the deadline for transposition had not yet passed and the interpretative result was clearly to the detriment of the asylum seeker involved.[170]

---

165 Rt-2004-610 A (*Bølgepapp*); H.H. Fredriksen and G. Mathisen, *EØS-rett* (Fagbokforlaget, 2018), p. 386.

166 And in the EFTA States, also prior to the transposition period for regulations: as mentioned previously, according to Art. 7 of the EEA Agreement, unlike the situation under EU law, both directives and regulations incorporated into the EEA Agreement are to be transposed into the national law of the EEA EFTA States. This is a direct result of the lack of transfer of national legislative competence under the EEA Agreement itself.

167 Case C-129/96, *Inter-Environnement Wallonie*, ECLI:EU:C:1997:628; Case C-212/04, *Adeneler*, ECLI:EU:C:2006:443.

168 Slovenia, pp. 432–34.

169 *Decision Up-2012/08* of 5 March 2009 (Uradni list RS, št. 22/2009; OdlUS XVIII, 65).

170 *Judgment U 713/2007* of 6 February 2008.

The UK contribution also points to an interesting example in this regard. In *EBR Attridge Law LLP v. Coleman*, the Employment Appeal Tribunal dismissed arguments based on the precedent in *Lloyd-Briden v. Worthing College*, that consistent interpretation should be ruled out merely because the transposition deadline of the directive in question had not passed.[171] It is worth noting here, however, that a specific implementation measure had in fact been introduced prior to the transposition deadline – whether the court would have done the same in the event that no specific transposition measure had existed remains perhaps a more open question.

In *Nebojsa Micovic*, the Cypriot Supreme Court accepted in principle that national authorities should apply the principle prior to expiration of the transposition period.[172] This general understanding was subsequently confirmed by the Supreme Court in *Vera Joudine*, although application of the principle was deemed irrelevant in that case.[173] The duty appears to be similarly accepted – in principle, if not yet in practice – in Finland. Although the obligation is noted in several recent decisions of the Market Court under reference to the ECJ's decision in *Adeneler*, conforming interpretations were in any event not required in any of these cases as the objectives of the directives at issue were deemed not to be seriously compromised.[174]

The examples mentioned so far should be compared with experiences in France, where the courts appear to categorically refuse to perform consistent interpretations before the end of the transposition period.[175] Case-law of national courts in other countries reveals a more conflicted view. In Italy, the contributors point on the one hand to examples of the Criminal Divisions of the Court of Cassation not endorsing interpretations in conformity with an EU directive on linguistic assistance in trials on grounds that national courts are not required to do so until the time-limit for implementation has expired.[176] On the other hand, in a more recent judgment, the same Court adopted the opposite course, in recognising the obligation to translate a sentence (with either a written translation or an oral interpretation) in favour of a detained defendant who cannot understand or speak Italian.[177] According to the contributors, this

171 UK, pp. 238–41, *EBR Attridge Law LLP v. Coleman* [2010] 1 CMLR 28; *Lloyd-Briden v. Worthing College* [2007] 3 CMLR 27.

172 Cyprus, pp. 515–16, Supreme Court, Administrative Case No. 1012/2005, *Nebojsa Micovic v. The Republic* [2005] 4 CLR 890.

173 Supreme Court, Administrative Case No. 1632-3/2005, *Vera Joudine v. The Republic* [2006] 4 CLR 430.

174 Finland, p. 310, MAO:403/14, MAO:733-748/14 MAO:652/15.

175 France, pp. 174–75, *Lego v. Klip* [2002] Cour de cassation, chambre commerciale 99-13774; *Robert X v. Thomas X* [2012] Cour de cassation, criminal chamber 12-85645; *M. X. et al.* [2015] Cour de cassation, criminal chamber 14-87403.

176 Court of Cassation, III Criminal Division, 07.07.2011, no. 26703, and Court of Cassation, I Criminal Division, 16.02.2012, no. 10296.

177 Court of Cassation, III Criminal Division, 04.02.2013, no. 5486.

"remarkable overruling is based on the very obligation on the part of every national court to interpret domestic law consistently with an EU directive, *even if* the EU directive has not yet been transposed into Italian law and the period for its transposition has not yet expired".[178] The latter approach seems more in tandem with practice of the Italian Civil Divisions of the Court of Cassation – in a case concerning the burden of proof for the purposes of recognition of the status of political refugee, it was asserted that the duty of conforming interpretation limits the national courts even when the deadline for implementation of the directive has not yet expired.[179]

A similar duty of abstention to that imposed in *Adeneler* may also potentially exist under EEA law.[180] In *Liechtensteinische Gesellschaft für Umweltschutz*, the EFTA Court held that Art. 3 EEA imposes a duty on national courts of the EFTA States to apply, as far as possible, the methods of interpretation recognised by national law in order to achieve the result sought by the EEA measure in question, from the date upon which it is made part of the EEA Agreement (i.e. the date on which the directive or regulation is adopted by the EEA Joint Committee, or alternatively at a later date owing to fulfilment of national constitutional requirements following Art. 103 EEA).[181] It is nevertheless not entirely clear whether the EFTA Court had the ECJ's decision in *Adeneler* specifically in mind in reaching its decision in this case. The fact that the EFTA Court chose to address the duty in terms of the positive duties of action under the first sentence of Art. 3 EEA is probably not decisive in itself, as an abstention could arguably be viewed as one of the particular measures which national authorities must take in order to fulfil their EEA obligations. Yet an application of the principle of consistent interpretation prior to expiry of the transposition deadline may arguably go even further than current requirements under EU law: In light of the ECJ's stipulation that the national measure must be liable to "seriously compromise" attainment of the directive's objective, it remains uncertain whether it was applying the principle of consistent interpretation, or a similar (yet nevertheless distinct) duty grounded (in part, at least) in Art. 4(3) TEU. And unlike in *Adeneler*, the transposition deadline in the case facing the EFTA Court coincided with the directive's entry into force

---

178 Italy, p. 210.

179 Court of Cassation, Joint Civil Division, 17.11.2008, no. 27310.

180 Case C-212/04, *Adeneler*, ECLI:EU:C:2006:443, para. 123.

181 Case E-3/15, *Liechtensteinische Gesellschaft für Umweltschutz* [2015] EFTA Ct. Rep. 512, paras. 74–75. See also the EFTA Court's earlier indications to much the same effect in Case E-4/01, *Karlsson*, at para. 28: "... it is inherent in the general objective of the EEA Agreement of establishing a dynamic and homogeneous market, in the ensuing emphasis on the judicial defence and enforcement of the rights of individuals, as well as in the public international law principle of effectiveness, that national courts will consider any relevant element of EEA law, whether implemented or not, when interpreting national law."

under the EEA Agreement; meaning that since the transposition deadline had in fact passed, the principle of consistent interpretation would in any event have kicked in. There does not seem to be any practice from the EFTA States to date shedding light on how their national courts view this particular duty.

4.6. *EX OFFICIO* APPLICATION OF THE PRINCIPLE

According to the EU principles of equivalence and effectiveness, if national courts may or must raise points of national law *ex officio* (i.e. of their own motion) in proceedings or in their decisions, they may or must do the same in cases where points of EU law are at issue.[182] As pointed out in the Norwegian contribution, in light of the demands of homogeneity, these principles clearly apply under EEA law, and presumably entail much the same duties (with the general proviso that such application would not be irreconcilable with the peculiarities of the EEA Agreement).[183] The question as to whether – and if so, to what extent – national courts may or must apply the principle of consistent interpretation *ex officio* will therefore ultimately turn on the application of national procedural rules. Of course, finding examples of cases where national courts perhaps have overlooked the issue of consistent interpretation may not always be that easy, which may also serve to explain why this particular issue has remained somewhat unanswered in most of the individual contributions. The Slovenian account nevertheless points out more generally that national courts are obliged to discuss all relevant arguments raised by the parties to a case, including any arguments based on EU law, as failing to do so would amount to a Constitutional violation.[184] And even where none of the parties to a case have argued for a specific interpretation, national judges must still adhere to the *iura novit curia*-maxim, and interpret national provisions in accordance with EU law requirements of its own motion. The contribution on Norway further calls attention to a case where the Supreme Court seemed completely unaware of the EEA law aspects, including potential application of the principle of consistent interpretation.[185] Another decision is also mentioned, where the Norwegian Supreme Court sidestepped potential application of the

182 Case C-72/95, *Kraaijeveld*, ECLI:EU:C:1996:404; Case C-126/97, *Eco Swiss*, ECLI:EU:C:1999:269; Joined Cases C-222-225/05, *Van der Weerd and others*, ECLI:EU:C:2007:318. Generally concerning the authority of national courts to consider EU law of their own motion, see e.g. P. Craig and G. de Búrca, *EU Law – Text, Cases, and Materials* (n. 6) pp. 239–41.

183 Norway, p. 353, with further reference to Case E-11/12, *Koch* [2013] EFTA Ct. Rep. 272, paras. 121–25; Case E-07/13, *Creditinfo Lánstraust* [2013] EFTA Ct. Rep. 970, para. 45.

184 Slovenia, pp. 418–19.

185 Rt-1998-1809 (*BUD*).

principle entirely – even though the parties to the case had raised and argued the point before it.[186]

4.7. EFFECTS OF PARTY CONSTELLATION TO A CASE – HORIZONTAL, VERTICAL AND INVERSE VERTICAL APPLICATION

Longstanding case-law of the ECJ shows that the duty of consistent interpretation may clearly apply in cases involving both classic vertical (individual v. state) and horizontal (individual v. individual) party constellations.[187] The same may also be implied from the EFTA Court's practice as far as the EEA principle of consistent interpretation is concerned.[188] The question as to whether the principles are to apply with *equal force* in both vertical and horizontal situations has nevertheless been subject to a great deal of debate. The ECJ's case-law is somewhat unclear on this point, and the issue has not been ventured at all by the EFTA Court to date. Whilst the ECJ in certain (earlier) decisions appeared to indicate that application of the principle could not lead to the imposition of civil obligations on private parties,[189] other decisions show how the effects of applying the principle could (and did) lead to precisely such a result.[190] There seems to be general academic consensus today that consistent interpretations may (and often will) lead to the imposition of obligations which otherwise would not have existed – even in cases involving private parties.[191] Without definitive clarification by the ECJ, however, the question as to whether a distinction should be drawn between various types of legal disadvantages (i.e. "obligations" as opposed to "mere adverse repercussions") in applying the principle in cases involving private parties, remains open.

---

186 Rt-2014-1192 (*Sør Aurdal*). It is worth pointing out, however, that a result consistent with Norway's EEA obligations was ultimately achieved in the end in this case, albeit by different means.

187 See e.g. Case 14/83, *Von Colson*, ECLI:EU:C:1984:153 (vertical); Case 79/83, *Harz*, ECLI:EU:C:1984:155 (horizontal).

188 See e.g. Case E-01/07, *Criminal proceedings against A* [2007] EFTA Ct. Rep. 246 (vertical); Case E-28/13, *Merrill Lynch*; and Case E-06/13, *Metacom* [2013] EFTA Ct. Rep. 856 (horizontal).

189 See e.g. Case C-168/95, *Arcaro*, ECLI:EU:C:1996:363, para. 42; Case C-321/05, *Kofoed*, ECLI:EU:C:2007:408, para. 45.

190 See e.g. Case C-456/98, *Centrosteel*, ECLI:EU:C:2000:402; Case C-291/13, *Papasavvas*, ECLI:EU:C:2014:2209.

191 See e.g. S. Prechal, (n. 6), p. 213; P. Craig and G. De Búrca (n. 6) Sometimes accused of (and confused with) allowing horizontal direct effect through the backdoor, it is important to remember one very significant difference here: whereas direct effect will see the application of EU law itself to resolve the issue, consistent interpretations will always lead to national law being applied to resolve the case. The practical effects may well be same – but then again, that is the whole point.

It is not therefore surprising to see in the individual contributions how national courts at times have come to struggle with the issue, and how approaches may differ from one country to the next when it comes to application of the principle in horizontal situations. As we have already seen in France, according to the *Cour de cassation*, consistent interpretation is not possible in proceedings between individuals if the provision provides an option to waiver when transposing EU law into national law.[192] The Danish contributors note a general scepticism in Danish courts in applying the principle in horizontal situations, as contrary to notions of legal certainty as defined as a matter of national law.[193]

In the Netherlands, initial reluctance in performing consistent interpretations in earlier cases such as *Asseldonk-Ter Schure* and *Pink Floyd/Rigu Sound* was also explained by the horizontal relationship they revolved around.[194] As pointed out by the contributor, the Dutch Supreme Court seems to have proceeded with caution in these cases out of fear of imposing obligations on individuals without sufficient basis in national law.[195] The Supreme Court appears to have changed course in more recent case-law, however, as can be seen, for example, in *Thuiskopie* (2012), where it showed an increasing willingness to apply the principle in horizontal relationships.[196]

The practice of the Norwegian courts seems far from uniform on this point. In certain cases where the Norwegian principle of presumption of compliance with international obligations has been expressly applied in an attempt to resolve potential conflicts between international (including EEA) obligations and Norwegian law, the mere existence of a horizontal party constellation has provided (partial) grounds for ruling out consistent interpretations.[197] In *Lifebuoy*, however, the Supreme Court arrived at an interpretation of Norwegian Trademark law consistent with EEA law through application of the national principle of presumption, notwithstanding the fact that the case concerned a dispute between two private parties.[198] The same can be seen in certain other cases, where neither the principle of presumption nor the EEA principle of consistent interpretation was expressly applied or mentioned.[199] Interestingly,

---

192 France, p. 169/(n. 159).

193 Several examples are referred to – such as *U 2014.914 H* (*Compensatory Vacation*), and *UfR A 2017.824* (*Ajos*).

194 *Asseldonk/Ter Schure* (n. 130); Supreme Court 15 October 1996, ECLI:NL:HR:1996:ZC2177, *NJ* 1997/649 (*Pink Floyd/Rigu Sound*).

195 The Netherlands, p. 82.

196 Supreme Court 21 September 2012, ECLI:NL:HR:2012:BW5879, *NJ* 2012/532, *AB* 2012/367.

197 See e.g. Rt-2000-1811 (*Finanger I*). See also Rt-2007-234 (*Care Expenses*), where the Supreme Court ruled out consistent interpretation in a case between two public parties, partially on the grounds that this was a horizontal situation – which is surprising, to say the least, since such cases obviously raise no issue concerning the imposition of obligations on individuals in the first place.

198 Rt-2006-1473.

199 See e.g. the Supreme Court in Rt-1997-1965 (*Stavanger Catering*); the Court of Appeal in RG-2004-187 (*Topshop*); and the District Court in RG-2005-597 (*Tripp Trapp*).

in all of these latter cases, the interpretative results reached by the courts did not appear to impose hefty obligations on any of the private parties involved – potentially indicative therefore of a greater understanding of the EU/EEA principles scope of application. As pointed out by the contributor, however, whether Norwegian courts by placing less emphasis on party constellation in certain cases can be understood as having modified their application of the national principle of presumption, or whether the change in attitude may be due to implied direct application of the EEA principle of consistent interpretation, seems rather difficult to say.[200]

Finally, it would seem as though Finnish courts do not bear any general reservations to applying the principle in horizontal situations. The Finnish narrative provides a number of examples in this regard,[201] including *KKO:2006:17*, where the Supreme Court – following a request for a preliminary ruling in the case – interpreted national trademark law restrictively, and hence in line with the corresponding EU directive, so that protection which might have been available under the national provision alone was no longer available. Although the Supreme Court made reference to primacy and as to whether this interpretation imposed new obligations on a private individual, in the same paragraph it went on to state that there was no obstacle to interpreting national law in line with the directive.

Interestingly, the individual contributions also expose many examples of cases where national courts perform EU/EEA-consistent interpretations to the benefit of the state, consequently leading to an imposition of obligations on individuals – i.e. so-called inverse vertical application. As we recall, the ECJ has generally ruled out that Member States may rely on the principle of direct effect against individuals – which is logical, as states should not be able to rely on their own failure to transpose certain EU measures correctly (or at all) in causing legal disadvantages to private individuals.[202] Similarly, the ECJ has made clear that public authorities should not generally be able to rely on the EU principle of consistent interpretation in order to impose criminal liability on private individuals.[203] In other types of public cases, however, the situation may prove

200 Norway, pp. 335–36.

201 Finland, p. 308, with further reference to the Supreme Court's decisions in e.g. *KKO:2005:145 30.12.2005* (*Candolin*), which also involved a preliminary reference to the ECJ (Case C-537/03, *Candolin*, ECLI:EU:C:2005:417, and has been observed as a situation where conforming interpretation took place in a dispute between two private parties; and *KKO:2010:20*, where it seemed prepared to apply the principle of consistent interpretation to a horizontal dispute, but came to the conclusion that national law already satisfied the requirements of the directive in question.

202 See e.g. Case 14/86, *Pretore di Salò*, ECLI:EU:C:1987:275; Case C-168/95, *Arcaro*, ECLI:EU:C:1996:363; and Joined Cases C-387, 391 and 403/02, *Berlusconi and Others*, ECLI:EU:C:2005:270.

203 See e.g. Case 80/86, *Kolpinghuis Nijmegen*, ECLI:EU:C:1987:431.

different. In *Kofoed*, the ECJ accepted (in principle) that national authorities may rely on consistent interpretations in administrative proceedings, in order to prevent private individuals from otherwise improperly or fraudulently taking advantage of (i.e. abusing) EU law provisions.[204] Having opened the door to inverse vertical application in certain scenarios, the contributors were therefore asked whether – and if so to what extent – national courts in their countries have applied the principle to the benefit of the state (and consequently) to the detriment of individuals, and whether there might be any general patterns emerging in practice.

Many interesting examples of national courts applying the principle to the benefit of the state in tax cases are provided in the Polish contribution.[205] A number of dissenting opinions in these cases also go some way in showing how further clarity might be needed from the ECJ on the issue of where the line is to be drawn more generally. Much the same can be seen in the Netherlands, in light of the Dutch Supreme Court's seminal decision in *Vierdaagse* (2007).[206] The case involved a situation where certain national tax provisions pointed towards application of a lower tariff, whereas an interpretation of these in conformity with the EU directive at issue seemed potentially to lead to taxation based on a higher tariff. The Court of Appeals declared a consistent interpretation as impossible, and in violation of the principle of legal certainty, as the legislator had presumably intended to deviate from the directive. The Supreme Court nevertheless arrived at a different conclusion, with the argument based on legal certainty failing to alter the Court's judgment. In several cases since, Dutch national courts have continued to perform consistent interpretations leading to higher tax duties being imposed than would otherwise have been the case under national law viewed in isolation.[207] Another interesting example beyond the realm of taxation is provided in *Hees/EPON*, an administrative case where consistent interpretation led to a private individual's wood burning activities no longer being allowed under a licence, thereby clearly leading to a deterioration of its legal position – although this case might well be seen to fall within the exception set out in *Kofoed*.[208]

---

204 Case 321/05, *Kofoed*, ECLI:EU:C:2007:408, para. 45: "although it is true that the requirement of a directive-compliant interpretation cannot reach the point where a directive, by itself and without national implementing legislation, may create obligations for individuals or determine or aggravate the liability in criminal law of persons who act in contravention of its provisions, *a Member State may nevertheless, in principle, impose a directive-compliant interpretation of national law on individuals*" (emphasis added). Confirmed in Case C-53/10, *Mücksch*, ECLI:EU:C:2011:585, paras. 33–35.

205 Poland, pp. 484–90.

206 Supreme Court 10 August 2007, ECLI:NL:HR:2007:AZ3758, *AB* 2007/291.

207 The Netherlands, p. 90 with further reference to e.g. Supreme Court 6 June 2008, ECLI:NL:HR:2008:BD3139 *AB* 2008/214 (*Joustra*).

208 Administrative Jurisdiction Division of the Council of State 20 June 2001, ECLI:NL:RVS:2001:AB2437, *AB* 2001/260.

As far as the outcome in *Kofoed* itself is concerned, the case was dropped by the Danish Ministry following the ECJ's preliminary ruling in the case, and hence before the Supreme Court had the chance to render a final verdict.[209] The Danish contributors nevertheless point to two further judgments concerning value added tax (VAT), which seem to point in different directions. *U 2000.1000 Ø* concerned a bowling facility's alleged obligation to pay VAT on income generated from non-professional sports activities. Whilst such income would attract VAT according to Art. 13 (a)(1)(m) of the Sixth VAT Directive,[210] it was not required under Section 13 of the Danish VAT Act. The Eastern High Court decided not to interpret the national legislation consistently with the VAT Directive in this case, finding that the VAT Directive's requirement that only non-profit companies were exempt from the VAT obligation was not enshrined in Danish law. The High Court's decision to rule out consistent interpretation to the benefit of the private individual involved should nevertheless be compared with the Supreme Court's approach many years later in *U 2011.1099 H*. In this second case, consistent interpretation was again not applied, yet this time to the benefit of the State (and consequent detriment to the private individual involved). The case concerned a dispute between the Danish tax authorities and the private "Roskilde Festival" association, again centring on Section 13 of the Danish VAT Act, this time in the context of the use of profits from the festival for charitable purposes. The Association argued that the Directive's rules placed it in a better legal position than under Danish law viewed in isolation, and should therefore be applied. The Supreme Court held that the conditions for VAT exemption under Section 13 of the Danish VAT Act had not been complied with. An EU-consistent interpretation could not lead to a different conclusion either, according to the Supreme Court, as the Directive did not support activities partly open to profitable purposes. The Danish Supreme Court did not refer the case to the ECJ and did not argue on the ground of the *acte clair* principle.

Moving beyond tax cases, the narrative on Cyprus provides many potential examples of application of the principle leading to interpretative results ultimately favourable to the state in decisions involving residence permit rights.[211] The Slovenian account also provides a rather striking example from the Administrative Court (upheld by both the Supreme Court and Constitutional Court), of an asylum seeker who wanted to rely on a literal interpretation of national law to his benefit, but where the national court instead performed a consistent interpretation in line with an EU directive to his detriment – even though the deadline for transposition of the directive

---

209 Denmark, p. 281.

210 Council Directive 2006/112/EC of 28 November 2006 on the common system of value added tax [2006] OJ L347/1.

211 Cyprus, pp. 515–20.

in question had not yet passed.[212] The Administrative Court also applied the principle in another case (as a supplementary argument) in upholding a Slovenian State ban on the advertising of e-cigarettes.[213] A further possible example is provided in the Finnish contribution.[214] Finnish national authorities had refused to issue a driving licence to an individual, due to vision requirements set out in an EU directive. The Directive had not been transposed correctly under national law, as the domestic provisions allowed the authorities discretion in such matters where the directive left none. The individual in question brought administrative proceedings against the State. Despite the express plea that a Member State should not be able to rely on its own failure to implement the Directive, and referring to the EU duty of loyal cooperation, the Finnish Supreme Administrative Court upheld the administrative authority's refusal to grant a licence. Finally, the Norwegian contribution provides one example where national authorities clearly sought an interpretation of domestic law consistent with Norway's EEA obligations in a manner directly detrimental to the interests of the private parties involved in the case. *Aluminium (State Aid Recovery)* concerned a claim for repayment by the Norwegian State against certain companies which had received state aid contrary to EEA law.[215] Whilst undoubtedly imposing hefty financial obligations on the companies involved, the decision nevertheless seems in line with EEA (and EU) law in light of the ECJ's decision in *Kofoed*, as any other result would have led to the companies obtaining an unfair financial and competitive advantage.[216]

5. RECEPTION AND UNDERSTANDING OF THE LIMITS TO THE PRINCIPLE OF CONSISTENT INTERPRETATION

The standard mantra of the ECJ and EFTA Court today is that national courts are required to interpret and apply national law consistently with their EU/EEA obligations "*as far as possible*".[217] Questions as to what might be possible or not, are obviously not solely related to the limits of the principle – in defining its limits we are thereby naturally also defining the principle's (outer) scope, and

---

212 Slovenia, p. 428, *Judgment U 713/2007* of 6 February 2008.

213 *Judgment of the Administrative Court I U 1561/2011* and *I U 1562/2011* of 15 September 2011; *Judgment of the Supreme Court III U 389/2013* of 8 January 2015.

214 Finland, p. 306, with further reference to *KHO 26.04.1999/889*.

215 Rt-2013-1665; Joined Cases E-5-7/04, *ESA v. Norway* [2005] EFTA Ct. Rep. 117.

216 Case 321/05, *Kofoed*, ECLI:EU:C:2007:408, para. 45 – even though this case was not mentioned in the Norwegian court's decision, or raised by either party to the case.

217 See e.g. Case C-106/89, *Marleasing*, ECLI:EU:C:1990:395, para. 8; Case C-240-248/98, *Océano Grupo*, ECLI:EU:C:2000:346, para. 30; Case E-1/07, *Criminal proceedings against A*, para. 39; Case E-15/12, *Wahl* [2013] EFTA Ct. Rep. 534, para. 54.

vice-versa. Some issues and observations already covered in the foregoing sections might therefore just as readily have been included in the present section concerning the principles' limits. We shall not spend a great deal of time rehashing such points – suffice to recall them where appropriate, and to focus instead on certain other issues concerning the "as far as possible" requirement and what it entails which have not been raised so far. These may generally be sorted under two different headings – as related to the perceived role and authority of national courts under their national legal systems (section 5.1), or adherence to general principles of law (section 5.2), particularly including legal certainty and the famed *contra legem* limit (section 5.3). Underlying all of the various issues raised in this part is nevertheless the key issue of who ultimately decides what is possible and not – the ECJ, EFTA Court or national courts of the EU/EEA Member States? At times, the answer may seem rather clear. On certain points where there seems to remain a lack of guidance from the ECJ and EFTA Court, however, the views of the national courts may prove even more illuminating as to where the boundaries may perceivably lie.

5.1. THE ROLE AND FUNCTION OF NATIONAL COURTS

The "as far as possible"-requirement may at times be seen as related to issues concerning the role and authority of national courts, and their place and function within their national legal orders. Indeed, certain earlier statements of the ECJ clearly stipulated that the duty to perform consistent interpretations only imposed obligations on the national court "in so far as it is given discretion … under national law".[218] Viewed in isolation, one might therefore be forgiven in thinking that it would be left entirely to the national courts to decide whether they had the necessary competence to construe national law consistently with EU law in a given case. The specific reference to the "discretion" of national courts has nevertheless been replaced in later case-law with the general reference to the duty applying "as far as possible".[219] And as we have seen, the ECJ has seemed content and willing to interfere more specifically with constitutional doctrines of the separation of powers in the Member States in many different ways – requiring national courts to ignore expressions of legislative intent set out in preparatory works if necessary,[220] to adopt strong(er) presumptions of parliamentary intent to legislate in tune with EU obligations to begin with,[221] and to change previous case-law in order to

[218] Case 14/83, *Von Colson*, ECLI:EU:C:1984:153, para. 28.

[219] As consistently noted in case-law since Case C-106/89, *Marleasing*, ECLI:EU:C:1990:395.

[220] Section 4.2 above.

[221] See e.g. Case C-334/92, *Wagner Miret*, ECLI:EU:C:1993:945, para. 20: "… it should be borne in mind that when it interprets and applies national law, every national court must presume

arrive at EU-conform interpretations of national law.[222] We have seen how national courts in countries with strong traditions of historical or genetic interpretations of national law (e.g. Holland) have come to accept limitations to the judicial function in this regard. Concerning the obligation to change or challenge findings in past case-law and to presume legislative compliance with EU law, the lengths to which national courts in, for example, the UK have appeared willing to go also seem rather astounding, bearing in mind the fundamental constitutional doctrine of parliamentary sovereignty and the common law system of precedence. On the whole, it seems as though national judiciaries in these – and many other – EU Member States have largely come to accept that they may not therefore have the last word on what is possible in these contexts, and that certain limits as to the judicial function may well be imposed by the ECJ in practice.

That is not to say that all national courts in the countries covered by our study have proven equally accepting of the ECJ or EFTA Court effectively (re)defining the competences and prerogatives of national authorities through its decisions. The Danish Supreme Court, for example, made clear in *Ajos* that performing a consistent interpretation of national law would not be possible in the case, amongst other reasons as contrary to the limits of its function.[223] The Norwegian Supreme Court has similarly had pause to refer to considerations based on the separation of powers doctrine in ruling out EEA conform interpretations of national law, on the grounds that this would amount to an effective usurpation of legislative power by the courts.[224] Far from feeling a sense of empowerment by virtue of the principle as some courts might naturally do, the argument here is essentially that changing the law is the legislator's job, and not that of the courts.[225] Looking at the EFTA Court's case-law, the contention may indeed be more understandable as far as national courts in the EFTA States are concerned. Although the same reference to the duty applying "as far as possible" has become standard fare in the EFTA Court's findings, it is often followed up with a statement echoing the earlier case-law of the ECJ: that the EEA principle of consistent interpretation requires the referring court to do whatever lies within its "competence" or "jurisdiction".[226] Given the already rather strained relationship between the EFTA Court and the national courts

---

that the State had the intention of fulfilling entirely the obligations arising from the directive concerned"; confirmed in e.g. Joined Cases C-397–403/01, *Pfeiffer*, ECLI:EU:C:2004:584, para. 112.

222 Section 4.1 above.

223 Denmark, p. 287.

224 Norway, p. 344, and further in Rt-2000-1811 (*Finanger I*).

225 See also e.g. Germany, p. 121, with reference to the German Federal Constitutional Court's decision in *Doorstep Selling Directive* [2011] ECLI:DE:BVerfG:2011:rk20110926.2bvr221606.

226 Case E-18/11, *Irish Bank*, para. 124; Case E-25/13, *Engilbertsson*, para. 163.

of the EFTA States, and recalling that its Advisory Opinions are not formally binding, the EFTA Court has also yet to embark upon the same route as the ECJ in effectively instructing the national courts as to the results to be achieved by way of consistent interpretation in specific cases (discussed directly below). Whilst this has been taken by some in EEA academic circles as meaning that the limits to the EEA principle of consistent interpretation are thereby determined under reference to national law alone, such a conclusion seems questionable from the perspective of ensuring homogeneity with developments under EU law.[227]

Furthermore, whilst the ECJ in many cases seems relatively content to leave questions concerning how national law might possibly be interpreted in order to arrive at an EU-conform result to the national courts alone, in certain cases it has proven much more forceful in its guidance – sometimes going so far as to effectively instruct the national court to arrive at a particular interpretative outcome in the case. The individual contributions point to several examples of such cases,[228] and many more may also be gleaned from the case-law of the ECJ.[229] This is obviously contentious, as contrary to the fundamental division of competences foreseen under the preliminary ruling procedure in Art. 267 TFEU: the interpretation of EU law is the ECJ's sole prerogative, whilst the interpretation of national law is to be left to the national courts. In most cases, however, it seems as though the national courts – perhaps wary of otherwise causing a breach of EU law by not following the ECJ's ruling – will somehow find a way to reach the mandated outcome. The national court's understanding of the conceptual nature of the duties imposed may be telling in this regard: whilst some would appear to view the principle as imposing an obligation of process (a procedural duty), some view it more clinically as an obligation of result alone – others still as both. According to the Italian contributors, the principle should be understood as imposing mainly an obligation of process, and not result – a mandatory step to be taken by courts, but not necessarily the destination to be reached.[230] This is nevertheless seemingly based on the premise that there will always be another way to reach the desired result, in

---

227 Norway, pp. 355–56.

228 Such cases will commonly "preclude" a particular (non-conform) interpretation – at times without even expressly mentioning the principle of consistent interpretation itself. See e.g. Slovenia (Case C-162/13, *Vnuk*, ECLI:EU:C:2014:2146); the Netherlands (Case C-242/09, *Albron*, ECLI:EU:C:2010:625); UK (Case C-32/93, *Webb*, ECLI:EU:C:1994:300); Italy (Case C-7/11, *Caronna*, ECLI:EU:C:2012:396); Denmark (C-203/99, *Veedfald*, ECLI:EU:C:2001:258); Poland (Case C-3/14, *T-Mobile Polska*, ECLI:EU:C:2015:232).

229 See e.g. Case C-106/89, *Marleasing*, ECLI:EU:C:1990:395; Case C-37/92, *Vanacker*, ECLI:EU:C:1993:836; Case C-215/97, *Bellone*, ECLI:EU:C:1998:189, Case C-456/98, *Centrosteel*, ECLI:EU:C:2000:402; Case C-408/01, *Adidas-Solomon*, ECLI:EU:C:2003:582; Case C-105/03, *Pupino*, ECLI:EU:C:2005:386; Case C-404/06, *Quelle*, ECLI:EU:C:2008:231; Case C-12/08, *Mono Car Styling*, ECLI:EU:C:2009:466.

230 Italy, p. 193.

the event that it will prove impossible to achieve the result by way of consistent interpretation – i.e. direct effect, or referral to Italian Constitutional Court for a declaration of unconstitutionality (setting aside provision in case at hand). The contributors do therefore also point to exceptions where Italian courts will apparently view their obligation as one of result, but only apparently in cases where support for the EU-friendly outcome can be found in at least two of three particular reference parameters: constitutional law, EU law and/or the ECHR.[231] The German contributor on the other hand points out how the German Federal Constitutional Court seems to view the principle as merely entailing an obligation of result:

> As the ECJ is not entitled to apply and interpret national law, it may not decide on the issue if there is space in national law to interpret in consistency with EU law. This autonomy of interpretation has been acknowledged by the ECJ ... The identification as well as the utilisation of methodological space of the national law is a question – even if it is determined by EU directives – decided by national institutions bound by Basic Law.[232]

According to the UK contributor, for the UK courts, the focus is similarly trained on achieving an EU-compliant outcome rather than on the process of interpretation itself – as reflected in the questions they refer to the ECJ, which tend to focus on how the EU measure in question is to be understood, rather than asking specific questions concerning the scope of the principle itself.[233] In the view of the Dutch contributor, although consistent interpretation is still first and foremost a best efforts obligation to reach a certain result, using all methods available under national law, the case-law of the ECJ does dispute the classically held view that national methods of interpretation remain untouched.[234]

One final point concerning the role and function of judges in this context is how different methodological approaches applied by national courts may also prove a rather significant barrier to achieving interpretative results consistent with EU/EEA obligations in practice. In cases where the courts appear inclined to perform a consistent interpretation, it seems that they will often start by assessing how the relevant EU/EEA law must be interpreted first, prior to

231 Italy, pp. 210–11, with further reference to the decision in Court of Cassation, Joint Criminal Division, 30.01.2007, no. 4614, concerning the European Arrest Warrant.

232 *Doorstep Selling Directive* [2011] ECLI:DE:BVerfG:2011:rk20110926.2bvr221606, Germany, p. 122. Norwegian courts seem to share the view that the (EEA) principle only imposes obligations of result, and not of method – although the EFTA Court appears to be of a different opinion. See Norway, pp. 327–29.

233 UK, p. 235.

234 The Netherlands, p. 79.

examining the national law at issue. In many cases where national courts contend that a consistent interpretation is not possible, however, they will often reach this conclusion having interpreted national law in isolation first, before posing the question as to whether it might be open to further interpretation(s) in light of any relevant EU/EEA law obligations. The latter approach is innately negative, and clearly geared more towards the result than the process of interpretation – in fact, the process of interpretation is not touched upon at all here, as the meaning of national law is established in isolation prior to attempting to view it through the lens of EU/EEA law. The methodological approach adopted by a national court may therefore often be quite revealing and predictive of the interpretative results reached in individual cases.

Several of the individual contributions spy certain trends in the national case-law of their countries in this regard. The Dutch contributor, for example, notes how the Supreme Court in early cases focused on a "means of choice-approach".[235] The meaning of the Dutch law would be established first, with an EU-consistent interpretation only proving possible in situations where national law proves ambiguous – thereby serving as a means of choosing competing interpretations (i.e. the one in line with EU law).[236] This has been changed over time, however, as one can see in the Dutch Supreme Court's decision in *Vierdaagse*.[237] The account on Cyprus also notes indications of a more positive approach, with Cypriot courts looking to interpret the EU law obligation in question first, before moving on to interpret national law in light thereof.[238] The Italian contributors note a potentially different attitude of certain Italian courts looking at national law in isolation first, thereby in turn negating the possibility of consistent interpretation (or at least application of the principle).[239] And in Norway, although academic consensus is that EEA law ought to be interpreted first before viewing Norwegian law in the light thereof, Norwegian courts appear to have adopted both approaches in different cases, with varying end results, in practice.[240]

---

235 The Netherlands, p. 80.

236 Supreme Court 20 October 1995, ECLI:NL:HR:1995:ZC1846, *NJ* 1996/330 (*Asseldonk/Ter Schure*); Supreme Court 15 October 1996, ECLI:NL:HR:1996:ZC2177, *NJ* 1997/649 (*Pink Floyd/Rigu Sound*).

237 Supreme Court 10 August 2007, ECLI:NL:HR:2007:AZ3758 *AB* 2007/291 (*Vierdaagse*).

238 Cyprus, p. 517, with further reference to Supreme Court (full bench), Administrative Case No. 673/2006, *Cresencia Cabotaje Motilla v. The Republic* [2008] 3 CLR 29.

239 Italy, p. 203. The contributors point out that when the state refers questions to the Italian Constitutional Court regarding a regional law affecting both the separation of competences and conformity with European law, the Court tends to examine firstly the internal complaints, with the result that the EU law issue is often absorbed (thereby also absorbing the possible issue of consistent interpretation).

240 Norway, pp. 357–58.

5.2. GENERAL PRINCIPLES OF LAW

The ECJ has repeatedly held since its ruling in *Kolpinghuis Nijmegen* that the duty of national courts to apply the principle is limited by general principles of law.[241] Yet exactly what general principles the Court had in mind is not always so clear.

Firstly, one might ask whether the ECJ meant general principles of national law or EU/EEA law, or some mix of both. In certain cases, it has referred specifically to general principles of EU law,[242] whilst in others it says merely that application of the principle is limited by general principles of law.[243] The EFTA Court for its part appears to have remained silent on this particular issue to date. In situations where general principles of EU/EEA law and national law appear synonymous, the issue may naturally seem rather academic – as the same limits would then apply as a matter of EU/EEA and national law. Yet the question as to whether the content and scope of the general principles is to be defined as a matter of EU/EEA law or under national law may also naturally be of more practical import. As much was illustrated in *Ajos*, where competing views of the definition and scope of the general principle of legal certainty and the *contra legem* limit as a matter of EU and Danish law led the ECJ and Danish Supreme Court to different conclusions as to whether a consistent interpretation might be possible or not.[244] The same can be seen in Norway, where practice of the national courts reveals that in cases where the national principle of presumption is applied, general principles of national law will exclusively determine its limits.[245] Much the same approach appears to be adopted by Icelandic courts, too. The Icelandic contributors, for example, point out that where fundamental rights and principles of criminal law are relied upon in ruling out consistent interpretations, the Supreme Court refers to Constitutional provisions as the source in doing so.[246] The Dutch contributor similarly points out that in the case-law of Dutch courts where the principle of legality is used as an argument in ruling out a consistent interpretation, they tend to refer to its codified version under national law or to Art. 7 ECHR, but not to EU law itself – and further how explicit references to the EU principles of legality or legal certainty are seldom

241 Case 80/86, *Kolpinghuis Nijmegen*, ECLI:EU:C:1987:431, para. 13.

242 Ibid., para. 13. Joined Cases C-189, 202, 205–208, and 213/02 P, *Dansk Rørindustri and others*, ECLI:EU:C:2005:408, para. 220.

243 See e.g. Case C-105/03, *Pupino*, ECLI:EU:C:2005:386, para. 44; C-268/06, *Impact*, ECLI:EU:C:2008:223, para. 100; Case C-441/14, *Ajos*, ECLI:EU:C:2016:278, para. 32; see also Joined Cases C-74 and 129/95, *X*, ECLI:EU:C:1996:491, paras. 24–25, where further reference is made to Art. 7 ECHR, and the common constitutional traditions of the Member States.

244 The case is returned to in more detail in section 5.3 below.

245 Norway, p. 357.

246 Iceland, pp. 407–08, with further reference to e.g. Supreme Court Case No. 15/2000 of 14 April 2000 *Stjörnugrís hf. v. the Icelandic State*; and Supreme Court Case No. 92/2013 of 14 October 2014 *the Icelandic State v. Atli Gunnarsson*.

made in the case-law of the criminal courts.[247] Further clarity may therefore be required on this issue, perhaps especially from the EFTA Court.

The second issue, which is inherently related to the first, concerns which specific general principles of EU/EEA and/or national law may be applied by national courts to limit application of the duty. The ECJ has, for example, specifically referred to the principles of legal certainty, non-retroactivity, *nulla poena sine lege* and *nullum crimen sine lege* in its case-law to date.[248] The individual contributions also provide several examples where these particular general principles have been relied upon by national courts in ruling out consistent interpretations, especially where application of the duty might otherwise be seen to lead to an aggravation of criminal liability or the establishment of a new criminal offence.[249] The French and Danish accounts also refer to cases where the principle of non-retroactivity barred consistent interpretations.[250]

The lack of a more elaborative list propounded by the ECJ has nevertheless naturally left national courts somewhat at liberty in applying other general principles in ruling out consistent interpretations in practice. The principle of legal certainty itself may, for example, be seen to have many different connotations, leading national courts to refuting the possibility of consistent interpretations for a wide range of reasons related thereto – for example for breach of legitimate expectations and foreseeability,[251] and due to deterioration of the individual's position in administrative cases or under private law.[252]

Similarly to the French contributor's observation concerning the reluctance of French courts in applying the principle when an option is offered by the directive to the Member State, the Dutch account points to several decisions where minimum harmonisation directives were viewed as barring consistent interpretations. The Administrative Jurisdiction Division of the Council of State has ruled that in situations where a directive leaves room for more stringent national regulation, but this discretion has not been used by the legislator, that no stricter rules may be imposed upon individuals as this would violate legal certainty.[253] The Dutch Supreme Court appears to have implied that the same

---

247 The Netherlands, p. 93, with further reference to District Court of Rotterdam 20 December 2007, ECLI:NL:RBROT:2007:BC0861, *JOR* 2008/46.

248 Joined Cases C-74 and 129/95, *X*, ECLI:EU:C:1996:491; Case C-60/02, *X*, ECLI:EU:C:2003:326.

249 See e.g. Iceland (Supreme Court Case No. 181/2006 of 25 January 2007 *Criminal Proceedings against Jóhannesson and Others*; Supreme Court Case No. 251/2004 of 28 October 2004 *Criminal proceedings against X*), Finland (*KKO:2013:90*), the Netherlands (Court of Appeals of Arnhem-Leeuwarden 23 April 2014, ECLI:NL:GHARL:2014:3361); and Italy (Court of Cassation, Joint Criminal Division, 19.01.2012, no. 22225).

250 France (*Mme X v. Institut Pasteur* [2006] Cour de cassation, 1st civil chamber 03-20178); Denmark (*U 2014.914 H (Compensatory Vacation)*.

251 See e.g. Denmark – *UfR A 2017.824*, (*Ajos*); and Norway – Rt-2000-1811 (*Finanger I*).

252 The Netherlands – ABRvS 20 June 2001, ECLI:NL:RVS:2001:AB2437, *AB* 2001/260 (*Hees/EPON*); UK – *White v. White* [1999] 1 CMLR 1251.

253 ABRvS 17 April 2013, ECLI:NL:RVS:2013:BZ7904, *AB* 2014/75.

limit will apply as far as minimum harmonisation directives in the field of criminal law are concerned.[254]

The Finnish narrative further explains how in some academic accounts the national principle of legality is considered as a limit to consistent interpretation, pointing to a case where the national principle of legality of taxation was relied upon to refuse to apply a conforming interpretation.[255] The Dutch contributor also calls attention to a specific example in the field of criminal law in this regard.[256]

Fundamental rights have also been called upon in some cases in order to rule out consistent interpretations, with national courts in such cases commonly referring to constitutional rules as the basis in doing so. The Icelandic Supreme Court's decision in *Stjörnugrís* concerning an administrative decision to conduct an environmental impact assessment, for example, demonstrates how the principle of legality and constitutional provisions on protection of property rights and freedom to conduct economic activity may limit the effects of EEA law.[257] In Poland, the Constitutional Tribunal in *K18/04* held that the principle of consistent interpretation could not lead to results contradicting the explicit wording of constitutional norms, or an outcome irreconcilable with the minimum guarantee functions recognised by the Constitution.[258] The norms of the Constitution within the field of individual rights and freedoms indicated a minimum and unsurpassable threshold which could not be lowered or questioned as a result of the introduction of EU provisions.

5.3. SPECIFICALLY CONCERNING LEGAL CERTAINTY AND THE *CONTRA LEGEM* LIMIT

The ECJ has repeatedly held that the duty to perform consistent interpretations does not require national courts to perform interpretations *contra legem* – which literally means "against the law".[259] Whilst this is the limit most commonly relied upon by national courts in ruling out application of the principle, we also find many examples of national courts performing what could only be described as heroic acts of creative or strained interpretation to bring national law in line with EU/EEA law commitments – both in cases where pressed or urged (often indirectly) by the ECJ to do so, and also of their own accord. The reason

254 The Netherlands, p. 97, Supreme Court 9 July 2002, ECLI:NL:HR:2002:AD7737, *NJ* 2005/569.

255 Finland, p. 314, *KHO:2014:190*.

256 The Netherlands, pp. 92–3, with further reference to the decision of the District Court of Amsterdam 3 December 2004, ECLI:NL:RBAMS:2004:AR6884 and ECLI:NL:RBAMS:2004:AR6888 *JOR* 2005/13.

257 Iceland, pp. 407–08, Supreme Court Case No. 15/2000 of 14 April 2000 *Stjörnugrís hf. v. The Icelandic State*.

258 Poland, pp. 462–63, see also *P1/05*.

259 Implied in Case C-334/92, *Wagner Miret*, ECLI:EU:C:1993:945, and first explicitly stated in Case C-105/03, *Pupino*, ECLI:EU:C:2005:386.

for this seems directly connected to the fact that the very term *contra legem* has until recently remained largely undefined by the ECJ, thereby leaving national courts free to interpret and apply the limit more or less as they pleased. Similarly to the rather "hands-off" approach of the ECJ, beyond tacit acceptance of the *contra legem* limit, the EFTA Court has not provided much guidance on this issue, either.[260] This is perhaps not so surprising, however, as national courts in at least Iceland and Norway do not tend to refer questions concerning the content, remit or application of any EEA principles, including the principle of consistent interpretation and its limits – they merely ask how particular provisions of EEA law are to be understood.

In academic circles, the term *contra legem* has generally been understood as referring to a construction of a national legislative provision which its wording cannot bear, or which deviates from an initial literal reading of the national provision in question.[261] According to this view, the focus of the limit is primarily (at times perhaps exclusively) directed towards the wording of the legislative provision at issue. If the wording of the national provision is unambiguous, and points to a different solution than that provided for under EU/EEA law, then the *contra legem* limit will often be triggered and consistent interpretation ruled out. There are several examples in the individual contributions of national courts applying the limit in this way. Whilst therefore helpful to a certain extent in seeking to explain what the *contra legem* concept means and may entail, the definition does not seem wholly adequate to reflect the realities often facing courts in practice. Even if the very wording of the national provision is unambiguous, as we have seen, national courts are also under a duty to actively seek the use of other tools in an attempt to arrive at a consistent interpretation – such as, for example, its preparatory works, (mandatory) presumptions of intent to legislate in line with EU/EEA obligations, and other recognised methods of interpretation and/or conflict-resolving principles. And in situations where the text of the provision seems ambiguous, and therefore potentially open in and of itself to interpretation in conformity with EU/EEA law, national courts may sometimes revert to these very same tools as grounds for applying the *contra legem* limit. In short, sometimes national courts may have to do more than simply focus on the wording off the national provision at issue, whilst other times they may have to do less.

Rather than seeking out a conclusive definition, it may therefore prove more helpful to think of the various approaches of national courts in defining the scope of the *contra legem* limit as falling somewhere between two opposite

260 Case E-18/11, *Irish Bank*, para. 125; Case E-28/13, *Merrill Lynch*, para. 45.

261 See e.g. S. Prechal, *Directives in EC Law* (2nd ed., Oxford University Press, 2005), p. 207; P. Craig and G. de Búrca, *EU Law: Text, Cases and Materials* (3rd ed., Oxford University Press, 2003), p. 216; M. Dougan, "When worlds collide! Competing visions of the relationship between direct effect and supremacy" 44 (2007) *Common Market Law Review* 931–63.

points of a spectrum – the two points represented on the one hand by a narrow understanding of the scope of the limit (i.e. providing limited scope for its application), and a broad understanding of the scope (i.e. providing an expansive scope for application of the limit) on the other. Crudely put, the narrower the understanding, the more likely a national court will be able to escape or circumvent the *contra legem* barrier; the broader the understanding, the more likely it will be deemed to apply. Looking at the individual contributions, it seems as though approaches may differ significantly – both as between different countries, and as between different courts within specific countries. Whilst one should therefore be slightly cautious in seeking to draw too many conclusions from the snapshots of case-law provided in the individual contributions, a few general observations may nevertheless be made in the following.

Looking at experiences in the Netherlands, the *contra legem* limit seems generally understood by the courts as meaning an interpretation going against the very wording of a provision. In *Pink Floyd/Rigu Sound*, the Dutch Supreme Court, for example, ruled out a consistent interpretation, since this would go against the "unambiguous wording" of the national provision at issue, and would therefore not be in line with the principle of legal certainty.[262] An EU-conform interpretation was also ruled out in *Asseldonk/Ter Schure*, where the Dutch Supreme Court in arriving at its result lay great emphasis on the need to interpret the national provision at issue in light of its preparatory works.[263] Following the seminal decision in *Thuiskopie*, however, it appears as though a much narrower view of the scope of the limit has been adopted. The Dutch Supreme Court held here that:

> Whenever the Dutch legislature, when enacting transposing legislation, has given a certain interpretation of the law which appears to be in contravention of the directive, the national court may not, because of this legislative history, set aside the duty of consistent interpretation ... because of legal certainty, if the legislature has had the intention of transposing the directive faithfully and the text of the national provision allows for an interpretation in conformity with the directive.[264]

As contended by the Dutch contributor, the passage suggests that reliance on legal certainty will be categorically ruled out where the wording of the national provision seems open to a consistent interpretation, and a faithful transposition

---

262 Supreme Court 15 October 1996, ECLI:NL:HR:1996:ZC2177, *NJ* 1997/649 (*Pink Floyd/Rigu Sound*). As pointed out by the Dutch contributor, though, the Court's decision in this case has been heavily criticised by several commentators in the doctrine, since the wording of the provision may arguably have seemed more pliable than the Supreme Court was willing to admit.

263 Supreme Court 20 October 1995, ECLI:NL:HR:1995:ZC1846, *NJ* 1996/330 (*Asseldonk/Ter Schure*).

264 Supreme Court 21 September 2012, ECLI:NL:HR:2012:BW5879, *NJ* 2012/532, para 5.1.3, Dutch contributor's translation.

was intended by the legislature. The focus is thereby shifted more firmly over to the question of whether there are any national interpretative methods which might lead to a result consistent with EU law. This rather functional approach is interesting, since it may potentially contribute to narrowing the scope of the *contra legem* prohibition in the eyes of national courts.[265]

Drawing inferences from academic writings and national case-law, the Slovenian contributors similarly define the term *contra legem* as meaning whatever lies outside the approved methods of interpretation.[266] Whilst interpretations *contra legem* national law would be considered unconstitutional under Slovenian law, the very scope of the prohibition seems to be narrowed from the outset, by requiring courts to look beyond the wording of the provision alone. Slovenian courts also appear to go very far in practice in seeking EU-conform interpretations of national law – in certain cases, arguably beyond the limits allowed under national law. In *Judgment II Ips 228/2013*, for example, a case concerning a tourist agency's liability for damage caused to its customers by a subcontractor, the Supreme Court went well beyond the wording of the provision at issue, and seemed to add words to the provision which were not there. And in *Decision VIII IPS 191/2010*, concerning compensation for unused annual leave, the Supreme Court relied on consistent interpretation as a tool to fill a void in Slovenian law, in a manner arguably *contra legem* the Constitution (i.e. breaching the principle of the separation of powers).[267]

The civil courts in Germany also appears to have adopted a rather unique, functional approach to the *contra legem* limit, thereby narrowing its potential scope of application. As explained by the German contributor, in the German legal culture, the interpretative competences of the courts comprises *Auslegung* (a more text oriented method of interpretation), and *Rechtsfortbildung* (a more text-detached, constructive method of interpretation). Recourse to *Rechtsfortbildung* nevertheless only comes into play when a legal provision is not considered open to an EU-conform interpretation in light of its wording, its positioning in the system of law, its historic background or its purpose, and is further preconditioned on the existence of a gap in the statute's underlying purpose:

> In case of a national statute implementing a directive, such an underlying purpose can be reconstructed so as to serve the correct implementation of the respective directives.[268]

---

[265] The Netherlands, pp. 95–7, with further reference to District Court of Amsterdam 2 September 2015, ECLI:NL:RBAMS:2015:5712.

[266] Slovenia, pp. 439–40.

[267] Slovenia, pp. 446–47, with further reference to Administrative Court decisions which (arguably) "reconstructed" national provisions to make them EU-compliant.

[268] For example in the *Quelle* case, §439.4 Civil Code as a part of national legislation attempting to correctly implement Directive 1999/44/EC including its attribution of consumer rights "free of charge" (see Art. 3.3).

> Therefore, whenever there are new insights on the basis of ECJ judgments with regard to the interpretation of a directive, it can be presumed that the legislator would not have issued such national legislation if it had known it to be at odds with EU law.[269] Thus, a gap contrary to purpose as a requirement for *Rechtsfortbildung* can almost always be supposed whenever legislation is (also) intended to implement a directive. As the Federal Civil Court understands the *contra legem* prohibition functionally as a reference to whatever lies outside the approved methods of interpretation, it consequently does not hinder such *Rechtsfortbildung* after the assessment that its requirements are met.[270]

According to the case-law of the Federal Civil Court, the limits of consistent interpretation will only be considered transgressed when an interpretation results in a change of the discernible will of the legislator and does not still (somehow) conform to its will.[271] German civil courts therefore appear to have adopted a relatively relaxed approach with regard to methodological constraints under the *Rechtsfortbildung* approach in practice, although they have suffered criticism from certain voices in legal doctrine for doing so, as arguably transgressing constitutional limits.[272] The case-law of the Federal Administrative Court is similarly characterised by ample space allowing for interpretations in conformity with EU law – administrative legal provisions are often open to dynamic interpretation,[273] and the Court is also open to interpretation via *Rechtsfortbildung*.[274] According to the German account, however, the Federal Finance Court appears more strictly oriented on the wording of the national law in question. As explained by the contributor:

> in a case concerning the preconditions for a reduced rate of value added tax, the Federal Finance Court did not deem it possible to interpret in accordance to the ECJ's understanding of the respective directive which provided for a dual requirement.[275]

---

269 For example in the *Quelle* case effectively negating the right to compensation following from §439,4 (now clarified by statute in §474 section 2 of the Civil Code); see also Federal Justice Court: BGHZ 201, 101; cf. K. Kroll-Ludwigs and M. Ludwigs, 'Die richtlinienkonforme Rechtsfortbildung im Gesamtsystem der Richtlinienwirkungen' [2009] *ZJS* 7.

270 Germany, p. 123.

271 The German contributor calls attention in this regard to a case where an interpretation in conformity with EU law was deemed impossible due to a lack of legislative intent (NJW 2016, 1718, 1722).

272 See Federal Justice Court: BGHZ 150, 248 (*Heininger*) [2002]; BGHZ 179, 27 (*Quelle*) [2008]; BGHZ 192, 148 (*Weber*) [2011]; BGHZ 201, 101 [2014]; similar Federal Labor Court: BAGE 130, 119 [2009].

273 With regard to §34 of the Federal Building Statute, see *Mücksch/Merck* [2012] DE:BVerwG:2012:201212U4C11.11.0; see also the cases deeming an interpretation in conformity possible in *Altrip* [2015] DE:BVerwG:2015:221015U7C15.13.0; *Dentist* [2004] DE:BVerwG:2004:290104U3C39.03.0.

274 See e.g. *Approval of Prices to electronic communication networks* [2017] ECLI:DE:BVerwG:2017:310117U6C2.16.0.

275 See Federal Finance Court: DStR 2012, 1177; DStRE 2006, 1534; Council Directive 2006/112/EC on the common system of value added tax [2006] OJ L347/1; Case 492/08, *Commission v. French Republic*, ECLI:EU:C:2010:348, para. 43.

> As there was no adequate indication in the respective national law text, the Court deemed the second requirement for a reduced rate of value added tax for being engaged in "welfare or social security work" as not being a possible requirement under German Tax law. The court did not even explicitly consider an interpretation by way of *richtlinienkonformer Rechtsfortbildung*, even though it has acknowledged the method in its jurisprudence.[276]

Somewhat ironically, in light of Brexit, the narrowest understanding of the *contra legem* limit at national level (at least of the countries covered by this book) appears to be that adopted by the UK courts in practice. Following a process of assimilation with the approach adopted under section 3 of the Human Rights Act, it seems clear today that EU-consistent interpretations of legislative provisions will only be considered *contra legem* if they go against the thrust, aim or grain of the statute of which they form part.[277] Furthermore, application of the principle is not constrained by conventional rules of construction, meaning that courts can (and often do) imply or read words into a statute in order to give effect to EU measures by way of consistent interpretation.[278] As noted earlier, certain decisions of the French courts (e.g. *Dorries* and *Bitouzet*) also appear to implicitly adopt much the same approach – yet only apparently where provisions in the EU Treaties are at stake, and not where conformity with secondary EU measures is at issue.[279]

Whilst the threshold therefore generally seems high, this does not mean that the *contra legem* limit has never been relied upon by UK courts to rule out consistent interpretations in practice. In *Google v. Vidal-Hall* (2015), an EU-consistent interpretation was, for example, refused as going against the grain of the Data Protection Act – the national provision in question was considered a central feature of the legislation, there was no suggestion that this was a mere drafting error and Parliament had deliberately sought to limit the compensation available in the event of a breach.[280]

The narrow view as to what will be considered as "against the law" by UK courts must nevertheless be compared with the broader understanding of the

---

276 Federal Finance Court: BFHE 243, 8 [2013].

277 UK, pp. 236 and 243, with further reference to *Ghaidan v. Godin-Mendoza* [2004] UKHL 30; [2004] 2 AC 557; *Vodafone 2 v. Revenue and Customs Commissioners* [2009] EWCA Civ 446, at paras. 37–38; *Jessemey v. Rowstock Ltd* [2014] 3 CMLR 24; endorsed by the UK Supreme Court in *Swift v. Robinson* [2014] UKSC 50 and *United States of America v. Nolan* [2015] UKSC 63.

278 Even in earlier years, the House of Lords had considered itself competent to imply the words necessary to construe national law in accordance with EU law, see e.g. *Litster v. Forth Dry Dock and Engineering Co Ltd* [1990] 1 AC 546. For other examples, see e.g. *EBR Attridge Law LLP v. Coleman* [2010] 1 CMLR 28.

279 Section 3.2 above.

280 *Google Inc v. Judith Vidal-Hall* [2015] EWCA Civ 311. See also *UK Insurance Ltd v. Holden* [2016] EWHC 264 (2016), where the national court refused to apply an interpretation which would "go against the grain" of the statute in question.

limit's scope adopted by national judiciaries in certain other countries. Case-law of the Icelandic courts, for example, appears to show an approach focused more directly on the wording of the national provision – where unambiguous, and at odds with EEA obligations, the courts have in many cases seemed to immediately rule out consistent interpretation as *contra legem*, without looking much further.[281] The Supreme Court further appears to say in *Merrill Lynch* that, regardless of whether the wording of the provision is equivocal, a clear statement set out in preparatory works to the effect that the legislator intended to violate EEA law (i.e. by not implementing EEA rules correctly, or at all) would not be disregarded.[282] Although the Icelandic courts have yet to face such a situation in practice, it may potentially broaden the scope of the limit even further.

Whilst Finnish courts also generally appear to understand the term as meaning interpretation contrary to the wording of the relevant legal provision, we also find certain cases where the limit appears extended to black letter law as further explained in the light of legislative preparatory works.[283] This is not apparently followed in all cases, though – in a case concerning a national provision on data processing, which the ECJ had declared incompatible with an EU directive, the Finnish Supreme Administrative Court relied on the national provision's preparatory works as grounds for performing a consistent interpretation.[284] According to the contributor, "[t]he case has been criticised by some as a *contra legem* interpretation of national law to the detriment of a private individual. After all, the national law expressly excluded data that had been published in media and yet the outcome of the judgment was that the processing of such data was subject to restrictions".[285] Where national courts decide to change an established interpretation of national law (i.e. changing earlier case-law precedents), however, this will not apparently be considered *contra legem*.[286]

Other national courts seem to stretch the scope of the *contra legem* limit even further. One can, for example, infer from the case-law of the Norwegian Supreme Court that it has at times adopted a very broad understanding the *contra legem* limit's scope. Its approach seems generally focused on the wording of the provision, and whether it is unambiguous or not – and the Supreme Court has on several occasions ruled out consistent interpretations on this basis.

---

281 Supreme Court Case No. 79/2010 of 9 December 2010, *Biðskýlið í Njarðvík ehf. and CU 2 ehf. v. Írena Rut Sigríðardóttur*; Supreme Court Case No. 10/2013 of 24 January 2013, *Landsbankinn hf. v. Flugastraumur ehf*; Supreme Court Case No. 92/2013 of 14 October 2014, *The Icelandic State v. Atli Gunnarsson*; Supreme Court Case No. 160/2015 of 13 May 2015, *Gunnar V. Engilbertsson v. Íslandsbanki hf.*

282 Supreme Court Case No. 250/2015 of 21 April 2015, *Kaupþing hf. v. Merrill Lynch International.*

283 Finland, p. 311, with further reference to *KKO:2005:139*.

284 *KHO:2009:82*; Case C-73/07, *Satakunnan markkinapörssi*, ECLI:EU:C:2008:727.

285 Finland, p. 310.

286 See e.g. *Liskojärvi v. Juntunen*, Vantaa District Court, case 95/9236, judgment of 17 June 1996; and the Finnish Supreme Court in *KKO:2005:145 (Candolin)*.

And even in cases where the wording of the national provision appeared open on its face to a consistent interpretation, both clear and equivocal expressions of legislative intent set out in preparatory works, and the way in which national courts have interpreted the provision in prior case-law, have led to the *contra legem* limit being relied upon to rule out application of the principle (or its national equivalent).[287] The use or disregard of preparatory works and discounting of prior case-law by Norwegian courts in certain "soft cases" (i.e. where the potential barriers seemed easily surmountable) does little to change the overall impression of a generally broad perception as to the scope of the *contra legem* limit. One interesting exception where a much narrower understanding appears to have been adopted in a "hard(er) case", is *Wullum Amcar* – where the Court of Appeal performed a remarkably strained interpretation of Norwegian law in order to achieve conformity with an EEA directive.[288]

A similarly broad understanding as to the scope of the *contra legem* limit appears to have been adopted in Denmark, where the term seems to be understood as meaning not only where contrary to unambiguous black letter law,[289] but also as contrary to ambiguous national provisions as further interpreted (and thereby clarified) by national courts. The question as to whether or not the *contra legem* limit could be defined and applied in such an expansive fashion, and who may ultimately decide the issue more definitively, was brought to a head in *Ajos* – a case originating in a referral for a preliminary ruling by the Danish Supreme Court, and described in detail in the Danish contribution.[290] In short, the Danish Supreme Court had interpreted a provision of national law in a particular way for more than 40 years, in a long line of case-law. Following an earlier decision of the ECJ, however, it turned out that the way in which the Supreme Court had construed the provision was incompatible with EU law.[291] In its referral to the ECJ, the Supreme Court nevertheless indicated that it would not be possible to interpret the national provision in conformity with EU law, as this would amount to an interpretation *contra legem*. The ECJ's response was emphatic: Having recalled that the principle cannot serve as the basis for an interpretation of national law *contra legem*, it held that a national court cannot validly claim that it is impossible for it to interpret the national provision at issue in a manner that is consistent with EU law by mere reason of the fact that it has consistently interpreted that provision in a manner that is incompatible with EU law – in such cases, they are obliged to change their case-law.[292]

---

287 Rt-2000-1811 (*Finanger I*), Rt-2007-234 (*Care Expenses*); HR-2016-2591-A (*Legal Capacity of A*).

288 Norway, p. 358, with further reference to LF-2010-21736 (*Wullum Amcar*).

289 Denmark, p. 266, with further reference to the Eastern High Court's decision in *U 2000.1000 Ø*.

290 Denmark, pp. 281–88, Case C-441/14, *Ajos*, ECLI:EU:C:2016:278.

291 Case C-499/08, *Ingeniørforeningen i Danmark*, ECLI:EU:C:2010:600.

292 Case C-441/14, *Ajos*, ECLI:EU:C:2016:278, para. 33.

Essentially, the ECJ was saying that if the very wording of a national provision seems open to an interpretation in conformity with EU law, then national courts must disregard the way in which it has been understood and applied in the past, and focus on the wording alone. By clarifying – and effectively restricting – the scope of the *contra legem* limit, the ECJ was thereby also making clear that it is legal certainty as a general principle of EU law, and therefore as defined as a matter of EU law, which acts as a limit to the principle of consistent interpretation, and not any notions of legal certainty as these might be understood under the national laws of the Member States alone. Notwithstanding the Danish Supreme Court's controversial final decision in the case, in which it refrained from following the ECJ's ruling,[293] the ECJ's decision in *Ajos* has been confirmed in a later case.[294]

There is one general exception to the picture painted so far, which deserves specific mention. It seems apparent from several of the individual contributions that national courts will generally seem more prepared to narrowly interpret the scope of the *contra legem* limit in criminal law cases, where a strained or creative interpretation of national law could benefit the defendant's legal position. Indeed, where this is possible under national law, the ECJ does not appear to have any issue with this, and has remained silent on the issue. The Dutch contribution, for example, calls attention to two very clear examples in this regard, where a district court added a condition to a criminal offence so as to avoid a prohibited restriction on the internal market,[295] and where the Court of Appeals interpreted "50 mg/kg" as "100 mg/kg" to avoid a violation of European law.[296] Both cases seem rather obvious examples of interpretations *contra legem*, yet ultimately justifiable as potentially beneficial to the defendants on charge. Another example is provided in *Árnason*, where the Icelandic Supreme Court appears to have performed an interpretation clearly contravening the wording of a national provision in order to ensure that the defendants in the case could rely on rights granted to them under EEA law.[297]

---

293 For the Danish Supreme Court's final decision in the case, see *Højesteret, 1. afdeling, dom af 06/12/2016 (Sag 15/2014).*

294 Case C-554/14, *Ognyanov*, ECLI:EU:C:2016:835, para. 67: "it must be made clear that the requirement to interpret national law in conformity with EU law includes the obligation, on national courts, including those ruling as courts of last instance, to alter, where necessary, settled case-law if that case-law is based on an interpretation of national law that is incompatible with the objectives of [the EU measure in question]; and Case C-614/14, *Ognyanov*, ECLI:EU:C:2016:514, paragraph 35".

295 The Netherlands, p. 93, with further reference to District Court of Den Bosch 7 December 2006, ECLI:NL:RBSHE:2006:AZ3896 / ECLI:NL:RBSHE:2006: AZ3897 / ECLI: NL:RBSHE:2006:AZ3903 / ECLI:NL:RBSHE:2006:AZ3905 / ECLI:NL:RBSHE: 2006:AZ3934 / ECLI:NL:RBSHE:2006:AZ3935, *JGR* 2007/1 and 2007/2.

296 See Supreme Court 23 December 2003, ECLI:NL:HR:2003:AL4343, para 7.

297 Iceland, p. 404, Supreme Court Case No. 842/2014 of 4 February 2016, *Criminal proceedings against Árnason and Others*; endorsed in Supreme Court Case No. 498/2015 of 6 October 2016, *Criminal proceedings against Sigurðsson and Others.*

6. A FEW FINAL OBSERVATIONS BY WAY OF CONCLUSION – AND LOOKING AHEAD

It might seem strange to some that we have attempted to synthesise our collective findings in the very first contribution to this book – one might perhaps usually expect to find such an exposé appended at the very end. The hope is nevertheless that readers will find this effort to broadly summarise the main themes and issues – both those more and/or less resolved – from the very outset, and calling attention to certain strands of the case-law of national courts covered, as providing a useful framework of reference in reading the individual contributions which follow. As readers will see, the individual contributions are indeed written in their own style, following variable structures, in an attempt to truly reflect developments at national level in their countries. Since providing a set of conclusions on what has essentially already been a summary of sorts seems rather superfluous at this stage, we shall instead look to focus on one final issue in this section, which will hopefully provide even more food for thought when moving through the contributions to come.

Picking up the thread from the last section: being the most commonly referred to limitation relied upon by national courts in ruling out consistent interpretations of national law in practice, the guidance provided by the ECJ in *Ajos* on what the *contra legem* limit entails – or more precisely, what it does not cover – certainly seemed both long overdue and welcome. And in providing more clarity as to the limits, the Court was naturally also providing more clarity as to the scope of the duties entailed by the principle. Yet how do we explain why certain courts or judges adopt a narrower or broader understanding of the principle's scope/limits? Why do certain courts or judges seem prepared to stretch themselves further than others in seeking EU/EEA-consistent interpretations of national law? Although a plurality of approaches may be considered a mere and natural corollary to issues which remain unresolved, we have also seen how a lack of uniformity may persist even with regard to certain questions long since answered by the ECJ and/or EFTA Court.

Whilst we may ultimately only guess as to the reasons why divergent approaches are adopted, as we have seen, legal culture may at times certainly seem to play an important role. Several of the contributors also offer other suggestions in their accounts – such as the extent of ownership, responsibility or empowerment with respect to the principle and the duties it entails, which may be felt differently by the courts and judges tasked with dealing with such cases. Varying levels of knowledge of, schooling in and exposure to EU/EEA legal issues in practice might also play a part. Perhaps economic obligations under EU/EEA law are not considered as important and worthy of protection as other (fundamental) rights. Or maybe it simply boils down to a lack of specific guidance provided by the ECJ and/or EFTA Court on particular issues.

To the extent that the latter may be said to play a part, the solution may naturally prove rather simple in the end – if in doubt, national courts can always ask the ECJ or the EFTA Court for guidance. Indeed, it seems clear to me that increased dialogue and awareness of developments at ground level in the EU/EEA Member States – both in the ECJ, EFTA Court and national courts – is key to achieving greater balance and cohesion in practice. As to the reasons why such questions still seem to persist, however, the relationship and dialogue between the national courts and the ECJ/EFTA Court may naturally be rather telling.

First, in order to provide the necessary answers, the ECJ and EFTA Court must obviously be asked the questions to begin with. Yet referrals are not always forthcoming, even in cases where one might expect them to be made. The Finnish contributor, for example, notes how courts in Finland generally seem to adopt a very Eurocentric approach, with national case-law revealing a remarkably clear understanding of the ECJ case-law requirements concerning the scope and content of the principle. Yet we also see how the majority in *KKO:2015:74* decided not to request a preliminary ruling on how to interpret the term "proceeds of crime", and instead found that in the absence of judgments from the ECJ that there was no reason to conclude certain assets should be regarded as such.[298] Whilst Slovenian courts in the vast majority of decisions touching upon the principle have adopted an EU-friendly approach to potential conflicts between Slovenian and EU law, only 14 referrals (four of which specifically concerned the principle of consistent interpretation) have been made to the ECJ since it joined the EU. A similar reticence in referring to the ECJ is also noted in the Cypriot account, and how the Supreme Court in the controversial *Motilla* case – where consistent interpretation was ruled out – did not even appear to discuss the issue concerning a potential referral. The Cypriot contribution further suggests that there may potentially be a link between the low number of references for preliminary rulings by national courts in Cyprus (only seven to date), and their generally rather narrow view of the principle's scope. Although there appears to be a growing number of arguments put before courts to refer, these are apparently "all too often not submitted to the ECJ by the national court, usually acting without sufficient justification for doing so".[299] Even in countries whose national courts appear willing to stretch themselves very far in interpreting national law consistently with EU obligations, there is sometimes a reluctance to refer such questions to the ECJ. For example, in earlier (i.e. pre-*Marleasing*) years, in cases where UK courts had refused to interpret pre-existing national legislation to comply with EU law enacted at a later date, no references for preliminary rulings were made.[300] Not to mention

298 Finland, p. 313.

299 Cyprus, p. 515.

300 UK, p. 228.

of course the alarmingly low number of references by Icelandic and Norwegian courts to the EFTA Court, noted earlier. Even though there is no formal duty for national courts (even of last instance) to refer questions to it, there seem to be very few convincing arguments why they should not choose to exercise their right to do so more regularly.

Second, even if certain national courts sometimes might want to, they may not always have the possibility of making referrals. In certain countries, lower national courts are in fact fettered in their discretion in referring questions concerning the interpretation and application of EU and EEA law to the ECJ and EFTA Court, thus preventing them from taking a more active role in the dialogue. In Denmark, for example, the State Prosecutor plays a significant role in deciding whether references should be made.[301] Furthermore, in the event that a referral is made by a Danish court, the Ministry of Foreign Affairs will apparently also be in a position to considerably influence how the questions referred should be drafted by the referring court. In Iceland, orders by lower courts requesting Advisory Opinions from the EFTA Court under Art. 34 SCA may be appealed and hence vetted by the Icelandic Supreme Court before they get sent. The Icelandic contributors note an interesting example here of the Supreme Court rejecting a request for an Advisory Opinion in a case where the dispute concerned the issue of how precedents of the Supreme Court should be interpreted.[302] It should be noted however that Art. 34 SCA itself allows the EFTA States to limit the right to refer cases to the EFTA Court to courts of last instance.

Finally, even in cases where referrals are in fact made by national courts to the ECJ or EFTA Court, they may not always be asking the right – or most pertinent – questions. As we have seen, several of the contributors note how national courts in their countries routinely only ask questions specifically concerning the interpretation of the EU/EEA law provisions at issue in the cases they are dealing with, and generally refrain from asking questions concerning the scope of any relevant or applicable principles beyond this. Of course, although the ECJ and EFTA Court will seldom feel limited by the actual questions posed by referring national courts, the reluctance of many national courts and judges to engage in a dialogue concerning the "big" issues – including matters related to the principle of consistent interpretation – is rather worrisome from the perspective of uniformity/homogeneity. The Finnish contributor, for example, notes in this regard an innate reluctance of

[301] Denmark, p. 271. The Danish contributors here point to the example of *Bang and Grøngaard*, where a decision by the Copenhagen City Court to make a reference for a preliminary ruling was appealed to the Eastern High Court (which upheld the City Court's decision), and could (but was not granted leave) to be appealed further to the Supreme Court.

[302] Iceland, p. 381, with further reference to Supreme Court Case No. 10/2013 of 24 January 2013 *Landsbankinn hf. v. Flugastraumur ehf.*

Finnish courts to push the marker beyond what is known, and to ask more pressing questions concerning particularly the limits.[303] The same general approach is clearly adopted by Norwegian courts: in the *Finanger I* case, where consistent interpretation was ultimately ruled out, a referral was made to the EFTA Court – yet not one of the questions raised concerned the principle of consistent interpretation. For reasons unknown, the EFTA Court did not attempt to broach the issue of its own accord, either.[304] The Danish Supreme Court's referral in *Ajos* nevertheless seems to buck the trend in this regard. Far from shying away from matters, the Danish Supreme Court seemed almost intent on drawing the ECJ to answer certain questions directly concerning the scope, content and limits of the principle of consistent interpretation. As we have seen however, in light of the reply received, and the Supreme Court's final decision in the case, it remains to be seen whether national courts will feel encouraged to ask similarly brazen questions of the ECJ in the foreseeable future.

---

303 Finland, p. 304. "The references to the ECJ in Finnish conforming interpretation cases concern the interpretation of relevant EU law but not the interpretation of the principle of conforming interpretation as such."

304 Case E-01/99, *Finanger* [2000] EFTA Ct. Rep. 119.

CONSISTENT INTERPRETATION IN THE NETHERLANDS

A Theoretical Perspective on the Principle and its Use by the Dutch Supreme Court

Judit ALTENA-DAVIDSEN

1. INTRODUCTION

The Netherlands were one of the six states founding the European Community on Coal and Steel, the first of the European Communities, back in 1951.

The Netherlands have been very active in shaping the European Community and later the European Union legal order, with the conclusion of the Maastricht Treaty (1992) and the Amsterdam Treaty (1999) under Dutch presidency of the Council. According to the European Commission Database on infringement decisions,[1] of the six founding members, the Netherlands have attracted the fewest infringement decisions and are among the Member States that generally comply well with European Union (EU) legislation. Courts seem well aware of their duties and comply fairly conscientiously with their European duties.[2]

At the risk of stating the obvious, this does not mean that inconsistencies between EU and national law do not occur. Delays in transposition occur frequently, and transposition is by no means flawless. In some cases, national legislation is found wanting but is not repaired by the legislature, or only after a long time. Traditionally, the Dutch legal order is characterised by openness towards influences of international law.[3] According to Art. 93 of the Dutch Constitution, "[p]rovisions of treaties and of resolutions by international institutions which may be binding on all persons by virtue of their contents shall become binding after they have been published".[4] According to Art. 94 of the Constitution, national laws shall not be applicable if their application is in conflict with such binding treaty provisions and resolutions. These Articles are the result of constitutional amendments made in the 1950s, which were intended to accommodate the growing impact of international and European law on the Dutch legal order.[5] In a judgment from 2005, however, the Dutch Supreme Court stated that European law can impact Dutch law not because of the Dutch Constitution, but because of European law itself. In other words, the Supreme Court accepted the autonomy and supremacy of European law vis-à-vis national law.[6] This position was supported by mainstream Dutch constitutional theory at that time.[7] It must be noted, however, that the status of this case-law is at present disputed: it is contested whether it really means that Art. 93 and 94 of

---

1 See the database with Commission decisions on infringements, available online at <http://ec.europa.eu/atwork>.

2 B. de Witte, "Do Not Mention the Word: Sovereignty in Two Europhile Countries, Belgium and the Netherlands" in N. Walker (ed.), *Sovereignty in Transition* (Hart Publishing, 2003), p. 352.

3 For a more detailed rendering of the constitutional implications of European law for Dutch law, see de Witte (n. 2).

4 A translation of the Constitution into English provided by the Ministry of the Interior and Kingdom Relations is available online at <www.rechtspraak.nl/SiteCollectionDocuments/Constitution-NL.pdf>.

5 M.L. van Emmerik, "De Nederlandse Grondwet in een veellagige rechtsorde" [2008] 4 *RM Themis* 135, 139; de Witte (n. 2), pp. 362–63.

6 Supreme Court 2 November 2004, *NJ* 2005/80 with case note by E.A. Alkema (*Verplichte rusttijden*).

7 de Witte (n. 2), pp. 361–64.

the Constitution are of no relevance for the interaction between European and national law, and even more whether this *should* be the case.[8]

Besides direct application of international law, the principle of consistent interpretation has traditionally been an accepted way of giving effect to international law in the Dutch legal order. It has also been accepted as a means of decentralised enforcement of European law. Research conducted by Betlem and Nollkaemper comparing the Dutch principle of consistent interpretation with the European version of it, concluded that the national mechanism is less far-reaching than the European principle. Courts have more latitude when deciding on the scope and limits of the national mechanism when applied to international law than they have when exercising their duty of consistent interpretation under European law. However, they saw no fundamental distinction between the two mechanisms, only a distinction of degree.[9] The principle of consistent interpretation in relation to European law is applied by Dutch courts as a European principle, based upon a European mandate. This can be considered a logical consequence of the acceptance of the power of European law to decide how it takes effect in the Dutch legal order.

Against the backdrop of the openness of the Dutch legal order and the Dutch acceptance of the supremacy of European law, it is interesting to look into how Dutch courts fulfil their obligation to interpret national law in line with European law.[10] This contribution will describe how consistent interpretation as a mechanism of decentralised enforcement plays out in the Dutch legal order and, in the wake thereof, how this duty relates to national methods of interpretation and how it affects the division of powers between the legislature and the courts.

In order to do so, this contribution will, in section 2, present a concise conceptual framework that will make it possible to study how the interpretation of national law is affected by European law and how interpretation can be bound by rules. On this basis, some general impressions can already be presented on the impact of consistent interpretation *in abstracto*. In section 3, an overview is given of the Dutch Supreme Court's case-law in which it has dwelt upon the implications of consistent interpretation for Dutch courts. This section shows considerable changes over time in the Supreme Court's understanding of the duty. Section 4 will deal with the limits of consistent interpretation, and

---

8 For a short overview of the debate, see W. Geelhoed, *Het opportuniteitsbeginsel en het recht van de Europese Unie: een onderzoek naar de betekenis van strafvorderlijke beleidsvrijheid in de geëuropeaniseerde rechtsorde* (Kluwer, 2013), pp. 25–32.

9 G. Betlem and A. Nollkaemper, "Giving effect to public international law and European Community law before domestic courts. A comparative analysis of the practice of consistent interpretation" [2003] 14 *EJIL* 569.

10 Generally, this contribution will refer to interpretation in conformity with directives, but substantially, this applies equally to interpretation in conformity with framework decisions.

will discuss these in relation to private law, administrative law and criminal law respectively, as the limits of the duty are dependent upon the legal relationship central to the case. The fourth section will also deal with the applicability of the duty in the case of minimum harmonisation, a problem that is of particularly high relevance in relation to substantive criminal law, where minimum harmonisation is the rule.

Before presenting the material, some general comments must be made on the research methods used for this contribution. The most important source for case-law analysis used by Dutch scholars is the database of the judicial system itself, which can be found at <www.rechtspraak.nl>. Criteria for publication can be accessed through the website of the judiciary.[11] To name a few criteria that might be relevant in the context of this contribution, judgments of the Supreme Court are always published, as well as every judgment in which a preliminary reference is made to the Court of Justice of the European Union (ECJ). Furthermore, cases that are expected to have informal precedent effect[12] or that deal with a question not previously dealt with by courts will be published. Approximately 1.5 per cent of District Court judgments are published, and approximately 12 per cent of the judgments handed down by Courts of Appeal.[13] Cases can be found by entering their ECLI or one or more search term(s) in the search engine of the website.

Researching how the duty of consistent interpretation is carried out by Dutch courts through this database is no easy task for several reasons. First, it is difficult to find all of the potentially relevant cases. Courts do not always refer to the duty of consistent interpretation explicitly, and if they do, they use different formulations or expressions to refer to it. In addition, they do not refer consistently to the case-law of the ECJ it stems from, such as *Von Colson and Kamann*. Even though the fact that they apply the duty of consistent interpretation is in no way obscured, the different formulations in the judgments make them more difficult to find: the search engine yields few results for keywords relating explicitly to the duty of consistent interpretation. This means it is impossible to get a complete overview of all the cases in which the duty is in fact applied. Second, in many cases it also remains unclear how exactly European law has influenced the outcome of the case. This means that even when the duty is applied (albeit perhaps implicitly), it is not always possible to draw any conclusions as to how and within what boundaries it is applied. Third, it does not often happen that the duty and its limits must be explored. In a great deal of cases, the Dutch legislature transposes EU law correctly and in a timely

11 Besluit selectiecriteria uitsprakendatabank Rechtspraak.nl (Decision selection criteria judgments database <Rechtspraak.nl>), available online at <www.rechtspraak.nl> (enter "besluit selectiecriteria" in the search box).

12 Courts are not formally bound to precedents in the Dutch legal system.

13 See *Kengetallen gerechten 2015*, available online at <www.rechtspraak.nl/SiteCollection Documents/Kengetallen-2015.pdf>.

manner. In these cases, of course, national provisions must be interpreted in line with European law, but this will usually be relatively straightforward and unproblematic. It is only when discrepancies exist, and only when they are of such a nature that they may or may not be overcome through consistent interpretation, that courts must explore the boundaries of their discretionary powers.

Given these methodological problems, it is self-evident that the case-law analysis conducted for the purposes of this contribution could not be fully comprehensive. The contribution focuses on a selection of cases that are good examples of a certain problem or way of reasoning. These cases were found through the search engine, through references in academic literature, and by using the "snowball method". To a great extent, the contribution relies on research done by the author for a doctoral thesis on the principle of legality and the effects of European law on Dutch substantive criminal law.[14]

2. CONSISTENT INTERPRETATION – A THEORETICAL PERSPECTIVE

The first step to be taken is providing basic analytical concepts that can be used to describe and evaluate the impact of consistent interpretation on a national system, *in casu* the Dutch legal system. These concepts aim at enabling an analysis of how the duty of consistent interpretation affects the activities of courts, and, in the wake of this, how the duty affects constitutional relations between the Dutch legislature and Dutch courts. After sketching the framework, these concepts will be used to give a very short description of the duty of consistent interpretation.

2.1. A CONCISE CONCEPTUAL FRAMEWORK FOR ANALYSING THE IMPACT OF CONSISTENT INTERPRETATION ON NATIONAL SYSTEMS

The framework comprises three elements: first, concepts that relate to the process of interpretation; second, an analysis of the ambiguity of the concept of interpretation; and, third, a succinct typology of ways in which judicial discretion can be subject to limitations.

First, the process of interpretation can be dissected in the interpretive methods courts must or may use, and the hierarchy that exists between these methods of interpretation. Regarding methods of interpretation, it is sometimes

---

14 J.G.H. Altena-Davidsen, *Het legaliteitsbeginsel en de doorwerking van Europees recht in het Nederlandse materiële strafrecht* [The Principle of Legality and the effects of European Law on Dutch Substantive Criminal Law] (Wolters Kluwer, 2016).

asked whether consistent interpretation constitutes a method of interpretation in and of itself, but there is no consensus as to what exactly constitutes an independent method of interpretation. The relevance of the question whether consistent interpretation must be seen as a method of interpretation lies in the question behind it, namely whether taking European law into account is possible and obligatory if none of the "national" methods of interpretation point in the direction of the EU obligation in question. If consistent interpretation is a derivative of historical interpretation, for example, it cannot apply to legislation enacted prior to the directive. Regarding the hierarchy of interpretive methods, the question is whether European law establishes such a hierarchy. This could be done, for example, by never allowing the court to disregard the wording of the national statute, or by deciding that whatever method of interpretation produces a result consistent with a directive must prevail over the others.

Second, the duty of consistent interpretation and its limits can refer to various aspects of interpretation. The reason it is necessary to clarify some concepts regarding consistent interpretation lies in the well-known observation that the concept of interpretation suffers from so-called "process-product ambiguity".[15] The word "interpretation" can refer to the process of finding out the meaning of an act, a provision or a part thereof, as well as to the result of this activity, i.e. the meaning given by the court. In a similar fashion, the duty of consistent interpretation can be understood to refer to a certain way of interpreting (the process), as well as to reaching a certain result (the product). So what is the nature of the duty: is it a duty to proceed in a certain way when interpreting national law, or is it (merely) a best efforts obligation that is based on purely national methods of interpretation?

When discussing the limits of the duty of consistent interpretation, this scheme can get complicated further. First, it is important to stress that it is for pragmatic reasons that we speak of "limiting" judicial discretion: the way in which judges reach a decision cannot really be limited or governed by norms; rather it is the justification of choices as laid down in the judgment which is subject to norms and which can hence be limited. In a certain legal system, courts may be said to be limited regarding the process (i.e. they may not or must use certain interpretive methods in a certain order), or regarding the product (i.e. the results they reach may not violate legal certainty). This corresponds to the concepts as discussed in the previous paragraph. However, in the context of limits to judicial discretion, a third possibility must be added, and that is limiting the *application* of this product in the concrete case (i.e. extending criminal

15 H.T.M. Kloosterhuis, *Van overeenkomstige toepassing. De pragma-dialectische reconstructie van analogie-argumentatie in rechterlijke uitspraken* (diss. Amsterdam UvA) (Thela Thesis, 2002), pp. 165–66; M.A. Loth, *Recht en taal. Een kleine methodologie* (Gouda Quint, 1984), p. 45.

liability in case-law is acceptable, but in some situations this new interpretation may not be applied in the concrete case).[16] Limits to (consistent) interpretation can hence refer to limits regarding its process (both the methods used and the hierarchy between them), its product, and its application in a concrete case.

2.2. THE NATURE OF THE DUTY OF CONSISTENT INTERPRETATION

When reading the case-law of the ECJ, at first sight it may seem that the duty refers only to a certain effort to be made to reach a certain *result*. National courts must, according to the Court in the *Von Colson and Kamann* case, "interpret their national law in the light of the wording and the purpose of the directive" with a view to reaching the result prescribed by that directive.[17] This the national court must do "in so far as it is given discretion to do so under national law".[18] In the *Pfeiffer* judgment, the ECJ states that national courts must abide by their national law not only regarding the scope of their discretion, but also regarding the use of interpretive methods.[19] This entails a limitation, but also a strong requirement: if courts have the possibility of applying interpretive methods under national law, they are held to apply these to European law as well. Nevertheless, the important thing to note here is that the Court formulates a duty to try to reach a certain *result*, but it does not affect the ways in which this result is reached.

Or so it seems. In later case-law, the ECJ has given much more concrete pointers to national courts as to how to fulfil their duties under European law. An important question courts are confronted with is how they should weigh statements from their national legislature against the wording and purpose of the relevant directive. This is especially so in systems where legislative history and legislative intent are important sources for the interpretation of statutes, such as in the Netherlands.[20] An important instruction was given in the *Wagner Miret* case: national courts "must presume that the State had the intention of fulfilling entirely the obligations arising from the directive concerned".[21] Next, from the

---

16 An example of this last restriction of the powers of courts can be found in the ECtHR case-law, see *Contrada v. Italy*, 14 April 2005, appl. no. 66655/13, para. 71.

17 Case 14/83, ECLI:EU:C:1984:153, *Von Colson and Kamann v. Land Nordrhein-Westfalen* [1984] ECR 1892, para. 26.

18 Ibid., para. 28.

19 Joined Cases C-397 to 403/01, ECLI:EU:C:2004:584, *Pfeiffer and Others v. Deutsches Rotes Kreuz* [2004] ECR I-8878, para. 116.

20 M.J. Borgers, "Wetshistorische interpretatie in de strafrechtspraak" in M.S. Groenhuijsen and J.B.H.M. Simmelink (eds.), *Glijdende schalen* (De Hullu-anthology, Wolf Legal Publishers, 2003), pp. 51–69.

21 Case C-334/92, ECLI:EU:C:1993:945, *Wagner Miret v. Fondo de garantia salarial* [1993] ECR I-6913, para. 20.

Björnekulla Fruktindustrier case, it becomes clear that this presumption may trump concrete remarks on the correct interpretation uttered by the national legislature. The ECJ asserts that the duty applies "notwithstanding any contrary interpretation which may arise from the *travaux préparatoires* for the national rule."[22] This may be seen as a form of teleological interpretation, whereby a general purpose is abstracted from preparatory documents, which may in turn be used to trump more concrete statements in those very same preparatory documents. It greatly reduces, but does not completely deny, the relevance of national legislative history: the presumption regarding the intent to fulfil the relevant obligations may be rebutted by legislative history.

Another case that must be mentioned in this context is the *Pupino* case, in which the ECJ reminded the national court of the fact that a consistent interpretation is only required if national law so allows: a consistent interpretation "cannot serve as the basis for an interpretation of national law *contra legem*".[23] The precise meaning of this limitation has been widely debated and will be discussed in more depth in section 4.2, but it is generally taken to refer to the wording of the national provision.

These cases show that the duty of consistent interpretation does indeed potentially impact the process of interpretation, in spite of its abstract formulation only referring to the results thereof. As Prechal remarks subtly but sharply, consistent interpretation is only required when possible within the limits of national law, but "[b]e this as it may, it seems that national courts are no longer entirely free to determine the parameters of what is 'possible' and what not".[24] First, the duty of consistent interpretation affects the methods of interpretation in the sense that European law must always be involved when interpreting national statutes falling under the scope of European law, also in case none of the national methods refers to it. Courts must – at least in certain cases – refer to European law in their judgments.[25] Also, European law may be decisive for which of the possible interpretations enabled by the wording of the statute is the "right" one. Second, consistent interpretation establishes a hierarchy between interpretive methods. The text of the national statute is

---

22 Case C-371/02, ECLI:EU:C:2004:275, *Björnekulla Fruktindustrier AB v. Procordia Food AB* [2004] ECR I-5811, para. 13.

23 Case C-105/03, ECLI:EU:C:2005:386, *Criminal proceedings against Pupino* [2005] ECR I-5309, para. 47.

24 S. Prechal, *Directives in EC Law* (OUP, 2005), p. 199.

25 Whether and in which circumstances courts must raise points of EU law of their own motion cannot be said in general: this depends on the field of law (private, administrative or criminal law) and of which provisions of European law are relevant to the individual case. For the line of reasoning, it is important whether this *can* be the case. In the author's view, in criminal law it is indeed obligatory to raise points of EU law ex officio if these deny the validity and applicability of the criminal provision. This follows not only from EU law, but also from Art. 350 of the Dutch Code of Criminal Procedure.

determinative of the range of meanings that can be attributed to the statute. Moreover, legislative intent, in its abstract form of an intention to fulfil European obligations, trumps other sources of information, including concrete remarks on the part of the legislature.

In the view of the present author, consistent interpretation is still first and foremost a best efforts obligation to reach a certain result, using any methods that are available under national law. But the case-law discussed here does dispute the view that national methods of interpretation, and hence constitutional relations between the national legislature and courts, remain untouched.[26] Consistent interpretation indeed also relates to and affects the *process* of interpretation. Whether and how much the duty in practice really impacts interpretation in national law depends on the customs and norms governing the interpretation of national law in a specific system.

3. THE DUTCH SUPREME COURT'S APPROACH TO CONSISTENT INTERPRETATION

Over the course of the last 20 years, the Dutch Supreme Court has given several rulings in which it has dwelt upon the duty of consistent interpretation and its implications for Dutch courts. They are of a more general and principled character, in the sense that general remarks are made on the scope of duties for courts deciding on facts, even though these remarks more often than not bear no relevance to the outcome of the case at hand. Together, these judgments picture how the Supreme Court usually understands the duty of consistent interpretation and its limits.[27] The discussion of this case-law in this contribution is spread out over three sub-sections, the first dealing with older, more resilient case-law; the second with a tax case that, in the view of the present author, was a turning point for the case-law; and the third dealing with recent case-law that represents the current approach of the Supreme Court. The case-law shows a gradual development from a national law-oriented approach towards a European law-oriented approach. Although most of the judgments concern private law cases, the field of administrative law has also generated some important judgments that have impacted the case-law on consistent

26 This view is defended by C.W. Canaris, "Die richtlinienkonforme Auslegung und Rechtsfortbildung in System der juristischen Methodenlehre" in H. Koziol and P. Rummel (eds.), *Im Dienste der Gerechtigkeit* (Bydlinski-anthology, Springer Verlag, 2002), p. 56.

27 This section presents a general overview. The Supreme Court is not always consistent in its approach, therefore examples can be found that may not entirely fit the picture presented here. The cases discussed here are selected because of their general reflection on the duty of consistent interpretation.

interpretation in horizontal relationships. In the field of criminal law, no such general and principled judgments have been handed down. The case-law on consistent interpretation in private law is, however, also referred to in criminal cases.[28] In addition, the Supreme Court itself refers in criminal cases to its earlier case-law concerning other areas of law. A joint discussion of the Supreme Court's case-law is therefore justified.

3.1. CONSISTENT INTERPRETATION AS A MEANS OF CHOICE

An important Supreme Court ruling was given in the *Asseldonk/Ter Schure* case.[29] The case concerned the Dutch transposition of Art. 2(2) of Directive 76/207/EEC (the "Equal Treatment Directive"), in which it is stated that exceptions to equal treatment are possible for occupational activities for which "by reason of their nature or the context in which they are carried out, the sex of the worker constitutes a determining factor".[30] The Dutch legislature had interpreted this exception as allowing the categorical exclusion of women from church offices or other religious offices. Hence, there was an intention to transpose, but a discussion arose whether this intention could possibly have been misguided, as it was debated whether EU law indeed allowed this type of sex discrimination on religious grounds. The Supreme Court stated that because of the wording and parliamentary history, the relevant national provisions could not be understood in any way other than in the sense that they excluded religious offices. The Dutch Equal Treatment Act explicitly mentions religious offices as a possible exception to the right to equal treatment of men and women, which exception is, according to legislative history, based on the right to religious freedom. Therefore, the Supreme Court did not deem it necessary to establish whether the national law provisions indeed violated the Equal Treatment Directive – even if they did, an interpretation in line with the Directive would be impossible to reach. The possibility of seeking damages because of state liability was, according to the case note, mentioned by the complainants, but was not mentioned in the judgment.

28 District Court of Rotterdam 20 December 2007, ECLI:NL:RBROT:2007:BC0861, *JOR* 2008/46, with case note by M. Nelemans. In this case, the criminal court refers to the *Vierdaagse* judgment (Supreme Court 10 August 2007, ECLI:NL:HR:2007:AZ3758, *AB* 2007/291 with case note by R.J.G.M. Widdershoven). See also the advisory opinion of AG Wortel in Supreme Court 31 May 2005, ECLI:NL:HR:2005:AR8021, *NJ* 2005/458, which refers to the case *Pink Floyd/Rigu Sound* (Supreme Court 15 October 1996, ECLI:NL:HR:1996:ZC2177 *NJ* 1997/649 with case note by D.W.F. Verkade).

29 Supreme Court 20 October 1995, ECLI:NL:HR:1995:ZC1846, *NJ* 1996/330 (*Asseldonk/Ter Schure*), with case note by E.A. Alkema, para. 3.5.

30 Council Directive 76/207/EEC of 9 February 1976 on the implementation of the principle of equal treatment for men and women as regards access to employment, vocational training and promotion, and working conditions [1976] OJ L39/40, Art. 2(2).

The *Asseldonk-Ter Schure* case was the forerunner to the judgment in *Pink Floyd/Rigu Sound* from 1996, which counted as the main ruling on consistent interpretation for over a decade. The case concerned the consequences of Council Directive 92/100/EEC on rental right and lending right and on certain rights related to copyright in the field of intellectual property (the "Rental Directive") for a private dispute, hence again a horizontal relationship in which the Directive did not have direct effect. The case dealt with the question whether the right to sell a certain Pink Floyd CD had been exhausted. Art. 9(2) of the Rental Directive states that distribution rights "shall not be exhausted within the Community in respect of an object as referred to in paragraph 1, except where the first sale in the Community of that object is made by the rightholder or with his consent". Rigu Sound was sued for having sold a CD in contravention of distribution rights. This had taken place both before and after expiration of the transposition deadline, but before the actual transposition of the Directive into Dutch law. The relevant Dutch provision, in the Neighbouring Rights Act, stated only that the producer of phonograms (i.e. sound recordings) has the exclusive right to bring the product on the market, and that this right is exhausted whenever a first sale is made by the rightholder with his consent. The provision contains no geographical limitations to this exhaustion, hence the right is considered to be exhausted whenever a sale is made by the rightholder *anywhere in the world* – and not just within the Community, as stated by the Rental Directive in Art. 9. This interpretation of Dutch law is based on the fact that the statute mentions no geographical limitation, and on the fact that the preparatory documents from the legislature contain no implications that despite this omission, the exhaustion was meant to be limited to the European Economic Community (EEC). The complainants sought to rely on the Directive to argue that their distribution rights had not been exhausted, as the phonograms were brought on the market in the US, not in the EEC. The question whether the Directive actually *obliges* Member States to geographically limit the exhaustion of rights to the EEC was not dealt with in depth by the Court of Appeals, but was answered in the positive for the sake of argument. For the Court of Appeals argued that even when national law is interpreted in line with the Directive "as far as possible" (as follows from the *Marleasing* judgment of the ECJ[31]), it cannot be read as meaning that exhaustion is limited to the EEC. A consistent interpretation would be *contra legem*, and would furthermore violate the principle of legal certainty. The question central to the cassation proceedings was then whether such interpretation was indeed impossible. This meant that the question whether national law violated European law at all was – again – never answered (and could, at the time, presumably only be answered by

[31] Case C-106/89, ECLI:EU:C:1990:395, *Marleasing SA v. La Comercial Internacional de Alimentación SA* [1990] ECR I-4156, para. 8.

the ECJ based on preliminary questions).[32] The Supreme Court ruled that a consistent interpretation would go against the "unambiguous wording" of the national provision, and that it would therefore not be in line with the principle of legal certainty.[33]

These two judgments reflect an early (mis)understanding of the duty of consistent interpretation. The Supreme Court seems to assume that a consistent interpretation is only possible whenever the national provision is in and of itself ambiguous. In *Pink Floyd/Rigu Sound*, the wording is unambiguous; in *Asseldonk/Ter Schure*, it is the combination of the wording and legislative history that leads to only one possible interpretation of the provisions. This presupposes an approach whereby the court first establishes the meaning of the provision purely on the basis of national arguments (the wording, legislative history, the broader system of which the provision forms part, and the aim of the provision). If there is any ambiguity or uncertainty regarding this meaning, the one most in line with European law must be chosen. This was termed the "means of choice" approach by Wissink: consistent interpretation serves as a means of choosing between competing interpretations of Dutch law.[34] In this approach, consistent interpretation has no impact on the process of interpretation, only on the result. The reluctance towards a consistent interpretation in these cases has been explained in the literature by the horizontal relationship they revolved around: the Supreme Court may have proceeded with caution in these cases out of fear of imposing obligations on individuals without sufficient basis in national law.[35]

Both judgments were met with criticism. First of all, the outcome of the cases was criticised. Swaak argues that the national provisions central to the *Pink Floyd/Rigu Sound* were not as unambiguous as they were said to be, but instead left enough room for an interpretation in line with the Directive. Second, Swaak is not convinced by the argument based on legal certainty, as it is the *national law* imposing obligations, not European law itself.[36] Furthermore, it was argued that the Supreme Court had attributed too much weight to national parliamentary history and national legislative intent.[37] This point of critique was voiced most

---

32 The present author has not been able to find any follow-up to this case, but considering the fact that no violation of European law was ever established, it seems unlikely that any action in damages was raised against the state. The possibility of state liability was not mentioned in the judgments discussed here.

33 Supreme Court 15 October 1996, ECLI:NL:HR:1996:ZC2177, *NJ* 1997/649 (*Pink Floyd/ Rigu Sound*) with case note by D.W.F. Verkade, para. 3.4.

34 M.H. Wissink, *Richtlijnconforme interpretatie van burgerlijk recht* (Kluwer, 2001), pp. 115–21, 163–64.

35 As to the *Pink Floyd/Rigu Sound* judgment, see C.R.A. Swaak, "Consistent interpretation of national law: Dutch courts on the wrong track?" [1996] 2 *European Public Law* 219, 220–21. As to the *Asseldonk/Ter Schure* judgment, see the case note by E.A. Alkema in *NJ* 1996/330.

36 Swaak (n. 35), pp. 222–23.

37 J.M. Smits and E.A. van Schagen, "De Hoge Raad als Europese rechter: mag het ietsje meer zijn?" [2009] 25 *BW-krant jaarboek* 79, 81; M.H. Wissink (n. 34), pp. 163–64.

clearly by Wissink, who explicitly opposes the means of choice approach. According to Wissink, the Supreme Court pays too little attention to European law: if national law is straightforward, its conformity with European law is no longer a relevant argument for the Supreme Court, as its meaning is already established. This is illustrated in the cases described above, as the conformity of national law with European law is not even considered relevant. Therefore, no inquiry is done into the exact meaning of the relevant EU law provisions. According to Wissink, European law should on the contrary always play a role in determining the meaning of national law (stating the obvious: in so far as it falls under the scope of European law).[38] The third, repeated, criticism regarding the Supreme Court's approach to consistent interpretation in these early cases has been that it is insufficiently consistent, in the sense that it is unpredictable whether a consistent interpretation will be deemed possible or not.[39]

3.2. ADMINISTRATIVE LAW CASES PAVING THE WAY FOR A STRONGER APPROACH TOWARDS CONSISTENT INTERPRETATION ACROSS THE BOARD

Later judgments show a bolder approach. In 2007, a judgment of the Supreme Court in a tax case (the *Vierdaagse* case) spawned debate and a series of judgments on the duty of consistent interpretation.[40] At the time, the leading case (although rendered in civil proceedings) was *Pink Floyd/Rigu Sound*, discussed earlier. In the *Vierdaagse* case, the tax chamber of the Supreme Court, in the opinion of the present author, limited the possibilities for lower courts to render a consistent interpretation impossible, by denying validity to certain arguments that could be used to refuse to interpret national law in line with European law. The facts of the case revolved around the amount of tax due for the organisation of a public event, depending on whether the organised activities should be taxed according to a low or a high tariff. The relevant tax provisions pointed in the direction of the low tariff, but an interpretation of these provisions in conformity with the relevant directive could possibly lead to taxation based on the high tariff. The Court of Appeals declared such interpretation impossible and in violation of the principle of legal certainty,

38 M.H. Wissink (n. 34), pp. 152–67 and more generally on the different approaches pp. 111–41. For further reference on these approaches, see the book that inspired Wissink on this point: W. Brechmann, *Die richtlinienkonforme Auslegung: zugleich ein Beitrag zur Dogmatik der EG-Richtlinie* (Beck, 1994).

39 J.H. Even, "Richtlijnconform of contra legem: that's the question" [2012] *Tijdschrift Arbeidsrechtpraktijk* 104, 110. M.H. Wissink (n. 34), pp. 163–64; Smits and van Schagen (n. 37).

40 Supreme Court 10 August 2007, ECLI:NL:HR:2007:AZ3758, *AB* 2007/291, with case note by R.J.G.M. Widdershoven (*Vierdaagse*).

as the legislature had presumably intended to deviate from the Directive. The Advocate General at the Supreme Court[41] agreed with this line of reasoning, although he based his interpretation on the text of the national provision, and not on the legislative intent. The Supreme Court came to a different conclusion. It referred to the assumption formulated by the ECJ in the *Wagner Miret* case, according to which the court must presume that the legislature has intended to transpose the Directive correctly, unless explicitly stated otherwise.[42] It continues by stating that if the wording allows for a consistent interpretation, legislative history leading to another interpretation may not be invoked in order to refuse reaching a result in conformity with the directive. This train of thought echoes the *Björnekulla Fruktindustrier* judgment,[43] which was however not referred to by the Supreme Court. The judgment concluded with a treatment of the argument based on legal certainty, which will be discussed in section 4, but this argument does not alter the Court's judgment.

The approach of the Supreme Court differs from that of the Court of Appeals and from the Advocate General in that it takes the result, and not the process of interpretation, as a point of departure. The Court of Appeals and the Advocate General use different interpretive methods to find out which is the best interpretation of the national provision. Both thus take the national provisions as their point of departure and see in either their formulation or their legislative history a hindrance to a consistent interpretation.[44] The Supreme Court, on the contrary, first establishes what result would be in line with the objectives of the directive, before moving on to analyse whether the text of the national provision makes reaching such result impossible. If the text of the provision is no hindrance for a consistent interpretation, the next question is whether such interpretation would lead to a violation of legal certainty of one of the parties. In principle, this is not the case, as tax payers may not rely solely on national law – unless this explicitly expresses the intention of deviating from European law. Preparatory documents can therefore only limit the possibilities for a consistent interpretation inasmuch as they reveal an explicit intention to not adhere to European law – which will be a rarity. Although a consistent interpretation was deemed possible by the Supreme Court, it was not applied as the Supreme Court understood the Directive in such a way that the lower tax tariff was to be applied in the case at hand.

---

41 Advocates General in the Dutch legal system play a role comparable to their counterparts at the ECJ: they provide the Supreme Court with independent advisory opinions on the case pending before the Court.

42 See para. 3.4 of the Vierdaagse judgment, referring to Case C-334/92, ECLI:EU:C:1993:945, *Wagner Miret v. Fondo de garantia salarial* [1993] ECR I-6913 This assumption was already being used by Dutch courts long before that, see Supreme Court 2 May 1984, ECLI:NL:HR:1984:AW8625, *BNB* 1984/295 with case note by A.L.C. Simons.

43 Case C-371/02, ECLI:EU:C:2004:275, *Björnekulla Fruktindustrier AB v. Procordia Food AB* [2004] ECR I-5811, para. 13.

44 See the case note by R.J.G.M. Widdershoven at 4.

3.3. A RESULT-ORIENTED APPROACH TO CONSISTENT INTERPRETATION

Two recent judgments took this approach further and applied the new line of case-law to civil proceedings. The first is the *Thuiskopie* judgment from 2012. The case deals with the compatibility of the Dutch rules concerning private copying, as laid down in the Copyright Act, with Directive 2001/29/EC of the European Parliament and of the Council of 22 May 2001 on the harmonisation of certain aspects of copyright and related rights in the information society (the "Copyright Directive"). The question revolves around the "fair compensation" that Member States may require to be paid according to Art. 5(2) of the Copyright Directive. More specifically, the case deals with the question whether this fair compensation may include the damages suffered when a private copy is made from an illegal (internet) source. According to the Dutch Copyright Act, as can be derived from the preparatory works, making a copy from an illegal source is not illegal in itself and hence the fair compensation does not include damages resulting from the illegality of the source itself. It was – and remained – unclear throughout the case whether this was in line with the Copyright Directive. The Court of Appeals had summarised the existing case-law on consistent interpretation as follows: "the wording of the national provision viewed in conjunction with the legislative history thereof, may entail that an interpretation in conformity with a directive is not possible, especially when also the principle of legal certainty resists such an interpretation".[45] However, the Court of Appeals also referred to the *Vierdaagse* judgment discussed above, which was delivered in an administrative case, and deduced from it that a consistent interpretation will be possible, as a rule, unless the distance between national and European law is so great that it cannot be bridged through means of interpretation.[46] The Court of Appeals did not establish whether indeed the Copyright Act violated the Copyright Directive, as this would not alter the outcome of the case: if the Copyright Act were in line with the Directive, the Dutch provisions would be applied in line with it, but if the Act were to violate the Copyright Directive, the gap could not be bridged and the Dutch provisions would still be applied in the same manner.

According to the Supreme Court, however, the wording *could* be interpreted in line with the Directive, even if the Dutch system indeed opposed that of European law. Like in the *Vierdaagse* case just discussed, even though the

---

[45] Author's translation of Court of Appeals of 's-Gravenhage 15 November 2010, ECLI:NL:GHSGR:2010:BO3982, para. 2.11: "de bewoordingen van de nationale bepaling in samenhang bezien met de totstandkomingsgeschiedenis daarvan [kunnen] met zich ... brengen dat richtlijnconforme interpretatie niet mogelijk is, met name wanneer ook het rechtszekerheidsbeginsel zich daartegen verzet."

[46] Supreme Court 21 September 2012, ECLI:NL:HR:2012:BW5879, *NJ* 2012/532 *AB* 2012/367 with case note by R.J.G.M. Widdershoven (*Thuiskopie*), para. 2.11.

legislature might have given an interpretation of national law in contravention of European law, it cannot be inferred from the legislative history that the legislature has intended anything else than faithfully transposing the Directive. Therefore, the statements from the legislature do not stand in the way of a consistent interpretation. If the wording allows a reading in line with the directive, a consistent interpretation is possible and hence required, according to the Supreme Court. Therefore, the Court of Appeals could not have left the question of compatibility unanswered. As the Supreme Court also had no answer to the question of compatibility, it initiated a preliminary procedure in which the ECJ decided that the Dutch Copyright Act did, indeed, not correctly transpose the Copyright Directive.[47] It is not clear what has happened to the case since. What is interesting about the case is that the judgment shows an increasing willingness on the part of the Supreme Court to apply the instrument of consistent interpretation in horizontal relationships.

The second judgment went further still. In the early cases discussed previously, the text of the law seemed to function as an insuperable hurdle to a consistent interpretation. However, in the more recent *Albron* case from 2013, things turned out to be even more complicated than that.[48] The case dealt with the question of who counts as an "employer" (in the words of Dutch law) or "transferor" (in the words of European law). The case leading to the Supreme Court ruling concerned the Heineken International company, which comprised several subsidiary companies. One of these subsidiaries, HNB, employed all of the company's workers, who were seconded to other subsidiary companies, including "Heineken Nederland". Catering activities at Heineken Nederland were originally carried out by people employed at HNB, but Heineken Nederland decided to outsource its catering activities to another company, Albron. The question was whether Heineken Nederland was the 'transferor' in the sense of Directive 2001/23/EC of 12 March 2001 on the approximation of the laws of the Member States relating to the safeguarding of employees' rights in the event of transfers of undertakings, businesses or parts of undertakings or businesses (the "Transfers of Undertakings Directive"), in which case the people working there would enjoy the protection granted by the Transfers of Undertakings Directive, consisting in the preservation of their employment and employment conditions. The reason this was unclear, was that the people working at Heineken Nederland were not formally employed by that company (as they were employed by the other subsidiary, HNB). According to established case-law in the Netherlands at the time, Heineken Nederland would not be the 'employer' and its workers would not enjoy the protection granted by EU law. This established case-law was based

---

47 Case C-435/12, ECLI:EU:C:2014:254, *ACI Adam BV and Others v. Stichting de Thuiskopie* [2014] ECR I-5331.

48 Supreme Court 5 April 2013, ECLI:NL:HR:2013:BZ1780, *NJ* 2013/389 with case note by E. Verhulp (*Albron*).

on a literal interpretation of Art. 7:663 of the Dutch Civil Code, which refers to rights and obligations ensuing from an employment contract. A preliminary procedure was initiated in order to ask the ECJ about the correct explanation of the Directive, so that the conformity of Dutch law could be assessed.[49] The ECJ ruled that Heineken Nederland could be seen as the "transferor", even though the employees did not have an employment contract with this subsidiary.

The cassation proceedings following the Court of Appeals judgment concerned the question whether the Dutch provisions could indeed – as had been done by the Court of Appeals – be read in conformity with the Directive as explained in the *Albron* judgment (this question had not been raised in the preliminary procedure). According to Albron, who compared his case to *Pink Floyd/Rigu Sound* and *Asseldonk/Ter Schure* (the early cases discussed in section 3.1), this was not the case. The Supreme Court, however, agreed with the Court of Appeals and with Advocate General Wissink, who had given the Supreme Court his advisory opinion.[50] The discrepancies between European and national law were not intentional, but based on a misunderstanding of the Directive on the part of the national legislature. Hence, the presumption that the legislature has had the intent of transposing the Directive correctly is valid in this case and thus it cannot be said that parliamentary history only allows the interpretation leading to a result contrary to the directive. The Supreme Court continued by stating that the appeal to the wording of the statute was unsuccessful, as "the wording of the law is not always decisive for its interpretation".[51] According to the Supreme Court, the wording of the statute is even less important in light of the intent to transpose correctly, as the preparatory works show that the legislature has chosen these words precisely with the purpose of transposing EU law faithfully.

In both these cases, it was not the purely national interpretation of Dutch law that was taken as a point of departure, but rather the result that is to be reached because of European law. This means that the directive will always play a certain role for the interpretation of national law, even in the case where none of the traditional sources to be consulted[52] refers to the directive. Also, a contrary interpretation given by the legislature is no longer a valid ground for not reaching a result in conformity with the directive, at least not when the legislature has had the intention of transposing faithfully. A shift can therefore be observed from a national approach in which European law may only play a role

49 Case C-242/09, ECLI:EU:C:2010:625, *Albron* [2010] ECR I-10309.

50 This is the same Wissink as the author of the book referred to in fn 34.

51 Author's translation of Supreme Court 5 April 2013, ECLI:NL:HR:2013:BZ1780, *NJ* 2013/389, with case note by E. Verhulp (*Albron*), para. 3.7: "De formulering van de wet is … niet steeds beslissend voor de uitleg daarvan".

52 The methods of interpretation used in Dutch law are inspired by the four classical methods as presented by Von Savigny: grammatical, historical, systematic and logical (teleological, in modern words) interpretation. See C.F. von Savigny, *System des heutigen Römischen Rechts* (Veit, 1840).

if national law is ambiguous, towards a more European law oriented approach, in which the result to be reached is the starting point. This development is in line with the development in the ECJ's case law towards a stronger duty of consistent interpretation. Accepting this European law oriented approach means accepting greater influence of European law on the methods of interpretation used and their hierarchy.

4. THE LIMITS TO CONSISTENT INTERPRETATION IN DUTCH CASE-LAW

This section will turn to the limits of the duty of consistent interpretation and how they manifest themselves in the case-law of Dutch courts. This section will set out discussing the most important limit: the general principles of European law, of which the principle of legal certainty is in turn the most important. For the field of substantive criminal law, this translates further into the principle of legality.[53] This limit refers to the result of interpretation: a national court may not reach a result that contravenes the principle of legal certainty. This means that bigger discrepancies between European and national law cannot be overcome through means of consistent interpretation, and that in case of serious discrepancies, the legislature will have to take action. The *contra legem* limit, as discussed previously in this contribution and central to section 4.2, establishes a primacy of literal interpretation over the other interpretive methods and thus relates to the process of interpretation. The last part of this section discusses the question whether minimum harmonisation stands in the way of a consistent interpretation.

4.1. GENERAL PRINCIPLES OF EUROPEAN LAW, ESPECIALLY THE PRINCIPLE OF LEGAL CERTAINTY

Contrary to the general approach to the duty of interpretation, the limits to consistent interpretation must be discussed in relation to the different legal fields in which consistent interpretation is applied. This is because those limits play a different role according to the legal relationship central to the case.

4.1.1. Private Law

Even in its early case-law, the Dutch Supreme Court applied the limits to consistent interpretation to private law cases, even though these limits were

---

[53] Case 80/86, ECLI:EU:C:1987:431, *Criminal proceedings against Kolpinghuis Nijmegen BV* [1987] ECR 3982.

originally formulated by the ECJ in the context of criminal law. In the *Pink Floyd/Rigu Sound* case analysed earlier in this contribution, the Court of Appeals had stated that a consistent interpretation would be *contra legem*, even though the *contra legem* boundary had not even been formulated in European case-law at that point.[54] The Supreme Court implicitly accepted this viewpoint, and added that a consistent interpretation would violate the principle of legal certainty.[55] Only in the *Adeneler* case from 2006, the ECJ mentioned the principle of legal certainty for the first time as a principle relevant to private law.[56] It can thus be observed that in the early case-law the Dutch courts were keen to stress the limits to the principle of consistent interpretation.

In its more European law oriented later case-law, the Supreme Court also instructs courts when not to accept an appeal to the principle of legal certainty. The *Thuiskopie* judgment discussed in the previous section contained a much-cited passage on the duty of consistent interpretation in relation to legal certainty: "Whenever the Dutch legislature, when enacting transposing legislation, has given a certain interpretation of the law which appears to be in contravention of the directive, the national court may not, because of this legislative history, set aside the duty of consistent interpretation ... because of legal certainty, if the legislature has had the intention of transposing the directive faithfully and the text of the national provision also allows for an interpretation in conformity with the directive."[57] The passage suggests that application of the principle of legal certainty is categorically ruled out if the wording of the national law allows for a consistent interpretation and a faithful transposition was intended by the legislature.

4.1.2. *Administrative Law*

Whereas the Supreme Court has been criticised in earlier years for not attributing enough weight to European law in its case-law and for not being consistent in its approach,[58] the *Afdeling Bestuursrechtspraak van de Raad van State*

54 It was first accepted in Case C-105/03, ECLI:EU:C:2005:386, *Criminal proceedings against Pupino* [2005] ECR I-5309.

55 Supreme Court 15 October 1996, ECLI:NL:HR:1996:ZC2177, *NJ* 1997/649 with case note by D.W.F. Verkade (*Pink Floyd/Rigu Sound*), para. 3.4.

56 Case C-212/04, ECLI:EU:C:2006:443, *Adeneler and others v. Ellinikos Organismos Galaktos* [2006] ECR I-6091, para. 110.

57 Author's translation of Supreme Court 21 September 2012, ECLI:NL:HR:2012:BW5879, *NJ* 2012/532, para. 5.1.3: "Wanneer de Nederlandse wetgever bij de totstandkoming van de implementatiewetgeving een bepaalde uitleg aan de wet heeft gegeven die in strijd met de richtlijn blijkt te zijn, kan de nationale rechter niet vanwege die totstandkomingsgeschiedenis met een beroep op het rechtszekerheidsbeginsel afzien van de ... verplichting tot richtlijnconforme uitleg, indien de wetgever heeft beoogd de richtlijn getrouw om te zetten en de tekst van de wettelijke regeling ook een richtlijnconforme uitleg toelaat."

58 Swaak (n. 35), pp. 222–23; M.H. Wissink (n. 34), pp. 163–64; Smits and van Schagen (n. 37); M.H. Wissink (n. 34); J.H. Even (n. 39) 104, 110 (all discussed in the previous section).

(the Administrative Jurisdiction Division of the Council of State – *ABRvS*, the highest administrative court in some types of administrative procedures) was criticised for the opposite, namely not observing the boundaries to the duty of consistent interpretation.[59] This criticism related to the *Hees/EPON* case, which in an earlier stage had led to a preliminary ruling procedure at the ECJ about the correct interpretation of the term "waste".[60] The answers provided by the ECJ showed that the government had granted permits in contravention of a directive. The conditions attached to these permits allowed the burning of "clean wood", but not the burning of waste. However, according to the ECJ, what was called "clean wood" in the permit conditions had to count as "waste". As it turned out, the granting of the permits had been based on an incorrect interpretation of the term "waste". The Administrative Jurisdiction Division of the Council of State interpreted the licence conditions in conformity with the Directive, as a consequence of which the activities of EPON were no longer permitted.[61]

Likewise, in the *Vierdaagse* case the result of consistent interpretation could potentially have led to a deterioration of the position of a legal person.[62] The reasoning of the Supreme Court in that case implied that a conforming interpretation of tax law may lead to higher tax duties being imposed. This was confirmed in a later judgment handed down by the same tax chamber of the Supreme Court,[63] in the aftermath of the *Joustra* judgment from the ECJ.[64] Joustra had imported wine from France for himself and for his circle of wine-loving friends. Excise duties had been levied over these products in France, but then Dutch authorities also levied excise duties and a conflict arose. In order to establish whether excise duties should be levied by the Dutch authorities in this situation, the ECJ was asked whether this situation fell under Art. 7, 8 or 9 of Council Directive 92/12/EEC of 25 February 1992 on the general arrangements for products subject to excise duty and on the holding, movement and monitoring of such products. The ECJ ruled that it fell under the scope of Art. 7 of the Directive, according to which excise duties must be levied in the state in which

---

59 F.G.H. Kristen, *Misbruik van voorwetenschap naar Europees recht: een onderzoek naar de grondslag en de werking van het Europese verbod van misbruik van voorwetenschap, met aandacht voor de doorwerking van EG-richtlijnen in het strafrecht* (Wolf Legal Publishers, 2004), p. 79; M.P. Jongma and J.R.C. Tieman in their case note to ABRvS 20 June 2001, ECLI:NL:RVS:2001:AB2437 *AB* 2001/260 (*Hees/EPON*).

60 Joined Cases C-418 and 419/97, ECLI:EU:C:2000:318, *Archo Chemie Nederland and others* [2000] ECR I-4512.

61 ABRvS [Administrative Jurisdiction Division of the Council of State] 20 June 2001, ECLI:NL:RVS:2001:AB2437, *AB* 2001/260 with case note by M.P. Jongma and J.R.C. Tieman (*Hees/EPON*).

62 Supreme Court 10 August 2007, ECLI:NL:HR:2007:AZ3758, *AB* 2007/291 with case note by R.J.G.M. Widdershoven (*Vierdaagse*).

63 Supreme Court 6 June 2008, ECLI:NL:HR:2008:BD3139, *AB* 2008/214 with case note by R.J.G.M. Widdershoven.

64 Case C-5/05, ECLI:EU:C:2006:733 *Joustra* [2006] ECR I-11075.

the products are held: in this case, the Netherlands. The excise duty paid in the first state must be reimbursed.[65] This judgment led to the question whether Dutch law could indeed be read in line with the Directive, so as to achieve the prescribed result. Several possible legal bases that were scrutinised could not be used to levy the taxes, as they were only applicable to entrepreneurs. There was one article that could possibly be used (Art. 2c(2) of the Excise Duty Act), but this was meant to transpose Arts. 8 and 9 of the Directive, not Art. 7, which was the relevant directive provision in this case. An interpretation of these provisions in line with their legislative history would lead to the conclusion that the provisions did not apply, as they were meant to apply only to the situation where the products were transported by the private person, whereas in the case at hand the wine was transported by a transport company. Para. 1 of Art. 2c also mentioned explicitly that it applied to cases where the products were brought to the Netherlands by the private party. Hence, both the text and the legislative history of Art. 2c(2) implied that the article did not apply to the case at hand. However, para. 2 of this article, whilst referring to and expanding the scope of application of para. 1, did not repeat the demand from para. 1 concerning by whom the products were transported. Hence, the wording of the text of para. 2 did not in and of itself explicitly prevent it from being applied to the situation at hand. Referring to the *Vierdaagse* judgment and the statement therein that legislative history does not stand in the way of a consistent interpretation, the Supreme Court decided that the article could be used as a legal basis for levying the excise duties, albeit only for the wine imported not for own use but for the members of the circle of wine friends. A consistent interpretation of the Excise Duty Act thus led to the imposition of tax duties which would otherwise not be imposed. Again, the consequences of this argumentation were mild, as the excise duties paid in France had to be reimbursed.

In the *Vierdaagse* case, the Supreme Court made it clear that the principle of legal certainty can seldom bring solace. This principle does not, according to the Supreme Court, imply that individuals must be able to rely solely on the text and legislative history of their national provisions. Such a conclusion on the principle of legal certainty would be in denial of Art. 249 EC Treaty, which states that directives are binding as to their result.[66] It follows from the Supreme Court case-law that individuals may not rely solely on national law, but must consult European law as well in order to assess their duties and obligations.

Of course, this does not mean that "anything goes" in administrative law. The imposition of sanctions must always have a clear basis in national law.

---

65 Ibid., para. 53.

66 Supreme Court 10 August 2007, ECLI:NL:HR:2007:AZ3758, *AB* 2007/291 with case note by R.J.G.M. Widdershoven (*Vierdaagse*), para. 3.4.

Hence, a consistent interpretation may not lead to the extension of a prohibition which is enforced by means of administrative sanctions.[67]

4.1.3. Criminal Law

The question of the limits to consistent interpretation is, in the present author's view, most pressing for the field of substantive criminal law. Unfortunately, there is no case-law from the Supreme Court that explains these boundaries and provides guidance to lower courts. There is some case-law, mostly on money laundering, that has spawned criticism because the Supreme Court did not involve European law at all in its interpretation of national law.[68] Indeed it may be expected of the Supreme Court that it accounts for the European dimension of national provisions wherever relevant. However, this case-law cannot directly inform us on the limits to consistent interpretation in the opinion of the Supreme Court.

Case-law from the courts deciding on facts shows a varying picture. In some cases, a consistent interpretation was refused as it would lead to the defendant being held liable under criminal law, even though the acts were not criminal according to Dutch law at the time of their commission.[69] In another case, Directive 2003/6/EC of the European Parliament and of the Council of 28 January 2003 on insider dealing and market manipulation (market abuse) was invoked by the defendant (further details on the content of the claim are not specified in the judgment).[70] At that time, the Directive had not yet been transposed into Dutch law, but a legislative proposal was pending before the Parliament. The Directive would be further clarified and specified in a comitology procedure, and since it was going to be transposed, a debate had arisen as to the scope and meaning of the substantive norms in the Directive. Because of the uncertainty still surrounding the Directive, it could not serve as the basis for direct effect or a consistent interpretation, according to the Amsterdam District Court. This reasoning was criticised in the case note, both regarding the Court's claim that the market abuse directive was insufficiently clear, and regarding the conclusion that in that case the duty of consistent interpretation

---

67 ABRvS 28 February 2007, ECLI:NL:RVS:2007:AZ9494, *AB* 2007/183 with case note by R.J.G.M. Widdershoven; ABRvS 4 March 2009, ECLI:NL:RVS:2009:BH4621, *AB* 2009/156 with case note by R.J.G.M. Widdershoven.

68 Supreme Court 6 February 2007, ECLI:NL:HR:2007:AY6713, *NJ* 2008/467 with case note by F.G.H. Kristen; Supreme Court 26 October 2010, ECLI:NL:HR:2010:BM4440, *NJ* 2010/655 with case note by N. Keijzer; Supreme Court 17 April 2012, ECLI:NL:HR:2012:BW1481; Supreme Court 8 January 2013, ECLI:NL:HR:2013:BX6910, *NJ* 2013/266 with case note by M.J. Borgers.

69 Court of Appeals of Arnhem-Leeuwarden 23 April 2014, ECLI:NL:GHARL:2014:3361.

70 District Court of Amsterdam 3 December 2004, ECLI:NL:RBAMS:2004:AR6884 and ECLI:NL:RBAMS:2004:AR6888, *JOR* 2005/13.

no longer applies. What is striking in the case-law is that when the principle of legality is used as an argument to refuse a consistent interpretation, courts refer to its codification in Art. 1 of the Dutch Penal Code or Art. 7 of the European Convention on Human Rights (ECHR), but not to European law itself.[71] Explicit references to the EU principle of legality or the principle of legal certainty are seldom found in the case-law of the national criminal courts.

Some of the decisions delivered by courts do seem to stretch the duty of consistent interpretation quite far. The Den Bosch Court of Appeals added a condition to a criminal offence, so as to avoid a prohibited restriction on the internal market.[72] The Court read a provision prohibiting the selling, delivering or trading of certain unregistered pharmaceutical medicines and preparations in such a manner that this was only prohibited inasmuch as these medicines and preparations are destined for distribution to final consumers in the Netherlands. In another case, a Court of Appeals read the maximum of "50 mg/kg" of cadmium allowed in toys as "100 mg/kg", to avoid a violation of European law.[73] This had no consequences for the case at hand, as the amount of cadmium found exceeded both limits. In the view of the present author, these interpretations are obvious examples of interpretations *contra legem*. In both cases, however, these interpretations are (potentially) beneficial to the defendant, as a result of which the principle of legal certainty in its manifestation as a right pertaining to the defendant is not under serious pressure. The same result could have been reached by setting aside the national provisions in so far as they contravene European law.

Generally, the duty of consistent interpretation causes no problems in the field of criminal law. In a rare case, however, courts are tempted to an extensive interpretation based on European law. This was the case with the Dutch provision on human trafficking, which is drafted very broadly and which therefore has led to several convictions for conduct not usually understood as human trafficking.[74] One of the problems with the Dutch provision is that it has literally taken over the description of exploitation used in the Palermo Protocol on human trafficking, which states: "exploitation shall include", after which several

---

71 District Court of Rotterdam 20 December 2007, ECLI:NL:RBROT:2007:BC0861, *JOR* 2008/46 with case note by M. Nelemans.

72 District Court of Den Bosch 7 December 2006, ECLI:NL:RBSHE:2006:AZ3896 / ECLI:NL:RBSHE:2006: AZ3897 / ECLI:NL:RBSHE:2006:AZ3903 / ECLI:NL:RBSHE:2006: AZ3905 / ECLI:NL:RBSHE: 2006:AZ3934 / ECLI:NL:RBSHE:2006:AZ3935, *JGR* 2007/1 and 2007/2 with case note by M. Claessens.

73 As described in the Opinion of AG W.H. Vellinga for Supreme Court 23 December 2003, ECLI:NL:HR:2003:AL4343, para. 7.

74 L.B. Esser and C. Dettmeijer-Vermeulen, "Mensenhandel op een tweesprong. De omgang van rechters met de ruim geformuleerde mensenhandelgedraging in de delictsomschrijving van artikel 273f lid 1 sub 4 Sr" [2014] 7 *Delikt en Delinkwent* 512.

forms of exploitation are listed.[75] The United Nations Office on Drugs and Crime stated that because of the legality principle, Member States must spell out all forms of exploitation in national law,[76] which the Netherlands had not done. The 2011 Council Directive on human trafficking added new forms of exploitation to the framework decision it replaced, among which was the exploitation of criminal activities.[77] A suspect was convicted of human trafficking because of the exploitation of criminal activities, which took place before the Directive was transposed in Dutch law when the exploitation of criminal activities was added to the list of forms of exploitation.[78] The court takes the view that this interpretation is not *contra legem*, as the list is non-exhaustive. This argument is logically correct, but challenges the spirit of the ECJ's case-law on the limits to consistent interpretation and the obligation to safeguard the principle of legality.[79]

In the present author's view, it is crucial, for reasons of legality but also with a view to the legitimacy of European law, that courts stress that the duty of consistent interpretation is a limited duty. The principle of legality precedes over the duty to give effect to European law – according to European law, that is. It would be incomplete to state that the duty of consistent interpretation conflicts with the duties of states under their national (constitutional) law or the ECHR, without referring to the limits of the duty accepted in European law.

4.2. NO DUTY TO INTERPRET *CONTRA LEGEM*

In the description of the case-law of the Supreme Court, some references as to what is considered an interpretation *contra legem* have already been provided. Generally, an interpretation *contra legem* is understood as an interpretation going against the wording of the provision. As interpreting a law in a manner at odds with its wording is not categorically prohibited in Dutch law (see the *Albron* judgment discussed above, where the Supreme Court states that the wording of a provision is not always decisive for its meaning), it is sometimes questioned whether such an interpretation is categorically prohibited,

75 Art. 3 of the Palermo Protocol (the 2000 United Nations Protocol to Prevent, Suppress and Punish Trafficking in Persons, Especially Women and Children).

76 UNODC, Model Law against Trafficking in Persons, United Nations Publication 2009, p. 35 (available online at <www.unodc.org/documents/legal-tools/Model_Law_TiP.pdf>).

77 Directive of the Council and of the European Parliament 2011/36/EU of 5 April 2011 on preventing and combating trafficking in human beings and protecting its victims and replacing Council Framework Decision 2002/629/JHA [2011] OJ L101/1.

78 District Court of Midden-Nederland 9 July 2013, ECLI:NL:RBMNE:2013:2679.

79 See for another example in which European law seemingly inspires an extensive interpretation District Court of Maastricht 22 March 2012, ECLI:NL:RBMAA:2012:BV9705.

or only not obliged.[80] This debate is however not as vivid as in Germany, where the distinction between interpretation and *Rechtsfortbildung* is drawn more clearly.[81] In practice, for example in the *Albron* case discussed earlier, it seems accepted that an interpretation *contra legem* is not mandated, not even if it is possible according to national law, but that it is not ruled out either. It must be mentioned, however, that it is not always so easy to discern whether a certain outcome of the case would breach the wording of the provision.

Aside from question whether an interpretation would be *contra legem* or not, the question arises whether *contra legem* only refers to the wording of national law. This question turned out to be pressing in a series of judgments concerning the interpretation of criminal procedural law on the European Arrest Warrant. The Overleveringswet (the Dutch Surrender Act – OLW) transposes the Framework Decision on the European Arrest Warrant (FD EAW) into Dutch law.[82] This transposition has failed in different ways. Over the course of years, the Amsterdam District Court (ADC) has found several discrepancies between the Framework Decision and the OLW. As the wording of the OLW is clearly in contradiction with the FD EAW, the ADC has never asked preliminary questions but has simply declared Dutch law to be in contravention of the Framework Decision. The discrepancies were thought unresolvable through means of consistent interpretation. In a recent case, the ADC was confronted with the fact that Art. 7(1) OLW makes surrender for crimes not listed in Art. 2(2) of the Framework Decision conditional upon the requirement that the conduct must be punishable according to Dutch law with at least 12 months' imprisonment. Surrender for all facts not meeting this requirement must be refused. According to the Framework Decision, the possibility of surrender depends only upon the sentence in the issuing state, not in the executing state. If the court were to follow national law, it would have to refuse to surrender a Moroccan convict to Belgium for the execution of a prison sentence for a fact not meeting this criterion. This time, the court decided to start a preliminary procedure asking whether the requirement laid down in Art. 7(1) OLW constitutes a breach of the FD EAW.[83] The ECJ explained that the requirement of double criminality is unproblematic in light of Art. 2(4) of the FD, but that no requirement may be added that it must

---

80 See F.G.H. Kristen (n. 59), pp. 68–70.

81 See, among others, K. Riesenhuber and R. Domröse, "Richtlinienkonforme Rechtsfindung und nationale Methodenlehre" [2005] *Recht der Internationalen Wirtschaft* 52–54; W. Dänzer-Vanotti, "Die richtlinienkonforme Auslegung deutschen Rechts hat keinen rechtlichen Vorrang. Zugleich eine Erwiderung auf den Beitrag von Spetzler, RIW 1991 S. 579" [1991] *Recht der Internationalen Wirtschaft* 754; A.J. Kaiser, "Richtlinienkonforme rechtsfortbildung. Unionsrechtliche und nationale Methodik der Rechtsfindung" [2010] *Zeitschrift für Europarechtliche Studien* 219.

82 Council Framework Decision 2002/584/JHA of 13 June 2002 on the European arrest warrant and the surrender procedures between Member States [2002] OJ L190.

83 District Court of Amsterdam 2 September 2015, ECLI:NL:RBAMS:2015:5712.

be punishable with a custodial sentence of at least 12 months.[84] No remarks were made regarding the way this outcome had to be incorporated into the Dutch legal system, as the Court only stipulated how the FD EAW was to be interpreted.

With the judgment of the Court, the discrepancy between national law and EU law is indisputable. The ADC once again tried to resolve this discrepancy through means of consistent interpretation, and this time with more success. How can the possibility of reaching a consistent result have changed, given the fact that the laws have not? The ADC first recounts that the legislature has intended to transpose the FD EAW faithfully, and that Art. 7(1) OLW does not deviate from the FD EAW on purpose. The intention to introduce an extra condition for surrender in contravention of the FD EAW, does therefore not in itself make a consistent interpretation impossible. Then comes the *pièce de resistance* of the judgment: according to EU law, national courts must do whatever lies in their power to reach a result that conforms to EU law, considering the whole of national law. That last part of the sentence is of crucial importance, for the ADC places Art. 7 OLW in a systematic relationship to Art. 2 OLW. Art. 2 OLW explains the scope of the FD EAW by stating in what cases a EAW may be issued and in what cases it may be executed. In this article, the conditions for issuing a EAW are stated in accordance with the FD EAW (unlike in Art. 7 OLW). Because Art. 28 OLW states that courts must consider both Art. 2 and Art. 7 OLW, the ADC must reconcile the two. According to the ADC, a systematic interpretation of the entire act prevails in this case over one specific provision of the act. Hence, the ADC considers it possible to reach a result consistent with the FD EAW that is not *contra legem*.

A shift in the ADC's case-law on what counts as an interpretation *contra legem* can be seen here. A systematic interpretation permits the District Court to take into account the whole of national law. Whereas the court earlier saw every interpretation contravening the text of the national provision as an interpretation *contra legem*, the criterion now seems to be whether there are any *national* interpretive methods leading to a result consistent with EU law. If so, the interpretation is not *contra legem*. This approach was termed "primacy of conformity with European law" by Wissink, which means that if one of the available national interpretive methods makes it possible to reach a consistent result, this method takes primacy over all other interpretive methods.[85] In this approach, the main effect of consistent interpretation is establishing a hierarchy of methods of interpretation, albeit a flexible one that varies from case to case. The present author does not believe the shift in approach is based on a theoretical

---

84 Case C-463/15 PPU, ECLI:EU:C:2015:634, *A*, para. 31; Case C-463/15, ECLI:EU:C:2015:634, *Openbaar Ministerie v. A* [2015], para. 31.

85 M.H. Wissink (n. 34), pp. 121–41. Wissink further distinguishes approaches according to whether this primacy is based on national or on European law, but this distinction is not necessary for our present purposes.

reflection on the nature of the duty of consistent interpretation; rather this case shows that courts are willing to stretch their possibilities more when faced with acute problems.

4.3. NO CONSISTENT INTERPRETATION IN CASE OF MINIMUM HARMONISATION OR DISCRETION?

On occasion, the question has risen whether the duty of consistent interpretation applies in cases where the directive leaves discretion to the Member States. If, for example, the directive leaves room for more stringent regulations in national law, but the directive was transposed *verbatim* into national law, may national law be interpreted in a stricter manner than the directive?

In several administrative cases, the Administrative Jurisdiction Division of the Council of State has ruled that no stricter rules may be imposed upon individuals if the discretion has not been used when transposing the directive.[86] In those cases, a consistent interpretation would violate legal certainty. An optional provision in EU law may not be used against the individual, unless transposed by the legislature in a manner that respects the principle of legal certainty. This reasoning is based on the *Accardo* judgment of the ECJ.[87]

The reasoning in the few criminal cases dealing with this issue is slightly different. As directives enacted on the basis of Art. 82 and 83 TFEU usually aim only at minimum harmonisation, the issue often arises whether consistent interpretation is still compulsory. The Supreme Court has suggested, albeit implicitly, that this is not the case. The Supreme Court denied an appeal to a directive in a case where it was unsure whether national law was in line with the Directive, because the directive left room for discretion.[88] The Supreme Court seemed to imply that because the Directive enabled more stringent regulations under national law, it was not necessary to assess whether the legislature had sought to create more stringent regulations. Even if the Directive were to be narrower in its scope, the defendant could never benefit from it, because the legislature may vest more criminal liability than obliged. Hence, the Court does not actively investigate whether the legislature has had the intention of enacting a wider criminal offence compared to the Directive. This approach deviates slightly from the assumption that national law meant to transpose a directive has the same meaning and scope as the directive, unless explicitly stated otherwise by the legislature.

---

86 ABRvS 17 April 2013, ECLI:NL:RVS:2013:BZ7904, *AB* 2014/75 with case note by R. Ortlep and M.J.M. Verhoeven.

87 Case C-227/09, ECLI:EU:C:2010:624, *Accardo and Others v. Comune di Torino* [2010].

88 Supreme Court 9 July 2002, ECLI:NL:HR:2002:AD7737, *NJ* 2005/569.

In another criminal case, Advocate General Wortel advised the Supreme Court not to interpret national law in line with a directive, as the Directive aimed at minimum harmonisation. He stated that the court did not need to decide whether a consistent interpretation could benefit the defendant. His statement is somewhat ambiguous, as it seems to be partly informed by the opinion that national law does indeed not deviate from the Directive, but it implies again that consistent interpretation is not mandatory in case of minimum harmonisation. The most explicit utterance comes from Kristen, who states that minimum harmonisation not only allows the legislature to pose stricter norms, it also allows the court to interpret the provision in such a manner that more protection is granted in national law than in European law.[89]

The view that can be observed in the field of criminal law, entailing that courts do not need to pay attention to European law seeking minimum harmonisation, greatly diminishes the harmonising potential of such instruments. The present author would adhere to a more strict conception of the duty of consistent interpretation or, rather, a more strict conception of the principle of minimum harmonisation. In the view of the author, minimum harmonisation allows the *legislature* to raise the level of protection in national law compared to European law. If the legislature has not chosen to do so, the presumption of a correct implementation applies. This position is supported by para. 112 of the *Pfeiffer* judgment, in which the ECJ states that courts must presume that the Member State "following its exercise of the discretion afforded it under that provision" had the intention of faithfully transposing the Directive.[90] This consideration, even though it was given in a slightly different context,[91] implies that discretion is either used or not by the legislature, and not by the courts. Therefore, the present author believes that the *Wagner Miret* presumption applies to this situation as well. However, this presumption may be rebutted more easily in this context: leaving out a constituent element in a criminal provision would, also without the explicit utterance that national law thereby deviates from EU law, be sufficient to decide that the legislature has used its discretionary powers.[92] But if a directive or framework decision has been transposed into national law *verbatim*, the meaning and scope of European law provides guidance to national courts as to the meaning and scope of the relevant national provisions.[93] In the present author's view, in these cases courts must interpret

89 F.G.H. Kristen (n. 59), p. 77.

90 Joined Cases C-397 to 403/01, ECLI:EU:C:2004:584, *Pfeiffer and Others v. Deutsches Rotes Kreuz* [2004] ECR I-8878, para. 112.

91 The question was whether national law had managed to reach the minimum level of protection prescribed by the directive.

92 Not only is the meaning of minimum rules unclear, the meaning of minimum harmonisation in the context of substantive criminal law is unclear. The present author finds the interpretation that it allows for a wider scope of the criminal offence most convincing.

93 See to this effect also Case C-306/12, ECLI:EU:C:2013:650, *Spedition Welter GmbH v. Avanssur SA* [2013].

national law in line with the directive, irrespective of the fact that it leaves discretionary powers to the Member States.

5. CONSISTENT INTERPRETATION IN THE NETHERLANDS – MORE INFLUENCE OF EU LAW ON INTERPRETATION, LESS DISCRETION FOR COURTS

It can be observed that in line with the case-law of the ECJ, the duty of consistent interpretation exercises an increasing influence on the interpretation of Dutch statutory provisions. Whereas in the 1990s the Supreme Court only accepted consistent interpretation as a means of choosing between two interpretations enabled by a purely national interpretation, its later case-law is much more oriented towards reaching the result prescribed by the directive. Canonical ways of interpretation must be bent and stretched in order to achieve this goal. The way a directive or national provision was interpreted by the legislature in preparatory documents is not decisive. Especially in the field of substantive criminal law, the role of legislative intent is diminished compared to its usual importance. Indeed, the duty of consistent interpretation has a significant impact on the task of courts and the exercise of their discretion.

However, the duty is not stretched beyond the realms of possibility. What is considered possible is decided mainly on the basis of the wording of national law, even though the wording need not be an insuperable barrier either. Due attention is paid to legal certainty, especially in vertical relationships, although negative consequences for individuals are not categorically ruled out. Individuals may no longer solely rely on their national law and its legislative history, as they must take European law into account as well.

Overall, the evaluation of this contribution is that Dutch courts pay due attention to European law when interpreting national law in the cases where they exercise the duty explicitly. The case-law of the Supreme Court providing guidance to lower courts is in broad agreement with the case-law of the ECJ. However, the principle of legality is seldom referred to in its quality of a principle of European law that limits the ways in which European law may take effect in the national legal order. A second mild criticism is that the duty is not often exercised explicitly. It is not always mentioned explicitly, and the way in which European law has influenced the outcome of the case remains unspecified more often than not. Therefore, it is difficult to establish the exact parameters and boundaries of the duty in Dutch law. There is room for improvement on these points.

In some ways, national courts have become more independent vis-à-vis their national legislature as a consequence of their role in the decentralised enforcement of European law, especially the duty of consistent interpretation.

According to Léger, national courts have as a consequence gained a more autonomous position regarding the law: "the national judge is no longer necessarily, as Montesquieu was able to say in earlier times, the mouthpiece of the law".[94] That courts become more autonomous in relation to national legislation, is fairly undisputed.[95] Barents has, however, added that they may have become autonomous in relation to national law, but not in relation to European law.[96] What courts gain in return for their freedom vis-à-vis the national legislature, is an even more strict hierarchical relationship with European law. Therefore, constitutional relations between the legislature and the judiciary at the national level are indeed impacted by the duty of consistent interpretation. But contrary to what one might expect, the discretionary powers of the Dutch judiciary have diminished rather than increased.

94 Case C-244/01, ECLI:EU:C:2003:513, *Gerhard Köbler v. Republik Österreich* [2003] ECR I-10243, Opinion of AG Léger, para. 59.

95 W. Brechmann, (n. 38), pp. 25–30; M.H. Loth, *De Hoge Raad in dialoog; over rechtsvorming in een gelaagde rechtsorde* (Tilburg, 2014).

96 R. Barents, "Enkele kanttekeningen bij de autonomie van de nationale rechter in het Unierecht" [2013] *Trema* 128, 130.

EFFECTIVENESS AND APPLICATION OF EU LAW IN GERMAN COURTS

A Constitutional Perspective

Nils Grosche

1. INTRODUCTION

European integration is developed and consolidated through law.[1] Its implementation and effectiveness thereby essentially depend on the functionality of a multi-component system comprising European Union (EU) and national law. In this context, national courts are a keystone in the legal order of the EU due to their function of applying the law. This entanglement implies a decentralisation of the enforcement of law.[2] Whilst from the perspective of EU law all national courts are equal in terms of their general duties, their jurisprudence is nevertheless entrenched in historically distinct legal structures, cultures and traditions.[3]

Part of this entrenchment is how Member States model the role of national courts in general, and consequently their specific relationship to the effectiveness and application of EU law when applying the law. This contribution focuses on the domestic legal structure governing jurisprudence of German courts when the application of law is connected to the effectiveness of EU law. In this structure, consistent interpretation is one *modus operandi* serving effectiveness of EU law in the German legal system.

Although the understanding of the German framework to a great extent results from the jurisprudence of the *Bundesverfassungsgericht* (German Federal Constitutional Court – GFCC),[4] a chronological case overview is not provided here. The description rests on the constitutional building blocks laid out in the GFCC's jurisprudence. In a first step, three broader issues are addressed to highlight the general framework of the relationship of international as well as EU law and national jurisprudence according to the legal system of Germany (section 2). Against this background, the contribution discusses how the effectiveness and application of EU law are generated by constitutional

1 W. Hallstein, *Der unvollendete Bundesstaat* (Econ, 1969) 33, famously called the European Community a "*Schöpfung des Rechts, ... Rechtsquelle und ... Rechtsordnung*" (a creation of law,, a source of law and a legal system).

2 K. Lenaerts and P. Van Nuffel, *European Union Law* (3rd ed, Sweet & Maxwell, 2010), paras. 13-078 and 14-013; see also A. Voßkuhle and M. Lange, "Die Rolle der nationalen Gerichte im Europarecht" in S. Leible and J.P. Terhechte (eds.), *Europäisches Rechtsschutz- und Verfahrensrecht* (Nomos, 2014), p. 153.

3 These differences can be decisive even from an EU perspective in terms of assessing the concrete dimension of duties provided by EU law. For instance, when the ECJ requires national courts "to interpret it [i.e. domestic law], so far as possible" in conformity with EU law: Case C-212/04, *Adeneler*, ECLI:EU:C:2006:443, para. 108.

4 The GFCC's jurisprudence has a dominant role not only for German courts in general, but also regarding its dominant position as a point of reference in the German scientific community concerned with public law, see C. Schönberger, *Der "German approach"* (Mohr Siebeck, 2015), p. 30 *et seq*; on the expanding nature of the course of reception of EU law in the German academic profession see A.K. Mangold, *Gemeinschaftsrecht und deutsches Recht* (Mohr Siebeck, 2011), p. 187 *et seq*.

mechanisms on the one hand, and constrained by constitutional limits on the other (section 3).

2. BACKGROUND

The question of effectiveness and application of EU law in German courts is linked to the role of autonomous legal sources outside the national legal order, and the role of courts when referring to these. Three topics provide the necessary background for understanding the German approach: First, the general conceptual approach to the relationship between German and public international law; second, the specific conceptual approach to the relationship between German and EU law; and, finally, the structure of the German national court system.

2.1. DUALIST CONCEPTION OF PUBLIC INTERNATIONAL LAW AND THE PRINCIPLE OF OPENNESS

In *Görgülü*, a case concerning the scope of the binding effect of the European Convention on Human Rights (ECHR) as interpreted by the European Court of Human Rights, the GFCC explicated the constitutional understanding of the relationship of public international and domestic law:

> The Basic Law is clearly based on the classic idea that the relationship of public international law and domestic law is a relationship between two different legal spheres and that the nature of this relationship can be determined from the viewpoint of domestic law only by domestic law itself; …[5]

It derived this conclusion from the wording of Art. 25 and Art. 59.2 of the *Grundgesetz* (Basic Law – GG). The message is clear: the German legal order frames the influence of international law through a constitutional lens. Thus, there is a sharp division between questions of public international law and questions concerning their impact on the national legal order. As a consequence of this, effectiveness (or the ranking of international treaties within the national legal order) depends on the design of the constitutional framework provided by the Basic Law. In its design, the Basic Law treats different sources of public international law differently. For example, in a case concerning the relevance of

[5] *Görgülü* [2004], DE:BVerfG:2004:rs20041014.2bvr148104, para. 34 – the translations are largely based on the translations available at the homepage of the GFCC (<www.bundesverfassungsgericht.de>). The GFCC translates some but not all of its decisions. Only German versions are authoritative.

a bilateral treaty aimed at avoiding double taxation, the Federal Constitutional Court held that the Basic Law does not preclude more recent federal statutes from superseding treaty provisions of public international law in conflict with them.[6] Having regard to principles of democracy and parliamentary discontinuity, legislation can generally deviate from international treaties, and is not constrained to do so only when protecting fundamental constitutional principles.[7] Such legislative deviation by statute is not possible with respect to general rules of public international law,[8] however, as they rank above statutory law yet below the constitution.[9]

As there is no general constitutional obligation under the Basic Law to schematically comply with public international law obligations, there is always a risk that acts of the state may breach such obligations, with all of the possible consequences under public international law that may entail. However, according to constitutional doctrine, the Basic Law implies an unwritten open stance towards public international law circumscribed as *Grundsatz der Völkerrechtsfreundlichkeit*, thereby mitigating the risk of conflict whilst at the same time ensuring that the German State's commitment to international law does not override the democratic and constitutional system of the Basic Law.[10] The characteristics of this affirmative stance lie in the idea of *offene Staatlichkeit* (open statehood), meaning openness to international law through a legal structure enabling the exercise of sovereign power through international agreements and cooperation, and the integration of general rules of public international law. In the words of the GFCC:

> The Basic Law is intended to achieve comprehensive commitment to international law, cross-border cooperation and political integration in a gradually developing international community of democratic states under the rule of law.[11]

The principle of openness to international law derives from a systematic synopsis of the constitutional provisions governing issues related to public

---

6 In consequence, the court reiterated the applicability of the *Lex posterior derogat legi priori*-rule: *Treaty Override* [2015], DE:BVerfG:2015:ls20151215.2bvl000112, para. 50.

7 Justice König filed a separate opinion entailing a proposition for a more international law-oriented reading of the constitution in *Treaty Override* [2015] (n. 6).

8 This is a domestic legal term encompassing rules of universally applicable customary international law, supplemented by the traditional general legal principles of national legal orders: *State Insolvency* [2007], DE:BVerfG:2007:ms20070508.2bvm000103, para. 34.

9 Art. 25 sentence 2 of the Basic Law; on the position in the constitutional hierarchy of sources of law, see M. Herdegen in T. Maunz and G. Dürig (eds.), *Grundgesetz: Kommentar* (Beck, 2017), Art. 25 para. 78.

10 The Basic Law's openness can accurately be described as a reflective approach against the background of both traditional and innovative features in the constitutional tradition of Germany, see F. Schorkopf, *Grundgesetz und Überstaatlichkeit* (Mohr Siebeck, 2007), p. 33 *et seq.*, 61 *et seq.*

11 *Görgülü* [2004] (n. 5), para. 36.

international law.[12] Its most distinctive normative feature results from its role as a guideline in matters of interpretation:[13] international public law must be taken into consideration when interpreting fundamental rights, constitutional principles derived from the rule of law, and statutory law. National statute law must – if possible – be interpreted in a manner to avoid conflict with public international law.[14] Thus, national courts are generally obliged to choose an interpretation favourable to international law, as long as it appears justifiable according to the recognised methods of statutory and constitutional interpretation, and does not lead to a restriction of fundamental rights under the Basic Law.[15] With regard to provisions of the Basic Law, the GFCC emphasises a results-oriented approach, not allowing a schematic parallelisation, but requiring a system-adequate integration into the context of the German basic rights system.[16] For example, in a case concerning preventive detention, the GFCC ruled in accordance with the ECHR as interpreted by the European Court of Human Rights by accounting for its assessment in the context of the proportionality test – a principle inherent to the basic rights doctrine under the Basic Law.[17] The GFCC clarified that when taking into account judgments of the European Court of Human Rights beyond the scope of application of Art. 46 ECHR, an interpretation must give due consideration to the specific circumstances of the domestic law in question in order to achieve an adequate contextualisation.[18]

---

12 I.e. the Preamble, and Arts 1.2; 23; 24, 25, 26 and 59.2 of the Basic Law.

13 The dimensions of openness to international law listed by the GFCC are: the goal that all state institutions must follow public international law obligations of the Federal Republic of Germany and if possible prevent breaches; legislation must correct breaches by state institutions; and state institutions – under specific circumstances – have the duty to enforce public international obligations breached by other states. See *Treaty Override* [2015] (n. 6), para. 70.

14 *Treaty Override* [2015] (n. 6), para. 71.

15 The GFCC notes that this "obstacle to the reception of law may become relevant above all in multi-polar fundamental rights relationships in which the increase of liberty for one subject of a fundamental right at the same time means a decrease of liberty for the other": *Preventive Detention of G.* [2011], DE:BVerfG:2011:rs20110504.2bvr236509, para. 93. See with respect to decisions of international courts: A. Proelß, *Bundesverfassungsgericht und überstaatliche Gerichtsbarkeit* (Mohr Siebeck, 2014), p. 107 *et seq.*

16 The GFCC in *Preventive Detention of G.* [2011], ibid., para. 92, sees a parallel with regard to interpretation by means of comparing constitutions: "Against this background something similar is true of an interpretation of the concepts of the Basic Law that is open to international law as of an interpretation based on a comparison of constitutions: similarities in the text of the norm may not be permitted to hide differences which follow from the context of the legal systems: the human rights content of the agreement under international law under consideration must be 'reconceived' in an active process (of reception) in the context of the receiving constitutional system."

17 *Preventive Detention of G.* [2011], ibid.

18 *Ban on Strike Action for Civil Servants* [2018] DE:BVerfG:2018:rs20180612.2bvr.173812, para. 132.

When preventing and removing violations of public international law obligations by German courts the GFCC deems itself "indirectly in the service of enforcing international law".[19] For example, a constitutional claim can in principle be filed when international public law or decisions of international courts are not taken into consideration when applying statute law, thereby violating the so-called *Berücksichtigungspflicht* (duty to take into consideration).[20] It must be noted, though, that the constitutional duty to interpret in a manner that avoids conflict with international law does not apply universally and blindly to all sources of public international law. It depends on whether their respective content corresponds to the concept laid down by the Basic Law.[21] Conceptual correspondence with regards to human rights enshrined in public international law is reflected by Art. 1.2 of the Basic Law, a provision calling for the protection of the central stock of international human rights.[22]

The moderate dualist conception of the Basic Law with its openness to international law sets up the basic constitutional framework, encompassing a far-reaching receptiveness for public international law on the one hand, whilst safeguarding basic constitutional principles on the other. However, the constitutionally derived linkage of sources of public international law, including jurisprudence of international courts, to the application of the law by national courts, creates a scenario of constant reassurance and adjustment, presenting national courts with quite a challenge in their daily work. Although the rather unspecific concept of a "dialogue of courts"[23] certainly appeals to

---

19 *Görgülü* [2004] (n. 5), para. 61; see generally in regard to the application of the openness-principle by all state institutions: *Treaty Override* [2015] (n. 6), para. 66.

20 So-called "*Görgülü*-Rüge":, see K. Schneider, "§1" in C. Burkiczak, F.-W. Dollinger and F. Schorkopf (eds.), *Bundesverfassungsgerichtsgesetz* (C.F. Müller, 2015), paras. 136 *et seq.* On the other hand, if a public authority applies public international law schematically, this also amounts to a breach of rights as well. Another constitutional complaint serving correspondence of international and domestic law is an interpretation of basic rights provisions in conformity with parallel provisions enshrined in international or supranational law (called "*Verfassungsgerichtsverbundrüge*"), ibid., paras. 140 *et seq.*

21 *Land Reform III* [2004] DE:BVerfG:2014:rs20141022.2bvr066112, para. 92; this differentiation is not emphasised in later decisions such as *Treaty Override* [2015] (n. 6), para. 71 *et seq*, although the decision refers to the prohibition of schematic parallelisation.

22 The GFCC also deems such correspondence in the area of consular law resulting in a constitutional duty of regular courts to take into consideration in their decisions of the International Court of Justice, see *Consular Relations* [2013] DE:BVerfG:2013:rk20131105.2bvr157911, para. 11; and with regard to the Geneva Refugee Convention, see *Refugee Convention* [2014] DE:BVerfG:2014:rk20141208.2bvr045011, para. 36.

23 *Preventive Detention of G.* [2011] (n. 15), para. 89: "... even the 'last word' of the German constitution is not opposed to an international and European dialogue of courts, but is the normative basis for this". On the idea of dialogue with respect to Art. 4.2 TEU and Art. 79.3 of the Basic Law, see T. Wischmeyer, "Nationale Identität und Verfassungsidentität. *Schutzgehalte, Instrumente, Perspektiven*" [2015] *AöR* 415, 426; cf. M. Wendel, "Richterliche Rechtsvergleichung als Dialogform" [2013] *Der Staat* 339.

an idea of creating a pluralistic forum for deliberation, it nevertheless poses a challenge to aspirations of legal certainty and clarity.[24] The most salient effect can be witnessed in the higher courts practice of reasoning and its tendency of cascading paraphrases and citations.

2.2. OPENNESS TO EU LAW

The Federal Republic of Germany is a founding member of the ECSC, EURATOM and the EEC Treaty. The participation was part of a policy determined to commit the young West German democratic republic to *Westbindung* (western values).[25] In the past, advancing European integration has been a central and largely uncontested pillar of German foreign policy underlined by vast majorities voting for accession legislation of European treaties,[26] and founded on bipartisan support.[27]

Germany's active role in the continuous development of the European integration process is not only a question of political discretion with regards to economic and commercial intertwining, and later with regards to political unification. It is also envisioned in the Preamble of the Basic Law, which calls for a "determination to promote world peace as an equal partner in a united Europe", a provision shaping the moral foundation for the German constitutional order as well as a constant implicit reminder of the devastating wars endured by the European peoples.[28] In conjunction with the power transfer clause

---

24 An even greater problem when considering the fragmentation debate and its consequences for clarity. See the report by M. Koskenniemi, *Fragmentation of International Law* [2006] ILC General Assembly A/CN.4/L.682.

25 A. Wirsching, "Europa als Wille und Vorstellung" [2005] *ZSE* 488 (494).

26 For example, the Maastricht Treaty – entailing the replacement of the German Deutsche Mark with the Euro – was supported by 543 of 568; the Lisbon Treaty was supported by 515 of 611 members of the *Bundestag* (Federal parliament).

27 J. Ipsen, *Der Staat der Mitte* (C.H. Beck, 2009), p. 93 *et seq*. The ongoing Eurozone crisis as well as the refugee crisis have, however, caused discussions regarding the public perception of the role of Germany in the EU due to the fact that the development of these policy areas is in large part attributed to dysfunctional EU rules. Against this background, Germany's crisis management in EU matters is becoming a more visible and controversial factor: see J. Janning, "Suche nach Gestaltungsmacht" [2016] *APuZ – Deutsche Außenpolitik* 13.

28 The Parliamentary Council abstained from an explicit reference in order to not constitute an "eternal monument" of national-socialist power, see P. Häberle (ed), *Neuausgabe des Jahrbuch des öffentlichen Rechts der Gegenwart* (2nd ed., Mohr Siebeck, 2010), p. 27. In *Treaty of Lisbon* [2009] DE:BVerfG:2009:es20090630.2bve000208, para. 223, the GFCC derived a specific concept of sovereignty: "The Basic Law abandons a self-serving and self-glorifying concept of sovereign statehood and returns to a view of the state authority of the individual state which regards sovereignty as freedom that is organised by international law and committed to it. It breaks with all forms of political Machiavellianism and with a rigid concept of sovereignty which until the beginning of the 20th century regarded the right to wage war – even a war of aggression – as a right due to a sovereign state as a matter of course ...".

in Art. 23.1 of the Basic Law,[29] the constitution adopts an affirmative, open stance towards European integration, thereby echoing the abovementioned openness to international law, as well as underlining a more special relationship with regard to matters of European integration:

> The Basic Law calls for European integration and an international peaceful order. Therefore, not only the principle of openness towards international law, but also the principle of openness towards European law (*Europarechtsfreundlichkeit*) applies.[30]

Although the principle of openness towards EU law is a constitutional feature that impacts on the relationship between the German and EU legal orders, this relationship is entrenched in a highly sophisticated constitutional architecture that has evolved against the backdrop of an unprecedented transfer of power. This provokes questions of constitutional constraints when transferring such power, as well as questions concerning the possibilities of domesticising acts exercised in the name of transferred power. Although up to this point there has not been a constitutional halt to ratification of a treaty revision, or a declaration of inapplicability of an act of power by the EU, there are significant requirements laid out in the jurisprudence of the GFCC. From a narrative-driven point of view, the emerging pattern can be described as a recursive "yes, but ..." line of argument.

By permitting the transfer of sovereign powers, including their direct exercise within the national legal system, Art. 23.1 of the Basic Law generally "contains a promise of effectiveness and implementation corresponding to the primacy of application of Union law".[31] However, just like the openness towards international law, openness towards European integration is not tantamount to unconditional submission.[32] To the contrary, according to the GFCC, a constitutional prerequisite for participation under the Basic Law is that the EU is not in its treaty design or *de facto* a federal union with *prima facie* unlimited power, but an organisation to which power is conferred by the Member States.[33] With respect to applicability in Germany, EU power is

29 In the Basic Law's original design, the transfer of power to the European Communities was based on Art. 24.1, a provision not specifically tailored to European integration.

30 *Treaty of Lisbon* [2009] (n. 28), para. 225.

31 *Honeywell* [2010] DE:BVerfG:2010:rs20100706.2bvr266106, para. 53 *et seq.*

32 The GFCC connotes this idea to the preservation of sovereign statehood: *Treaty of Lisbon* [2009] (n. 28), para. 226. See also *Gauweiler* [2016] DE:BVerfG:2016:rs20160621.2bvr272813, para. 134.

33 To conceptually capture this idea as well as to emphasise the uniqueness of the European Union compared to a *Staatenbund* (a confederation), the GFCC refers to the European Union as a *Staatenverbund* (an association of sovereign states). This referral to statehood is criticised, see C. Möllers and D. Halberstam, "The German Constitutional Court says 'Ja zu Deutschland!'" [2009] *GLJ* 1241, 1247. The GFCC recently inflated the *Verbund*-conjunction when representing the relationship as a *Staaten-*, *Verfassungs-*, *Verwaltungs-* und *Rechtsprechungsverbund* (association of states, constitutions, administrations and jurisprudence): *Gauweiler* [2016] ibid., para. 140.

considered to be derived, and – seemingly contrary to the assertion of the Court of Justice of the European Union (ECJ) in *Costa v. ENEL* – not autonomous.[34] In consequence, its (democratic) legitimacy with regard to its impact in the domain of the Basic Law is necessarily connected to mechanisms enshrined in the Basic Law itself.[35] One major pillar is that supranational power must be exercised on the basis of an integration program approved and accounted for by the *Bundestag*. This does not mean that it is necessary to prescribe all steps of the integration process in detail, but rather to lay out a range of possibilities beforehand,[36] thereby fending off the issue of EU institutions deciding on their own competences, whilst simultaneously allowing ample space for them to effectively interpret their respective powers.[37] Another pillar of the legitimacy of the exercise of EU power in the German legal order follows from its compliance with Art. 79.3 of the Basic Law, a provision highlighting substantive features that are *verfassungsänderungsfest* (non-disposable even by constitutional amendment). *Mutatis mutandis*, these features may not be altered in the process of European integration and are *integrationsfest* (non-disposable even by transfer of powers to the EU), as reiterated by Art. 23.1 sentence 3 of the Basic Law. For example, according to the GFCC, the preservation of the principle of democracy requires that a transfer of power may not result in curtailing the *Bundestag*'s competences by essentially negating its substantial decision-making power. The point which the GFCC has in mind here is that the election to the *Bundestag* must be a reliable source of power, and that it may not serve as a mere façade whilst in substance all relevant decisions take place on a European level.[38]

34 *Treaty of Lisbon* [2009] (n. 28), para. 339: "The primacy of application of European law remains ... a derived concept which will have legal effect in Germany only with the order to apply the law given by the Act Approving the Treaty of Lisbon".

35 Consequently, the Basic Law prohibits citizens from being subject to political authority that they cannot avoid and where they cannot participate in its decision-making process equally and freely: *Gauweiler* [2016] (n. 32), para. 128. In a recent judgment, the GFCC coined the new term "*Einflussknick*" (drop in influence) to describe a democratic deficit of supranational measures due to the fact that they cannot directly be linked to approval of the national parliament (e.g. majority rule in the council, or independence of the ECB), and points to other factors of legitimisation. The standard is pretty steep because such a legitimacy claim is not even constitutionally ensured where national organs operate outside the scope of democratically approved law, see K. Schneider, "Der Ultra-vires-Maßstab im Außenverfassungsrecht" [2014] *AöR* 1, 25.

36 Conceptually, a difference can be made between the concrete process of integration and the program, see clearly elaborated by Schneider, ibid., 15 *et seq.*

37 Therefore, in the prospect of entering into new treaties, it is constitutionally forbidden to agree to treaty provisions that can be used in any possible manner (i.e. provisions of a blanket character). *Treaty of Lisbon* [2009] (n. 28), para. 239; *Gauweiler* [2016] (n. 32), para. 134.

38 Although this does not mean that "a pre-determined number or certain types of sovereign rights should remain in the hands of the state", it does require that "sufficient space is left to the Member States for the political formation of the economic, cultural and social living conditions". The GFCC connects the requirement of the ability of a constitutional state to democratically shape itself with specific areas: substantive and formal criminal law;

Constitutional complaints regarding the transgression of constitutional pillars can be raised through a multitude of different procedures before the GFCC.[39] The most controversial (but now well established) of these was first recognised in the GFCC's *Maastricht*-jurisprudence.[40] It concerns *Verfassungsbeschwerde* (i.e. the citizens' right to constitutional complaint pursuant to Art. 93.1 no. 4a of the Basic Law). The basic idea is founded on the prospect of lasting democratic self-government, and derived from the German citizen's rights set out in Art. 38.1 and Art. 38.2 of the Basic Law, a provision guaranteeing aspects of participation in the elections to the *Bundestag*. According to the GFCC, the function of the provision also entails a substantive claim, meaning that the act of voting must – in essence – necessarily refer to a (lasting) sufficient degree of responsibilities and competences at the hands of the Bundestag:

> Without the free and equal election of the body that has a decisive influence on the government and the legislation of the Federation, the constitutive principle of personal freedom remains incomplete. ... The citizens' right to determine in respect of persons and subjects, in freedom and equality by means of elections and other votes, public authority is the fundamental element of the principle of democracy. The right to free and equal participation in public authority is enshrined in human dignity (Art. 1.1 of the Basic Law).[41]

The transfer and exercise of EU power therefore has the potential to constitute a basic rights question.[42] The GFCC recently called the construction a "*right to democracy*" on the basis of Art. 38 of the Basic Law.[43] Although the wording of Art. 38 of the Basic Law is at best inconclusive, the GFCC's conceptual reading is nevertheless persuasive on another level, as it recognises the game-changing nature of a transfer of power for the democratic process.[44] Whilst the democratic

---

the disposition of the monopoly on the use of force by the police within the state and by the military; fundamental fiscal decisions on public revenue and public expenditure; decisions on the shaping of living conditions in a social state and decisions of particular cultural importance, e.g. on family law, the school and education system and dealing with religious communities, see *Treaty of Lisbon* [2009] (n. 28), para. 248 *et seq.*

39 See for an overview of admitted claims in the GFCC's jurisprudence, Schneider, "§1" (n. 20), para. 120 *et seq.*

40 Critics see an abolishment of the distinction between matters concerning the organisation of state power and individual rights.

41 *Treaty of Lisbon* [2009] (n. 28), para. 210 *et seq.*

42 By reviewing a law approved by a vast majority of the *Bundestag* in the name of democracy and by prescribing possible limits of European integration under the Basic Law the court's jurisprudence provokes a counter-majoritarian difficulty of a special kind. It limits the power of democratic disposal under Basic Law to ensure the continuation of a specific democratic framework in its scope of application.

43 *Gauweiler* [2016] (n. 32), para. 147.

44 Its essential premises are that public authority needs a forum fully accountable to the Basic Law where decisive power is exercised (theoretically unhindered), and where the people

texture of the Basic Law spelled out by the GFCC is accompanied by some inflexibility, it can be considered a form of lasting transparency with regard to the relevant rules governing public authority under the Basic Law.[45]

One ongoing constitutional issue concerns whether or not EU power is in accordance with the abovementioned constitutional pillars, and if, and under what circumstances, an individual can file a constitutional complaint. More detailed features of the GFCC's jurisprudence will be discussed below, as they are closely linked to the role of national courts and their contribution to the effectiveness of EU law – including the principle of consistent interpretation.[46]

2.3. COURT SYSTEM AND THE PRELIMINARY REFERENCE PROCEDURE

Chapter IX of the Basic Law contains provisions on the act of judging. Art. 92 of the Basic Law states that judicial power shall be vested in the judges, and shall be exercised by the Federal Constitutional Court, by the federal courts provided for in the Basic Law and by the courts of the *Länder* (the federal states). The provision reveals the differentiated institutional design triggered by the German federal system, as well as the special role of the constitutional court.

participate equally (i.e. by the principle of one man, one vote) and freely. If these premises are met, people are, first, not at risk of being stripped of their capacity to equally and freely decide on public affairs although they are primary subjects of the respective public authority (they qualify as primary subjects of the public authority because the territory where power is executed has a unique link to their citizenship). And, second, they are not stripped of the effective governing role of their constitution. Thus, with regard to the substantial space, measures of public authority are inevitably shaped by the Basic Law's conditions with regard to the democratic process, be it the limits or functional output derived from fundamental rights or be it formal requirements laid out in the constitution. This, of course, cannot be explained by the assertion that a democratic process in a forum not fully accountable to the Basic Law would *per se* be inferior, much rather, the Basic Law – due to its scope of application – does not commit to a promise of democracy it cannot uphold on its own terms.

45 In its Lisbon jurisprudence, the GFCC by essentially allowing a constitutional complaint against a change of the Basic Law in disguise even takes into consideration the requirements for a replacement of the Basic Law, an outlook originally foreseen for the case of reunification in Art. 146 of the Basic Law and afterwards maintained in a modified version (see M. Herdegen, *Die Verfassungsänderungen im Einigungsvertrag* (Decker & Müller, 1991)). The GFCC refers to a "pre-constitutional right" to release the state constituted by the Basic Law on behalf of the constituent authority, and not on behalf of the constitutional authority emanating from the constitution. In its *Lisbon* decision, the GFCC rejected the plaintiff's notion that the Treaty of Lisbon constituted such a step, see *Treaty of Lisbon* [2009] (n. 28), para. 179. See further on the issue H. Grefrath, "Exposé eines Verfassungsprozessrechts von den Letztfragen?" [2010] *AöR* 221; and M. Nettesheim, "Wo 'endet' das Grundgesetz? Verfassungsgebung als grenzüberschreitender Prozess" [2012] *Der Staat* 313.

46 See section 3.3.

The GFCC's jurisprudence is restrained to specific constitutional matters, as it does not serve as the supreme appellate court on non-constitutional issues. However, under certain circumstances interpretation of non-constitutional statute law constitutes a constitutional matter.[47] There is no monopolisation on the application of the constitution at the hands of the GFCC, especially as regards basic rights. Art. 1.3 of the Basic Law states that the basic rights bind the legislature, the executive and the judiciary as directly applicable law. Thus, all courts can be considered as courts with an equal responsibility to apply the constitution. However, the GFCC has specific competences beyond those of regular courts. For example, Art. 100.1 of the Basic Law stipulates a referral procedure to the GFCC when a court is convinced that a parliamentary law on whose validity its decision depends is unconstitutional. Similar special competences are also put in place to protect the effectiveness of EU law.[48] Constitutional complaints by individuals pursuant to Art. 93.1 no. 4a of the Basic Law are considered an extraordinary remedy outside of the regular court system.

The courts' role for the individual is mainly related to two basic right-pillars. First, Art. 19.4 of the Basic Law provides recourse to the courts should one's rights be violated by executive power. Second, *Justizgewährleistungsanspruch*, a more general right of access to courts, including matters of civil dispute, is derived from Art. 2.1, in conjunction with Art. 20.3 of the Basic Law.[49] The established right to recourse also encompasses the efficiency of such recourse. By and large it can be considered the foundation for setting up a system of judicial review that is primarily tailored to serve the bearer of an individual right, and not a somehow detached public interest therein.[50]

The structure of the regular court system in Germany is divided into five branches, each consisting of a Federal Supreme Court.[51] The federal courts

47 The leading case is the famous *Lüth*-decision BVerfGE 7, 198 [1958].

48 See the constraint mechanisms discussed below, section 3.3.3.

49 BVerfGE 107, 395, 401 [2003].

50 For a general discussion in the context of the *OMT* case deemed to introduce an *actio popularis*, see K.F. Gärditz, "Beyond Symbolism: Towards a Constitutional Actio Popularis in EU Affairs? A Commentary on the OMT Decision of the Federal Constitutional Court" [2014] *GLJ* 183, 197. With respect to administrative jurisdiction, see K.F. Gärditz, "Funktionswandel der Verwaltungsgerichtsbarkeit unter dem Einfluss des Unionsrechts?" [2016] *NJW Beilage (2)* 61. Structural tensions therefore seem to appear whenever EU law calls for a more functional approach to individual rights, i.e. by a tendency to mobilise the *Citoyen* to enforce law as an agent of the public good, see for example, with regard to the environmental impact assessment pursuant to the Århus Convention: Case C-115/09, *BUND v. Trianel*, ECLI:EU:C:2011:289; Case C-72/12, *Altrip v. Rheinland-Pfalz*, ECLI:EU:C:2013:712; and Case C-137/14, *Commission v. Germany*, ECLI:EU:C:2015:683.

51 The Federal Court of Justice deals with ordinary jurisdiction, the Federal Administrative Court with administrative jurisdiction, the Federal Finance Court with tax jurisdiction, the Federal Labour Court with labour jurisdiction and the Federal Social Court with social jurisdiction (Art. 95 of the Basic Law); Art. 96 of the Basic Law establishes other federal courts.

are at the top of a hierarchically organised system with an underlying state court system. The so-called ordinary jurisdiction covers civil, family as well as criminal matters, and has the highest number of courts by far.[52]

Between 1952 and 2015, German courts have filed more than one-fifth of all referrals for preliminary rulings to the ECJ (2,216 of 9,146 cases).[53] The vast majority were filed by courts other than the abovementioned federal courts (1,481). The highest number of referrals for a preliminary ruling to the ECJ by a federal court originate from the Federal Finance Court (307), followed by the Federal Court of Justice (202) and the Federal Administrative Court (117).[54] Referrals for a preliminary ruling to the ECJ cover a multitude of fields. For example, the Federal Administrative Court has referred important questions with regard to the free of movement of persons,[55] services and goods,[56] state aid,[57] EU citizenship,[58] environmental law[59] and migration law.[60] The example of state aid illustrates a case where the effectiveness of EU law led to a curtailment of individual rights.[61]

In 2014, in the *OMT* case the GFCC made a reference for a preliminary ruling for the first time in its history.[62] Though foreseeable following its decision in *Honeywell*, where it called for the ECJ "to be afforded the opportunity to

52 The term "ordinary" reveals a traditional role of the judiciary in these areas of law as they were disconnected to the executive power even before a democratic system with separation of powers was set up.

53 In 2015 German Courts referred 79 cases for a preliminary ruling (in comparison: France – 25; Italy – 47; Netherlands – 40; Belgium – 32); in 2014, 87 cases (in comparison: France – 20; Italy – 52; Netherlands – 30; Belgium – 23); in 2013, 97 cases (in comparison: France – 24; Italy – 62; Netherlands – 46; Belgium – 26), in 2012, 68 cases (in comparison: France – 15; Italy – 65; Netherlands – 44; Belgium – 28), see Court of Justice of the European Union, *Annual Report 2015*, 100.

54 Federal Social Court (76); Federal Labour Court (32), see Court of Justice of the European Union, *Annual Report 2015*, 97.

55 On applicability with regard to a trainee teacher, see Case 66/85, *Lawrie-Blum v. Baden-Württemberg*, ECLI:EU:C:1986:284.

56 On human dignity as fundamental value enshrined in the national constitution as a justification for affecting freedom, see Case C-36/02, *Omega-Spielhallen v. Bonn*, ECLI:EU:C:2004:614.

57 On the recovery of unlawful state aid, see Case C-24/95, *Rheinland-Pfalz v. Alcan*, ECLI:EU:C:1997:163; on allowed compensation for the services provided by a recipient undertaking in order to discharge public service obligations, see Case 280/00, *Altmark Trans*, ECLI:EU:C:2003:415.

58 On loss of citizenship with retroactive effect of nationality acquired on account of deception, see Case C-135/08, *Rottmann v. Bayern*, ECLI:EU:C:2010:104.

59 See the cases in n. 50.

60 See for example Case C-670/16, *Tsegezab Mengesteab v. Germany*, ECLI:EU:C:2017:587.

61 It concluded that there is no room to invoke the time limit pursuant to §48.4 of the Federal Administrative Code for a recovery of state aid violating EU law, BVerwGE 106, 328 [1998].

62 *Gauweiler Reference* [2014] DE:BVerfG:2014:rs20140114.2bvr272813; see U. Di Fabio, "Karlsruhe Makes a Referral" [2014] *GLJ* 107. The GFCC's second referral 2017 also concerned the ECB mandate, see *Gauweiler Reference II* [2017] ECLI:DE:BVerfG:2017:rs20170718.2bvr085915.

interpret the Treaties, as well as to rule on the validity and interpretation of the legal acts in question" before concluding an act to be *ultra vires*,[63] the GFCC's stance nevertheless posed the question whether the accustomed role of the ECJ with respect to referrals for preliminary rulings was hijacked. The referral itself was contested on grounds of the relevance of the ECJ's ruling in the case. The GFCC had strongly argued in its referral that the European Central Bank (ECB) was acting outside its mandate and therefore *ultra vires*. This assertion seemed to entail the conclusion that granting the ECJ the chance to rule in the case was a mere act of courtesy. However, the ECJ did not see the presumption of relevance being sufficiently challenged by the *ultra vires* setting. Contrary to the GFCC's assumption, the ECJ held that the *OMT* announcement was within the ECB's mandate.[64] In its final decision, the GFCC accepted the Court of Justice's interpretation with regards to the ECB's mandate, notwithstanding serious objections on the part of the Senate.[65] Although there has never been a referral for a preliminary ruling to the ECJ by the GFCC outside the context of the mentioned *ultra vires*-complaint, the GFCC has considered referral obligations numerous times, but refrained as it deemed the questions at hand to be *acte clair* or *acte éclair*.[66]

3. EFFECTIVENESS AND APPLICATION OF EU LAW IN GERMAN COURTS

3.1. BOUNDED PROMISE OF THE PRIMACY AND EFFICIENCY OF EU LAW

The German legal system opens itself up to the application of acts of supranational law through the parliamentary treaty approval system under Art. 23 and Art. 59.2 of the Basic Law. This makes the direct exercise of transferred powers within the legal system possible. Consequently, regarding this function, the GFCC has stated that the Basic Law "contains a promise of effectiveness and implementation corresponding to the primacy of application of Union law".[67] Thus, all state institutions are in principle obliged to fulfil this promise.

---

63 *Honeywell* [2010] (n. 31), para. 60.

64 Case C-62/14, *Gauweiler et al*, ECLI:EU:C:2015:400.

65 *Gauweiler* [2016] (n. 32).

66 See e.g. with regard to the Counter-Terrorism Database Act: *Counter-terrorism Database* [2013] DE:BVerfG:2013:rs20130424.1bvr121507, para. 90; with regard to congruent requirements with respect to human dignity when being convicted without knowledge (in a case of extradition pursuant to the Framework Decision on the European Arrest Warrant), see *Extradition* [2015] DE:BVerfG:2015:rs20151215.2bvr273514, para. 125.

67 *Honeywell* [2010] (n. 31), para. 53.

However, the promise of effectiveness and implementation corresponding to the primacy of EU law is not construed in such a way as to rigorously enforce whatever the addressed obligation may be as long it can be attributed to institutions acting under EU law. Instead, it is a bounded promise that derives its shape from the integration program provided by the parliamentary Act approving a European treaty and the restraints of the constitutional identity set out in Art. 79.3 of the Basic Law.[68]

The idea of a bounded promise begs the question what mechanisms ensure that both the promise and its boundaries are kept, and what the implications are with respect to the everyday application of EU law by national courts and their judicial relationship to the jurisprudence of the ECJ. This is the decisive constitutional background underlying the principle of consistent interpretation in the German legal order.

3.2. CONSTITUTIONAL MECHANISMS GENERATING APPLICATION AND EFFECTIVENESS BY COURTS

With regard to the constitutional mechanisms generating application and effectiveness of EU law by German courts, two dimensions can be distinguished: the objective duty of court action under the Basic Law on the one hand (section 3.2.1), and the subjective rights with respect to court action under the Basic Law on the other (section 3.2.2).

3.2.1. Obligation under the Constitution to Apply EU Law

According to Art. 20.3 of the Basic Law the judiciary is bound by law and justice. Therefore, whatever qualifies as law within the meaning of the respective Article has to be applied by national courts. With respect to supranational EU law, it is the parliamentary Act of approving a European treaty pursuant to Art. 23 and 59.2 of the Basic Law that provides the respective quality as binding law within the meaning of Art. 20.3 of the Basic Law. Therefore, the legislature principally bears the responsibility to decide whether or not to integrate into a European system that provides for primacy of its own sources of law. Against this background, the Basic Law is open to accepting *Anwendungsvorrang des Unionsrechts* (i.e. a precedence of application of EU law), or a specific principle of consistent interpretation, as long as there is a parliamentary decision opening for this. Although there may be some doubt that the evolution of primacy laid down by the ECJ in its famous *Costa v. ENEL* and *van Gend en Loos*

68 This dependency is also a reason for the fact that supranational law transports no derogating effect to the extent that conflicting law of the *Länder* is void in light of conflicting federal laws (Art. 31 of the Basic Law).

jurisprudence was fully anticipated by the prior parliamentary act of approving the European treaties, there is little doubt that such integration has been subsequently validated by parliamentary acts approving the European treaties up to and including the Lisbon Treaty.[69]

3.2.1.1. Direct Applicability

a) Generally Accepted Precedence Over Rules of National Law

German entities that implement EU law are obliged to give effect to the primacy (precedence) of EU law according to Art. 20.3, in conjunction with Arts. 23 and 59.2 of the Basic Law. This implies that a German court has to derogate from the application of national law whenever such law conflicts with the law of the EU insofar as required by the Treaties.[70] In contrast to Art. 100.1 of the Basic Law, concerned with matters regarding the constitutionality of statute law, there is no special procedural requirement for a national court to derogate in the light of conflicting EU law even if it means not applying parliamentary statute law. Thus, every national court – in principle – has the competence to determine whether or not a provision of national law is inapplicable due to the primacy of EU law.[71]

b) Precedence Over or Consistent Interpretation of Guarantees of the Basic Law?

Although constitutional provisions have been reshaped to comply with EU law (for example Art. 12a.4 and Art. 28.1 sentence 3 of the Basic Law), its provisions have not been rendered inapplicable *expressis verbis* by national courts due to conflicting EU law.[72] In a prominent case regarding Art. 19.3 of the Basic Law – a case clearly provoking the question of precedence – the court took a rather questionable approach of securing compliance by way of interpretation.[73]

---

69 Critical towards this development of constitutionalisation by the ECJ, see D. Grimm, *Europa ja – aber welches?* (C.H. Beck, 2016), pp. 12 *et seq*. As a matter of fact the scope of the primacy of application envisioned by declaration no. 17 was a crucial point of discussion in the Lisbon case, see *Treaty of Lisbon* [2009] (n. 28), para. 342 *et seq*.

70 For a detailed analysis of the jurisprudence of administrative and finance courts, see T. Kruis, *Der Anwendungsvorrang des EU-Rechts in Theorie und Praxis* (Mohr Siebeck, 2013), p. 263 *et seq*.

71 This can cause problems insofar as the question whether or not there is a conflict is not settled, and divergent opinions of courts emerge. However, the constitutional mechanism enshrined in Art. 101.1 of the Basic Law can effectively curtail fragmentation tendencies. Against this construction *de lege ferenda*, see C. Burkiczak, "Eine neue Zuständigkeit für das BVerfG?" [2015] *ZRP* 21.

72 U. Volkmann, *Grundzüge einer Verfassungslehre der Bundesrepublik Deutschland* (Mohr Siebeck, 2013) 124, speculates over such conduct in between the EJC decision (*Tanja Kreil*) and the constitutional amendment of Art. 12a of the Basic Law.

73 See in detail section 3.2.1.2.

The reluctance to rely openly on the doctrine of precedence in such a case generates a lack of clarity concerning the relationship of the two major pillars of effectiveness of EU law (i.e. direct effect and consistent interpretation) when it comes to questions governed by the Basic Law. Thus, effectiveness seems to significantly depend on the prospects of consistent interpretation in constitutional matters.

However, in recent cases where the issue was not material, the GFCC explicitly held – in line with a longstanding claim formulated by the ECJ[74] – that the acceptance of primacy extends to where the scope of concurring guarantees of the Basic Law are altered or supplemented, thereby principally in line with Art. 23.1 sentence 3 of the Basic Law overriding the requirement in Art. 79.1 sentence 1 of the Basic Law which provides for explicit amendments to the Basic Law.[75] However, the not fully elaborated but – without being specific – widely accepted idea,[76] of inapplicability of constitutional law based on the constitutional authorisation in Art. 23 and 59.2 of the Basic Law, raises questions with regard to its assumptions and implications, and may be misleading. First, the assumption of a possible suppression of constitutional guarantees by EU law outside of Art. 79.3 of the Basic Law and barriers following from the integration program can gradually ridicule the foundations of the idea that the text of the Basic Law can be considered a reliable source of law.[77] As the primacy of EU law is not limited to an excerpt of core features but entails the entire corpus of EU law, the reference to the Basic Law's black letter as a governing factor would come with a major *caveat* when deeming it inapplicable. Although the Joint Constitutional Commission explicitly stated the inapplicability of Art. 79.1 sentence 1 of the Basic Law to "avoid technical legal complications"[78] with regard to the transfer of powers on the basis of Art. 23.1 of the Basic Law, there is a difference between curtailing an all-embracing approach on making alterations of the constitution explicit and rendering the substance of features inapplicable due to an alleged conflict.

---

74 Case 11/70, *Internationale Handelsgesellschaft*, ECLI:EU:C:1970:114.

75 *Legal Entities Domiciled outside Germany* DE:BVerfG:2011:rs20110719.1bvr191609, para. 81; *Gauweiler* [2016] (n. 32), para. 118.

76 See for example H.-G. Dederer, "Die Grenzen des Vorrangs des Unionsrechts – Zur Vereinheitlichung von Grundrechts-, Ultra-vires- und Identitätskontrolle" [2014] *JZ* 313, 313; T. Kingreen, "Vorrang und Vorbehalt der Verfassung" in J. Isensee and P. Kirchhof (eds.), *Handbuch des Staatsrechts der Bundesrepublik Deutschland* XII (3rd ed., C.F. Müller, 2015), para. 38.

77 A feature that was central when founding the constitution due to experiences with the fragmentation of the substance of the *Weimarer Reichsverfassung* by overriding statute law without a change in the constitutional texture, see the discussion of the founders referenced in Häberle (ed.) (n. 28), p. 574.

78 The *Gemeinsame Verfassungskommission* (Joint Constitutional Commission) was a body examining the demand for revision in the aftermath of reunification. See Joint Constitutional Commission of 5 November 1993, Bundestag document 12/6000, 21.

Secondly, there is an argument concerning the structure of the Basic Law's openness with regard to European integration. What if it does not resolve a possible conflict between EU law and constitutional provisions – as suggested when purporting a general primacy of application? The idea of a conflict is based on the premise of the EU to be bound in the execution of its powers (when executed by German entities) under the EU treaties by guarantees set out in the Basic Law. However, the Basic Law does not generally apply to external public authority,[79] and it does not require participation in supranational organisations only when identical standards concerning public authority exist.[80] To the contrary, in the GFCC's own jurisprudence there is evidence of a nuanced approach, primarily in regard to basic rights under the Basic Law.[81] Integration on the basis of Art. 23 of the Basic Law requires a guaranteed level of protection for basic rights essentially comparable to the level afforded by the Basic Law. Though it can be argued that only the human dignity substance of basic rights as set out in Art. 79.3 of the Basic Law is hereby referenced,[82] the emphasis in Art. 23.1 sentence 1 of the Basic Law standing next to the reference to Art. 79.3 in Art. 23.1 sentence 3 can also be understood as stipulating a more independent requirement.[83] Be that as it may, it was created in the aftermath of, and in an attempt to mirror, the traditional *Solange* reservation of the GFCC,[84] which provides a structure securing the integrity of both the unity of EU law and the basic right promises of the Basic Law with regard to the exercise of external power by internal public authority. Thus, rather than framing the problem as a conflict of law situation, it is convincing to assume that the basic rights under

---

79 See Schneider, "§1" (n. 20), para. 147; apparently assuming a violation of the Basic Law by acts of EU institutions though *Gauweiler* [2016] (n. 32), para. 135; see on this, H. Sauer, "Der novellierte Kontrollzugriff des Bundesverfassungsgerichts auf das Unionsrecht" [2017] *EuR* 185, 192 *et seq*.

80 *Treaty of Lisbon* [2009] (n. 28), para. 266.

81 In its first *Solange* decision (BVerfGE 37, 271, 278 [1974]) the court stated that it is simply not enough to assert the primacy of application against concurring constitutional law with the argument that otherwise the integrity of EU law would be endangered; see also *Treaty of Lisbon* [2009] (n. 28), para. 266, where the court states that no "structural congruence" is required concerning requirements of democratic legitimacy of EU powers.

82 Purporting a unification of standards (including the *Solange* reservation) based on the early references to the essential structure of the Basic Law and its identity founded in Art. 79.3 of the Basic Law, see Dederer (n. 76), p. 316. However, there is an argument against the conceptual integration of the *Solange* reservation into Art. 79.3 of the Basic Law. Although in its first decision concerning the *Solange* reservation the GFCC referred to the term identity and basic structure of the constitution, it separated this from the non-alterable substance of the Basic Law in Art. 79.3 of the Basic Law by highlighting that any change of the identity and the basic structure requires a constitutional amendment (BVerfGE 37, 271, 279 [1974]). As Art. 79.3 of the Basic Law concerns non-disposable content even by constitutional amendment, the respective reference to identity most likely has a different meaning than today.

83 In order to be essentially comparable, the integration program may even provide for a higher standard than the guaranteed level of protection of basic rights.

84 Joint Constitutional Commission (*Gemeinsame Verfassungskommission*) of 5 November 1993, Bundestag document 12/6000, 21.

the Basic Law simply do not apply to external acts even when these are executed by national institutions, or – more precisely – that they are applicable yet only in a modified function in order to not unnecessarily endanger the constitutional promise of effectiveness and uniform implementation of Union law.[85] Whilst it can be said that the distinction between inapplicability and modified application is a mere matter of semantics when considering the consequences, it accurately highlights the balancing approach under the Basic Law, and bridges an otherwise questionable approach towards its governing role. In sum, the Basic Law neither deems itself applicable nor inapplicable with regard to external acts of sovereignty. It only controls their claim of implementation in the domain of the Basic Law,[86] especially, but not only, when implementation is accounted for by its own public authority.[87]

In any case, the relationship between the doctrine of precedence over and consistent interpretation of constitutional law requires clarification in cases where the GFCC has committed itself to a specific constitutional doctrine that is contradictory to the interpretation of EU law and this interpretation must be effectively implemented in the national legal order, either by means of consistent interpretation or by means of disapplication of any contrary provision of national law. The stage for such clarification has recently been set by exposed differences between an interpretation by the GFCC on the one hand and by the ECJ on the other hand.[88] The conflict in question concerns the GFCC`s understanding of the constitutionally enshrined churches' right of self-determination guaranteed by Art. 140 of the Basic Law in conjunction with Art. 137.3 of the Weimarer Reichsverfassung and the ECJ`s interpretation of the prohibition of all discrimination on grounds of religion provided for in Directive 2000/78. The conflict arises due to the fact that the latter is deemed by the ECJ to not establish a principle by itself but only to reframe an existing general principle of EU law, thus requiring it disapply any contrary provision of national law (including the GFCC`s interpretation of the churches' right of self-determination).

3.2.1.2. Principle of Interpretation of National Law in Conformity with EU Law

Another dimension of EU law influence relevant to national courts, and the central focus of this contribution, concerns the interpretation of national law.

---

85 For this reason constitutional complaints are inadmissible to the extent that they directly challenge acts of the European Union, see *Gauweiler* [2016] (n. 32), para. 97 *et seq.*

86 See Schneider, "§1" (n. 20), para. 147.

87 On the duties of state institutions with regard to ECB policy decisions, see *Gauweiler* [2016] (n. 32).

88 See on the one side *Churches' Right of Self-determination* [2014] ECLI:DE:BVerfG:2014:rs20141022.2bvr066112 and on the side Case C-414/16, *Egenberger v. Evangelisches Werk für Diakonie* ECLI:EU:C:2018:257; see also pending Case C-68/17, *IR v. JQ*.

According to the ECJ, Art. 4.3 of the Treaty on European Union (TEU) places a duty on all public authorities including the national courts to interpret applicable national law as far as possible in conformity with the requirements of EU law,[89] with a view to avoiding a conflict of laws. The mechanism of interpreting in accordance with higher ranked legal sources is familiar to the German legal system, as there is a longstanding duty to interpret lower ranked law in conformity with the Basic Law.[90] Such interpretation requires the possibility of different interpretations in line with the wording, legislative history and position in the legal system as well as purpose of the respective provision.[91]

Whilst the duty to interpret in conformity refers to all sources of EU law and is implemented accordingly by German courts, the field of its original development and the main area of its application relates to directives.

a) Interpretation Consistent with a Directive

In its famous *Kloppenburg* decision, the GFCC concluded that the ECJ's position on the nature of directives in terms of their normative implications – including the principle of consistent interpretation (and the exceptional case of direct effect) – is within the scope of the integration program of the treaty.[92] Consequently, the duty is to be fulfilled by German authorities as it is part of their objective duty under Art. 20.3 of the Basic Law in conjunction with the parliamentary Act of approving to a European treaty in line with Arts. 23 and 59.2 of the Basic Law.

In practical terms, it has become quite a common feature in the case-law of the German courts to refer to an interpretation consistent with a directive.[93]

---

89 Case C-157/86, *Murphy v. An Bord Telecom Eireann*, ECLI:EU:C:1988:62, para. 11; Case C-60/02, *X*, ECLI:EU:C:2004:10, para. 59 *et seq.*

90 See BVerfGE 2, 262, 282 [1953]; 122, 39, 61 [2008].

91 BVerfGE 112, 164, 182 f. [2005]; concerning the limits, see *Damages caused by planning* [2014] ECLI:DE:BVerfG:2014:rs20141216.1bvr214211.

92 BVerfGE 75, 223, 240 [1987]. In this case, the GFCC in the light of the direct effect of directives acknowledged a competence of the ECJ to develop the law *via Rechtsfortbildung*, a methodological approach rooted in the Member States tradition. Although not clearly transparent in the national court's practice, with respect to the functional features of the directive as an integrative measure, direct effect is – compared to an interpretation in conformity – a subsidiary mechanism of EU-law efficiency, see W.-H. Roth and C. Jopen, “Die richtlinienkonforme Auslegung” in K. Riesenhuber (ed.), *Europäische Methodenlehre* (3rd ed., de Gruyter, 2015), para. 12 *et seq.*

93 See e.g. Federal Labour Court: BAGE 105, 32 [2003]; Federal Justice Court: BGHZ 195, 135 [2012]; Federal Administrative Court: *Altrip* [2015] ECLI:DE:BVerwG:2015:221015U7C15.13.0; *Mücksch/Merck* [2012] ECLI:DE:BVerwG:2012:201212U4C11.11.0; Federal Finance Court: BFHE 201, 359 [2003], BFHE 252, 171 [2015]; see J. Suhr, *Richtlinienkonforme Auslegung im Privatrecht und nationale Auslegungsmethodik* (Nomos, 2011); W.-H. Roth and C. Jopen, ibid.; P. Reimer, “Richtlinienkonforme Rechtsanwendung: Spielräume und Bindungen nach mitgliedstaatlichem Recht” [2015] *JZ* 910; A. Funke, *Umsetzungsrecht* (Mohr Siebeck, 2010), p. 130 *et seq.*

In scholarship it is occasionally even considered a somehow independent method of interpretation, in the sense that it does not merely result from implementing the classical canons of interpretation, giving due consideration to the EU law background of the respective national law in question.[94] Whilst it can be said that this perception is backed by the fact that national courts generally refer to consistent interpretation as a genuinely self-contained question of interpretation, and not as an appendix to other interpretation methods, it can also be attributed to the fact that the *modus operandi* of interpretation differs when consistent interpretation is in play: interpretation is matched to a known result (the meaning of the directive in question), and not only the pathway to an unknown meaning of the law.

As the duty to interpret in conformity with the requirements of EU law only requires an interpretation *as far as possible*, its structure not only largely seems to respect methodological peculiarities of the Member States with respect to interpretation, but its consequences in a given case also strongly depend on the methodological approach in the national legal order. In the German legal culture, the competence of interpretation by courts comprises *Auslegung*, as a more text-oriented method of interpretation; as well as *Rechtsfortbildung*, as a more text-detached, constructive method of interpretation, requiring an unintentional gap in the textual structure. Whilst the terminological distinction may not be familiar in all legal cultures,[95] the underlying question concerning the binding effect of a statutory text on the one hand, and the judge's competence to make the law on the other, surely is. Recourse to *Rechtsfortbildung* as a method of interpretation only comes into play when a text is not considered open to the specific interpretation result due to the fact that it is not in line with the wording of the text, its position in the system of law, its historic background, or its purpose (general interpretation guidelines). Where it is possible to read the statute in line with the general interpretation guidelines, the principle of consistent interpretation forces the national court to give preference to such a reading to ensure the constitutionally backed promise of effectiveness.[96]

However, interpretation may not lead to an undermining of the legislative agenda and to a court taking the role of legislator.[97] National courts are only

94 See F. Reimer, *Juristische Methodenlehre* (Nomos, 2016), p. 282 *et seq.*; Roth and Jopen (n. 92), para. 42 *et seq.*; see the discussion by C.-W. Canaris, "Die richtlinienkonforme Auslegung und Rechtsfortbildung im System der juristischen Methodenlehre" in *Festschrift für Franz Bydlinski* (Springer, 2002), p. 47. C. Höpfner, *Die systemkonforme Auslegung* (Mohr Siebeck, 2008), p. 216 *et seq.*

95 For a detailed overview, see N. Grosche, *Rechtsfortbildung im Unionsrecht* (Mohr Siebeck, 2011), p. 28 *et seq.*

96 Thus, court decisions refer to consistent interpretation as supporting or not standing in the way of a specific interpretation resulting from the application of standard interpretation guidelines, see for example Federal Justice Court: BGHZ 201, 290 [2014]; BGHZ 201, 168 [2014].

97 See *Doorstep Selling Directive* [2011] ECLI:DE:BVerfG:2011:rk20110926.2bvr221606, para. 45.

obliged to choose an interpretation favourable to the directive as long as it appears justifiable according to the recognised methods (including *Rechtsfortbildung*). This general constitutional structure is decisive "irrespective of the fact if the national law in question is intended to implement an EU directive or not".[98] The GFCC sees this approach as in conformity with EU law, because it is at the hands of national courts to determine if and how far national law is open to an interpretation consistent with EU law:

> This conforms to the division of competencies between the national and EU judiciary laid out in Art. 267 TFEU. As the ECJ is not entitled to apply and interpret national law, it may not decide on the issue if there is space in national law to interpret in consistency with EU law. This autonomy of interpretation has been acknowledged by the ECJ ... The identification as well as the utilization of methodological space of the national law is a question – even if it is determined by EU directives – decided by national institutions bound by Basic Law.[99]

From the ECJ's perspective, a question posed in a preliminary reference procedure concerning the meaning of a directive normally implies that the court referring the case assumes methodological space with regard to the interpretation of the national law in question due to the requirement of relevance of the answers of the ECJ in the national court's case.[100] However, in the *Pfeiffer* decision,[101] a labour law conflict concerning emergency workers' rights under Directives 89/391 and 93/104, the ECJ – asked by the referring local labour court whether the conditions for direct applicability were met – pointed to the

98 Ibid., para. 47.

99 Ibid., para. 48.

100 For example in the *Quelle* case, a case concerning compensation for the usage of goods lacking conformity, this space, though initially not obvious, derived from the possibility of an interpretation *via Rechtsfortbildung*, see Federal Justice Court, BGHZ 179, 27 (*Quelle*) [2008]. At first glance the *Spedition Welter* case of the ECJ appears to be an outlier since the ECJ, asked whether the conditions for direct applicability of a directive were met, unequivocally pointed to the principle of consistent interpretation, see Case C-306/12, *Spedition Welter v. Avanssur*, ECLI:EU:C:2013:650. However, the case concerned a word-for-word implementation of the Directive into national law. Thus, there was no ground to preclude the possibility of consistent interpretation unless one assumed German courts and the ECJ operated in totally different universes in terms of their respective methodological approaches. A theoretical possibility that under these circumstances consistent interpretation is not possible requires a context of contradictory national rules interpreted as to actively preclude alterations of the subject matter they govern even when alterations are established by interpretation of a source of law on an equal level (effectively constituting a self-contained regime concerning a legal topic). In the *Spedition Welter* case the ECJ had no indication that such rigid interpretative inflexibility existed with regard to the provisions on the service of judicial documents (i.e. §171 Civil Procedure Code). Thus, pointing to consistent interpretation in the case may be no more than a gentle reminder of interpretative capabilities.

101 Joined Cases 397–403/01, *Pfeiffer et al v. Deutsches Rotes Kreuz*, ECLI:EU:C:2004:584.

principle of consistent interpretation to reiterate the national court's obligations in this regard.[102]

Although it is in principle clear that national judges must achieve conformity with the requirements of EU law by means of *Auslegung* as well as *Rechtsfortbildung*, the particulars of the latter are often contested.[103] Disputes concern the limits of such interpretation under the *contra legem* theme. The civil courts, in particular, have by and large taken a relatively permeable approach with regard to methodological constraints,[104] and it has been noted by some that this approach has been taken too far, thus transgressing constitutional limits allegedly constituted by the separation of powers.[105] The reason for the extensive openness to interpreting in conformity with EU law derives from a specific line of argument with respect to the methodological requirements for a text transcending *Rechtsfortbildung* of national law made by the Federal Justice Court: *Rechtsfortbildung* requires a gap in the texture of the statute – meaning a particular deficiency regarding its underlying purpose. In case of a national statute implementing a directive, such an underlying purpose can be reconstructed so as to serve the correct implementation of the respective directives.[106] Therefore, whenever there are new insights on the basis of ECJ judgments with regard to the interpretation of a directive, it can be presumed that the legislator would not have issued such national legislation if it had known it to be at odds with EU law.[107] Thus, a gap contrary to purpose as a requirement for *Rechtsfortbildung* can almost always be supposed whenever legislation is (also) intended to implement a directive. As the Federal Civil Court understands the *contra legem* prohibition functionally as a reference to whatever lies outside the approved methods of interpretation, it consequently does not hinder such *Rechtsfortbildung* after the assessment that its requirements are met.[108]

---

102 However, in its final decision the referring Court in Lörrbach (Case 5 Ca 145/01) refrained from considering the normative impact of the Directive, as it deemed it not decisive for the financial compensation claim.

103 See *Doorstep Selling Directive* [2011] (n. 97), para. 45; *Assurance Directive* [2016] ECLI:DE:BVerfG:2016:rk20160523.1bvr223015, para. 37.

104 See Federal Justice Court: BGHZ 150, 248 (*Heininger*) [2002]; BGHZ 179, 27 (*Quelle*) [2008]; BGHZ 192, 148 (*Weber*) [2011]; BGHZ 201, 101 [2014]; similar Federal Labour Court: BAGE 130, 119 [2009].

105 L. Michael, "Verfassungsrechtliche Grenzen richtlinienkonformer Rechtsfortbildung" [2015] *Der Staat* 349.

106 For example in the *Quelle* case, §439.4 Civil Code as a part of national legislation attempting to correctly implement Directive 1999/44/EC including its attribution of consumer rights "free of charge" (see Art. 3.3).

107 For example in the *Quelle* case effectively negating the right to compensation following from §439,4 (now clarified by statute in §474 Section 2 of the Civil Code); see also Federal Justice Court: BGHZ 201, 101; cf. K. Kroll-Ludwigs and M. Ludwigs, "Die richtlinienkonforme Rechtsfortbildung im Gesamtsystem der Richtlinienwirkungen" [2009] *ZJS* 7.

108 Federal Justice Court: BGHZ 179, 27 [2008].

The uniqueness of the methodological approach when EU obligations are in play can best be seen in cases where interpretation in consistency beyond the actual scope of the respective directive is at issue, i.e. when the legislator's adaptation of the national law involves more than required by the directive. For example, German legislation incorporated the Directive on certain aspects of the sale of consumer goods by applying the national rules to all sales of goods – thereby triggering the question whether or not a business-to-business sale is also governed by the principle of consistent interpretation. In a case concerning the seller's obligation to bear the costs of removing non-conforming goods and installing replacement goods, the Federal Justice Court held that the legislator originally misunderstood the meaning of the Directive when implementing the sales law – specifically the Directive's impact on the seller's obligations and that, had it known better, it would have abstained from applying such rules to all sales.[109] As there was no superseding will to act in compliance with EU obligations due to the fact that business-to-business relations fell outside their scope, the Federal Justice Court gave credit to the misconceived perception by calling for a split interpretation of the text, thereby fragmenting the sales law regime.

The often-expressed criticism of cases involving *richtlinienkonforme Rechtsfortbildung* – that they do not picture the common standard for interpretation and thereby displace traditional methods – is true in one sense and false in another. It is true that there are no similar instances of attributing an underlying (often only hypothetical) purpose of correct implementation by a statute, and assuming it to effectively override all the other legislative intentions attributed to the legislation in question. However, it is false to assume this unfamiliarity to be an impediment to such conduct, which can be deduced from a methodological standard.[110] The standards for the assumption of a gap contrary to the statutory purpose are not established in a clear and testable manner, so as to preclude the Federal Justice Court from dealing with them as a matter of *richtlinienkonforme Rechtsfortbildung* – or, from another perspective: the dimension of a binding effect of statute law is not always as clear as it might seem. There is no methodological standard according to which a court may only assume a gap contrary to a purpose when such purpose can be traced to the explicit conduct of the legislator;[111] neither is there a methodological standard according to which in situations of competing purposes a court cannot assume

---

109 Federal Justice Court: BGHZ 195, 135 [2012].

110 For a different opinion, see J. Höft and N. Grosche, "Richtlinienkonforme Rechtsfortbildung ohne Grenzen?" [2009] *NJOZ* 2294, 2306 *et seq.*

111 Generally, the *travaux préparatoires* can be considered a supporting but not a decisive factor when interpreting the law. In *Damages caused by planning* [2014] DE:BVerfG:2014:rs20141216.1bvr214211, the GFCC held that a combination of wording, systematical positioning and *travaux préparatoires* may preclude an interpretation which is consistent with the Basic Law. In any case, there is no rule giving special preference to the *travaux préparatoires* in the event of conflicting obligations, as purported by Case C-371/02, *Björnekulla v. Procordia*, ECLI:EU:C:2004:275, para. 13; for an assessment on the development in the

overriding preferences with regard to a specific purpose.[112] Finally, there is no methodological standard that interpretation may not lead to a derogating effect of a particular part of a statute *in toto*,[113] or be detached from its wording.[114] Of course, the implications may hamper the element of trust with respect to statute law,[115] but this effect is not induced by European law but rather a consequence of the development of the particular methodological setting in German doctrine.[116] When comparing consistent interpretation with an EU directive and consistent interpretation with the constitution, one has to bear in mind that there is not so much a difference with regard to the relevant methodological framework but rather with the situation of its implementation. This is due to the fact that in the case of an interpretation consistent with a directive, the object of interpretation (i.e. the national law in question) regularly provides a background not comparable to other scenarios of interpretation, for it is genuinely set up to correctly implement the directive.[117]

However, in a case not relating to EU law (the *Vaterschafts* case),[118] the First Senate of the GFCC has recently indicated a more substantive approach to the permissibility of *Rechtsfortbildung* under the Basic Law, especially regarding basic rights,[119] thereby echoing a dissenting opinion in a Second Senate decision (the so-called *Rügeverkümmerung* case).[120] The main suggestion is that the likelihood of *Rechtsfortbildung* being permissible corresponds to the question of whether or not its implications fulfil a constitutional goal, especially by promoting individual rights. Conversely, the likelihood of impermissibility

GFCC's jurisprudence on the *travaux préparatoires*, see C. Burkiczak, "§1", in C. Burkiczak, F.-W. Dollinger and F. Schorkopf (eds), *Bundesverfassungsgerichtsgesetz* (C. F. Müller, 2015), para. 76.

112 See *Doorstep Selling Directive* [2011] (n. 97), para. 51.

113 Different Michael (n. 105); Reimer (n. 94), p. 96; apparently, but rather unspecific, W. Durner, *Verfassungsrechtliche Grenzen richtlinienkonformer Rechtsfortbildung* (ZEW Bonn, 2010), p. 29.

114 In line with the presented argumentation, see *Assurance Directive* [2016] (n. 103), para. 50, where it was held that the competences of the judiciary according to Art. 20.3 of the Basic Law are not limited to interpretations prescribed by the wording of a statute. On the discrepancies in literature with regard to the handling of the 'clear wording' argument, see T. Vesting, *Rechtstheorie* (2nd ed., Beck, 2015), para. 198.

115 This is true whenever permissibility refers to a rather open plethora of factors, for example when the permissibility of interpretation is considered to also depend on the legislators reaction *ex post facto* to an ECJ interpretation, see *Assurance Directive* [2016] (n. 103), para. 49. This can be considered a problem of democracy because such dependency overrides the formal requirements for normative impact of a legislator's conduct.

116 Similar Reimer (n. 94), p. 919; and Durner (n. 113), p. 13.

117 Funke (n. 93), p. 117 calls this the prime example of *Umsetzungsrecht* (implementation law).

118 The case referred to the question of a child's right against its mother for disclosure of the identity of its father: *Identity of Presumed Father* [2015] DE:BVerfG:2015:rs20150224.1bvr047214.

119 *Identity of Presumed Father* [2015] ibid., para. 41.

120 Dissenting opinion of Justices U. Di Fabio, A. Voßkuhle and L. Osterloh in *Atrophied Objection* [2011] DE:BVerfG:2009:rs20090115.2bvr204407, para. 105.

increases correspondingly to the curtailment of individual rights. Though the argument has been made that this line of case-law points to further limits in the context of *richtlinienkonforme Rechtsfortbildung*,[121] when considering the full context of the jurisprudence, there are quite convincing arguments purporting just the opposite. The central idea regarding the substantive approach to limits of *Rechtsfortbildung* is to synchronise legal requirements binding the legislator, and – where case-law in some respect amounts to a similar normative impact – legal requirements binding the courts.[122] Considering this background, according to which *Rechtsfortbildung* may not transcend what the legislator is constitutionally obliged to do, it is quite clear that *richtlinienkonforme Rechtsfortbildung* cannot entail the envisioned problem as long as the legislator is not constitutionally prevented from correctly implementing the respective directives. To the contrary, as Art. 23.1 of the Basic Law generally contains a promise of effectiveness and implementation of Union law, there is a constitutional pull towards compliance regarding conformity with EU law. Hence it is more likely to be permissible on constitutional grounds as its implications fulfil a constitutional goal.[123]

According to the jurisprudence of the Federal Civil Court, the limits of an interpretation in conformity with EU law are only transgressed when an interpretation results in a change of the discernible will of the legislator and does not still (somehow) conform to its will. For example, in a recently decided case the Federal Civil Court held that an interpretation in conformity was not possible due to the fact that the legislator did not aim to implement the relevant provisions of the directive.[124] In this case, national legislation allowing for the adjustment of the price for the supply of electricity and gas in consumer contracts did not provide any requirements regarding adequate notice of the consumers confronted with such adjustment, thus failing to meet the requirements of two directives.[125] The Federal Civil Court held that the rule generally allowing a price adjustment could not be interpreted in a consistent manner so as to also entail the transparency requirements, since the legislator in the

---

121 L. Michael and M. Payandeh, "Richtlinienkonforme Rechtsfortbildung zwischen Unionsrecht und Verfassungsrecht" [2015] *NJW* 2392, 2397.

122 The *Dissenting opinion* in the *Rügeverkümmerung* decision even starts the remarks referred to with the conclusion that regardless of competence issues the same substantive constitutional guidelines binding the legislator apply to interpretation via *Rechtsfortbildung* by the courts. Similarly in its *Vaterschaft* case the GFCC sees the substantive requirements as constitutional guidelines "also binding the legislator".

123 Although in *Assurance Directive* [2016] (n. 103), the court once again dismissed the notion that *richtlinienkonforme Rechtsfortbildung* transcends the constitutional limits of judicial interpretation, it did not base its arguments on the constitutional promise of effectiveness and implementation of EU law.

124 Federal Civil Court: NJW 2016, 1718, 1722.

125 Directive 2003/54/EC of the Parliament and Council concerning common rules for the internal market in electricity [2003] OJ L176/37, Art. 3.5; Directive 2003/55/EC of the European Parliament and of the Council concerning common rules for the internal market in natural gas [2003] OJ L176/57, Art. 3.3.

travaux preparatoires expressly conceived this question to be addressed by way of decree.[126]

In comparison to the Federal Civil Court's relatively high threshold for conceding to the limits of consistent interpretation, the Federal Finance Court appears much more strictly oriented on the wording of the national law in question. Thus, its argumentation when deeming that an interpretation in conformity is not possible does not generally rely on the conduct of the legislator (essentially asking whether legislation attempted to comply), but focuses only on the structure of the legal text. For example, in a case concerning the preconditions for a reduced rate of value added tax, the Federal Finance Court did not deem it possible to interpret in accordance to the ECJ's understanding of the respective directive which provided for a dual requirement.[127] As there was no adequate indication in the respective national law text, the Court deemed the second requirement for a reduced rate of value added tax for being engaged in "welfare or social security work" as not being a possible requirement under German Tax law. The court did not even explicitly consider an interpretation by way of *richtlinienkonformer Rechtsfortbildung*, even though it has acknowledged the method in its jurisprudence.[128]

Similar to that of the Federal Civil Court, the case-law of the Federal Administrative Court is characterised by ample space allowing for interpretations in conformity with EU law. The argument of national law being closed to an interpretation in conformity with EU law may normally be rejected due to the fact that administrative national law frequently has rules open to dynamic interpretation that can be used as a platform to interpret in conformity with EU law by means of the general interpretation guidelines.[129] The Federal Administrative Court is also in principle open to an interpretation via *richtlinienkonformer Rechtsfortbildung*, as illustrated by its decision on the interpretation of national law concerning the procedure of the approval of prices for access to electronic communication networks.[130]

---

126 Astonishingly, the court considered the respective price adjustment clause itself not to constitute a sufficient basis for a price adjustment (although not deeming it inapplicable when dealing with the issue of consistent interpretation) due to its incompatibility with the directives – without elaborating on the question on what grounds national legislation shall not apply (and discussing the issue of direct applicability of the directive and negating it in the case at hand), Federal Civil Court: NJW 2016, 1718, 1721, 1724.

127 See Federal Finance Court: DStR 2012, 1177; DStRE 2006, 1534; Council Directive 2006/112/EC on the common system of value added tax [2006] OJ L347/1; Case 492/08, *Commission v. French Republic*, ECLI:EU:C:2010:348, para. 43.

128 Federal Finance Court: BFHE 243, 8 [2013].

129 With regard to §34 of the Federal Building Statute, see *Mücksch/Merck* [2012] DE:BVerwG: 2012:201212U4C11.11.0; see also the cases deeming an interpretation in conformity possible in *Altrip* [2015] DE:BVerwG:2015:221015U7C15.13.0; *Dentist* [2004] DE:BVerwG:2004:290 104U3C39.03.0.

130 *Approval of prices to electronic communication networks* [2017] ECLI:DE:BVerwG:2017: 310117U6C2.16.0. The question was whether or not every single price approval requires

b) Interpretation of Conformity of Guarantees of the Basic Law?

The basic mechanism of the *Solange* reservation in principle prevents the development of conflicts between EU-law obligations on the one hand and the basic rights laid out in Arts. 1–19 of the Basic Law on the other.[131] Therefore, there is – in principle – no need to interpret these guarantees in accordance with EU law obligations in order to avoid such conflict. However, this initial position changes when the obligation of EU law itself concerns the application of basic rights enshrined in a national legal order – for example by calling for their application towards EU citizens or legal entities from the Member States in the light of the ban on discrimination set out in Art. 18 TFEU.[132]

In a case concerning the application of the substantive fundamental rights for foreign legal entities in general, the GFCC provided an interpretation in contrast to the wording of Art. 19.3 of the Basic Law. The First Senate – without explicitly referring to the principle of consistent interpretation – based its argument on the Basic Law's drafters' lack of desire "to permanently exclude legal entities from Member States of the European Union", since they could not have foreseen such a high level of integration. The result of this historical reflection is openness towards interpreting the constitution in a way which avoids conflicts between the obligations of Germany under EU law from arising:

> The expansion of the scope of application of the protection of fundamental rights to cover legal entities from the European Union corresponds to the contractual obligations taken on through the European Treaties, as they are expressed in particular in the European fundamental freedoms and – in a subsidiary fashion – the general ban on discrimination contained in Art. 18 TFEU.[133]

The GFCC's jurisprudence thereby in principle appears to follow the same line of argument as outlined in the *Görgülü* and *Preventive detention* decisions:[134] when there is (due to the historic background) methodologically legitimate space for interpretation, there is room for an impact on the content of basic rights

---

a procedure in accordance with Art. 7.3 of Directive 2002/21/EC of the Parliament and Council on a common regulatory framework for electronic communications networks and services [2002] OJ L108/33.

131 See below, section 3.3.2.

132 For example, the ECJ's stance with respect to application of guarantees provided only to the EU Member States' own citizens facing extradition (see Case C-182/15, *Petruhin*, ECLI:EU:C:2016:630), could trigger this question, as the GFCC in a chamber decision concluded that questions of extradition with states outside the EU do not fall in the scope of the treaties; see *Extradition* [2014] (n. 66), with further reference to BVerfGK 14, 113.

133 *Legal Entities Domiciled outside of Germany* [2011] ECLI:DE:BVerfG:2011:rs20110719.1bvr191609, para. 75; see M. Ludwigs, "Grundrechtsberechtigung ausländischer Rechtssubjekte" [2013] *JZ* 434.

134 See above, section 2.2.

of the Basic Law in the light of obligations derived from EU law or the ECHR by means of constitutional interpretation.[135] However, there appear to be two differences with regard to the presuppositions of constitutional interconnectivity in this context.

First, whilst the Second Senate has emphasised that outside influence on the interpretation of the fundamental rights must be integrated as carefully as possible, and depends on the recognised methods of interpretation of the constitution,[136] the First Senate is more at ease in overriding the wording with an argument that poses questions. This is due to the fact that the First Senate implies a pretty low methodological and procedural hurdle. Methodologically, the conclusion that the drafters of the Basic Law did not want to "permanently exclude" a specific obligation under EU law is hardly convincing as such lack of specific anticipation can be assumed with regard to virtually every case interpreting originally drafted constitutional law. Procedurally, the GFCC gives the question whether it has dealt with foreign legal entities domiciled in the European Union as holders of substantive basic rights of the Basic Law the doubtful appearance of being unsettled.[137] With regard to the methodological argument, there are already signs of the Second Senate steering away from such a low threshold by referring to a *contra legem* argument in a similar case. In a non-acceptance decision (pursuant to §93b of the Federal Constitutional Court Act), a Chamber of the Second Senate held that even though the (in the case at hand non-decisive) question as to whether legal entities or citizens of the European Union can invoke basic rights explicitly applicable only to German citizens was not resolved in its case-law, there are serious doubts concerning a reading of the constitutional provision in conformity with EU law due to its wording.[138] It must be highlighted that with respect to the basic rights section in the Basic Law there is – contrary to statute law meant to implement directives – no plausible argument for a presumption of conformity with EU standards.[139]

Second, there is another striking discrepancy when comparing the approach in the *Görgülü* and *Preventive detention* decisions and in the case of extending the scope of Art. 19.3 of the Basic Law. Whilst the former emphasises the restriction of fundamental rights under the Basic Law as an

135 In a case concerning the German exit from nuclear energy the GFCC likewise referred to EU Law in an unspecific manner pointing to Art. 49 TFEU to argue for a Basic Right of a state-owned Swedish entity, see *Vattenfall* [2016] DE:BVerfG:2016:rs20161206.1bvr282111, para. 197.

136 GFCC in *Preventive Detention of G.* [2011] (n. 15), para. 91.

137 It admits that the GFCC has so far ruled that foreign legal entities may not invoke substantive fundamental rights. Thereby, its argument is like saying, the court has ruled on animals but not on house pets.

138 *Price regulations on medicine* [2015] DE:BVerfG:2015:rk20151104.2bvr02821, para. 11.

139 Thus, even a conceptual parallel to the described framework of *Rechtsfortbildung* by the Federal Court of Justice seems misplaced.

obstacle to reception of international law obligations,[140] the latter completely fails to elaborate on this point. The case at hand certainly provoked further clarification as it concerned a constitutional claim against a Civil Court ruling. Therefore, whilst any reading of the constitution which is *in accordance with international law* automatically leads to an increase of liberty for one subject of a fundamental right, it at the same time inevitably causes a decrease of liberty for the other party. It is not clear if the First Senate implicitly makes a special case concerning the interpretation of basic rights in conformity with EU law (due to the constitutionally promised primacy of application and effectiveness of EU law) or avoids this implication by the assumption that this is not even a case of reception of international law but some sort of original interpretation of Art. 19.3 of the Basic Law. The former would most definitely trigger disorder with respect to the distribution of power between the two Senates, for the Second Senate is traditionally and legally competent for issues mainly involving the interpretation of public international law and Arts. 23, 24 and 59 of the Basic Law.[141]

In sum, the GFCC's jurisprudence on the impact of EU law on the interpretation of basic rights of the Basic Law is not settled with respect to the derivative application of EU law obligations. There is no detailed framework explicitly expressed in the court's jurisprudence as to what extent EU law serves as a guideline in matters of interpretation similar to the framework which can be seen in relation to public international law obligations. Consequently, it is an open question how the GFCC will resolve manifest differences with regard to its own interpretation of basic rights enshrined in the Basic Law that contradict the interpretation of EU law laid out by the ECJ.[142]

3.2.2. Individual Rights Generating Application and Effectiveness by National Courts

Pursuant to Art. 101.1 sentence 2 of the Basic Law, no one may be deprived of their "lawful judge". Although a genuine standard of the Basic Law, the mechanism enshrined in the guarantee of the lawful judge is linked to the

---

140 *Preventive Detention of G.* [2011] (n. 15), para. 93; *Church Privilege in Labour Law* [2014] DE:BVerfG:2014:rs20141022.2bvr066112, para. 128 *et seq.*

141 §14.4 Federal Constitutional Court Act in conjunction with the decision of the Plenum, see C. Burkiczak, "§14" in C. Burkiczak, F.-W. Dollinger and F. Schorkopf (eds.), *Bundesverfassungsgerichtsgesetz* (C. F. Müller, 2015), para. 24.

142 Such manifest differences are apparent with regard to the GFCC`s interpretation of the churches' right of self-determination guaranteed by Art. 140 of the Basic Law in conjunction with Art. 137.3 of the Weimarer Reichsverfassung on the one hand (see *Churches' Right of Self-determination* [2014] (n. 88)) and the ECJ`s interpretation of the prohibition of all discrimination on grounds of religion provided for in Directive 2000/78 on the other hand (Case C-414/16, *Egenberger v. Evangelisches Werk für Diakonie* ECLI:EU:C:2018:257).

application and efficiency of EU law as it allows for a subjective complaint with regard to the handling of EU law by national courts. Specifically with regard to consistent interpretation, this means that a national court's failure to comply with the principle of consistent interpretation can amount to a violation of a constitutional right.

The general idea of Art. 101.1 sentence 2 of the Basic Law is to ensure the integrity of law by providing that the decision on who is to judge in a case is not influenced in an objectionable manner.[143] The nexus to EU law is as follows: Art. 267(3) TFEU is a rule on jurisdiction within the meaning of Art. 101.1 sentence 2 of the Basic Law, as the ECJ – whilst not a German public authority – can be the lawful judge in a case at hand. This means that a national court has an *ex officio* obligation to refer the matter to the ECJ.[144] Hence, an unconstitutional denial of the lawful judge can be established if a German court does not comply with the obligation to make a submission to the ECJ in preliminary ruling proceedings according to Art. 267(3) TFEU.[145] In case of such a breach, the GFCC does not itself file a preliminary reference procedure. Instead it declares the respective decision of a lower court void and obliges it to adjudicate in compliance with constitutional standards.[146]

However, just as not every violation of jurisdiction rules in statutes *via* interpretation will breach the right to the lawful statutory judge, not every violation of the EU law standard of Art. 267 TFEU in light of the ECJ's interpretation[147] breaches the right to the lawful statutory judge.[148] To constitute a constitutional breach, the obligation to make a submission must have been dealt with in a manifestly untenable manner. The GFCC recognises and distinguishes the following scenarios:

- *fundamental disregard of the obligation to make a submission*, i.e. "cases in which a court of last instance deciding on the merits does not at all consider

143 BVerfGE 4, 412, 416 [1956]. Whilst this entails constitutional requirements with regard to the design of rules on competences (see BVerfGE 95, 322, 327 *et seq* [1997]), it also implies a regulative effect on the way the respective rules on competences are applied by national courts (*Damages caused by planning* [2014] DE:BVerfG:2014:rs20141216.1bvr214211, para. 69). Pursuant to established jurisprudence of the GFCC this does not mean that all violations of rules of competences in statute law on behalf of the courts *via* interpretation automatically constitute a breach of the constitutional right to the lawful judge. A violation is constituted only if the interpretation and application of rules on jurisdiction no longer appear to be comprehensible and are manifestly untenable bearing in mind a sensible interpretation of the concepts determining the Basic Law, see also D. Wolff, "Willkür und Offensichtlichkeit – Die verfassungsgerichtliche Prüfung einer Verletzung von Art. 101 Abs. 1 S. 2 GG i. V. m. Art. 267 Abs. 3 AEUV" AöR 40, 58 *et seq.*

144 BVerfGE 73, 339, 367 *et seq* [1986].

145 See BVerfGE 73, 339, 366 *et seq* [1986]; Proelß (n. 15), 172 *et seq.*

146 Schneider, "§1" (n. 20), para. 143.

147 Case 283/81, *CILFIT*, ECLI:EU:C:1982:335.

148 *Honeywell* [2010] (n. 31), para. 88.

making a submission despite the question of Union law being – in its view – material to the ruling although it itself has doubts as to the correct answer to the question";
- *deliberate deviation without a willingness to make a submission*, i.e. cases "in which the court of last instance deciding on the merits deliberately deviates in its ruling from the case law of the Court of Justice regarding questions which are material to the ruling and nonetheless does not make a submission or refrains from making a renewed submission";
- *deviation in case of incompleteness of case-law and unjustifiable transgression of the evaluation framework*, i.e. "in cases in which material case law of the Court of Justice is not yet available with regard to a question of Community law which is material to the ruling, or if existing case law has possibly not yet exhaustively answered the question which is material to the ruling, or if a further development of the case law of the Court of Justice not only appears as a distant possibility", and a court has "unjustifiably transgressed the evaluation framework".[149]

Although there have been some diverging views between the Senates as to whether or not the last of these three scenarios of an unjustifiable transgression of the evaluation standard refers to the handling of the substantive EU law calling for interpretation or the handling of the Art. 267 TFEU mechanism itself by the national court, the *Filmfördergesetz* decision has cleared the way for a more unified approach.[150]

Whilst there is no necessary congruence between the obligations under EU law and those following the constitutional right enshrined in Art. 101.1

149 Ibid., para. 90; *Legal Entities Domiciled outside Germany* [2011] ECLI:DE:BVerfG:2011:rs20110719.1bvr191609, para. 98. As to the question of whether further development of the case law is not merely a distant possibility, the GFCC takes into account the interdependence of the understanding of the ECHR by the European Court of Human Rights and the understanding of fundamental rights enshrined in the Charter, *Violation of the duty to submit a request for a preliminary ruling* [2017], ECLI:DE:BVerfG:2017:rs20171219.2bvr042417, para. 48.

150 *Honeywell* [2010] (n. 31), para. 90: "This may particularly be the case if possible counterviews to the question of Union law that is material to the ruling are to be clearly preferred over the opinion put forward by the court." Compare with *Legal Entities Domiciled outside Germany* [2011] DE:BVerfG:2011:rs20110719.1bvr191609, para. 98: "In such cases, the review of a violation of Article 101.1 sentence 2 of the Basic Law does not primarily depend on the justifiability of the ordinary courts' interpretation of the substantive Union law which is material to the dispute, but on the justifiability of the handling of the obligation to submit under Article 267.3 TFEU." According to the GFCC's ruling it is decisive whether "a national court comes to the arguable conclusion that the question of correct application of EU law is obvious from the outset ("*acte clair*") or has been settled by the ECJ's jurisprudence in a manner leaving no reasonable doubt ("*acte éclairé*")", *Film Subsidy law* [2014] DE:BVerfG:2014:rs20140128.2bvr156112, para. 184; see Wolff (n. 143), p. 48 *et seq.*; E. Wagner and C. Finck, "Eine schrittweise Annäherung des BVerfG an den unionsrechtlichen Maßstab der Vorlagepflicht nach Art. 267 III AEUV beim gesetzlichen Richter?" [2014] *NVwZ* 1268.

sentence 2 of the Basic Law,[151] the constitutional mechanism effectively ensures the correct implementation of EU law *via* national courts and the fulfilment of their constitutional obligation to give effect to the primacy of EU law according to Art. 20.3 in conjunction with Art. 23 and 59.2.[152] An aggrieved party can successfully file a constitutional complaint claiming that a court has not submitted an issue to the ECJ in accordance with the preliminary reference procedure.

The mechanism protects the uniform application of EU law by constitutional means and indirectly triggers a unique standard of constitutional review of national courts due to the design of the rules on jurisdiction of the ECJ pursuant to Art. 267 TFEU. This is highlighted by comparing the basic standard of constitutional review of judicial acts in the German court system, which follows from the distinction between constitutional law interpretation matters and interpretation matters of law not primarily related to the constitution which are to be settled in the forum of the lower courts (so called *Fachgerichtsbarkeit*). Usually it is the responsibility of the lower courts to deal with questions of interpretation concerning aspects of the law ranking below the constitution. The GFCC's constitutional standard of review with regard to the practice of the lower courts usually only concerns whether the application of law as such amounts to a violation of Art. 3.1 of the Basic Law (equality before the law) on the grounds that it is *willkürlich* (arbitrary) – a high threshold even tolerating errors and intended principally to balance the respective roles in the court system.[153] As to rules on jurisdiction of national courts, these are – in the national context – designed as somewhat independent issues: the distribution of jurisdiction is not constructed in a way to control matters of interpretation with regard to substantive issues by means of precluding certain courts from autonomously applying the law (outside the narrow area of application pursuant to Art. 100 of the Basic Law). For example, the Federal Civil Court does not have to refer a question to the Federal Administrative Court in order to engage in an administrative law question raised in a civil law dispute; just as the appellate courts of the *Länder* do generally not have to refer to a higher federal court in order to proceed with their cases. By largely not reserving an exclusive interpretative jurisdiction for a specific court for a particular subject matter, questions on rules of court jurisdiction are not interrelated with their power to autonomously interpret questions concerning aspects of the law raised in cases before them. Consequently, the principal threshold of *arbitrary* application as

---

151 See Schneider, "§1" (n. 20), para. 146.

152 See in recent jurisprudence *DB Prelimary Reference* [2015] DE: *DB Prelimary Reference III* [2015] DE:BVerfG:2015:rk20151008.1bvr350913.

153 BVerfGE 81, 132, 137 [1989]. See on similarities with respect to the standard of the rule of law in conjunction with Art. 2.1 of the Basic Law (as well as Art. 101.1 sentence 2) with further references, H. Bethge in T. Maunz, B. Schmidt-Bleibtreu, F. Klein and H. Bethge (eds.), *Bundesverfassungsgerichtsgesetz* (Beck, 2017), §90 para. 294.

the (unspecific) relevant constitutional limit remains decisive when assessing the practice of national courts with regard to their interpretation of aspects of the law ranking below the constitution. In contrast, in order to prevent fragmentation of EU law, the rule on ECJ jurisdiction pursuant to Art. 267 TFEU precludes the national court's power to autonomously interpret EU law. The question of the national court's jurisdiction thereby essentially depends on whether and how a court will be materially engaged in the application of EU law. Thus, when determining the limits of a national court's practice regarding the application of EU law, including the principle of consistent interpretation, constitutional rules on the application of rules on jurisdiction play the decisive role, thereby crowding out the question and limits of review of constitutionality of the court's application of substantive EU law itself. Although the constitutional standard under Art. 101.1 sentence 2 of the Basic Law does not seek to ensure errorless application of jurisdictional rules and is only triggered by a manifestly untenable application[154] it may (and in the case of EU law, does) nevertheless control the national court's practice with regard to the application EU law in a much stricter manner than when considering the constraints to which a national court is held when applying the law in general.[155]

3.3. CONSTITUTIONAL MECHANISMS CONSTRAINING THE APPLICATION OF EU LAW IN COURTS

Constitutional constraints on the application of EU law result from three standards of review: the preservation of constitutional identity,

---

154 Due to the functional distinction between the constitutional court and lower courts, see BVerfGE 82, 159 (194) [1990]; Wolff (n. 143), p. 51 *et seq.*, does not see this distinction as a question of standard but of *Prüfdichte*, i.e. the rules for applying the standard by the GFCC. This assessment can be questioned as it is based on the premise that the GFCC tolerates basic rights violations *en masse*. The background for this assertion is a parallel view to a widespread understanding of the GFCC's groundbreaking *Elfes* decision (BVerfGE 6, 32 [1957]), to imply a violation of Art. 2.1 of the Basic Law whenever a court acts wrongfully, for there is no statute legitimising such curtailment of freedom. However, the *Elfes* decision's vital conclusion was only that the general freedom of action is guaranteed by Art. 2.1 of the Basic Law and not merely specific highly relevant areas of conduct. However, it did not state that the general freedom of action is violated by every wrongful act of the judiciary, nor is this a necessary conclusion. Whilst the latter can of course be considered a possible dimension of the GFCC's general freedom of action, it has never implemented it in its practice. To the contrary, it has repeatedly pointed out that a Basic Right violation does not flow from a merely debatable application of non-constitutional law (see the so-called and highly discussed *Hecksche* formula in BVerfGE 18, 85, 92 *et seq.* [1964]; 128, 193, 209 [2011]). The most relevant dimension of the *Elfes* doctrine concerns its implications for administrative and government action.

155 The original standard of the Second Senate (*Honeywell* [2010] (n. 31), para. 90), referring to the national court's handling of the law that is material, smoothed the tension between the general control level towards judicial acts when applying law ranking below the constitution, and the indirectly higher control level provoked by Art. 267 TFEU.

the *Solange* reservation, and the *ultra vires* concept. These constraints apply equally to all EU acts, thus encompassing direct effect as well as the principle of consistent interpretation. It may well be true that the principle of consistent interpretation in itself only theoretically touches upon the constitutional constraints,[156] but it is certainly not true with regard to its function as a medium transporting EU normativity. In other words: the duty of national courts to interpret in consistency with EU law can and has triggered the issue of constitutional constraints in practice as well.

3.3.1. Preservation of Constitutional Identity

The notion of "constitutional identity" provided for by Art. 23.1 sentence 3 in conjunction with Art. 79.3 of the Basic Law, presents a generic and static barrier to European integration.[157] The reference to identity, although challenged as implying a meta-normative plus,[158] can be described as the idea of a normative minimum which cannot be impinged without abandoning the governing role of the Basic Law as a whole.[159] Identity review by the GFCC may ultimately result in declaring measures of EU law inapplicable within the scope of the Basic Law, thereby creating a tension towards the claim for uniform application of EU law including *via* consistent interpretation. According to the GFCC's assessment, the identity review is a concept inherent in Art. 4.2 sentence 1 TEU, and does not violate the principle of sincere cooperation within the meaning of Art. 4.3 TEU.[160]

With respect to the implementation of the identity review *via* the plethora of national courts in Germany, the GFCC does see the potential for disruption

156 For example, if the ECJ developed a concept of consistent interpretation obliging a court to take the role as if it were legislator, or if the integration program adopted by parliament specifically excludes consistent interpretation.

157 This is contested due to its implicit self-centered sovereignty approach, see e.g. M. Wendel, *Permeabilität im europäischen Verfassungsrecht* (Mohr Siebeck, 2011), p. 572 *et seq.*; Wischmeyer (n. 23), p. 437 *et seq.*, suggests a dialogue-based approach.

158 A. Ingold, "Die verfassungsrechtliche Identität der Bundesrepublik Deutschland" [2015] *AöR* 1, 3, 7 *et seq.*

159 The dimension of the petrification clause of Art. 79.3 of the Basic Law is central when discussing the boundaries of integration in the light of treaty amendments and revisions on the one hand, and when assessing acts of EU law established under a treaty regime in force (as these acts may possibly transgress the respective limits) on the other. If institutions of the European Union could decide on treaty interpretation without any outside oversight, the conservation of the constitutional identity would rely on the conduct of actors not bound by the Basic Law.

160 *Extradition of R.* [2015] ECLI:DE:BVerfG:2015:rs20151215.2bvr273514, para. 47. The court stressed the prevalence of similar mechanisms in other Member States, referring to jurisprudence of courts in 10 other countries; in its Lisbon jurisprudence, the GFCC also formulated a comparison to the ECJ's *Kadi* case in order to underline the structure of its argumentation (*Treaty of Lisbon* [2009] (n. 28), para. 340); on the European perspective, see A. Haratsch, "Nationale Identität aus europarechtlicher Sicht" [2016] *EuR* 131.

and fragmentation of the uniform application of EU law. Thus, it monopolises the identity review procedure and reserves the power to declare a violation of the constitutional identity for itself. This prevents German authorities and courts from simply disregarding EU law's claim to uniform application.[161]

Procedurally, identity review can follow different paths, including the constitutional complaint procedure under Art. 93.1 no. 4a of the Basic Law (*Verfassungsbeschwerde*). Thus, if a national court refers to the primacy of EU law in a manner which is not in line with the constitutional identity under Art. 79.3 of the Basic Law, the aggrieved party can in principle successfully file a constitutional complaint.[162] The not yet elaborated requirements for raising a complaint without infringement of the complainant's basic rights beyond Art. 38.1 sentence 1 of the Basic Law need to be determined against the backdrop of the issue of preventing an overreaching *actio popularis* in disguise.[163]

According to recent developments in the GFCC's case-law, the most relevant practical aspect of Art. 79.3 of the Basic Law as a factor when assessing supranational acts under a treaty regime, concerns the reference to human dignity in Art. 1.1 of the Basic Law. In this context, it appears as though the principle of consistent interpretation is effectively superseded by a principle of conformity with the constitutional identity. The GFCC held that a Higher Regional Court transgressed the limits of Art. 1.1 in conjunction with Art. 23.1 sentence 3 and Art. 79.3 of the Basic Law, by allowing the execution of a European Arrest Warrant extraditing a person convicted *in absentia* in Italy without knowledge, and in whose case it was unclear whether or not there was

161 The court derives the approach from *Europarechtsfreundlichkeit*, i.e. the principle of openness towards EU law, and compares it to the legal concept expressed in Art. 100.1 of the Basic Law with regard to the claim of unconstitutionality of parliamentary law and to Art. 100.2 of the Basic Law. Furthermore, the ECJ is to be given the opportunity to adjudicate and prevent a possible fragmentation of EU law by declaring an act void for the whole EU area: *Extradition of R.* [2015] ibid., para. 46. Regarding the requirement's function often only being connected to the principle of openness, see Schneider, "§1" (n. 20), para. 171; regarding obstacles with respect to the implementation of the GFCC's monopoly concerning national agencies, see Sauer, "Der novellierte Kontrollzugriff des Bundesverfassungsgerichts auf das Unionsrecht" (n. 79), pp. 185, 199 *et seq.*

162 Although not clearly expressed, the questionable and undifferentiated line of argument in the OMT decision, where the violation of the "right to democracy" was connected to a possible undermining of the democratic decision-making process through supranational acts, may suggest that a complaint against an act of the EU violating the constitutional identity (structurally) can be filed by individuals on the grounds of Art. 38.1 of the Basic Law, even without further individual implications of this act (in its final OMT decision the GFCC held the identity complaint referring to the lasting parliamentary budget admissible but without merit: *Gauweiler* [2016] (n. 32)). Such a broad approach would *de facto* amount to a kind of *actio poularis*; with regard to the *ultra vires* complaint as a procedural anomaly, see Gärditz, "Beyond Symbolism: Towards a Constitutional Actio Popularis in EU Affairs? A Commentary on the OMT Decision of the Federal Constitutional Court"(n. 50).

163 In *Extradition of R.* [2015] (n. 160), the complainant itself was the aggrieved party. On the issue, see Sauer, "Der novellierte Kontrollzugriff des Bundesverfassungsgerichts auf das Unionsrecht" (n. 78), pp. 185, 202.

an effective judicial remedy. The Court concluded that extradition under such circumstances would be incompatible with the principle of individual guilt as part of the human dignity clause in Art. 1.1 of the Basic Law. Whilst the case at first glance seemed to trigger the identity reservation with the result of declaring an act (the issued Arrest Warrant) inapplicable, and with the line of argument in the decision clearly heading in this direction,[164] the GFCC's reasoning took a rather astonishing turn. It held that its understanding of incompatibility with human dignity is mirrored by and consistent with fundamental rights under EU law, thereby effectively negating any potential conflict with the Council Framework Decision on the European Arrest Warrant.[165] The GFCC refrained from requesting a preliminary ruling from the European Court of Justice under Art. 267 TFEU on the ground that the matter was *acte clair*; the guarantees of the Basic Law were in tune with fundamental rights enshrined in EU law in prohibiting the extradition in the case at hand. The decision not to refer seemed highly questionable in light of the ECJ's *Melloni* case.[166] The GFCC's remarks with regard to the identity review can be considered a giant *obiter dictum* which is surprising in light of the line of reasoning by the Court. It nevertheless lies in the logic of this line of reasoning that an interpretation in consistency with EU law has to be considered *en quelque faćon nulle* when the content of EU law is effectively overridden by constitutional law's identity reservation.

However, the issue of incompatibility only arises where EU law is clearly in conflict with Art. 1.1 of the Basic Law. This is not the case when a development of the case law of the ECJ is capable of nullifying possible normative tensions and appears as more than a distant possibility, thus calling for the necessary activation of the reference procedure under Art. 267 TFEU by the national courts. The abovementioned constitutional mechanism in Art. 101.1 sentence 2 of the Basic Law therefore essentially ensures the ECJ`s active role before rendering EU law inapplicable as the last resort on behalf of the GFCC.[167]

An important aspect derives from the GFCC's rather unconditional readiness to accept complaints against the implementation of supranational acts based on violations of Art. 1.1 of the Basic Law. Its eagerness to do so seems somewhat surprising, as this cannot be realised without simultaneously trimming the *Solange* doctrine in a significant manner. This is due to the fact that human dignity in Art. 1.1 of the Basic Law has a specific dimension. First, there is formally no room for balancing rights where human dignity is involved, as it is declared "inviolable". Second, as illustrated in the ECJ's *Omega* case,[168] the

---

164 *Extradition of R.* [2015] (n. 160), para. 35–84.

165 Ibid., para. 84 *et seq.*

166 Case C-399/11, *Melloni v. Ministerio Fisca*, ECLI:EU:C:2013:107.

167 See *Violation of the duty to submit a request for a preliminary ruling* [2017] (n. 149) para. 35 *et seq.*

168 Case C-36/02, *Omega v. Bonn*, ECLI:EU:C:2004:614.

instances of reference in German law are rather frequent compared to other legal systems.[169] Third, the GFCC understands human dignity to be the foundation of all basic rights,[170] and attributes *Menschenwürdegehalt* (i.e. an underlying essence of human dignity) to the content of other basic rights.[171] Therefore, the readiness to accept complaints against the implementation of supranational acts based on violations of Art. 1.1 of the Basic Law may provoke a rather broad field of complaints in the future. In the scope of the evolving field, the new identity-doctrine will trump the limited approach of review under the *Solange* reservation.[172] The court itself, however, does not address the implications for its traditional *Solange* jurisprudence.

*3.3.2. The "As Long As" Reservation (*Solange*)*

In the early stages of European integration, questions arose concerning the status of basic rights under the Basic Law when European Community law was applied by German authorities, as the Basic Law provides no exemption with regard to the binding effect of basic rights on the exercise of public authority under Art. 1.3. However, tackling this issue by simply requiring full compliance and otherwise declaring acts executing EU law inapplicable would have burdened the process of EU integration. It could potentially trigger a fragmentation of the EU legal order,[173] which in turn would hamper the Basic Law's promised openness to European integration.[174] The GFCC addressed this difficulty of balancing constitutional imperatives by constructing the so-called "as long as ..." reservation.[175] The main feature of this reservation is: as long as EU law

---

169 Another question is whether there is a comprehensible approach to the application of human dignity – e.g. BVerfGE 30, 1, 25 [1980] required that public authority must act disdainful towards a human being, whilst in *Extradition of R.* [2015] (n. 160), an extradition due to a conviction *in absentia* without knowledge and chance to face trial in person amounted to a breach of human dignity.

170 See BVerfGE 107, 275, 284 [2003].

171 See BVerfGE 109, 279, 311 [2004]; M. Herdegen in T. Maunz and G. Dürig (eds.), *Grundgesetz: Kommentar* (Beck, 2017), Art. 1 Abs. 1 para. 26 *et seq.*

172 As the *Solange* doctrine serves as a building block for the integrity of EU law, the consistency of such an approach seems highly doubtful, see below section 3.3.2.

173 See *Treaty of Lisbon* [2009] (n. 28), para. 337: "With the idea of a Union-wide legal community inherent in the Basic Law's mandate of integration and in currently applicable European treaty law, these require the restriction of the exercise of Member States' judicial power. No effects endangering integration should occur because the uniformity of the Community's legal order is called into question by divergent decisions as to applicability on the part of Member State courts." The validity of EU law is not touched upon by its inapplicability under the Basic Law, see BVerfGE 37, 271, 281 *et seq.* [1974] and *Gauweiler* [2016] (n. 32), para. 157.

174 Described as an instance of constitutional tension by Schneider, "§1" (n. 20), para. 158.

175 Schneider, "§1" (n. 20), para. 159, stresses that this approach does not – contrary to a widespread belief – result in a decline of constitutional standards, because it is the constitutional standard specified for taking part in supranational integration.

generally ensures effective protection of fundamental rights against measures of the EU which are to be regarded as substantially similar to the protection of fundamental rights required unconditionally by the Basic Law, the GFCC will not exercise its jurisdiction to decide on the applicability of EU law serving as the legal foundation obliging certain acts of German courts or authorities within the sovereign jurisdiction of the Federal Republic of Germany, and will no longer review by the standard of fundamental rights contained in the Basic Law.[176] The general idea of the "as long as ..." approach is considered to be mirrored by the European Court of Human Rights in its *Bosphorus* decision.[177]

The GFCC set out the key elements of the reservation for the first time in its 1974 *Solange I* decision. In this case, the GFCC concluded that there was no substantially similar protection of fundamental rights on the European Community level.[178] In its 1986 *Solange II* decision, the GFCC arrived at a different result when assessing whether European Community law provided an adequate substitute to the catalogue of fundamental rights contained in the Basic Law, thereby triggering a significant shift in the role of national authorities.[179] The court's line of argument was essentially reiterated in its *Maastricht* decision, and implicitly approved by the amendment of Art. 23.1 sentence 1 of the Basic

---

176 This is a slight modification of the GFCC's condensed summary of the *Solange II* decision in *EC Banana Market Regulation* [2000] ECLI:DE:BVerfG:2000:ls20000607.2bvl000197, para. 36. In *Greenhouse Gas Emission* [2007] ECLI:DE:BVerfG:2007:fs20070313.1bvf000105, the court clarified that the doctrine which was unfolded against the background of regulations applies to directives as well. This means that basic rights are only relevant insofar as the directive leaves decisions to the Member States. A prominent example is featured in the GFCC's case on Precautionary storage of telecommunication data under Directive 2006/24/EC, see *Telecommunication Data* [2010] ECLI:DE:BVerfG:2010:rs20100302.1bvr025608.

177 F. Schorkopf, "The European Court of Human Rights' Judgment in the Case of Bosphorus Hava Yollari Turizm v. Ireland" [2005] *GLJ* 1255, 1264.

178 To underline this assessment, the court pointed out that Community law contained no codified catalogue of fundamental rights adopted by a Parliament and of settled validity, a factor not attributed the same relevance in later decisions. As a consequence of the gap with regard to the protection of basic rights, the GFCC regarded the reference by a national court pursuant to Art. 100 of the Basic Law admissible and necessary if the German court was of the opinion that the rule of Community law relevant to its decision was inapplicable, because and in so far as it conflicted with one of the fundamental rights of the Basic Law. However, the GFCC did not concur with the national court's assessment of a basic rights violation (BVerfGE 37, 271, 288 *et seq.* [1974]), and thus avoided a conflict.

179 BVerfGE 73, 339, 381 [1986]. The development of such a level of fundamental rights protection in the EU is attributed to the jurisprudence of the ECJ and its development of fundamental rights as unwritten general principles of EU law (following the Lisbon Treaty, now as referred to in Art. 6.3 TEU) as the driving force (e.g. the GFCC cites ECJ cases *Nold*, Case 4/73, ECLI:EU:C:1974:51; *Hauer*, Case 44/79, ECLI:EU:C:1979:290; *Agricola Commerciale and SAVMA*, Case 232/81, ECLI:EU:C:1981:191). Thus, the *Solange II* decision implied that an adequately consolidated standard no longer depended on the codification of fundamental rights, the latter being an approach vested too greatly in a civil law tradition. As a consequence of deeming the standard adequate, the GFCC held that it will no longer review in light of the standard of basic rights contained in the Basic Law, and that constitutional complaints and submissions by courts are therefore inadmissible.

Law in 1992. In a ruling concerning the organisation of the banana market by an EU regulation, the GFCC restated the "as long as" reservation and clarified the conditions necessary to rebut the presumption of limited review. A constitutional complaint or a submission by courts:

> must state in detail that the protection of fundamental rights required unconditionally by the Basic Law is not generally assured in the respective case. This requires a comparison of the protection of fundamental rights on the national and on the Community level similar to the one made by the Federal Constitutional Court in [the *Solange II* decision].[180]

The conditions for a rebuttal of adequacy are considered to practically rule out review by the GFCC.[181] A collision between, for example, the duty to interpret national law in consistency with EU law and basic rights of the Basic Law therefore appears merely theoretical.

Presuming an institutional desire on behalf of the GFCC to act as an important forum of judicial discourse, this result might seem surprising – and even more so taking into account the fact that the increasing number of acts by national authorities (including national courts) which are predetermined by EU law naturally leads to a decline of the relevance and visibility of basic rights – i.e. as long as the "as long as" standard is upheld. Critical voices have been raised in this context, especially with regard to the tendency in the ECJ's jurisprudence to expand the implications of EU law, thereby questioning the space for applicable standards of basic rights.[182] However, the "as long as"

---

180 *EC Banana Market Regulation* [2000] ECLI:DE:BVerfG:2000:ls20000607.2bvl000197, para. 39. Therefore, it is not enough to point to a singular instance such as a particular ECJ judgment as failing the adequacy test. To successfully invoke basic rights before the GFCC in the context of binding EU measures, a general drop of the rights standard is required – although it is not yet clear if this requires showing that the standard of all basic rights in general is inadequate, or if demonstrating a drop concerning particular rights is already sufficient, see Schneider, "§1" (n. 20), para. 160.

181 C. Goos and C. Hillgruber, *Verfassungsprozessrecht* (4th ed., C.F. Müller, 2015), para. 965d.

182 J. Masing, "Einheit und Vielfalt des Europäischen Grundrechtsschutzes" [2015] *JZ* 477, 485 *et seq.*; M. Bäcker, "Das Grundgesetz als Implementationsgarant der Unionsgrundrechte" [2015] *EuR* 389, who proposes two solutions to regain ground in the development of fundamental rights. The GFCC could interpret basic rights under the Basic Law and take fundamental rights of the EU into consideration as an interpretation aid, or it can broaden its standard of review and review EU fundamental rights next to the basic right guarantees of the Basic Law against its wording (p. 405 *et seq.*). *Bäcker* suggests the latter "radical approach" to be necessary in order to avoid a conflict with the principle of non-discriminatory enforcement (in the sense purported by the ECJ in Case 33/76, *Rewe*, ECLI:EU:C:1976:188, para. 5) as only basic rights are reviewed by the GFCC. However, this argument is not convincing. Its understanding of implementing in a non-discriminatory fashion would first not reflect the fact that fundamental rights under EU law are not independently implemented, but only implemented in conjunction with applicable EU law. Second, the idea of applying national law in a non-discriminatory fashion is connected to a comparability with regard

approach of the GFCC remarkably abstains from a self-centred approach in order to take the Basic Law's imperative of openness to European integration seriously: the main role of fundamental rights is not defined by a specific forum ("Who is in charge?"), but rather by a specific outcome ("What protection is effectively realised?").[183] From this perspective, it is less astonishing that the GFCC's implicit deficiency guarantee with regard to basic rights standards is not already triggered by a single act failing the adequacy standard, because such singular inadequacy can be considered a general risk in every system of law placing basic rights protection in the hands of an institution (including the GFCC). The realisation of such a risk is tolerable, as it simultaneously preserves the integrity of the EU legal order. In contrast, if there were a *modus vivendi* implying a permanent comparison of every singular case by a German court (i.e. the GFCC), a serious risk of putting the integrity of the EU law at risk would arise by complaints alleging a divergence of the relevant standard applied in their particular case, thereby paving the way to indirectly challenge the applicability of EU law. Of course, in the best-case scenario, decisions in which the primary fundamental rights protection at the EU level failed can be filtered out, and do not remain unchallengeable. However, in most cases, i.e. when the system of EU law adequately protects fundamental rights, answers to basic right questions are merely duplicated. This expands the timeframe of the legal dispute, seriously impairing the functioning of EU law, since individual certainty on the applicability of EU law is not provided. Against this background it is quite surprising that the GFCC's recent case-law concerning the European Arrest Warrant basically seems to require such duplication with regard to human dignity in Art. 1.1 of the Basic Law, irrespective of the inadequacy of protection of fundamental rights on the EU level in general, or their protection concerning particular rights or their protection in a particular case at hand.[184] Whilst some see an important new "*divide et impera*" approach with a federal impetus as to who shall decide on fundamental rights questions,[185] others are

to its function as an overarching basic infrastructure serving the implementation of law (with regard foremost to the executive). A procedural safeguard specifically concerning the protection of requirements pursuant to the Basic Law lacks such similarity (and the ECJ has never proposed this dimension, and would most likely abstain from assuming this dimension as it would not necessarily provide efficiency benefits). Finally, it could – taking its premises one step further – lead to absurd results. For example, the Basic Law also allows for anticipatory review of international agreements by the GFCC –, could this following Bäcker's argument's premises mean that the GFCC must also review the EU's international agreements against the TFEU standard to escape the trap of non-discriminatory implementation of EU law.

183 Schneider, "§1" (n. 20), para. 158; this of course implies a trade-off producing a unitisation-tendency, see Bäcker (n. 182).

184 *Extradition of R.* [2015] (n. 160).

185 M. Nettesheim, "Annotation to 2 BvR 2735/14" [2016] *JZ* 424, 425; in this direction, see C.D. Classen, "Zu wenig, zu fundamentalistisch – zur grundrechtlichen Kontrolle 'unionsrechtlich determinierter' nationaler Hoheitsakte" [2016] *EuR* 304.

rather astonished by the court's unnecessary intervention in settled doctrine.[186] As the implications of the "as long as" approach are not made explicit in the GFCC's ruling, there remains some undesirable ambiguity.

The "as long as" reservation reshapes the role of national courts with regard to the consideration of basic rights under the Basic Law. First, the declaration of inapplicability of binding EU law is a reserved competence of the GFCC, in accordance with the basic notion in Arts. 100.1 and 100.2 of the Basic Law, thereby protecting EU law from fragmentation caused by German courts invoking basic rights against it.[187] Second, references under Art. 100.1 of the Basic Law concerning national measures are only admissible when unconditional fundamental rights required by the Basic Law are not generally assured at the EU level. Third, according to EU law, German courts are not competent to disregard binding EU law on the grounds of an alleged fundamental rights violation by themselves, since this is a reserved competence of the ECJ pursuant to Art. 267 TFEU. Finally, any attempt to autonomously disregard binding EU law on the grounds of an alleged fundamental rights violation will usually amount to a violation of Art. 101.1 sentence 2 of the Basic Law – either by not referring to the ECJ in accordance with Art. 267 TFEU because the German court considers the standard of the protection of basic rights on the EU level adequately sufficient, yet deems a violation of this standard with respect to a specific EU measure; or by not referring to the GFCC when it considers the general standard of protection to be inadequate.

3.3.3. Ultra Vires

The term "*ultra vires*" is used to describe the situation of acts "beyond the powers" of the relevant actor.[188] With regard to European integration, the specification of conferred powers is shaped by an integration program (integration agenda) adopted by the *Bundestag* in the Act of Approval (Arts. 23 and 59.2 of the Basic Law).[189] Acts cannot be considered *intra vires* and thus applicable within the sovereign jurisdiction of the Federal Republic of Germany unless the constitutional prerequisite of the existence of an integration program is met.[190]

---

186 C. Schönberger, "Annotation to 2 BvR 2735/14" [2016] *JZ* 422, 424; Sauer, "Der novellierte Kontrollzugriff des Bundesverfassungsgerichts auf das Unionsrecht" (n. 79), 186, 202 *et seq.*

187 See BVerfGE 37, 271, 285 *et seq.* [1974]; generally with regard to inapplicability, see *Treaty of Lisbon* [2009] (n. 28), para. 241; cf. *Extradition of R.* [2015] (n. 160), para. 36.

188 When transferring sovereign powers to international organisations in general, the Basic Law requires such powers to be conferred in a specific manner (Art. 24, 59.2 of the Basic Law), and even more specifically when it comes to matters of European integration (Art. 23, 59.2 of the Basic Law); see BVerfGE 68, 1, 97 [1984] – decision on the deployment of nuclear bombs under the NATO treaty; see with regard to European integration, *Gauweiler* [2016] (n. 32), para. 115.

189 See the conceptual distinction between program and process for the first time clearly unfolded by Schneider, "Der Ultra-vires-Maßstab im Außenverfassungsrecht" (n. 35), p. 16.

190 Schneider, "Der Ultra-vires-Maßstab im Außenverfassungsrecht" (n. 35), p. 46.

Hence, by adopting an integration program, the *Bundestag* can principally tailor the possible range of acts that are supposed to be applicable within the sovereign jurisdiction of the Federal Republic of Germany.[191] In its *OMT* case the GFCC even proclaimed that the *ultra vires* review's constitutional basis is essentially linked to the fundamental elements of the principle of democracy (Arts. 20.1 and 20.2 of the Basic Law) as part of the constitutional identity of the Basic Law (Art. 79.3 of the Basic Law),[192] and *Rechtsstaat* (the principle of the rule of law).[193] It must be noted though that despite their common background, the GFCC emphasises that its *constitutional identity* review and its *ultra vires* review are independent instruments of control.[194]

In its jurisprudence, the GFCC has repeatedly alluded to the effect of non-application on the development of the European integration under the Basic Law.[195] Nevertheless, taking into account the openness towards European integration, the GFCC is reluctant to monopolise the review procedure,[196] and has held that *ultra vires* review must be exercised in a reserved was so as not to endanger supranational integration.[197] This outset has led to a nuanced development of the *ultra vires* concept, as seen in its decisions in the *Honeywell* case and the *OMT* case, the latter following the GFCC's first reference to the ECJ.[198]

The 2010 *Honeywell* decision concerned the implications of the ECJ's jurisprudence in the *Mangold* case, where it held that although the Directive 2000/78 was not yet applicable, given that the transposition period had not yet expired, the Member States nevertheless had a duty to ensure non-discrimination on the grounds of age as a general principle of EU law – an interpretation highly contested in German literature.[199] The constitutional

191 It must be noted though that the approval of an integration program is formally not distinct from the approval to the treaty in question. Thus, the same act can in principle serve more than one function if and insofar as an integration program can be verified as to its content, see Schneider, "Der Ultra-vires-Maßstab im Außenverfassungsrecht" (n. 35), pp. 48, 55. However, this distinction has never been explicitly referred to in the GFCC's jurisprudence.

192 *Gauweiler* [2016] (n. 32), para. 127 *et seq.*

193 Ibid., para. 152; it held that the principle of sovereignty of the people (*Volkssouveränität* – Art. 20 sec. 2 sentence 1 of the Basic law) was violated if institutions, bodies, offices and agencies of the European Union exercised public authority even though they were not adequately democratically legitimised through the integration program laid down in the Act of Approval.

194 Ibid., para. 154.

195 BVerfGE 89, 155, 188 [1993] – coined as acts breaking out; *Treaty of Lisbon* [2009] (n. 28), para. 240 *et seq.*

196 *Gauweiler* [2016] (n. 32), para. 155.

197 Ibid., para. 154 *et seq.*

198 *Honeywell* [2010] (n. 31); *Gauweiler* [2016] (n. 32); a second preliminary reference was filed by the GFCC with regard to the ECB's expanded asset purchase programme *Gauweiler Reference II* [2017] (n. 62).

199 Case C-144/04, *Mangold v. Helm*, ECLI:EU:C:2005:709. For further references, see Grosche (n. 95), p. 281 fn. 21.

issue of an *ultra vires* act arose with regard to the implementation of this jurisprudence by the Federal Labour Court, which found the incompatibility of a fixed term on the basis of §14.3 sentence 4 of the Federal Law on Part-Time Working and rejected its application referring to the primacy of EU law. The GFCC rejected the alleged basic rights violation,[200] since the prerequisites for a finding of an *ultra vires* act in line with the openness towards EU law were not met. The GFCC elaborated on the prerequisites: first, prior to the finding of an *ultra vires* act, the ECJ is "to be afforded the opportunity to interpret the Treaties, as well as to rule on the validity and interpretation of the legal acts in question, in the context of preliminary ruling proceedings according to Art. 267 TFEU".[201] Second, a qualified transgression of the integration program by acts of the European bodies and institutions was also required, comprised of two components:

> This means that the act of the authority of the European Union must be manifest in violation of competences and that the impugned act is highly significant in the structure of competences between the Member States and the Union with regard to the principle of conferral and to the binding nature of the statute under the rule of law.[202]

The GFCC even conceded that it would tolerate errors with regard to the ECJ's interpretation, thereby implicitly echoing a similar standard applied when assessing acts of the national judiciary.[203] Against this background, the GFCC did not deem the case-law of the ECJ (*Mangold*) to violate the principle of conferral in a manifest and structurally relevant manner, regardless of whether the outcome found in the *Mangold* ruling could be achieved by recognised methods of interpretation, and of whether any existing shortcomings would be sufficiently clear.[204]

---

200 The complainant burdened by this decision alleged a violation of his right under Arts. 2.1 and 12.1 in conjunction with Art. 20.3 of the Basic Law.

201 *Honeywell* [2010] (n. 31), para. 60; a convincing reason is given by Schneider, "Der Ultra-vires-Maßstab im Außenverfassungsrecht" (n. 35), p. 57, pointing out that the integrity of EU law would be better if the ECJ invalidates a measure EU-wide, since the GFCC can only rule on the applicability in the sovereign jurisdiction of the Federal Republic of Germany.

202 *Honeywell* [2010] (n. 31), para. 61. The dissenting opinion of Justice Landau regarded the majority to have placed excessive requirements on the finding of an *ultra vires* act.

203 "It is hence not a matter for the Federal Constitutional Court in questions of the interpretation of Union law which with a methodical interpretation of the statute can lead to different outcomes in the usual legal science discussion framework, to supplant the interpretation of the Court of Justice with an interpretation of its own. Interpretations of the bases of the Treaties are also to be tolerated which, without a considerable shift in the structure of competences, constitute a restriction to individual cases and either do not permit impacts on fundamental rights to arise which constitute a burden or do not oppose domestic compensation for such burdens." *Honeywell* [2010] (n. 31), para. 66. The GFCC also calls for "respect for the Union's own methods of justice to which the Court of Justice considers itself to be bound".

204 *Honeywell* [2010] (n. 31), para. 80 *et seq.*

However, the latter point concerning interpretation was a decisive factor in the GFCC's 2016 decision in *OMT*. This case concerned a policy decision of the ECB (the OMT programme) and its not yet initiated implementation.[205] The circumstances of the case, particularly the fact that the specific conduct of the ECB was only announced and not implemented,[206] posed questions as to what specific obligations German authorities would be under following an alleged *ultra vires* act, and under what circumstances an individual could file a constitutional complaint.[207] The GFCC construed a right of citizens derived from Art. 38.1 sentence 1 of the Basic Law, a concept originally adopted to review treaty modifications.[208] It is an innovation of the OMT jurisprudence to assume an inevitable connection between qualified transgressions and the constitutional identity in Art. 79.3 of the Basic Law, and to note that – although self-contained – *ultra vires* review is a special case of the protection of the constitutional identity.[209] Astonishingly, in this context the GFCC deems it possible that acts of institutions of the European Union themselves breach the core of the principle of sovereignty of the people, and thereby also of Art. 1.1 of the Basic Law in case of transgressions.[210] However, it is highly questionable that the public authority of the European Union can and should be considered bound by guarantees enshrined in the Basic Law.[211] Be that as it may, by allowing

---

205 ECB President Draghi famously remarked: "Within our mandate, the ECB is ready to do whatever it takes to preserve the euro. And believe me, it will be enough", see <https://www.ecb.europa.eu/press/key/date/2012/html/sp120726.en.html>.

206 As a matter of fact, the ECB only announced what conduct it was not willing to undertake: K. Schneider, "Questions and Answers: Karlsruhe's Referral for a Preliminary Ruling to the Court of Justice of the European Union" [2014] GLJ 217, 227 *et seq.*

207 Issues leading to the two dissenting opinions in the GFCC's ruling on referral from Justices G. Lübbe-Wolff and M. Gerhard in *Gauweiler Reference* [2014] (n. 62).

208 The GFCC deems the "unilateral usurpation of powers by institutions and other agencies of the European Union" to be an instance similar to the transfer of powers by the *Bundestag* requiring a basic right safeguard of democratic influence of citizens in the process of European integration (the "claim to democracy"). Otherwise, according to the GFCC the principle of sovereignty of the people enshrined in Art. 79.3 in conjunction with Art. 20.2 sentence 1 of the Basic Law could be violated, see *Gauweiler* [2016] (n. 32) para. 82, 121 *et seq.*, cf. 123, 128. In her dissenting opinion in *Gauweiler Reference* [2014] ibid., Justice G. Lübbe-Wolff called it "an originally bold, now established doctrine of the Court's case-law" (para. 15).

209 This connection was especially not aesserted in the referral decision, see dissenting opinion from Justice G Lübbe-Wolff in *Gauweiler Reference* [2014] ibid., para. 16: "the Senate now holds that Art. 38 sec. 1 GG also allows to address the Federal Constitutional Court with the assertion of a qualified *ultra vires* act ... which does not necessarily include a violation of constitutional identity", see *Gauweiler* [2016] (n. 32), para. 153.

210 *Gauweiler* [2016] (n. 32), para. 135. According to the GFCC transgressing acts would amount to an exercise of power not democratically legitimised and – on the basis of the institutional shape of the EU – not sufficiently influenceable in a free and equal manner by the German people. See the critique by Sauer, "Der novellierte Kontrollzugriff des Bundesverfassungsgerichts auf das Unionsrecht" (n. 79), pp. 185, 192 *et seq.*

211 Schneider, "§1" (n. 20), para. 149 points out that the *ultra vires*, *Solange* and identity objections serve only to fend off basic rights violations by German public authority when they implement

a complaint under Art. 38 of the Basic Law and linking it to the constitutional identity without a connection to a fundamental right aside from Art. 38 itself, it appears as if every individual can act as a watchdog with regard to manifest and structural transgressions (including those *via* the principle of consistent interpretation).[212]

The corresponding claim in the OMT case concerned the mere inactivity of the Federal Government as well as the *Bundestag* aiming to force these to "actively deal with the question of how the distribution of powers entailed in the treaties can be restored".[213] The GFCC then mentions a plethora of possible actions at the discretion of the state institutions and compares their situation to when *Schutzpflichten* (i.e. positive duties of the state to protect basic rights) are adjudicated.[214]

With respect to the first part of the *Honeywell* standard,[215] requiring the act of the authority of the European Union to be manifestly in violation of its competences,[216] the GFCC took the stance that this will be the case when the alleged competence can under no legal point of view be argued for when applying common methodological standards.[217] The GFCC clarified that this does not mean that the requirement is not met when legal opinions on the question are in existence – indicating the otherwise imminent hijacking of what counts as sound argumentation by "interested circles". Hence, the finding of a manifest

supranational public authority; regarding the GFCC's – due to the nature of the referenced cases, perhaps only seemingly – changing stance on EU acts as the subject matter in dispute of a basic right claim, see Sauer, "Der novellierte Kontrollzugriff des Bundesverfassungsgerichts auf das Unionsrecht" (n. 79), pp. 185, 187, 189 *et seq.*

212 The GFCC points out to the subsidiary nature of its *ultra vires* review: *Gauweiler* [2016] (n. 32), para. 84.

213 *Gauweiler* [2016] (n. 32), para. 80 *et seq.*; in her dissenting opinion in *Gauweiler Reference* [2014] (n. 62), Justice G Lübbe-Wolff called this a "blatant innovation" (para. 17).

214 *Gauweiler* [2016] (n. 32), para. 169. The concept essentially implies a wide margin of appreciation to the question how the duty is fulfilled and a duty to protect is violated only if no protective measures are taken at all, if measures taken are manifestly unsuitable or completely inadequate, or if they fall considerably short of the protection's aim. Measures mentioned by the GFCC in the *OMT* case are: for the Federal Government, a legal action in front of the ECJ, the objection of the questionable act towards EU authorities, measures with regard to votes in EU institutions and invoking the Luxembourg Compromise from 1966; for the *Bundestag*, the parliamentary right to question, debate and adopt resolutions.

215 With respect to the second part of the *Honeywell* standard requiring that the act of the authority of the European Union must be highly significant in the structure of competences between the Member States and the Union the GFCC holds that the transgression must carry significant weight with regard to the principle of democracy and the principle of sovereignty of the people: *Gauweiler* [2016] (n. 32), para. 151.

216 In its referral decision *Gauweiler Reference* [2014] (n. 62), the GFCC only assumed that "it would have to be considered a manifest and structurally significant transgression of its mandate if the European Central Bank acted beyond its monetary policy mandate ..., or if the prohibition of monetary financing of the budget was violated by the OMT program ...", and thus effectively did not commit.

217 *Gauweiler* [2016] (n. 32), para. 149.

transgression can be the result of thoughtful deliberation.[218] However, in order to apply the *ultra vires* review in accordance with the Basic Law's openness to European integration, the GFCC approaches the resulting methodological review of ECJ decisions by emphasising the peculiarities of interpretation of EU law whilst at the same time trying to avoid a methodological "anything goes": although methodological standards must not perfectly mirror those valid for national courts, they cannot simply disregard them either. Nevertheless, the special features of EU law allow for a "not insignificant deviation" in terms of relevance of the particular means of interpretation (i.e. wording, history, systematic context and purpose), whilst a manifest disregard of interpretation methods common in the European legal systems or of generals principles common in the Member States is not permitted.[219] This "ping-pong" sequence of the court is evidently not leading to a feasible and transparent methodological standard, and can be considered to provide a rather unclear situation.[220] In its own conclusion, the GFCC is inclined to accept an interpretation by the ECJ even if there are good reasons to consider another legal interpretation, as long it is traceable to recognised methodological standards and not arbitrary. It thereby essentially offers an additional layer of EU Treaty review. By adopting such a standard, the GFCC's finding of an *ultra vires* act depends on how the ECJ decides its cases with respect to the interpretation of EU treaties. This disconnects the *ultra vires* review from the idea that the integration program adopted by the *Bundestag* is fixed when entering into a treaty and thereby serves as a standard which can be tested against in order to create continuous democratic accountability of the *Bundestag*.[221] Thus, an intricate but central pillar of the *ultra vires* doctrine, i.e. that it serves to preserve the parliamentary adopted integration program when entering into a treaty, is implicitly called in question.

According to the developed standard, the GFCC held that the policy decision of the ECB – which the ECJ had held in its OMT decision to be within

[218] Ibid., para. 150. The GFCC refers to its equal understanding of "manifest" in other circumstances (i.e. §24 and §93c of the Federal Law on the Procedure of the GFCC).

[219] Ibid., para. 160.

[220] The abovementioned discussion on the issue of *richtlinienkonforme Rechtsfortbildung* illustrates the methodological leeway even in German court practice, see above section 3.2.1.2.

[221] Clearly envisaged by Schneider, "Der Ultra-vires-Maßstab im Außenverfassungsrecht" (n. 35), p. 53. If the *Bundestag* were to consent to all acts of an authority of the European Union as long as the ECJ's alleges a competence traceable to methodological standards and not arbitrary the shape of the resulting integration program is anybody's guess for only a modus of exercise of power is fixed irrespective of its particular outcome. Whilst it is questionable if it is possible to consider this fixation of a modus itself as the relevant integration program without effectively transferring the competence-competence, it would certainly deviate from the supposed and verified integration program the GFCC assessed before allowing the approval to the Lisbon treaty. Pointing out that the GFCC has used this program in its Maastricht and Lisbon decisions, ibid., p. 54.

the bounds of the ECB's competence and not in violation of the prohibition of monetary financing of the state budget – did not constitute a manifest transgression of competences. Although the Senate had "serious objections" regarding the ECJ's interpretation of the TFEU,[222] it concluded that the ECJ's approach was acceptable due to the fact that it had essentially performed the restrictive interpretation envisaged by the GFCC in its referral decision[223] – an assessment on behalf of the GFCC which is found (only) by relying on a relative unspecific overall picture of the ECJ jurisprudence on the matter.[224]

222 *Gauweiler* [2016] (n. 32), para. 181 *et seq.*

223 See *Gauweiler Reference* [2014] (n. 62), para. 100.

224 *Gauweiler* [2016] (n. 32), paras. 193, 201. A second preliminary reference was filed by the GFCC with regard to the ECB's expanded asset purchase programme: *Gauweiler Reference II* [2017] (n. 62).

CONSISTENT INTERPRETATION IN FRANCE

Revealing the Duality of the Judicial System

Vincent Couronne

1. INTRODUCTION

A former president of the *Conseil d'État*'s litigation division said: "We interpret the law in accordance with general interest".[1] According to Judge Genevois, this statement shows that interpretation is "the expression of a judicial policy",[2] and it is undoubtedly also true when consistent interpretation is applied in relation to European Union (EU) law. This contribution therefore intends to show that while consistent interpretation is generally applied in France in conformity with EU case-law, there are still remnants of judicial policy that make the overall situation unsatisfactory.

Before diving into a substantive analysis of relevant French case-law, it is important to outline its scope, as well as to recall some France-specific characteristics. Due to insufficient data in legal databases, the analysis must be limited to decisions from the *Cour de cassation* (the supreme court of the judicial order), and from the *Conseil d'État* (the supreme court of the administrative order). Indeed, while all recent decisions from the *Cour de cassation* and the *Conseil d'État*, as well as all decisions from the *Conseil constitutionnel*, are available online, only a limited number of decisions ruled in first instance and by lower courts of appeal are made available.[3]

The scope of the decisions analysed is partly affected by the reasoning used by the judge. The French way of reasoning favours short decisions in which a syllogistic form is most likely the most prominent characteristic. This reasoning is not France-specific, but is commonly found in civil law systems. As Lord Justice Cooper said, "The civilian naturally reasons from principles to instances, the common lawyer from instances to principles".[4] The brevity of the decision is more problematic for scholars who intend to work on case-law, because the opinions of the judges, the Advocate General and the Public Rapporteur are not made public. The same applies as far as the arguments presented by the applicants and defendants are concerned. This brevity often leads to highly technical, cryptic decisions written in one, single sentence. Therefore, only using keywords to search for decisions will never be sufficiently comprehensive. Using a keyword search must be accompanied by an analysis of legal doctrine.

Be that as it may, the *Cour de cassation* now commonly uses the expression "*interprété à la lumière de*" ("interpreted in the light of") in its decisions. The wording is exactly the same as that used in the French version of the

---

1 As former Judge B. Genevois reports in "Le Conseil d'État et l'interprétation de la loi" [2002] *RFDA* 877.

2 Ibid.

3 After gathering decisions from the following databases: *Legifrance.gouv.fr, Doctrine.fr, Dalloz.fr, LexisNexis.fr, Lextenso.fr* and *Lexbase.fr*.

4 1950, "Address to Edinburgh University", cit. in E. Steiner, *French Law* (OUP, 2010), p. 140.

Von Colson judgment.[5] The expression has been used 340 times by the *Cour de cassation* since 1998,[6] however its first decision applying consistent interpretation in relation to EU law dates back to 1990.[7] It must be noted that the expression is used much more often by the appellant or the defendant than by the judge. In most cases, the judge dismissed the argument brought by the parties as inadmissible or irrelevant. Therefore, one cannot consider all 340 decisions as relevant for the investigation at hand. When using the same keywords "interpreted in the light of" and "European" on the same databases as for the previous search, but restricting the new search to case-law from the *Conseil d'État*, 105 decisions are shown, three of which come from the *Tribunal des conflits*,[8] addressing conflicts of competence between the ordinary courts and the administrative courts. Also, one must not forget that the *Conseil constitutionnel* plays a role in assessing the compliance of parliamentary statutes with EU directives, and therefore its case-law might require some attention.

Finally, after studying each of the decisions collected, and after adding decisions found by a search of legal doctrine, more than 200 judgments from both the ordinary and the administrative courts have been deemed relevant, and therefore selected for analysis.

As case-law makes up the large part of the data set on which this contribution is based, it has to be said that precedents do not constitute official sources of French law. However, a sort of pattern emerges from case-law which ultimately turns some decisions into a rule that judges will then follow. This pattern appears to be especially strong in some areas such as administrative law, where codification is mostly absent, and where precedents therefore play a leading role.

Limiting the following analysis to supreme court decisions has only a minor impact on the overall picture due to the decentralised structure of the judicial system. The decisions of the *Cour de cassation* are binding for lower judges.[9] The same rule does not expressly exist for the administrative courts, but the decisions of the *Conseil d'État* are generally followed by lower court judges – if not immediately, then at least after a transition period. The same observation can be made in relation to constitutional law: the French Constitution itself provides that the decisions of the *Conseil constitutionnel* are vested with absolute *res judicata*.[10]

---

5 Case EU:C:1984:153, *Von Colson and Kamann* [1986] para. 26.

6 As of 1 July 2018.

7 *Société nîmoise de tauromachie et de spectacles v. Bodrero Sereu* [1990] Cour de cassation, plen assembly 86-40686, Bulletin AP n° 4, 6.

8 As of 1 July 2018.

9 Art. L431-6 of the Judicial Organisation Code.

10 Art. 62 of the Constitution: "No appeal shall lie from the decisions of the Constitutional Council. They shall be binding on public authorities and on all administrative authorities and all courts."

2. EMBRACING CONSISTENT INTERPRETATION

Now that statistical data and a general presentation of the French judicial system have been provided, scrutiny of the case-law can be handled. In this respect, referrals to the Court of Justice of the European Union (ECJ) may help transition between statistics and substantive study. Nine cases were referred to the ECJ by the *Cour de cassation* and the *Conseil d'État* relating to consistent interpretation.[11] In each case, the referring court applied the decision of the ECJ.

The 2012 decision of the *Cour de cassation* in *Dominguez* is a case in point. Not only is it a landmark decision for consistent interpretation, but it is also an example more generally of the reasoning used by the French courts. The case dealt with a national statute (Art. L3141-3 of the Labour Code), which provides that the right to paid leave is conditional on a minimum 10-day working period. On referral, the ECJ stated that the provision did not comply with Art. 7 of Directive 2003/88 on the organisation of working time, because the Directive entitles the worker to annual leave where Member States cannot make the existence of that right "subject to any preconditions whatsoever".[12] In the subsequent decision of the *Cour de cassation*, the ECJ's *Dominguez* judgment was rigorously applied: as Art. 7 of the Directive precluded the 10-day working period precondition, national law had to be interpreted in the light of the wording and the purpose of the Directive. When interpreting the national provision "as far as possible" in the light of the EU directive, the *Cour de cassation* took "the whole body of domestic law into consideration".[13] The problem was that interpreting Art. L3141-3 in the light of the Directive would have resulted in a *contra legem* interpretation. Unfortunately, as the Advocate General highlighted, neither the parties nor the order for reference to the ECJ gave any information or thought as to whether it might be possible to interpret the national law in the light of the Directive.[14] However, case-law of the *Cour de cassation* shows that interpreting a national provision so that time limits are no longer enforced is clearly a *contra legem* interpretation.[15] According to the ECJ, if consistent interpretation cannot be performed, national judges must then let the applicant benefit from the direct effect of the directive's provision. However, as the situation before the *Cour de cassation* was horizontal (i.e. between two private parties), direct effect could not be applied.

---

11 As of 24 May 2016.

12 Case EU:C:2012:33, *Maribel Dominguez* [2012] para. 18, recalling the outcome in the decision of the ECJ in ECLI:EU:C:2001:356, *BECTU* [2001] para. 53.

13 Ibid., para. 27. The requirement is recalled by the Cour de cassation itself in its subsequent decision.

14 See the Opinion of Advocate General Trstenjak delivered on 8 September 2011, para. 68.

15 *Mme X v. Institut Pasteur* [2006] Cour de cassation, 1st chambre civile 03-20178.

Nevertheless, the factual situation aided the *Cour de cassation* in abiding by consistent interpretation requirements. The applicant, Maribel Dominguez, had been refused the benefit of annual leave because she had been absent from work due to an accident sustained on her commute between home and her workplace. The factual situation must then be considered together with the statutes at stake: first, Art. L3141-3 provides for a 10-day effective working period, then Art. L3141-5 provides elements that constitute "effective working days". Fortunately, Art. L3141-5 of the Labour Code provides that the 10 effective working days take into account absence from work due to workplace accidents. Such accidents are not considered the same as accidents that occur while commuting to or from the workplace. However, unlike Art. L3141-3, consistent interpretation of which would lead to a *contra legem* interpretation, Art. L3141-5 could certainly be interpreted in a way to better achieve the purpose of Art. 7 of the Directive. As the *Cour de cassation* stated, Art. L3141-5 could be interpreted so that an accident on the journey from home to work was considered as a workplace accident. Consequently, Maribel Dominguez could benefit from annual leave despite her absence from work.[16]

The *Dominguez* case, while important in terms of relying on EU law, also provides insights into the ability and willingness of French courts to comply with consistent interpretation requirements. Not only is priority given to consistent interpretation over direct effect, the *contra legem* limits set out by the ECJ are also handled.

Indeed, while consistent interpretation has been accepted by the courts and is broadly applied, this process was no doubt facilitated by long-standing case-law in relation to national and international law. Reasoning by consistent interpretation, whatever law is at stake, has become common practice, even for the *Conseil constitutionnel*.[17]

The doctrine is also quite open to the application of consistent interpretation. Before courts began to apply consistent interpretation to their reasoning, a number of academics maintained that consistent interpretation worked much like a blood transfusion – taking the prevailing norm and "transfusing" it into the norm to be interpreted, thereby treating the "illness" affecting the internal order.[18] A more conventional definition was given by Viala in 2011, which is applicable to all cases including those pertaining to EU law, describing it as

---

16 See comments by S. Laulom, "Le droit aux congés annuels payés: les limites de l'obligation l'interprétation lonforme" [2013] *Droit social* 564.

17 A. Viala, *Nature de l'office du juge de 1ère instance et d'appel dans l'appréciation du caractère sérieux d'une QPC: filtrage ou contrôle de constitutionnalité?* (Université Montpellier 1 CERCOP, 2012), p. 965.

18 Y. Galmot and J.-C. Bonichot, "La CJCE et la transposition des directives en droit national" [1988] *RFDA* 1.

an "intellectual mechanism used by judges in order to interpret a text in a way that is conform with a norm".[19]

As of the end of the 1980s, French courts changed how they put consistent interpretation into practice. The *Conseil d'État*, familiar with the reasoning, was the first to apply it when EU law was at stake, as can be seen in the *Ministre du Budget v. Cercle militaire mixte de la caserne Mortier* judgment from 1989.[20] In this case, the *Conseil d'État* had to apply the Sixth Directive on VAT to a statute of the General Tax Code.[21] The provision of the Directive at issue in the case had been held to be capable of producing direct effects by the ECJ.[22] The factual situation was to determine whether or not a refreshment bar in a military facility should be subject to VAT. The problem was that back in 1989, the *Conseil d'État* had not yet accepted the application of directly effective provisions of EC law. The solution was to apply consistent interpretation reasoning to the national statute at stake. As such, the *Conseil d'État* ruled that a refreshment bar had to be interpreted as being a "staff shop" as provided by the Sixth Directive.[23]

A few months later, in the 1990 *Société nîmoise de tauromachie et de spectacles v. Bodrero Sereu* judgment, the *Cour de cassation* also decided it was time to give life to the *Von Colson* case-law.[24] In this case, the supreme court of the judicial order interpreted a national statute in the light of Directive 77/187 relating to the safeguarding of employees' rights in the event of transfers of undertakings, businesses or parts of businesses.[25] Thus, 1989 and 1990 were major turning points, with national courts beginning to embrace consistent interpretation. As the *Cour de cassation*'s decision in the *Dominguez* case shows, application is generally in line with EU case-law. Judges of the ordinary courts now go so far to interpret national law in line with EU framework decisions as well, and therefore comply with the *Pupino* judgment of the ECJ.[26] Not only did

---

19 A. Viala, *Nature de l'office du juge de 1ère instance et d'appel dans l'appréciation du caractère sérieux d'une QPC: filtrage ou contrôle de constitutionnalité?* (Université Montpellier 1 CERCOP, 2012), p. 965.

20 *Ministre du Budget v. Cercle militaire mixte de la caserne Mortier* [1989] Conseil d'État 86113.

21 Art. 4, para. 5 of the Council Directive (EC) (Sixth Directive) 77/388 [1977] OJ L145/1; and Art. 256 B of the General Tax Code.

22 Case ECLI:EU:C:1989:381, *Comune di Carpaneto Piacentino et al.* [1989] para. 31. The Advocate General before the *Conseil d'État* referred to this decision but admitted that direct effect was not yet applied by administrative courts.

23 As enshrined in the Council Directive (EC) (Sixth Directive) 77/388 [1977] OJ L145/1, Annex D para. 12.

24 *Société nîmoise de tauromachie et de spectacles v. Bodrero Sereu* [1990] Cour de cassation, plen assembly 86-40686, Bulletin AP n° 4, 6.

25 Council Directive (EC) 77/187 on the approximation of the laws of the Member States relating to the safeguarding of employees' rights in the event of transfers of undertakings, businesses or parts of businesses [1977] OJ L61/26.

26 Respectively: *Pedja X* [2014] Cour de cassation, criminal chamber 13-80161; and Case EU:C:2005:386 *Pupino* [2005].

the *Conseil d'État* appropriate consistent interpretation, it turned it into a tool that can be used to protect the administration.

The general goodwill shown by courts does however conceal certain pockets of resistance. While the boundaries of consistent interpretation drawn by the ECJ – such as *contra legem* limitations – seem correctly applied, courts still refuse to perform consistent interpretation before the end of the transposition period.[27] For the principle to apply in horizontal situations, courts also require conditions which go beyond the requirements of direct effect. In fact, the ordinary courts state that consistent interpretation is not possible "in proceedings between individuals" if the EU provision provides Member States with an option when transposing it into national law.[28] This observation means that French courts do not completely abide by the requirements of consistent interpretation.

3. GENERALLY ACCEPTED RULE OF INTERPRETATION

The *Conseil d'Etat* was the first to perform consistent interpretation when EU law is at stake. This is surprising, because the *Cour de cassation* had been the first to accept both the primacy of EU law and the possibility for an applicant to invoke the direct effect of a provision of a directive.[29] However, considering the *Conseil d'État*'s long-standing experience with consistent interpretation in general, and that such reasoning enables the judge to resolve a conflict of laws through the application of national provisions without claiming primacy of the "external" law, it is in fact surprising that the *Conseil d'État* did not apply the principle earlier. Be that as it may, since consistent interpretation is accepted by both ordinary and administrative judges as a rule of interpretation (see section 3.1), it has been progressively applied to national law as a whole. However, there are still some exceptions – such as the application of said legal reasoning to international conventions duly integrated within the national legal order (see section 3.2).

3.1. RECOGNISING CONSISTENT INTERPRETATION AS A RULE OF INTERPRETATION

One of the most interesting aspects of consistent interpretation in relation to EU law is that it was made easier by a similar, established, legal practice in

---

27 See, for the ordinary courts: *Lego v. Klip* [2002] Cour de cassation, chambre commerciale 99-13774; and *X et al.* [2015] Cour de cassation, chambre criminelle 14-87403. See under 4.2.2 for a detailed presentation of these cases.

28 *Ferring SAS* [2007] Cour de cassation, 1st chambre civile 05-10234.

29 See, respectively: *Smissaert* [1978] Cour de cassation, chambre criminelle 77-93026; and *Mme Perreux* [2009] Conseil d'État 298348.

the fields of national and international law. From the moment consistent interpretation was used vis-à-vis EU law, it in turn enabled judges to reinforce requirements for consistent interpretation in relation to national law. Thus, we observe a form of cross-fertilisation between national, international and EU law (see section 3.3.1). Moreover, general application of consistent interpretation by the *Cour de cassation*, the *Conseil d'État*, and more marginally by the *Conseil constitutionnel*, appears therefore to be respectively horizontal, vertical and abstract (see section 3.3.2).

3.1.1. Cross-Fertilisation between National, EU and International Law

For the time being, consistent interpretation does not seem to be considered as a principle. Simply, it is a rule of conflict which allows two norms to remain in force.[30] While some tribunals of first instance refer to the consistent interpretation as a "principle established by the Court of Justice in the *Von Colson & Kamann* decision",[31] this wording has not been used by the *Cour de cassation* or the *Conseil d'État*.

However, the administrative courts have a long-standing experience in performing consistent interpretations, which began with national law and was later extended to EU law. The *Conseil d'État* opened the door to consistent interpretation in 1957, long before applying it in cases governed by EU law.[32] From 1957 onwards, many examples can be found where the judge has performed consistent interpretation between two national norms.[33] For instance, in 1977, the *Conseil d'État* interpreted an opinion of the *Direction générale des impôts* in the light of a parliamentary statute.[34] A step towards applying such reasoning to EU law was made in the 1975 *Mathis* case, where consistent interpretation was applied for the first time to resolve a conflict between a national decree and an international convention.[35] Interpretation of national law in the light of EU law was first allowed by the *Conseil d'État* in 1989, in the

---

30 V. Bouhier, "Interprétation conforme en droit de l'Union et réserves d'interprétation du Conseil constitutionnel: regards croisés" [2013] *Constitutions* 195.

31 For a recent example: *Cuirco Diffusion SAS v. American Apparel Deutschland GmbH* [2016] Tribunal de grande instance de Paris 2014/16995.

32 *Syndicat autonome du personnel enseignant des Facultés de droit* [1957] Conseil d'État Recueil 9 [1957] RDP 673. The appellant brought an action against a decree which makes every international conference subject to government authorisation. The Conseil d'État interpreted the decree in such a way that authorisation is required only when the conference is publicly subsidised.

33 See references given by A. Viala, *Les Réserves d'interprétation dans la jurisprudence du Conseil constitutionnel* (LGDJ, 1999), p. 32 *et seq.*

34 *Sieur X.* [1977] Conseil d'État 96456.

35 *Mathis* [1975] Conseil d'État 86685.

Cercle militaire mixte de la caserne Mortier decision.[36] Since then, decades of decisions have expressly applied consistent interpretation.[37]

Even though it did so later than the *Conseil d'État*, the *Cour de cassation* also performed consistent interpretation in relation to national law before EU law was taken into account. In a series of decisions during the 1980s, it applied this reasoning to bypass bans on constitutionality reviews of parliamentary statutes.[38] It has to be said that despite the *Cour de cassation*'s relatively late acceptance of such reasoning, in a previous case from 1931, *Sanchez v. Gozland*, the Public *Rapporteur* Paul Matter suggested that interpreting a national statute in accordance with a French-Spanish treaty would be a solution for the conflict of laws.[39] While the *Cour de cassation* did not follow the *Rapporteur*'s suggestion, it represented a first attempt at applying consistent interpretation within the ordinary courts. It was only in 1990 that the Ordinary Supreme Court first applied consistent interpretation in the field of EU law.[40] The ordinary courts now undertake inclusion of the purpose of EU law.[41] More recently, the *Cour de cassation* also used the consistent interpretation method to assess the compatibility of statute and the fundamental rights enshrined in the French Constitution so as to avoid a referral to the *Conseil constitutionnel*.[42] This particular use shows how commonplace this practice has become for the *Cour de cassation*.

---

36 *Ministre du Budget v. Cercle militaire mixte de la caserne Mortier* [1989] Conseil d'État 86113.

37 Meaning decisions using the "interpreted in the light of" formula. Since 2010, more than 10 decisions per year can be found using this expression.

38 M. Jeol, "Les techniques de substitution", *La Cour de cassation et la Constitution de la République* (PUAM, 1995), p. 69. The first decisions cited are from 1985, when the Cour de cassation added a condition to the 1946 Foreigners control Act so that it can comply with Art. 66 of the Constitution. Jeol, then first Advocate General at the Cour de cassation, cites several decisions between 1985 and 1993.

39 P. Matter, "Conclusions dans l'affaire Sanchez v Gozland" [1932] *JDI* 683. The decision then applied another solution suggested by Matter, the so-called "doctrine Matter", by virtue of which the *lex posterior* prevails over the treaty: Cour de cassation, 22 December 1931, *Sanchez v. Gozland.*

40 In three decisions of the same day: *Société nîmoise de tauromachie et de spectacles v. Bodrero Sereu* [1990] Cour de cassation, plen assembly 86-40686, Bulletin AP n° 4, 6; *SARL Onet v. Mallet et al.* [1990] Cour de cassation 85-44.518; *Société d'exploitation du Touring club de Paris-Ouest v. Appart et Schwinding* [1990] Cour de cassation 89-45730. See G. Couturier, "L'article L122-12 du code du travail: la nouvelle jurisprudence de la Cour de cassation" [1990] *Droit social* 412; and X. Prétot, "L'article L122-12 du code du travail: la nouvelle jurisprudence de la Cour de cassation" [1990] *Droit social* 416.

41 For example: *Mme X v. association des combattants prisonniers de guerre de la Seine* [2009] Cour de cassation, social chamber 08-40375.

42 [2011] Cour de cassation, criminal chamber 11-90087 and [2012] Cour de cassation, criminal chamber 12-90004. This can only be recent case-law given the fact that the so-called French ex-post preliminary reference to the Conseil constitutionnel, "question prioritaire de constitutionnalité", has been in force since 2010.

Remarkably, the *Conseil constitutionnel* applies the rule of conflict through what are called "interpretation reservations", described by the doctrine as being similar to consistent interpretation.[43] The *Conseil constitutionnel* uses interpretation reservations in order to avoid the annulment of an Act due to its unconstitutional nature. It may carry out such an interpretation even *ex officio*.[44] This reasoning was applied when assessing a transposition statute of a directive from 2004.[45]

3.1.2. Horizontal, Vertical and Abstract Application

Litigation before the ordinary courts is, by its very nature, between individuals. As a result, the high number of cases involving consistent interpretation before the *Cour de cassation* is self-explanatory: horizontal application of the principle is not problematic for the judge. Moreover, as the ECJ maintains, it is the main way to circumvent the lack of direct effect of a directive's provisions in cases between individuals.[46] It is clear that horizontal direct application in the event of a late or failing transposition is usually impossible. For example, in a case where a court of appeal had interpreted national law *contra legem*, the *Cour de cassation* said that the interpretation in question led to new obligations for the company being created,[47] and then to a horizontal application of the directive. In this case, employment contracts of two employees had been transferred from one company to another without duly informing the employees, although Directive 2001/23 would require such employees to be informed.[48] The Directive not having been transposed into national law, the court of appeal interpreted the relevant national statute, which provided only that in the event of an employee transfer, the employment contract had to be upheld. The court of appeal said that this provision could be interpreted in line with Directive 2001/23 in a way that contained the obligation to inform employees in the event of a transfer. The provision of the Directive clearly satisfied the conditions for direct effect,[49] and the interpretation of the national statute was a *contra legem* interpretation.

---

43 G. Drago, "Procédures du contrôle de constitutionnalité" [2015] *JCl Administratif* [192].

44 *Loi relative à la prévention de la corruption et à la transparence de la vie économique et des procédures publiques* [1993] Conseil constitutionnel 92-316 DC.

45 Further elaborated on in the next section.

46 Case EU:C:1984:153, *Von Colson* [1984] ECR 1891.

47 *Open cascade* [2009] Cour de cassation, social chamber 08-43397, Bulletin V 256.

48 Directive 2001/23 (EC) relating to the safeguarding of employees' rights in the event of transfers of undertakings, businesses or parts of undertakings or businesses [2001] OJ L82/16.

49 Art. 7, para. 6 provides: "Member States shall provide that, where there are no representatives of the employees in an undertaking or business through no fault of their own, the employees concerned must be informed in advance of: the date or proposed date of the transfer; the reason for the transfer; the legal, economic and social implications of the transfer for the employees; any measures envisaged in relation to the employees."

The *Cour de cassation* overruled the court of appeal's judgment, stating that the reasoning was erroneous. The court ruled that

> far from interpreting the national statute, [the court of appeal] has actually imposed upon the defendant, an individual, an obligation of information [and therefore] has breached both Article 249 EC and [Article L122-12 of the Labour Code].[50]

It is clear therefore that consistent interpretation – as long as it does not reach the limits of *contra legem* interpretation – is by default the preferred way of applying a directive which is not duly transposed.

Consistent interpretation by the *Conseil d'Etat* is by nature vertical. Given its competency to annul and amend regulations of the administration,[51] and to receive applications for remedies where a public contract is at stake,[52] litigation before the administrative courts opposes an individual on the one hand, and the State or an individual acting on behalf of the State on the other. When an action for annulment of a regulation is made before the *Conseil d'État*, the appeal is made against the State. The litigation is therefore always vertical. However, the administrative courts also consider that when an individual is in charge of a public service, decisions connected to this service are of a public nature and can then be subject to annulment.[53] It must be said that no instance of consistent interpretation of such decisions was found in the *Conseil d'État* case-law. Nevertheless, applying consistent interpretation to these decisions would be a vertical application and perfectly coherent with the administrative courts' case-law.

However, consistent interpretation performed by the *Conseil constitutionnel* is neither horizontal nor vertical. When applying consistent interpretation requirements in the event an appeal is made prior to a law being promulgated, there is no defendant and no applicant is affected by this law. The reason is

50 *Open cascade* [2009] Cour de cassation, chambre sociale 08-43397, Bulletin V 256.

51 *Conseil de la concurrence* [1987] Conseil constitutionnel DC-86-224, para. 15: "[I]n last instance administrative courts have the competence to annul and amend decisions made, within the exercise of prerogative of the public powers, by the authorities of the executive, their agents, the local governments of the Republic or by the public bodies they either control or which are under their authority".

52 A contract is of a public nature when for instance it is concluded between two public bodies unless it only creates obligations of private nature (*UAP* [1983] Tribunal des conflits 2256); it is a public contract also when it is concluded between a public body and an individual if it either contains prerogatives of the public powers or concerns the execution of a public service (respectively: *Société des granits porphyroïdes des Vosges* [1912] Conseil d'État 30701, and *Époux Bertin et Ministre de l'agriculture v. Consorts Grimouard* [1956] Conseil d'État 98637). A public contract can also be concluded between two individuals, when one of the co-contractors acts on behalf of a public body (see for instance: *Commune de Boulogne-Billancourt* [2007] Conseil d'État 281796).

53 See the comprehensive case-law deriving from the decision *Caisse primaire "Aide et protection"* [1938] Conseil d'État 57302 Lebon 417.

that, under Art. 61 of the Constitution, only the President of the Republic, the Prime Minister, the presidents of both houses of Parliament, or 60 members from either of the two houses may bring appeals before the *Conseil constitutionnel*. This *ex ante* appeal – meaning before promulgation – is thus an abstract review, where the situation is neither horizontal nor vertical. It is therefore more unusual for the *Conseil constitutionnel* to use consistent interpretation regarding a directive. In a 1975 decision, the *Conseil constitutionnel* refused to assess the compatibility between Acts and international conventions, including EU law.[54] However, EU law was vested with a new status by a 1992 constitutional amendment which added Art. 88-1, providing that "The Republic shall participate in the European Union". As such, this provision was taken into account in 2004 by the *Conseil constitutionnel*, which drew the conclusion that "transposition of directives is a constitutional requirement".[55]

In its case-law concerning Acts that serve to transpose directives, the *Conseil constitutionnel* established a specific reasoning: when the *Conseil constitutionnel* is called upon to assess the constitutionality of an Act that transposes an EU directive, it ensures that the transposition is effective, and if it is not, the Act will be struck down. This means that the constitutional judge has to make sure that the Act complies with the directive's requirements, and thus complies with Art. 88-1 of the Constitution, which makes the transposition of directives a "constitutional requirement".[56] In this respect, the *Conseil constitutionnel* has on occasion had to interpret a parliamentary statute in the light of a directive, in order to avoid the statute being annulled. These are known as the "interpretation reservations" of the *Conseil constitutionnel*.

The *Conseil constitutionnel* used this method in a landmark decision from 2004. In a nutshell, the Act at stake provided that legal persons providing an information society service could not be held responsible for storing unlawful information given by recipients of the service, when the service providers were not aware of the unlawfulness of these pieces of information. The *Conseil constitutionnel* held that as long as the Act did not allow for the responsibility of the provider of an information society service to be called into effect when he did not withdraw the piece of unlawful information in circumstances described in the decision, it complied with Directive 2000/31 on electronic commerce.[57] Thus, "subject to this reservation", the plea was rejected. The term consistent interpretation, meaning the expression "interpreted in the light of" as used by both the ordinary and the administrative courts, is not used by the *Conseil constitutionnel*. Yet it is without a doubt applying the same rule of interpretation.

---

54 *Interruption volontaire de grossesse* [1975] Conseil constitutionnel 74-54 DC.

55 *Loi pour la confiance dans l'économie numérique* [2004] Conseil constitutionnel 2004-496 DC.

56 Ibid.

57 Ibid., para. 9. See also, for the detailed circumstances, Art. 14(1) of Directive 2000/31 (EC) on electronic commerce [2000] OJ 178/1.

Viala calls "interpretation reservations" a "third decision-making path",[58] which sits between the two more common paths: either rejecting the appeal, or annulling the judgment or the national regulation. Albeit unconventional, it allows the judge to formally reject the appeal while applying the newly interpreted norm to the applicant. As such, according to Viala, it acts like "venom withdrawal", and can be compared with consistent interpretation as applied by the administrative courts.[59] The *Conseil constitutionnel* later used the same reasoning in another major decision in 2006, showing that this way of adapting national law to EU laws (and particularly directives) has become common practice.[60]

Therefore, the *Conseil constitutionnel* – a typical body of the European model of constitutional justice – and its interpretation of Art. 88-1 of the Constitution, gives rise to a consistent interpretation that it is neither horizontal nor vertical, but abstract. Consequently, all three courts – *Conseil constitutionnel*, *Cour de cassation* and *Conseil d'État* – would appear to have all the necessary tools to apply consistent interpretation to "national law as a whole" in their respective fields of competence.

3.2. APPLICATION TO NATIONAL LAW (ALMOST) "AS A WHOLE"

The ECJ requires that consistent interpretation extends to national law "as a whole".[61] While both the ordinary and the administrative courts are broadly willing to apply the reasoning (see section 3.3.1), application to international treaties duly integrated into national law has not been seen yet. Given the position of both EU directives and international law under the French Constitution, application of consistent interpretation to international treaties appears to be foreseeable (see section 3.3.2).

3.2.1. A Broad Application to National Law

Both the administrative and the ordinary courts apply consistent interpretation to national law as a whole, with a few exceptions. The *Cour de cassation* supports a broad application: the judge "is required to interpret national law in the light of the wording and the purpose of the directive".[62] This is the exact same wording

[58] A. Viala, *Les réserves d'interprétation dans la jurisprudence du Conseil constitutionnel* (LGDJ, 1999), p. 32 *et seq.*

[59] Ibid.

[60] *Droits d'auteur et droits voisins dans la société d'information* [2006] Conseil constitutionnel 2006-540 DC para. 40.

[61] Case EU:C:2004:584, *Pfeiffer* [2004] ECR I-8835 para. 115.

[62] *Les Laboratoires Servier* [2009] Cour de cassation, 1st civil chamber 08-12777.

used by the ECJ in *Von Colson*;[63] and the *Cour de cassation* uses it to specify that consistent interpretation is applicable to *national law* – not just statues or decrees.

As can be expected, interpretation of parliamentary statutes accounts for the overwhelming majority of cases.[64] The explanation is purely statistical. As a matter of fact, the administrative courts have almost sole jurisdiction over appeals made against decrees. In 2014, the *Conseil d'État* and its lower courts issued approximately 230,000 decisions, of which 12,200 were from the *Conseil d'État*.[65] In the ordinary courts, where litigation between individuals is the core activity, the *Cour de cassation* and its lower courts issued more than 2.6 million decisions in civil matters alone. The *Cour de cassation* handed down decisions in 28,700 cases in 2014. This means that decisions from the ordinary courts far outweigh decree-based appeals before the administrative courts in case-law analysis. Nevertheless, it is interesting to study case-law involving decrees, because the *Cour de cassation* also plays a role in some decree-based appeals. Moreover, the *Conseil d'État* not only differentiates between types of decrees, it is probably the most committed to taking into account national law "as a whole"; this includes the Constitution itself.

In some cases, decrees were subjected to consistent interpretation. In 1957, a decree was at the heart of the very first decision implying consistent interpretation made by the *Conseil d'État*.[66] A decree was again at stake in the first case in which the *Conseil d'État* used the consistent interpretation method within the field of international law in the 1975 *Mathis* decision.[67] After opening up consistent interpretation to the scope of EU law in its 1989 decision,[68] the *Conseil d'État* applied it to decrees for the first time in 1995 in the *Association Artus* case.[69] Since then, interpretation of decrees has common practice within the *Conseil d'État*.[70]

However, individual administrative decisions are not subject to consistent interpretation. This type of decree only targets a single person and does not have general effect. Appointment of a magistrate or a grant of a subsidy are examples of individual decisions. As explained by Viala, writing about the general reasoning of interpretation reservations before the administrative judge, interpretation "is performed on general and impersonal regulations, as their application

63 Case EU:C:1984:153, *Von Colson* [1984] ECR 1891.
64 It represents more than three quarters of the decisions found.
65 Conseil d'État, *Rapport public 2015* (La documentation française 2016), p. 17.
66 *Syndicat autonome du personnel enseignant des Facultés de droit* [1957] Conseil d'État Recueil 9 [1957] *RDP* 673.
67 *Mathis* [1975] Conseil d'État 86685.
68 *Ministre du Budget v. Cercle militaire mixte de la caserne Mortier* [1989] Conseil d'État 86113.
69 *Association Artus* [1995] Conseil d'État 154401.
70 See, for recent instances: *Société Neptune Distribution* [2016] Conseil d'État 351618; *Jansseng-Cilag* [2015] Conseil d'État 379389.

measures derive only from them".[71] It is true that individual decisions can only be either legal or illegal. Applying consistent interpretation to such a regulation would have no effect when the individual is already affected by the decision, and no measure applying the decision is expected. As a consequence, no decision can be found where the *Conseil d'État* has applied consistent interpretation to an individual decision of the administration. It is one of the reasons behind the impact of the 2009 landmark decision in the *Mme Perreux* case, where the *Conseil d'État* finally accepted the direct effect of a directive in cases involving individual decisions.[72] In the case, Judge Perreux appealed a decision made by the Justice Minister to refuse her appointment to a teaching position at the National Magistates' School, on the grounds of her being a member of a trade union. As such, no interpretation in accordance with Directive 2000/78 on equal treatment in employment and occupation was possible, thus direct effect was the only path to complying with EU law.[73]

As a consequence, in the event that an individual decision infringes upon EU law provisions which are not of vertical direct effect, or takes place in a horizontal litigation, the only remedy would be to invoke the principle of Member State liability. However, this does not appear to weaken the obligation of sincere cooperation, which underlies consistent interpretation of national law "as a whole", as interpreting an individual decision in the light of EU law would have harsher consequences than not interpreting at all. As a matter of fact, interpreting a national regulation would fall in favour of the applicant; but as we already saw, it would also sometimes allow the judge to dismiss the application. In these circumstances, it would be excessively difficult for the applicant to recover damages by way of Member State liability.

Consistent interpretation is obligatory for more than just the judges. The administration, including all administrative bodies, has a duty to comply with

---

71 A. Viala, *Les réserves d'interprétation dans la jurisprudence du Conseil constitutionnel* (LGDJ, 1999), p. 35.

72 *Mme Perreux* [2009] Conseil d'État 298348.

73 Yet, D. Ritleng in its comment on *Mme Perreux* ("L'arrêt Perreux ou la fin de l'exception française" [2010] *RTD eur.* 228) wrote that direct effect against individual decisions has a "widely symbolic impact" as the *Conseil d'État* made it possible to perform consistent interpretations of decrees. However, the present author does not agree with this statement because no judgments involving individual decisions were found. Furthermore, the decisions D. Ritleng cites do not relate to individual decisions. While in the decision *SARL La Biomécanique intégrée* [2003] Conseil d'État 231126, a homologation decision was at stake, case-law shows that it is a regulation of a general effect, not an individual decision: *Groupement Qualité Cocorette* [2011] Conseil d'État 321975, according to B. Seiller (ed.), *La rétroactivité des décisions du juge administratif* (Economica, 2012), para. 378. The two other judgments cited also did not involve individual decisions: in *Ministre du Budget v. Cercle militaire mixte de la caserne Mortier* [1989] Conseil d'État 86113, a parliamentary statute was at stake; in *Association pour la protection des animaux sauvages* [2005] Conseil d'État 271216, a ministerial ruling authorising the culling of wolves in certain areas was appealed.

EU directives through an interpretation of national law in the light of their wording and purpose. The *Conseil d'État* has recalled this obligation on many occasions. For instance, in a 2012 opinion, it stated that in order to comply with Directive 2008/115 on common standards for returning illegally staying third-country nationals,[74] and when enforcing Art. L. 511-1 of the French Code on the Entry and Residence of Foreign Nationals and the Right of Asylum, the administrative body is required, in line with Directive 2008/115, to take into account the best interest of the child, family life and the state of health of the third-country national concerned.[75] This reasoning was later repeated in subsequent judgments.[76]

Arguably the most significant consistent interpretation to date came in 1999, when the *Conseil d'État* was asked to interpret the Constitution in the light of Directive 79/409 on the conservation of wild birds.[77] In a spectacular turn of events,[78] the *Conseil d'État* stated that the Prime Minister must seek a referral before the *Conseil constitutionnel* whenever a parliamentary statute is passed in a field where the executive is the sole competent body, and whenever the statute infringes upon an EU directive. As it is written, the Constitution states that the Prime Minister can appeal a statute.[79] The *Conseil d'État*, however, stated that the Prime Minister must appeal a statute that infringes upon the executive's jurisdiction and an EU directive. The Prime Minister must first refer to the *Conseil constitutionnel*, and then adopt a decree which replaces the statute and which is expected to comply with EU obligations. More precisely,

---

74 Directive (EC) 2008/115 of the European Parliament and of the Council on common standards and procedures in Member States for returning illegally staying third-country nationals [2008] OJ L348.

75 [2012] Conseil d'État (Opinion) 356505. Art. 5 of Directive 2008/115 requires that when Member States implement it, they "shall take due account of: (a) the best interest of the child; (b) family life; (c) the state of health of the third-country national concerned".

76 *Mme B. A. et Mme A* [2014] Conseil d'État 365054; *Ordre national des chirurgiens-dentistes v. Agence nationale de sécurité du médicament et des produits de santé* [2015] Conseil d'État 372718.

77 *Association ornithologique et mammalogique de Saône-et Loire et rassemblement des opposants à la chasse* [1999] Conseil d'État 164789 and 165122.

78 This decision was criticised by prominent academics: D. de Béchillon, "Courte reaction en forme de grimace" [2000] *RFDA* 676; L. Favoreu, "L'interprétation de l'article 37, alinéa 2 de la Constitution par le Conseil d'Etat" [2000] *RFDA* 664. It was also endorsed by not less prominent academics: B. Genevois, "Conditions d'exercice du pouvoir réglementaire et compétence de la juridiction administrative" [2000] *RFDA* 668. See also P. Cassia and E. Saulnier, "La loi du 3 juillet 1998 sur la chasse et le droit communautaire: 'error communis facit jus'?" [1999] 7 *Europe* 5 *et seq.*

79 Art. 37, sub-para. 2 of the Constitution: "Provisions of statutory origin enacted in such matters may be amended by decree issued after consultation with the Conseil d'État. Any such provisions passed after the coming into force of the Constitution shall be amended by decree only if the Constitutional Council has found that they are matters for regulation as defined in the foregoing paragraph."

Art. 37 sub-para. 2 provides that statutes impinging on governmental competence "shall be amended by decree only if the Constitutional Council has found that they are matters for regulation as defined in the foregoing paragraph". Hence, the Government has a duty to amend the statute by decree, but does not have such an obligation when deciding to refer to the *Conseil constitutionnel*. Yet for the *Conseil d'État*, if the provision is taken within the scope of EU law and does not comply with its requirements, this possibility of referral becomes an obligation.

The *Cour de cassation* also interprets collective bargaining agreements, but it does so while interpreting statutes. The first time, in 2011, was where an agreement was consistent with the EU Directive, but the national statute that served as a pivot between the two was in fact in breach of the Directive.[80] Consistent interpretation targeted first the law, then the agreement. Later, in 2015, consistent interpretation was applied in the same way to both a collective bargaining agreement and a national statute.[81] The first case, in 2011, was in relation to a series of dismissals within a company as well as a string of contracts being terminated by mutual consent. The case gave rise to the question whether terminations by mutual consent must be included in a collective redundancy plan as provided by Directive 98/59 relating to collective redundancies.[82] Neither the statute nor the collective bargaining agreement provided for such inclusion. However, the *Cour de cassation* interpreted the two norms in line with the Directive in such a way that terminations of employment contracts by mutual consent were included and must then benefit from information obligations. In the second case, in 2015, the *Cour de cassation* interpreted Art. L3141-5 of the Labour Code – the same national provision at issue in the *Dominguez* case – and a collective bargaining agreement on social security in the light of Directive 2003/88. As a result, periods of sick leave due to workplace accidents or occupational diseases are to be treated as time at work when calculating entitlement to paid leave.

French courts are nevertheless still reluctant to interpret collective bargaining agreements in the light of EU law unless a national statute is also considered. This may be due to the fragile balance of such agreements that arise from industrial relations negotiations. Changing a single provision may displace the balance of the entire bargaining agreement as a result. Thus, there is more legitimacy in interpreting a national statute jointly with the collective agreement. As discussed below, the same reluctance applies to international treaties, which bear similar fragilities.

---

80 *Norbert Dentressangle* [2011] Cour de cassation, social chamber 10-11581.

81 *Société Yacco* [2015] Cour de cassation, social chamber 13-26317.

82 Council Directive 98/59 (EC) on the approximation of the laws of the Member States relating to collective redundancies [1998] OJ L226/16.

3.2.2. *A Foreseeable Application to International Treaties*

The relationship between French and international law is predominantly monist. Art. 55 of the French Constitution provides that "[t]reaties or agreements duly ratified or approved shall, upon publication, prevail over Acts of Parliament". For the application of the latter, it is up to both the ordinary and the administrative courts to assess the compatibility between Acts and international conventions,[83] since the *Conseil constitutionnel* stated in 1975 that it was not competent.[84] If a court wants to interpret an international treaty in the light of EU law, the provisions of the international treaty need to be of direct effect so that it can first be relied upon by the applicant.[85] Therefore, when such a provision is invoked before the court, it is difficult to see what would prevent the court from applying consistent interpretation to a provision of an international treaty in the scope of EU law.

Such an application is not entirely improbable. In a 2011 decision, the Appeal Court of Colmar interpreted the European Convention on Human Rights in the light of the Convention on the Rights of the Child, resulting in the granting of a family allowance to a child of Iranian citizenship.[86] The *Cour de cassation* subsequently dismissed the decision of the Appeal Court, but not because the court had applied consistent interpretation to the two treaties. The reasoning does not therefore appear to be called into question, and the case shows that an international treaty may in fact be subject to consistent interpretation. Considering the position of directives in French law, the transposition of which is a "constitutional obligation", added to the fact that the Constitution takes precedence over international treaties, there is little doubt that one day French courts may be called upon to interpret an international treaty provision in the light of an EU directive.

4. REASONABLY ACCEPTABLE LIMITS

As discussed so far, except for application to international treaties before a court, which does not yet appear to have occurred, national judges in France generally seem to accept the reasoning of consistent interpretation. The national courts

83 For the ordinary courts: *Société Jacques Vabre* [1975] Cour de cassation, joint chambers 73-13556; and for the administrative courts: *Alitalia* [1989] Conseil d'État 74052.

84 *Interruption volontaire de grossesse* [1975] Conseil constitutionnel 74-54 DC.

85 The *Conseil d'État* accepts direct effect of an international treaty's provision since its decision *GISTI* [1997] Conseil d'État 163043. The criteria of direct effect have been updated and approximated with EU law criteria in *GISTI et FAPIL* [2012] Conseil d'État 322326.

86 *Caisse d'allocation familiale du Bas-Y* [2011] Cour d'appel de Colmar 10/03326.

have done so mainly due to previous experience in applying similar reasoning in relation to other legal orders. Yet certain limitations to consistent interpretation have been expounded by the ECJ, and are now also applied by French judges in practice. According to the *Conseil d'État*, consistent interpretation is a means to protect the administration, as its application avoids an annulment of the national provision. However, due to the fact that it deals mostly with horizontal situations, the *Cour de cassation* faces other concerns. Beyond their diverging purposes, both the administrative and the ordinary courts have maintained certain pockets of resistance, refusing for example a preventive application of consistent interpretation in certain cases, and performing bold interpretations in others. Hence, while the goals of administrative and ordinary courts differ (see section 4.1), they behave similarly when it comes to certain aspects of applying consistent interpretation, be it with reluctance or audacity (see section 4.2).

4.1. DIFFERING COURTS, DIFFERING GOALS

One must not lose sight of the fact that the administrative courts deal primarily with vertical situations, that is to say situations where an individual brings an action against the State. The very nature of this litigation, combined with a long-standing experience with consistent interpretation, leads the *Conseil d'État* to favouring this form of reasoning, which protects the administration against its regulations being annulled (see section 4.1.1). However, the *Cour de cassation* does not share such goals, as it faces mostly horizontal situations, where the direct effect of EU directives is not applicable. Thus, ordinary courts require that directives do not offer an option to the State when transposing the provision into national law (see section 4.2.2).

4.1.1. Priority Given to Consistent Interpretation Over Direct Effect by the Administrative Courts in Order to Protect the Administration

The ordinary courts do not give priority to consistent interpretation over direct effect, as consistent interpretation is applied by default in horizontal situations, without any reference to direct effect. However, due to long-standing reasons, the *Conseil d'État* is much more at ease than the *Cour de cassation* with this reasoning. This is the case especially in vertical situations when the option exists between direct effect and consistent interpretation.

On the one hand, priority is given to consistent interpretation by the *Conseil d'État*, probably because it prevents lawmakers from amending national law. It allows courts to favour the individual while protecting the administration's integrity. As Waline wrote in relation to consistent interpretation, by leaning in favour of the applicant while dismissing the application, the *Conseil d'État* is "charitable towards the administration".[87] In this respect, when applying consistent interpretation instead of setting aside national law, the judge achieves the same goal as the *Conseil constitutionnel* when it issues "interpretation reservations": in all these situations, national law complies with EU law, and needs no amendment.

The *Conseil d'État* gave an example of this priority in the 2015 *Jansseng-Cilag* case.[88] The court prioritised consistent interpretation even though the provision of the directive was sufficiently clear and unconditional. Art. 11 of Directive 2001/83 on the Community code relating to medicinal products for human use provided detailed information that the summary of the product characteristics had to contain: dates, names, particulars, properties and more were required, in a specific order.[89]

For its part, the *Cour de cassation* only applies the principle of consistent interpretation in horizontal situations when the directive is not duly transposed. In such cases, direct effect is not an option. As a matter of fact, the *Cour de cassation* drew a line between direct effect and consistent interpretation in the *Open Cascade* case in 2009: in litigation between individuals, the provisions of a directive can only be relied on through consistent interpretation. Furthermore, the directive cannot create new obligations for individuals. In any event, only national law can be applied, and if possible interpreted in the light of the directive.[90]

The limit between direct effect and consistent interpretation also appears in the 2014 *Pedja X.* judgment. In this case, the *Cour de cassation* dismissed an appeal made by an individual who sought to combine three distinct prison sentences from three Member States. The *Cour de cassation* wrote that the court of appeal had correctly interpreted the national provision of the Criminal Code in the light of Framework Decision 2008/675, "*qu'elle n'a pas directement appliquée*" (without "applying [it] directly").[91]

---

87 Waline, [1957] *Revue du droit public* 673, on *Syndicat autonome du personnel enseignant des Facultés de droit* [1957] Conseil d'État Recueil 9.

88 *Jansseng-Cilag* [2015] Conseil d'État 379389.

89 Art. 11 states: "The summary of the product characteristics shall contain, in the order indicated below, the following information: 1. name of the medicinal product followed by the strength and the pharmaceutical form. 2. qualitative and quantitative composition in terms of the active substances and constituents of the excipient, knowledge of which is essential for proper administration of the medicinal product. The usual common name or chemical description shall be used. 3. pharmaceutical form. 4. clinical particulars: [*a list of 9 particulars follows*]. 5. pharmacological properties: [*a list of 3 properties follows*]. 6. pharmaceutical particulars: [*a list of 6 particulars follows*]. 7. marketing authorisation holder. 8. marketing authorisation number(s). 9. date of the first authorisation or renewal of the authorisation. 10. date of revision of the text ...".

90 *Open cascade* [2009] Cour de cassation, social chamber 08-43397, Bulletin V 256.

91 *Pedja X* [2014] Cour de cassation, criminal chamber 13-80161.

4.1.2. *Inapplicability of Consistent Interpretation by the Ordinary Courts When an Option is Offered, Showing the Limit of Horizontal Situations*

It appears that the ordinary courts are more rigorous in applying consistent interpretation in horizontal situations. Indeed, the *Cour de cassation* writes that consistent interpretation is not possible "in proceedings between individuals" if the EU provision is not "binding", meaning "when an option is offered" by the directive to the Member State.[92] It is unclear as to what extent the requirement of a binding provision concerns only "proceedings between individuals", because the *Cour de cassation* applies consistent interpretation mainly in horizontal situations.

Be that as it may, when the ordinary courts question the binding nature of a directive's provisions, the *Cour de cassation*'s case-law does not meet with the requirements of the ECJ. Normally speaking, the binding criterion should not be raised before the court, as consistent interpretation need only take into account the wording and purpose of the directive. However, one could argue that an EU provision, even for consistent interpretation, must be binding to produce effects. Hence, the question would be "according to the *Cour de cassation*'s criteria, what fulfils the binding requirements?" The *Cour de cassation* usually writes that the provision should not provide the Member State "an option when transposing EU law into national law".[93] Some decisions have been given where such an option was under scrutiny, involving the compatibility between national law and Directive 85/374 concerning liability for defective products.[94] More precisely, Art. 7(e) of the Directive provides that "[t]he producer shall not be liable as a result of this Directive" if the producer proves "that the state of scientific and technical knowledge at the time when he put the product into circulation was not such as to enable the existence of the defect to be discovered". Art. 15(1) goes on to state that Member States are allowed to waive Art. 7(e) – a right France has not made use of, as Art. 7(e) has never been duly transposed. According to the *Cour de cassation*, when a right to waiver is offered to a Member State, the absence of transposition means the provision is not binding. As a matter of fact, it is impossible to know whether France would have chosen to use this right or not. Consequently, in decisions involving Art. 7(e),

92 The Cour de cassation writes "c'est à la condition que celle-ci soit contraignante pour l'Etat membre et ne lui laisse pas une faculté d'option pour l'adaptation de son droit national au droit communautaire": *Ferring SAS* [2007] Cour de cassation, 1st civil chamber 05-10234.

93 *Les Laboratoires Servier* [2009] Cour de cassation, 1st civil chamber 08-12777; *Ferring SAS* [2007] Cour de cassation, 1st civil chamber 05-10234; *GAN v. Christophe X.* [1996] Cour de cassation, 1st civil chamber 93-19160.

94 Council Directive (EEC) 85/374 on the approximation of the laws, regulations and administrative provisions of the Member States concerning liability for defective products [1985] OJ L210.

the French courts have maintained that consistent interpretation of national law is impossible.[95] Similar outcomes occurred in relation to Directive 2000/29 on protective measures against organisms harmful to plants.[96]

This requirement for a provision free from option goes beyond what is necessary to consider the direct effect of a provision. Willing to extend direct applicability as much as possible, the ECJ found in *Kügler* that once the transposition period is over, it cannot be argued that the Member State would have chosen to waive the directive's provisions.[97] After the *Kügler* decision, the ECJ has recalled the requirement on many occasions.[98] The fact that Art. 15(1) of Directive 85/374 concerning liability for defective products and Art. 5(3)(c) of Directive 2000/29 on protective measures against organisms harmful to plants would both benefit from direct effect in a vertical situation, but not from consistent interpretation in a horizontal one, is therefore illogical.

Yet consistent interpretation enables courts to bypass the absence of direct effect.[99] It is therefore surprising, and difficult to justify, that the judge requires that the EU provision fulfils obligations which go beyond the direct effect criteria itself. The repeated use of this reasoning is itself in contradiction with the *Cour de cassation*'s case-law which sometimes applies consistent interpretation in horizontal situations where the EU provision is not vested with direct effect. In many decisions, the fact that there was no provision that was either unconditional or sufficiently precise was not seen as an obstacle.[100] The binding provision requirement appears to be above all a protection of the State's choice not to transpose the directive on time.

Fortunately, this restrictive criterion is not required by the *Conseil d'État*. Contrary to the practice of the ordinary courts, it applies EU case-law on derogations in the absence of transposition. For instance, in the judgment *Association CIMADE* in 2013, the *Conseil d'État* applied consistent interpretation of national law, even though the provisions of Directive 2003/9

---

95 *Les Laboratoires Servier* [2009] Cour de cassation, 1st civil chamber 08-12777; *Ferring SAS* [2007] Cour de cassation, 1st civil chamber 05-10234; *GAN v. Christophe X.* [1996] Cour de cassation, 1st civil chamber 93-19160.

96 *Société de conception de presse et d'édition v. société 1633* [2009] Cour de cassation, 1st civil chamber 07-21063.

97 Case EU:C:2002:473, *Kügler* [2002] ECR I-6833 paras 59–60. See L. Coutron, "Retour fataliste aux fondements de l'invocabilité des directives. Du cartésianisme au pragmatism" [2005] *RTD* eur. 39.

98 Case EU:C:2005:92, *Linneweber and Akritidis* [2005] ECR I-1131, para. 35; Case EU:C:2008:429, *Flughafen Köln/Bonn GmbH* [2008] ECR I-5999, para. 32.

99 L. Coutron, "Retour fataliste aux fondements de l'invocabilité des directives. Du cartésianisme au pragmatism" [2005] RTD eur. 39; A. Rosas and L. Armati, *EU Constitutional Law. An Introduction* (2nd ed., Hart Publishing, 2012), p. 72; D. Simon, *Le système juridique communautaire* (3rd ed., Presses Universitaires de France, 2001), p. 439.

100 See for a recent example: *Motorolla Mobility France v. Copie France* [2016] Cour de cassation, 1st civil chamber 15-10896.

for the reception of asylum seekers made it possible for the Member State to limit the rights of said asylum seekers. According to the *Conseil d'État*, the simple fact that France did not transpose the directive did not mean that it chose to limit the rights of asylum seekers.[101]

4.2. COURTS CAUGHT BETWEEN RELUCTANCE AND BOLDNESS

As Judge Genevois wrote, consistent interpretation "may lead to bold legal constructions".[102] This assertion is supported by case-law from both the *Conseil d'État* and the *Cour de cassation* when they are called on to interpret national law "as far as possible" in relation to the EU Treaty. In other regards, (1) the "as far as possible" requirement is read in conformity with EU case-law, and (2) both courts still refuse preventive application of consistent interpretation, i.e. application before the end of the transposition period.

4.2.1. A Rigorous Reading of the "As Far As Possible" Requirement ... Unless the EU Treaty is at Stake

Both the *Conseil d'État* and the *Cour de cassation* practise a rigorous reading of the "as far as possible" requirement. On many occasions, the courts consider the passing of a national law in order to transpose the directive as a prerequisite for drawing the limits of consistent interpretation. It appears that the purpose of national transposition provisions is to facilitate conciliation between a national provision and EU law. Both the administrative and the ordinary courts take the purpose of legal texts into consideration. For instance, in one case, the *Conseil d'État* took the purpose of an Act transposing a directive into account, with the result that the Act was interpreted as repealing a previous provision of the General Tax Code.[103] The administrative courts provide many further examples in which the purpose of an Act has led them to the presumption that the Member State intended to correctly transpose the directive.[104]

In this respect, their interpretation is consistent with EU case-law concerning the *contra legem* and legal certainty limitations. There is one exception, however: when conformity with the EU Treaty is at stake, the *Conseil d'État* seems more willing to extend the boundaries of the *contra legem* limitation, effectively

[101] *Association CIMADE* [2013] Conseil d'État 350191.
[102] B. Genevois, "Le Conseil d'État et l'interprétation de la loi" [2002] *RFDA* 877.
[103] *Banque Populaire de la Côte-d'Or* [1991] Conseil d'État 71041.
[104] *Ministre du Budget v. Cercle militaire mixte de la caserne Mortier* [1989] Conseil d'État 86113; *Ministre de l'économie v. SA Le Brevent* [2001] Conseil d'État 219443; *Ministre de l'économie v. Société Monte Dei Paschi Di Siena* [2001] Conseil d'État 169692.

rewriting the national law at issue. Such cases are rare, but find their historical rooting in cases involving interpretation of national law in the light of the European Convention on Human Rights.

Indeed, in one particular case where national law had to be reconciled with the European Convention on Human Rights, the outcome was unexpected. Of course, the national judge would have normally applied consistent interpretation in such a situation, as they do when international law is at stake.[105] However, in the *Bitouzet* judgment, where the judge had to assess the compatibility of a national Act with Art. 1 of the First Protocol of the European Convention on Human Rights, this rule of conflict led to a peculiar outcome.[106] In French law, one of the provisions of the Urbanism Code states that no damages can be granted in cases of easement, except in two specific situations. In the *Bitouzet* case, the *Conseil d'État* found that the provision under scrutiny could be easily interpreted as including a third exception to the principle of non-compensation. By doing so, the judge gave an interpretation of the law consistent with Art. 1 of the First Protocol of the ECHR. The practical consequence was that the *Conseil d'État* had effectively rewritten the provision of French law.[107]

Later practice of the *Conseil d'État* shows a zealous application of the "as far as possible" requirement where EU law is at stake.[108] In the 2003 *Dorries* decision, an appeal was raised by an applicant arguing that a 1985 decree did not comply with Art. 45 TFEU (ex Art. 39 EC) on the free movement of workers. Although the EU provision is directly effective[109] the *Conseil d'État* chose to perform a consistent interpretation, and applied the national law to resolve the case. The national provision – Art. 4 of the Decree of 26 April 1985 – outlines criteria which will be taken into account when appointing a higher education teacher. However, in this provision, there is no indication of whether professional experience in another Member State will be considered. The *Conseil d'État* nevertheless added this criterion in handing down its decision. It wrote that Art. 4 "shall be interpreted as taking into account services of the same nature accomplished in another EU Member State".[110] According to Gautier and Melleray, with the *Dorries* decision, as well as with the *Bitouzet* decision, the *Conseil d'État* rewrote a national provision.[111] In the *Dorries* decision, the leeway left for administrations to identify a service as being "of the same nature" as

105 *Association Ekin* [1997] Conseil d'État 151064, where national law is interpreted in the light of Arts. 10 and 14 of the European Convention on Human Rights.

106 *Bitouzet* [1998] Conseil d'État 158592.

107 M. Gautier and F. Melleray, *JCl Administratif*, Fasc. 22, para. 54.

108 Case EU:C:1990:395, *Marleasing SA* [1990] ECR I-4135, para. 8.

109 Case EU:C:1974:133, *van Duyn v. Home Office* [1974] ECR 1337, para. 6.

110 *Dorries v. Ministère de la jeunesse, et l'éducation nationale et de la recherche* [2003] Conseil d'État 239085.

111 M. Gautier and F. Melleray, *JCl Administratif*, Fasc. 22, para. 54.

one in France, is indeed a significant addition to the Decree. The Decree clearly outlines which professional experience is to be taken into account and how this should be done in order to determine whether the applicant will join the French civil service as category A, B or C. Comparing these categories with those of other Member States might be challenging. However, Gautier and Melleray's assessment should be carefully considered, as the purpose of the Decree at stake in the *Dorries* decision was to help temporary employees to become permanent civil servants. There is no doubt that interpreting the Decree in a way that ensured that professional experience in another Member State had to be taken into account helped in achieving the purpose of this Decree.

While the administrative courts may be inclined to distort national law in order to bring it in line with EU primary law requirements, such goodwill seems to disappear when the Treaty is not at stake. In the decision *Ambulances de France* from 2013, the *Conseil d'État* refused to interpret the General Tax Code in accordance with Directive 90/434 on the common system of taxation applicable to mergers, divisions and transfers of assets,[112] because it would result in "an interpretation contrary to the wording" of the national statute.[113] Clearly, the *Conseil d'État* used the *contra legem* limitation, writing it explicitly in the judgment.[114] More precisely, the national statute provided that, in order to be exempted from corporate tax on added value in the event of a corporate spin-off, each of the newly created companies must receive an entire branch of the original company.[115] The *Conseil d'État* considered that the statute was too "clear" to allow an interpretation which was different to its exact wording.[116] The Paris Administrative Appeal Court did much the same in a 2008 judgment. The court ruled the national provision in question as "too contrary to EC law to be subject to consistent interpretation".[117] As such, the only tool available for the judge in order to conform to the framework decision was to set aside national law.[118]

---

112 Directive (EC) 90/434 on the common system of taxation applicable to mergers, divisions and transfers of assets [1990] OJ L58.

113 *Ambulances de France* [2013] Conseil d'État 346683.

114 The *Conseil d'État* states that it is impossible to give "an interpretation contrary to the letter" of the statute ("ne saurait conduire à donner des dispositions précitées une interprétation contraire à leur lettre").

115 Art. 210 B of General Tax Code: "Les dispositions de l'article 210 A [prévoyant l'exonération] s'appliquent à la scission de société comportant au moins deux branches complètes d'activités lorsque chacune des sociétés bénéficiaires des apports reçoit une ou plusieurs de ces branches".

116 On top of that, the EU provision was not precise enough to make it possible for the court to apply direct effect, and state liability for a violation of EU law was not invoked. When it came to the argument of setting aside the national provision, the *Conseil d'État* answered that the corporate spin-off was not in the field of the directive, which then was not applicable.

117 P. Cassia [2008] *RFDA* 1054.

118 *Mme de Caupenne d'Aspremont* [2008] Cour administrative d'appel de Paris 7PA00057, J-D. Chétrit and M. Pons-Sarradeil [2008] *BJCL* 325.

Without expressly saying so, the *Cour de cassation* does not want to perform consistent interpretation of national provisions when the interpretation would lead to a retroactive application and therefore be in breach of legal certainty. The ordinary courts do not use the "legal certainty" wording, but their case-law is clear on this issue: retroactive application is a limitation to consistent interpretation. In the case *Mme X v. Institut Pasteur* in 2006, an individual had died from a disease contracted in a public hospital, and the heirs brought an action claiming state liablity. The appellant, which was one of the public bodies held responsible, argued before the *Cour de cassation* that according to Directive 85/374 concerning liability for defective products, national law should have been interpreted in a way whereby the prescription period to sue the State had been exceeded. National law provided for a 30-year prescription period,[119] while Directive 85/374 provided either a 3-year or a 10-year prescription period.[120] According to the court, where the compliance requirement concerns limitation periods, and the national provisions provide a precise period, "there is no reason for interpretation of national law in the light of" a directive.[121] The reason to address this specific procedure is because it "operates retroactively by nature". Therefore, the case-law of the *Cour de cassation* is perfectly in line with the *Adeneler* decision of the ECJ, where it held that applying consistent interpretation of national law "is limited by general principles of law, particularly those of legal certainty and non-retroactivity".[122]

4.2.2. No Preventive Application for Any Court

In many decisions, the *Cour de cassation* recalled that the transposition deadline had expired, thus allowing it to proceed to consistent interpretation.[123] Indeed, according to the ordinary courts, there cannot be any preventive application of the directive through consistent interpretation. In 2015, the *Cour de cassation* dismissed interpretation of the Criminal Procedure Code in the light of Directive 2012/13 on the right to information in criminal proceedings, on the grounds that the transposition deadline had not yet expired at the time the conflict arose.[124] The *Cour de cassation* regularly upholds that there cannot be

119 Art. 2262 of Civil Code.

120 Art. 10 and Art. 11 of Council Directive 85/374 (EEC) on the approximation of the laws, regulations and administrative provisions of the Member States concerning liability for defective products [1985] OJ L210/29.

121 *Mme X v. Institut Pasteur* [2006] Cour de cassation, 1st civil chamber 03-20178.

122 Case EU:C:2006:443, *Adeneler e. a.* [2006] ECR I-6057, para. 110.

123 For an example: *Société de conception de presse et d'édition v. société 1633* [2009] Cour de cassation, 1st civil chamber 07-21063.

124 *M. X. et al.* [2015] Cour de cassation, criminal chamber 14-87403.

any consistent interpretation in a preventive situation.[125] Likewise, in a 2012 decision, the *Cour de cassation* stated that because Directive 2012/13 on the right to information in criminal proceedings was not yet in force, consistent interpretation could not be applied.[126] But it has to be noted that in this specific case, the appellant did not ask for consistent interpretation of national law, but of the EU Charter of Fundamental Rights.

In line with the ordinary courts, the administrative courts are not willing to apply consistent interpretation before the end of the transposition period of a directive. Naturally, the *Conseil d'État* refuses the applicability of a proposed directive, that is to say before its entry into force.[127] However, the *Conseil d'État* applies the outcome of the 1997 *Inter-Environnement Wallonie* ECJ decision, according to which Member States "must refrain from taking any measures liable seriously to compromise the result prescribed" by the directive before the end of the transposition period.[128] No further examples seem to exist in which the *Conseil d'État* complied with the *Adeneler* decision, which requires the judge to interpret national law in order to avoid a breach of the purpose of the directive before the end of the transposition period.

5. CONCLUSIONS

To conclude, there is no doubt that the long-standing practice of French courts vis-à-vis consistent interpretation reasoning made it easier for them to apply the ECJ's requirements. The general acceptance of the *Von Colson* principle is the result of a cross-fertilisation of reasoning between national, European and international law. However, different approaches by courts reveal the duality of the French judicial system, distinguishing the ordinary courts from the administrative courts. Horizontal litigation – i.e. between individuals – before the ordinary courts sees consistent interpretation as being one of the few ways to comply with EU law requirements, for as long as horizontal direct effect of directives is not an option. The *Cour de cassation* being forced to apply consistent interpretation has led the ordinary courts to a broad application of *contra legem* limits. The *Conseil d'État*, however, does not consider consistent interpretation

---

125 For a previous decision on the same ground, see: *Lego v. Klip* [2002] Cour de cassation, chambre commerciale 99-13774.

126 *Robert X v. Thomas X* [2012] Cour de cassation, criminal chamber 12-85645. In this case, the appellant argued that Art. 7 of Directive 2012/13 would lead to interpreting national law as requiring that the lawyer could have access to all records relating to the time spent by the client in custody.

127 *Société KPMG* [2006] Conseil d'État 288460.

128 Case EU:C:1997:628, *Inter-Environnement Wallonie* [1997] ECR I-7411, followed by *France Nature Environnement* [2001] Conseil d'État 217237, D. Simon [2001] Europe, comm. 152.

to be a constraint. In vertical situations – i.e. between individuals and the administration – the administrative courts can often choose between direct effect and consistent interpretation. The latter is more advantageous in that the pre-eminence of EU law over national law is less conspicuous when interpreting domestic norms. Furthermore, it favours the administration, because the national norm will be interpreted as complying with the EU norm. In this situation, it is virtually impossible to sue the State for damages. Finally, there are two different approaches of consistent interpretation by either the ordinary or the administrative courts: the ordinary courts feel forced to apply the reasoning of consistent interpretation, while the administrative courts sometimes use it to protect the administration. This may provide insight into why French courts persist in refusing to apply consistent interpretation preventively before the end of the transposition period is reached.

INTERPRETATION IN CONFORMITY WITH EU LAW IN THE ITALIAN LEGAL SYSTEM

Tatiana GUARNIER and Elisabetta LAMARQUE*

1. INTRODUCTION

A very popular topic in Italian academic literature in recent years is that concerning the influences and effects in the domestic legal system of EU law and the decisions of the Court of Justice of the European Union (ECJ) on the one hand, and of the European Convention on Human Rights (ECHR) and the decisions of the European Court of Human Rights (ECtHR) on the other. The subject of analysis and reflection has especially focused on the dense intertwining among the Charters that ensure human rights at various levels – the Italian Constitution, the EU Charter of Fundamental Rights and the ECHR; and even other international conventions establishing specific bills of rights, such as the New York Convention on the Rights of the Child – as well as the external and internal courts that are called on to apply these Charters in various ways.

---

* This chapter is the result of the joint reflection of the authors. Nevertheless, sections 1, 2, 3, 4 should be attributed to Tatiana Guarnier and sections 5, 6, 7, 8 should be attributed to Elisabetta Lamarque.

For legal practitioners, the issues raised by the overlapping of national, European and international legal sources and judicial decisions have now become very urgent. Some authors refer to them as a "labyrinth" for the interpreter,[1] who is frequently asked to choose among several possible directions, and is often not equipped with adequate tools to navigate between them. In this situation, the temptation may be, of course, to avoid obstacles, to take unorthodox shortcuts, to skip the necessary logical and argumentative passages, and to rely on vague principles and values in order to achieve a solution in the case at hand.

However, it should be stressed that in the Italian legal system, the Constitutional Court (ItCC) has created a "map", setting out "the logical path for the decision of national proceedings involving fundamental rights" guaranteed by international and supranational sources.[2] In fact, the interpretation and the application of the constitutional norms that function as a connection between the "inside" and the "outside" of the legal system are up to the ItCC to determine. Therefore, over the years, the ItCC has created the "instructions for use" of supranational and international norms, and indicated the logical path to follow in each case.[3]

This is precisely what it did in the 1980s with reference to Art. 11 of the Constitution,[4] establishing the connecting rules between the Italian and European legal systems; rules that will be analysed immediately below, and which are still used by all legal practitioners.[5] The same task was carried out in the same period with reference to international customary law, clarifying the content of Art. 10(1) of the Constitution.[6] More recently, with the so-called "twin sentences",[7] the same Court has outlined the way in which Art. 117(1) of the Constitution works with regard to international conventional norms.[8] The ItCC affirmed that when it is impossible to interpret Italian law in conformity with an international norm, the ordinary judge may not set aside the Italian law and directly implement that norm. Instead, he has the power and the

---

1 V. Manes, *Il giudice nel labirinto. Profili delle intersezioni tra diritto penale e fonti sovranazionali* (Dike, 2012).

2 This is the term used in the document, available online at <www.eui.eu>, prepared by a group of researchers of the European University Institute of Fiesole, containing the guidelines for the national courts of European countries, when facing rights guaranteed by both internal and external Charters.

3 See T. Groppi, "The Constitutional Court of Italy: Towards a multilevel system of constitutional review?" (2008) 3(2) *Journal of Comparative Law* 116.

4 "Italy agrees, on conditions of equality with other States, to the limitations of sovereignty that may be necessary to a world order ensuring peace and justice among the Nations".

5 More details in section 2 below.

6 "The Italian legal system conforms to the generally recognised rules of international law".

7 ItCC, dec. no. 348 and no. 349 of 2007. See section 2 below.

8 "Legislative powers shall be vested in the State and the Regions in compliance with the Constitution and with the constraints deriving from EU legislation and international obligations".

duty to refer the question to the ItCC itself, assuming the international norms (ECHR included) as an interposed parameter of constitutionality.

Very different and much more complex is the solution suggested with regard to EU law. So, the analysis of this peculiar area of supranational relations needs to be developed in several passages. First of all, it should be stressed that the Italian Constitution preceded the creation of the EEC (European Economic Community), which later became the European Community (EC) and now the EU. It is therefore necessary to move from the norms in the Italian Constitution that, in general, allowed an always increasing intertwining of national legal orders, considering that obviously, there were no explicit constitutional references to the European legal system in the Italian Constitution of 1948, but only some provisions that, in the intention of the framers, were devoted to expressing an international and European openness.[9]

As mentioned, Art. 11 of the Constitution is pivotal for these issues. The interpretation of this provision has been the subject of great debate, until the ItCC definitely construed it as a "European clause".[10] This interpretation gave rise to several effects: above all, the recognition of the primacy of European law, with the only exception of counter-limits (i.e. the fundamental principles of the Italian legal order and the essential nucleus of fundamental rights guaranteed by its Constitution),[11] the non-application of Italian norms conflicting with directly effective EU norms, and the unconstitutionality of domestic norms in contrast with EU obligations which do not have direct effect.

The judges' duty to interpret Italian norms in conformity with EU law is indeed another consequence (perhaps preliminary, as will be demonstrated in section 4 below) of the aforesaid effects. Unlike the other effects, however, it did not seem to pose complicated facets or give rise to big questions concerning the approach of the ItCC. This impression seems further confirmed by an almost

---

9 See V. Onida, *La Costituzione ieri e oggi* (Il Mulino, 2008).

10 As noted, among others, by G. Martinico and O. Pollicino, "Report on Italy" in G. Martinico and O. Pollicino (eds.), *The National Judicial Treatment of the ECHR and EU Laws. A Comparative Constitutional Perspective* (Europa Law Publishing, 2010), p. 271, "this acceptance, however, did not come about immediately. On the contrary, it was the result of a long series of judgments. One of the reasons for this can be attributed to the absence of a written European clause in the Italian text. As a matter of fact, Art. 11 was originally conceived to explain the Italian membership to organizations like the United Nations rather than for justifying the consequence of supranationalism (phenomenon not yet known when the Italian Constitution came into force)". This said, it should also be noted that other authors underline how the European project was considered by the Framers, during the preparatory debates on the contents of Art. 11 of the Constitution: see L. Carlassare, "L'articolo 11 della Costituzione nella visione dei Costituenti" in N. Ronzitti (ed.), *L'articolo 11 della Costituzione. Baluardo della vocazione internazionale dell'Italia* (Editoriale Scientifica, 2013), p. 11; T. Guarnier, *Interpretazione costituzionale e diritto giurisprudenziale. Specificità e problemi dell'interpretazione costituzionale nell'ordinamento giuridico integrato* (Editoriale Scientifica, 2014), p. 214 ff.

11 See section 3 below.

absolute silence in the Italian doctrine on this topic,[12] while certainly there are more studies that address the issue from the perspective of the ECJ.

2. THE "EUROPEAN CLAUSES" IN THE ITALIAN CONSTITUTION

As outlined in the introduction above, the "European-friendly" interpretation of Art. 11 of the Constitution provided by the ItCC plays a crucial part in the definition of the relations among norms of the domestic and European legal systems. But, as also mentioned, this interpretation was quite difficult and debated. The reasons for the original resistance of the ItCC were, very likely and to a great part, tightly linked to the consequences that the opening of the Italian legal order to the EC might have for the functioning and the position of the ItCC itself:

> It is no surprise … that the Italian Constitutional Court – like higher courts in other Member States – firmly resisted the principles of supremacy and direct effect of European law, since those principles implied a veritable revolution of the role of the judiciary and required national constitutional courts to hand over an important portion of their most crucial function to other non-specialised lower courts. Indeed, the Constitutional Court was fully aware of the consequences of dealing with cases that involved the effects of the European law.[13]

Therefore, while the ECJ for its part always supported a monist approach, with priority to be accorded to the EC legal system, the ItCC at the beginning did not recognise the special nature of the EC. It asserted that the founding Treaties should be assimilated into every other international treaty. Therefore, the traditional "pure" dualist approach governing the relations of the Italian legal system with international norms was extended also to them. Emblematic of this phase of the ItCC's case-law is dec. no. 14 of 1964, in which the ItCC interpreted the relationship between national and EC acts in the light of the chronological criterion (on the basis of the argument that the enabling act of ratification of the Treaties was an ordinary legislative act).

It was only when the *sui generis* nature of the European order was recognised, together with the fact that the EU – unlike traditional international organisations – had the goal of founding a new legal system, equipped with

---

[12] Apart from some isolated studies: see G. Pistorio, *Interpretazione e giudici. Il caso dell'interpretazione conforme al diritto dell'Unione europea* (Editoriale Scientifica, 2012), pp. 259–341, who dedicates considerable space to the perspective of the ItCC and E. Lamarque, "L'interpretazione conforme al diritto dell'Unione europea secondo la Corte costituzionale italiana" in A. Bernardi (ed.), *L'interpretazione conforme al diritto dell'Unione europea. Profili e limiti di un vincolo problematico* (Jovene editore, 2015).

[13] V. Barsotti, P. G. Carozza, M. Cartabia and A. Simoncini, *Italian Constitutional Justice in Global Context* (OUP USA, 2016), p. 108.

its own powers and its own legal sources, that the ItCC consequently had to admit that its foundation was not only poised on the ratification law, but also on Art. 11 of the Constitution.[14] EU legislation was therefore recognised as having a higher rank: set at a *quasi*-constitutional level, and hence "superseding domestic ordinary law in case of conflict".[15] This reconstruction nevertheless assured the ItCC a central role – because the respect for the primacy of EU law, construed as an indirect violation of a constitutional article, always required its intervention to declare the (indirect) unconstitutionality of domestic law. In other words, this interpretation did not allow for the direct intervention of every judge in the verification and declaration of the contrast: the existence of the contrast would always have to be verified by the ItCC, and the consequence of this verification had to be a declaration of unconstitutionality.[16]

The ECJ subsequently objected that this reconstruction nullified the direct and immediate applicability of Community law, and consequently its uniform application within the Member States.[17] These considerations "forced" – in the famous *Granital* case of 1984 – the ItCC to recognise, without any barriers or controls whatsoever, the immediate entry into and direct application of Community legal sources within the Italian legal system at the aforementioned *quasi*-constitutional level, finally admitting an unusual sphere of diffused control of constitutionality which is shared among all the Italian judges: namely conformity of Italian norms with directly effective supranational rules.[18] Therefore, the consequence of the verification of a conflict between Italian and EU law with this characteristic is the non-applicability of the domestic norm, and every judge has to set aside the latter.

The situation partially changed in 2001, when constitutional law no. 3 of 2001 introduced a new paragraph in Art. 117 of the Constitution, which (as mentioned above) expressly codified that the Italian legislative power belonging to State and Regions should be exercised not only in accordance with the Constitution, but also within the limits and duties set by European law and with respect to international obligations. The most innovative part of this provision is surely that concerning the introduction of international obligations as limits for the legislature. The part concerning EU law nevertheless also assumes great importance, since both the prevalent Italian literature and the ItCC itself have considered it to constitute an explicit constitutionalisation of the pre-existing situation: "a sort of *a posteriori* assent to the European primacy".[19]

---

14 ItCC, dec. no. 183 of 1973.

15 In these terms, V. Barsotti, P.G. Carozza, M. Cartabia and A. Simoncini, *Italian Constitutional Justice in Global Context* (OUP USA, 2016), p. 106.

16 See ItCC dec. no. 230 del 1975; no. 205 del 1976 and no. 163 del 1977.

17 CGE, dec. 9.03.1978, *Simmenthal*, C 106/77.

18 ItCC, dec. no. 170 of 1984, *Granital*.

19 Martinico and Pollicino (n. 10), p. 271. Other scholars, soon after the reform, tried to emphasise the importance of the new constitutional *status* of European primacy, stating

While international obligations in fact became sources of indirect control of the constitutionality of Italian statutes,[20] this possibility still remained impracticable for directly effective European legal sources for the reasons outlined by the ECJ. In this case, Art. 117(1) of the Constitution should therefore be interpreted together with Art. 11, still imposing a direct intervention of each national judge when facing a conflict between a national statute and a directly effective EU norm. On the other hand, where non-directly applicable EU norms are concerned, the introduction of Art. 117(1) of the Constitution lets us undoubtedly use them as interposed parameters of constitutionality,[21] and, where needed, justifies the referral for a preliminary ruling to the ECJ by the ItCC.[22]

All things considered, what took place through Art. 117(1) is a partially innovative collocation of the Italian legal system in the supranational normative and judicial net, that still assumes supervision by the ItCC, but in very different ways for each type of supranational legal source. Albeit sometimes with some delays, the vast potential of the reform has also found an implementation in the ItCC case-law. The first occasion in which the new provision was applied as a parameter of constitutionality for EU law dates back to 2005. In a judgment referred by the state against a regional law, the ItCC established the illegitimacy of the latter because of a conflict with EU law.[23] From that moment on, use of the provision by the ItCC has gradually increased. It represented a strong support to move some important steps in the construction of relations between legal orders, outlining a path that redesigned the ItCC's role and its position within

that it paved the way for the acceptance of the monist thesis. But this approach has been constantly rejected by the ItCC, which has always preferred a dualist approach, even if softened and modulated in an "integrative" approach. On the interpretation of Art. 117(1) It. Const., see E. Lamarque, "Il vincolo alle leggi statali e regionali derivante dagli obblighi internazionali nella giurisprudenza comune" in *Corte costituzionale, giudici comuni e interpretazioni adeguatrici. Atti del seminario svoltosi in Roma, Palazzo della Consulta, 6 novembre 2009* (Giuffrè, 2010), p. 97 ff.; A. D'Atena, "La nuova disciplina costituzionale dei rapporti internazionali e con l'Unione europea" [2002] *Rassegna parlamentare* 913 ff.; C. Panara, "I vincoli derivanti dall'ordinamento comunitario cinque anni dopo: quid novi?" [2006] *Quaderni costituzionali* 796 ff.; G. D'Alessandro, "Prime impressioni sull'impatto della costituzionalizzazione del 'vincolo comunitario' sulla giurisprudenza costituzionale" [2003] *Le istituzioni del federalismo* 210 ff.; C. Pinelli, "I limiti generali alla potestà legislativa statale e regionale e i rapporti con l'ordinamento internazionale e con l'ordinamento comunitario" [2001] *Il Foro italiano V* 195.

20 Leading cases are decisions no. 348 and no. 349 of 2007.

21 ItCC, decc. no. 406 of 2005; no. 129 of 2006; no. 284 of 2007; no. 28 of 2010; no. 227 of 2010; no. 75 of 2012; no. 207 of 2013.

22 ItCC, dec. no. 207 of 2013 and 24 of 2017. On these decisions and their impact in the relationship between the courts involved, see T. Guarnier, "La Corte costituzionale: organo giurisdizionale dinnanzi al suo primo rinvio pregiudiziale alla Corte di giustizia europea. Contraddizione, apertura o 'dissociazione'?" [2009] *Giurisprudenza italiana* 40–47; Ead., "Rinvio pregiudiziale interpretativo e giudizio di legittimità costituzionale. Nuovi scenari e nuove prospettive nel crocevia sopranazionale" [2013] *Diritto e Società* 237–89. See also section 3.

23 ItCC, dec. no. 406 of 2005.

the integrated system, and allowing a crescent dialogue with supranational and international courts.

3. EUROPEAN DIMENSION AND CONSTITUTIONAL IDENTITIES

There is another aspect which is worth studying a little more. In fact, the analysis of supranational integration would be incomplete if it did not take into account the liminal areas of dialogue – i.e. the boundaries, the limits that it meets. One of the fundamental points of differentiation between Kelsenian monism and the integration model adopted by the ItCC is indeed the necessity for mutual recognition by both of the legal orders involved, and this recognition is effective only if supported by respect for the identities and fundamental elements of each level and each legal system. Therefore, even on this point, it is very important to stress that the dialoguing courts firmly posed the conditions under which the opening to supranational orders can be considered compatible with state identity and fundamental principles of the state.

It is well known that the ItCC has been one of the promoters (together with the German Constitutional Court) of the issue of the limitations to this dialogue, and that it elaborated the "counter-limits" theory. The first decision in this sense dates back to 1965,[24] when it stated that: "it would not be acceptable for our legal order to join a supranational organization where the respect for inviolable rights guaranteed by Art. 2 of the Constitution is not properly ensured". A more complete formulation of the theory of counter-limits may be found in decision no. 183 of 1973, where the ItCC introduced an exception to the aforesaid diffused control of the contrast between internal and directly effective European norms, by maintaining an "exclusive competence" for the ItCC: the verification of EC law's compatibility with the supreme principles and inviolable rights guaranteed by the Constitution.

In this first phase, the existence of counter-limits was justified on the grounds that the limitations of sovereignty provided by Art. 11 of the Constitution are conditioned to the goals pursued by the international organisations considered: the purpose of ensuring peace and justice between Nations.[25] In other words, on the basis of the identified constitutional foundations of European integration, it was asserted that if the European Communities acted against fundamental principles and inviolable human rights, they would also act against the goals of peace and justice, and that this would justify a revocation of Italian membership to the organisation.

---

24 ItCC, dec. no. 98 of 1965.

25 See section 1 above.

Later on, in decision no. 232 of 1989, the ItCC amended its position, by introducing a more moderate and dynamic way of applying the counter-limits theory. Without discussing its unique competence on the conflict between EU provisions and fundamental constitutional principles, it admitted that the eventual verification of such a conflict would not necessarily provoke the drastic effect of membership revocation, but could rather limit its effects to the relevant individual provision, as interpreted and applied by EU authorities.[26] In other words, it affirmed that a potential declaration of unconstitutionality of the European norm would imply only its unenforceability within the Italian legal system.

The issue of compatibility of this approach with the requirement of uniform and complete implementation of EU law is evident, and is today one of the main unresolved knots of the "Italian way" of integration. Moving from these reflections, however, some authors have identified a further element of centrality of the role of interpretation in the connection between legal systems, which finds the interpretative solution as the only possible way out of the *impasse*: according to this perspective, the interpretation of the European norm in conformity with constitutional requirements on the one hand, and the progressive "harmonisation" of state laws and constitutions on the other, appears to be the only way capable of descrambling the possible conflict between EU provisions and fundamental principles of the state. This orientation now seems to find support in Art. 4(2) of the Treaty on European Union (TEU), which amplified the European duty to respect national identities.[27] It will nevertheless still worry those concerned for the guarantee of uniform application of EU law within the Member States: the concern is naturally that if each state was allowed to implement EU law interpreting it consistently with its fundamental principles, then the very rationale of European intervention would be affected because the precise objective of the EU legal system is to uniformly discipline matters that (according to the principle of subsidiarity) need to be regulated at the supranational level.[28]

---

26 See M. Cartabia, *Principi inviolabili e integrazione europea* (Giuffrè, 1995); E. Cannizzaro, "Tutela dei diritti fondamentali e garanzie costituzionali secondo le Corti costituzionali italiana e tedesca" [1990] *Rivista di diritto internazionale* 372 ff.; G. Gaja, "La sentenza della Corte costituzionale n. 232 del 1989 e i 'controlimiti' alla superiorità del diritto comunitario", in *La Corte costituzionale tra diritto interno e diritto comunitario. Atti del seminario svoltosi in Roma, Palazzo della Consulta, nei giorni 15 e 16 ottobre 1990* (Giuffrè, 1991), pp. 81 ff.; A. Tizzano, "Ancora sui rapporti tra Corti europee: principi comunitari e c.d. controlimiti costituzionali" [2007] *Rivista di diritto pubblico europeo* 734 ff.

27 Some authors emphasise the possible use of this norm as a tool for a "Europeanisation" of counter-limits. See A. Von Bodgandy and S. Schill, "Overcoming absolute supremacy: Respect for national identity under the Lisbon Treaty" 48 [2011] *Common Market Law Review* 1417 ff.; B. Guastaferro, *Legalità costituzionale e legalità sopranazionale. Tensioni costitutive e giunture ordinamentali* (Giappichelli, 2013), pp. 190 ff.

28 See Case C-11/70, *Internationale Handelsgesellschaft*, ECLI:EU:C:1970:114. In literature, the concept of *primauté existentiel* outlined by P. Pescatore should be recalled: see P. Pescatore,

So the assertion of counter-limits, far from having a merely protectionist scope, rather implies the need for a dialogue – for a judicial network which is able to come to a shared interpretation of European provisions. More precisely, an interpretation shared not only between the state in which there is the problem of existence of a counter-limit and the European legal order, but among all the various EU Member States and the ECJ: in performing its function of "standardisation" of interpretations, the latter must ensure that those interpretations can be shared and compatible with the fundamental principles and the essential nucleus of rights guaranteed by the Constitutions of each Member State.

However, it should be recalled that there are very few possibilities of impacting in these delicate and very fundamental areas. In the internal legal system, it has indeed, to the contrary, encouraged a sort of "team play" in the internal legal system between the ItCC and the Italian Supreme Courts (i.e. the supreme ordinary court, the Court of Cassation, Civil and Criminal Divisions, and the supreme administrative courts, the Council of State and the Court of Accounts), aimed at – and making a shared task of – defending the national identity. The scheme looks like the one that American detective films call "good cop and bad cop": whenever possible, the ordinary and administrative supreme jurisdictions do not hesitate to play the part of the "bad cop", reacting or resisting in the face of EU law, while the ItCC plays the part of the milder and more open jurisdiction.

Indeed, the only occasion in which an Italian judge has actually opposed counter-limits to the entrance of EU law is the Italian State Council's debated decision of 2005 in the *Federfarma* case.[29] On that occasion, the Supreme Administrative Court avoided setting aside a national legislative provision which had been introduced by a manipulative decision of the ItCC that implemented a fundamental right, but the State Council did so independently, without referring the question to the ItCC.[30]

Le droit de l'intégration (Bruylant, 1972) and P. Pescatore, *L'ordre juridique des communautés européennes* (Bruylant, 1975). See also H. Gaudin, "Primauté 'absolue' ou primauté 'relative'?" in H. Gaudin (ed.), *Droit constitutionnel droit communautaire vers un respect réciproque mutuel?* (Economica – Droit Public Positif, 2001), p. 97 ff. and O. Dord, "Ni absolue, ni relative, la primauté du droit communautaire procède de la Constitution", ibid., p. 121 ff.

29 State Council, V Division, 08.08.2005, no. 4207, commented by G. Morbidelli, "Controlimiti o contro la pregiudiziale comunitaria?" [2005] *Giurisprudenza costituzionale* 3404 ff.

30 But also the Court of Cassation has sometimes used a similar protective shield in favour of the ItCC, exposing itself alone to the direct clash with the other European court: that of Strasbourg. See, in particular, Cass., I Civil Division, 06.05.2009, no. 10415 and the reconstruction of the whole affair in E. Lamarque, "Il vincolo alle leggi statali e regionali derivante dagli obblighi internazionali nella giurisprudenza comune" in *Corte costituzionale, giudici comuni e interpretazioni adeguatrici. Atti del seminario svoltosi in Roma, Palazzo della Consulta, 6 novembre 2009* (Giuffrè, 2010), p. 160 ff.

Much more relevance may attach to another recent case in which the ItCC has threatened the application of these limits: the *Taricco* case, which has already been the subject of great attention in Italian doctrine.[31] The issue arose following an ECJ decision that declared the Italian prescription period system for VAT fraud incompatible with Art. 325 of the Treaty on the Functioning of the European Union (TFEU), which requires Member States to prevent fraud that could affect the EU's financial interests. In applying that decision, some judges decided to set aside the internal rules, even though this implied an *in malam partem* treatment of the defendants in the case. They affirmed that this solution was possible because they considered that the norms involved pertained to criminal procedural law and not to substantive criminal law.[32] Other judges disagreed with this assumption, considering it impossible to set aside the internal norms censored by the ECJ. They therefore referred the case to the

---

31 See e.g. A. Albano "Il termine assoluto (o relativo?) di prescrizione dei reati tributari alla luce della sentenza '*Taricco*': profili sistematici" [2016] *Rivista di diritto tributario* 45 ff.; A. Bargi, "Il singolare funambolismo interpretativo dei rapporti tra diritti dell'UE, diritto nazionale e tutela dei diritti fondamentali nella sentenza '*Taricco*' della Corte di giustizia dell'Unione europea" [2016] *Archivio della nuova procedura penale* 327 ff.; M. Bassini, "Prescrizione e principio di legalità nell'ordine costituzionale europeo. Note critiche alla sentenza Taricco" [2016] *Consultaonline* 103 ff. <http://www.giurcost.org/studi/bassini.pdf>; R. Bin, "Taricco, una sentenza sbagliata: come venirne fuori?" [2016] *Rivista di diritto penale contemporaneo* 1 ff.; M. Luciani, "Il brusco risveglio. I controlimiti e la fine mancata della storia costituzionale" (15.04.2016) *Rivista AIC* 11 ff. <http://www.rivistaaic.it/il-brusco-risveglio-i-controlimiti-e-la-fine-mancata-della-storia-costituzionale.html>; V. Maiello, "Prove di resilienza del '*nullum crimen*': Taricco '*versus*' controlimiti" [2016] *Cassazione Penale* 1250 ff.; V. Manes, "La 'svolta' Taricco e la potenziale 'sovversione di sistema': le ragioni dei controlimiti" [2016] *Rivista di diritto penale contemporaneo*; R. Mastroianni, "Supremazia del diritto dell'Unione e 'controlimiti' costituzionali: alcune riflessioni a margine del caso *Taricco*" [2016] *Diritto penale contemporaneo* <https://www.penalecontemporaneo.it/d/5043-supremazia-del-diritto-dellunione-e-controlimiti-costituzionali-alcune-riflessioni-a-margine-del-ca>; F. Rossi, "L'obbligo di disapplicazione '*in malam partem*' della normativa penale interna tra integrazione europea e controlimiti. La problematica sentenza '*Taricco*' della Corte di Giustizia" [2016] *Rivista italiana di diritto e procedura penale* 376 ff.

32 Court of Cassation, III Criminal Division, 17.09.2015–20.01.2016; Court of Cassation, IV Criminal Division, 25.01.2016–26.02.2016, with comments by R. Bin, "La prima sentenza 'post Taricco' della Cassazione" [2016] *Archivio penale* 1 ff.; G. Fiorentino, "La Corte di cassazione e la resistibile ascesa della giurisprudenza Taricco" [2016] *Questione Giustizia* <http://www.questionegiustizia.it/articolo/la-corte-di-cassazione-e-la-resistibile-ascesa-della-giurisprudenza-taricco_01-02-2016.php>; M. Gambardella, "Caso Taricco e garanzie costituzionali ex art. 25 Cost." [2016] *Cassazione penale* 1445 ff.; G. Repetto, "La Cassazione sul caso 'Taricco', tra disapplicazione con effetti retroattivi '*in malam partem*' e mancata attivazione dei controlimiti" [2016] *Rivista AIC* no. 2 <http://www.rivistaaic.it/la-cassazione-sul-caso-taricco-tra-disapplicazione-con-effetti-retroattivi-in-malam-partem-e-mancata-attivazione-dei-controlimiti.html>; F. Rossi, "La Cassazione disapplica gli artt. 160 e 161 c.p. dopo la sentenza 'Taricco'" [2016] *Giurisprudenza italiana* 965 ff.; F. Viganò, "La prima sentenza della Cassazione *post* Taricco: depositate le motivazioni della sentenza della Terza Sezione che disapplica una prescrizione già maturata in materia di frodi IVA" [2016] *Diritto penale contemporaneo*.

Constitutional Court, asking for an evaluation of the constitutionality of the law that gave execution to the TFEU, regarding the part in which it allows the entry into the Italian legal system of a provision (i.e. Art. 325 TFEU, as interpreted by the ECJ) in potential conflict with the constitutional principles of legality and *favor rei*.[33]

Responding to the referral, the ItCC decided to refer a preliminary question of interpretation to the ECJ, foreseeing the possibility of a clash between the *Taricco* decision and state counter-limits.[34] The reasoning of the ItCC begins: "if the application of Art. 325 TFEU may imply the entry into the legal order of a rule contrary to the principle of legality in criminal matters ... the Court would have to prevent it".[35] It continued by affirming that "the European Union law and the decisions of the Court of Justice that specify its meaning to ensure its uniform application, cannot be interpreted as imposing on the Member State the sacrifice of the supreme principles of its constitutional order".[36]

In the light of these assertions, the ItCC suggested and asked the ECJ for an interpretation of its decision which might be consistent with the intangible core of the basic principles and values of Italian constitutional identity ("The conviction of this Court, of which is demanded a confirm by the European Court of Justice, is that ... it intended to affirm that the norm extracted by Art. 325 TFEU may be applied only if it is compatible with the constitutional identity of the Member State and that it is up to the competent State authorities to make such an assessment"),[37] and with the duty of sincere cooperation ("This Court wants to stress that the interpretation just outlined,

---

33 Milan Court of Appeal, II criminal section, 18.09.2015, with comments by F. Bertolino, "La Corte d'Appello di Milano sollecita la Corte Costituzionale a vagliare la compatibilità dell'obbligo di disapplicazione imposto al giudice italiano dalla sentenza 'Taricco' della Corte di Giustizia con il principio di irretroattività '*in malam partem*.'" [2016] *Diritto del commercio internazionale*, 205 ff.; P. Faraguna and P. Perini, "L'insostenibile imprescrittibilità del reato. La Corte d'appello di Milano mette la giurisprudenza 'Taricco' alla prova dei controlimiti" [2016] *Diritto penale contemporaneo* 9 ff.; Court of Cassation, III criminal section, 08.07.2016.

34 ItCC, dec. no. 24 of 2017, with comments by M. Bassini and O. Pollicino, "The Taricco Decision: A last attempt to avoid a clash between EU law and the Italian Constitution" [2017] *Verfassungsblog on Matters Constitutional* <http://verfassungsblog.de/the-taricco-decision-a-last-attempt-to-avoid-a-clash-between-eu-law-and-the-italian-constitution>; A. Celotto, "Caso Taricco: un rinvio pregiudiziale 'muscoloso' e costruttivo (a prima lettura sulla ord. n. 24 del 2017 della Corte costituzionale)" [2017] <www.giustamm.it>; M.L. Ferrante, "L'ordinanza della Corte costituzionale sull'*affaire* Taricco: una decisione 'diplomatica' ma ferma" [2017] *Dirittifondamentali* <http://www.dirittifondamentali.it/fascicoli/anno-2017/numero-1/massimo-luigi-ferrante-l-ordinanza-della-corte-costituzionale-sullaffaire-taricco-una-decisione-diplomatica-ma-ferma>. See also A. Bernardi and C. Cupelli (eds.), *Il caso Taricco e il dialogo tra le Corti. L'ordinanza 24/2017 della Corte costituzionale* (Jovene, 2017).

35 ItCC, dec. no. 24 of 2017, §2 (translation by the author).

36 ItCC, dec. no. 24 of 2017, §6 (transation by the author).

37 ItCC, dec. no. 24 of 2017, §7 (translation by the author).

while preserving, on the one hand, the Italian constitutional identity, does not undermine, on the other, the requirements of uniform application of European Union law and is, therefore, proposed as a solution consistent with the duty of sincere cooperation and proportionality").[38]

In conclusion, on this occasion the ItCC has chosen to firmly claim its crucial role on fundamental rights issues, by standing before the ECJ as an authoritative and necessary interlocutor when this special area of rights – which is the essential core of the intangible principles and values of the constitutional order – is at stake; and by promoting the interpretation of counter-limits not in a rigid and exclusive direction, but rather as a place of discussion that requires hermeneutic efforts of "conformity with", which also have to be accomplished by the ECJ.[39]

The answer of the ECJ in the *Taricco II* case was equally open to this debate,[40] notwithstanding the opposing Opinion of Advocate General Bot,[41] and allowed an "exception" to the rule posed in the *Taricco I* case when its application could

---

38 ItCC, dec. no. 24 of 2017, §8 (translation by the author).

39 For in-depth reflections on this point, see M. Cartabia, *Principi inviolabili e integrazione europea* (Giuffrè, 1995) 242 ff.; A. Ruggeri, "'Tradizioni costituzionali comuni' e 'controlimiti', tra teoria delle fonti e teoria dell'interpretazione" [2003] *Diritto pubblico comparato ed europeo* 110.

40 ECJ, Great Chamber, M.A.S. and M.B., 5 December 2017, Case C-42/2017. On that decision, and on the real existence of a dialogue between the ItCC and the ECJ, the opinions of the Italian scholars are different. See M. Bassini and O. Pollicino, "Defusing the Taricco Bomb through Fostering Constitutional Tolerance: All Roads Lead to Rome" [2017] *VerfBlog*; V. Manes, "Some lessons from the Taricco saga" (2018) 9 *New Journal of European Criminal Law*, 12 ff.; N. Lupo, "La sentenza europea c.d. Taricco-bis: risolti i problemi per il passato, rimangono aperti i problemi per il futuro" [2017] *Diritto penale contemporaneo*; M. Nisticò, "Taricco II: il passo indietro della Corte di giustizia e le prospettive del supposto dialogo tra le Corti" [2018] *Osservatorio Aic*; G. Repetto, "Quello che Lussemburgo (non) dice. Note minime su Taricco II" [2017] *Diritticomparati.it*; F. Urbinati, "L'epilogo di 'Taricco bis': la Corte di Giustizia cede all'ordinanza della Consulta" [2017] *Archivio penale*; V. Marcenò, "La sentenza Taricco-bis. Conseguenze di una sovranità non decisa" [2018] *forumcostituzionale.it*; V. Valentini, "Sweetening the pill. Il caso Taricco e l'illusionismo prospettico della Consulta" [2017] *Questione Giustizia*; A. Longo, "Taricco-bis: un dialogo senza comunicazione" [2018] *Archivio penale*. The final act of the *Taricco* saga was obviously played by the ItCC (judgment no. 115 of 2018). On that last decision, see C. Amalfitano and O. Pollicino, "Two Courts, Two Languages? The Taricco Saga Ends on a Worrying Note" [2018] *VerfBlog*.

41 Opinion of Advocate General Bot, 18.07.2017, C-42/17, with comments by A. Ruggeri, "Rapporti interordinamentali e conflitti tra identità costituzionali (traendo spunto dal caso Taricco)" [2017] *Diritto penale contemporaneo* <https://www.penalecontemporaneo.it/d/5631-rapporti-interordinamentali-e-conflitti-tra-identita-costituzionali-traendo-spunto-dal-caso-taricco>; M. Bassini and O. Pollicino, "The Opinion of Advocate General Bot in Taricco II: Seven 'deadly' sins and a modest proposal" [2017] *Verfassungsblog on Matters Constitutional* <https://www.penalecontemporaneo.it/d/5631-rapporti-interordinamentali-e-conflitti-tra-identita-costituzionali-traendo-spunto-dal-caso-taricco>; L. Daniele, "Il seguito del caso Taricco: l'Avvocato generale Bot non apre al dialogo tra Corti" [2017] *European Papers* <http://europeanpapers.eu/en/europeanforum/il-seguito-del-caso-taricco-lavvocato-generale-bot-non-apre-al-dialogo-tra-corti>.

imply the violation of state constitutional rights. Finally, the ItCC affirmed the *erga omnes* value of this exception in decision no. 115 of 2018.[42]

Moreover, it must be noted that the ItCC has tried to play an even more central role in protecting fundamental rights in another recent decision. It is worth quoting part of the very long *obiter dictum* of judgment no. 269 of 2017, because it may inaugurate the most significant shift of its jurisprudence since the *Granital* case of 1984, since it suggests that, when fundamental rights protected by both the EU Charter and the Italian Constitution are at stake, every Italian court should *first* refer to the ItCC rather then the ECJ:[43]

> Granted the principles of the primacy and direct effect of European Union law as consolidated in both European and constitutional case law, it bears considering that the aforementioned Charter of Rights is a part of Union law that is endowed with particular characteristics due to the typically constitutional stamp of its contents. The principles and rights laid out in the Charter largely intersect with the principles and rights guaranteed by the Italian Constitution (and by other Member States' constitutions). It may therefore occur that the violation of an individual right infringes, at once, upon the guarantees enshrined in the Italian Constitution and those codified by the European Charter ... Therefore, violations of individual rights posit the need for an *erga omnes* intervention by this Court, including under the principle that places a centralized system of the constitutional review of laws at the foundation of the constitutional structure (Article 134 of the Constitution). The Court will make a judgment in light of internal parameters and, potentially, European ones as well (per Articles 11 and 117 of the Constitution), in the order that is appropriate to the specific case, including for the purpose of ensuring that the rights guaranteed by the aforementioned Charter of fundamental rights are interpreted in a way consistent with constitutional traditions, which are mentioned in Article 6 of the Treaty on

---

42 See C. Amalfitano, "Jusqu'ici tout va bien ... ma non sino alla fine della storia. Luci, ombre ed atterraggio della sentenza n. 115/2018 della Corte costituzionale che chiude (?) la saga Taricco" [2018] *Diritticomparati.it*; P. Faraguna, "*Roma locuta*, Taricco finita" [2018] *Diritticomparati.it*.

43 See P. Faraguna, "Constitutional Rights First: The Italian Constitutional Court fine-tunes its 'Europarechtsfreundlichkeit'" [2018] *VerfBlog*; A. Ruggeri, "Svolta della Consulta sulle questioni di diritto eurounitario assiologicamente pregnanti, attratte nell'orbita del sindacato accentrato di costituzionalità, pur se riguardanti norme dell'Unione self-executing (a margine di Corte cost. n. 269 del 2017)" [2017] *Diritticomparati.it*; G. Pistorio, "Conferme e precisazioni nel «cammino comunitario» della Corte costituzionale. Commento a prima lettura della sentenza n. 269 del 2017" [2018] *Diritticomparati.it*; A. Guazzarotti, "Un 'atto interruttivo dell'usucapione' delle attribuzioni della Corte costituzionale? In margine alla sentenza n. 269/2017" [2018] *Forumcostituzionale.it*; L.S. Rossi, "La sentenza 269/2017 della Corte costituzionale italiana: obiter 'creativi' (o distruttivi?) sul ruolo dei giudici italiani di fronte al diritto dell'Unione europea" [2018] *Federalismi.it*; A. Anzon Demmig, "La Corte riprende il proprio ruolo nella garanzia dei diritti costituzionali e fa un altro passo avanti a tutela dei 'controlimiti'" [2018] *Forumcostituzionale.it*; G. Scaccia, "Giudici comuni e diritto dell'Unione europea nella sentenza della Corte costituzionale n. 269 del 2017" [2018] *Rivistaaic.it*.

> European Union and by Article 52(4) of the EUCFR as relevant sources in this area … In keeping with this line of reasoning, this Court holds that, where a law is the object of doubts concerning the rights enshrined in the Italian Constitution or those guaranteed by the Charter of Fundamental Rights of the European Union in those contexts where EU law applies, the question of constitutionality must be raised, leaving in place the possibility of making a referral for a preliminary ruling for matters of interpretation or of invalidity of Union law, under Article 267 TFUE.[44]

In other words, the last step of the "European pathway"[45] made by the ItCC is a delimitation of the widespread constitutional review and disapplication of national norms, when the latter are in potential contrast with the EU Charter of Fundamental Rights. Therefore, the final outcome of the combination of the more recent decisions of the ItCC is a reappropriation of constitutionality issues in the areas of fundamental constitutional principles and fundamental rights. This reappropriation – as sharply noted – passes both through the "right to the *last* word", in the *Taricco case*, and through the "right to the *first* word", in decision no. 269 of 2017.[46] Indeed, according to the latter, the right to speak first (and not only to speak second, using the brutal weapon of counter-limits) means activating an interpretative dynamic in which the respect for the constitutional identity is not only seen as the extreme border of the interpretative discretion of the Luxembourg Court, but also as an essential hermeneutical reference in the interpretation of the provisions of the EU Charter of Fundamental Rights.[47]

It is worth noting, in conclusion, that this last step has already been received and accepted by the Italian Supreme Court of Cassation, that referred a case to the Constitutional Court in which fundamental rights were concerned and both levels of protection were involved, stating the "suspension" of its power and duty to refer the interpretative question to the ECJ until the answer of the ItCC.[48] But it is also true, as someone has noted, that a collateral effect of ItCC's decision no. 269 of 2017 could be an exponential increase of consistent interpretation.[49]

---

44 Translation by the ItCC staff.

45 The Italian expression "*cammino comunitario*", by now irreplaceable in the Italian reflections, dates back to P. Barile, "Il cammino comunitario della Corte" [1973] *Giurisprudenza costituzionale* 2406 ff., in comment to ItCC, dec. no. 183 of 1973.

46 A. Guazzarotti (n. 43), p. 2.

47 G. Scaccia (n. 43), p. 7.

48 Court of Cassation, II Civil Division, 16.02.2018, no. 3831, with comments by A. Ruggeri, "Una prima, cauta ed interlocutoria risposta della Cassazione a Corte cost. n. 269/2017 (a prima lettura di Cass., II sez. civ., 16 febbraio 2018, n. 3831, *Bolognesi c. Consob*)" [2018] *Consultaonline.it*; D. Tega, "Il seguito in Cassazione della pronuncia della Corte costituzionale n. 269 del 2017: prove pratiche di applicazione" [2018] *Questionegiustizia.it*. More problematic than other susequent questions. See, f.i., Court of Cassation, Labour Division, 30.05.2018, no. 13678.

49 V. Piccone "A prima lettura della sentenza della Corte di Cassazione n. 4223 del 21 febbraio 2018. L'interpretazione conforme come strumento di "sutura" post Corte costituzionale n. 269/2017" *Diritticomparati.it*, no. 1/2018 and A. Ruggeri "Corte europea dei diritti

4. THE BRIDGING ROLE PLAYED BY THE ITALIAN CONSTITUTIONAL COURT

The two cases analysed above shows how even if, "as a matter of principle, in a centralised system like the Italian one, the Constitutional Court is endowed with the exclusive power of reviewing legislation ... as a matter of fact, however, the Italian Constitutional Court shares its authority with other judicial bodies, whose importance has grown over time".[50] This sharing of authority rests foremost on the ground of interactions between Italian and supranational and international legal systems, as designed by the ItCC itself, according to the suggestions coming from the ECJ, on the one hand, and of the Strasbourg Court, on the other one. In carrying out this function of connection and junction, in fact, it is quite evident that the ItCC had to address not only the external sources of law, but also the external decisions of the courts called on to apply those sources (albeit from their point of view, and according to the specific function that the relative system assigns to them).

With regard to these issues, the ItCC has also taken on the task of establishing what the implications, impact and effects of the decisions of international and supranational courts are within the Italian legal system. This task has given rise to a permanent confrontation between the ItCC and those Courts: the ECJ, the relations with which – as discussed above – has been recently revived by choosing to refer for a preliminary ruling directly by the ItCC itself[51] and by the abovementioned ItCC decision no. 269 of 2017; the International Court of Justice, with which it has recently collided on the question of damages compensation for Nazi war crimes;[52] and the Strasbourg Court, whose relation with the ItCC was defined by the "twin sentences", but was gradually modified until a partial new framework was established in 2015, where it is enhanced the importance of appreciating the constitutional protection of rights and principles before evaluating and balancing this protection with the one accorded in Strasbourg.[53]

---

dell'uomo e giudici nazionali, alla luce della più recente giurisprudenza costituzionale (tendenze e prospettive)" RivistaAIC, 2018, 1.

50 V. Barsotti, P.G. Carozza, M. Cartabia and A. Simoncini, *Italian Constitutional Justice in Global Context* (OUP USA, 2016), p. 104.

51 ItCC, dec. no. 103 of 2008, no. 207 of 2013 and the mentioned no. 24 of 2017.

52 ItCC, dec. no. 238 of 2014. See E. Lamarque, "Some WH questions about the Italian Constitutional Court's judgment on the rights of the victims of the Nazi crimes" [2015] 2 *Italian Journal of Public Law* 197 ff. <http://www.ijpl.eu>.

53 See ItCC, dec. no. 49 of 2015. On that important judgment, see A. Pin, "A jurisprudence to handle with care: The European Court of Human Rights' unsettled case law, its authority, and its future, according to the Italian Constitutional Court" (1 May 2015) *Int'l J. Const. L. Blog* and D. Tega, "A national narrative: The Constitution's axiological prevalence on the ECHR – A comment on the Italian Constitutional Court judgment no. 49/2015" (1 May 2015) *Int'l J. Const. L. Blog*, both <http://www.iconnectblog.com/2015/04/mini-symposium-on-cc-judgment-49-2015>.

On the other hand, from the internal point of view, it should also be noted that the openness towards international and supranational law is achieved jointly by the ItCC, which dictates the criteria and the conditions to be fulfilled, and by the other Italian national courts – in particular by the ordinary and administrative Supreme Courts – which adopt the criteria dictated by the ItCC with regard to a particular case and even possibly develop them, sometimes creatively, alongside the direction traced by the ItCC. In fact, one of the most interesting features of the Italian system of constitutional justice is the progressive sharing of tasks and responsibilities between the ItCC and the other national courts in the judicial review of legislation and in the implementation of fundamental rights. The first 40 years of Italian preliminary judgments of constitutionality (1956–1996) may be compared to long "orchestra rehearsals", in which the ItCC and the judges have gradually tuned the procedural tools at their disposal by filling the blank spaces in the referred norms. The last 20 years, and particularly the first years of the new millennium, have instead been devoted to a strengthening of the judicial rules of connection, and above all to confirming the collaboration between the two entities, the mutual interdependence of their work and the sharing of their goals.[54] So when the supranational and the international norms came into the Italian legal system at the beginning of the new century, the special relationship of brotherhood between the ItCC and Italian ordinary judges was already consolidated, and the European dimension enhanced it.

Watching from outside the Italian legal system, this cooperation has manifested itself in several ways. First of all, it can be certainly affirmed that the "rules of engagement" proposed by the ItCC for the entry of human rights into the Italian legal system, and the relative border controls, are closely followed by the Italian ordinary judges. Under the guidance of the higher courts, the ordinary judges have for many years complied with the rules dictated by the ItCC: confronted with directly effective norms, they proceed independently by setting aside the internal norm conflicting with EU law; confronted with norms without direct effect, they refer the case for a preliminary ruling of constitutionality for violation of Art. 11 and/or Art. 117(1) of the Constitution.

Moreover, as will be more closely analysed later on, the ordinary courts accepted and implemented another important "lesson" patiently taught by the ItCC: that interpretation in conformity with ECHR and EU law is *a duty* for each and every judicial body. More precisely, it is a duty that should be fulfilled *before* deciding whether it is necessary to set aside the national norm or to refer the preliminary ruling of constitutionality to the ItCC, as the ItCC itself construed it as a *procedural* obligation. In fact, the common feature of all of the forms of

[54] E. Lamarque, *Corte costituzionale e giudici nell'Italia repubblicana* (Editori Laterza, 2012), p. 101 ff. and, in particular, p. 132 ff.

consistent interpretation recognised and imposed by the ItCC in the Italian legal system is their mandatory nature for the courts. National courts are therefore subject to a genuine duty to elaborate the rule of each case by taking into account all the different effective, relevant and non-invalid sources – i.e. the Italian Constitution and the supranational and international obligations – rather than picking just one and neglecting the rest.[55] Thus, according to the ItCC, judges are under an obligation that regards the means used, and not the result achieved.[56] This means that the ordinary judges are required not only to try to read the legislation in a manner which does not conflict with the Italian Constitution, EU law and international obligations, but also to take all possible actions, exhaust all interpretative powers available to them, or indeed avoid leaving anything unaddressed. However, they may – and indeed *must* – desist when confronted with an evident solution; that is, when it is almost certain – notwithstanding their best efforts – that consistent interpretation is not practicable in the particular case. The duty of consistent interpretation is therefore a *procedural* duty: the attempt on the part of the judges to interpret the Italian law must be carried out in a very serious way, but it is only a "mandatory step" which every judge must demonstrate to have taken, and not necessarily the destination that has to be reached. When judges start looking into the possibility of performing consistent interpretation, they are not yet supposed to know if that will be their point of arrival or just a stage of their line of reasoning.

The fact that the obligation is only procedural is also proven *a contrario* by the circumstance that in case of failure of the attempt of conforming interpretation, there are *other* instruments and measures provided for remedying the overlap between the two heterogeneous normative levels which have been demonstrated to be irreconcilable – i.e. the setting aside of, or the declaration of unconstitutionality of, the national norm.

A ruling of incompatibility between normative spheres is thus always the last resort.[57] More precisely, it is always an ancillary measure,[58] which must admittedly be adopted, but only when the principal measure (i.e. consistent interpretation) is not feasible. In that case, it will be adopted either by the ordinary judges when setting aside national legislation on grounds of

---

55 This is the appropriate definition of the judicial duty formulated by O. Chessa, "Non manifesta infondatezza *versus* interpretazione adeguatrice?" in M. D'Amico and B. Randazzo (eds.), *Interpretazione conforme e tecniche argomentative* (Giappichelli, 2009), p. 273.

56 A. Celotto and G. Pistorio, "Interpretazioni comunitariamente e convenzionalmente conformi" [2010] *Giurisprudenza italiana* 1980.

57 This is noted, among others, by F. Modugno, *Scritti sull'interpretazione costituzionale* (Editoriale Scientifica, 2010), p. 222; F. Modugno, "Sul problema dell'interpretazione conforme a Costituzione: un breve *excursus*" [2010] *Giurisprudenza italiana* 1964.

58 S. Rodin, "Back to the square one – the past, the present and the future of the Simmenthal mandate" in J.M. Beneyto and I. Pernice (eds.), *Europe's Constitutional Challenges in the Light of the Recent Case Law of National Constitutional Courts* (Nomos Publishers, 2011), p. 300.

incompatibility with EU law, or by the ItCC when striking down legislation as unconstitutional on grounds of breach of the Constitution or of the interposed rule under EU law or the ECHR.

Using a metaphor, this technique of interpretation is used as a *hinge*, or a *zip*, between two normative levels – or even between two logics or two worlds – that sometimes are far from each other, but that should be always taken into consideration simultaneously to adjust the case at hand.[59] Such a mechanism is proving more and more necessary because of the complexity, intertwining and overlapping of legal sources with different origins and legitimacy that populate contemporary legal systems, and that influence the everyday activity of interpreters of the law. The metaphor may even suggest that when two fabrics of different quality and consistency have to be kept together, it is indeed always convenient to try to first use a zip that leaves the tissues intact, and that can always later be re-opened and then closed with one simple gesture. Or it may also suggest that it is only when the zip does not work that one of the two fabrics should, even if reluctantly, be cut to sew it to the other.

Metaphors aside, it could be said that the ItCC has simply affirmed that when a conflict between an internal norm and a European one is glimpsed, it is better first of all to make every effort to try to compose the antinomy in the softest way, using a tool – i.e. consistent interpretation – that does not question either the validity or the enforceability of the internal norm.[60] Only if (and when) this way proves impracticable the drastic and severe measures mentioned above become inevitable.

5. THE FOUNDATIONS OF THE DUTY OF CONSISTENT INTERPRETATION IN THE ITALIAN LEGAL SYSTEM

While the orientations discussed in sections 2 and 3 were developed over several years and needed many pronunciations by the courts involved before achieving firm anchorage, the interpretation of domestic laws in conformity with EU law was developed like a marginal landmark, confined to few, rare and sparse beats within the ItCC rulings where its "European pathway" was traced. Perhaps it

---

59 E. Lamarque, "I giudici italiani e l'interpretazione conforme al diritto dell'Unione europea e alla Convenzione europea dei diritti dell'uomo" in L. Cappuccio and E. Lamarque (eds.), *Dove va il sistema italiano accentrato di controllo di costituzionalità? Ragionando intorno al libro di Victor Ferreres Comella Constitutional Courts and Democratic Values* (Editoriale Scientifica, 2013), pp. 244–58.

60 R. Bin, *A discrezione del giudice. Ordine e disordine una prospettiva "quantistica"* (FrancoAngeli, 2013), p. 49 ff., notes that a similar "deferent" attitude towards the law, typical of every European Court and aimed to preserve their legitimacy towards the sovereignty of Parliament, has also been a character of the US Supreme Court since the beginning of the eighteenth century.

may be that this passage constituted the less problematic of the whole "journey": a peaceful transition on both the domestic and external fronts because, unlike other orientations of the ItCC, it has never created misunderstandings or frictions with the ECJ – at least from a theoretical point of view.[61]

The duty of interpretation in conformity with EU law in fact emerged in the ItCC's case-law during the 1980s, in parallel with the ECJ case-law, and gave rise to a progressive joint action of encirclement of the Italian courts. The first formulation of this obligation dates back to the *Von Colson* decision in 1984, in which the ECJ held for the first time that

> the Member States' obligation arising from a directive to achieve the result envisaged by the directive and their duty ... to take all appropriate measures, whether general or particular, to ensure the fulfilment of that obligation, is binding on all the authorities of Member States including, for matters within their jurisdiction, the courts. It follows that ... the national court is required to interpret its national law in the light of the wording and the purpose of the directive.[62]

On the internal front, the leading case is the *Granital* decision (also symbolically dated 1984, and adopted only two months after *Von Colson*), in which the ItCC asserted that

> at the hermeneutic level, it is in force the presumption that national legislation is compatible with Community law: out of the possible interpretations of the legislative text adopted by the national organs it is necessary to select that which is compatible with the requirements of Community law, and thereby also with the Constitution, which guarantees compliance with the Treaty of Rome and the law derived from it.[63]

Actually, there were some traces of this orientation before 1984. In two judgments from 1981, the ItCC itself acceded to an interpretation consistent with EU law of an Italian law, declaring that: "ultimately, it is to adopt, among the possible interpretations of the law ... the one consistent both with the requirements of the EU authorities, and to the principles of our own system, which guarantee the observance of the Treaty and the norms derived from it".[64] In light of this, it may be said that the Italian constitutional case-law is quite different from the ECJ's case-law, setting out a separate rationale and an *internal* foundation for the duty of interpretation in conformity with EU law. While the ECJ is concerned about

61 E. Lamarque, "L'interpretazione conforme al diritto dell'Unione europea secondo la Corte costituzionale italiana" in A. Bernardi (ed.), *L'interpretazione conforme al diritto dell'Unione europea. Profili e limiti di un vincolo problematico* (Jovene editore, 2015), 91 ff.

62 Case C-14/83, *Von Colson*, ECLI:EU:C:1984:153.

63 ItCC, dec. no. 170 of 1984 (translation by the author). The statement is repeated also in the following constitutional case-law. See G. Pistorio, "La prevalenza ermeneutica del diritto comunitario" in *Studi in onore di Franco Modugno* (III, Editoriale Scientifica, 2011), pp. 2623.

64 ItCC, dec. no. 176 of 1981, §6, and no. 177 of 1981, §5 (translation by the author).

the urgency of finding a judicial remedy for the infringement by the Member States' political bodies of an EC norm without direct effects or unable to affect horizontal relations between citizens,[65] the ItCC presents this duty as a species of the more general duty of interpretation in conformity with the Constitution (i.e. in that "phase" of the "European pathway", with Art. 11 of the Constitution).

The historical moment at which this constitutional orientation was born in fact confirms that the ItCC's concern was the *purely internal* need to ensure the adaptation of legislation to superior constitutional rules: a requirement that also implied compliance with Community law, as one of the constraints descending from Art. 11 of the Constitution and from Italian participation in the EC. Another confirmation of this peculiarity may also be found in the *Granital* judgment of 1984, since that decision referred to directly effective European norms (i.e. to a case different from the one considered by the ECJ in its leading case). Thus, in the logic of the ItCC, the presumption of conformity is to be preferred to a declaration of unconstitutionality (1981) and to the non-application of the law (1984), only because it is a judicial measure that is less traumatic than the other two aimed at ensuring compliance with Art. 11 of the Constitution.

Following the *Granital* decision, the ItCC thereby definitely overcame the "weak" paradigm of the *presumption* of conformity with EU law, to embrace more clearly the *duty* of consistent interpretation – the latter being stronger and more binding as hooked to Art. 11 of the Constitution. This is particularly well demonstrated by the fact that the ItCC manages the duty of EU consistent interpretation in exactly the same way as it manages the duty of constitutional consistent interpretation: by affirming that the judge may refer a preliminary issue of constitutionality only when a consistent interpretation is impossible,[66] or – with an equivalent expression – when the contrast "may not be prevented by interpretation".[67] Consequently, the judge will be sanctioned with an inadmissibility ruling if he does not demonstrate properly that he has looked for an interpretation in conformity with the Constitution (or, in this case, a European directive or a framework decision), and could not find it.[68]

However, above all, in cases involving EU law which is directly applicable or has direct effect, it is the ECJ which imposes the requirement of consistent interpretation of national law, as a measure which must under all circumstances

---

65 M. Cartabia and M. Gennusa, *Le fonti europee e il diritto italiano* (Giappichelli, 2009), p. 48 ff.; M.P. Iadicicco, "Integrazione europea e ruolo del giudice nazionale" [2001] *Rivista italiana diritto pubblico comunitario* 405, and V. Piccone, "L'interpretazione conforme nell'ordinamento integrato" in R. Cosio and R. Foglia (eds.), *Il diritto europeo nel dialogo delle corti* (Giuffrè, 2013), pp. 291 ff.

66 F.i., ItCC, dec. no. 454 of 2006.

67 ItCC, dec. no. 227 of 2010, §7.1. and no. 222 of 2011 (translation by the author).

68 ItCC, dec. no. 28 of 2010, §4.

be preferred to the setting aside of the national law.[69] Moreover, in cases involving EU law without direct effect, consistent interpretation is classified as the "indirect effect" of such legislation,[70] having been imposed in the name of the effectiveness of EU law.[71] It is to be preferred *inter alia* to damages claims by individuals,[72] which are premised on a finding that the state has breached EU law. With regard to this, it may be important to stress that the ECJ is institutionally capable of imposing the attempt of consistent interpretation at the very least on the referring court, as an effect of its interpretative judgments. Furthermore, if the methodological requirement to attempt a consistent interpretation of the national law is also binding upon all of the courts throughout the other Member States, this will naturally depend upon which answer is given to the long-standing question regarding the general effects of the judgments of the ECJ.[73] Whichever answer is provided – and this is not the appropriate forum to consider these answers – it is nonetheless clear that if such an interpretative judgment is issued by the ECJ, no national court will be able to avoid the requirement to give reasons (even if only in summary form) as to how it is impossible to read its own national law in such a manner as to ensure

---

69 See, e.g., Case C-60/02, *X*, ECLI:EU:C:2004:10; Case C-555/07, *Kücükdeveci*, ECLI:EU:C:2010:21; Case C-282/10, *Dominguez*, ECLI:EU:C:2012:33, which strongly insists on stating that, among the obligations of a national judge – when acting as a judge of the EU – the obligation relative to an interpretation that is consistent with internal law retains precedence over any obligation for its disapplication.

70 In Italian legal theory the expression "indirect effect" is not frequently used to specify the result of an interpretation of the national law in conformity with EU law. Explicit use of the term is found, however, in M. Cartabia and M. Gennusa, *Le fonti europee e il diritto italiano* (Giappichelli, 2009), p. 48 ff. and G. Tesauro, *Diritto dell'Unione europea* (6th edn., Cedam, 2010), p. 196. The case-law of the ECJ concerning the obligation of interpretation of national law in conformity with EU law without direct effect is extensive: in addiction to the above cited *Von Colson* of 1984 and the other judgments cited in the previous note, reference can also be made, among others, to Case C-106/89, *Marleasing SA*, ECLI:EU:C:1990:395 and Case C-397/01, *Pfeiffer*, ECLI:EU:C:2004:584.

71 The fact that this is a fundamental element of the doctrine of indirect effect – despite certain ambiguities in ECJ case-law – is almost universally recognised. See, in particular, S. Drake, "Twenty tears after Von Colson: the impact of 'indirect effect' on the protection of the individual's Community rights" [2005] 30 *European Law Review* 329 ff.

72 Case C-378/07–C-380/07, *Angelidaki*, ECLI:EU:C:2009:250, but see also *Dominguez* (n. 69).

73 With regard to this point refer to R. Caponi, "Corti europee e giudicati nazionali" in *Corti europee e giudici nazionali* (Bononia University Press, 2011), p. 290 ff.; E. D'Alessandro, *Il procedimento pregiudiziale interpretativo dinanzi alla Corte di Giustizia. Oggetto ed efficacia della pronuncia* (Giappichelli, 2012), p. 245 ff.; G. Gaja and A. Adinolfi, *Introduzione al diritto dell'Unione europea* (Editori Laterza, 2012), p. 116; F. Ghera, "Pregiudiziale comunitaria, pregiudiziale costituzionale e valore di precedente delle sentenze interpretative della Corte di Giustizia" [2000] *Giurisprudenza costituzionale* 1204 ff.; G. Martinico, "Le sentenze interpretative della Corte di giustizia come forme di produzione normativa" [2004] *Rivista di diritto costituzionale* 249 ff.; G. Martinico, *L'integrazione silente. La funzione interpretativa della Corte di Giustizia e il diritto costituzionale europeo* (Jovene, 2009), pp. 91 ff.; T. Guarnier (n. 10), pp. 309 ff.

the *effet utile* of EU law in relation to which the ECJ has already adopted a position. A national court of last instance is no less able to avoid the requirement to give reasons on this point – and, it could be specified, no less is an Italian Court of last resort able to do so. As well known, the stringent approach followed by the ECJ in recent years was adopted in relation to certain Italian cases where it held that the Member State is liable "for damage caused to individuals by an infringement of the European law attributable to a court of last resort", and insofar as may be of interest for the purposes of this contribution, "from an interpretation of provisions of law".[74]

From the national point of view it could be simply said that in accordance with the ECJ, the ItCC both in preliminary judgments and in judgments referred to it by the State and Regions not only practices the technique of consistent interpretation, but also always recommends it (when feasible) even to its interlocutors (i.e. State, Regions and ordinary judges).

6. THE LOGICAL LIMIT OF CONSISTENT INTERPRETATION

Beyond its mandatory nature, one further element which is common to all the current forms of consistent interpretation is the requirement that it involves genuine interpretation – either of an individual provision or of the entire system of primary legislation – and cannot be transformed through distortion into the correction or manipulation of the actual legislation. Indeed, when imposing this procedural obligation, the ItCC and the ECJ speak with one voice. They maintain that not only its mandatory nature but also the very possibility for every court to engage in consistent interpretation will cease if the literal meaning of the law is not amenable to be stretched to achieve the result sought by the reference norm, according to letter of the law, as read together with – and in the light of – constitutional, supranational and international principles, rights and duties. This has been significantly identified as the "logical limit" of the technique:[75] as a matter of principle, consistent interpretation *contra legem* is not permitted.

---

[74] Case C-379/10, *European Commission v. Italian Republic*, ECLI:EU:C:2011:775; Case C-173/03, *Traghetti del Mediterraneo*, ECLI:EU:C:2006:391 and Case C-224/01, *Köbler*, ECLI:EU:C:2003:513 (where it is specified that the liability of the state will apply only in the exceptional case that the judge has manifestly violated EU law). With regard to this issue, refer in particular to M. Luciani, "Funzioni e responsabilità della giurisdizione. Una vicenda italiana (e non solo)" 3 [2012] *RivistaAIC*; R. Bifulco, "La responsabilità del giudice tra principi dell'unione europea e applicazioni nazionali" [2012] *astrid-online.it*; and M.A. Sandulli, "Riflessioni sulla responsabilità civile degli organi giurisdizionali" 10 [2012] *federalismi.it*.

[75] See F. Viganò, "Il giudice penale e l'interpretazione conforme alle norme sovranazionali" in *Studi in onore di Mario Pisani* (Vol. II, La Tribuna, 2010), p. 649 ff.; and V. Manes, "Metodo

Logically speaking, it would no longer amount to interpretation. In reality, it would conceal an operation (i.e. the setting aside of the clear textual provision of the law) under the guise of interpretation. Depending upon the circumstances, such setting aside of national law will be prohibited; or, if permitted, such as in cases involving directly applicable EU law, must be conducted in the full light of day, and called by its true name.

Is it all well therefore? Not entirely. The unstoppable tendency – which once again brings together the three current forms of consistent interpretation (i.e. interpretation in conformity with the Constitution, EU law and international obligations, including the ECHR) within the same destiny – is to see the technique stretched beyond the logical and structural limit mentioned above. In other words, the extraordinary qualities of malleability and flexibility with regard to the harmonisation of the various normative levels offered by the technique of consistent interpretation, which are so precious within a complex framework of sources of law as the current one, result in an inexorable tendency to degenerate into different operations. Indeed, in the experience of all legal practitioners – or at the very least those working in Italy – the technique lends itself to be used in an non-rigorous, elusive and intangible manner, as a pretext for achieving the result sought, without getting to the more drastic measures mentioned above. In this way, however, consistent interpretation stops being an element of "pacification" between sources and legal systems, instead turning into a cause of "upheaval in the operational mechanisms of one source or the other source, of one legal system or the other legal system".[76]

Nonetheless, it must be said that the interpretations in conformity with EU law suggested by the ItCC are never impossible, bold or *contra legem*. The ItCC does not dare, does not go too far, and never comes to suggest a reading of Italian law so creative as to substantially become a non-application of the text. A completely different attitude from the one manifested by the ItCC concerning interpretation in conformity with the Constitution can therefore be seen. According to the ItCC, it is evidently worth sacrificing the letter of the national law only on the altar of the constitutional provision, and not on that of EU law, which already has other more orthodox ways through which to prevail.

On the other hand, however, although it is the ECJ which asserts and imposes the logical limit of consistent interpretation, it is also often the first to suggest

---

e limiti dell'interpretazione conforme alle fonti sovranazionali in materia penale" [2012] *Archivio penale* 17 ff., who distinguish between the "logical" limit of any type of conforming interpretation, and the "axiological" limits that are present only in interpretations in conformity with EU law in criminal matters.

[76] See M. Luciani, "Le funzioni sistemiche della Corte costituzionale, oggi, e l'interpretazione 'conforme a'" [2007] *federalismi.it* (translation by the author). See also Id., "Interpretazione conforme a Costituzione" in *Enciclopedia del diritto*, Ann. IX, 2016, 391 ff. and especially 453 ff.

interpretations of the law in individual cases which are seemingly impossible, or at the very least acrobatic (i.e. difficult to reconcile with the literal wording).[77] In other words, the ECJ does not practice what it preaches; that is to say, it specifies the logical limit, but breaches it in concrete cases. This sets a bad example for other courts, which will in turn feel that they are authorised to proceed in the same brazen manner.

There are at least three reasons why the ECJ acts in this way. First and foremost, consistent interpretation assures flexibility in the relations between different normative levels, and neutralises (or takes the sting out of) the ever possible conflicts between national law and European law. The more rigid measure of setting aside legislation exacerbates these conflicts, always portraying a winner (the EU) and a loser (the Member State).[78] In order to ensure peace of mind for all, including the ECJ, it is therefore better to rely on indirect effect rather than on direct effect.

---

77 The adjective has been used by G. Gaja, "Il processo di armonizzazione e la sua incidenza sull'ordinamento italiano" in *L'ordinamento italiano dopo 50 anni di integrazione europea* (Giappichelli, 2004), p. 44. However, the awareness that both the ItCC as well as the ECJ do not hesitate to propose hermeneutical excesses is widespread in legal theory. In particular, refer – with regard to the first court – to E. Lamarque, "Interpreting statutes in conformity with the Constitution: The role of the Constitutional Court and ordinary judges" 2 [2010] 2 *Italian Journal of Public Law* 197 ff. <http://www.ijpl.eu>; E. Lamarque, "La fabbrica delle interpretazioni conformi a Costituzione tra Corte costituzionale e giudici comuni" in B. Biscotti, P. Borsellino, V. Pocar and D. Pulitanò (eds.), *La fabbrica delle interpretazioni. Atti del VI convegno della Facoltà di Giurisprudenza. Università degli studi di Milano-Bicocca 19–20 novembre 2009* (Giuffrè, 2012), p. 43 ff.; R. Pinardi, "L'interpretazione adeguatrice tra Corte e giudici comuni: le stagioni di un rapporto complesso e assai problematico" in G. Brunelli, A. Pugiotto and P. Veronesi (eds.), *Il diritto costituzionale come regola e limite al potere* (Vol. IV, Jovene Editore, 2009), p. 1527 ff.; R. Romboli, "Qualcosa di nuovo … anzi d'antico: la contesa sull'interpretazione conforme della legge" in *Studi in memoria di Giuseppe G. Floridia* (Jovene, 2009), p. 677 ff.; R. Romboli, "L'applicazione della Costituzione da parte del giudice comune" in S. Panizza, A. Pizzorusso and R. Romboli (eds.), *Testi e questioni di ordinamento giudiziario e forense* (Pisa University Press, 2002); R. Romboli, "L'interpretazione della legge alla luce della Costituzione tra Corte costituzionale e giudice comune" in E. Navarretta and A. Pertici (eds.), *Il dialogo tra le Corti* (Pisa University Press, 2004); G. Sorrenti, *L'interpretazione conforme a Costituzione* (Giuffrè, 2006), p. 177 ff. and *passim*; G. Sorrenti, "Corte costituzionale giudici e interpretazione ovvero … l'insostenibile leggerezza della legge" in A. Ruggeri (ed.), *La ridefinizione della forma di governo attraverso la giurisprudenza costituzionale* (Edizioni Scientifiche Italiane, 2006), p. 465 ff.; G. Sorrenti, "La Costituzione 'sottintesa'" in *Corte costituzionale, giudici comuni e interpretazioni adeguatrici. Atti del seminario svoltosi in Roma, Palazzo della Consulta, 6 novembre 2009* (Giuffrè, 2010), p. 15 ff. With regard to the second Court, see G. Pistorio, *Interpretazione e giudici. Il caso dell'interpretazione conforme al diritto dell'Unione europea* (Editoriale Scientifica, 2012).

78 G. Martinico, "The importance of consistent interpretation in subnational constitutional contexts: Old wine in new bottles?" 4 [2012] 2 *Perspectives on Federalism* 283; G. Martinico, "Is the European Convention going to be 'supreme'? A comparative-constitutional overview of ECHR and EU Law before national courts" 23 [2012] 2 *EJIL* 409.

Second, if the national legislation develops jurisprudential guidelines requiring the interpretation of existing national laws in conformity with a directive that has direct effect, the legislative or administrative implementation of that directive becomes unnecessary, because the state's obligation can be deemed to have been fulfilled. On the other hand, if the national judge chooses to set aside national law, action by the political bodies will remain essential. Here again, the result achieved through a "soft" approach is more worthwhile than that achieved through the more drastic measures.

Lastly, there is one additional possible reason which might induce the ECJ to suggest a consistent interpretation that is risky and of dubious compatibility with the statute's wording: the awareness that in some cases consistent interpretation can achieve a practical result which even the more invasive judicial instruments are not able to achieve, and it may be also the only option available for ensuring effectiveness of the EU norm.

In fact, the ECJ is often led to suggest an interpretation in conformity with national law without paying heed to its feasibility when a case pending before the national judges involves a relationship between private parties. Given that it is impossible to ensure direct effect, the only way of guaranteeing that EU law prevails in such cases is to require indirect horizontal effect. Compared to this possibility, the payment of damages is nothing more than a pale surrogate available to the few, which is incapable of guaranteeing the effectiveness and superiority of EU law. In that case, consistent interpretation is embraced, not so much as the best and more desirable measure (i.e. as a mandatory step in order to avoid a declaration of incompatibility between two normative systems), but rather as the only way available to achieve a result which could not otherwise be achieved without legislative action. This may again help us to understand why the ECJ dares to propose consistent interpretation even in the context of a legislative framework which could only with difficulty be lent to interpretation in conformity with constitutional or EU law.

However, the breach by the ECJ of the textual limit of the law is supported by a justification which would not apply to similar action by the ItCC, or by another national court. It may in fact be reasonably supposed that out of the other 27 legal systems at which the judgments of the ECJ are directed, there will always be at least one – although perhaps not that of the referring court! – in which the framework of internal sources lends itself to interpretation in conformity with EU law. Moreover, the institutional task of the ECJ is to interpret EU law, and not the individual national laws into which it often strays in order to ensure the efficacy of EU law (even though it does not bear any responsibility for their correct operation; the national courts being the only bodies responsible for the interpretation of national law).[79]

[79] See now the Grand Chamber decision of the ECJ in Case C-441/14, *Ajos*, ECLI:EU:C:2016:278: "EU law is to be interpreted as meaning that a national court adjudicating in a dispute

7. INTERPRETATION IN CONFORMITY WITH EU LAW IN CONSTITUTIONAL CASE-LAW

The ItCC refers to interpretation in conformity with EU law only in a few of its decisions, especially when compared to the hundreds of cases in which it refers to interpretation in conformity with the Constitution, and very few even where compared with the many important judgments of the ECJ. In the present authors' opinion, this is especially due to the fact that not many cases engaging EU law in various ways arrive before the ItCC at all. As previously mentioned, the possibility for the ordinary judge to refer questions where EU law is concerned was only recognised in 1984, and only where there may be a concrete risk of application of a national law contrary with a European norm which is not directly effective (but now, according to the ItCC's decision no. 269 of 2017, the ordinary judge has to *first* refer to the Constitutional Court every question where a right under the EU Charter of Fundamental Rights is concerned, together with a right under the Italian Constitution). Another possibility is the referral of an incorrect implementation of a legislative delegation aimed at transposing an EU directive. In this case, the ItCC may suggest an interpretation of the legislative decree that complies with the law of delegation, and is therefore compliant with the EU legislation – the principles and guiding criteria of which the delegation law aimed to transpose into the Italian legal system. In this case, the doctrine talks about *indirect* or *improper* interpretation in conformity with EU law.[80]

More generally, with regard to the indirect way of constitutional judgment (the one solicited by each judge of the legal system), it should be noted that the persistent refusal of the ItCC to appeal directly to the ECJ for preliminary rulings,[81] combined with the explicit request addressed to the common judges to refer interpretative question to the ECJ before interrogating the ItCC (as an implementation of the duty of attempting, with every means, the consistent interpretation), certainly did not favour the Court using the technique itself.[82] To the contrary, as is well known and often repeated, such an attitude has

---

between private persons falling within the scope of Directive 2000/78 is required, when applying provisions of national law, to interpret those provisions in such a way that they may be applied in a manner that is consistent with the directive or, if such an interpretation is not possible, to disapply, where necessary, any provision of national law that is contrary to the general principle prohibiting discrimination on grounds of age."

80 P. Ivaldi, "Diritto dell'Unione europea e processo costituzionale" [2013] *Diritto dell'Unione europea* 218; A. Longo, "Alcune riflessioni sui rapporti tra l'interpretazione conforme a diritto comunitario e l'utilizzo del canone di equilibrio finanziario da parte della Corte costituzionale" [2011] *Consulta on line*.

81 Since the important overrulings made by the named decisions no. 207 of 2013 and no. 269 of 2017, that are giving rise to a different attitude of the Court.

82 See T. Guarnier, "Rinvio pregiudiziale interpretativo e giudizio di legittimità costituzionale. Nuovi scenari e nuove prospettive nel crocevia sopranazionale" [2013] *Diritto e Società*.

encouraged the maximum devolution of questions of compatibility between Italian and EU norms to the ordinary judges, possibly in connection with the ECJ, with the consequence of depriving the ItCC of the very opportunity to rule on the interpretation of national law in light of EU law. In other words, until a few years ago, the real "EU ordinary judges" have been the ordinary courts. As such, only they were invited by the ECJ to deal with consistent interpretation with European law,[83] while the ItCC in its voluntary isolated position has had a very little voice on this regard. After ItCC decision no. 269 of 2017, things will probably change, but it is too early to say how at this stage.

Moreover, with reference to constitutional judgments in cases referred directly either by the State or Regions under Art. 127 of the Constitution, there are some obstacles to the raising of EU interpretative issues before the ItCC. First of all, Regions cannot pose questions concerning Arts. 11 or 117 of the Constitution, the only exception being where the violation of EU law implies a breach of their competences. This limit naturally impedes them from fully reporting possible conflicts between EU law and the state law object of scrutiny. Second, on the opposite side, when the state refers to the ItCC a question regarding a regional law affecting both the separation of competences and European compliance, the ItCC usually examines the "internal" complaints first, with the result that the supranational issue is often absorbed (consequently thereby absorbing also the possible issue of consistent interpretation).[84]

That said, the few cases in which the ItCC itself has fulfilled the duty of interpretation in conformity with EU law can now be examined. First of all, as previously mentioned, a common feature of all these cases is a tendency to absorb the interpretation in conformity with EU law within the broader interpretation in conformity with the Constitution. Indeed, in the reasoning of those constitutional judgments, the two parameters (i.e. the domestic and the supranational) are always used together, and tend to be confused.[85] This inevitably makes a reading of the contested law different to the one proposed by the judge.

The expressions used by the ItCC are unequivocal. In one case the ItCC states that the "preferential canon of interpretation in conformity with the

83 See B. Guastaferro, "La Corte costituzionale ed il primo rinvio pregiudiziale in un giudizio di legittimità costituzionale in via incidentale: riflessioni sull'ordinanza n. 207 del 2013" [2013] in *www.forumcostituzionale.it*.

84 See e.g. ItCC, dec. no. 245 del 2013, commented by A. Ruggeri, "A proposito dell'ordine giusto col quale vanno esaminate le questioni di costituzionalità e le questioni di 'comunitarietà' congiuntamente proposte in via d'azione (a prima lettura di Corte cost. n. 245 del 2013)" [2013] *Consulta on line – Studi e commenti*.

85 A. Bernardi, "Interpretazione conforme al diritto UE e costituzionalizzazione dell'Unione europea. Brevi osservazioni di un penalista" in A. Bernardi (eds.), in *L'interpretazione conforme al diritto dell'Unione europea. Profili e limiti di un vincolo problematico* (Jovene editore, 2015), p. 10.

Constitution" is "reinforced by the concurring canon of interpretation in conformity with the EU law",[86] and therefore overrules an interpretation made by the Supreme Court of Cassation explicitly because it is in conflict with EU law. The case concerned a succession through the years of several statutes on collective dismissal of transport workers that, according to the Court of Cassation, excluded the applicability of a particular EU directive. Instead, the ItCC suggested another interpretation of the statutes in order to avoid the alleged inapplicability of the directive: it held that, in the light of the European law, the national statutes should be considered as referring only to common dismissal and not to collective dismissal, the latter being disciplined by the directive. Therefore, by limiting the extent of national law, the ItCC prevented the conflict with the EU norms and the consequent liability of the state.

In another case, the ItCC rejected an interpretation of the law in order to support "a systematic criterion, able to take into account the rationale of the provision, and to avoid an incongruous attribution of sense, which would be in contrast with constitutional and European principles".[87] On another occasion, it held that the interpretation of a regional norm proposed by the state "could not be accepted", "also in the light of the European and domestic normative framework".[88] Finally, in yet another case, the ItCC said that "basing on a due systematic, and constitutionally oriented, reconstruction", it is possible to achieve "a regulatory framework perfectly coherent with the (even European) required levels of environmental protection".[89]

8. THE CASE-LAW OF THE ITALIAN COURTS AND INTERPRETATION IN CONFORMITY WITH EU LAW

Given the theoretical framework and the foundations of the duties enshrined by the ItCC as analysed so far, it is now time to answer some practical questions about interpretation in conformity with EU law. How do the Italian ordinary judges actually act? Do they make excessive use of the technique? And consequently, can the fear that the ItCC may be sidelined by an uncontrolled increase of decentralised forms of review of laws, hidden under the veil of consistent interpretation, be considered to be justified?

---

86 ItCC, dec. no. 190 of 2000, §5 (interpretative decision of rejection, made under the referral by the Court of Cassation; translation by the author).

87 ItCC, dec. no. 86 of 2004, §2 (interpretative decision of rejection, made under the referral by the Council of State; translation by the author).

88 ItCC, dec. no. 7 of 2004, §2 (translation by the author).

89 ItCC, dec. no. 145 of 2013, §2.3. (interpretative decision of rejection, made under direct referral by the state; translation by the author).

These are very weighty questions. Before trying to formulate any answer, it must be pointed out that the vast case-law of the ordinary Italian judges dealing with EU law (and particularly the EU Charter of Fundamental Rights), the ECHR and the Constitution itself, in support of interpretative choices which have already been made independently, cannot be included in a single chapter.

The style of argumentation which refers to fundamental rights asserted in those bills of rights, or in the case-law of the ItCC or of the two European courts, is very widespread throughout the Italian courts – although this is by no means an indicator of the application of the technique of consistent interpretation within specific individual cases. Indeed, it only arises when a judge declares that the choice between more than one interpretation, all initially considered to be viable, is resolved or significantly affected by a consideration of the reference parameter, in the absence of which the choice would have been different.

That clarified, it is now possible to try to answer those demanding questions, step by step. First of all, there is no doubt that the Italian ordinary judges – from both the higher and lower courts – know well and apply without any difficulty all of the possible rules and facets of the technique of consistent interpretation. For instance, they have learned from the ECJ that an obligation of conforming interpretation exists even within the old framework decisions on police and judicial cooperation in criminal matters.[90] Further, that setting aside is a secondary measure, since a conforming interpretation must always be preferred, where possible.[91] That in the criminal sector, the interpretation in conformity with EU law cannot have effects *in malam partem*.[92] That in cases involving horizontal relationships, directives cannot produce direct effects, and an interpretation of internal law in conformity with the directive is required whenever compatible with the textual meaning of the internal law.[93] That the "principle of conforming interpretation of national law – despite essentially referring to internal norms that are introduced in order to incorporate EU directives – places overall internal law, however, within a hermeneutical circuit which aims to generate an application that is not in conflict with the result that the directive itself is aiming at".[94]

---

90 For an important application of this principle, see Court of Cassation, III Criminal Division, 04.03.2010, no. 10981, pertaining to juvenile pornography; see also among others Court of Cassation, IV Criminal Division, 23.09.2011, no. 39240.

91 This is the reasoning, for example, of the Council of State, V Division, 14.12.2011, no. 6543, concerning public work contracts.

92 See e.g. Court of Cassation, Joint Criminal Division, 19.01.2012, no. 22225, and other references within the text.

93 In this sense, see among others the sentence of the Court of Palermo no. 42 of 26 March 2010, pertaining to bank account contracts.

94 As stated by the former First President of the Court of Cassation, E. Lupo, "Pluralità delle fonti ed unitarietà dell'ordinamento" in E. Falletti and V. Piccone (eds.), *Il nodo gordiano tra diritto nazionale e diritto europeo* (Cacucci editore, 2012), p. 13, with reference to Court of Cassation, Joint Civil Division, 13.01.2010, no. 355 (translation by the author).

And another lesson learned by Italian judges is that it is mandatory to attempt consistent interpretation, in the wake of the strong insistence of the ItCC and the ECJ.[95]

Moreover, there is no doubt that they largely use this technique not only in "easy" cases, but also where the intersection between sources and legal systems is more intricate. Indeed, when pursuing this path they are able to resolve very "hard" cases wisely and in a balanced manner, avoiding choices which would be needlessly more expensive or painful both for the national and for external legal systems.

Again, there is no doubt that each time the ItCC or the ECJ suggest an interpretation which departs from the literal wording of the law, the regular courts feel authorised to ignore the law with which they would have most likely complied in the absence of the judgment by the ItCC or the ECJ. It is nevertheless necessary to draw a distinction on this point. As regards the reactions of the ordinary courts to the "bolder" interpretations of the law proposed by the ItCC, a fairly recent study has demonstrated that almost every judicial authority complies with the ItCC's indications, although subject to a condition: that these indications be specified in ItCC judgments which are well documented and duly supported by reasons, and not in summary constitutional orders supported by sparse argumentation.[96] Therefore, common judges will also follow the interpretations in conformity with the Constitution suggested by the ItCC, even when the interpretation suggested is difficult to reconcile with the letter of the law, although such adherence is never noncritical and only occurs if the ItCC has used convincing interpretative arguments.

By contrast, adherence by the Italian ordinary courts to the "acrobatic" interpretations of Italian law which emerge in the light of the judgments of the ECJ is automatic, and practically independent of the reasons given. A significant example of this is provided by the follow-up of the well-known *Pupino* judgment,[97] in which the Italian referring court – without a comment –[98] followed a judgment in which the ECJ requested the Italian courts to order the taking of evidence according to special pre-trial procedures (*incidente probatorio*) in a case not included within the closed list laid down in the Code of Criminal

95 See Court of Cassation, Joint Criminal Division, 21.01.2010, no. 18288; Court of Cassation, Joint Criminal Division, 19.01.2012, no. 14484, moving from a duty of interpretation in conformity with ECHR.

96 E. Lamarque, "Il seguito delle decisioni interpretative e additive di principio della Corte costituzionale presso le autorità giurisdizionali (anni 2000–2005)" [2008] *Rivista Trimestrale di Diritto Pubblico*.

97 Case C-105/03, *Pupino*, ECLI:EU:C:2005:386.

98 The follow-up of the *Pupino* decision of the ECJ reached by the Tribunal of Florence is referred to in F. Viganò, "Il giudice penale e l'interpretazione conforme alle norme sovranazionali" in *Studi in onore di Mario Pisani* (Vol. II, La Tribuna, 2010), p. 621.

Procedure, by virtue of a provision of EU law contained in a framework decision which certainly lacked direct effect.[99]

A judgment of the Court of Cassation from 2011 provides another important example – out of the many available – of this way of thinking.[100] This case draws a line under the long-standing issue of study grants for trainee specialist doctors between the years 1983 and 1991, during which – in breach of a European directive governing the matter[101] – no national legislation was enacted to recognise their economic rights. Indeed, arguing in a manner which was far from convincing, the judgment ended up recognising the *effet utile* of the directive through a mix of consistent interpretation of national legislation and the direct application of EU law, as suggested by two judgments of the ECJ.[102]

In this sense, those who criticise the excessive nonchalance with which the ECJ invites the national courts to accept consistent interpretations of national laws which are not adequately supported by the literal wording of such legislation are right. In fact, such invitations induce national courts to cast aside cognitive style in justifying their decisions because they appear to authorise them – although inadmissibly – to refrain from providing adequate reasons in support of the real possibility offered by the national legislation to follow the interpretation of the law suggested by the ECJ.[103]

On the bright side, however, it must be said that when the ECJ speaks, the reasoning of its judgments is always well understood and appreciated by the Italian courts. The Italian Supreme Courts in particular often refer to ECJ judgments in order to interpret in the light of EU norms even other Italian laws, not already considered by the ECJ. In this regard, for example, a judgment of the Labour Division of the Court of Cassation refers to a statement of the ECJ that equates a harassment for disability with discrimination.[104] The Court applied this in a very extensive way, stating that "the duty of interpreting EU law as interpreted by the ECJ imposes to equate a sexual harassment to a gender discrimination as far as the burden of proof is concerned".[105]

---

99 See R. Calvano, "Il Caso Pupino: ovvero dell'alterazione per via giudiziaria dei rapporti tra diritto interno (processuale penale), diritto UE e diritto comunitario" [2005] *Giurisprudenza costituzionale* 4030. On the *Pupino* case see also P. Craig and G. de Bùrca, *EU Law: Text, Cases and Materials* (5th edn., OUP, 2011), p. 204.

100 Court of Cassation, III Civil Division, 29.08.2011, no. 17682.

101 EU Directive 82/76/EEC.

102 Case C-131/97, *Carbonari and Others*, ECLI:EU:C:1999:98 and Case C-371/97, *Gozza*, ECLI:EU:C:2000:526.

103 M. Caianello, "Il caso 'Pupino': riflessioni sul nuovo ruolo riconosciuto al giudice alla luce del metodo adottato dalla Corte di Giustizia" in F. Sgubbi and V. Manes (eds.), *L'interpretazione conforme al diritto comunitario in materia penale* (Bononia University Press, 2007), p. 97 ff.

104 Case C-303/06, *Coleman*, ECLI:EU:C:2008:415 on Directive 2000/78/EC establishing a general framework for equal treatment in employment and occupation.

105 Court of Cassation, Labour Division, 15.11.2016, no. 23286.

Finally, there is no doubt that the ordinary judges frequently adopt, albeit without an explicit invitation from the ItCC or the ECJ, "suspect" instances of consistent interpretation, i.e. readings of the statute law which appear to ignore its literal wording. The reasons why the judicial authorities may prefer a consistent interpretation to a different measure, even when the wording of the law would appear to oppose such an interpretation, are entirely comprehensible. This kind of approach is favoured first and foremost by the desire to make a "fair" decision in the individual case. In this regard, some commentators have asserted (although with perhaps excessive rigidity) in relation to interpretations in conformity with the Constitution that "within this perspective the Constitution does not count for what it actually states in the text of its articles considered overall: it is only a pretext for legitimising actions carried out for the purposes of material justice".[106]

Moreover, the tendency to go to extremes in performing conforming interpretations is also fuelled by the growing anti-formalism which inspires judicial activity, and by recognition of the fact that a dose of creativity is inevitably contained in all judicial choices. It is also assisted by the legitimate desire to achieve justice and to swiftly protect the rights of the parties – without waiting for example for the conclusion of constitutionality proceedings, the outcome of which is considered to be a foregone conclusion. In this framework, the repeated encouragement by the ItCC and the ECJ naturally has the more general effect of enticing otherwise reticent courts to proceed more boldly along the road of conforming interpretation whenever they see the possibility.

However, an examination of the case-law over recent years, above all from the Court of Cassation, suggests that a distinction between various forms of conforming interpretation should be drawn. Indeed, interpretation in conformity with the Constitution is the one that the ordinary judges engage with the least (formal) scruples, considering themselves as joint custodians (along with the ItCC), albeit naturally using different instruments.[107] As regards interpretation in conformity with EU law, the ordinary judges instead adopt a more prudent approach.[108] It is therefore a fairly rare occurrence that they spontaneously accept interpretations of national law in the name of those external norms which are so "stretched" as to be essentially equivalent to a correction or an amendment of the law itself.

---

106 M. Manetti, "La delega al giudice dell'applicazione della Costituzione come sistema di governance" [2011] *Democrazia e diritto* 135 (translation by the author).

107 See E. Lamarque, "I giudici italiani e l'interpretazione conforme al diritto dell'Unione europea e alla Convenzione europea dei diritti dell'uomo" in L. Cappuccio and E. Lamarque (eds.), *Dove va il sistema italiano accentrato di controllo di costituzionalità? Ragionando intorno al libro di Victor Ferreres Comella Constitutional Courts and Democratic Values* (Editoriale Scientifica, 2013), p. 255 ff.

108 See F. Mannella, *Giudici comuni e applicazione della Costituzione* (Editoriale Scientifica, 2011), p. 175.

The judges thereby demonstrate their awareness of the mandatory status of consistent interpretation, while also having perfectly understood its procedural nature and "logical" limit. When accepting it, they very often specify that when national law does not allow an interpretation in accordance with the supranational law, the subsidiary alternatives (depending upon the circumstances) of setting aside the national law,[109] or referring a question of constitutionality to the ItCC,[110] should necessarily be followed.

Analogously, Italian courts show some difficulty in following the ECJ when it imposes a further limit on them – although this time of an "axiological" nature – suggesting "bold" interpretations of national law in conformity with EU law.[111] Examples of this are once again provided by the judgments of the Joint Divisions of the Court of Cassation relating to the confiscation of equivalent assets,[112] and the acquisition of items of suspect origin.[113] In these cases, while concluding in favour of a "bold" interpretation of national law, it is asserted and repeated that the use of supranational legislation is precluded when "the result of such an interpretation translates into an interpretation *contra reum* of the criminal national law".

Expressions of the same spirit of prudence may be seen in the judgments of the Criminal Divisions of the Court of Cassation. Following the indications of the ECJ as to the time when the obligation of conforming interpretation arises,[114] notwithstanding that the ECJ's decisions are not entirely clear in this regard,[115] the Court of Cassation did not endorse interpretations in accordance with the EU directive on linguistic assistance in trials (not yet transposed into Italian law) on the grounds that national courts are not required to do so until the time limit for implementation has expired.[116] Yet it is important to note that in a more recent judgment, the same Supreme Court has recognised the obligation to translate a sentence (with either a written translation or an oral interpretation) in favour of a detained defendant who cannot understand

109 See e.g. Council of State, V Division, 14.12.2011, no. 6543.

110 Among the numerous examples, Council of State, IV Division, 02.09.2011, no. 4960 and Court of Cassation, Labour Division, 22.02.2012, no. 2632.

111 See among others, Case C-7/11, *Caronna*, ECLI:EU:C:2012:396.

112 Court of Cassation, Joint Criminal Division, 25.06.2009, no. 38691. With regard to this point, and on this decision, see V. Manes, "Metodo e limiti dell'interpretazione conforme alle fonti sovranazionali in materia penale" [2012] *Archivio penale* 17, 19 ff.; V. Manes, "Nessuna interpretazione conforme al diritto comunitario con effetti in malam partem" [2010] *Cassazione penale* 101 ff. and A.M. Maugeri, "La confisca per equivalente – ex Art. 322-ter – tra obblighi di interpretazione conforme ed esigenze di razionalizzazione" [2011] *Rivista italiana di diritto e procedura penale* 791 ff.

113 Court of Cassation, Joint Criminal Division, 19.01.2012, no. 22225.

114 Case C-212/04, *Adeneler*, ECLI:EU:C:2006:443 and *Angelidaki* (n. 72).

115 D. Chalmers, G. Davies and G. Monti, *European Union Law* (2nd edn., Cambridge University Press, 2010), pp. 297–300.

116 Court of Cassation, III Criminal Division, 07.07.2011, no. 26703, and Court of Cassation, I Criminal Division, 16.02.2012, no. 10296, both relative to the translation of the sentence.

or speak Italian, and that this remarkable overruling is based on the very obligation on the part of every national court to interpret domestic law consistently with an EU directive, *even if* the EU directive has not yet been transposed into Italian law and the period for its transposition has not yet expired.[117]

It must also be noted that various judgments of the Civil Divisions of the Court of Cassation – among which the important judgment on the burden of proof for the purposes of recognition of the status of political refugee is prominent – assert that the duty of conforming interpretation limits the national courts even when the deadline for implementation of the directive has not yet expired.[118] On this issue, a recent judgment of the Italian Supreme Administrative Court recalls that the Member States to which a directive is addressed must refrain, during the period laid down therein for its implementation, from adopting measures liable to seriously compromise the result prescribed also as far as judicial activity is concerned. So national courts, during that time, must prefer the interpretation of national laws more adequate to the directive. Nevertheless, it clarifies that if the EU directive inserts a totally new concept, such as the possibility for an economic operator to rely on the capacities of other entities under Art. 63 of Directive 2014/24/EU on public procurement, the interpretative activity of the national courts cannot be bound to that result.[119]

Before examining the reasons for such caution by the Italian courts in interpreting in accordance with EU law, it must be pointed out that a prudent approach is not always adopted and that there are exceptions. The cases in which judges act on their own (even when perhaps they should not) are however rare, and moreover feature one common characteristic: in support of their bold interpretation of the legislation, the reasons given by the judges refer jointly to at least two, if not all three, reference parameters (i.e. Constitutional law, EU law and the ECHR).[120] In other words, it is only the total sum of various converging indications which forms an explosive mixture. In cases involving such a convergence of parameters, no form of literal wording will hold good, and the courts will end up construing their duty of conforming interpretation not so much as a procedural obligation but rather as an obligation of result. Emblematic of this issue is the case involving the European Arrest Warrant, which culminated in the 2007 judgment of the Joint Criminal Divisions of the Court of Cassation. The case concerned the rule precluding surrender in cases in which, according to the Italian law implementing the Framework Decision,

117 Court of Cassation, III Criminal Division, 04.02.2013, no. 5486.

118 Court of Cassation, Joint Civil Division, 17.11.2008, no. 27310. With regard to the latter guidelines, also with reference to other decisions, see R. Conti, *La Convenzione europea dei diritti dell'uomo. Il ruolo del giudice* (Aracne, 2011), p. 307 ff.

119 Council of State, III Division, 25.11.2015, no. 5359.

120 In this sense S. Cassese, "La giustizia costituzionale in Italia: lo stato presente" [2012] *Rivista trimestrale di diritto pubblico* 610.

no provision was made in the legislation of the issuing state for maximum limits to pre-trial custody.[121] In that judgment, no referral was made to the ItCC, as would perhaps have been necessary given the literal wording of the law which appeared to introduce a preclusionary condition not stipulated and hence prohibited under the European legislation.[122] Instead, the Joint Divisions interpreted domestic legislation in conformity with EU law, and at the same time with Art. 5 of the ECHR (as interpreted by the Strasbourg Court), thereby successfully executing the acrobatic operation of reconciling three different and apparently irreconcilable indications of differing origin and provenance upon application.[123] Moreover, it must be stressed that, at the first opportunity, the ItCC approved without hesitation the operation carried out by the Court of Cassation.[124]

In other cases, national judges proved themselves able independently to perform EU-consistent interpretations – that is, without any suggestion or imposition by the ItCC or the ECJ – when EU directives were at stake. But, as previously mentioned, it should also be stressed that this "bolder" attitude is usually related to cases where there is a conjunction of different parameters of consistent interpretation (constitutional law, EU law, ECHR). An important example is given by some decisions concerning the renewal of residence permits for non-EU citizens. The Council of State, called to judge on the denied renewal of a residence permit motivated by the lack of the required minimum income, nullified the decision. It stated that other parameters indicated by EU norms should also be taken into consideration (e.g. long-stay residence and family situation, with particular reference to the presence of children integrated in the Italian legal system).[125] Similarly, deciding on an appeal against a refusal of residence permit by a male applicant married in Spain to an Italian man, the Court of Reggio Emilia affirmed the need for a reinterpretation of the term "family" used by Italian norms in light of the European Charter of Fundamental Rights and the ECHR,[126] without any indication to such effect by the ItCC.[127]

---

121 Court of Cassation, Joint Criminal Division, 30.01.2007, no. 4614.

122 This is argued for example by F. Viganò, "Il giudice penale e l'interpretazione conforme alle norme sovranazionali" in *Studi in onore di Mario Pisani* (Vol. II, La Tribuna, 2010), pp. 622 and 654.

123 The decision of the Joint Divisions is very appreciated by R. Mastroianni, "Il dialogo tra la Corte costituzionale e le corti europee: dal conflitto alla contaminazione" in *Corti europee e giudici nazionali* (Bononia University Press, 2011), pp. 414–20, who considers it a sign of "the capacity of our legal system, beyond formalisms, to be open to a common constitutional scope", as well as a demonstration of the fact that, in practice, the case-law of Strasbourg in any case plays a decisive role.

124 ItCC, dec. no. 109 of 2008.

125 Council of State, VI Division, no. 7200/2010.

126 See Court of Reggio Emilia, I civ. div., 13.02.2012.

127 Indeed, the ItCC, in dec. no. 310 of 2010 was far more prudent at this regard.

THE UK PERSPECTIVE ON THE PRINCIPLE OF CONSISTENT INTERPRETATION

Sara DRAKE*

* I am grateful to James Davey, Pauline Roberts, Melanie Smith and Keith Syrett, for their comments on an earlier version of this chapter, and to Hedydd Phylip for her research assistance. Diolch yn fawr! The usual disclaimer applies.

1. INTRODUCTION

This study of the principle of consistent interpretation, more commonly referred to as the *Marleasing* principle in UK law,[1] demonstrates the striking degree to which this method of statutory interpretation has been embedded in the practice of the UK national courts. Originating in the jurisprudence of the Court of Justice of the European Union (ECJ), and based on the principle of loyal co-operation set out in Art. 4(3) of the Treaty on European Union (TEU), the principle of consistent interpretation consists of a duty incumbent on all public authorities including national courts to interpret national law "as far as is possible to do so" in conformity with European Union (EU) law.[2] The principle of consistent interpretation plays a fundamental role in securing the effective enforcement of individual rights derived from EU law before a national court.[3] This study reveals that the principle has been invoked in a wide range of policy areas including tax, employment, intellectual property, data protection, and health and safety in the UK. More recently, the application of this method of statutory interpretation has been consciously "assimilated" by the judiciary with the application of s. 3 of the Human Rights Act 1998 (HRA) despite their separate theoretical and schematic underpinnings.[4]

1 Other English language terms used by academics and the UK judiciary include indirect effect, conform interpretation, and sympathetic interpretation.
2 Case 14/83, *Von Colson*, [1984] ECR 1891.
3 See further S. Drake, "Twenty years after Von Colson: The impact of 'indirect effect' on the protection of the individual's Community rights" (2005) 30(3) *European Law Review* 329–48.
4 This convergence was predicted by Betlem: G. Betlem, "The doctrine of consistent interpretation – Managing legal uncertainty" (2002) 22(3) *Oxford Journal of Legal Studies* 397–418, at p. 417.

This chapter makes an important contribution to the literature in three respects. First, it explores the conceptual basis and scope of application of the principle of consistent interpretation by the UK courts in a systematic manner.[5] There has been very limited exploration of its application before UK courts by either EU or public law scholars in more recent years,[6] and a notable absence of detailed discussion of its symbiotic relationship with s. 3 HRA.[7] The chapter identifies three different phases in the approach of the UK judiciary, and considers (briefly) the implications of the UK's withdrawal from the EU, and predicts the emergence of a fourth phase. It is argued that the three phases in the evolution of the application of the principle of consistent interpretation by the UK courts reflect the changing perception of parliamentary sovereignty in the UK by the judiciary. Indeed, it is the tension between the traditional and "New View" of parliamentary sovereignty and its relationship with the supremacy of EU law which is the common thread in these three periods.[8] The traditional view, embodied in the works of Dicey[9] and Wade,[10] advocates that Parliament is the supreme law-maker and cannot bind its successors. Proponents of the "New View" accept that Parliament is no longer the sole law-maker, and that it may be bound by international Treaty obligations (including those set out in the EU Treaties and European Convention on Human Rights), and that some law-making powers have been devolved to Scotland, Northern Ireland and Wales.[11]

---

5 This analysis is qualitative in nature and broadly responds to the questionnaire distributed by the primary investigator. A quantitative study would have been too onerous within the timeframe of the study. When "*Marleasing*" is used as a search term (since the UK courts commonly use the term "*Marleasing* principle" and deem this judgment to be the leading ECJ case on the doctrine) in the Westlaw database, as of January 2017, it reveals just over 600 results.

6 For some examples, see Lord Mance, "The interface between national and European law" (2013) 38(4) *European Law Review* 437–56; W. Twining and D. Miers, *How to Do Things with Rules* (5th ed., Butterworths, 2010), pp. 321–25. For some analysis of earlier UK court decisions, see A. Arnull, "The Law Lords and the European Union: Swimming with the incoming tide" (2010) 35(1) *European Law Review* 57–87; Drake (n. 3); P. Craig, "Directives: Direct effect, indirect effect and the construction of national legislation" (1997) 22(6) *European Law Review* 519–38.

7 This is in marked contrast to the amount of ink spilt by public law scholars on the operation of s.3 (and s.4) HRA.

8 For more discussion of the academic debate amongst UK constitutional lawyers, see for example, P. Craig, "Britain in the European Union" in J. Jowell, D. Oliver, C. O'Cinneide (eds.), *The Changing Constitution* (8th ed., Oxford University Press, 2015), pp. 114–24; P. Craig, "Parliamentary sovereignty of the United Kingdom parliament after Factortame" (1991) 11 *Year Book of European Law* 221.

9 A. Dicey, *An Introduction to the Study of Law of the Constitution* (10th ed., Palgrave Macmillan, 1967).

10 H.W.R. Wade, "The basis of legal sovereignty" [1955] *Cambridge Law Journal* 172.

11 A process of devolution to local government is underway in England.

Second, the chapter considers the more problematic application of the principle in two policy areas which are regulated to some degree by EU directives, namely motor insurance liability and annual leave. Third, the chapter allows for comparison with the application of the principle by the judiciary of the other Member States of the EU and EEA discussed in this volume. Over the past 40 years, there has been a gradual acceptance by the UK judiciary of its interpretative obligation under EU law. This has culminated in an approach which is more far-reaching than any of the other Member States discussed in this volume. Lord Mance has described the UK courts as being, "… more catholic than the Pope in their understanding of this interpretative duty".[12] This has been accompanied by the increasing knowledge and expertise of lawyers who have recognised that the principle of consistent interpretation can be a formidable weapon when seeking to assert EU rights on behalf of an applicant against the mightier state or an employer. It is noteworthy that the arguments of legal counsel have had a significant influence on the development of the jurisprudence.[13]

This contribution will first, and very briefly, set out the UK's position in (with) the EU in the rest of this section before exploring the nature of its constitutional settlement including the relationship between UK law and EU law (section 2). The contribution then sets out the three different phases in the application of the principle of consistent interpretation by the UK judiciary (section 3). This provides the foundation for a more detailed exploration of how the UK courts have determined the scope of their duty and applied the principle of consistent interpretation (section 4). The final section focuses on two substantive areas of EU policy where the application of the principle of consistent interpretation in relation to certain EU rights has been more problematic (section 5) before some concluding remarks are made. At the time of writing, the UK remains a full member of the EU, but is engaged in negotiating its withdrawal from EU in accordance with Art. 50 TEU. Where appropriate and possible to do so at a time of great uncertainty, reference will be made to the UK's withdrawal from the EU and the future application of the principle of consistent interpretation in the UK courts.

1.1. THE UK AS A MEMBER STATE OF THE EUROPEAN UNION

In his famous Zurich Speech in 1946, Sir Winston Churchill, who had been the UK's Prime Minister during the Second World War, called for "a kind of United States of Europe" to secure peace, safety and freedom on mainland

12 Lord Mance (n. 6), 450.

13 See the impact of counsel's summary of the scope of the principle in *Vodafone 2 v. Revenue and Customs Commissioners* [2009] EWCA Civ 446, at paras. 37 and 38.

Europe. At that time, he did not envisage the UK being part of this political construct: the UK still had strong links with the Commonwealth. In 1960, the UK joined the European Free Trade Association (EFTA) with six other European states who were unable or unwilling to join the then European Economic Community (EEC).[14] The UK finally joined the original six Member States to become a member of the EEC on the 1 January 1973 at the same time as the Republic of Ireland and Denmark. Two previous attempts to join in 1961 and 1963 had been vetoed by France.[15] The UK, which consists of four countries, England, Wales, Scotland and Northern Ireland,[16] is one of the largest Member States of the EU with a population of just over 65 million.[17] To reflect its status, it has the same number of votes as France, Italy and Germany in the Council of the European Union[18] and 73 MEPs[19] in the European Parliament.

The UK's relationship with the EU has been complex and it has not followed the same path of integration as the other Member States. Some key developments are charted below. Not long after accession in 1973, a referendum was held on EU membership in 1975 resulting in a "yes" vote by 67 per cent with a 65 per cent turnout. In 1984, Margaret Thatcher, the British Prime Minster, successfully negotiated what has been termed the "UK rebate", a complex financial correction to the UK's annual contribution to the EU budget. In the negotiations leading up to the Maastricht Treaty, the UK secured opt-outs from Economic and Monetary Union (EMU) and the Social Chapter and was instrumental in incorporating the principle of subsidiarity into the Treaties to prevent "competence creep". The election of a new Labour Government in 1997 led to the adoption of the Social Chapter under the Treaty of Amsterdam and three opt-outs relating to the Area of Freedom, Security and Justice (AFSJ). A referendum was promised in the Labour Party manifesto on the

---

14 EFTA, an intergovernmental organisation, which promotes free trade and economic integration, was established in 1960 by Austria, Denmark, Norway, Portugal, Sweden, Switzerland and the United Kingdom. Finland became an associate member in 1961 and a full member in 1986. Iceland joined in 1970. Liechtenstein joined in 1991. Many members subsequently left to join the EU. Current membership comprises of Iceland, Norway, Liechtenstein and Switzerland. To participate in the EU's Single Market, Iceland, Liechtenstein and Norway are also members of the European Economic Area (EEA) and subject to the authority of the EFTA Surveillance Authority and EFTA Court. Switzerland has a bilateral agreement with the EU.

15 The French President Charles de Gaulle was suspicious of the UK's close relationship with the US.

16 Note that Great Britain (GB) refers to England, Wales and Scotland.

17 The UK's Office for National Statistics annual mid-year estimate released on 23 June 2016 stood at 65,110,000 as of 30 June 2015. <https://www.ons.gov.uk/peoplepopulationandcommunity/populationandmigration/populationestimates>.

18 29 votes each. See also the Committee of the Regions and the Economic and Social Committee with 24 votes each.

19 The 73 MEPs are divided as follows: Wales (4), Scotland (6), Northern Ireland (3) and England (60).

Constitutional Treaty 2004, but this was withdrawn once France and the Netherlands had failed to ratify the Treaty. A similar promise to offer a referendum was not pursued for the Treaty of Lisbon 2009.[20] The UK secured opt-ins in relation to the AFSJ and Schengen. A Protocol was agreed on the application of the EU Charter of Fundamental Rights in the UK courts.[21] With the new Conservative-Liberal Democrat Coalition Government 2010–2015, the European Union Act 2011 was passed, which requires any amendment to the TEU or Treaty on the Functioning of the EU (TFEU) made by Treaty, and any use of the *passerelle* provisions,[22] to be approved by an Act of Parliament at least, and that a referendum should be held in a number of cases where this would enlarge EU competence or reduce safeguards such as unanimous voting.[23]

1.2. THE UK'S EXIT FROM THE EUROPEAN UNION

In January 2013, the British Prime Minister, David Cameron delivered his "Bloomberg speech" in which he promised to seek renegotiation of the UK's membership of the EU and subsequently hold a referendum on UK membership if a Conservative Government was elected to office in 2015. This was indeed the case and the European Union Referendum Act 2015 was enacted committing to an advisory referendum to be held by the end of 2017.[24] In November 2015, David Cameron presented his proposals for renegotiation to the EU. These were accepted by Donald Tusk, President of the European Council, in February 2016. This arguably "minimalist" new settlement for the UK within the European Union centred on four themes: economic governance, competitiveness, sovereignty and immigration. A referendum was held on 23 June 2016 which asked voters whether they wished to remain as a member of the EU or leave the EU. It is no exaggeration that the result in which 51.9 per cent voted to

---

20 The European Union (Amendment) Act 2008 was enacted to give effect to the Treaty of Lisbon.

21 Protocol 30 which also applied to Poland.

22 A number of new *passerelle* provisions were inserted into the Treaties by the Treaty of Lisbon. They allow for revision of the voting requirements (e.g. from unanimity to QMV) or legislative procedures (from special legislative procedure to the ordinary legislative procedure) by the European Council or Council without having to resort to Treaty revision. The Treaties now contain a general *passerelle* provision (Art. 48(7) TEU) and six sectoral *passerelle* provisions (Art. 153(2), last subpara., TFEU; Art. 192(2) last subpara., TFEU; Art. 31(3) and (4) TEU; Art. 312(2) 2nd subpara., TFEU; Art. 81(3) TFEU; Art. 333 TFEU.

23 For consideration of the legal and political complexities of the Act, see P. Craig, "The European Union Act 2011: Locks, limits and legality" (2011) 48 *Common Market Law Review* 1915–44.

24 The Act did not contain any provisions setting out the procedure for leaving the EU if this was the result of the referendum vote.

leave and 48.1 per cent to remain with a 71.8 per cent[25] turnout sent shockwaves throughout the world and had immediate economic, political, constitutional, sociological, cultural and psychological ramifications for the four countries which make up the UK, with the potential for further tremors hitting the UK and rest of the EU for some time, probably years.

The UK will be the first Member State to leave the EU (often referred to as "Brexit"). Art. 50 TEU is the Treaty provision introduced by the Treaty of Lisbon which sets out the procedure for withdrawal by a Member State from the EU. Art. 50(1) TEU states that "Any Member State may decide to withdraw from the Union in accordance with its own constitutional requirements". In the aftermath of the referendum result, a legal vacuum was revealed in the UK constitutional settlement, and different political and legal views emerged as to the nature of the UK's "constitutional requirements" in this situation,[26] and the scope of parliamentary sovereignty. The UK Government considered that it had the power to invoke Art. 50 TEU and inform the European Council of its intention to withdraw from the EU triggering the negotiation process through the exercise of its prerogative (executive) powers in international affairs. This view was challenged successfully before the High Court of England and Wales in *Miller v. Secretary of State for Exiting the European Union.*[27] In a surprise decision, the court ruled that the Government could not proceed without the prior authorisation of Parliament.[28] A leap-frog appeal directly to the Supreme Court was permitted. In January 2017,[29] the Supreme Court upheld the decision of the High Court confirming that the Government could not trigger Art. 50 TEU unilaterally and needed the authority of the Westminster Parliament. However, it ruled that the consent of the three devolved assemblies was not required. The Government promptly introduced the European Union (Notification of Withdrawal) Bill 2017, a mere 133 words. It was passed by both Houses of Parliament and received Royal Assent on 16 March 2017. Its enactment paved the way for the Prime Minister to inform

25 More than 30 million people voted and it was the highest turnout in a UK-wide vote since the 1992 general election.

26 For a range of views, see S. Douglas-Scott, "Brexit, Article 50 and the contested British Constitution" (2016) 79(6) *Modern Law Review* 1019–40; R. Craig, "Casting aside clanking medieval chains: Prerogative statute and Article 50 after the EU referendum (2016) 79(6) *Modern Law Review* 1041–63; G. Phillipson, "A dive into deep constitutional waters: Article 50, the prerogative and Parliament" (2016) 79(6) *Modern Law Review* 1064–89.

27 *Miller v. Secretary of State for Exiting the EU* [2016] EWHC 2768 (Admin). The judgment was delivered on 3 November 2016, and its light of its huge importance, it was made available immediately online at <www.judiciary.gov.uk>.

28 Both parties in the proceedings agreed that it was not possible for Art. 50 TEU to be revoked once triggered. This common agreement was accepted by both the High Court and the Supreme Court, and no referral for a preliminary ruling was made to the ECJ under Article 267 TFEU.

29 The fully televised hearing was held for four days in December 2016: <www.supreme court.uk>.

the European Council on the 29 March 2017 of the UK's intention to leave the EU in accordance with Art. 50 TEU triggering the two-year timeframe for negotiating a withdrawal agreement by 29 March 2019. At the time of writing, this complex and highly political process is on-going, and a detailed account is outside the scope of this contribution.

2. THE UK AND ITS CONSTITUTIONAL SETTING

The constitutional setting of the UK has some unique characteristics which need to be considered in order to appreciate the context within which the principle of consistent interpretation has been applied by the UK judiciary, and to allow for comparison with the application of the principle in other Member States as set out in this volume.

2.1. A CONSTITUTIONAL MONARCHY

The UK can be characterised as having a constitutional monarchy similar to some other EU Member States: Belgium, Denmark, the Netherlands, Spain and Sweden.[30] The monarch is nominally the head of government, but the incumbent, currently Queen Elizabeth II, does not exercise any effective political power in reality.[31]

2.2. AN UNWRITTEN CONSTITUTION

One of the most striking characteristics of the UK's constitutional settlement is the absence of a codified constitution: there is no one document which sets out the authority of the main organs of government or the relationship between these organs or with the people. The UK is "virtually unique" in this respect[32] and it reflects "the absence of a historical break such as a civil war or independence" which elsewhere has normally led to a new written constitutional settlement.[33] That said, the UK does have a constitution in the much wider sense in that it has a whole system of government established and regulated by a collection of rules.[34] The system is founded on a complex mix of statutes, court judgments, constitutional principles, constitutional conventions and international treaties.

---

30 K. Syrett, *The Foundations of Public Law: Principles and Problems of Power in the British Constitution* (2nd ed., Palgrave, 2014), p. 132.

31 Ibid., p. 132.

32 Ibid., p. 9.

33 Ibid. Syrett also notes that although the English Civil War of the 1640s did see the adoption of two successive documents which could have been described as constitutions, these did not survive the restoration of the monarchy in 1660.

34 Bradley and Ewing, *Constitutional and Administrative Law* (14th ed., Pearson, 2007), p. 4.

The written constitution of the majority of the EU's Member States set out a number of key features including the division of tasks of government, whether unitary or federal, a list of fundamental rights beyond the reach of the organs of government and adhere to the separation of powers. In the UK, these gaps are filled by the doctrine of the legislative supremacy of Parliament and the rule of law. Fundamental rights protection was enhanced by the introduction of the Human Rights Act 1998. It made the fundamental rights set out in the European Convention on Human Rights (ECHR) legally enforceable before UK courts for the first time.

2.3. LEGISLATIVE SUPREMACY OR PARLIAMENTARY SOVEREIGNTY

The concept of legislative supremacy is of fundamental importance. It is also referred to as the doctrine of parliamentary sovereignty. Traditionally, Parliament is deemed to be the supreme law-maker. Importantly, this concept is encapsulated by the common law doctrine of implied repeal.[35] This means that any Act of Parliament may be changed by a subsequent Act on the same subject matter without the need to explicitly repeal the earlier statute. In essence, Parliament cannot bind it successors. This raises the question as to how the doctrine of parliamentary sovereignty can be reconciled with EU law, particularly where it has been well established by the ECJ that in the event of a conflict between EU and national law, EU law is supreme.[36] This is discussed below in section 2.6.

2.4. DEVOLUTION

The Blair Administration 1997 introduced devolution in Scotland and Wales and was committed to a peace deal for Northern Ireland under the terms of The Good Friday Agreement (1998). There are now three devolution settlements which differ quite considerably in nature, and which confer law-making powers on the Scottish Parliament, the Welsh Assembly and the Northern Ireland Assembly. The legislative power of Parliament can extend to all of the UK (or just to Great Britain or just to one or more of the countries within the UK).

The UK referendum on withdrawal from the EU has given rise to political tensions between the Westminster Government and its devolved counterparts. The majority of voters in England and (surprisingly) Wales voted to leave

---

35 *Ellen Street Estates v. Minister for Health* [1934] 1 KB 590.

36 Case 6/64 *Costa v. ENEL* [1964] ECR 585.

the EU.[37] In contrast, in both Scotland and Northern Ireland, the majority of the electorate voted to remain a member of the EU.[38]

2.5. A COMMON LAW SYSTEM

The UK, together with the Republic of Ireland, were the first countries with common law legal systems to join the EEC.[39] A common law system is where court judgments are a source of the constitution. It is accepted that judges make law through the development of the case-law. This judge-made law can take the form of common law (laws and customs declared to be law by judges since early times) and interpretation of statute law. Different rules on statutory interpretation have emerged from the case-law, including their interface with the EU principle of consistent interpretation. In accordance with the doctrine of precedent, the decisions of the superior courts are binding on inferior courts (and may bind other superior courts). It should be noted that within the hierarchy of legal norms, legislation takes precedence over common law because Parliament is supreme.[40]

There are three different legal systems in the UK. Scotland and Northern Ireland have their own legal systems/jurisdiction. At present, England and Wales have a combined legal jurisdiction, although there is a continuing debate about whether Wales should have a separate jurisdiction in view of the emergence of Welsh law post-devolution.[41]

The UK has a unitary court system,[42] but there are specialised courts and tribunals in the fields of employment, immigration, tax, intellectual property and competition which have all embraced the application of the principle of consistent interpretation.[43] The Supreme Court (since 2009, formerly the

---

37 England: Remain 46.6% (13,266,996); Leave 53.4% (15,188,406); Turnout 73%; Wales: Remain 47.5% (772,347); Leave 52.5% (854,572); Turnout 71.7%. The result in Wales came as a surprise to the political establishment since Wales is a net beneficiary of EU funding.

38 Scotland: Remain 62% (1,661,191); Leave 38% (1,018,322); Turnout 67.2%. Northern Ireland: Remain 55.8% (440,707); Leave 44.2% (349,442); Turnout 62.7%.

39 They have since been joined by Cyprus. Note that Scotland has a hybrid system which is a mix of common law and civil law elements.

40 Syrett (n. 30), p. 214.

41 See further, Alan Trench, "A legal jurisdiction for Wales?" at <www.devolution.matters.wordpress.com> accessed 06.11.17.

42 High Court of England and Wales, Court of Appeal of England and Wales, Supreme Court, Senior Courts in Northern Ireland (High Court and Court of Appeal) and Scotland (High Court of the Justiciary and Court of Sessions). Other jurisdictions: Isle of Man, Channel Islands, Privy Council – Commonwealth countries elect to use this body, whose members are made up of Supreme Court judges, as a final court of appeal.

43 Employment Appeal Tribunal, VAT and Duties Tribunal, Crown Court, Immigration Appeals Tribunal, employment tribunals, magistrates, Social Security Commissioner and specialist competition courts.

House of Lords) is the final and highest court in the UK (in all matters bar criminal law in Scotland). Only the higher courts (the High Court, Court of Appeal and Supreme Court in England and Wales) have powers of judicial review. There are some cases in which the principle of consistent interpretation has been applied in the Northern Irish and Scottish courts and the approach taken by the judiciary is the same.

2.6. THE RELATIONSHIP BETWEEN UK LAW AND INTERNATIONAL LAW (INCLUDING THE EU TREATIES AND THE EU ACQUIS)

The UK has a dualist system requiring an Act of Parliament to be adopted in order for an international treaty to have legal effect. The European Communities Act (EC Act) 1972 was enacted to give internal effect to EU law in the UK and has been amended on subsequent occasions to give effect to all the amendments to the original EEC Treaty. Section 2(1) states that:

> All such rights, powers, liabilities, obligations and restrictions from time to time created or arising by or under the Treaties, and all such remedies and procedures from time to time provided for by or under the Treaties, as in accordance with the Treaties are without further enactment to be given legal effect or used in the United Kingdom shall be recognised and available in law, and be enforced, allowed and followed accordingly; and the expression "enforceable Community right" and similar expressions shall be read as referring to one to which this subsection applies.

This provision makes the concept of direct applicability and direct effect part of UK law and places an obligation on the UK courts to enforce any directly effective EU measures without any further acts of implementation.

Section 2(2) provides for the implementation of EU obligations (such as directives), even where this requires national legislation and Acts of Parliament to be replaced by an Order in Council or statutory instrument rather than by primary legislation.

Section 3 amounts to a constitutional instruction to the domestic courts to act as "Union courts"[44] and renders judgments of the ECJ authoritative in the UK courts. It states that:

> For the purposes of all legal proceedings any question as to the meaning or effect of any of the Treaties, or as the validity, meaning or effect of any Community instrument, shall be treated as a question of law (and, if not referred to the European Court, be for

---

44 See T. Horsley, "Brexit and the UK courts" in M. Dougan (ed.), *The UK after Brexit: Legal and Policy Challenges* (Intersentia, 2017).

> determination as such in accordance with the principles laid down by and any relevant decision of the European Court or any court attached thereto).

There is no provision in the EC Act 1972 which declares that EU law is supreme in the event of a conflict. Instead, there is a "rule of construction" contained in s. 2(4). The relevant part states that "any enactment passed or to be passed [subject to certain exceptions] … shall be construed and have effect subject to the foregoing provisions of this section". This section, in conjunction with s. 2(1), has enabled the UK courts to interpret national law to comply with EU law.

In relation to the principle of consistent interpretation, Arden LJ in *IDT Card Services* stated that "The 1972 Act thus contains the mandate for the English courts to interpret domestic legislation in accordance with applicable Union directives".[45]

There has been considerable debate in the UK as to how parliamentary sovereignty can be reconciled with the supremacy of EU law. Prior to the *Factortame*[46] judgment of the House of Lords, the approach of the UK courts and the extent to which they felt bound to apply the principle of consistent interpretation was directly entwined with their view of parliamentary sovereignty, and is reflected in the first period of case-law identified in this contribution and discussed below (section 3.1). A direct conflict between the doctrine of parliamentary sovereignty and (putative) directly effective EU law rights emerged during the *Factortame* litigation and had been the subject of a preliminary ruling.[47] Lord Bridge famously stated that:

> Some public comments on the decision of the Court of Justice, affirming the jurisdiction of the courts of member states to override national legislation if necessary to enable interim relief to be granted in protection of rights under Community law, have suggested that this was a novel and dangerous invasion by a Community institution of the sovereignty of the United Kingdom Parliament. But such comments are based on a misconception. If the supremacy within the European Community of Community law over the national law of member states was not always inherent in the EEC Treaty it was certainly well established in the jurisprudence of the Court of Justice long before the United Kingdom joined the Community. Thus, whatever limitations of its sovereignty Parliament accepted when it enacted the European Communities Act 1972 was entirely voluntary. Under the terms of the 1972 Act it has always been clear that it was the duty of a United Kingdom court, when delivering final judgment,

---

45 *R (IDT Card Services Ireland Ltd) v. Customs and Excise Commissioners* [2006] EWCA Civ 29, at [74].

46 *Factortame Ltd v. Secretary of State for Transport* [1991] 1 AC 603.

47 Case C-213/89, *R v. Secretary of State for Transport, ex parte Factortame Ltd and Others* [1990] ECR I-2433.

> to override any rule of national law found to be in conflict with any directly enforceable rule of Community law. Similarly, when decisions of the Court of Justice have exposed areas of United Kingdom statute law which failed to implement Council directives, Parliament has always loyally accepted the obligation to make appropriate and prompt amendments. Thus there is nothing in any way novel in according supremacy to rules of Community law in those areas to which they apply and to insist that, in the protection of rights under Community law, national courts must not be inhibited by rules of national law from granting interim relief in appropriate cases is no more than a logical recognition of that supremacy.[48]

Thus, the conceptual basis for the acceptance of the supremacy of EU law lies with national constitutional law rather than an acceptance of the monist view of supremacy of the EU's Court of Justice.[49] EU law is supreme over conflicting national law on the basis of the Parliament's enactment of the EC Act 1972.

In the subsequent case of *Thoburn*,[50] (also known as the "Metric Martyrs case"), Laws LJ considered that some statutes have special significance. These so-called "constitutional statutes" are not subject to the doctrine of *implied* repeal (discussed earlier) and must be *expressly* repealed in a later statute with the clear intention of Parliament. This approach was confirmed by the Supreme Court in its *HS2* judgment.[51] The EC Act 1972 and HRA, as well as the statutes setting out devolution are considered to fall within this category of "constitutional statutes" and must be expressly repealed by Parliament.

2.7. THE STATUS OF EU LAW FOLLOWING THE UK'S WITHDRAWAL FROM THE EU

Withdrawal from the EU requires Parliament to expressly repeal the EC Act 1972. The Prime Minister, Theresa May, announced plans for a "Great Repeal Bill" at the Conservative Party Conference in October 2016 which would repeal the EC Act 1972 on the date that any withdrawal agreement with the EU comes into force. The Government introduced the European Union (Withdrawal) Bill to Parliament in July 2017. It received Royal Assent on 26 June 2018. The main aim of the Act is to put in a place a legal framework which will maximise legal

48 Ibid., 658.

49 See P. Craig and G. de Búrca, *EU Law: Text, Cases and Materials* (6th ed., Oxford University Press, 2015), p. 300.

50 *Thoburn v. Sunderland City Council* [2003] QB 151.

51 *R (HS2 Action Alliance Ltd) v. Secretary of State for Transport* [2014] UKSC 3, [79], [203]–[205]. See further P. Craig, "Constitutionalizing constitutional law: HS2" [2014] *Public Law* 373; M. Elliott, "Constitutional legislation, European Union law and the nature of the United Kingdom's contemporary constitution" (2014) 10 *European Constitutional Law Review* 379.

certainty on the day that the UK leaves the EU (exit day). In summary, the key features of the Act are as follows:

- It repeals the EC Act 1972 on exit day.
- It incorporates the EU acquis in force in the UK on exit day into national law.
- It grants delegated powers to Ministers to amend/repeal retained EU law which does not operate effectively or is deemed deficient.
- It allows the UK Government to freeze the power for the devolved assemblies to amend retained EU law.
- It removes the jurisdiction of the Court of Justice of the European Union.
- It removes the general principle of supremacy of EU law.
- It removes the EU Charter of Fundamental Rights.
- The principle of state liability will expire two years after exit day.

In November 2017, the Minister for Exiting the European Union announced that a separate Withdrawal Agreement and Implementation Bill would be enacted in order to give effect to the final Withdrawal Agreement between the UK and the EU in domestic law including any implementation (or transition) period that is agreed.

It is unsurprising that huge political and constitutional controversy afflicts each stage of the UK's exit from the EU.[52] Withdrawal from the EU represents a new chapter in the history of the UK. It requires the UK's constitutional framework to be re-drawn and new relationships with the EU and non-EU States to be forged. This will not only pave the way for the "de-Europeanisation" of UK law, but also the development of new regulatory frameworks. In the 2017 Queen's Speech, the UK Government announced that it would introduce a number of Bills to re-regulate key policy areas such as immigration and trade in order to ensure that the UK "makes a success of Brexit".[53]

3. THE APPLICATION OF THE PRINCIPLE OF CONSISTENT INTERPRETATION IN THE UK COURTS

It has been asserted by Sir Rupert Cross that the approach of members of the judiciary to statutory interpretation at any one time will reflect their own

52 Over 400 amendments to the Bill were tabled by parliamentarians as it proceeded through the House of Commons.

53 The Queen's Speech 2017 includes proposals for a Customs Bill, Trade Bill, Immigration Bill, Fisheries Bill, Agriculture Bill, Nuclear Safeguards Bill and International Sanctions Bill.

perception of their constitutional role.[54] This study identifies three phases in the application of the principle of consistent interpretation by the UK courts.

3.1. PHASE ONE: INITIAL REACTION OF THE UK COURTS POST-*VON COLSON*

This first phase illustrated the challenge facing the judiciary and its approach to statutory interpretation where there was a conflict between a literal reading of national law and EU law. Where the national law at issue had been enacted expressly by Parliament to give effect to EU law, the UK courts followed the *Von Colson* judgment and interpreted national law to comply with the later EU law. The principle was first applied by the House of Lords in *Pickstone v. Freemans plc* in 1989,[55] to bring the Equal Pay Act 1970 which had been amended by the Equal Pay (Amendments) Regulations[56] in line with the (broader) interpretation of the principle of equal pay enshrined in Art. 157 TFEU[57] and fleshed out in Directive 75/117 (the "Equal Pay Directive"). The use of the principle was confirmed by the House of Lords in *Litster* in 1990[58] in which the TUPE (the Transfer of Undertakings (Protection of Employment)) Regulations 1981) had been expressly enacted to give effect to Directive 77/187 (the "Acquired Rights Directive").[59] The House of Lords had no qualms in adapting the national law to give effect to the Directive and where necessary "implying words which would achieve that effect".[60]

In contrast, and at the same time, the House of Lords refused to interpret *pre-existing national legislation* to comply with EU law that had been enacted at a later date. While the court recognised the interpretative duty, in both *Duke v. GEC Reliance* in 1988[61] and *Finnegan v. Clowney Youth Training Programme Ltd* in 1990,[62] the House of Lords denied any role to the Equal Treatment Directive 76/207 in the interpretation of the Sex Discrimination Act 1975 because it had been adopted *after* the enactment of the Act of Parliament,

---

54 J. Bell and G. Engle (eds.), *Cross's Statutory Interpretation* (3rd ed., Butterworths, 1995), p. 10.

55 [1989] AC 66.

56 The Equal Pay Act 1970 had been amended by the Equal Pay (Amendment) Regulations 1983 in order to bring UK law in line with EU law. The Regulations had been presented to Parliament as intending to give effect to the ECJ's ruling in Case 61/81, *Commission v. UK* where the ECJ had ruled that the UK law did not comply with EU law in place.

57 Previously Art. 119 EEC and Art. 141 EC.

58 *Litster and Others v. Forth Dry Dock & Engineering Co Ltd (In Receivership) and Another* [1990] 1 AC 546.

59 This provides for the safeguarding of employees' rights on the transfer of a business.

60 Indeed, the House of Lords implied words into the national regulations.

61 [1988] 1 All ER 626.

62 [1990] 2 AC 407.

even though the UK accepted that the 1975 Act represented fulfilment of its obligations under the 1976 Directive.[63] As a consequence of this policy by the UK courts (and the lack of horizontal direct effect of directives), in both cases the female employees were denied their EU rights as they were unable to rely on the Directive against their *private* employer's retirement policy which they claimed was discriminatory. These gaps in the protection of individuals' EU rights were compounded by a failure to refer to the ECJ for a preliminary ruling under Art. 267 TFEU. Docksey and Fitzpatrick argued that "the House of Lords has ensnared itself in a principle of statutory interpretation which is entirely, [and now after ... *Marleasing*,] erroneously dependent upon notions of parliamentary intent which are inconsistent with the principle of supremacy of Community law".[64] For them, the House of Lords had failed to appreciate that a new canon of construction had been introduced by the ECJ in *Von Colson* which overrides both constitutional limitations and the doctrine of *stare decisis*[65] and which takes precedence over other canons of interpretation.[66] It is for this reason that the judiciary entered into a second phase in its relationship with the principle of consistent interpretation.

3.2. PHASE TWO: ACCEPTANCE OF THE PRINCIPLE POST-*MARLEASING*

Following the judgment of the House of Lords in *Factortame* in October 1990 and the ECJ's ruling in *Marleasing* the following month, in which it expressly confirmed that the interpretative obligation set out in *Von Colson* applied to *pre-existing* national law, the full scope of the obligation as a method of statutory interpretation being accepted by the UK judiciary can be seen. This is illustrated by the House of Lords 1993 decision in *Webb (No. 2) v. EMO Air Cargo (UK) Ltd*,[67] a legal dispute between two private parties involving the correct interpretation of the Equal Treatment and Pregnancy Directives. Following a referral to the Court of Justice,[68] the House of Lords interpreted the Sex Discrimination Act 1975 to include direct discrimination on the grounds of pregnancy. Significantly, the House of Lords was required to ignore any reference to a male comparator in discrimination cases, as required by national law. This was despite the fact that the Court of Appeal had earlier considered

[63] Ibid., 115.

[64] C. Docksey and B. Fitzpatrick, "The duty of national courts to interpret provisions of national law in accordance with Community Law" (1991) 20 *Industrial Law Journal* 113.

[65] A. Arnull, "The incoming tide: Responding to *Marshall*" (1987) *Public Law* 383.

[66] Ibid., p. 117.

[67] [1993] 1 CMLR 259, at paras. 19–21 (Lord Keith of Kinkel).

[68] Case C-32/93, *Webb v. EMO Air Cargo (UK) Ltd* [1994] ECR I-3567.

that this could only be achieved "by distorting the meaning of the British statute",[69] a view not expressly rejected by the House of Lords prior to making a reference.

3.3. PHASE THREE: IMPACT OF SECTION 3 OF THE HUMAN RIGHTS ACT 1998

A third phase can be identified in the approach of the UK courts since the House of Lords 2004 judgment in *Ghaidan v. Godin-Mendoza.*[70] This case concerned the scope of another new interpretative obligation placed on UK courts by s. 3 of the Human Rights Act 1998 (HRA), which requires UK legislation to be interpreted in a manner which is compliant with the HRA.[71] The House of Lords considered at length the scope of the interpretative obligation set out in s. 3 and drew parallels with the EU principle of consistent interpretation. Lord Steyn referred expressly to the fact that the drafters had modelled s. 3 on the EU interpretative obligation.[72] He also recalled the judgments of the House of Lords in *Pickstone* and *Litster* to illustrate the strength of the interpretative obligation.[73] For Lord Rodger, it was significant that Parliament had adopted the same wording for the HRA as that expounded by the Court of Justice in *Marleasing* and he considered that the judiciary should follow a similar approach to that adopted in *Pickstone* and *Litster*. Consequently, *Ghaidan* is now seen by the judiciary as the leading authority on the EU principle of consistent interpretation in the UK courts. In its 2014 decision in *Jessemey v. Rowstock Ltd*, the Court of Appeal referred to the fact that the decision of the House of Lords in *Ghaidan* amounts to an "assimilation" of the interpretative obligations set out in *Marleasing* and s. 3 HRA.[74]

This assimilation is interesting given that there are differences in the construction and operation of the interpretative obligations. The EU principle of consistent interpretation is a judge-made constitutional principle of EU law established by the ECJ. It does not have an explicit legal basis in the Treaties, but the Court has based its reasoning on the rule of law, Art. 4(3) TEU (together with Art. 288 TFEU), the principle of *effet utile*, and in *Pfeiffer*, it even went as far as to say that the duty was "inherent in the system of the [Treaties]".[75]

---

69 *Webb v. EMO Air Cargo (UK) Ltd* [1992] 1 CMLR 793, para. 53.
70 [2004] UKHL 30, [2004] 2 AC 557.
71 There is also a duty to ensure that all new law enacted is compliant with the HRA.
72 Per Lord Steyn, para. 45.
73 Per Lord Steyn, para. 48.
74 Per Underhill LJ, para. 40.
75 Joined Cases C-397/01–403/01, *Pfeiffer* [2004] ECR I-8835. See further, S. Drake, "Twenty years after *Von Colson*: The impact of 'indirect effect' on the protection of the individual's Community rights" (2005) 30 *European Law Review* 329–48.

The ECJ has recognised its limitations, particularly where it may conflict with general principles of law (e.g. non-retroactivity in criminal matters),[76] or where an outcome compliant with EU law would require the court to overstep its interpretative role and venture into the domain of policy-making which would be contrary to the doctrine of the separation of powers. In *Wagner Miret*, the ECJ implied that a national court is not required to interpret national law *contra legem*.[77]

In contrast, the HRA was enacted by Parliament in 1998 to enable national courts to give effect to the ECHR and came into force in 2000. An election manifesto commitment of the Blair Administration, it required national courts to interpret national law "as far as possible" in compliance with the ECHR. Where an interpretation is not "possible" under s. 3, the national court[78] has a discretionary power to make a "declaration of incompatibility". It is then for Parliament to remedy any failure of compliance on the part of national law with the "Convention right" set out in the HRA. The legislation in question remains valid and there is no obligation on Parliament to take any action.[79] Thus, in direct contrast to directly effective EU law under the EC Act 1972 (and more recently the EU Charter of Fundamental Rights), national courts do not have the power to set aside primary legislation emanating from the Westminster Parliament, only devolved legislation. O'Cinneide describes the HRA as achieving a "delicate constitutional balance: it leaves parliamentary sovereignty intact, while modifying the legal framework which governs how British courts interpret and give effect to primary legislation".[80]

To date, the courts have refuted any arguments put forward by legal counsel which try to differentiate between the two methods of interpretation in terms of their scope. It is suggested that the extent to which the principle of consistent interpretation has been embedded in the practice of the UK courts reflects the fact that the judiciary are more comfortable anchoring a method of statutory interpretation derived from EU law, with its contested legal basis and fluid nature, to a national method which has a statutory basis in an Act of Parliament. The national courts are impliedly reinforcing the view of the centrality of the Parliament in the UK constitutional system, particularly in determining the UK's relationship with the EU.

---

76 Case 80/86, *Kolpinghuis Nijmegen* [1987] ECR 3969.

77 Case C-334/92, *Wagner Miret* [1993] ECR I-6911.

78 Not all of them.

79 Nevertheless, it is intended that Parliament respond to the declaration of incompatibility. The HRA makes provision for the offending legislation to be amended by a fast-track parliamentary procedure: s. 10 of, and Sched. 2 to, the Act. It is important to note that a declaration of incompatibility does not prevent an individual from pursuing their claim in Strasbourg in an attempt to seek a determination from the European Court of Human Rights that the UK has breached the European Convention on Human Rights.

80 Ibid., 82. For an insight into the drafting of the HRA, see F. Klug, *Values for a Godless Age: The Story of the UK's New Bill of Rights* (Penguin, 2000).

3.4. PHASE FOUR: THE APPLICATION OF THE PRINCIPLE OF CONSISTENT INTERPRETATION POST-BREXIT

Since the UK's withdrawal from the EU will entail the express repeal of the EC Act 1972, the current mandate on the UK judiciary to interpret national law to comply with EU law will disappear. There is no doubt that a fourth phase in the application of the principle of consistent interpretation by the UK judiciary will emerge post-Brexit. It is argued that this will be predicated on the judiciary's understanding of Parliament's intention as expressed in the EU (Withdrawal) Act 2018. It is possible to discern some broad guidance on how the national courts should interpret "retained EU law" in the Act itself.

The EU (Withdrawal) Act provides for the EU acquis which is in force in the UK on exit day to be retained in the UK legal order. This "nationalised" law will be called "retained EU law". It includes directly applicable law including regulations, decisions, delegated and implementing acts, domestic law enacted to give effect to EU directives, and directly effective (Treaty) rights. It also includes the jurisprudence of the ECJ as on exit day, and general principles of EU law as recognised by the ECJ. The Act expressly excludes the application of the principle of supremacy to any law made on or after exit day, but it continues to apply in the event of a conflict between national law and retained EU law. The Act expressly excludes the EU Charter of Fundamental Rights and the principle of state liability has been strictly curtailed. Despite giving the appearance that the existing EU acquis will be retained providing legal certainty, it is highly likely that it will be substantially amended to give effect to the Withdrawal Agreement, either through primary or secondary legislation.

One major concern has been the potential loss of rights which have been enjoyed by individuals as a result of the UK's membership of the EU. The Act expressly provides that directly effective rights in force before exit day will remain part of UK law. However, the Act expressly excludes rights which are derived from EU directives and which are "not of a kind" recognised by the ECJ or a national court in a case decided before exit day. This clause could limit the protection of individuals' rights if interpreted as meaning that provisions which are sufficiently clear and precise to be justiciable may not be enforceable by an individual *simply because this status had not yet been recognised by the ECJ or national court on exit day.*

The Act, when read in conjunction with the Explanatory Notes, includes a new mandate for the national judges to continue to apply the principle of consistent interpretation when interpreting retained EU law. The Explanatory Notes state that:

> The principle of supremacy … means that domestic law must be interpreted, as far as possible, in accordance with EU law. So, for example, domestic law must be interpreted, as far as possible, in light of the wording and purpose of relevant

> directives. Whilst this duty will not apply to domestic legislation passed or made on or after exit day, subsection (2) preserves this duty in relation to domestic legislation passed or made before exit.[81]

The Act also states that the principle of supremacy (and, it is argued the principle of consistent interpretation), applies to pre-exit law which is amended on or after exit day if that is the intention of the modifications. This would be in keeping with the UK courts' approach to statutory interpretation which is to give effect to Parliament's intention.

The Explanatory Notes state further that when interpreting retained EU law, national court can adopt

> … a purposive approach to interpretation where the meaning of the measure is unclear (i.e. considering the purpose of the law from looking at other relevant documents such as treaty legal base for a measure, its recitals and preambles, and the '*travaux preparatoires*' (working papers) leading to the adoption of the measure). It also means applying an interpretation that renders the provision of EU law compatible with the treaties and general principles of EU law. Non-binding instruments, such as recommendations and opinions, would still be available to a court to assist with interpretation of retained EU law after exit. In these circumstances, the principle of supremacy continues to apply to EU retained law *enacted before exit day*.[82]

Pre-Brexit case-law of the ECJ will be considered binding precedent for the lower courts. The Supreme Court will not be bound to follow retained EU case-law, but if it wishes to depart from it, it must follow the same (strict) rules that apply when it wishes to depart from one of its own precedents.

There is less certainty with regard to the status of the post-Brexit case-law of the ECJ. This jurisprudence will no longer bind the UK courts, and they will not be able to request a preliminary ruling from the ECJ if they require assistance in interpreting retained EU law. The original version of the Bill permitted national courts to refer to ECJ case-law if it considers it "appropriate to do so". In response to calls for clearer instructions by senior members of the judiciary[83] and legal scholars,[84] the Government agreed to amend the text to state that national courts could refer to ECJ judgments where "relevant." There was clearly a concern

---

81 Explanatory Notes, at para. 104.

82 Explanatory Notes, at para. 111. Para. 112 states that the UK courts will also be required to interpret retained EU law by reference to the limits of the EU competence.

83 Lord Neuberger (out-going President of the Supreme Court), "UK judges need clarity after Brexit", *BBC News*, 8 August 2017; Lady Hale (incoming President of the Supreme Court), "UK's new supreme court chief calls for clarity on ECJ after Brexit", *The Guardian*, 8 October 2017.

84 T. Horsley, "In (domestic) courts we trust: The European Union (Withdrawal) Bill and the interpretation of retained EU law" *UK Constitutional Law Blog* (27 November 2017). Available at <https://ukconstitutionallaw.org>.

that any reference to judgments of the ECJ by the UK judiciary, however "appropriate" from a legal perspective, could be deemed politically unacceptable.

4. THE SCOPE OF THE DUTY OF CONSISTENT INTERPRETATION IN THE UK COURTS

4.1. STATUTORY INTERPRETATION IN THE UK COURTS

Historically, three common law methods of statutory interpretation have evolved before the UK courts: (a) the literal rule in which the normal meaning is conferred on the statutory words; (b) the golden rule which starts with a literal approach, but it is amended if the result would be absurd or inconsistent with the rest of the statute; (c) the mischief rule whereby the court identifies a deficiency (or "mischief") in the law and interprets the rule to stop the mischief reoccurring.[85] More contemporary practice also incorporates a fourth method, (d) the purposive approach where if the wording is unclear or ambiguous,[86] the contested provision(s) should "be read in the context of the statute as a whole, and the statute as a whole should be read in the historical context of the situation which led to its enactment".[87] In *Pepper v. Hart*,[88] the House of Lords ruled that a broad range of materials may be taken into account to ascertain the true meaning of a provision as intended by Parliament, including the official record of parliamentary proceedings in *Hansard* subject to certain limitations.[89]

The principle of consistent interpretation derived from EU law is seen as *additional* to the standard rules on statutory interpretation which have developed through the case-law. It is also broader and more flexible going beyond the limitations set out in *Pepper v. Hart*, and may apply even if the national law is not ambiguous.[90] It has been considered by Arden LJ to be the standard approach to interpreting legislation enacted to give effect to international treaties.[91]

---

85 Syrett (n. 30), p. 215. For a brief discussion of their evolution, see *Cross* (n. 55), Chapter 1.

86 This adoption of the purposive approach followed a proposal made by the Law Commission in 1969 following a review of statutory interpretation: *The Interpretation of Statutes* (Law Com no 21; Scottish Law Com no 11).

87 See Lord Bingham in *R (Quintavalle) v. Secretary of State for Health* [2003] 1 AC 687, para. 8.

88 [1993] AC 593.

89 Parliamentary materials (which are limited to clear statements by the minister or other promoters of the Bill directed to the very point in question in the litigation) are admissible only where (1) the question in issue between the parties is the true construction of a provision in the relevant statute; (2) the provision is ambiguous or obscure or its literal meaning leads to an absurdity; or (3) the statements are directed to the specific statutory provision under consideration.

90 *Three Rivers District Council v. Governor of the Bank of England (No. 2)* [1996] 2 All ER 363, per Clarke J.

91 Arden LJ in *IDT Card Services Ireland Ltd v. Customs and Excise Commissioners* [2006] EWCA Civ 29, at para. 75.

The most recent UK cases refer to *Pfeiffer*[92] and accept the full scope of the obligation imposed on them under EU law. In the latter case, the ECJ clearly stated that the interpretative obligation applies not only to national law that implements the directive, but to the national legal system as a whole. It held that to ensure that a directive is fully effective: "… the principle of interpretation in conformity with Community law thus requires the referring court to do *whatever lies within its jurisdiction, having regard to the whole body of rules of national law.*"[93]

The UK courts also adopt a number of presumptions when engaging in statutory interpretation including the principle of legality which assumes that legislation created by Parliament is in accordance with the rule of law and does not infringe fundamental principles of constitutional or administrative law. It is now accepted that there is a parallel presumption that assumes that legislation is adopted to comply with international treaties and EU law (unless there is an express intention to the contrary).[94]

There has been some confusion in the UK case-law before the Supreme Court on the application of the *Pupino* variant of the principle of consistent interpretation.[95] In *Assange*,[96] the Supreme Court found that the *Pupino* judgment was not binding on UK courts and could not be applied to interpret national law (Extradition Act 2003) in line with the European Arrest Warrant (EAW) Framework Decision despite having been applied in previous decisions of the final court in *Dabas* and *Calderelli*.[97] The EAW had been adopted under Title VI of the Third Pillar, and had not been given effect under s. 2 of the EC Act 1972. At the time, it constituted an intergovernmental measure subject to domestic methods of statutory interpretation including the presumption that Parliament has legislated to give full effect to the UK's international legal obligations. So while the adoption of the domestic approach did not change

92 Cases C-397-403/01, *Pfeiffer* [2004] ECR I-8835.

93 Ibid., para. 118. Emphasis added.

94 *Assange v. Swedish Prosecution Authority* [2012] UKSC 22.

95 Case C-105/3, *Criminal proceedings against Pupino* [2005] ECR I-5285. In this case, the ECJ extended the principle of consistent interpretation to Framework Decisions which had been enacted under the Third Pillar in accordance with Art. 34(2)(b) TEU, an analogous provision to Art. 249 EC (now Art. 288 TFEU) which defines the characteristics of directives. The ECJ based the obligation on the principle of loyalty set out in Art. 10 EC (now Art. 4(3) TEU). The judgment was of significant constitutional importance as the Member States had expressly prohibited Framework Decisions from having direct effect. See M. Fletcher, "Extending 'indirect effect' to the third pillar: the significance of *Pupino*?" (2005) 30(6) *European Law Review* 862–77.

96 *Assange v. Swedish Prosecution Authority* [2012] UKSC 22, per Lord Mance, paras. 198–218.

97 *Dabas v. High Court of Justice in Madrid, Spain* [2007] 2 AC 31, per Lord Bingham at para. 5; *Calderelli v. Judge of Preliminary Investigations of the Court of Naples, Italy* [2008] UKHL 51, per Lord Bingham at para. 22.

the outcome of the case itself, it reveals the constitutional complexities arising from the UK's differentiated integration with the EU in some policy areas.[98]

4.2. METHODOLOGY OF THE UK COURTS IN CASES INVOLVING EU LAW

It is important at the outset to understand the approach of the national judge when engaging in interpretation in a case involving EU law. First, the judge will be required to ascertain the correct meaning of the EU source of law at issue. This may (but not always) require a reference under Art. 267 TFEU to the ECJ if the meaning is unclear.[99]

It is at the second stage that the national judge will need to give effect to EU law. Early on in the UK literature, Docksey and Fitzpatrick argued that the principle of consistent interpretation should be the first obligation that the national court must address.[100] It is only if it fails that resort should be had to direct effect.[101] They concluded that "… the application of the indirect effect principle can be perceived as the natural basis upon which the rights in a directive reach Community citizens. It can also be seen as a significant alternative to direct effect, given that it is untrammelled by the vertical/horizontal effect distinction".[102] However, in general, the approach of the UK courts is to first consider whether the application of direct effect is possible before turning to the principle of consistent interpretation. In later cases, there tends to be no mention of the doctrine of direct effect if the dispute arises between two private parties.[103]

For the most part, the UK courts have embraced their EU interpretative duty and have not referred questions to the ECJ specifically on the scope of the principle itself. For the UK courts, the focus is very much on achieving an EU-compliant outcome rather than on the process of interpretation itself.[104] Further, following a preliminary ruling on an interpretation of a substantive provision, the national courts have followed the interpretation set out by the ECJ. There is some evidence in the case-law that where possible, judges may

98 Post-Lisbon, and following the expiry of the transitional five-year period in Protocol 36, the UK opted-in to the European Arrest Warrant (along with 34 other police and criminal justice measures) on 1 December 2014, and currently accepts the full jurisdiction of the Court of Justice and the sanctioning power of the European Commission under Art. 258 TFEU.

99 Case 283/81, *CILFIT* [1982] ECR I-3415.

100 C. Docksey and B. Fitzpatrick, "The duty of national courts to interpret provisions of national law in accordance with Community Law" (1991) 20 (2) *Industrial Law Journal* 113–120.

101 Ibid., 117–18.

102 Ibid. 118.

103 See e.g. *Attridge*, *Jessemey* and *Google*.

104 See discussion of the "process-product" dichotomy in the Dutch report.

determine that it is more legitimate to adopt a national statutory method of interpretation, as was the case in *White v. White* (discussed in section 5). It is not clear why this is the case, although it was suggested in *Jessemey* obiter by Underhill LJ that this would avoid future litigation, for example, where a dispute arises over the same part of the statute but in a domestic only case which would need to be re-litigated.

4.3. THE RELATIONSHIP BETWEEN THE EU DUTY OF CONSISTENT INTERPRETATION AND SECTION 3 HRA

It is in determining the scope of the obligation of the duty of consistent interpretation that an "assimilation" with the approach adopted under s. 3 of the HRA can be seen. A summary given by legal counsel on the scope of the duty was approved by Sir Andrew Morritt C in the Court of Appeal in *Vodafone 2 v. Revenue and Customs Commissioners*[105] and has since become the principal reference point for the judiciary.[106] It was endorsed by the Supreme Court in *Swift*[107] and *Nolan*.[108] It stated that:

> In summary, the obligation on the English courts to construe domestic legislation consistently with Community law obligations is both broad and far-reaching. In particular:
>
> (a) It is not constrained by conventional rules of construction (per Lord Oliver in *Pickstone* at 126B);
> (b) It does not require ambiguity in the legislative language (per Lord Oliver in *Pickstone* at 126B; Lord Nicholls in *Ghaidan* at 32);
> (c) It is not an exercise in semantics or linguistics (see *Ghaidan* per Lord Nicholls at 31 and 35; Lord Steyn at 48–49; Lord Rodger at 110–115);
> (d) It permits departure from the strict and literal application of the words which the legislature has elected to use (per Lord Oliver in *Litster* at 577A; Lord Nicholls in *Ghaidan* at 31);
> (e) It permits the implication of words necessary to comply with Community law obligations (per Lord Templeman in *Pickstone* at 120H–121A; Lord Oliver in *Litster* at 577A); and
> (f) The precise form of the words to be implied does not matter (per Lord Keith in *Pickstone* at 112D; Lord Rodger in *Ghaidan* at para. 122; Arden LJ in *IDT Card Services*, at 114).

105 [2009] EWCA Civ 446, paras. 37–38.

106 The summary is restated in full by Underhill LJ in the Court of Appeal in 2014 in *Jessemey v. Rowstock Ltd* [2014] 3 CMLR 24.

107 *Swift v. Robinson* [2014] UKSC 50.

108 *United States of America v. Nolan* [2015] UKSC 63.

It is also clear to the UK judiciary that it is for them to determine whether or not domestic legislation can be interpreted in a way which conforms with the applicable EU law.[109] Limitations on this interpretative duty are recognised by the national judiciary, and these are a matter for the national court. In *Vodafone 2 v. Revenue and Customs Commissioners*, it was held that:

> The only constraints on the broad and far-reaching nature of the interpretative obligation are that:
>
> (a) The meaning should "go with the grain of the legislation" and be "compatible with the underlying thrust of the legislation being construed." (per Lord Nicholls in *Ghaidan* at 33; Dyson LJ in *EB Central Services*, at 81). An interpretation should not be adopted which is inconsistent with a fundamental or cardinal feature of the legislation since this would cross the boundary between interpretation and amendment; (see *Ghaidan* per Lord Nicholls at 33; Lord Rodger at 110–113; Arden LJ in *IDT Card Services* at 82 and 113) and
> (b) The exercise of the interpretative obligation cannot require the courts to make decisions for which they are not equipped or give rise to important practical repercussions which the court is not equipped to evaluate. (See *Ghaidan* per Lord Nicholls at 33; Lord Rodger at 115; Arden LJ in *IDT Card Services* at 113.)

4.4. APPLICATION OF THE DUTY IN PRACTICE

The strong interpretative obligation set out in EU law has led the UK courts to what may seem to some to be surprising results. To illustrate the strength and lengths to which the UK courts are prepared to interpret national law, a few examples are given. What is clear is that (i) the principle is applied in parallel with s. 3 of the HRA and (ii) the scope of the duty is broader and more flexible than methods of interpretation set out in national law. Lord Mance, writing extra-judicially, considers that the *Marleasing* principle goes beyond the domestic (common) law presumptions, and allows a "quite radical reading in, out or down of words in legislation in the field of EU law".[110]

4.4.1. Writing New Provisions into a Statute

When exercising their interpretative duty, national courts are permitted to add words to a statute which are not there. This is not considered by the

109 See *IDT Card Services Ireland Ltd v. Customs and Excise Commissioners* [2006] EWCA Civ 29.
110 Ibid.

UK judiciary as going beyond a court's interpretative role (i.e. interpretation *contra legem*) as long as the interpretation is consistent with the "grain" of the legislation (discussed below). It was evident from the earliest phase that the House of Lords[111] considered it within its remit to imply the words necessary to construe national law in accordance with EU law. The *Litster* case concerned the correct interpretation of Acquired Rights Directive[112] which safeguards the rights of employees when their employer's undertaking is transferred to another company. The UK implementing legislation protected persons who were "employed immediately before the transfer". The employer in question had become insolvent and had entered receivership. At issue was whether the national provision set out above covered employees who were dismissed by receivers one hour before the transfer. The House of Lords held that, to give effect to the underlying directive as interpreted by the Court of Justice, there had to be read into the words "a person so employed immediately before the transfer" the words "or who would have been so employed if he had not been unfairly dismissed in the circumstances described in regulation 8(1)".[113] A literal interpretation would not suffice. In other words, the House of Lords made a significant change to the wording of the legislation by adding words that were not there, even where the wording of national law was not ambiguous. Arden LJ later noted that this would not be possible under purely domestic law and would probably be regarded as "impermissible judicial legislation."[114]

Moving to our third phase, the judgment in *EBR Attridge Law LLP v. Coleman*[115] is a good example of how far the national courts are willing to go to give full effect to EU law. In this case, the national court was prepared to write a new paragraph into the statute in order to give full effect to the principle of non-discrimination on grounds of disability in a dispute between an employee and her employer.

Mrs Coleman worked for a law firm and was the principal carer for her disabled son. She had resigned from her post claiming that she had been the victim of unlawful discrimination by her employer on account of her son's disability (so-called "associative discrimination"). Mrs Coleman brought legal proceedings in 2005 against her employer for unlawful discrimination contrary to the Disability Discrimination Act 1995 (DDA) and unfair dismissal. The DDA did not apply to associative discrimination, but Mrs Coleman argued the statute should be construed to include associative discrimination which, in her view, was unlawful under Directive 2000/78, which establishes a general

---

111 *Litster v. Forth Dry Dock & Engineering Co Ltd* [1990] 1 AC 546.

112 Directive 77/187/EEC.

113 *Litster v. Forth Dry Dock & Engineering Co Ltd* [1990] 1 AC 546, at 577.

114 *IDT Card Services Ireland Ltd v. Customs and Excise Commissioners* [2006] EWCA Civ 29, Arden LJ.

115 *EBR Attridge Law LLP v. Coleman* [2010] 1 CMLR 28.

framework for equal treatment and occupation (the "Framework Directive").[116] The DDA had been amended to give effect to the Framework Directive with effect from 1 October 2004.[117]

The Employment Tribunal (ET) referred the matter to the ECJ[118] which confirmed that the effectiveness of the Directive would be undermined if it did not outlaw associative discrimination.[119] On return to the ET, and in line with her original decision, the judge was of the view that the DDA could be interpreted to give effect to the Directive by "supplying words if necessary" unless it contained "an express and unambiguous indication to the contrary".[120]

This judgment was appealed to the Employment Appeal Tribunal (EAT) on the grounds that (a) the judge had "distorted and rewritten" the DDA by reading in words to render associative discrimination unlawful; and (b) the judge had erred in stating that the duty to interpret applied from the date that the UK had given effect to the Directive through the enactment of amending legislation (1 October 2004) and that any duty arose only after the final and extended date for implementation of the Directive which was later (2 December 2006). In their view, this date had not passed at the time of the alleged acts or omissions took place.[121]

The EAT dismissed both grounds of appeal.[122] With regard to the principle of consistent interpretation, Underhill J referred to *Marleasing* as the leading authority from the ECJ. He acknowledged that the UK courts and tribunals had accepted that the duty may in certain circumstances allow the national court to "read words into a statute in order to give effect to EU legislation which the statute was evidently intended to implement"[123] and cited the earlier cases of *Pickstone* and *Litster*. Yet, he also acknowledged that such an approach is not always legitimate and that determining what is or is not possible is a difficult task.[124] The judge considered in depth the approach of the House of

---

116 Council Directive 2000/78/EC. Member States had until 2 December 2003 to implement the Directive, subject to a right to an extension, "in order to take account of particular conditions" for a further three years. Hence, the final date for implementation was 2 December 2006.

117 Disability Discrimination Act 1995 (Amendment) Regulations 2003 (SI 2003/1673) which came into effect on 1 October 2004. As a consequence, the claimant was required to rely on acts or omissions which occurred after this date to substantiate her claim.

118 The respondents' appeal against the order to refer to the ECJ was dismissed by the Employment Appeal Tribunal: [2007] ICR 654.

119 Case 303/06, para. 48.

120 November 2008.

121 The respondents relied on *Lloyd-Briden v. Worthing College* [2007] 3 CMLR 27.

122 *EBR Attridge Law LLP v. Coleman* [2010] 1 CMLR 28. Although the case was remitted back to the employment tribunal to consider the merits of the claim by Mrs Coleman, the case was settled. The settlement agreement included terms requiring no further appeals to be made and for payment to Mrs Coleman of an undisclosed sum for "injury to feelings", see <www.cloisters.com>.

123 Para. 11.

124 Para. 11.

Lords in *Ghaidan* referring to the judgments of Lords Nicholls, Steyn and Rodgers, and noted that the *Ghaidan* approach had been applied subsequently by the Court of Appeal in the context of an EU law case, *IDT Card Services Ireland Ltd v. Customs and Excise Commissioners*. He applied the approach to the *EBR Attridge Law LLP v. Coleman* case and confirmed the duty to interpret the DDA in accordance with the meaning of the Directive as now interpreted by the ECJ. Underhill J stated that:

> there is nothing "impossible" about adding words to the provisions of the 1995 Act so as to cover associative discrimination. No doubt such an addition would change the meaning of the 1995 Act, but, as the speeches in *Ghaidan* make clear, that is not in itself impermissible (see, e.g. per Lord Nicholls as paras. 32-33). The real question is whether it would do so in a manner which is not "compatible with the underlying thrust of the legislation" (per Lord Nicholls at para.33) or which is "inconsistent with the scheme of the legislation or its general principles" (per Lord Rodger at para 121). In *Ghaidan* the majority were prepared to interpret the words "wife or husband" in Schedule 1 of the Rent Act 1977 as extending to the same-sex partners. That was plainly not the intention of Parliament when the act was enacted, nor does it correspond to the actual meaning of the words, however liberally construed; but the implication was necessary in order to give effect to Convention rights and it went "with the grain of the legislation" (in Lord Rodgers's phrase). In my view the situation with which I am concerned is closely analogous. The proscription of associative discrimination is an extension of the scope of the legislation as enacted, but it is in no sense repugnant to it. On the contrary, it is an extension fully in conformity with the aims of the legislation as drafted. The concept of discrimination "on the ground of disability" will remain central.[125]

The judge also referred to the fact that other discrimination statutes in the UK, as interpreted by the UK courts *without reference to EU law*, outlaw associative discrimination, which for him demonstrated that such a result was in line with UK policy on anti-discrimination legislation.[126] In relation to the actual text, the judge recommended inserting an additional and distinct provision to the statute to give effect to the ECJ's interpretation of the Framework Directive in the particular circumstances.

On the issue of when the duty arises, he dismissed the arguments based on the case of *Lloyd-Briden v. Worthing College* in which the ET and EAT had both refused to apply the ECJ's (controversial) decision in *Mangold*[127]

125 Underhill J, at para. 14.

126 Ibid., citing the EAT decision in *Showboat Entertainment Centre Ltd v. Owens* [1984] ICR 65 approved by the Court of Appeal in *Weathersfield Ltd v. Sargent* [1999] ICR 425. He noted that this view was not undermined by the fact that the Disability Discrimination Act referred to "a disabled person".

127 Case C-144/04, *Mangold v. Helm* [2005] ECR I-9981. In this case, the ECJ held that the principle of age discrimination at issue was not derived from the Directive but reflected the principle of equal treatment which is found in international instruments and in the

to disapply national law that conflicted with the principle of age discrimination in relation to events which occurred prior to the date for implementation of the Directive (i.e. 2 December 2006). In his view, *Mangold* was distinguishable. He also dismissed the argument that the interpretative duty did not arise until the date for implementation had passed as held by the ECJ in *Centrosteel*.[128] For Underhill J, these cases were distinguishable as the UK had implemented legislation purporting to give effect to the Directive within the implementation deadline. For him,

> the "*Marleasing* obligation" must bite at the moment when those Regulations came into force: it is logically irrelevant that the legislator chose to act rather sooner than he was obliged to. I would also add that it would be bizarre if the (amended) 1995 Act meant one thing on 2 December 2006 but something different on 3 December.[129]

The case was subsequently returned to the lower ET for damages to be assessed, but was settled out of court. The UK subsequently enacted the Equality Act 2010 which amalgamated all of the UK's discrimination legislation under one statute and expressly includes protection against associative direct discrimination.[130]

4.4.2. *Correcting Drafting Errors*

It is recognised that UK courts may not only engage in statutory interpretation to resolve ambiguities in statutes, but also to correct obvious drafting errors. This may include adding, substituting or omitting words.[131] In these circumstances, the judicial role is confined to construing the law and judges should not give the appearance of engaging in "judicial legislation".[132] In *Jessemey v. Rowstock Ltd*,[133] the principle of consistent interpretation was utilised by the Court of Appeal to correct drafting errors made by Parliament when consolidating legislation on discrimination in the shape of the Equality Act 2010 to bring it into line with EU law.[134]

Mr Jessemey had been dismissed by his employer, Rowstock Ltd, on the ground that he was over 65 years old. Mr Jessemey brought proceedings under

---

constitutional traditions of the Member States. As such, it could be relied upon by the individual litigant irrespective of the lack of horizontal direct effect of directives or the fact that the time limit for implementing directives had not passed.

128 Case C-456/98, *Centrosteel Srl v. Adipol GmbH* [2000] ECR I-6007, para. 21.

129 Ibid., para. 22.

130 See S. Fredman, "The reason why – unravelling indirect discrimination" (2016) *Industrial Law Journal* 231–43.

131 *Jessemey v. Rowstock Ltd* [2014] EWCA Civ 185, per Underhill LJ at p. 558.

132 See *Cross* (n. 54), p. 103.

133 *Jessemey v. Rowstock Ltd* [2014] EWCA Civ 185.

134 Note that the leading judgment was delivered by Underhill LJ, who was also the single judge who delivered the EAT decision in *ETR Attridge v. Coleman*, discussed above.

national employment law for unfair dismissal and age discrimination. When he tried to find another job, his former employer gave him a poor reference. Mr Jessemey believed that the poor reference was in response to the legal claims that he had brought and so instigated a further claim against his employer for victimisation.

The EAT[135] held that while post-employment discrimination and harassment was explicitly prohibited under the Equality Act 2010,[136] which implemented the Framework Directive and Directive 2006/54 on the implementation of the principle of equal opportunities and equal treatment of men and women in matters of employment and occupation (recast), post-employment victimisation was not. According to the EAT, there was no equivalent provision proscribing victimisation which was only referred to in s. 108(7). The EAT was of the view that it was not "possible" to interpret such behaviour as unlawful when the statute clearly states that is not unlawful. This would go beyond the duty to interpret "as far as possible" set out in *Ghaidan*. Two months later, in *Onu v. Akwiwu*,[137] a differently-constituted EAT held that the 2010 Act *did* prohibit acts of victimisation against former employees.

A clear lack of clarity had arisen in the law which may in itself seem surprising in light of the earlier decision of the Court of Justice in *Coote*.[138] In the latter case, the ECJ had held that protection from discrimination on grounds of equality in employment matters conferred on employees by the Equal Treatment Directive[139] also applied to victims of sex discrimination who had been victimised on account of making a claim of sex discrimination either while employed or after the employment relationship had ended. When the preliminary ruling returned to the EAT, the referring national court, the principle of consistent interpretation was utilised to interpret national law to comply with the Directive in this dispute between two private parties. It was held that the phrase "in the case of a woman employed by him" covered the case of a former employee. The interpretation of EU law set out in *Coote* had subsequently been applied by the House of Lords in a number of appeals heard together relating to all three "first generation" discrimination statutes – the Sex Discrimination Act 1975, the Race Relations Act 1976 and the Disability Discrimination Act 1995.[140]

When *Jessemey* came before the Court of Appeal, Underhill LJ, now promoted from the EAT, and clearly familiar with the scope of the principle of consistent interpretation, held that since post-employment victimisation was unlawful prior to the enactment of the Equality Act 2010, the failure of the

135 [2013] ICR 807.
136 See s. 108(1) and (2).
137 [2013] ICR 1039.
138 Case C-185/97, *Coote v. Granada Hospitality Ltd* [1998] ECR I-5199.
139 Council Directive 76/207/EEC.
140 *Rhys-Harper v. Relaxion Group plc* [2003] 1 CMLR 44.

statute to proscribe this behaviour was a drafting error and did not reflect the intention of Parliament.[141] Indeed, this would have been contrary to EU law as confirmed in *Coote*. The Court of Appeal was of the view that the *Ghaidan* approach permits words to be implied into the Equality Act 2010 to achieve the result of rendering post-termination employment victimisation unlawful since it would be "consistent with the fundamental principles of the Act itself and 'go with its grain'".[142] The Court of Appeal rejected the approach of the EAT and recalled the need to consider the flexibility of the *Ghaidan* approach and the broader context in which the law has evolved.[143]

4.5. LIMITATIONS: "GOING AGAINST THE GRAIN"

It is important to consider the circumstances in which the national courts have considered that it is not "possible" to interpret national law to comply with EU law and the legal and practical consequences that ensue. It should be recalled that in *Vodafone 2*, the Court of Appeal set out two key limitations. First, the national court should ensure that:

> The meaning should "go with the grain of the legislation" and be "compatible with the underlying thrust of the legislation being construed." (per Lord Nicholls in *Ghaidan* at 33; Dyson LJ in [*EB Central Services Ltd v. Revenue and Customs Commissioners* [2008] EWCA Civ 468] at 81). An interpretation should not be adopted which is inconsistent with a fundamental or cardinal feature of the legislation since this would cross the boundary between interpretation and amendment; (see *Ghaidan* per Lord Nicholls at 33; Lord Rodger at 110–113; Arden LJ in *IDT Card Services* at 82 and 113).

Second, that the:

> exercise of the interpretative obligation cannot require the courts to make decisions for which they are not equipped or give rise to important practical repercussions which the court is not equipped to evaluate. (See *Ghaidan* per Lord Nicholls at 33; Lord Rodger at 115; Arden LJ in *IDT Card Services* at 113.)

4.5.1. Determining the Boundaries

These limitations are clearly designed to preserve the boundaries between the role of the national courts as interpreters of the law rather than as law-makers.

---

141 The Court of Appeal confirmed at para. 32 that Explanatory Notes are in principle admissible as an aid to interpretation by the courts: *R (Westminster City Council) v. National Asylum Support Service* [2002] UKHL 38, per Lord Steyn at paras. 2–6 (pp. 2958–59).

142 *Jessemey v. Rowstock Ltd* [2014] EWCA Civ 185, at para. 42.

143 Ibid., at para. 44.

For the judiciary, the objective or purpose of the national legislation is paramount, and even if a consistent interpretation is possible in principle, if it entail practical consequences which the national court does not have the competence to address, the national court should refrain from adopting the *Marleasing* principle.

Where the boundary lies was discussed by the Court of Appeal in 2015 in *Google Inc v. Vidal-Hall*[144] in which it was held that the *Marleasing* principle could not be applied. In this case, a dispute had arisen between two private parties, and concerned the transposition of the Data Protection Directive into UK law. The Court first sought to determine whether on a literal interpretation, the national implementing law correctly transposed the relevant EU law. It considered that the national provision[145] was more restrictive than EU law,[146] i.e. that the term "damage" contained in the Data Protection Act should not be restricted to pecuniary damage only and prohibit claims for non-pecuniary loss or moral damages. It followed that the Directive had not been effectively transposed,[147] and denied the claimant of an effective remedy for breach of her privacy as protected by the Directive as well as Art. 7 and 8 of the EU Charter of Fundamental Rights. The second issue was whether it was possible to interpret national law in such way as to give full effect to Directive which it purported to implement. The Court of Appeal was of the view that the application of the *Marleasing* principle in this case was not possible. In her judgment, Sharp LJ recalled Lord Rodger's phrase in *Ghaidan*,[148] namely that the interpretation should not led to a change that "goes against the grain" of the legislation. She went on to set out the litmus test:

> The question must always be whether the change that would result from the proposed interpretation (whichever interpretative technique is adopted) would alter a fundamental feature of the legislation. It will not be "possible" to interpret domestic legislation, whether by reading in, reading down or disapplying a provision, if to do so would distort or undermine some important feature of the legislation.[149]

The Court of Appeal held that the exclusion of the right to damages for distress where certain conditions are not satisfied is a fundamental feature of the statute, and this reflected a deliberate intention on the part of Parliament to limit the compensation available in the event of a breach. The national court could not find an explanation in the statutory text itself or in Hansard to explain the restriction. There was no evidence that could be provided that could indicate

---

144 *Google Inc v. Judith Vidal-Hall* [2015] EWCA Civ 311.

145 Section 13(2) of the Data Protection Act.

146 Art. 23 of Directive 95/46/EC.

147 See *Google Inc. v. Judith Vidal-Hall* [2015] EWCA Civ 311, at para. 84.

148 See Lord Rodger at para. 121, restated by Sharp LJ in *Google Inc v. Judith Vidal-Hall* [2015] EWCA Civ 311, para. 89.

149 *Google Inc. v. Judith Vidal-Hall* [2015] EWCA Civ 311, at para. 90.

to the court what Parliament had intended on this issue and which could give the national court some scope for interpretation.[150] While the national court accepted that the interpretative duty may involve disapplying a part of national law to make it compatible with EU law,[151] it held that this would be a step too far in this case. The provision was considered to be a central feature of the legislation and it was clear that Parliament had enacted a "carefully calibrated scheme" which restricted the compensation available to victims.[152] Nevertheless, an alternative method of securing Ms Vidal-Hall's right to damages for distress was possible in this case (see below).

4.5.2. *What Happens When a Consistent Interpretation is Not "Possible"?*

In the absence of direct effect, if a consistent interpretation is not possible, this may leave a gap in the judicial protection that an individual can obtain where their EU right has been breached. It should be noted that unlike the HRA, there is no power imposed on national courts by EU law or national law to make a declaration of incompatibility stating that national law incompatible with EU law will trigger an amendment to national law.

4.5.2.1. Principle of State Liability

In EU law, the ECJ has long held the view that the alternative remedy is to bring an action for damages against the state for breach of EU law.[153] This approach is recognised by the UK courts as illustrated in *Google Inc v. Vidal-Hall.* The option was not explored any further as it was not necessary to secure an outcome for the case.[154] Yet, it is also well established that an action for damages is no panacea and subject to conditions and limitations which curtail its effectiveness as an alternative remedy.[155] It should be noted that the European Union (Withdrawal) Act expressly provides for the removal of the *Francovich* remedy from UK law after two years.

4.5.2.2. EU Charter of Fundamental Rights

Prior to the UK's EU referendum result, it is argued that the UK courts had been adopting a very *communautaire* approach when interpreting and applying

---

150 Ibid., para. 91.

151 Ibid., para. 90.

152 Essentially, the relevant provision only permitted compensation for distress for breach of privacy to be awarded if economic loss had also been sustained.

153 See *Wagner Miret* and more recently *Dominguez.*

154 *Google Inc v. Judith Vidal-Hall* [2015] EWCA Civ 311, para. 86.

155 See T. Lock, "Is private enforcement of EU law through state liability a myth?: An assessment 20 years after *Francovich*" (2012) 49 *Common Market Law Review* 1675–1702.

the EU's Charter of Fundamental Rights. In *Google Inc*, the Court of Appeal held that the *Marleasing* principle was not applicable, and relied on Art. 47 of the EU Charter of Fundamental Rights (EUCFR) to disapply the offending primary legislation. The same approach had been utilised by the Court of Appeal in an earlier case, *Benkharbouche v. Sudan* and *Janah v. Libya*,[156] where Art. 47 was used to disapply the State Immunity Act 1978 which denied the claimants a right of access to a court for alleged breaches of the national law giving effect to the Working Time Directive.

There is evidence that following the EU referendum result, the Supreme Court is adopting a more cautious approach and moving away from reliance on Art. 47 EUCFR to secure individuals' rights. On appeal in *Benkharbouche v. Secretary of State for Foreign and Commonwealth Affairs, Secretary of State for Foreign and Commonwealth Affairs and Libya v. Janah*,[157] the Supreme Court relied on customary international law and Art. 6 ECHR to grant the claimants the *procedural* right of access to a court. The Supreme Court referred to Art. 47 EUCFR very briefly, stating that it did not raise a separate issue to be addressed. It did acknowledge that where there is a conflict with national law, EU law must prevail and the former disapplied, and that, in contrast, where there is a breach of Art. 6 ECHR, a declaration of incompatibility is the only remedy (under s. 4 HRA). However, EU law was not relied upon to resolve the dispute. Similarly, in *Unison*, the Supreme Court briefly referred to Art. 47 EUCFR before relying on common law principles to reach the same result.[158] The European Union (Withdrawal) Act removes the EU Charter of Fundamental Rights from UK law. Yet, the role of the EU Charter of Fundamental Rights before UK courts is in decline even before the UK has withdrawn from the EU. In both cases discussed above, the Supreme Court was able to guarantee fundamental rights of individuals independently of EU law.

4.6. LEGAL CERTAINTY

A degree of legal uncertainty is inherent in the operation of the principle of consistent interpretation.[159] One of the criticisms of the EU principle is its strength and breadth. To what extent can it be considered acceptable that the employers in *Webb*, *Coote*, *Attridge* and *Jessemey* were subject to legal obligations of which they would have been unaware? Is this consistent with the rule of law? There is a view that this level of legal uncertainty is an acceptable

156 *Benkharbouche, Janah v. Embassy of the Republic of Sudan*: [2015] EWCA Civ 33.
157 [2017] UKSC 62.
158 *R (on the application of Unison) v. Lord Chancellor* [2017] UKSC 51.
159 Betlem (n. 4), p. 417.

trade-off between, "on the one hand, the legitimate expectations of the individual seeking to have purely national law applied, and, on the other hand, the need to ensure the widest enforcement possible of Community law, along with the protection of the rights of individuals originating in Community law".[160] Furthermore, the limitations on interpreting national law *contra legem* or in breach of general principles of law could be considered to be sufficient safeguards in respecting the rule of law. It could also be argued that much of the litigation would not arise if the Member States implemented EU law in their own legal orders correctly (estoppel argument).

The UK judiciary seems have some sympathy with concerns about legal certainty for parties who may be subject to unforeseen legal obligations, but it is limited and, in general, it has not been sufficient to override their duty to apply a consistent interpretation. In *IDT Card Services,*[161] the principle of consistent interpretation was adopted in a complex case concerning the interpretation of national law purporting to implement the Sixth EC VAT Directive[162] which raised an issue of "novelty and difficulty". Essentially, as the rules in the UK and Republic of Ireland differ, they had given rise to circumstances in which a VAT-free scenario had arisen. Arden LJ acknowledged that there was an argument against applying the *Marleasing* principle based on legal certainty and the legitimate expectations of the taxpayer. However, she was of the view that it was well known that the VAT Act 1994 had to be interpreted in conformity with the Sixth VAT Directive and that the supply of telecommunications services amounts to a taxable supply for the purposes of the Directive.[163] In *British Gas Trading v. Lock,*[164] Sir Colin Rimer expressed some sympathy for the fact that the "correct" interpretation of Art. 7 of the Working Time Directive had emerged several years after it had come into force through a later interpretation of the EU provision by the ECJ, but proceeded to interpret national law in line with EU law. In 2002, Betlem argued that if the legislature "voluntarily" accepted the levels of legal uncertainty created by s. 3 HRA, which had in turn been inspired by the EU interpretative principle, then the same acceptance should be accorded to legal uncertainty resulting from the application of the *Marleasing* principle. This is even more compelling given that the UK legislature considered the insertion of an interpretative obligation into the HRA preferable to permitting courts to set aside conflicting legislation as in the case of direct effect.[165]

---

160 K. Lackhoff and H. Nyssens, "Direct effect of directives in triangular situations" (1998) 23 *European Law Review* 397, at 411.

161 *R (IDT Card Services Ireland Ltd) v. Customs and Excise Commissioners* [2006] EWCA Civ 29.

162 Directive 77/338/EC.

163 Arden LJ, at para. 110.

164 *British Gas Trading v. Lock, Secretary of State for Business, Innovation and Skills* [2016] EWCA Civ 983.

165 Betlem (n. 4), p. 417.

5. THE EFFECTIVENESS OF THE PRINCIPLE OF CONSISTENT INTERPRETATION IN THE UK COURTS

There are two specific policy areas where the effectiveness of the UK courts' approach in relation to the principle of consistent interpretation has been called into question. This undermines its potency as a key weapon in the armoury of individuals who are seeking to invoke or protect their EU rights before national courts which have been infringed, and particularly in the absence of direct effect.

5.1. MOTOR INSURANCE DIRECTIVES

The *nature* of the implementation of the EU Motor Insurance Directives[166] into UK law is unconventional and includes relying on existing statutes such as the Road Traffic Act 1988, and the continued use of historic *private law* agreements between the Department of Transport and the Motor Insurance Bureau.[167] This hotchpotch legal framework has given rise to many of the deficiencies in the transposition of EU law into national law and resulted in extensive litigation before the UK and the emergence of specialist lawyers in the field.[168] The application of the principle of consistent interpretation has had mixed results. In this policy area, there seems to be a more cautious approach on the part of the judiciary to using the *Marleasing* principle. Compared to the field of employment law, the UK courts seem much more reluctant to insert new provisions into national law to ensure compliance with EU law even where this would seem to be demanded by interpretations of the law delivered in the judgments of the ECJ. In contrast, where there has been a referral by a UK court, the referring court has been more willing to adopt a conform interpretation of national law in line with EU law.[169]

One restriction on the use of the principle of consistent interpretation arose in the House of Lords 2001 decision in *White v. White*. The case involved

---

166 The five Motor Insurance Directives enacted between 1972 and 2005 have now all been consolidated into a single instrument: Directive 2009/103/EC.

167 The first agreement of this nature dates back to 1945. See further J. Davey and C. Richards, "Direct but ineffective? The Second Motor Insurance Directive" (1999) *Journal of Business Law* 157.

168 See e.g. specialist UK solicitor firms like Nicholas Bevan and Leigh Day solicitors.

169 See e.g. in *Churchill Insurance Company Ltd v. Fitzgerald Wilkinson; Evans v. Cockayne & Equity Claims Ltd v. Secretary of State for Transport* [2012] EWCA Civ 1166 where following a referral to the ECJ in Case C-442/10, *Churchill*, the court (and all the parties including the intervening Secretary of State for Transport) accepted that an interpretation conforming to EU law was possible, but the disagreement centred on the form of the words to be inserted into the Road Traffic Act 1988.

a number of disputes (joined on appeal) concerning the enforcement of the EU's Second Motor Insurance Directive[170] which requires Member States to establish a compensation fund for the victims of uninsured drivers and "hit and run" accidents. In the UK, these obligations were given effect through private law contractual arrangements between the Department for Transport and the Motor Insurance Bureau, the body responsible for paying compensation claims. The litigation reflects the general approach to the enforcement of EU rights before national courts with direct effect being considered first, followed by the principle of consistent interpretation, and finally the principle of state liability.[171] At first instance, the trial judge resolved the issue through recourse to the doctrine of direct effect.[172] The Court of Appeal[173] held that the trial judge had erred in law in relying on direct effect. Further, it refused to adopt the principle of consistent interpretation on the grounds that the private law contractual arrangements purporting to give effect to the Directive could not be categorised as "national law" for the purpose of the *Marleasing* principle. Similarly, the House of Lords declared that the relevant provisions of the Directive were insufficiently precise to have direct effect, and then considered that the *Marleasing* principle could not be used as an alternative method of giving effect to the Directive. Lord Nicholls held that the principle of indirect effect "cannot be stretched to the length of requiring contracts to be interpreted in a manner that would impose on one or other of the parties obligations which, the *Marleasing* case apart, the contract did not impose".[174] Fortunately for the claimant, Lord Nicholls resolved the dispute by drawing on a domestic variant of statutory interpretation. He held that, even though the *Marleasing* principle could not apply in this context, "I consider that the application of the conventional [contract law] principles of interpretation of documents arrives at the same result".[175] Lord Cooke argued that the EU version could have been used.

Although the practical result for the claimant was the same, the UK's unconventional transposition of the Directive through non-legislative means

---

170 Directive 84/5/EEC of 30 December [1984] OJ L8/17.

171 For further discussion and a comparison of how a similar dispute was resolved before the Irish courts by recognising that the Motor Insurance Bureau of Ireland was jointly liable for damages with the State for mal-implementation of the Directive in accordance with the *Francovich* principle: C. Costello and S. Drake "Enforcing EC Motor Insurance Directives: Navigating the Maze" (2003) 9(3) *European Public Law* 371–98.

172 Judgments of 13 March 1997 and 12 March 1998 unreported.

173 *Mighell v. Reading; Evans v. MIB; White v. White* [1999] 1 CMLR 1251. It should be noted in Case C-413/15, *Farrell*, ECLI:EU:C:2017:745, the Motors Insurers' Bureau of Ireland was deemed to be an emanation of the state. It is argued that the same interpretation should be applied to the MIB in the UK which would mean that the judgment of the Court of Appeal is no longer good law.

174 *White* [2001] 2 All ER 43, para. 22.

175 Ibid., para. 23.

combined with the refusal by the House of Lords to apply the *Marleasing* principle to private law agreements created unacceptable levels of legal uncertainty and a lacuna in the effective protection of individuals' rights before the national courts. It was hoped that the ECJ would chastise the UK's method for transposing the Directive into national law in *Evans*.[176] The Advocate General had been highly critical of the UK's implementing approach and considered it to be "fraught with so many imponderables that it fails to satisfy the requirements of legal certainty ...".[177] He called on the national courts to use the *Marleasing* principle to rectify this legal uncertainty.[178] In his view, failing to do so because of the constraints of national law meant that the Directive had not been implemented correctly into UK law.[179] Unfortunately, the ECJ adopted a more deferential and pluralist approach and made no direct reference to the *Marleasing* principle. The Court clearly did not want to be drawn on the UK's implementation of the Directive by a private law agreement, or on the reliance of the national courts on domestic principles of interpretation. It is argued by this author that the ECJ would prefer the UK courts to resolve the issues themselves. Indeed, in *White*, the end result for the claimant was the same. Nevertheless, in the interests of legal certainty, the effective judicial protection of the individual's Union rights, and to avoid unnecessary litigation, there have been calls for the ECJ to be more explicit to avoid any confusion on the part of the national court in the future.[180]

Further legal uncertainty has arisen in this area of law in more recent litigation. For example, in *Bristol Alliance Partnership v. Williams, EUI Ltd*,[181] the *Marleasing* principle was adopted by the High Court to interpret the Road Traffic Act 1988 and the 1999 MIB Agreement to bring national law in line with the EU Motor Insurance Directives as interpreted by the ECJ in *Bernaldez*.[182] However, this ruling was overturned by the Court of Appeal which held that the ECJ ruling was not of "general application."[183] A subsequent successful *Francovich* damages claim in *Delaney II*[184] casts doubt on this view and lawyers

176 Case C-63/01, *Evans v. Secretary of State for the Environment, Transport and the Regions and Motor Insurers' Bureau* [2004] 1 CMLR 47.

177 Opinion of Advocate General Alber, C-63/01 *Evans v. Secretary of State for the Environment, Transport and the Regions and Motor Insurers' Bureau* [2004] 1 CMLR 47 at para. 131.

178 Ibid., para. 132.

179 Ibid., para. 133.

180 Betlem (n. 4).

181 [2011] EWHC 1657 (QB).

182 Case C-129/94, *Ruiz Bernaldez* [1996] ECR I-1929. The ECJ held that the EU Motor Insurance Directives could not be interpreted to allow an insurance contract to exclude liability to pay compensation for damage to property caused by an intoxicated driver. The exceptions listed in the relevant directive are exhaustive.

183 *EUI Ltd v. Bristol Alliance Ltd Partnership* [2012] EWCA Civ 1267. For criticism of this decision, see N. Bevan, "Marking the Boundary" (2013) 3 *Journal of Personal Injury Law* 151.

184 See *Delaney v. Secretary of State for Transport* [2014] EWHC 1785 (QB).

have called for the Department of Transport's systemic failure to fully implement the Motor Insurance Directives to be addressed.[185] An investigation for non-compliance by the European Commission under Art. 258 TFEU is not yet complete.

A great deal of legal uncertainty has arisen following the ECJ's judgment in *Vnuk*[186] in which the Court held that the concept of "use of vehicles" as set out in the First Motor Insurance Directive[187] which covers "the use of a vehicle that is consistent with the normal function of that vehicle" includes the use of a tractor with a trailer attached, in a farmyard, in order to reverse into a barn. Furthermore, it is *implicit* in *Vnuk* that the liability extends to private land such as the farmyard in the main proceedings. This means that UK motor insurance law as it currently stands is incompatible with EU law. In a UK case, *UK Insurance Ltd v. Holden*,[188] a claim was brought in which a car had caught fire while being repaired on private land and had spread to an adjacent building causing extensive damage. The insurer of the property paid out over £2million and then sought an indemnity from the car owner, Mr Holden, and his motor insurer, UK Insurance Ltd. The motor insurer claimed that the policy did not cover the claim as the incident took place on private land and did not entail the "use" of the car. In accordance with national law, third party liability only arises in relation to accidents when the car is being driven or used on a public road or other public place. Before the High Court, the judge denied the claim on the basis that the repair of the car did not amount to use. However, the judge considered obiter that the Road Traffic Act 1988 (s. 145(3)) which refers to the use of vehicle "on a road or other public place" did not comply with EU law following *Vnuk*. He did not consider it appropriate to apply the principle of consistent interpretation in this case since to even insert the word "including" before "on a road" into the Act to bring it in line with EU law would "go against the grain" of the Act of Parliament and amount to an amendment rather than an interpretation of the law. He held obiter that

> The addition of that single word belies … the scale of the change. It may be that extending the ambit of the Act in this way does not in practice lead to many more claims especially given the need to have requisite use of the vehicle but nonetheless, this is potentially a significant additions to the scope of the Act and it is in a different league to importing the ECJ's definition of "use".[189]

---

185 See e.g. N. Bevan, in his article, "A world turned upside down" (2014) 3 *Journal of Personal Injury Law* 136.

186 Case C-162/13, *Vnuk v. Zavarovalnica d.d.*, ECLI:EU:C:2014:2146.

187 Art. 3(1) "covers any use of a vehicle that is consistent with the normal function of that vehicle".

188 [2016] EWHC 264.

189 Ibid., para. 38.

The issue was addressed directly by the High Court in an action for judicial review brought by Roadpeace, a charity which promotes road safety and provides support for crash victims. In *Roadpeace v. Secretary of State for Transport, Motor Insurer's Bureau*,[190] the claimant argued that various provisions of national law are inconsistent with EU law. The High Court accepted that national law is not compliant with the ECJ's ruling in *Vnuk*, but also refused to adopt the *Marleasing* principle on the grounds that it would run counter to the principles set out in *Vodafone No. 2*. The court was cognisant of its duty to provide effective remedies in line with Case C-432/05, *Unibet*, but considered that the only remedy available was to issue a Declaration. It was willing to accept submissions by the parties on whether more was required once the judgment has been handed down, e.g. a timetable for legislative amendment.[191]

This author argues that the recognition by the judiciary of the potentially wide-reaching implications of interpreting national law in compliance with *Vnuk* for the insurance industry and its business model explains their more cautious approach in this field compared to employment policy. For Davey, this resistance to "Europeanisation" in the field of motor insurance by some of the judiciary, demonstrates a commitment to the model of insurance (and tort) law as separate in nature and subject to the market.[192]

Nevertheless, the inconsistency between EU law and national law exposes the UK to a *Francovich* damages claim.[193] Given that the full implications of the *Vnuk* ruling are far-ranging and unforeseen by the Court of Justice, the European Commission[194] and the UK Government[195] have launched consultations to consider the appropriate (legislative?) response.

190 [2017] EWHC 2725. Roadpeace is a national charity which promotes road safety and provides support for road crash victims.

191 In *R (ClientEarth) v. Secretary of State for the Environment, Food and Rural Affairs* [2015] UKSC 28, the Supreme Court issued a mandatory order requiring the Secretary of State to prepare new air quality plans which should be delivered to the European Commission in accordance with a defined timetable.

192 J. Davey, "A compulsory diet of chickens and eggs: The EU Motor Insurance Directives as a shadow tort regime" in P. Giliker, *Research Handbook on EU Tort Law* (Edward Elgar, 2017).

193 In December 2016, a claim brought by a motor trade dealer who traded from his farm in Wales and was injured by a customer test-driving a 4X4 quad bike was settled. The barrister for the claimant indicated that if the claim had gone to trial and the national court not construed UK law to comply with EU law, the claimant would have instigated a *Francovich* claim: "Andrew Ward obtains settlement in a *Vnuk* type personal injury claim" 3 January 2017. Accessed at <www.exchangechambers.co.uk> on 9 January 2017.

194 See Inception Impact Assessment, "Adaptation of the scope of Directive 2009/103/EC on motor insurance: Roadmap" (8 June 2016).

195 Department for Transport, Technical consultation on motor insurance: Consideration of the European Court of Justice ruling in the case of *Damijan Vnuk v. Zavarovalnica Triglav d. d*, (C-162/13), published 20 December 2016. Consultation ends on 31 March 2017.

5.2. WORKING TIME DIRECTIVE

Another area of legal uncertainty has revolved around the correct interpretation of the national law purporting to implement the Working Time Directive,[196] particularly the provisions on annual leave.[197] A preliminary reference was sent to the ECJ by an ET to ascertain the correct interpretation of Art. 7(1) with regard to holiday pay. The case concerned a salesman, whose remuneration package included a basic salary plus results-based commission depending on the number and type of contracts he persuaded customers to enter into. However, his holiday pay consisted only of his basic salary and any commission which had been earned at an earlier date but had not been paid at that time. Since he was not working he could not earn any commission while he was on holiday. He claimed that his rights under EU law had been infringed and that the relevant national law[198] should be interpreted in light of the Directive. The ECJ held in *Lock v. British Gas Trading Ltd*[199] that the right to paid annual leave is an important principle of EU social law and further, is set out in Art. 31(2) of the Charter of Fundamental Rights.[200] Accordingly, Art. 7(1) requires that results-based commission paid to an employee which is not dependent on the amount of work done by that employee must be taken into account in the calculation of pay for annual leave (otherwise employees may be deterred from taking leave). On referral back to the ET, it was held that it was possible to interpret the relevant national law to comply with EU law by "reading words" into the applicable statute.[201] This approach was confirmed on appeal to the EAT[202] (following the earlier EAT decision in *Bear Scotland and Others v. Fulton and Others*).[203]

---

196 Council Directive 93/104/EC and amended by Council Directive 2000/34/EC. These two directives have since been consolidated into Council Directive 2003/88/EC which came in force on 2 August 2004.

197 Art. 7: "(1) Member States shall take the measures necessary to ensure that every worker is entitled to paid annual leave of at least four weeks in accordance with conditions for entitlement to, and granting of, such leave laid down by national legislation and/or practice. (2) The minimum period of paid annual leave may not be replaced by an allowance in lieu, except where the employment relationship is terminated."

198 Section 221 of the Employment Rights Act 1996 and Regulation 16 of the Working Time Regulations 1998, as amended. The current version came into force on 1 October 2013.

199 Case C-539/12 *Lock v. British Gas Trading Ltd* [2014] ICR 813.

200 Art. 31(2) EUCFR states that every worker has the right to limitation of maximum working hours, to daily and weekly rest periods and to an annual period of paid leave.

201 The employment tribunal considered four alternatives and opted for the national law being construed as if an additional paragraph had been added to the implementing law.

202 *British Gas Trading Ltd v. Lock, Secretary of State for Business, Innovation and Skills*, EAT, 22 February 2016. It should be noted that this claim had been selected as the lead claim for over 900 claims against British Gas and for thousands of other similar claims that have been stayed pending the outcome of this claim.

203 *Bear Scotland and Others v. Fulton and Others* [2015] ICR 221. Although not bound to follow its own decisions, the EAT will find them of persuasive authority and generally will follow

On appeal before the Court of Appeal,[204] the leading judge, Sir Colin Rimer was also prepared to interpret national law to comply with EU law. He dismissed the argument that such an interpretation would be *contra legem* as held in case-law pre-dating the jurisprudence of the ECJ on Art. 7. He added that in light of the recent judgment in Case C-441/14, *Dansk Industri*,[205] the existence of conflicting domestic case-law does not prevent a conform interpretation being adopted by a national court. In his view, the case fell within a set of circumstances referred to by Arden LJ in *IDT Card Services Ltd*[206] whereby the correct interpretation of the law could not have been envisaged by Parliament when adopting the domestic implementing legislation, but that there was no conflict with the "grain or thrust" of the national legislation.[207] In an interesting development, the judge confined *Lock* to its facts. He also held that a narrower interpretation of national law should be adopted which referred to results-based commission only. The conforming interpretation originally adopted by the ET had referred to all forms of commission. Deep concerns about the implications of such a broad interpretation were raised during the proceedings as this could include, *inter alia*, bankers' bonuses![208] Permission to appeal against the Court of Appeal ruling to the Supreme Court was refused, paving the way for payment of compensation for Mr Lock and thousands of employees in a similar position.

6. CONCLUDING REMARKS

This contribution explores the application and the effectiveness of the principle of consistent interpretation by the UK courts since its inception by the ECJ in *Von Colson* in 1984. Three phases are identified in the application of this

---

them. There are four exceptions to this general principle: (1) where the earlier decision was per incuriam, in other words, where a relevant legislative provision or binding decision of the courts was not considered; (2) where there are two or more inconsistent decisions of the Appeal Tribunal; (3) where there are inconsistent decisions of the Appeal Tribunal and another court or tribunal on the same point, at least where they are of co-ordinate jurisdiction, for example the High Court; (4) where the earlier decision is manifestly wrong; (5) where there are other exceptional circumstances.

204 *British Gas Trading v. Lock, Secretary of State for Business, Innovation and Skills* [2016] EWCA Civ 983.

205 Case C-441/14, *Dansk Industri (DI), acting on behalf of Ajos A/S v. Estate of Karsten Eigil Rasmussen* ECLI:EU:C:2016:278, judgment of 19 April 2016 (Grand Chamber). This judgment and the response of the Danish courts is discussed elsewhere in this volume.

206 Sir Colin Rimer refers to Arden LJ at para. 113.

207 Ibid., paras. 109–12.

208 Ibid., paras. 114–16.

EU method of statutory interpretation by the UK courts. They broadly reflect a shift from a traditionalist view of parliamentary sovereignty, where Parliament is deemed to be the supreme law-maker, to the New View, where it is accepted that parliamentary sovereignty has to be reconciled with the UK's international law obligations stemming from its membership of the European Union and as a signatory to the European Convention of Human Rights. The first phase immediately follows the establishment of the duty in *Von Colson* and demonstrates a cautious approach: where national legislation had been enacted to give effect to EU law, the national courts were prepared to apply the principle of consistent interpretation to read words into a statute where a literal reading was not ambiguous, but would not be sufficient to comply with EU law; yet where national legislation pre-dated an EU directive, the UK courts refused to interpret it in light of a later EU directive. This initial reluctance and arguably deference to parliamentary sovereignty and its legislative intentions changed following the *Marleasing* ruling in 1990 (and the ruling of the then House of Lords in *Factortame*), where the ECJ was unequivocal in stating that the duty of consistent interpretation imposed on national courts required them to consider all national law, even if it pre-dated the conflicting EU law. At this point, the UK courts entered into a second phase in which they broadly accepted the full nature of the duty imposed on them by EU law. Indeed, from this point onwards, the principle of consistent interpretation was more commonly referred to by legal counsel and the judiciary as the "*Marleasing* principle". This phase continued until the House of Lords delivered its decision in *Ghaidan*. This was a judgment on the interpretation of a statute in light of the HRA and it explored in depth the duty of interpretation incumbent on national courts to interpret national law in compliance with the ECHR. It was later claimed by the Court of Appeal that it was at this point that the UK judiciary "assimilated" their duty under s. 3 of the HRA with their duty under EU law under the *Marleasing* principle (or vice versa). There is now no discernible difference in the application of the principle of consistent interpretation when determining its scope, namely whether a consistent interpretation is "possible". The UK courts are confident in complying with the interpretative obligation derived from EU law and are clear as to the boundaries between interpretation and amendment of the law. The courts have consistently refused to "go against the grain" of national legislation enacted by Parliament and venture into the field of policy-making. The contribution draws attention to the areas of motor insurance law and annual leave where the use of the principle of consistent interpretation has been more cautious and contested before the UK courts. This uncertainty in the law has arguably led to unnecessary and costly litigation for individuals seeking to assert their EU rights where national implementing legislation is deemed out of line with EU law, sometimes as a result of later ECJ rulings. There remains a great deal of legal uncertainty surrounding the UK's departure from the EU. Nevertheless, on the basis of this contribution, it can predicted that the UK judiciary will interpret in accordance with Parliament's intentions. For this reason, it is essential that the EU (Withdrawal) Act 2018 (and any other Acts of Parliament related to Brexit) clearly stipulate the obligations of the judiciary to interpret national law to comply with EU law as it evolves post-Brexit either through legislation or judgments of the ECJ.

CONSISTENT INTERPRETATION IN DENMARK

Christina D. Tvarnø and Grith Skovgaard Ølykke

1. INTRODUCTION

This contribution will look at EU-consistent interpretation in Denmark. It is structured as follows: in section 2, a thorough background on the Danish legal system is provided; in section 3, the methodology applied in the more empirical part of the contribution is accounted for; in section 4, national case-law on EU-consistent interpretation, where no preliminary reference has been made, is analysed, with a special focus on the issue of limits to consistent interpretation; in section 5, the Danish courts' use of the preliminary reference procedure is described and preliminary rulings on questions from Danish courts concerning consistent interpretation are discussed in detail; and section 6 rounds off with a set of conclusions.

2. THE DANISH LEGAL SYSTEM

Denmark, Greenland, and the Faroe Islands constitute the Kingdom of Denmark, which has a total population of approximately 5.8 million inhabitants.[1] The first Danish Constitution from 1241 was the *Jyske Lov* (Law of the Jutes), and laid down the principle that no one must judge contrary to the law which was issued by the king and adopted by the people.

The chosen king and the nobles jointly held the formal power in government affairs in an aristocracy. In 1660 and 1665, King Frederik III changed the Danish legal system to absolute monarchy through the – *Lex Regia* (King's Act). *Lex Regia* was the legal foundation of *jura majestatis* (the king's power).

This regime lasted until the Danish Constitution was adopted in 1849. The King's Act was a constitutional act and is the only written constitution for an autocratic regime in Europe. As a direct result of the absolute monarchy in 1660, King Christian V initiated the national unification of law implementing the absolute monarchy in the substantive law, accomplished in 1683 by *Danske Lov* (the Danish Code) of King Christian V. Important principles of the Danish Code are still in force, for example fundamental rules of the law of contract and principles of liability for damages.

The Danish *Grundloven* (Constitution) of 1849 abolished the absolute monarchy and made Denmark a constitutional monarchy in accordance with Section 3 of the Constitution.[2] The Constitution has been amended three times since 1849.

The Danish political system is a multi-party structure, where several parties are represented in the *Folketinget* (Danish Parliament). Eight parties are currently represented in the Parliament, which consists of 179 members,

---

1 <https://www.dst.dk/da/Statistik/emner/befolkning-og-befolkningsfremskrivning/folketal>.
2 Act 169/1953. <http://www.grundloven.dk>.

of whom 175 are from Denmark and two delegates each from the Faroe Islands and Greenland.

2.1. THE DIVISION OF POWERS UNDER THE DANISH CONSTITUTION

In accordance with Section 3 of the Danish Constitution, power is divided under three branches of government; the legislative (the parliament), the executive (the ministers and public government) and the judicial power. Due to the wording of Section 3 of the Danish Constitution, the king/queen is involved in the legislative and executive power, but according to Section 13 of the Constitution, the king/queen has no legal power; legal power rests solely with the Ministers and Parliament. Hence, Parliament votes for and adopts the acts, the ministers propose the acts and the king/queen approves the proposals and signs the acts.[3] The Ministers and the Government hold the executive power to implement and enforce the laws, and to establish public orders, and other legally binding administrative regulations. The courts hold the judicial power.

The administration of Denmark is divided between the state, five state regions and 98 municipalities. The Government forms the top of the hierarchy of the administration. Each Minister in the Government is chief executive within his/her field. The state administration is organised in a hierarchical system directed by the government with each minister as a top executive within a certain field. Each ministry is organised in departments that are divided into subsections.

The five state regions are: The Capital Region, Region of Zealand, Region of Southern Denmark, Region of Mid-Jutland, and Region of North-Jutland. The Regions' main task is to manage the Danish healthcare system, but they are also responsible for parts of the social sector and development of the Regions. The state Regions are funded through contributions from the state, and the municipalities are funded by tax payments and subsidies from the government. According to Section 82 of the Constitution, the municipalities are entitled to manage their own affairs independently; however, they are still under the supervision of the state.

Local government is executed on the municipal level. The municipal government is in principle autonomous. The extent of self-government is

---

[3] Legislation can be initiated by a bill introduced by a member of the Parliament, in accordance with Section 41(1) of the Constitution. Most commonly, the relevant minister will introduce a bill. Before being passed, the bill must be read and negotiated three times in the *Folketing* (Parliament), and must receive Royal Assent countersigned by the minister: see Section 42 of the Constitution. In accordance with Section 21 of the Danish Constitution, any member of the Parliament can introduce a bill in Parliament.

regulated by statute, whereas the execution of autonomy is submitted to control by the state, according to Section 82 of the Constitution.

The Parliament elects an Ombudsman, who supervises the public administration, making inquiries upon complaint or on his/her own initiative.[4]

The courts have an independent position. According to Section 62 of the Danish Constitution, judicial procedure must be regulated by statute and must be separated from the executive power. Section 64 of the Constitution provides that the judges must be directed only by the law in performance of their duties, and that judges can only be removed for misconduct. The courts decide private conflicts and impose penal sanctions. According to Section 63 of the Danish Constitution, the courts control the limits of the competence conferred on the administration. Furthermore, the courts are competent to decide the compatibility of a statute with the Constitution. Thus, all levels of Danish courts (City Courts, High Courts and the Supreme Court) have general competence in disputes concerning civil law and administrative law; however, the Maritime and Commercial Court is a specialised court at the same level as the High Courts.

Danish courts make *ratio decidendi* decisions. Normally, court decisions do not contain *obiter dicta*. When a general principle or solution of dubious legal value is expressed or may be deduced from the court's reasoning, the decision is important and useful even if it is not a Supreme Court decision, but is issued by a lower court.

2.2. DENMARK AND THE EUROPEAN UNION

Following a referendum, Denmark and Greenland acceded to the European Community (EC) on 1 January 1973. The Faroe Islands chose not to join the EC. By the Treaty of 13 March 1984, Greenland withdrew from the EC. Upon withdrawal, Greenland obtained an agreement on fisheries and adhesion to the Overseas Countries and Territories associated with the EC. The Treaty on the relationship between Greenland and the EC came into force on 1 January 1985.

The Danish Government signed the Maastricht Treaty and thereby entered the European Union (EU) on 7 February 1992; however, this ratification was rejected by a referendum on 2 June 1992. Consequently, the European Council agreed on a set of arrangements in Edinburgh on 12 December 1992 concerning the problems raised by Denmark. Following a referendum on 18 May 1993, Denmark adopted the Treaty on European Union, supplied by the Edinburgh

4 The activities of the Ombudsman of the Danish Parliament are regulated by law: Bekendtgørelse af lov om Folketingets Ombudsmand, LBK nr. 349 af 22/03/2013.

Agreements including four opt-outs (concerning the Monetary Union (EMU), the Common Security and Defence Policy (CSDP), Justice and Home Affairs (JHA), and EU Citizenship).

Denmark has subsequently signed the Nice, Amsterdam and Lisbon Treaties. Denmark is not a member of the EURO, but did join the EURO PLUS Pact 2012, thereby agreeing to a budgetary discipline and economic coordination to ensure public finances in a long-term perspective. The EURO PLUS Pact requires Denmark and the other participating countries to have a government budgetary position in balance or surplus. In 2015, Denmark voted "no" in a referendum regarding an opt-in model on JHA.

In general, EU legislation is implemented by parliamentary acts and by executive orders authorised by such acts, and Danish law must be interpreted in conformity with EU law. It is a general understanding that, according to Art. 288 of the Treaty on the Functioning of the European Union (TFEU), Art. 4 of the Treaty on European Union (TEU) and the Court of Justice of the European Union (ECJ) in the *Von Colson* case, Danish national courts are obliged to carry out "EU conform" (also known as "EU consistent") interpretation in vertical cases (i.e. disputes between private parties and the state).[5] The Danish courts have in several cases used EU-consistent interpretation, and hence interpreted Danish law in light of a provision of an EU directive. Thus, in vertical cases, EU directives and regulations will be placed on par with Danish statutes in the legal structure of sources, and judgments from the ECJ are therefore regarded as of the same legal value as a legal source as Danish court judgments. The situation is nevertheless different in horizontal cases, following the Supreme Court ruling in the *Ajos* case, discussed below in section 5.2.4.

2.3. DANISH LEGISLATION AND LEGAL SOURCES

Legislation in the form of statutes lay down general rules within a certain area of law. When a statute has been amended several times, it is frequently updated and published in consolidated form, where the amendments are incorporated into the text of the original statute.[6]

The provisions of a statute may or may not be mandatory. When a provision is mandatory, everybody has to comply with it, whereas there may be deviation from provisions that are not mandatory by agreement or by usage.[7] In commercial matters, the traditional legal regulation is generally not

---

5 C. D. Tvarnø and R. Nielsen, *Retskilder og retsteorier* (5. udg., København, 2017), Neergaard and Nielsen, *EU ret* (2016) and J. Kristiansen, "Grænser for EU-konform fortolkning i lyset af nyere højesteretspraksis" (2014) 1 *Juristen* 19.

6 Such a consolidated act is designated "*lovbekendtgørelse*" or "*bekendtgørelse af lov*".

7 Tvarnø and Nielsen (n. 5).

mandatory, whereas for public law a widespread set of mandatory legislation exists.

For the interpretation of statutory texts, in order to clarify the conception of the legislator indications may be found in the preparatory works of the statute, for example reports from an expert commission, comments to a bill introduced in Parliament, and the parliamentary debates. Interpretation by analogy can be used when there is a lacuna in the statutes, and the reasons for regulation in the laws in question are the same.[8] When a provision enumerates specific deviations from a general rule, a conclusion to the contrary (if it is not restricted in the rule, it might be interpreted that it is allowed) can often be made. Furthermore, a provision may be interpreted in a restrictive sense or in a broader sense.

Statutes are published online at <www.retsinformation.dk> and in *Lovtidende* (the official Law Gazette) Section A, which also includes amendments and the updated texts of statutes, i.e. the *lovbekendtgørelse* (consolidated acts) mentioned above. The Law Gazette Section B contains the Finance Act related statutes and the statutes on citizenship. Section C publishes the treaties in which Denmark is engaged with other states. The official Law Gazette is available (in Danish only) at <www.lovtidende.dk>.[9]

Administrative rules by public orders form an important part of Danish legal regulation. Frequently, Parliament (as a legislative power) authorises the relevant minister to issue general rules in the form of executive orders. The statutes stipulate which rules the ministry is allowed to enforce and accordingly which specific provisions that can be issued by the administration. Thus, an order constitutes a general rule that binds the citizens in the same way as a statute would. Executive orders are also published in the official Law Gazette Section A.[10]

The superior administrative authorities issue binding circulars and instructions to subordinate authorities. These rules are intended for internal administrative use, and normally do not bind individuals or enterprises. A number of the internal rules are published at retsinformation.dk.[11] The relative importance of administrative practice depends on the authority that has issued the decision, as a subordinate authority has to follow instructions from a superior one. According to Art. 63 of the Constitution, the courts

8 Tvarnø and Nielsen (n. 5).

9 Translations of some of the central acts, etc. can in some cases be found online on the home page of the website of the relevant ministry.

10 Within very limited areas, a regulation may be issued by *kongelig anordning* (royal decree). The authorisation is based on custom and tradition established under the absolute monachy. Nielsen and Tvarnø (n. 5), p. 90.

11 From 2008–2012, public instructions can be found in the *Ministerialtidende* (the official Law Gazette), <https://www.ministerialtidende.dk>. Material from 1871–2007 can be found at public libraries.

may review the legality of administrative decisions, but this control is seldom executed. Administrative precedents are applied as indicators in the same way as court precedents. Important precedents are issued within the fields of tax law, environmental law, employment law and concerning social matters.

In a traditional sense, a legal custom constitutes a certain conduct which has been practised generally, continuously, and for a long period in the conviction that there is a legal obligation to do so. In regard to contract law, a long period of conviction is not necessary, if it is obvious that a firm persuasion of the legal rule has manifested itself. The courts consider a legal custom as a rule of law that is recognised when the customary rule fills in a statute (*custom praeter legem*). In general, a custom contrary to the law (*custom contra legem*) is not applicable. Mandatory legislative provisions take precedence over custom.

Collective agreements (within the field of labour law) constitute an alternative to legislation. Such agreements are binding on the employers who apply them or who are members of the organisations that have adopted them. Furthermore, they seem to be indicative for the interpretation of other contracts outside the system of collective agreements.[12]

General principles of law include the principle of legality, the principle of the binding effect of contracts and the principle of procedural negotiating in civil cases (the negotiation doctrine),[13] defined in Section 388 of the Administration of Justice Act.[14] The negotiation doctrine is a general legal principle of Danish civil justice and prescribes that the parties should be familiar with the legal matter of the case and the dispute, and that the parties bear the costs of the case.

2.4. MONISM VERSUS DUALISM IN DENMARK IN REGARD TO EU LAW

Neither the Constitution nor the Act on Denmark's accession to the EU contain rules on the relationship between Danish law and EU law. Hence, as in the other Nordic countries, Denmark has traditionally upheld a dualistic perspective on international legal sources, and thus considered national and international legal sources as separate systems. Therefore, a ratified treaty will only become national law when incorporated by national legal sources, e.g. a statute – otherwise national law will be superior to international law.

Unlike in Norway, where the dualist theory is still highly prioritised, it is debated in the Danish legal theory whether dualism is suited to describe the legal relationship between Danish law and EU law, due to the principles of

12 R. Nielsen, *Dansk Arbejdsret* (3rd ed., DJØF, 2016), pp. 152–58.
13 Tvarnø and Neilsen (n. 5), p. 192.
14 LBK nr. 1257 af 13/10/2016.

EU supremacy and consistent interpretation;[15] it may be argued that Denmark (to a certain extent) approaches the monistic theory in regard to EU law.[16]

Furthermore, in accordance with Art. 218(7) TFEU, the EU's treaties with third countries are binding on the EU institutions and the Member States as an integrated part of EU law. Due to the monistic theory adopted in the EU, a ratified EU treaty concerning a third country is automatically part of Union law and thus of national law in the Member States.

Today, Danish national law contains a relatively high proportion of EU legislation originating from either EU regulations or directives. Furthermore, the EU principles of supremacy and consistent interpretation are a substantial part of Danish law, applicable even in situations where the legislator has not implemented specific EU rules by statute or other binding legal sources.

3. METHODOLOGY FOR THE EMPIRICAL PART OF THE CONTRIBUTION

The data forming the basis of this contribution are High Court and Supreme Court judgments, decisions from the Ombudsman and preliminary rulings from the ECJ concerning Danish cases.

Significant court decisions are published in *Ugeskrift for Retsvæsen* (Weekly Law Report – *UfR*), which is made up of a collection of the decisions made from the Supreme Court and a selection of decisions from the High Courts and the Maritime and Commercial Court. The Weekly Law Report is not open to the public; however, recent Danish court decisions are available on several public websites.[17]

---

15 H. Zahle, *Dansk Forfatningsret* (bind 3, Copenhagen, 2001); J. Christoffersen, "Folkerettens virkning i dansk ret" *U 2001 B 143*; O. Spiermann, "Højesterets anvendelse af folkeret i det 20. århundrede" (2001) *Juristen* s. 1; Section 13 in *Kupferberg-sagen*, sag 104/81 (Hauptzollamt Mainz mod C A Kupferberg & Cie KG a A, Saml., 1982), s. 3641; H. Zahle, *Dansk Forfatningsret* (bind 3, Kbhvn., 2001); J. Christoffersen, "Folkerettens virkning i dansk, ret" *U 2001 B 143*; O. Spiermann, "Højesterets anvendelse af folkeret i det 20. århundrede", *Juristen* (2001), s. 1; N. Finn Seyersted i Mikkelsen (ed.), *The Implementation in National Law of the European Convention on Human Rights* (Copenhagen, 1989), s. 77; A. Ross, *Lærebog i Folkeret* (1. udgave, 1942); K. Eilschou, "Konventionens praktiske betydning i Danmark", i *NTfIR* (1981), s. 126 f; C. Gulmann, "The position of international law within the Danish legal order", i *NTfIR* (1983), s. 45, N. Madsen, *Festskrift til Højesteret* (1986), s. 33 f. Also see H. Zahle, *Dansk Forfatningsret 3* (Menneskerettigheder, Copenhagen, 2003), s. 235 ff. and regarding Norway, Helgesen, J. Erik, *Teorier om "Folkerettens stilling i norsk rett"* (Oslo, 1982); O. Espersen, *Indgåelse og opfyldelse af traktater* (Copenhagen, 1970), s. 164 and p. 491.

16 Tvarnø and Nielsen (n. 5), pp. 172–73.

17 <http://domstol.fe1.tangora.com/S%C3%B8geside---H%C3%B8jesteretten.31488.aspx>. <http://www.domstol.dk/oestrelandsret/nyheder/domsresumeer/Pages/default.aspx>.

The national sources in the examined data set were accessed through information from the Danish Supreme Court,[18] Karnov,[19] *UfR*[20] and the Ombudsman.[21]

The selection of data was made through manual investigation, based on the search function in the above-mentioned databases and supported by legal academic literature. Thus, court cases settled by the parties are not included in this contribution. The cases in the data set cover a wide range of topics and do not focus on specific legal themes.

EU case-law was accessed through the ECJ's website, and was manually registered to enable production of certain general statistics on preliminary references from Danish courts. Subsequently, the number of judgments was reduced by searches within the initial data set of EU judgments, narrowing the search result to only a few cases which were then individually assessed as to their content on consistent interpretation. As this contribution concerns consistent interpretation, only judgments concerning interpretation of *national law* were included in the final data set (irrespective of whether they actually "determined" the outcome of the case or some discretion was left to the national court); i.e. preliminary references solely concerning interpretations of EU law were excluded. In order to find the final judgment applying the preliminary ruling to the national case, searches were made on *UfR* and on *infomedia*.[22] In this way it was possible to find judgments and other accounts of the final outcome of the cases.

The selection of data was based on both search functions and decisions addressed in Danish academic literature. Thus, this contribution contains the published Danish cases and administrative decisions. It is not possible to provide a complete list of Danish court decisions or a specific number of cases concerning consistent interpretation of EU law; hence, the collection of data is not reliable from a statistical point of view. It will not be possible to estimate particular political or legal patterns from the cases used in this contribution.

4. DANISH PRACTICE ON EU-CONSISTENT INTERPRETATION

4.1. CONCEPTUAL BASIS AND GENERAL SCOPE FOR THE OBLIGATION TO APPLY CONSISTENT INTERPRETATION

Danish legal academic literature and the national courts speak of the concept of EU-consistent interpretation as *"EU konform fortolkning"*. Danish national

18 <www.hoejesteret.dk>.

19 <https://www.karnovgroup.dk/?gclid=COLr4dPZhNACFYPhcgod9G8Azg>.

20 Ibid.

21 <http://www.ombudsmanden.dk>. These decisions are available at <www.retsinformation.dk>.

22 Database covering all Danish printed media, etc.

courts apply the principle of consistent interpretation directly, as an EU obligation based upon EU law, without applying a Danish national legal method or principle.

As to the legal disputes where the principle of consistent interpretation is relied upon by the parties, there are examples of public authorities attempting to rely on the principle in order to benefit themselves, e.g. in criminal proceedings such as in the *Grøngaard and Bang* judgment, and in the *Kofoed* judgment mentioned in sections 5.2.2 and 5.2.3, and two judgments of the Eastern High Court, *U 2000.1000 Ø* and *U 2011.1099 Ø*, regarding VAT.

U 2000.1000 Ø concerned a bowling facility and the obligation to pay VAT on income generated from non-professional sports activities. In this case, there was a discrepancy between Section 13 of the Danish VAT Act and Art. 13 (a)(1)(m) of the Sixth VAT Directive. The income would give rise to a VAT charge under the Directive, but not under the Danish VAT Act. The Eastern High Court did not interpret the national Danish legislation on VAT in a manner consistent with the VAT Directive. The Court mentioned the principle of EU-consistent interpretation in the judgment and concluded that the EU Directive's requirement that only non-profit companies were exempt from the VAT obligation was not enshrined in Danish law. From a literal (black letter law) interpretation of the Danish VAT Act, the bowling facility was not liable to VAT.

U 2011.1099 H concerned a dispute between the tax authorities and the "Roskilde Festival" association. The issue before the Supreme Court concerned Section 13 of the Danish VAT Act and the use of the surplus from the festival for charitable purposes. The association wanted to use some of the surplus from the festival to support an establishment of a youth and community centre project including music activities, a café and a bar. The private association argued (among others) that the directive on the EU's common system of VAT resulted in a better legal position than the Danish law and thus should be applied.[23] The Supreme Court held that due to the business activities of the private association, the conditions for VAT exemption pursuant to Section 13(1)(18) of the Danish VAT Act had not been complied with, as the surplus from the festival could not be used for this purpose; also, the Directive did not support activities partly open to profitable purposes, and thus an EU-consistent interpretation could not lead to a different conclusion. The Danish Supreme Court did not refer the case to the ECJ and did not argue on the ground of the *acte clair* principle. The dissenting judge in the Eastern High Court concluded in favour of the private association, due to the Directive, but did not use EU-consistent interpretation as the decisive element.

In *U 2003.233/2 Ø* concerning equal treatment among A and B shareholders, the Eastern High Court denied referral of a preliminary question to the ECJ,

---

[23] Council Directive 2006/112/EC – the EU's common system of value added tax (VAT).

requested by the City Court. The Eastern High Court argued that the Second Company Law Directive concerned equal treatment among equal shareholders, and therefore did not concern the relationship between A and B shareholders in the specific case.[24] Thus, due to the *acte clair* principle, the case was not referred to the ECJ.

Several cases concern EU-consistent interpretation of national law with regard to the Treaties. *U 2004.1246 H* concerned the compatibility of the Danish regulation on guarantees with Arts. 12 and 49 of the Treaty Establishing the European Community (TEC); *U 2001.1249 H* concerned the previous provision in the Danish Land Act requiring residence as a key element to owning a farm in Denmark, and its consistency with the provisions on free movement of capital – directives (vertical) and general principles (vertical and horizontal).[25]

In *U 2012.2247 Ø*, the Eastern High Court noted: "private parties cannot rely on a directive directly in a case against another private party". The national courts apply EU-consistent interpretation in cases between public and private parties. In cases between private parties, the Danish courts apply the *contra legem* principle. In cases of general EU principles, the Supreme Court submitted a question to the ECJ in *Ajos*;[26] see section 5.2.4 below.

The Danish courts seem to be hesitant to give the principle of consistent interpretation a wide scope. In *U 2002.1047 H*, the Supreme Court concluded that a provision in a directive should not be applied because the case concerned a dispute in Greenland (which is not part of the EU); and in *U 1998.800 H*, the Danish Supreme Court concluded that Section 20 of the Danish Constitution provides the limit to EU-consistent interpretation of Danish law.

4.2. NATIONAL INTERPRETATION METHODS AND THE *CONTRA LEGEM* LIMITATION

As mentioned previously, neither the Constitution nor the Act on Denmark's accession to the EU contains rules on the relationship between Danish and EU law. Thus, the principle of EU-consistent interpretation is derived directly from the case-law of the ECJ. The principle of EU-consistent interpretation is applied by the Danish courts, even to the detriment of private parties. However, the Supreme Court stresses that EU-consistent interpretation must be undertaken within the context of the recognised principles of interpretation in Danish law.[27]

---

24 Directive 2012/30/EU (the "Capital Directive").

25 See e.g. *U 2012.2247 Ø*, *U 2012.3220 V*, Eastern High Court's judgment of 09.04.2013 in Case *B-1593-11*, Maritime and Commercial Court judgment of 14.01.2014 in *F-19-12* and *U 2014.914 HIn*.

26 Case C-441/14, *Ajos*, ECLI:EU:C:2016:278.

27 Kristiansen (n. 5).

The Danish national courts have used the term "*contra legem* interpretation" to describe situations in both vertical and horizontal cases, where an EU-consistent interpretation is in conflict with the broadest interpretation of national law. In horizontal cases, between private parties, the EU-consistent interpretation will not overrule the national law. In these situations, a potential "*Francovich*" compensation claim against the Danish government becomes relevant. Furthermore, the *contra legem* principle is a general principle of Danish law.

In *U 2014.2442 H*, a case concerning public broadcasting and copyright, the Supreme Court stated that Section 31(1) of the Danish Copyright Act should be interpreted in accordance with Art. 5(2)(d) of the InfoSoc Directive.

In *U 2016.1230 H*, which concerned a defendant whose Danish driving licence had been suspended for a five-year period due to drunk driving, the Supreme Court concluded that the EU's Third Driving Licence Directive[28] should be interpreted in an EU-consistent manner in criminal matters. In accordance with the Danish law, the defendant was required to pass a new driving test in order to obtain a valid Danish driving licence. The defendant was resident in France and had obtained a valid French driving licence. The Supreme Court stated that Art. 11(4) in the Directive was not correctly implemented in Danish law, implying that the defendant could not be penalised for having driven without a valid Danish driving licence, because Denmark, as an EU Member State, was obliged to acknowledge the valid French driving licence.

In general, preparatory works are not defined as a binding legal source, but as a source of interpretation. The courts refer to preparatory works in several cases, but the lack of legally binding content normally means that they, as stated in the *Björnekulla* case,[29] will not overrule a directive.[30] In case *104/2001*, the High Court used preparatory legislative works as basis for reaching *contra legem*, and thus refusing consistent interpretation. In 1998, the Maritime and Commercial Court in case *N3/97* interpreted the national legislation in accordance with the preparatory works. The preparatory works indicated that the relevant national provision implemented a provision of an EU directive, and the Court explained that the Danish rule had to be interpreted in a manner consistent with it. As described above in *U 2014.914 H*, the Supreme Court relied on the preparatory works and on the firmly settled understanding of the provision in order to establish a valid law, and as a consequence overruled the High Court's earlier judgment in the case, where consistent interpretation had been carried out, despite the directions provided by the preparatory works.[31] In a few cases,

28 Directive 2006/126/EC of the European Parliament and of the Council of 20 December 2006 on driving licences (Recast).

29 Case C-371/02, *Björnekulla*, ECLI:EU:C:2004:275.

30 In the *Ajos* case, the Supreme Court came to a different conclusion in regard to the preparatory work of the Act on Denmark's accession to the European Communities. See section 5.2.4.

31 Kristiansen (n. 5) points out at p. 24 that this was the first time the Supreme Court refused to apply consistent interpretation.

the Supreme Court has considered settled national case-law as part of the basis for establishing *contra legem*,[32] i.e. relying on a previous interpretation of a provision made contrary to EU law.[33] This approach was nevertheless firmly rejected by the ECJ in the *Ajos* judgment, discussed in section 5.2.4 below.

4.3. LEGAL CERTAINTY AND LEGITIMATE EXPECTATIONS

The principles of legal certainty and legitimate expectations are important in Danish law. For example, in *U 2014.914 H*, the legal certainty of the private party was decisive for the outcome of the case. In this case, the Supreme Court relied on the principles of legal certainty (horizontal case, i.e. legal certainty for one of the private parties) and non-retroactivity. The case concerned the right to compensatory vacation when an employee falls ill while on holiday. According to longstanding Danish practice, there was no right to compensation if the employee falls ill after the start of a vacation; the preparatory works of the Vacation Act, which implemented the EU Directive concerning certain aspects of the organisation of working time,[34] explicitly stated this and pointed out that the interpretative practice dated back to 1939. In the case itself, an employee had fallen ill while on vacation in July 2009. In September the same year, a judgment from the ECJ clarified that the Directive contained a right to replacement vacation if the employee falls ill after the beginning of the vacation. The High Court used consistent interpretation to interpret the implemented law and found that it could be interpreted to provide for a replacement vacation in that case, as required by the Directive. Before the High Court, there was a discussion whether the ECJ's judgments could be attributed legal value, due among other things to the lack of an Advocate General opinion in the case, to which the parties attributed different meanings.

When the case was appealed, the Supreme Court started by noting that there was no direct horizontal effect of directives. It was stated that giving a right to replacement vacation in the case – and probably all the way back to 2012, when the national law was changed – would be *contra legem*, in light of national practice and the preparatory acts. It also referred to the principle of legal certainty (for the employers) and the principle of non-retroactivity. There were some considerations of a possible *Defrenne*[35] issue in the argumentation

---

32 *U 2014.914 H*. In the judgment, it was decided to make a preliminary reference in the *Ajos* case, cf. section 5.2.4.

33 See C.D. Tvarnø and R. Nielsen, "Ajos-sagens betydning for rækkevidden af EU-konform fortolkning i forhold til det almindelige EU-retlige princip om forbud mod aldersdiskrimination" *U 2016.B 28*.

34 Directive 2003/88/EC of the European Parliament and of the Council of 4 November 2003 concerning certain aspects of the organisation of working time.

35 Case 43/75, *Defrenne*, ECLI:EU:C:1976:56.

of the parties in the case – the case was filed after the judgment from the ECJ, which, however, was not limited in time, as it was in *Defrenne*. The Supreme Court found for the defendant.

This was also the approach taken by the Supreme Court in the *Ajos* case.[36] In its preliminary reference to the ECJ, the Supreme Court suggested that legal certainty and legitimate expectations should be given (perhaps more) weight, when the principle of consistent interpretation is applied; the Supreme Court also suggested that state liability could mend any breach of rights derived from EU law in the case.[37] The ECJ completely rejected these considerations, probably because the Supreme Court had framed its reference to concern the impact of the general principle of prohibiting discrimination on the grounds of age (as it assumed a contra legem situation thereby ruling out a consistent interpretation, where the other principles might have carried greater weight). The ECJ disagreed with the Danish Supreme Court's assumptions and mandated consistent interpretation. As discussed further below in section 5.2.4, the Danish Supreme Court did not follow the judgment from the ECJ.

4.4. *FOLKETINGETS OMBUDSMAND* (OMBUDSMAN OF THE DANISH PARLIAMENT)

The Ombudsman of the Danish Parliament is chosen by Parliament to handle complaints regarding public authorities.[38] The decisions of the Ombudsman are perceived as a source of law in legal theory.[39] The practice of the Ombudsman regarding EU law is not voluminous; however in the existing cases where consistent interpretation is applied, the Ombudsman seems to be rather meticulous, placing significant weight on ensuring the effect of EU legal rights in Danish law.[40] Thus, the Ombudsman controls and supports the national authorities in their application of EU law and national implementing law.[41]

36 Case 441/14, *Ajos*, ECLI:EU:C:2016:278.

37 On 29 May 2018, in Case B-929-17, the Danish High Court ruled that no claim of damages could be made against the Danish state by the plaintiff in the *Ajos* case because the limitation period had expired.

38 The activities of the Ombudsman are regulated by law, *lov om Folketingets Ombudsmand, LBK nr 349 af 22/03/2013*. See further <http://www.ombudsmanden.dk>. In Denmark, there is also a Consumer Ombudsman handling complaints regarding marketing law and other consumer regulation: <http://www.forbrugerombudsmanden.dk>.

39 For example Tvarnø and Nielsen (n. 5), pp. 199 and 291.

40 See as an example the detailed analysis of the concept of "information on the environment", *Oplysningerne i Vetstat er miljøoplysninger*, FOU nr. 2011.1405. There are, however, also examples where the analysis of the EU law behind national implementing measures is seemingly less meticulously examined, e.g. *Arbejdsgivers ansættelse af medarbejder i flere tidsbegrænsede stillinger var ikke ulovlig. Impelmenting af EU-direktiv*, FOU nr. 2012.0022.

41 Among others, the Ombudsman has examined the compatibility with EU law of the immigration authorities' administrative practices: *Udlændingemyndighedernes vejledning om familiesammenføring efter EU-retten mv.*, FOU nr. 2008.238.

5. PRELIMINARY REFERENCES – THE EU PERSPECTIVE ON THE USE OF CONSISTENT INTERPRETATION IN DENMARK

5.1. PRELIMINARY REFERENCES IN GENERAL

In this section, a brief overview is provided regarding the use of the preliminary reference procedure by Danish courts. In 2010, Wind wrote a critical article concerning Danish courts' use of the preliminary reference procedure from a political science perspective.[42] Relying on data between the period of 1973–2010, she found that a total of 104 references had been made in those 37 years (on average 2.8 references per year). She gave two main explanations for the low number. First, that Denmark is a majoritarian democracy with no tradition of legal review; Wind gives the example that Danish courts as the consequence of a case concerning legal review (validity) of national legislation have set aside national legislation only once in 160 years. Second, the State Prosecutor in Denmark plays a significant role in deciding whether preliminary references should be made; and, if so, the Ministry of Foreign Affairs has significant influence on how the questions to the ECJ should be drafted.[43] The development in the number of references made since Denmark became a Member State is shown below (see Figure 1).

From 1973 to 2016, 182 references were made, thus increasing the average to 4.16 references per year. The average from 2000 to 2016 is 5.94 and from 2010 to 2016 it is 8.14, indicating a further increase in recent times, which is also evident from Figure 1.

The first Danish court to make a preliminary reference to the ECJ was the Maritime and Commercial Court in 1975. It is interesting that in the period 1975–1980, out of a total of eight preliminary references, Copenhagen City Court made three, signalling an initially positive attitude towards using the preliminary reference system to solve EU law disputes already in the first instance. Another interesting observation is that in total, 16 of the 182 preliminary references made (i.e. 8.8 per cent) were withdrawn or otherwise removed from the ECJ's register. The reason for the removal is typically not provided, but the urge to settle the case before it reaches the national court appears to be a plausible reason (see Figures 2 and 3). As shown in Figure 2, the High Courts make the highest number of references (57 per cent).

---

42 M. Wind, "The Nordics, the EU and the Reluctance Towards Supranational Legal Review" 48 (2010) 4 *Journal of Common Market Studies* 1039–63.

43 For a full account of these procedures; see Wind, ibid., pp. 1050–51.

Figure 1. Number of preliminary references per year in Denmark, 1973–2016

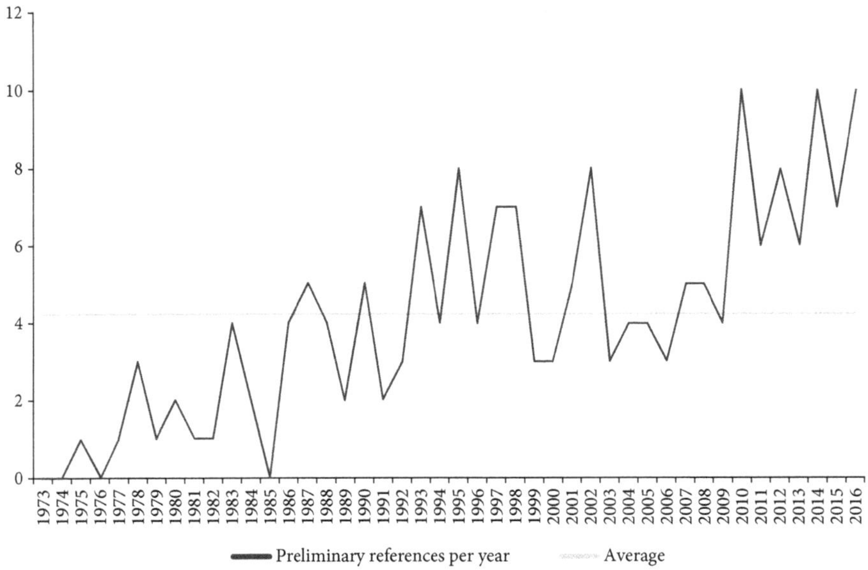

Source: Ølykke, Grith Skovgaard, 2017, based on official data from Curia.

Note: The horizontal line indicates the average of 4.23 preliminary references a year, from 1973 to 2016.

Figure 2. Preliminary references divided by referring court

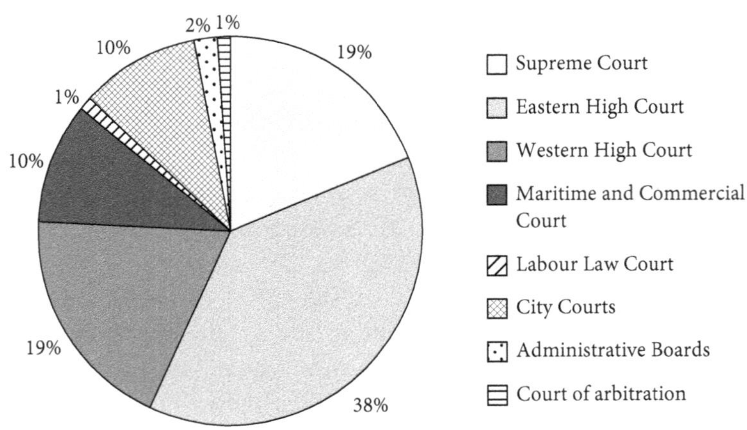

Source: Ølykke, Grith Skovgaard, 2017, based on official data from Curia.

Note: Preliminary references which were later joined by the ECJ are counted as separate references.

The two main topics giving rise to preliminary references from Danish courts are pecuniary and non-pecuniary measures affecting free movement of goods, i.e. customs, duties and restrictions (total 25 per cent), and social policy

Figure 3. Preliminary references from Danish courts categorized by topic

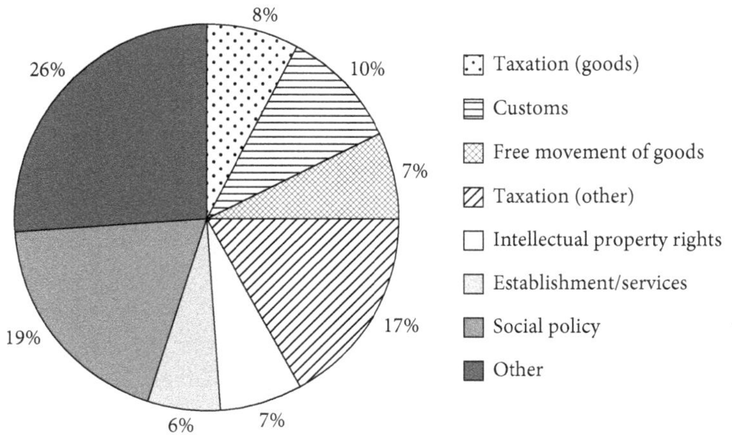

Source; Ølykke, Grith Skovgaard, 2017, based on official data from Curia.

Note: The categories are those provided at the website of the ECJ, only the first out of several labels are used in the figure. However, the categorisation has been simplified and changed to achieve informative categories; for example, where "harmonisation" is indicated as the first of several labels, label number two is preferred. Moreover, if more specific labels are available, they are used where possible, for example "customs" are preferred to "free movement of goods", whereas "free movement of goods" is preferred to "measure with equivalent effect". The purpose is to keep the labels general, but show, for example, the difference between pecuniary and non-pecuniary measures. Taxation (other) covers, for example, VAT on services, taxation in relation to mergers etc. The category "other" includes, in no particular order, competition law, consumer protection, environment, free movement of capital, harmonisation (where this was the only label provided), non-discrimination on grounds of nationality, telecom, transport, etc.

(19 per cent). Social policy covers a broad spectrum of issues, such as pensions, labour law and social security more generally.

5.2. PRELIMINARY REFERENCES CONCERNING OR INVOLVING CONSISTENT INTERPRETATION

A more detailed search was conducted on the ECJ's website (<curia.europa.eu>) of the 182 preliminary references to identify those concerned with consistent interpretation. The method used was to identify well-known judgments concerning all aspects of consistent interpretation and search for the number of those judgments in the wider dataset comprising of all preliminary references from Danish courts. Five judgments directly or indirectly concerned with consistent interpretation were identified: the Supreme Court made two of these preliminary references, while the Eastern High Court, the Maritime and Commercial Court and the Copenhagen City Court all made one preliminary reference each. The references concerned consumer protection, harmonisation, taxation, and social policy, respectively.

5.2.1. Henning Veedfald v. Århus Amtskommune[44]

In this case, Mr Veedfald was due to undergo a kidney transplant at Skejby Hospital and his brother had donated one of his kidneys for this purpose. When the kidney was being prepared for transplantation, it was flushed with a perfusion fluid produced by Århus Amts Hospital. The perfusion fluid was defective, making the kidney unsuitable for transplantation. Both Skejby Hospital and Århus Amts Hospital were owned by what is now the Region of Mid-Jutland. Veedfald asked for compensation under the implementing law on product liability. When this was denied, he filed a case for damages before the Western High Court, where the question of liability was separated from the other conditions that need to be fulfilled for damages to be incurred. Veedfald lost the case because the Western High Court found that the perfusion fluid had not been put into circulation and was not manufactured for an economic purpose – hence, the Region of Mid-Jutland was not liable, according to the Danish Product Liability Act.

Veedfald appealed the case to the Supreme Court, which made a preliminary reference to the ECJ. Before the ECJ, the Region of Mid-Jutland unsuccessfully argued – as it had successfully done before the Western High Court – that the transplantation was a service, not a product, and therefore was not within the ambit of the Product Liability Directive 1985;[45] that the perfusion fluid had not been put into circulation;[46] and that, in any event, the perfusion fluid was not manufactured for an economic purpose; hence, the exemptions provided in the Directive did not apply.[47]

---

44 Case C-203/99, *Veedfald*, ECLI:EU:C:2001:258.

45 Council Directive 85/374/EEC of 25 July 1985 on the approximation of the laws, regulations and administrative provisions of the Member States concerning liability for defective products [1985] OJ L210/29 (the Product Liability Directive 1985).

46 Art. 7 of the Product Liability Directive 1985 states: "The producer shall not be liable as a result of this Directive if he proves: (a) that he did not put the product into circulation; or (b) … (c) that the product was neither manufactured by him for sale or any form of distribution for economic purpose nor manufactured or distributed by him in the course of his business …".

47 Art. 9 of the Product Liability Directive 1985 concerned damages, and states: "For the purpose of Art. 1, 'damage' means: (a) damage caused by death or by personal injuries; (b) damage to, or destruction of, any item of property other than the defective product itself, with a lower threshold of [EUR] 500, provided that the item of property: (i) is of a type ordinarily intended for private use or consumption, and (ii) was used by the injured person mainly for his own private use or consumption. This Article shall be without prejudice to national provisions relating to non-material damage." The Danish implementation of that provision in the Product Liability Act states: "1. This Law covers compensation by way of damages for loss due to personal injury and loss of family support provided by the breadwinner. The Law also covers compensation for damage to material goods in the cases mentioned in subparagraph 2. Damage to material goods is covered by the Law if the object in question is, given its nature, normally intended for non-commercial use and is primarily used by the injured person in accordance with that purpose. The Law does not cover damage to the defective product itself."

The third preliminary question from the Supreme Court was whether Community law posed any requirements as to how the Member States should define the terms "damage caused by death or by personal injuries" and "damage to, or destruction of, any item of property other than the defective product itself". The ECJ stated that:[48]

> Although it is left to national legislatures to determine the precise content of those two heads of damage, nevertheless, save for non-material damage whose reparation is governed solely by national law, *full and proper compensation for persons injured by a defective product must be available in the case of those two heads of damage.* (emphasis added)

The ECJ pointed out that the application of national rules could not impair the effectiveness of the Directive and that the national court had to interpret its national law in the light of the wording and the purpose of the Directive.[49] The ECJ specified that "A Member State may not restrict the types of material damage, resulting from death or from personal injury, or from damage to or destruction of an item of property, which are to be made good".[50] Hence, the ECJ found that damages covered by product liability could not be restricted by national law – the coverage of such damages was only to be limited by the conditions stipulated in the Directive: the damage should be of an amount exceeding EUR 500; the item damaged must be of a type ordinarily intended for private use or consumption; and must have been used as such by the injured person. Thus, the ECJ more or less prescribed the result which should be reached by the national court on this point.

The fourth and fifth preliminary question from the Supreme Court sought to apply the text of the Directive to the facts of the case, essentially asking whether in relation to the person receiving the organ, the damage to the kidney should be categorised as "damage caused by personal injury" or "damage to, or destruction of, any [other] item of property". In this context, the ECJ explained that the Directive makes a producer liable for damage caused by a defect in his product and covers the two types of damage discussed above; the Directive thereby provides an exhaustive regulation of material damage (non-material damage is up to national law). The ECJ left the national court to decide under which category the specific damage belonged. However, it underlined that if the other conditions of liability were fulfilled, the national court could not decline to award *any* damages at all under the Directive, on the ground that the damage incurred did not fall under either of the two categories. Hence, the ECJ steered the Danish Supreme Court in the sense that, if the Region of Mid-Jutland was liable, it had to fit the damages into one of the two boxes provided by the Directive.

---

48 Case C-203/99 *Veedfald* (n. 44), para. 27.

49 In this context the ECJ referred to Case 14/83, *Von Colson*, ECLI:EU:C:1984:153, para. 26.

50 Case C-203/99, *Veedfald* (n.44), para. 28.

The Supreme Court only handled the liability issue of the damage claim; in another part of the suit, the Western High Court handled the questions of causation and foreseeability. Before the Supreme Court, the Region of Mid-Jutland decided – in the light of the preliminary reference from the ECJ – to acknowledge liability.[51]

5.2.2. *Criminal Proceedings Against Knud Grøngaard and Allan Bang*[52]

Mr Bang was the General Secretary of *Finansforbundet*, the professional trade union of employees in the financial sector. Mr Grøngaard was an elected member of the company *RealDanmark*, a major financial institution quoted on the stock exchange. Furthermore, he was appointed a member of the *RealDanmark Group*'s Liaison Committee (henceforth: "the Liaison Committee") by *Finansforbundet*. During the autumn of 2000, Mr Grøngaard attended several meetings with the board of directors of *RealDanmark* and of the Liaison Committee. During the meetings, the forthcoming merger between *RealDanmark* and *Danske Bank* was discussed. After each of the meetings, Mr Grøngaard disclosed information to Mr Bang, who in turn shared this information with (among others) his secretary – Mr Christensen. Mr Christensen used the information to purchase shares in *RealDanmark*, which were then sold immediately after the merger was announced, at which point the value of the shares had increased by 65 per cent. Mr Christensen was subsequently convicted for insider trading.

Criminal proceedings were raised before the Copenhagen City Court concerning the passing on of information by Mr Grøngaard and Mr Bang. The decision by the Copenhagen City Court to make a preliminary reference in the case to the ECJ was appealed to the Eastern High Court by the State Prosecutor. The decision of the City Court was upheld, and the Appeals Permission Board did not grant access to appeal the matter further to the Supreme Court.

In its reference, the Copenhagen City Court considered that the Directive on Insider Trading 1989 was relevant for the case.[53] The Directive prohibited insider trading by persons in possession of inside information with specific relations to the relevant issuer of shares.[54] The national law was stricter than

---

51 *U 2001.2338.H.*

52 Case C-384/02, *Grøngaard and Bang*, ECLI:EU:C:2005:708.

53 Council Directive 89/592/EEC of 13 November 1989 coordinating regulations on insider dealing [1989] OJ L334/30.

54 According to Art. 2 of the Directive: "Each Member State shall prohibit any person who: – by virtue of his membership of the administrative, management or supervisory bodies of the issuer; – by virtue of his holding in the capital of the issuer, or – because he has access to such information by virtue of the exercise of his employment, profession or duties, possesses inside information from taking advantage of that information with full knowledge of the facts by acquiring or disposing of for his own account or for the account of a third party, either directly or indirectly, transferable securities of the issuer or issuers to which that information relates." According to Art. 3(a) of the Directive: "Each Member State shall prohibit any

the Directive, as it covered *any person* in possession of inside information, and not just those covered by the Directive.[55] The national court asked several preliminary questions in order to find out whether the information passed on by Mr Grøngaard and Mr Bang was disclosed under the conditions mentioned in Art. 3(a) of the Directive. The ECJ provided the following general guidelines for the national court: first, the exemption to the prohibition on disclosing information must be interpreted strictly, i.e. a close link between the disclosure and the exercise of the employment, the profession or those duties, is required in order to justify such disclosure;[56] and, second, the national court must ensure compliance with the principle of legal certainty in the interpretation, in the light of the directive's wording and purpose, of the national law adopted in order to implement it.[57] Hence, the national implementing law should be interpreted consistently with the wording and purpose of the Directive. Then, the ECJ seems to put a limit to the scope for consistent interpretation in criminal proceedings, by stating that:[58]

> It is also appropriate to note that *the obligation on the national court to refer to the content of the directive when interpreting the relevant rules of its national law is not unlimited*, particularly *where such interpretation would have the effect, on the basis of the directive and independently of legislation adopted for its implementation, of determining or aggravating the liability in criminal law of persons who act in contravention of its provisions*. (emphasis added.)

This statement is explained by the fact that in this case, the state is enforcing the national implementing law and should not be able – by virtue of consistent interpretation – to sanction citizens for acts or by remedies more strict than those adopted in the implementing law, which the citizens acted in accordance with.

On the basis of these and other general remarks, the ECJ noted that the positions of Mr Grøngaard and Mr Bang and the question of what information would be disclosed in "the normal course of their employment, profession or duties" was a matter regulated by national law. It held that even if the relevant disclosures were allowed by the applicable national legal order, the national

---

person subject to the prohibition laid down in Art. 2 who possesses inside information from: (a) disclosing that inside information to any third party unless such disclosure is made in the normal course of the exercise of his employment, profession or duties; …".

55 The Danish implementing law (*Værdipapirhandelsloven*) stipulated among other things that: "Any person in possession of inside information may not disclose such information to any other person unless such disclosure is made in the normal course of the exercise of his employment, profession or duties."

56 Case C-384/02, *Grøngaard and Bang* (n. 52), para. 31.

57 Ibid., para. 29.

58 Ibid., para. 30.

court should find that the Directive precludes disclosure of information unless there is a close link between the disclosure and the exercise of his employment, profession or duties, and that the disclosure is strictly necessary for the exercise of that employment, profession or duties.[59]

Hence, in this judgment, at first glance, the ECJ merely guided the national court. However, it did note that "... it is appropriate to observe that inside information relating to a merger between two companies quoted on the stock exchange is in general particularly sensitive",[60] suggesting that the national court would not have much leeway to conclude otherwise.

In 2006, in accordance with the guidelines from the ECJ, the Copenhagen City Court found that information had been disclosed in breach of the rules in the directive and national law, and hence that Mr Grøngaard and Mr Bang had not passed on the information in "the normal course of their employment, profession or duties". Copenhagen City Court imposed fines of 5.000 DKK.

The case was appealed to the Eastern High Court, which in 2008 upheld the judgment of the City Court, albeit in a 4 to 2 majority decision, with dissent. In its judgment, the Eastern High Court found that it would be permissible to disclose the relevant information to the persons involved, but that the disclosure had been premature considering the specific facts of the case, in particular the information on the possible effect of the merger on the share value. The dissenting judges found that the information had been disclosed in the normal course of the employment, profession and duties, as traditionally such information had been disclosed by union representatives to their union in the auspices of mergers. However, the dissenting judges found that the disclosure of information on the possible effects of the merger on share value was not information disclosed in the normal course of employment. Thus, generally, the Eastern High Court leaned on the ECJ's guidance.

The judgment was appealed further to the Supreme Court, which overruled the first two instances and found that the information had been disclosed in the normal course of the employment, profession and duties of Mr Grøngaard

---

59 Ibid., para. 48. "... *precludes* a person, who receives inside information in his capacity as an employees' representative on a company's board of directors or in his capacity as a member of the liaison committee of a group of undertakings, *from disclosing such information* to the general secretary of the professional organisation which organises those employees and which appointed that person as a member of the liaison committee, *unless*: there is a close link between the disclosure and the exercise of his employment, profession or duties, and; that disclosure is strictly necessary for the exercise of that employment, profession or duties. As part of its examination, the national court must, in the light of the applicable national rules, take particular account of: the fact that that exception to the prohibition of disclosure of inside information must be interpreted strictly; the fact that each additional disclosure is liable to increase the risk of that information being exploited for a purpose contrary to Directive 89/592, and; the sensitivity of the inside information." (emphasis added.)

60 Case C-384/02, *Grøngaard and Bang* (n. 52), para. 38.

and Mr Bang.[61] As a union representative on the board, Mr Grøngaard was entitled to discuss the future merger with the General Secretary of the trade union – both in order to discuss which position to take strategically, and to make sure that the union was ready for the merger. Moreover, information on the possible effect of the merger on share value had been necessary to disclose in light of the discussions about any possible alternative bids for the company with similarly serious consequences for the labour force. The Supreme Court referred to the purpose of the provision, as set out in the preparatory works, and to the fact that such disclosure had traditionally been made under similar circumstances. Thus, this case is an example of the preparatory works being included in the argumentation of the Supreme Court to rule out consistent interpretation. Mr Bang had also been allowed to discuss this information with his closest staff (including Mr Christensen). At the end of the judgment, the Supreme Court noted that "In the Supreme Court's perception this result is within the boundaries of the ECJ's judgment of 22 November 2005; cf. e.g. paras 27–30 and 39–40".[62] Whereas the lower courts had concluded otherwise, it must be noted that in the first two instances there were dissenting judges, suggesting that the specific circumstances of the case were quite decisive.

5.2.3. Hans Markus Kofoed v. Skatteministeriet[63]

The case essentially concerned whether a share transaction was taxable under the Directive on Taxation of the Exchanges of Shares etc.[64] The defendant in the case, Mr Kofoed, had made some transactions with a business partner. Contrary to what was argued by the Danish Ministry of Taxation, the ECJ found that these did not qualify for taxation according to the Directive.[65] Art. 11 of the Directive made the tax exemption provided inapplicable in the case of abuse of rights; however, that provision was not explicitly implemented in national law. Thus, The Eastern High Court inquired whether a possible abuse of rights could be taken into account when deciding the case.

The ECJ explained that Art. 11 reflected the general Union law principle that abuse of rights is prohibited; individuals must not improperly or fraudulently take advantage of provisions of Union law. As for the question as to whether Art. 11 could be relied upon in absence of its implementation in Danish law,

61 *U 2009.2142.H.*

62 Authors' translation ("*Dette resultat må efter Højesterets opfattelse anses for at ligge inden for rammerne af EF-domstolens dom af 22. november 2005, jf. herved bl.a. dommens præmisser 27–30 og 39–40.*").

63 Case C-321/05, *Kofoed*, ECLI:EU:C:2007:408.

64 Council Directive 90/434/EEC of 23 July 1990 on the common system of taxation applicable to mergers, divisions, transfers of assets and exchanges of shares concerning companies of different Member States [1990] OJ L225/1.

65 Case C-321/05, *Kofoed* (n. 63), paras. 24–35.

the ECJ held that generally "... the principle of legal certainty precludes directives from being able by themselves to create obligations for individuals. Directives cannot therefore be relied upon per se by the Member State as against individuals."[66]

However, the ECJ also reminded the national court that:[67]

> ... according to the actual wording of the third paragraph of Art. [288 TFEU], Member States may choose the form and methods for implementing directives which best ensure the result to be achieved by those directives ... Accordingly, provided that the legal situation arising from the national transposition measures is sufficiently precise and clear and that the persons concerned are put in a position to know the full extent of their rights and obligations, transposition of a directive into national law does not necessarily require legislative action in each Member State.

Then, it stated that:[68]

> ... all authorities of a Member State, in applying national law, are required to interpret it as far as possible in the light of the wording and purpose of the Community directives in order to achieve the result pursued by those directives. Moreover, *although it is true that the requirement of a directive-compliant interpretation cannot reach the point where a directive, by itself and without national implementing legislation, may create obligations for individuals* or determine or aggravate the liability in criminal law of persons who act in contravention of its provisions, *a Member State may nevertheless, in principle, impose a directive-compliant interpretation of national law on individuals ... it is therefore for the national court to ascertain whether there is, in Danish law, a provision or general principle prohibiting abuse of rights or other provisions on tax evasion or tax avoidance which might be interpreted in accordance with Art. 11 [of the directive on taxation of shares etc.]* and thereby justify taxation of the exchange of shares in question. (emphasis added)

This statement seems to indicate a voluntary possibility to impose taxation for Member States. In this case, the Ministry of Taxation clearly wanted to impose such an interpretation, and tax the transaction. However, the wording "a Member State may ... impose ..." seems to suggest some kind of authorisation; it gives rise to considerations whether it is the legislator, the national authorities or the national courts that should impose such an interpretation.

In reality, the ECJ seems to be referring here to the general obligation of national courts and authorities to take all national legislation into account and interpret it in accordance with the relevant directive.[69] However, there

---

66 Ibid., para. 42; see also Advocate General Kokott's, Opinion in Case C-321/05, *Kofoed*, ECLI:EU:C:2007:86, para. 66.

67 Ibid., para. 43–44.

68 Ibid., para. 45–46.

69 See also Advocate General Kokott's Opinion (n. 66)., para. 65.

are some steps on the way which were important for the ECJ in this case: first, the announcing of a general principle in order to prevent the abuse of rights attributed by EU law; second, the lack of direct horizontal effect of the directives; third, the lack of an explicit obligation to take legislative action when implementing a directive; fourth, in such situations, the requirement for national law to be "precise and clear and that the persons concerned are put in a position to know the full extent of their rights and obligations"; and, fifth, the need for some national legislation or principles to tie the consistent interpretation to. In reality, the ECJ guided the national court so it would be able to achieve different outcomes, depending on whether it "decided" to impose a consistent interpretation, even in the absence of implementation, and on the character of the provisions already existing in national law that the national court might subject to consistent interpretation. The existing of provisions or principles in national law concerning abuse of rights in the context of taxation could thus justify the actual horizontal effect of the directive to the detriment of citizens, even where the Member State was responsible for implementing the provision needed for the desired outcome (for the state), hence, the reverse-vertical effect.

Subsequent to the preliminary ruling, the Danish Ministry of Taxation (*Skatteministeriet*) decided to withdraw the case. The reason was that the Danish Tax Appeals Agency (*Landsskatteretten*)[70] had already stated in 1999 that provisions on abuse of rights in an EU directive cannot be relied upon if the provision is not implemented in Danish law.[71]

5.2.4. Dansk Industri Acting on Behalf of Ajos v. Rasmussen *(the* Ajos *Case)*[72]

The *Ajos* case concerned a horizontal dispute and consistent interpretations of national law in line with general EU principles, not consistent interpretation of articles of a directive. The ECJ stated in the *Ajos* case that national Danish law must be consistent with general EU principles and thus must be interpreted consistent with the principle of non-discrimination on the ground of age. It should be noted that the ECJ in para. 30 of its preliminary ruling stated that that obligations may not be imposed on individuals by directives by way of direct effect:

> While it is true that, in relation to disputes between individuals, the Court has consistently held that a directive cannot of itself impose obligations on an individual and cannot therefore be relied upon as such against an individual (see, inter alia,

---

[70] The Tax Appeals Agency is the central administrative appeals authority for cases involving taxation, VAT, duties, customs duty, collection of public debts, and property assessment.

[71] A.M. Ottosen, "Kort nyt om skat", Jyllands-Posten, 03.12.2007, Erhverv and Økonomi, p. 7.

[72] Case C-441/14, *Dansk Industri acting on behalf of Ajos v. Rasmussen*, ECLI:EU:C:2016:278. The judgment setting out the facts of the case and deciding that a preliminary reference should be made is *U 2017.824*.

judgments in *Marshall*, 152/84, EU:C:1986:84, paragraph 48; *Faccini Dori*, C-91/92, EU:C:1994:292, paragraph 20; and *Pfeiffer and Others*, C-397/01 to C-403/01, EU:C:2004:584, paragraph 108), the fact nonetheless remains that the Court has also consistently held that the Member States' obligation arising from a directive to achieve the result envisaged by that directive and their duty to take all appropriate measures, whether general or particular, to ensure the fulfilment of that obligation are binding on all the authorities of the Member States, including, for matters within their jurisdiction, the courts (see, to that effect, inter alia, judgments in *von Colson and Kamann*, 14/83, EU:C:1984:153, paragraph 26, and *Kücükdeveci*, C-555/07, EU:C:2010:21, paragraph 47).

The Danish Supreme Court requested a preliminary ruling from the ECJ, which was handed down on 19 April 2016. In its final ruling in the case on 6 December 2016, the Danish Supreme Court did not follow the ECJ. This section will present the facts in the *Ajos* case, the ruling of the ECJ as far as consistent interpretation is concerned, and the final ruling of the Danish Supreme Court.

5.2.4.1. The Facts and the ECJ Ruling in the *Ajos* Case

Mr Rasmussen had worked for the private company *Ajos* in the period of 1984–2009, when he was laid off at the age of 60. He subsequently found new employment. After he passed away, his heirs filed a case for payment of a severance allowance in accordance with national law. Section 2a(3) of the *Funktionærloven* (Employers and Salaried Employees (Legal Relationship) Act) provided that:

> *No severance allowance shall be payable if, on termination of the employment relationship, the employee will receive an old-age pension from the employer* and the employee joined the pension scheme in question before reaching the age of 50. (emphasis added)[73]

The emphasised part of the cited provision – as interpreted by Danish courts – had previously been considered by the ECJ in *Ingeniørforeningen i Danmark*.[74] In that ruling, which concerned a vertical relationship (i.e. a public employer), the ECJ had held the national law to be contrary to the Equal Treatment Directive.[75] Danish courts had interpreted the national law as meaning that employees were deprived of the severance allowance *only* because they were entitled to an

73 Section 2a(1) is interpreted by Danish courts in practice as meaning: "In the event of the dismissal of a salaried employee who has been continuously employed in the same undertaking for 12, 15 or 18 years, the employer shall, on termination of the employment relationship, pay a sum to the employee corresponding to, respectively, one, two or three months' salary."

74 Case C-499/08, *Ingeniørforeningen i Danmark*, ECLI:EU:C:2010:600.

75 Council Directive 2000/78/EC of 27 November 2000 establishing a general framework for equal treatment in employment and occupation [2000] OJ L303/16.

old-age pension, irrespective of whether they continued to be in employment or not. Relying on *Ingeniørforeningen i Danmark*, the heirs of Mr Rasmussen brought a case before the Maritime and Commercial Court alleging that the severance allowance should be paid.

The Maritime and Commercial Court found for the applicants.[76] The case was appealed to the Supreme Court by *Ajos*, claiming that any interpretation of the national law (in accordance with the ECJ's judgment in *Ingeniørforeningen i Danmark*) would be *contra legem*, and that precluding the application of national law based on a general principle of EU law that prohibits discrimination on grounds of age would be contrary to the principles of legal certainty and legitimate expectations.

The Supreme Court noted the difference between vertical and horizontal cases. It pointed out that in a vertical case – as *Ingeniørforeningen i Danmark* – discrepancies between national law and EU law can be handled by disapplication of national law and the direct effect of the provision in EU law (if the conditions for direct effect are fulfilled). This is not possible in horizontal cases concerning directives, however, as directives do not have horizontal direct effect. Therefore, national law has to be interpreted in consistency with EU law, as far as possible (i.e. limited by e.g. *contra legem*).[77] The Supreme Court noted the discussion among various Advocates General concerning the direct effect of general principles following the *Mangold* and *Kücükdeveci* judgments.[78] Seemingly spurred on by legal policy, it appeared to be intending to test whether this case-law would still stand.[79] The preliminary reference is framed by two assumptions: first, as the relation in the main case is horizontal, it is not possible to give direct effect to the Equal Treatment Directive; and, second, an interpretation of the relevant national law in consistency with EU law would conflict with

---

76 See also the Eastern High Court's judgment *U 2012.2247 Ø*, where it stated that "private parties cannot invoke a directive directly in a case against another private party". However, the Eastern High Court furthermore stated "that prohibition of discrimination on grounds of age must be considered as a common principle of EU law" and the High Court awarded the employee severance payment despite the restriction in the Salaried Employees Act section 2a(3). See also for the same result *U 2012.3220 V*; Western High Court, judgment of 09.04.2013 in B-1593-11; and the Maritime and Commercial Court, judgment of 14.01.2014 in *F-19-12*. All of these judgments followed Case C-144/04 *Mangold*, ECLI:EU:C:2005:709 and/or *Ingeniørforeningen i Danmark*. This "EU obeying" practice of lower courts could have spurred the reference for a preliminary ruling by the Supreme Court.

77 See also G.S. Ølykke, and C.D. Tvarnø, "Pligten til EU-konform fortolkning – Efter EU-domstolens afgørelse i Dominguez-sagen" in J. Fejø, U. Neergaard, C.D. Tvarnø and G.S. Ølykke (eds.) *Liber amicora et amicorum in honour of Ruth Nielsen* (DJØF Publishing, 2013), pp. 411–30, at pp. 429–30.

78 Case C-144/04, *Mangold*, ECLI:EU:C:2005:709; Case C-555/07, *Kücükdeveci*, ECLI:EU:C:2010:21.

79 For critique, see C.D. Tvarnø and R. Nielsen, "Ajos-sagens betydning for rækkevidden af EU-konform fortolkning i forhold til det almindelige EU-retlige princip om forbud mod aldersdiskrimination" *U.2016B.28*.

national case-law, thereby giving rise to a *contra legem* situation.[80] The Supreme Court therefore focused its preliminary reference on whether, in the absence of a possibility to interpret national law in conformity with the Directive, the "unwritten" general principle prohibiting discrimination on the ground of age has horizontal direct effect, and how that principle should be balanced with the principles of legal certainty and legitimate expectations.[81] Lastly, the Supreme Court asked whether state liability should be taken into account in such a balancing exercise.[82]

The first preliminary question was whether the general principle prohibiting discrimination on grounds of age precluded the Danish legislation, as interpreted by national courts. The ECJ generally followed its previous case-law in *Kücükdeveci* (which was also a horizontal case), and started off by stating that the principle was founded in "various international instruments and in the constitutional traditions of the Member States", enshrined in Art. 21 of the Charter of Fundamental Rights, and a general principle of EU law according to the ECJ's case-law.[83] The ECJ then established a link to EU law by referring to its previous findings in *Ingeniørforeningen i Danmark*. In that case, it found that the severance allowance affected the conditions of the dismissal of workers which was regulated by the Equal Treatment Directive.[84] Hence, the national legislation was within the scope of EU law and the principle prohibiting discrimination on the grounds of age.[85] The ECJ then swiftly declared that since the national law was contrary to the Directive, it was also contrary to the principle prohibiting discrimination on the grounds of age (being a specific expression of the principle of equal treatment).[86] The ECJ concluded on the first question in the following way:[87]

> … the answer to the first question is that the general principle prohibiting discrimination on grounds of age, as given concrete expression by [the Equal Treatment Directive], must be interpreted as precluding, *including in disputes between private persons*, national legislation, such as that at issue in the proceedings before the referring court …

80 See Advocate General Bot's Opinion where it is argued that *contra legem* means "against the law", referring to the letter of the law, not to case-law which is a result of the national courts' (wrongful) interpretation of the law; Case C-441/14, *Dansk Industri on behalf of Ajos v. Rasmussen*, ECLI:EU:C:2015:776, paras. 69–73.

81 Case C-441/14 (n. 72), para. 15.

82 Ibid., paras. 17–19.

83 Ibid., para. 22.

84 Art. 3(1)(c).

85 Case C-441/14 (n. 72), para. 25.

86 Ibid., para. 26.

87 Ibid., para. 27.

The second preliminary question was whether, if national law was contrary to the principle of prohibiting discrimination on the grounds of age, the national court should balance this principle against the principle of legal certainty and legitimate interest, and whether the possibility of the state being held liable for the breach of EU law should be taken into account in that balancing. The ECJ started by emphasising that national courts must provide the legal protection which individuals derive from provisions of EU law and must ensure that those provisions are fully effective.[88] The ECJ then acknowledged that directives cannot have direct effect in horizontal cases, but that national courts are obliged to interpret national law in order to achieve the result envisaged by the directive (i.e. consistent interpretation).[89] The ECJ then pointed out that the requirement to interpret national law in conformity with EU law entailed an obligation for national courts to change their established case-law, if it is based on an interpretation of national law which is incompatible with a directive,[90] and hence:[91]

> Accordingly, the national court cannot validly claim in the main proceedings that it is impossible for it to interpret the national provision at issue in a manner that is consistent with EU law by mere reason of the fact that it has consistently interpreted that provision in a manner that is incompatible with EU law.

The Supreme Court's understanding of the term *contra legem* is thus contested by the ECJ. The ECJ continued:[92]

> That point having been made clear, it should be added that *even if a national court seised of a dispute that calls into question the general principle prohibiting discrimination on grounds of age, as given concrete expression in Directive 2000/78, does in fact find it impossible to arrive at an interpretation of national law that is consistent with the directive*, it is nonetheless under an obligation to provide, within the limits of its jurisdiction, the legal protection which individuals derive from EU law and to ensure the full effectiveness of that law, disapplying if need be any provision of national legislation contrary to that principle. (emphasis added)[93]

In this paragraph, the ECJ tauntingly respects the framing of the question as concerning a *contra legem* situation, but nevertheless implies that consistent interpretation should still be the point of departure for national courts.

88 Ibid., para. 29.
89 Ibid., paras. 30–31.
90 Ibid., para. 33; in this connection the ECJ refers to C-456/98, *Centrosteel*, ECLI:EU:C:2000:402, para. 17. See also Advocate General Bot's Opinion concerning C-441/14 (n. 80), paras. 59 ff.
91 Case C-441/14 (n. 72), para. 34.
92 Ibid, para. 35.
93 Emphasis added.

The ECJ states that if a situation should arise, where consistent interpretation would lead to a *contra legem* interpretation, the national court must provide the legal protection that individuals derive from EU law and, if necessary, neglect the national law.[94] The ECJ refers to *Association de mediation sociale* in order to stress that the principle prohibiting discrimination on the grounds of age confers an individual right on a private person which, even in horizontal disputes, requires national courts to neglect national provisions that do not comply to the principle.[95] Then, the ECJ made it very clear that neither the principle protecting legitimate expectations nor the principle of state liability could alter the obligation of the national court to strive for an interpretation of national law that is consistent with the Directive on equal treatment, or (if such an interpretation is not possible) its obligation to neglect a national provision which is at odds with the general principle prohibiting discrimination on the ground of age, as given concrete expression by that Directive. Moreover, the national courts cannot give precedence to the protection of the legitimate expectations of a private person, namely in this case the employer, who has complied with national law.[96] Hence, the ECJ clearly states that legitimate expectations of private individuals emanating from mal-application of national law cannot supersede the individual's right derived by private persons from EU law; in such cases, state liability can mend the damage suffered by persons (or undertakings) who in good faith adhered to national law.

5.2.4.2. The Danish Supreme Court's Verdict in the *Ajos* Case, 6 December 2016

The Danish Supreme Court did not follow the first instance ruling of the Danish Maritime and Commercial Court; nor did it follow the judgment of the ECJ. The Supreme Court concluded that, due to the state of Danish law and the established practice of the Danish Supreme Court, and due to the *contra legem* limitation, it was not possible to interpret Section 2a(3) of the Employers and Salaried Employees (Legal Relationship) Act in line with the Equal Treatment Directive.

The Danish Supreme Court emphasised its own established legal practice in its judgments of 4 October 1973,[97] 7 December 1988,[98] 14 February 1991,[99] 9 May 2008[100] and 17 January 2014.[101] In those cases, the Supreme Court had

94 Case C-441/14 (n. 72), para. 35.
95 Case C-176/12, *Association de mediation sociale*, ECLI:EU:C:2014:2.
96 Case C-441/14 (n. 72), paras. 41–42.
97 *UfR 1973.898.*
98 *UfR 1989.123* and *UfR 1989.126.*
99 *UfR 1991.314/1*, *UfR 1991.314/2* and *UfR 1991.317.*
100 *UfR 2008.1892.*
101 *UfR 2014.1119.*

ruled that an employee was not entitled to severance payment if the employee upon his resignation was entitled to a retirement pension from the employer, regardless of whether the employee chose to make use of the right to a pension.

The Danish Supreme Court recognised the jurisdiction of the ECJ to determine questions on the interpretation of EU law according to Art. 267 TFEU. With regard to the interpretation of general principles in EU law, the Supreme Court stated that the impact of EU rules on Danish law depends on the Act on Denmark's Accession to the European Union of 1972.[102] The Supreme Court concluded that it was not foreseen in the Act on Denmark's Accession to the European Union that the general principle of non-discrimination on grounds of age must be regarded as a principle on Treaty level with direct effect and primacy over conflicting Danish law in a horizontal dispute. Subsequent amendments to the Act on Denmark's Accession to the European Union had not changed the legal situation, and the Supreme Court therefore concluded that in a horizontal dispute, the Act on Denmark's Accession to the European Union did not provide the legal basis for a contra legem interpretation, and that it would be acting outside the limits of its judicial power if it violated this regulation as well as its own established practice.

5.2.4.3. Critique of the Danish Supreme Court's Judgment in the *Ajos* Case

The Supreme Court ruled contrary to the judgment of the ECJ, releasing a private employer from any obligation to comply with the general EU law principle prohibiting age discrimination. In this context, the wording of the Declaration concerning primacy (no. 17) in the Lisbon Treaty should be taken into account.[103] In this Declaration it is stated that:

> The Conference recalls that, in accordance with well settled case-law of the Court of Justice of the European Union, the Treaties and the law adopted by the Union on the basis of the Treaties have primacy over the law of Member States, under the conditions laid down by the said case-law. Furthermore, the Opinion of the Council Legal Service of 22 June 2007 was explicitly mentioned in the Lisbon Treaty.[104]
>
> It results from the case-law of the Court of Justice that primacy of EC law is a cornerstone principle of Community law. According to the Court, this principle is inherent to the specific nature of the European Community. At the time of the

[102] Act no 447 of October 11, 1972.

[103] See also R. Nielsen and C.D. Tvarnø, "Danish Supreme Court infringes the EU Treaties by its ruling in the Ajos Case" 2 (2017) *Europaraettslig Tidskrift*, s. 303–326, R. Nielsen and C.D. Tvarnø, "Præjudikat eller ikke præjudikat: Chartrets retsvirkning i dansk ret efter EU-domstolens og Højesterets afgørelser i Ajos-sagen" 130 (2017) 2–3 *Tidsskrift for Rettsvitenskap*, s. 218–46, C.D. Tvarnø and R. Nielsen, *Retskilder og retsteorier* (5. udg., København, 2017).

[104] Final Act. The Opinion of the Council Legal Service on the primacy of EC law as set out in 11197/07 (JUR 260).

> first judgment of this established case-law (Costa/ENEL, 15 July 1964, Case 6/641 [1]) there was no mention of primacy in the treaty. It is still the case today. The fact that the principle of primacy will not be included in the future treaty shall not in any way change the existence of the principle and the existing case-law of the Court of Justice.

According to footnote 1 in the EU Council Legal Service's Legal Opinion on the primacy of EC law,[105] national courts of the Member States must consider the principle of primacy, which in the opinion is defined in the following manner:

> ... that the law stemming from the treaty, an independent source of law, could not, because of its special and original nature, be overridden by domestic legal provisions, however framed, without being deprived of its character as Community law and without the legal basis of the Community itself being called into question.[106]

The Danish Supreme Court did not mention Declaration 17 in its judgment, and thus did not take the Lisbon Treaty into consideration as a legal argument countering the Act on Denmark's Accession to the European Union. Furthermore, it should be noted that subsequent to the *Ingeniørforeningen i Danmark* judgment, in 2015 Danish legislation was changed in order for it to be compatible with EU law.[107] On this basis, it may be wondered whether Denmark risks infringement proceedings before the ECJ because of the Supreme Court ruling, and also because the ECJ has reiterated its stance in subsequent case-law.[108]

6. CONCLUSIONS

On the basis of the analysis carried out in this contribution, a few general conclusions and observations may be made. First, it appears that since 2010, there has been an upward trend in the number of preliminary references made by Danish courts. The research shows an increase of almost a third in the average of questions referred per year since 1973, as compared to when Wind published her article in 2010. This contribution has not attempted to redo the empirical efforts made by Wind, as it is entirely outside the scope of the

---

105 The Opinion of the Council Legal Service on the primacy of EC law as set out in 11197/07 (JUR 260).

106 Ibid. and Case 6/64, *Costa/ENEL*, 5 July 1964, ECLI:EU:C:1964:66.

107 Cf. §1 in *Lov om ændring af retsforholdet mellem arbejdsgivere og funktionærer, LOV nr. 52 af 27/01/2015*, available at <https://www.retsinformation.dk/Forms/R0710.aspx?id=167733>. See the preparatory works, where reference is made to the judgment of the ECJ in *Ingeniørforeningen i Danmark*.

108 See e.g. Case C-554/14, *Ognyanov*, ECLI:EU:C:2016:835.

present contribution to do so, and so the reasons for the increase are not clear. Second, while it appears that there has traditionally been willingness to apply the principle of consistent interpretation in vertical cases by the Danish Supreme Court, there appears to be less willingness in horizontal cases – including horizontal cases regarding consistent interpretation of general principles of EU law according to the *Ajos* case. Third, it cannot be deduced from the empirical investigation that Danish courts follow an established methodology in national case-law when applying the principle of consistent interpretation as opposed to the method used in cases concerning direct effect and state liability.

THE PRINCIPLE OF CONSISTENT INTERPRETATION IN FINNISH COURTS

Samuli MIETTINEN*

* I wish to thank Joonas Tervo and Petri Freundlich for their efficient research assistance, and Tuukka Vähätalo, Christian N.K. Franklin and the participants of the Bergen symposium for their comments on earlier drafts.

1. INTRODUCTION

This contribution reviews the case-law of the Finnish courts applying the doctrine of consistent interpretation. Consistent interpretation is recognised as *the most important* way in which European Union (EU) law appears and is given effect before the national courts. However, Finnish writing on the subject emphasises the case-law of the Court of Justice of the European Union (ECJ) to the almost complete exclusion of national law. A small exception to this involves articles reviewing the case-law of the first years of EU membership. Overall, the case-law shows that the national courts follow ECJ jurisprudence quite closely. There may be cases at the margins where national principles appear in the reasoning which counterbalance EU-mandated conforming interpretations, but these are relatively few in number. Nevertheless, the case-law which is accessible is almost exclusively that of the courts of last instance. A complete review of the cases in which the principle is pleaded at first instance may reveal a different picture.

2. NOTES ON THE DATA

This contribution reviews key textbooks, citations in the EDILEX database containing references to consistent interpretation, and a significant but nevertheless incomplete set of judgments which contain such references. The material seeks to identify the cases cited in legal writing and supplement this with original research based on key words (full-text searches based, for example, on variants of the word "interpret" and "EU"). The primary sources are accessed and compiled through the online database Finlex, and where they involve very early judgments of the Finnish Supreme Administrative Court (FSAC) reported only in summary form, supplemented by longer judgments where they are available through the premium service EDILEX. In addition, the EDILEX portal was used to identify writings that touched upon the principle. The cited judgments are from the Finnish Supreme Court (FSC), FSAC and the Market Court.

In addition to the case-law of the FSC and FSAC, there are a handful of cases from lower general courts. None of these shed more light on the national court's appreciation of the concept of conforming interpretation as such, also because the electronically published summaries at best mention which provisions are used in arriving at a decision on conforming interpretation.

As of March 2017, all judgments cited in the literature and judgments which explicitly refer to the principle of *tulkintavaikutus* (conforming interpretation) have been surveyed. A further set, overlapping with these, involves all judgments that cite variants of the search terms "Europe" and "interpretation" in Finnish.

Two further caveats must be stated. The first is the limited range of judgments that are published in searchable form. The second is the discussion, noted above, that Finnish courts may be engaging (or refusing to engage in) consistent interpretation without making this connection explicit (and thus searchable). It is worth noting in this context that there is a pending EU PILOT proceeding in which the European Commission has asked for comments regarding the possibility that the FSAC is not referring questions of EU law to the Court of Justice.[1]

Lower court decisions are in practice unpublished in Finland, and they are difficult to acquire since they must be individually requested from the courts in question. They are not typically provided in a form that enables text-mining, and therefore are doubly inaccessible from the perspective of conducting a preliminary study such as this. The case-law which is reported in Finlex, the free online repository provided by the central government, forms the basis of this report. Searches were conducted using references to leading case-law on consistent interpretation, which appears regularly in headnote summaries – even where the term is not employed by the court in its judgment. This results in judgments of the FSAC (approximately 40 of the 51 are relevant) and the FSC (6 out of 8 are relevant) which are cited, as the brief summaries of lower instance judgments did not provide more data that would be relevant to the questions on which this contribution was based. The relative size of the sample is nevertheless quite small: According to estimates, there are thousands of cases in which EU law has at least been a factor, if not the decisive element. Of the 3,500–4,500 cases considered annually by the FSAC, one-third is estimated to involve EU law.[2] The FSAC and FSC choose their own cases and issue published yearbook decisions – the only which qualify as precedents in the Finnish legal system – of approximately 100–200 cases annually.

3. FINLAND AND EUROPEAN INTEGRATION IN A HISTORICAL AND CONSTITUTIONAL PERSPECTIVE

Finland has been a member of the EU since 1995, joining at the same time as Sweden and Austria. Finland is also a latecomer to the Council of Europe, and

---

1 EU PILOT 7890/15/SJUR; *Velvollisuus pyytää ennakkoratkaisua*, reported on p. 42 of the Foreign Ministry's annual report on EU litigation, *Suomen hallituksen toimet EU-tuomioistuinasioissa ja EU-rikkomusasioissa* 01.01.2016–31.12.2016.

2 T. Ojanen, "The Impact of EU Membership on Finnish Constitutional Law" 10 (2004) 3 *European Public Law* 531–64, 557. See also the most recent Annual report of the FSAC (2015), p. 37, available at <http://www.kho.fi/material/attachments/kho/vuosikertomukset/f0jNHr0lF/kho_vuosikertomus_2015_suomi.pdf>; H. Kanninen, "EY-oikeuden soveltamisesta korkeimmassa hallinto-oikeudessa" (2003) 7–8 *Lakimies*, p. 1257, notes that cases with EU links are not subject to official statistics as such.

did not join until 1989.[3] These moves followed economic integration in the form of free trade agreements and EFTA membership: in 1961, Finland became an associate member of EFTA,[4] a full member in 1986,[5] and in 1993 concluded a free trade agreement with the EEC.[6] In 1992, Finland applied for EC and EU membership.[7] It joined the European Economic Area (EEA) in 1994,[8] and in 1995 the European Community (EC) and EU.[9]

In principle, the Finnish Constitution embodies a dualist approach to the relationship between national and international law.[10] The question of undertaking external obligations (Art. 94 of the Finnish Constitution) is separate from the process of enacting them in the domestic legal order (Art 95. of the Constitution). However, in light of the regular use of "blanco" incorporating enactments, i.e. enactments simply stating that Treaty provisions "are in force" domestically, the outcome has been described as *de facto* monism.[11]

Finnish constitutional practice has only gradually evolved to fully account for EU membership.[12] In the process leading to EU accession, Finnish preparatory works emphasised the need to ensure that Finnish law was not only interpreted in line with EU law, but that it would be transformed so that the text of national law reflects the requirements of EU law and is therefore not misleading.[13] Nevertheless, the preparatory works also observed that it was not

---

3 21/1989, *Asetus Euroopan neuvoston perussäännön voimaansaattamisesta.*

4 16/1961, *Asetus Suomen tasavallan ja Euroopan vapaakauppaliiton jäsenvaltioiden välisen sopimussuhteen luomista koskevien sopimusten voimaansaattamisesta.*

5 38/1986, *Laki Euroopan talousyhteisön kanssa Euroopan talousyhteisön ja Suomen tasavallan välisen sopimuksen pöytäkirjan nro 3 tekstin yhdistämisestä ja muuttamisesta tehdyn sopimuksen eräiden määräysten hyväksymisestä.*

6 66/1973, *Laki Euroopan talousyhteisön kanssa tehdyn sopimuksen eräiden määräysten hyväksymisestä.*

7 *Valtioneuvoston tiedonanto* VNT 1/1992 and application of Finland for membership of the European Economic Community, available at: <https://www.eduskunta.fi/pdf/sekalaiset/Suomen_EU_jasenyyshakemus.pdf>.

8 *Sopimus Euroopan talousalueesta*, SopS ETA/1994.

9 102/1994, *Laki Suomen liittymisestä Euroopan unioniin tehdyn sopimuksen eräiden määräysten hyväksymisestä.*

10 See Ojanen (n. 2).

11 A. Rosas, "Finland - Finland's Accession to the European Union: Constitutional Aspects" 1 (1995) 2 *European Public Law* 167 with references, more recently; T. Ojanen, "EU law and the response of the Constitutional Law Committee of the Finnish Parliament", 52 (2007) *Scandinavian Studies in Law* 203–26, 205.

12 See introductory chapter by T. Heinonen and J. Lavapuro, "Suomen oikeuden eurooppalaistuminen ja valtiosääntöistyminen 1990–2012" in *Oikeuskulttuurin eurooppalaistuminen' Suomalaisen Lakimiesyhdistyksen julkaisuja* (Suomalainen Lakimiesyhdistys, 2012).

13 See the Report of the parliamentary Committee on Foreign Affairs on the effects of EC membership on Finland, UaVM 6/1992 – *Ulkoasiainvaliokunnan mietintö n:o 6 valtioneuvoston selonteosta eduskunnalle EY- jäsenyyden vaikutuksista Suomelle,*

necessary to incorporate specific references to, for example, primacy, because it was considered part of the acquis and applicable regardless of a reference in national law.[14] The Finnish approach to EU competence is generally permissive, and few issues arise either in parliamentary debates or before the courts which seriously call into question the application of EU law in Finland.[15]

Finnish law at first had no specific provisions on the relationship between EU law and Finnish law, and accession was effected by a law passed under a special procedure required for laws that constitute exceptions to the Constitution, many provisions of which were thought contrary to the Treaties.[16] The 1994 Act on joining the EEA contained express provisions on direct effect and primacy.[17] Section 2 of the EEA implementation law stated that a Finnish law may not be applied if it is contrary to (1) an unconditional and sufficiently precise provision of the EEA Agreement, its Protocols or Annexes; (2) an EC Directive referred to in an annex to the EEA Agreement, if the provision in question is unconditional and sufficiently precise and it concerns the relationship of a private person to public power or the disapplication of the law, or regulation is in the private interest; or (3) an EC Regulation referred to in an Annex of the EEA Agreement.[18] The subsequent government bill on the law effecting membership of the EC and EU clearly explained how these principles would

available at <https://www.edilex.fi/mt/uavm19920006>: "Valiokunta pitää välttämättömänä, että EY-oikeusjärjestyksestä aiheutuvat muutokset sisällytetään mahdollisuuksien mukaan lainsäädäntöömme, jottei siitä tule harhaanjohtava. Valiokunta korostaa erityisesti sitä, että suomalaisten tuomioistuinten pitää voida lähteä siitä, että kansallinen lainsäädäntömme vastaa EY-oikeuden vaatimuksia." [The Committee considers it necessary that the changes required by the EC legal order are as far as possible included in our legislation so that national law is not misleading. The Committee particularly emphasises, that Finnish courts should be able to take as a point of departure that national law fulfils the requirements of EC law] (translated by the author).

14 P. Aalto, "Accession of Finland to the European Union: First remarks", 20 (1995) *European Law Review* 626; Rosas (n. 11), p. 168.

15 Recently, S. Miettinen and A. Hyvärinen, "Finland: The division of competences between the European Union and its Member States", National report, FIDE Congress 2016, Budapest.

16 See Aalto (n. 14), pp. 620–23; N. Jääskinen, "The application of Community law in Finland: 1995–1998", 36 (1999) 2 *Common Market Law Review* 408–11; Rosas (n. 11), pp. 165–70.

17 *Laki Euroopan talousalueesta tehdyn sopimuksen eräiden määräysten hyväksymisestä ja sopimuksen soveltamisesta* (1504/1993).

18 In Finnish: "Lain tai asetuksen säännöstä ei saa soveltaa, mikäli se on ristiriidassa: 1) ETA-sopimuksen pääsopimuksessa, pöytäkirjassa tai liitteessä olevan ehdottoman ja riittävän täsmällisen määräyksen kanssa; 2) Euroopan talousyhteisön sellaisessa direktiivissä olevan säännöksen kanssa, johon viitataan ETA-sopimuksen liitteessä, jos direktiivin säännös on ehdoton ja riittävän täsmällinen sekä jos se koskee yksityisen suhdetta julkiseen valtaan ja lain tai asetuksen säännöksen soveltamatta jättäminen on yksityisen edun mukaista; tai 3) Euroopan talousyhteisön sellaisen asetuksen kanssa, johon viitataan ETA-sopimuksen liitteessä."

apply after accession.[19] The Act incorporating the Accession Treaty, however, did not expressly consider domestic effects or the status of EU law within the Finnish legal system.[20] One main issue attached to both EC and EU membership was the extent to which membership would affect the sovereignty clause in Section 1(1) of the Finnish Constitution. This was resolved by passing accession and some later Treaty amendments through this special procedure.[21] A redraft of the Constitution in 2000 better reflected the developing practice of international cooperation.[22] In 2011 the Constitution was amended (in force 2012) to include a specific reference to EU membership.[23] This amendment also included new provisions which made it unnecessary to use the procedure for laws that constitute exceptions to the Constitution in the context of international cooperation.[24] Although the current Constitution emphasises international cooperation, it nevertheless states that "[a]n international obligation shall not endanger the democratic foundations of the Constitution".[25]

4. PERCEPTIONS OF THE FINNISH COURTS' APPROACH TO DOCTRINES OF EU LAW

There have, according to the most recent statistics published by the ECJ, been 95 references from Finnish courts in the period ending 31 December 2015. 17 of these have been from the FSC, 47 from the FSAC, 3 from the Labour Court, and a total of 28 from other courts.[26] This compares favourably with Sweden, especially up to 2005, but is a small number given the high volume of EU-related proceedings in the Finnish Supreme Courts alone. Sankari notes in her 2006 review of preliminary references that the courts have had reservations, and that

---

19 *Hallituksen esitys* 135/1994 v p.23, and Kanninen (n. 2).

20 *Laki Suomen liittymisestä Euroopan unioniin tehdyn sopimuksen eräiden määräysten hyväksymisestä* (1504/1994).

21 See T. Ojanen, "Suomi on täysivaltainen tasavalta – Täysivaltaisuusarvioinnin lähtökohtia ja perusteita uuden perustuslain aikana", *Oikeustiede-Jurisprudentia* 2004:XXXVII.

22 On the role of the Committee, see Ojanen (n. 11).

23 *Laki Suomen perustuslain muuttamisesta* 1112/2011. For an overview and references, see A. Mutanen, *Towards a pluralistic constitutional understanding of state sovereignty in the European Union?: The Concept, Regulation and Constitutional Practice of Sovereignty in Finland and Certain Other EU Member States* (Uni. Helsinki, Doctoral dissertation – monograph, 2015), pp. 324–81.

24 See law 1112/2011, articles 94.2 ja 95.2; a two-thirds majority is still required under these new provisions.

25 Finnish Constitution 94.3§. See e.g. J. Husa and T. Pohjolainen, *Julkisen vallan oikeudelliset perusteet: johdatus julkisoikeuteen* (Talentum, 2014), p. 173.

26 Court of Justice of European Union, Annual Report 2015 Judicial Activity, available at: <https://curia.europa.eu/jcms/upload/docs/application/pdf/2016-08/rapport_annuel_2015_activite_judiciaire_en_web.pdf>.

the Finnish Parliament's Committee of the Constitution, asked to review draft legislative acts for their constitutionality, originally voiced concerns that the obligation to make references endangered the impartiality of the courts.[27] The figure demonstrates the cumulative number of references since 1996. In addition to these, an Advisory Opinion was received from the EFTA Court in 1994 in case E-01/94, *Ravintoloitsijain Liiton Kustannus Oy Restamark*.[28] No preliminary reference requests were made in 1995.

Figure 1. Finland Preliminary Rulings 1996–2015

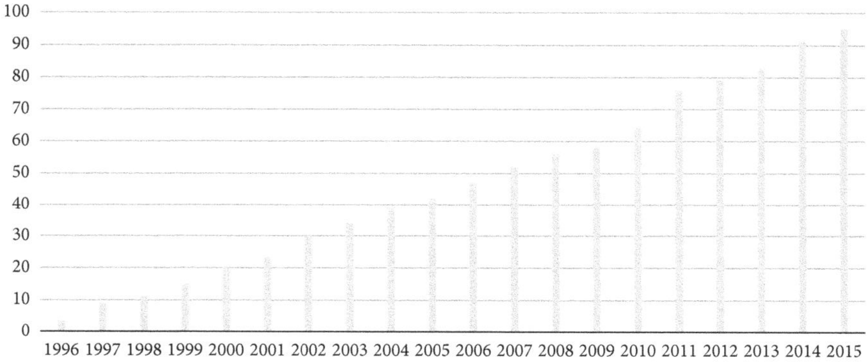

Source: Produced by the author.

According to a consensus presented in the relevant literature, the Finnish courts have generally not had difficulties in applying the key doctrines of EU law, including primacy.[29] It would be interesting to survey the circumstances in which the parties refer to consistent interpretation but where the courts decide the cases without reference to this. This study might reveal situations where national courts in practice avoid conforming interpretations in "hard" cases where the conflict between national law and EU law is irreconcilable. However, in cases where the principle is cited by the court, there does not appear to be any line of conflict between constructions of national law and the required conforming interpretation. It should be noted that Finland does not have a constitutional court; constitutionality reviews are carried out *ex ante* by the parliamentary Committee of the Constitution, and only very exceptionally by the national courts under Art. 106 of the Finnish Constitution.[30]

---

27 S. Sankari, "Ennakkoratkaisupyynnöt ja Suomi", 35 (2006) 1 *Oikeus* 54–72, 59.

28 Report of the EFTA Court 1 January 1994–30 June 1995. Available at <http://www.eftacourt.int/fileadmin/user_upload/Files/AnnualReports/Report-1994-01-01-1995-06-30-text.pdf>.

29 See Ojanen (n. 2), p. 559; and N. Jääskinen, *Eurooppalaistuvan oikeuden oikeusteoreettisia ongelmia* (University of Helsinki Press, 2008), p. 48.

30 Ojanen (n. 2), pp. 540–41.

5. CONFORMING INTERPRETATION IN FINNISH COURTS ACCORDING TO LEGAL WRITING

Conforming interpretation was used in case-law of the Finnish Supreme Courts at least as early as 1996,[31] and also in cases where the new interpretation changed an established interpretation under national law.[32] In a 1999 review, Jääskinen observed that Finnish courts typically sought conforming solutions and avoided reasoning which brought national and EU law into open conflict.[33] Haapaniemi's 1999 book on the obligation of national courts to apply EU law provides an outline of this requirement from the perspective of ECJ jurisprudence.[34] Jääskinen, writing in 2008, observed that the use of primacy by the Finnish courts went largely unnoticed: The ECJ doctrine was simply accepted at face value.[35] Indeed, the influence of both the ECJ and the European Court of Human Rights has been described as having developed the role and importance of case-law also in the national legal system.[36] Kanninen, summing up the first 10 years' practice before the FSAC, generally considered the relationship between EU law and national law unproblematic for national courts.[37] Ojanen, writing in 2004, observed that EU law predominantly enters Finnish courts in the form of questions concerning the effect of EU law on the interpretation of Finnish law.[38] He and Jääskinen note that the interpretation of national law in accordance with EU law involves a similar method to the national technique traditionally endorsed by the Finnish courts in situations involving the giving of judicial effect to constitutional provisions or international treaties.[39] Gräns, writing in 2009, reviews selected leading cases of the Supreme Court which had been referred to the ECJ and concludes that "the Finnish courts use the EC law as the dominant – or rather, one and only – legal source without taking any national legal sources into consideration other than the law

31 Jääskinen (n. 16), pp. 423–27, citing KHO 1996 B 527 17. September 1996, a VAT case, and a January 1996 judgment in the lower courts. Note that Jääskinen was later an Advocate General at the ECJ and served as a justice on the FSAC before and after his tenure as AG.

32 Jääskinen (n. 16), p. 425, citing *Liskojärvi v. Juntunen*, Vantaa District Court, case 95/9236, judgment of 17 June 1996.

33 Jääskinen (n. 16), pp. 605–06.

34 P. Haapaniemi, *Kansallinen tuomioistuin EU-oikeuden soveltajana* (Kauppakaari, 1999).

35 Jääskinen (n. 29), p. 49, referring to KHO 1996 B 577, continuing at p. 52 that primacy and direct effect were applied without questioning their normative basis.

36 T. Ojanen, "Eurooppa-tuomioistuimet ja Suomalaiset tuomioistuimet" (2005) 7–8 *Lakimies*, at p. 1214.

37 Kanninen (n. 2), p. 1253. Kanninen has been a judge at the FSAC, then from 2005 a judge at the Civil Service Tribunal of the ECJ, and from 2009 at the General Court.

38 Ojanen (n. 2), p. 560, see also N. Jääskinen, "Kolme aaltoa – Miten Suomen oikeusjärjestys eurooppalaistui?", 4 (2001) *Defensor Legis* 613.

39 Ojanen (n. 2), p. 650; N. Jääskinen,: "The Application of Community law in Finland: 1995–1998", 36 (1999) 2 *Common Market Law Review* at p. 423.

text as such".[40] Although most writings focus on the published decisions of Finnish courts which have precedent value, studies occasionally refer to conforming interpretation cases in lower courts.[41]

The material surveyed below does not suggest courts compromise on interpretations in line with EU law in order to achieve aims outside those found in EU law. Some authors have, however, criticised the lack of transparency in judicial reasoning, so it is likely those cases where references to case-law of the ECJ or explicit EU connections may exist but are missing from this data set.[42] This is evident in the earliest case-law: it is typical for published summaries in early years to refer to an application of the principle, but to publish no details of its content or how it was applied in the case. It may be worthwhile to explore the extent to which interpretations outside the judicial arena are less obviously conformist: it has been observed that the legislature is in some cases careful to implement EU law in a way that ensures the protection of fundamental rights,[43] an issue which continues to resonate also at EU level. Overall, in 2017, it is easy to agree with Ojanen's observation made in 2004 about the pragmatic approach of Finnish courts to indirect effect: "Each case is dealt with individually, without expressing any general views about the status of EU law. One looks in vain, therefore, for the kind of bold and sweeping observations on the relationship between EU law and national law that have been issued by certain English or German courts, for example."[44] Many of the cases involve a preliminary reference in order to ascertain how the EU rules themselves ought to be interpreted,[45] then followed by an application of this to the Finnish context, i.e. seeking an interpretation in line with the ECJ judgment.

---

40 M. Gräns, "Duty of Loyal Interpretation: Theoretical Structures and Practical Solutions" in L. Ervo, M. Gräns and A. Jokela (eds.), *Europeanization of Procedural Law* (Europa Law Publishing, 2009), pp. 43–86, at p. 84.

41 P. Haapaniemi, "EU-oikeuden vaikutus rikosasioissa – kehityskulkuja ja käytännön tapauksia" in P. Koponen, R. Lahti, and E. Konttinen-Di Nardo (eds.), *Kirjoituksia Rikos- ja Prosessioikeudesta* (Helsingin Hovioikeus/Helsinki District Court, 2016), pp. 11–28, at pp. 20–22.

42 Ojanen (n. 36), p. 1210.

43 Ibid., p. 1224, referring to *inter alia* data protection in the data retention directive and grounds of refusal in the EAW. It is worth noting that Finland was not behind, but ahead of the curve: Both instruments have since been successfully challenged, in the 2014 *Digital rights Ireland judgment*, and extradition, where the ECJ in 2016 finally applied additional fundamental rights refusal grounds in Case C-404/15 and Case C-659/15 PPU, *Aranyosi and Căldăraru*, ECLI:EU:C:2016:198, judgment 05.04.2016.

44 Ojanen (n. 2), p. 561.

45 For example *17.12.1999/4150 KHO:1999:68*, reference Case C-513/99, *Concordia Bus Finland*, ECLI:EU:C:2002:495; Case C-537/03, *Candolin*, ECLI:EU:C:2005:417, C-192/12 PPU, *West*, ECLI:EU:C:2012:404, *KKO:2008:118* also concerns a speciality principle, ECJ asked a reference on interpretation of the Framework Directive which is then applied (C-388/08 PPU, ECLI:EU:C:2008:669); *4.10.2010/2557 KHO:2010:58* refers to environmental obligations and involves *two* preliminary references: C-317/07, *Lahti Energia*, ECLI:EU:C:2008:684 and C-209/09, *Lahti Energia*, ECLI:EU:C:2010:98.

6. CONFORMING INTERPRETATION EXPLAINED IN FINNISH TEXTBOOKS

Textbooks generally offer a Eurocentric approach to defining the scope of the obligation. Legal writing considers the doctrine of consistent interpretation from the perspective of how it is seen in the case-law of the ECJ. Finnish courts have thus far not challenged this. They refer, via the case-law of the ECJ, to the obligation of courts to apply the EU principle of conforming interpretation,[46] but also to the possibility that other general principles of EU law such as legal certainty or non-retroactivity limit this obligation.[47] Textbooks consider consistent interpretation to be the primary way in which courts give effect to EU law:[48] and observe that whilst there have been cases involving direct effect or primacy, these are significantly outnumbered by the case-law on consistent interpretation.[49] The case-law in this contribution, for example, refers directly to ECJ case-law and does not anchor these in a domestic, internal perspective.

7. THE CONCEPT OF CONFORMING INTERPRETATION IN LEADING FINNISH CASES

The first case where conforming interpretation *as a concept* appears in the case-law of the Finnish Supreme Court continues to be referred to in recent case-law.[50] The case concerned the interpretation of national law in line with the EU Motor Vehicle Insurance Directives.[51] The case continues to be referred to in recent jurisprudence on these points.[52]

The case involved compensation for an injury suffered as a consequence of an accident in which the applicant was the passenger in a car driven by a drunk driver. Under the Finnish law which pre-dated EEA and EU membership,

---

46 T. Ojanen, *Eurooppaoikeuden perusteita* (Edita Publishing, Helsinki, 2010), p. 59; J. Raitio, *Eurooppaoikeus ja sisämarkkinat* (Talentum, 2013), p. 265.

47 Raitio, ibid. p. 266; Ojanen (n. 46), pp. 80–83.

48 Ojanen (n. 2), p. 198.

49 Ojanen (n. 2), p. 199. See also e.g. A. Maunu, "Direktiivien oikeusvaikutukset kansallisissa tuomioistuimissa: oireet, diagnoosi ja hoitokeinot" in H. Kaila, E. Pirjatanniemi and M. Suksi (eds.), *Yksilön oikeusasema Euroopan Unionissa- Individens rättställning inom Europeiska unionen* (Åbo Akademi, 2008), p. 606.

50 *KKO 2005:145*. This continues to be referred to in recent case-law, but see Jääskinen (n. 39) for references to less well-known, but earlier, occasions on which the principle is applied.

51 (Author's translation of excerpts from judgment below.) For a critical commentary, especially as regards the conforming interpretation, see M. Saarikoski, "EY-oikeuden vaikutuksesta keskeiseen vahingonkorvaus- ja vakuutusoikeuteen – Esimerkkinä matkustajan myötävaikutus liikennevahinkoon", 1 (2007) *Defensor Legis* 27–29, discussed below.

52 For example *KKO:2016:34* para. 24; *KKO:2016:35* para. 19.

damages could be reduced on account of the contributory negligence of the passenger. An express provision of national law stated that a passenger in a car driven by a drunk driver would be contributorily negligent "if he knew or should have known of the state of the driver".[53]

The courts had previously held that getting into the car amounted to contributory negligence when the passengers were aware of the driver's condition; there was an established line of case-law interpreting the national law in this way, an understanding which was also supported by the *travaux préparatoires* to the original national legislative text. This interpretation, however, was contrary to the Motor Vehicle Insurance Directives,[54] according to the ECJ in the preliminary reference which the national court requested in the case.[55] The national court's task was then to find a way to (re)interpret national law so as to allow compensation to be paid. Fortunately for the Court, the same provision of national law contained a reference to "special reasons" which could allow a claim to be successful despite any contributory negligence.

In *KKO:2005:14*, the FSC stated

> 19. The [CJEU] has in several of its judgments noted the duty of national courts in particular to ensure the legal protection granted to persons by provisions of Community law and the full effect of those provisions. The national court must therefore when applying national law interpret national law as far as possible in accordance with the wording and purpose of a directive regardless of whether the national rules precede the directive, in order to achieve the aims of the directive. The national court must interpret national law in this way especially when the state has already considered that the national rules are already in line with the requirements of the directive (references to C-106/89, *Marleasing*, 13.11.1990, C-397/01–C-403/01, *Pfeiffer* 5.10.2004, paragraphs 110 - 116)
>
> 20. According to the [CJEU] only if it is not possible to interpret national law in this way should the question of direct effect be examined (references to C-157/86, *Mary Murphy*, 4.2.1988, and C-262/97, *Engelbrecht*, 26.9.2000, para 40)[56]

---

53 Liikennevakuutuslaki 7 §3 mom (656/1994).

54 84/5/EEA, Art. 2(1); Directive 90/232/EEA, Art. 1.

55 C-537/03, *Candolin*, ECLI:EU:C:2005:417.

56 Author's translation. In Finnish: *19. Yhteisöjen tuomioistuin on useissa ratkaisuissaan todennut kansallisten tuomioistuinten tehtävänä olevan nimenomaisesti varmistaa, että oikeussubjektit saavat sen oikeusturvan, joka heille yhteisön oikeuden säännöksillä myönnetään, ja taata mainittujen säännösten täysi oikeusvaikutus. Kansallisen tuomioistuimen on sen vuoksi kansallista lainsäädäntöä soveltaessaan, riippumatta siitä, onko kyse direktiiviä edeltävästä vai sen jälkeen annetuista säännöksistä, tulkittava kansallista lainsäädäntöä mahdollisimman pitkälle direktiivin sanamuodon ja tarkoituksen mukaisesti, jotta direktiivillä tavoiteltu tulos saavutetaan. Kansallisen tuomioistuimen on tulkittava kansallista lainsäädäntöä tällä tavalla varsinkin silloin, kun jäsenvaltio on katsonut, että kansallisen oikeuden säännökset jo vastaavat kyseisessä direktiivissä asetettuja vaatimuksia (esim. asia C-106/89, Marleasing, tuomio 13.11.1990, Kok. 1990, s. I-4135 sekä yhdistetyt asiat C-397/01–C-403/01, Pfeiffer ym., tuomio 5.10.2004, Kok. 2004, s. I-8835, kohdat 110–116 ja siinä mainittu oikeuskäytäntö).*

The preparatory works to the national law (from 1978, and which therefore pre-dated EEA membership) also indicated that the purpose of the legislation was to ensure that even careless persons should be entitled to full compensation, but that "special" reasons would be required for a drunk driver and passenger to receive compensation (paras. 23–24). The national court then considered the drafting history of the national law, observed that no changes were made to these provisions on account of EEA membership (which already required the directive to be implemented), and as a consequence, the provisions were presumed compatible (para. 25 of the FSC judgment). Finally, the court stated (para. 28) that the objectives of the directive were to ensure the effective protection of passengers in the case of personal injuries, and that taking into account the Directives and their aims as the ECJ has interpreted them (this case also involved a reference in which such an interpretation had been requested),[57] it was not in accordance with the Directives to preclude the passengers from insurance compensation on the basis of formal grounds, based on the level of intoxication of the driver. When the passenger is contributorily negligent, this contributory negligence can be taken into account. However, according to EU law, the compensation can be limited only in exceptional circumstances and the limitation may not be disproportionate. The court went on to find that "special reasons" under national law had to be interpreted in accordance with EU law so that compensation was paid (para. 29), and that simply getting into the vehicle with a drunk driver could not be considered contributorily negligent. The national court thus used the doctrine of consistent interpretation in order to include a requirement of EU law as "special reasons" within the meaning of the national law which had not expressly provided for the contingency it faced in the case. This was contrary to established judicial practice, but hardly *contra legem* as regards the actual wording of the national law.

The most recent restatements of the FSC observe that national law must be interpreted in line with all Union law, including the case-law of the ECJ, not merely directives.[58] In other relevant FSC cases, it has also used an interpretation in line with a Framework Decision,[59] interpreted national employment law

---

20. Yhteisöjen tuomioistuimen oikeuskäytännön mukaan vasta sen jälkeen, kun kansallisen lain yhteisön oikeuden mukainen tulkinta ei ole mahdollista, on tutkittava, täyttyvätkö välittömän oikeusvaikutuksen edellytykset (asia C-157/86, Mary Murphy, tuomio 4.2.1988, Kok. 1988, s. 673 ja asia C-262/97, Engelbrecht, tuomio 26.9.2000, Kok. 2000, s. I-7321, 40 kohta).

57 ibid.

58 *KKO 2016:34*, 24–29, 20.5.2016; *KKO 2016:35*, 20.5.2016, 19–24 in identical terms.

59 *KKO 2007:1* paras. 8–10, citing *inter alia Pupino* to state the intention behind the Framework Decision was not to reduce the effectiveness of confiscation measures. Note here that the FSC declined to ask a reference because it considered the national provisions led to the conclusion required by the Framework Decision. See H. Lavonen, "Konfiskaatiopuitepäätöksen tulkintavaikutus ja menetettäväksi tuomittavan rikoshyödyn määrittäminen", 6 (2011) *Lakimies* 1215.

in line with the objectives of the EU succession directive[60] and observed that national patent law must, given the position of the Agreement on Trade-Related Aspects of Intellectual Property Rights (TRIPS) in the EU legal order and the intent to implement TRIPS obligations in the relevant provision of national law, be interpreted in line with relevant EU directives and also TRIPS itself.[61]

The very earliest case-law of the FSAC notes the obligation to interpret national law in line with, typically, a directive, but does not discuss the basis of the obligation. The first known case considers the VAT status of services provided by university libraries.[62] According to the FSAC, the preparatory works to the national VAT law considered such services to be exempt from tax because it was not undertaken as a business activity, and noted that the relevant EU directive also required the tax exemption of certain services. Thus the national law was to be interpreted in line with the Directive, and such services were to be exempted from VAT. The published text does not refer to the content or source of the duty of conforming interpretation.

The first published case before the FSAC in which *the concept* is examined in any detail involved the question of interpreting national law in line with relevant directives in the field of EU environmental law.[63] The FSAC stated, without reference to sources of law, that:

> regardless of whether a directive has direct effect, national law with relevance to EU law is to be interpreted in the light of the wording and the purpose of the directive. The directive must be considered as a source for interpretation even if the court considers the national legislature to have remained within its margin of discretion when implementing the directive. Even national law which was promulgated before the entry into force of the directive, or which does not seek to achieve the legal situation mandated by the directive, should where possible be interpreted in line with the wording and objectives of the directive.[64]

---

60 *KKO:2009:28* paras. 23–24.

61 *KKO:2015:51* paras. 9–15. Here, the obligation was stated but the source material, namely TRIPS and EU law, did not address that question.

62 *KHO:1997:147*, 30.12.1997.

63 *18.12.2002/3339 KHO:2002:86*. See the pleadings of the Environment ministry in point 5.2. Note that the case was decided without clear reference to a conforming interpretation – indeed a preliminary reference was refused because the FSAC considered the case to involve only the application of national law and thus outside the scope of 267 TFEU, and this was during pending related proceedings before the ECJ for an infringement action against Finland.

64 Author's translation. In Finnish: "*Siitä riippumatta, onko direktiivillä välitön vaikutus, yhteisöoikeudellisesti merkityksellistä kansallista lainsäädäntöä on tulkittava direktiivin sanamuodon ja päämäärän valossa. Direktiivi on otettava tulkintalähteenä huomioon siinäkin tapauksessa, että tuomioistuin katsoo kansallisen lainsäätäjän pysyneen harkintavaltansa rajoissa direktiiviä täytäntöönpannessaan. Myös sellaiselle kansalliselle oikeudelle, joka on säädetty jo ennen direktiivin voimaantuloa, tai jonka säätämisellä ei ole tavoiteltu direktiivin*

8. GENERAL FINDINGS

There is very little academic writing that directly addresses the questions posed in this book, and as a consequence many of the answers in this contribution are based purely on a review of the case-law; the academic literature typically addresses the obligations under EU law and not how they are in fact satisfied by national courts.[65]

The cases surveyed reveal two major connections to judgments which concern conforming interpretation. Tax cases, specifically the interpretation of national law in line with the VAT Directive, are the most significant set in the first set of case-law surveyed. Other cases cover a diverse range of topics, but simply the distribution of judgments that expressly refer to the concept of conforming interpretation in the case-law of the FSAC suggests that conforming interpretation arises most often in the public law context – i.e. proceedings where the issues can lead to an appeal in the administrative courts.

There is a clear trend to refer questions of interpretation to the ECJ where there is no relevant case-law on the interpretation of the EU instrument at issue. Thus, where the question of *how EU law should be interpreted* cannot be satisfactorily resolved without a reference, one is made before the court then considers the relationship between that interpretation and how national law can be interpreted within those parameters. The references to the ECJ in Finnish conforming interpretation cases concern the interpretation of relevant EU law but not the interpretation of the principle of conforming interpretation as such. The case-law surveyed suggests that where an answer is received on the interpretation of relevant EU law, this is then applied to achieve an interpretation of national law that conforms with the interpretation of EU law received in the preliminary ruling.

8.1. THE PREFERENCE FOR CONFORMING INTERPRETATION?

Is there a preference for conforming interpretation over other ways of achieving outcomes sought by EU law, such as the ECJ suggests in some of its case-law? Its preferred order of sequence for national courts requires first resorting to consistent interpretation, only then followed by direct effect, and finally state liability.[66] In legal literature, it can be seen that references to primacy are rare. The consensus is that Finnish courts resort primarily to consistent interpretation

mukaista oikeustilaa, on mahdollisuuksien mukaan annettava direktiivin sanamuodon ja päämäärän mukainen sisältö."

65 See, however, the references to the literature cited above.

66 For example C-282/10, *Dominguez*, ECLI:EU:C:2012:33. See also at least *El Corte Inglés* (C-192/94, ECLI:EU:C:1996:88, cited Saarikoski (n. 51)).

and avoid direct conflicts that would require references to primacy. None of the cases surveyed demonstrate a particular formula that has been used.

8.2. THE CONCEPTUAL BASIS FOR THE OBLIGATION TO PERFORM CONSISTENT INTERPRETATION

Many different terms are used in the English language to describe the principle being discussed, such as "consistent interpretation", "harmonious interpretation", "conform interpretation" and "indirect effect". What to call the principle in Finland is potentially complicated by the fact that it is a bilingual country, at least in principle: Finland has two national languages, Finnish and Swedish. Swedish is the main language of approximately 5 per cent of the population. Cases heard in Swedish are published in Swedish, whereas cases heard in Finnish are published in Finnish. Summaries are then published in the other national language. At the time of writing, there is no current Finnish textbook on EU law in Swedish. The most recent texts in Finnish were published in 2016.[67] *Euroopan Unionin Oikeus* defines "*Eurooppaoikeuden tulkintavaikutus*" (the principle of interpretation) as an interpretation under which rules of national law are sought to be interpreted so as to give them a meaning in conformity with EU law and the objectives of integration. The term "*tulkintavaikutus*" is also well-established in the case-law (see below), and appears as a heading in several last instance cases.[68] The term "indirect effect" is translated as "*välillinen oikeusvaikutus*",[69] but does not often appear in either literature or national case-law. *EU-Oikeuden Perusteita* deals with conforming interpretation at length.[70] It is notable that in both books the discussion focuses on the principle as it is expounded in ECJ case-law.[71]

The approach of the Finnish courts is Eurocentric, following the approach taken in the surveyed textbooks. The Finnish courts refer exclusively to case-law of the ECJ on consistent interpretation; no single case within the data set referred to any national principle of interpretation in the context of examining this question. There is therefore also no discernible attempt to assimilate this to national principles of interpretation, at least in the case-law that was examined.

The case-law begins with judgments that specifically address directives but without excluding the impact of other sources of EU law. Later case-law makes explicit reference to other sources, including judgments of the ECJ, international

---

67 See J. Raitio, *Euroopan Unionin Oikeus* (Talentum Pro, 2016), pp. 239–44.

68 See e.g. *KKO:2005:145*, where it appears in the title headnote and is explored in detail, paras. 19–29.

69 T. Ojanen, *EU-Oikeuden Perusteita* (3. Laitos, Edita Publishing, 2016), p. 78.

70 Ibid. pp. 90–98.

71 In addition to Ojanen (n. 69), and Raitio (n. 67), see e.g. Maunu (n. 49) p. 605.

agreements falling within the scope of EU law, and in some cases a very general duty of conforming interpretation which governs all EU law. The latter is the view expounded by modern doctrine,[72] and recent case-law.[73]

8.3. ARE INTERPRETATIONS SOUGHT TO THE DETRIMENT OF INDIVIDUALS?

Most of the case-law surveyed does not discuss any distinction between vertical and horizontal situations in consistent interpretation. The leading case which has also attracted some national attention, *KKO:2005:145* (discussed in detail below), resulted in horizontal effects on a motor vehicle insurer. The case-law generally juxtaposes the prohibition of horizontal direct effects with the requirement of consistent interpretation and comes to the conclusion that consistent interpretation is possible in such circumstances. A generalised difference in approach can be identified in the criminal case-law, discussed in detail below.

It is debatable whether Finnish courts have used consistent interpretation to the detriment of individuals in cases involving the state as one party. One leading case involved the interpretation of national law on drivers' licences. In *KHO 26.04.1999/889*, the FSAC interpreted national law on driving licences according to the requirements in an EU directive. The directive did not offer exceptions to the requirements concerning vision. Thus, under a conforming interpretation, national authorities ought not to have had discretion to issue a licence in circumstances where the vision requirements were not met. National law had not been amended in this respect to conform with the Directive. A provision in the relevant national law therefore allowed the authorities discretion to issue a licence also where this would not be possible under the directive. The FSAC referred to the EU duty of loyal cooperation and the Directive in upholding the administrative authority's refusal to grant a licence. This was despite the express plea that the Member State ought not to be able to rely on its own failure to implement the directive.[74] Even in the absence of the Directive, it should be noted that the national authorities would have had discretion to refuse, and that the outcome was therefore not solely dictated by application of the principle of conforming interpretation. This was also technically not a case brought against an individual, but involved a scenario where national law might be interpreted by a state authority to the detriment of the individual.

In *KKO:2005:139*, the FSC considered several questions of conforming interpretation, six months after the *Pupino* judgment to which the FSC also

72 e.g. Ojanen (n. 69), p. 91.
73 See e.g. *KKO:2016:35*.
74 See also Kanninen (n. 2), p. 1262, where the case is discussed.

refers. It should be recalled that in *Pupino*, the ECJ observed that it was not contrary to the principle of legality in EU law to interpret national law in line with Framework Decisions where the interpretation resulted in a *de facto* change to *procedural*, rather than *substantive criminal law*.[75] Thus, as explained in more detail below, when the national court refused to reach a conforming interpretation contrary to the preparatory legislative works, it was in practice expressing a national preference for the text of the national legislation and the preparatory works over the possible conforming interpretation. Nevertheless, the facts and outcome require a more detailed analysis.

The first question of interpretation involved whether psychiatric care was a penalty within the meaning of the European Arrest Warrant (EAW) Framework Decision, and which therefore entailed surrender. In principle, such an interpretation could be seen to reduce the rights of the surrendered person by increasing the range of circumstances that might entail surrender. That interpretation was accepted by the FSC. However, on the facts, an outcome which the surrendered person sought, namely refusal, was achieved by refusing to interpret the national implementing law *contra legem* on a later point, discussed in detail below.

The second question of interpretation involved a question of whether the national grounds for refusal should be interpreted as discretionary (optional) or as mandatory. Under the Framework Decision, the grounds were optional: judges should have discretion on whether to refuse surrender. However, under the national law, it appeared that refusal was mandatory. The preparatory legislative works noted that the government intended to implement that particular ground as mandatory.[76] Thus, the FSC declined, at least implicitly, to perform a conforming interpretation *contra legem* this provision. It nevertheless squared this particular circle by noting that the optional ground for refusal in the Framework Decision could be exercised when the refusing state undertook to execute the sentence – something the national law required when refusing to surrender. This leads to a third interpretation on the question of whether the sentence and its execution were subject to further discretion in line with one very likely interpretation of the national law.

National law suggested discretion to review the foreign penalty, but if this were allowed together with the mandatory refusal, it would lead to a situation the Framework Decision would not allow – namely refusal to surrender coupled

---

75 C-105/03 *Pupino* ECLI:EU:C:2005:386, para. 46.

76 In Finnish: "*13. Puitepäätöksen mukaan mainittu kieltäytymisperuste on siis harkinnanvarainen. EU-luovuttamislaissa kyseinen kieltäytymisperuste on kuitenkin haluttu säätää ehdottomaksi. Tämä ilmenee nimenomaisesti EU-luovuttamislain esitöistä, joiden mukaan Suomen kansalaisen pyytäessä saada suorittaa pidätysmääräyksessä tarkoitetun vapausrangaistuksen Suomessa luovuttamisesta olisi kieltäydyttävä, eikä tuomioistuimella olisi asiassa harkintavaltaa (HE 88/2003 vp s. 20).*"

with refusal to execute the sentence in lieu of surrender. The solution adopted by the FSC was to interpret the national law in line with the Framework Decision, and contrary to the position which would have maximised the defendant's rights, so that there would be no discretion to review the penalty after such a refusal to surrender. This was supported also with reference to the preparatory work.[77] It can therefore be concluded that the FSC refrained from a *contra legem* interpretation of national law, whilst at the same time partly interpreting national law against the interests of the individual in later cases and also arriving at an outcome that could be allowed by the EU legislation in question, bar the removal of judicial discretion to surrender envisaged by the Framework Decision.

8.4. PRIVATE PARTIES AND CONSISTENT INTERPRETATION

More than a few cases involve disputes between two private parties. The FSC case *KKO:2005:145 30.12.2005*, also involving a preliminary reference to the ECJ,[78] has been observed as a situation where conforming interpretation took effect in a dispute concerning the interpretation of national law in line with a directive but between two private parties.[79] So, too, in *KKO:2010:20*, the FSC appeared prepared to apply the doctrine of consistent interpretation to a horizontal dispute,[80] but came to the conclusion that national law already satisfied the requirements of the directive in question. In *KKO:2006:17*, it requested a reference from the ECJ on the interpretation of EU trademark rules,[81] and then applied this to the dispute between the private parties.[82] The FSC interpreted national trademark law restrictively and in line with the corresponding EU directive, so that protection which might have been available under the purely national provision was not available when interpreted in line with the Directive. In this case, as in some others, the Court makes reference to whether this interpretation imposes new obligations on a private individual (i.e. horizontal direct effect) and to primacy, but also in the same paragraph states that there is no obstacle to interpreting national law in line with the Directive.[83]

---

77 Points 14–18.

78 C-537/03, *Candolin*, ECLI:EU:C:2005:417.

79 Maunu (n. 49), p. 613. See also the similar *KKO:2007:34*, where a national judgment contrary to this interpretation was declared null despite being res judicata; the FSC referred to the duty to interpret the national law in line with the same directive. Here the FSC rectified its own judgment using extraordinary remedies on the basis that the first judgment involved a "manifestly incorrect application of the law".

80 Paras. 21–24.

81 C-228/03, *Gilette*, ECLI:EU:C:2005:177, 17.02.2005.

82 Paras. 40–44.

83 Para. 44.

23.9.2009/2303 KHO:2009:82 concerned the interpretation of provisions of national law implementing the first EU Data Protection Directive,[84] applied to a private enterprise (publishers of tax data, which in Finland is public). The FSAC had asked for an interpretation of the Directive from the ECJ.[85] After the ECJ judgment, it was clear that certain processing came within the scope of the EU data protection rules. The FSAC considered that national law sought to implement the Directive and should therefore be interpreted in accordance with it and ECJ judgments on the directive. A provision of national law on processing did not conform with the Directive because it completely excluded register entries which only included data as it was published in some media. These could *prima facie* therefore be processed without limitations, and therefore contrary to the requirements of the directive as interpreted by the Court of Justice.

The FSAC then continued:

> Because the data protection ombudsman's complaint concerns a situation between two private parties, the directive does not have direct effect. However, the [CJEU] has confirmed in its case-law that when interpreting national law national courts must as far as possible interpret national law in line with the wording and purpose of the directive in order to achieve the aims of the directive. According to the [CJEU] the national court can thus ensure within the scope of its jurisdiction the full effectiveness of [EU] law when it decides the case brought before it [referring to C-397/01–C-403/01, *Pfeiffer* paragraph 113]. The [national provision, *Henkilötietolaki* 2.4§] must be interpreted as far as possible in accordance with [EU] law, taking account of the case-law of the [CJEU].[86]

According to the FSAC, the preparatory works to the relevant provision did not mention the Directive, but this could nevertheless be used to interpret that provision (exceptions to protection). Taking into account the ECJ

---

84 Directive 95/46/EC of the European Parliament and of the Council of 24 October 1995 on the protection of individuals with regard to the processing of personal data and on the free movement of such data [1995] OJ L281/31.

85 Case C-73/07, *Satakunnan markkinapörssi*, ECLI:EU:C:2008:727.

86 In Finnish: "*Koska Tietosuojavaltuutetun viranomaisena tekemä hakemus koskee kahden yksityisen oikeussubjektin toimintaa, ei direktiivillä tässä asiassa ole välitöntä oikeusvaikutusta näiden yksityisten oikeussubjektien edun vastaisesti. Yhteisöjen tuomioistuin on kuitenkin oikeuskäytännössään vahvistanut, että kansallisen tuomioistuimen on kansallista lainsäädäntöä soveltaessaan tulkittava kansallista lainsäädäntöä mahdollisimman pitkälle kyseessä olevan direktiivin sanamuodon ja tarkoituksen mukaisesti direktiivillä tavoitellun tuloksen saavuttamiseksi. Yhteisöjen tuomioistuimen mukaan kansallinen tuomioistuin voi näin toimivaltansa rajoissa varmistaa yhteisön oikeuden täyden tehokkuuden, kun se ratkaisee käsiteltäväkseen saatetun asian (Yhdistetyt asiat C-397/01–C-403/01, Pfeiffer ym., tuomio 5.10.2004, Kok. 2004, s. I-8835, 113 kohta). Yhteisöjen tuomioistuimen oikeuskäytäntö huomioon ottaen esillä olevassa tilanteessa henkilötietolain 2§:n 4 kohtaa on tulkittava mahdollisimman pitkälti yhteensopivasti yhteisön oikeuden kanssa.*"

case-law, this provision had to be interpreted strictly, and could therefore not be interpreted so as to allow the free reprocessing of data that had already been published. The case has been criticised by some as a *contra legem* interpretation of national law to the detriment of a private individual.[87] After all, the national law expressly excluded data that had been published in media and yet the outcome of the judgment was that the processing of such data was subject to restrictions.

8.5. INTERPRETATIONS PRIOR TO THE DEADLINE FOR IMPLEMENTATION

Very recent case-law involves cases where the courts moot interpreting national law in line with directives prior to the deadline for implementation. The obligation not to seriously compromise achieving the directive's objectives is noted in the literature.[88] There are three citations for *Adeneler*, all in the lower courts and in fact all before the Market Court.[89] The judgments note the extent and limits of the duty but then conclude a conforming interpretation is not required because the objectives would not be seriously compromised.

8.6. LEGISLATIVE INTENT vs CONFORMING INTERPRETATION

Preparatory works are widely referred to in Finland in judicial proceedings as aids to interpretation, even where the works go far beyond the text of the legislation in question. Preparatory works may in many cases provide information that is decisive in interpreting provisions of statutes or the Constitution. In the consistent interpretation case-law surveyed, many cases involved a review of what the national legislature had considered and, in at least one case (*KKO:2005:145*), the literature claims the national legislature's views were sidelined by a consistent interpretation. However, the courts themselves do not seem to see this as problematic, or at least do not make their reservations known. The *Björnekulla* case itself is noted in the literature,[90] but is cited in only one case,[91] and not concerning this point.

At least one leading case on consistent interpretation has been criticised because a consistent interpretation may not be in line with the interpretation

87 For example R. Olilla, "Verotustietojen julkaiseminen", 16 (2009) *Edilex* 11–13.

88 Maunu (n. 49), p. 603 and C-212/04, *Adeneler*, 123–24.

89 MAO:403/14, MAO:733–748/14 MAO:652/15.

90 "… notwithstanding any contrary interpretation which may arise from the *travaux préparatoires* for the national rule" (C-371/02, *Björnekulla*, ECLI:EU:C:2004:275, para. 13) e.g. Maunu (n. 49), p. 614.

91 *KKO:2005:118*, citing paras 23–25 of the judgment.

invited by the preparatory works on the national law.[92] The critique is, in essence, that the ECJ requires national courts to reinterpret a provision in a way which contradicts the preparatory works and a prior, purely national interpretation of the relevant legal provision. Saarikoski has observed that in *KKO:2005:145*, the facts of which are discussed above, the Finnish Supreme Court interpreted national law in line with the motor vehicle insurance Directive even though the preparatory works on that particular provision called for another solution. In the case, the FSC concluded that a reference to "other particularly weighty reasons" in the national law should be interpreted so that, read together with this clause, the relevant substantive provision in the national law could be interpreted in line with the Directive. This was notwithstanding references in the preparatory works to the specific and contrary interpretation of that provision in the national law.[93] The critique is therefore in essence that national courts are doing precisely what EU law requires – asking for an interpretation of EU law, and applying this to national law that predates the applicability of those rules in Finland.

The national legislature's intent has been applied in at least one case despite the differences between this and a conforming interpretation.[94] In *KKO:2005:139*, discussed above, the preparatory works are cited in support of the ordinary meaning also found in the legislation, and which is not sidelined by the national court in its application of the principle of consistent interpretation. However, here the preparatory work was not decisive. This seems to be an unusual scenario.

Preparatory works would therefore seem to be largely ignored when they contradict later EU legislation. A recent set of cases involving the interpretation of EU Framework Decisions provides an interesting contrast.[95] In *KKO:2011:41*, the FSC considered aggravating factors when determining penalties for serious drugs offences. Here, national preparatory works, which pre-dated the relevant EU legislation, required that when organised crime was an aggravating factor, the criminal organisation's activities had to be connected to the crime for which the aggravating factor was applied (*KKO:2011:41*, point 20). The crimes were committed before a Framework Decision entered into force.[96] For this reason, the domestic *travaux préparatoires* were relevant in determining how the provisions should be interpreted. In contrast, in *KKO:2013:90*, the facts post-dated the Framework Decision; and as a consequence, this – rather than the national *travaux préparatoires* – was to be a main concern.[97] However, the

---

92 *KKO:2005:145.*

93 Saarikoski (n. 49), p. 27–29.

94 See the early case concerning the EAW and the national transposition of optional grounds of refusal as mandatory.

95 *KKO:2013:90. 16.12.2013; KKO:2011: 41.*

96 *2008/841; KKO:2013:90*, para. 10; *KKO:2011:41*, para. 8.

97 Para. 11.

FSC considered the Framework Decision could not be interpreted so as to require the aggravating factors to be applied, and declined to refer the case to the ECJ.[98]

Quite often conforming interpretation leads to a result that is favourable to the individual, particularly in criminal cases. For example, in a recent case of the FSC,[99] it considers the interpretation of national law under relevant EU rules as interpreted in a 2014 ECJ ruling.[100] This has the consequence that national regulatory practice preceding the reference can no longer be considered in line with the national law as interpreted in line with the Directive, and that therefore certain substances formerly classified as medicines could not be regarded as such even though the national law might have been capable, in the absence of the Directive, of a more permissive interpretation. The outcome in this case meant the discharge of the accused, because the smuggling offence was based on the classification of the substances as medicines.

9. LIMITS TO THE PRINCIPLE OF CONSISTENT INTERPRETATION

Given that the national courts derive the relevant rules of law directly from the ECJ case-law, there is little obvious resistance to the doctrine of consistent interpretation in terms of express references to *national* principles limiting consistent interpretation.[101] The limits to consistent interpretation are, as a consequence of the emphasis on EU doctrine rather than national canons of interpretation, generally also derived from EU law rather than national law,[102] although one possible exception is discussed below.

9.1. NATIONAL GENERAL PRINCIPLES AS LIMITS TO CONFORMING INTERPRETATION?

The principle of *rikosoikeudellinen laillisuusperiaate* (legality of criminal penalties) appears in case-law where EU-linked national provisions of criminal law are applied, but not in circumstances where the courts juxtapose the EU obligation to interpret in conformity solely with a *national* general principle. In some national literature, the national principle of legality is however

98 Paras. 12–14.
99 *KKO:2016:35.*
100 Joined cases C-358/13 and C-181/14, *Markus D.* and *G.*, ECLI:EU:C:2014:2060.
101 See e.g. *KKO:2016:35*: para. 24, referring to Case 28/62, *Da Costa en Schaake*, ECLI:EU:C:1963:6, and Case 157/86, *Mary Murphy*, ECLI:EU:C:1988:62, para. 11.
102 See e.g. *KKO:2015:74*, para. 12.

considered as a limit also to consistent interpretation.[103] For example, in *KKO:2015:32*, the court examined national law and found it did not criminalise the activity; whilst referring to directives, it did not explore the relationship between conforming interpretation and legality. In the lower court decision, the first instance court had referred to national law and a relevant EU directive.

In *KKO:2013:12*, the principle of legality was explored in both the national and EU legal context, after which the FSC concluded that on the facts, the offence was satisfactorily defined in the national law without recourse to consistent interpretation. Despite this, on the facts the defendant could not be regarded as having broken the law because he lacked the *mens rea* for the offence and the prosecution had not offered an alternative charge based on negligence rather than intent.[104]

The overall sense of the case-law is that the requirements of EU law, both in favour and restricting consistent interpretation, are observed. In very recent case-law, there have been debates about the extent to which effectiveness-driven interpretations ought to be entertained, particularly in the context of criminal prosecutions or confiscations. In *KKO:2015:74*, the majority decided not to ask for a preliminary ruling on the interpretation of proceeds of crime, and instead found that in the absence of judgments from the ECJ, there was no reason to conclude certain assets should be regarded as proceeds of crime.[105] In contrast, where an interpretation would have led to a judgment in favour of a defendant, the doctrine was applied.

There are also cases where the national court first states an obligation to interpret in line with e.g. a Framework Decision, tempered by general principles of law, and then comes to the conclusion that the effectiveness-enhancing outcome can be achieved.[106] In *KKO:2013:65*, the question arose whether forged passports had to be physically in the person's possession or whether the offence of possessing them was committed even where the forged passports were in fact intercepted by the customs authorities. The latter interpretation was applied taking account of the purpose of the relevant EU instrument and then continuing to observe that in analogous national case-law, actual physical possession was not required in order for the offence to have been committed.

There is also a significant body of case-law on the interpretation of EU procedural criminal law, especially the EAW. There, the Finnish courts do not at first appear to expressly acknowledge the ECJ distinction between legality in the substantive context and the rule following *Pupino:* that a change

---

103 For example S. Palo, *Järjestäytyneet rikollisryhmät ja rikollisvastuu* (Forum Iuris, 2010), p. 110; *Contra* S. Melander, *EU-rikosoikeus* (2nd ed., Alma Talent, 2015), p. 105, referring the ECJ case-law on the principle.

104 Paras. 11–16.

105 Para. 11; See also the dissenting opinion of Judge Kuparinen, advocating a preliminary reference.

106 *KKO:2013:65*.

to the *procedural rights of an individual* may not be contrary to the legality principle in the context of procedural law. In *KKO:2012:67*, the FSC, following a preliminary reference in that case, interpreted national law in line with the ECJ's judgment on onward surrender.[107] *KKO:2012:62* involved interpreting the national rules on detention to allow detention between the decision to surrender and the actual surrender. *KKO:2010:59* involved the speciality principle and the interpretation of the Framework Directive on surrender. The FSC referred to a previous preliminary reference to the ECJ and applied this interpretation to the facts.[108]

One case may be considered a judgment where national principles curtailed the requirement of conforming interpretation. *23.12.2014/4054 KHO:2014:190* concerned the return of VAT paid when goods were not delivered. The relevant provisions of the VAT Directive which could otherwise have been used to interpret national law had not been implemented by Finland. As a consequence, the FSAC considered that the tax authorities could not rely on a conforming interpretation of the national law to the detriment of the private individual. The Court referred to the principle of legality of taxation, thus arguably refusing to apply a conforming interpretation on the basis of a *national principle*.

9.2. *CONTRA LEGEM* AS A LIMIT

On *contra legem* and legal certainty in particular, national courts refer to an interpretation that is *sanamuodon vastaisesti* (contrary to the wording) of the relevant legal provision. The principle of legality in criminal law is well established, and precludes *contra legem* interpretations. The principle in national criminal law it is found in the Constitution (Section 8).[109] There is no corresponding principle of legality in national civil law. In public law, the acts of public authorities must be based on the law (Section 2 of the Constitution).

The *contra legem* limit has been used in national case-law involving criminal obligations. In *KKO:2015:60*, the FSC expressly declined to interpret national law so as to ensure the effectiveness of EU legislation on tachographs.[110] However, at least some case-law, for example *KHO:2009:82*, discussed above, has also been criticised as applying a consistent interpretation *contra legem*.[111] In the context

107 C-192/12 PPU, *West*, ECLI:EU:C:2012:404.

108 C-388/08 PPU, ECLI:EU:C:2008:669. The FSC judgment involves dissenting opinions, but not on the question of conforming interpretation.

109 In Finnish: "*Rikosoikeudellinen laillisuusperiaate. Ketään ei saa pitää syyllisenä rikokseen eikä tuomita rangaistukseen sellaisen teon perusteella, jota ei tekohetkellä ole laissa säädetty rangaistavaksi. Rikoksesta ei saa tuomita ankarampaa rangaistusta kuin tekohetkellä on laissa säädetty.*"

110 Para. 31.

111 *KHO:2009:82*.

of purely national law, there are also a handful of cases that authors consider *contra legem* decisions where national law is interpreted *contra legem* in line with other national law: Tapio Määttä notes *KHO:2007:28*, where he considers the appropriate court for appeals in specific cases was decided *contra legem*;[112] Kalle Määttä notes *KKO:1996:60*, involving the obligations flowing from the sale of a company as a going concern.[113] Tuula Linna notes *KKO:2011:100*, in which procedural time limits were set aside arguably *contra legem*.[114]

10. CONCLUSIONS

Conforming interpretation is in the judicial mainstream in Finland. The courts' approach appears to be quite Eurocentric, at least as seen from textbooks and the express views of the national courts. The Finnish courts as well as legal writings emphasise the doctrine as it is developed by the ECJ. Many of the cases which raise complex issues also involve references to the Court of Justice, and the interpretation which it gives is then applied by the national court in its interpretation of the national rules. Textbooks focus mostly on the requirements imposed by EU law on national judges.

This eurocentrism is underlined by the fact that it is the ECJ, rather than national canons of interpretation, which is expressly referred to when these sources explore the extent and limits to the principle. Very few cases can be identified in the data set on which this contribution is based which call into question a conforming interpretation clearly required by the doctrine as it is espoused by the ECJ. Rather, the criticism, when it does arise in the literature, occurs when the national courts – supreme courts in particular – do only that which is required by the case-law of the ECJ in applying the principle.

However, there are weaknesses in light of the incomplete methodology adopted in this contribution. First, the lack of access to first instance case-law means it is not possible to confirm that this approach prevails on all levels of the judicial system. Second, there are undoubtedly cases where conforming interpretation may have been appropriate but was raised neither by the parties nor by the courts *ex officio*. In principle Finnish courts have a duty to always know the law and which cases to apply, regardless of whether they are expressly

---

112 M. Tapio, "Lainsäätäjän Kunnioittamisasenne, Tavoitteellinen Laintulkinta Ja Lakien Tavoitesäännökset Vallitsevassa Tuomarinideologiassa" in A. Pakarinen, A. Hyvärinen and K. Ervasti (eds.), *Lainvalmistelu, Tutkimus, Yhteiskunta: Jyrki Talan Juhlakirja* (Turku University Faculty of Law, 2011), pp. 212–13.

113 K. Määttä, "Anekdootteja lain tulkinnasta" in H. Lindfors, E. Korkea-aho and S. Turunen (eds), *Kovia aikoja: riitoja ja maksukyvyttömyyttä Juhlakirja Risto Koulu 60 vuotta* (Edita, 2009) pp. 461–76, s. 463.

114 T. Linna, "KKO 2011:100 – Itse asetetun säännön seuraaminen contra analogiatulkinta' 1 (2012) *Lakimies* 177.

pleaded. Whether the court is also required to find facts or whether this is left to the parties depends in national law on the type of proceedings. Third, due to the data-mining approach adopted there may be cases that on a close reading prove to involve conforming interpretation but which were not caught by the search terms employed. The hypothesis that the doctrine as developed by the ECJ is faithfully applied by the Finnish courts is confirmed by the evidence reviewed thus far but, given the limitations of that evidence, a rebuttal may be forthcoming as research on this topic develops.

THE EEA PRINCIPLE OF CONSISTENT INTERPRETATION (OR SOMETHING THAT LOOKS LIKE IT) AND NORWEGIAN COURTS

Christian N.K. Franklin*

1. INTRODUCTION

This contribution will look at how courts in Norway approach and apply the European Economic Area (EEA) principle of consistent interpretation – or at least something which looks like it – in practice. As will be shown, although there may be many similarities to the way in which national courts in the

* Many thanks to Research Assistant Morten Henriksen for help in compiling certain parts of the data used in this contribution, and to Research Fellow Håvard Ormberg for comments on an earlier draft.

European Union (EU) Member States deal with such issues, there are also a number of peculiarities. Where some of these may be seen as connected to idiosyncrasies of the Norwegian legal culture, others may relate more to the particular nature of EEA law. After providing some important background information on Norway's legal system and its EEA context, and also looking at the methods applied in collecting the data used (section 2), this contribution will proceed to show how Norwegian courts generally seem to have received and understand the concept of consistent interpretation (section 3), the scope and criteria for its application (section 4) and its limits (section 5). Some concluding remarks will be provided at the end, to sum up the various findings (section 6).

2. METHOD AND BACKGROUND

Norway is a constitutional monarchy, with a democratic, representative parliamentary form of government. A relatively small country on a European scale, with a population of around 5.2 million people, it is nevertheless the largest of the three European Free Trade Association (EFTA) States party to the EEA Agreement, which allows Norway, Iceland and Lichtenstein to participate in the EU internal market.[1] Access to the internal market afforded to the EFTA States nevertheless comes at a price: EEA law must keep up to speed with developments in EU law. In light of the constantly evolving nature of EU law, certain mechanisms have therefore proven essential in seeking to ensure that EEA law has been developed dynamically in line with EU law. Key above all was the insertion of the fundamental principle of homogeneity into the Agreement, requiring the Contracting Parties (i.e. the EU and its institutions, the EU Member States and the EFTA States) to strive to ensure that identical rules under EU and EEA law are interpreted and applied in a uniform manner, on the basis of equality and reciprocity.[2]

1 [1994] OJ L1/3. Switzerland, although party to the EFTA Convention, is not party to the EEA Agreement. For simplicity's sake, however, the three EFTA States party to the EEA will hereinafter be referred to collectively as the EFTA States, in line with the definition provided for in Art. 2(b) EEA.

2 Arts. 1 and 6 EEA, and e.g. recitals 4 and 5 of the EEA Agreement's Preamble. It is worth noting that the precise nature and import of the EEA principle of reciprocity – according to which procedural and/or substantive rights conferred under EEA law should be the same for EU nationals under the EFTA pillar of the EEA as for EFTA nationals under the EU pillar of the EEA – is rather difficult to ascertain in practice. This is in no small part due to potentially divergent views held by the ECJ and EFTA Court as to how strictly its requirements ought to be understood. Adopting a seemingly less strict view, in Case 104/81, *Kupferberg*, ECLI:EU:C:1982:362, para. 18, the ECJ held that the fact that the courts of one of the parties to a free trade agreement between the European Economic Community (EEC) and Portugal considered certain of its provisions to have direct effect whereas the courts of the other party did not, "is not in itself such as to constitute a lack of reciprocity in the implementation of that agreement". Adopting a seemingly stricter understanding,

The EEA Agreement offers a high degree of integration and uniformity, especially since perceived gaps between the two legal orders are usually dealt with in a rather pragmatic way – and almost invariably in favour of EU or Court of Justice of the European Union (ECJ) (as opposed to national) sensitivities – by the EFTA Court in practice.[3] Yet it is important to bear in mind from the very outset here that the dialogue between the EFTA Court and national courts in the EFTA States, and any guidance provided by the former concerning the principle of consistent interpretation, is framed in a different way than under the EU legal system. EEA-cooperation rests on two pillars, and operates through a "mixity" of institutions.[4] Unlike the EU system where the ECJ acts as the ultimate arbiter in the interpretation and application of EU law, the EFTA Court is afforded no equivalent role as far as EEA law is concerned. Although the EFTA Court is naturally considered an authority on EEA questions, there is no duty for national courts in the EFTA States (of first or last instance) to refer questions on the interpretation and/or application of EEA law to it – merely a right to do so under an Advisory Opinion procedure.[5] And, as the name of the procedure itself suggests, the answers rendered are not binding on national courts of the EFTA States, either. The EFTA Court's Opinions are accorded significant weight, but they are still independently vetted by referring Norwegian courts. Relatively recent case-law of the Norwegian Supreme Court, for example, shows that it may well be prepared to deviate from an interpretation of EEA law spelt out by the EFTA Court in a given case, where it (rightly or wrongly) deems this necessary, usually in order to follow what it believes to be the ECJ's lead.[6] While it might therefore be contended that national judiciaries in the EFTA States enjoy more sovereignty vis-à-vis the EFTA Court than their

---

however, the EFTA Court held in Case E-14/11, *Schenker v. ESA* [2012] EFTA Ct. Rep. 1178, para. 121, that the EFTA Surveillance Authority was required "for reasons of reciprocity" to adopt certain rules concerning access to documents in competition cases corresponding to those applicable to the EU Commission under Regulation 1049/2001.

3 See generally e.g. H.H. Fredriksen and C.N.K. Franklin, "Of pragmatism and principles: The EEA Agreement 20 years on" 52 (2015) 3 *Common Market Law Review* 629–84, and C.N.K. Franklin, "Square pegs and round holes: The free movement of persons under EEA Law" 19 (2017) *Cambridge Yearbook of European Legal Studies* 165–86.

4 Generally on the two-pillar system and providing an overview of arrangements, see Synthesis in this book; further, the EFTA website <http://www.efta.int/eea/eea-institutions>, and e.g. G. Baur, "Decision-making procedure and implementation of new law", in C. Baudenbacher (ed.), *The Handbook of EEA Law* (Springer, 2016), pp. 45–68, at p. 45.

5 Art. 34 of the Agreement between the EFTA States on the Establishment of a Surveillance Authority and a Court of Justice [1994] OJ L344/3 (Surveillance and Court Agreement – SCA).

6 This was suggested in Rt-2000-1811 (*Finanger*), and unequivocally demonstrated in Rt-2013-258 (*STX*) and in the recent decision of the Court of Appeal in LF-2015-187242 (*Fosen-Linjen*). See also Rt-2009-839 (*Pedicel*), where the Supreme Court tacitly distanced itself from parts of the Advisory Opinion which the Norwegian Market Council had obtained from the EFTA Court.

counterparts under the EU system, the implicit deference paid by Norwegian courts to the ECJ in a bid to ensure homogeneity can naturally give a slightly different impression. And while there may not be a strict obligation to follow the EFTA Court's Opinions, the threat of infringement proceedings raised by the EFTA Surveillance Authority ("the ESA"), or one of the other EFTA States (although that would be unlikely), based *inter alia* on a breach of the duty of sincere cooperation under Art. 3 EEA and/or Art. 2 SCA will usually, and should, also entail a rather high threshold before national courts would consider arriving at a different result in practice. Indeed, the Norwegian Supreme Court has expressed as much of its own accord.[7] As may be further implied from the system of information exchange concerning judgments of the EFTA Court, ECJ and General Court and the courts of last instance of the EFTA States under Art. 106 EEA, national (and particularly the Supreme) courts of the EFTA States may therefore feel somewhat more entitled than national courts in the EU Member States to share the role as the ultimate arbiters on the interpretation and application of EEA law.[8]

Advisory Opinions are seldom requested by the Norwegian Supreme Court, which has only made seven requests to date, with two of these being withdrawn before the EFTA Court had a chance to respond to them. Numbers from other Norwegian courts, tribunals and complaint boards make for better reading, with around 50 requests being made. It is interesting to note for the purposes of this contribution that Norwegian courts usually only ask how particular provisions of EEA law – in the Main Part of the EEA Agreement, or a directive or regulation – are to be interpreted. Norwegian courts seldom if ever ask questions concerning the content, remit or application of any EEA principles, including the principle of consistent interpretation, even though certain cases would probably have benefitted from such guidance.[9] Barring a few general statements made by the EFTA Court concerning the EEA principle of consistent interpretation, the matter has fallen largely to national courts

7 Although the Norwegian Supreme Court has made it clear that it has the authority and a duty to consider independently whether and to what extent an Advisory Opinion is to be followed or not, it is settled Norwegian case-law that significant importance is to be attributed to the view of the EFTA Court – at least in cases where the Court itself has made the reference in question. See e.g. Rt-2000-1811, Rt-2004-904, Rt-2007-1003 and Rt-2013-258.

8 Although such claims seem slightly less convincing to my mind, at least as far as the Norwegian Supreme Court is concerned, given its apparent reluctance to entertain or answer relevant EEA law issues in certain cases – even where such arguments could serve to strengthen its findings, and the parties themselves have raised such questions directly before it. See e.g. Rt-2014-1192 (*Sør-Aurdal*), discussed in more detail below.

9 See e.g. the Supreme Court's decision in Rt-2000-1811 (*Finanger I*), dealt with in further detail in several places below, where neither the Supreme Court's request nor the reply received from the EFTA Court (Case E-01/99, *Finanger* [2000] EFTA Ct. Rep. 119) made any mention of the principle of consistent interpretation whatsoever, and an EEA-conforming result was ultimately ruled out by the Norwegian Court in its final decision.

in the EFTA States to develop at national level, through (non-)application of the principle (or as discussed below, a national equivalent) in specific cases. In light of the relatively low number of referrals and a seeming reluctance to ask the "bigger" questions, the relationship between the EFTA Court and the Norwegian courts may be viewed as somewhat strained.[10]

Norway maintains a strong, predominantly dualist view on the relationship between international and national law, which in turn has also influenced the way in which some Norwegian courts and judges approach EEA law issues in practice. Although the dualist principle is not expressly set out in any Norwegian law, Section 26 of the Norwegian Constitution, for example, implies a dualist approach in that international obligations must first be made part of Norwegian law before they will be deemed to impose obligations or create rights which individuals may rely on before national courts.[11] This is the case notwithstanding the international law principle that a state cannot invoke its national law as a reason for non-fulfilment of its international obligations – which also goes some way to explaining why Norway is not party to the Vienna Convention on the Law of Treaties.[12] The EEA Agreement was therefore made part of Norwegian law by virtue of the Norwegian EEA Act of 1992.[13]

The Norwegian judiciary is hierarchically structured, with the *Høyesterett* (Supreme Court) at the zenith, followed by six *lagmannsrett* (Courts of Appeal) and 63 *tingrett* (District Courts).[14] A number of administrative complaints boards also exist, exercising quasi-judicial jurisdiction on a range of issues also broaching EEA law matters, such as, for example, the Public Procurement Complaints Board. In order keep this contribution to manageable proportions, however, only the case-law of the ordinary Norwegian courts has been analysed. Although there is no strict system of precedent as found in common law systems, the rulings of the Norwegian Supreme Court carry substantial weight for lower courts – indeed, Norwegian lawyers are generally encouraged during their legal training to think and reason like the Supreme Court.

The sources used in the present contribution have been compiled through a number of systematic searches on *Lovdata* – a private foundation set up in 1981, providing access to all Supreme Court and Court of Appeal

---

10 For more on this troubled relationship, see e.g. Fredriksen and Franklin (n. 3), pp. 671–76.

11 The Norwegian Constitution, and several other important pieces of Norwegian legislation, are available in English at <https://lovdata.no/register/loverEngelsk>.

12 Arts. 27 and 46 of the Vienna Convention on the Law of Treaties, 23 May 1969, United Nations, Treaty Series, vol. 1155, p. 331. See nevertheless the Court of Appeal's rather interesting decision in LB-2014-26876; UTV-2015-953 (*Hallquist*), where it appears to accept Art. 27 as an expression of customary international law, and hence binding for Norway.

13 *Lov 27. nov 1992 nr. 109 om gjennomføring i norsk rett av hoveddelen i avtale om Det europeiske økonomiske samarbeidsområde (EØS).*

14 For more generally about the ordinary courts in Norway, see the Court Administration's webpage: <https://www.domstol.no/en>.

rulings, and many decisions of the lower courts.[15] The searches conducted have attempted to uncover all cases where the EEA principle of consistent interpretation (or something which looks like it) have been mentioned and/or applied by Norwegian courts. The terms used have for example included "*EØS konform fortolkning*", "*direktivkonform fortolkning*", "*EØS lov §2*", "*EØS lojalitetsplikt*", "*presumsjonsprinsipp*" and other variants thereto.

The search process proved rather challenging, and it is difficult to say exactly how many cases in which the principle of consistent interpretation has been at issue. First, because the Norwegian courts have never applied the EEA principle directly. In the few cases where a principle is relied upon or mentioned at all, they refer instead to a national equivalent – a point which will be discussed in further detail below. Second, because in many (if not most) cases, although it may seem apparent from the decision itself that the court has conducted a *de facto* evaluation of whether or not to perform a consistent interpretation, no principle is actually mentioned or referred to in the decisions. Bearing these caveats in mind, the list of cases compiled should nevertheless be considered as relatively comprehensive, and has aimed at covering decisions not only of the Supreme Court and Courts of Appeal, but also some decisions of the District Courts.

3. RECEPTION AND UNDERSTANDING OF THE PRINCIPLE OF CONSISTENT INTERPRETATION

In spite of the relatively few cases where the principle is touched upon, and the rather sparse guidance provided in these cases, the EFTA Court has referred to the concept in several different terms – as "the principle of conform interpretation",[16] a duty to interpret "in conformity with" EEA law,[17] or "in the light of the wording or purpose" of EEA law.[18] The very existence of the principle of consistent interpretation as a matter of EEA law is rooted in several authorities, including the EEA principle of loyal or sincere cooperation (Art. 3 EEA),[19]

15 <https://lovdata.no>. There are two versions available – *Lovdata* (which provides limited open access) and *Lovdata Pro* (which provides full access by paid subscription).

16 Case E-18/11, *Irish Bank* [2012] EFTA Ct. Rep. 592, para. 124.

17 Case E-1/07, *Criminal proceedings against A* [2007] EFTA Ct. Rep. 246, para. 39; Case E-28/13 *Merrill Lynch* [2014] EFTA Ct. Rep. 970, para. 42; Case E-25/13, *Engilbertsson* [2014] EFTA Ct. Rep. 524, para. 159; Case E-6/13, *Metacom* [2013] EFTA Ct. Rep. 856, para. 69.

18 Case E-18/11, *Irish Bank*, para. 123; E-28/13, *Merrill Lynch*, para. 42.

19 See e.g. Case E-01/07, *Criminal proceedings against A*, para. 39; Case E-6/13, *Metacom*, para. 69. For more generally on the remit and content of this principle in its EEA setting, see C.N.K. Franklin, "Article 3 – principle of loyalty" in H.H. Fredriksen *et al.* (eds.) *Agreement on the European Economic Area – A Commentary* (Beck/Hart/Nomos/Universitetsforlaget, 2018), pp. 180–96.

and the public international law principle of effectiveness.[20] The EFTA Court has stated further that the principle is to be considered as inherent in the Agreement's objectives of establishing a dynamic and homogenous EEA, and of ensuring equal treatment, equal conditions of competition and adequate means of enforcement for individuals and economic operators.[21] In *Irish Bank* it also added that the duty rests on the objectives sought by Arts. 7 and 104 EEA (the duty to implement EEA directives and regulations into national law), and Protocol 35 to the EEA Agreement (i.e. EEA quasi-primacy requirements).[22] The latter reference seems all the more interesting, given that the ECJ has never stated that the corresponding EU principle is based on the principle of primacy. In the most recent cases, however, the EFTA Court seems content on the whole to simply recall that the principle is "inherent in the objectives of the EEA Agreement".[23]

Norwegian courts for their part tend to mainly refer to the EEA principle as *direktivkonform tolkning* (directive conform interpretation). Which is something of a misnomer, in any event, since not only directives but also regulations must be transformed into Norwegian law in order to have full legal effect.[24] Given that the principle also applies to the provisions set out in the Main Part of the EEA Agreement, the term "EEA consistent" or "EEA conform" interpretation would seem more fitting.[25]

The Norwegian Supreme Court has willingly accepted that this unwritten principle is inherent in the EEA Agreement itself, and therefore legally binding for Norway – notwithstanding the dualist approach to international obligations under Norwegian law.[26] In spite of this, Norwegian courts have never (to date) expressly applied the EEA principle to resolve alleged conflicts between Norwegian and EEA law in practice. In the few cases where a specific principle or method of interpretation is referred to as potential grounds for arriving at a particular interpretative conclusion in line with Norway's international or EEA obligations, Norwegian courts rely instead on the national principle of presumption of compliance with international law (*presumsjonsprinsippet* – hereinafter referred to simply as the "principle of presumption"). And as mentioned above, in many cases, no principle is referred to whatsoever.[27]

---

20 Case E-04/01, *Karlsson* [2002] EFTA Ct. Rep. 240, para. 28.

21 Case E-01/07, *Criminal proceedings against A*, paras. 37–39.

22 Case E-18/11, *Irish Bank*, paras. 122–23.

23 Case E-25/13, *Engilbertsson*, para. 159; Case E-28/13 *Merrill Lynch*, para. 42.

24 Art. 7 EEA Agreement.

25 See e.g. Case E-04/01, *Karlsson*, para. 28, where the EFTA Court held that national courts have a duty to "consider any relevant element of EEA law, whether implemented or not, when interpreting national law"; and Case E-15/12, *Wahl* [2013] EFTA Ct. Rep. 534, para. 55.

26 See e.g. Rt-2000-1811 (*Finanger I*), p. 1827.

27 See e.g. the Supreme Court's decisions in Rt-1997-1965 (*Stavanger Catering*), Rt-2004-1474 (*Volvo*) and Rt-2006-1473 (*Lifebuoy*); and the Court of Appeal in RG-2004-187 (*Tripp Trapp*) and RG-2004-187 (*Topshop*).

The reason why Norwegian courts have refrained from express, direct application of the EEA principle of consistent interpretation were explained to a certain extent in the seminal *Finanger I* case.[28] This is the only decision to date in which the Supreme Court has set out its views on the principle of consistent interpretation at any length.[29] As discussed later, in spite of a tendency to downplay the importance of this decision in certain parts of the literature, it has not been overruled – to the contrary, later case-law reveals that it continues to have a marked impact on Norwegian court practice. The case essentially concerned a conflict between a provision of the Norwegian Automobile Liability Act (ALA) and several of the EU/EEA Motor Vehicle Insurance Directives.[30] Ms Finanger was a passenger in a car which spun off the road and crashed, killing another passenger and severely injuring both her and the driver. She was 17 years old at the time. The driver and all of the passengers were under the influence of alcohol, and Finanger also knew that the driver was intoxicated. Section 4 ALA set out the general rule that when a motor vehicle causes injury, injured parties may claim compensation from the insurance company of the vehicle in question. The insurance company which insured the car nevertheless rejected Finanger's claim for compensation, under reference to an exception set out in Section 7(3)(b) ALA. This provision ruled out compensation in the event that the injured party had allowed him/herself to be driven in the vehicle knowing that the driver was under the influence of alcohol.[31] Norwegian law viewed in isolation therefore barred Finanger from claiming compensation from the insurance company.

Both the District Court and the Court of Appeal nevertheless still found in favour of Finanger.[32] According to the Court of Appeal, the reason for

28 Rt-2000-1811.

29 Academic commentaries immediately following the decision seemed generally well-receptive of the Supreme Court's findings. See e.g. K. Krüger, "Finanger-dommen og den nye rettskildefaktor: frykten" (2001) 2 *Jussens venner*, 89–104; F. Arnesen, "Plenumsdommen i Finangersaken 16.11.2000, Rt 2000 s 1811" 27 (2000) 4 *Kritisk Juss*, 303–09. Greater awareness of and a more critical attitude towards the problems it raises, can nevertheless be traced in more recent writing, see e.g. C.N.K. Franklin, "Om innholdet i og rekkevidden av det EØS-rettslige prinsippet om direktivkonform fortolkning" (2012) 5 *Jussens Venner*, 269–317.

30 *Lov 3 feb 1961 om ansvar for skade som motorvogner gjer*; Council Directive 72/166/EEC on the approximation of the laws of Member States relating to insurance against civil liability in respect of the use of motor vehicles, and to the enforcement of the obligation to insure against such liability [1972] OJ L103/1; Second Council Directive 84/5/EEC on the approximation of the laws of the Member States relating to insurance against civil liability in respect of the use of motor vehicles [1984] OJ L8/17; Third Council Directive 90/232/EEC on the approximation of the laws of the Member States relating to insurance against civil liability in respect of the use of motor vehicles [1990] OJ L129/33.

31 A further exception to this exception nevertheless provided that compensation could still be awarded "in so far as special reasons are in favour of this" – a point returned to later in section 4.2.1 below.

32 LF-1998-998.

this was to be found in a combined reading of the three first EU/EEA Motor Vehicle Insurance Directives, which provided that the Member States could only exempt passengers travelling in stolen vehicles from compensation, and even then only in strictly defined circumstances. The exception set out in Section 7(3)(b) ALA was therefore clearly incompatible with the Directives – in spite of the Norwegian statute acting as implementing legislation for them.[33]

The case was appealed to the Supreme Court, which overruled the Court of Appeal in a majority decision (10-5). This was not altogether surprising, however, as the Court of Appeal had erroneously reached its decision by giving the Directives direct effect and setting aside the provisions of the ALA. Since membership in the EEA was not to entail any transfer of legislative sovereignty, there is no requirement of direct effect or primacy of EEA law – at least not in the way that these principles are understood as a matter of EU law.[34] Concerning the issue of what principle(s) might apply in seeking to resolve the conflict between national and EEA law in the case, the Supreme Court stated that there were no grounds for contending that the principle of consistent interpretation as developed in *EU law* stretched further than the Norwegian principle of presumption. The Supreme Court then said that, given its view, there was no reason to entertain the question of whether the principle of consistent interpretation under *EEA law* stretched as far as the EU law principle. Presumably, the Supreme Court felt that the Norwegian principle of presumption was adequate in itself to abide by the EEA standard – i.e. that the EEA principle stretched no further, and required Norwegian courts to do no more, than what was in any event required by the Norwegian principle. In other words, the Supreme Court was happy to apply the Norwegian principle alone to try to resolve the norm-conflict at issue in the case.

Notwithstanding the fact that the decision in *Finanger I* pre-dated the *Karlsson* case, where the EFTA Court formally established the existence of the EEA principle of consistent interpretation for the very first time, the Supreme Court's reluctance to apply the EEA principle directly is probably best understood in light of the rather longstanding (and unresolved) question as to

33 When implementing the Directives, the Norwegian Parliament had decided not to amend Section 7 as it (erroneously) considered the rule to concern tort law rules on contributory negligence, and hence as falling outside the scope of EEA law altogether.

34 Contrary to certain misguided statements made by the ECJ (see e.g. Case C-431/11, *UK v. Council*, ECLI:EU:C:2013:589, para. 54; and Case C-83/13, *Fonnship*, ECLI:EU:C:2014:2053, para. 2), the EFTA Court has repeatedly and correctly confirmed that the EEA Agreement does not require direct effect of non-implemented EEA provisions, although the EFTA States may naturally choose to apply such principles of their own accord (see e.g. Case E-18/11, *Irish Bank*, para. 122). Compare nevertheless the views of J. Kokott and D. Dittert, "European Courts in Dialogue" in EFTA Court (ed.), *The EEA and the EFTA Court – Decentred Integration* (Hart Publishing, 2014), pp. 43–52, at p. 46, with the views of D.T Björgvinsson ("Fundamental Rights in EEA Law", pp. 263–80, at p. 265) and H. Bull ("Shall be Made Part of the Internal Legal Order: The Legislative Approaches", pp. 203–13, at p. 211) in the same volume, and further with Fredriksen and Franklin (n. 3), pp. 669–70.

what the very nature of EEA law really is.[35] The EFTA Court has repeatedly stated that EEA law constitutes an autonomous legal order in its own right,[36] leading some to contend that certain legal consequences may be entailed from this fact alone.[37] In Norway, however, the EEA Agreement has generally been viewed much like any other treaty under public international law – albeit with a few special characteristics.[38] The Norwegian Supreme Court for its part seems rather divided on the issue. On the one hand, certain decisions indicate that the principle of presumption is to be applied in the same manner and extent to all international (including EEA) obligations. For example, in the *Care Expenses* case, the Supreme Court recalled and applied the very same "general principles" concerning the principle of presumption as set out in *Finanger I* in an (unsuccessful) attempt to interpret a provision of the Norwegian Social Services Act in light of Art. 11 of the European Council Charter of Local Self-Government.[39] On the other hand, in the recent *Sailors* case, in the course of explaining why the principle of state liability only applied to breaches of EEA law and not to any and all breaches of international law attributable to the Norwegian State, the Supreme Court said of the EEA Agreement: "We are not speaking of an ordinary international law obligation, but of an agreement which of itself [i.e. inherently] includes the principle that states may be held liable for defective implementation".[40] The fact that no uniform understanding seems to exist amongst Norwegian courts and judges as to whether EEA law is to be considered as merely public international law or perhaps something more, may also go some way in explaining why the principle of consistent interpretation seems to be understood, defined and implemented in different ways in different cases in practice.

---

35 Case E-04/01, *Karlsson*, para. 28.

36 Case E-9/97, *Sveinbjörnsdóttir* [1998] EFTA Ct. Rep. 95, para. 59: "... the EEA Agreement is an international treaty *sui generis* which contains a distinct legal order of its own. The EEA Agreement does not establish a customs union but an enhanced free trade area ... The depth of integration of the EEA Agreement is less far-reaching than under the EC Treaty, but the scope and the objective of the EEA Agreement goes beyond what is usual for an agreement under public international law." Reiterated in several cases since, e.g. Case E-4/01, *Karlsson*, para. 25, Case E-1/07, *Criminal proceedings against A*, para. 37.

37 See e.g. C. Baudenbacher, "Facets of an EEA Constitutional Order" in N. Colneric *et al.* (eds.), *Une Communauté de droit Festschrift für Gil Carlos Rodriguez Iglesias* (Berlin Wissenschaftsverlag, 2003), pp. 343–59.

38 See e.g. H.H. Fredriksen and G. Mathisen, *EØS-rett* (3rd ed., Fagbokforlaget, 2018), p. 38; and F. Arnesen and A. Stenvik, *Internasjonalisering og juridisk metode – særlig om EØS-rettens betydning i norsk rett* (2nd ed., Universitetsforlaget, 2015), p. 17.

39 Rt-2007-234. See also the Supreme Court's decision in HR-2016-2591-A (*Legal Capacity of A*), paras. 60–62, where both principled statements from the *Finanger I* case and the preparatory works to the Norwegian EEA Act were similarly directly relied upon to resolve a conflict between the Norwegian Guardianship Act and the UN Convention on the Rights of Persons with Disabilities in favour of the former. Both of these cases are returned to in more detail below.

40 HR-2016-296-A, para. 46 (author's translation).

In any event, had the Norwegian principle of presumption and the EEA (or EU) principle of consistent interpretation stretched equally far, then all would have been fine – the same interpretative result would then presumably be achievable regardless of which principle was applied, thus rendering the issue of the content and scope of the EEA principle perhaps more of academic than any real, practical interest. Indeed, in cases where the conflicts between Norwegian and EEA law prove easily resolvable (i.e. so-called "soft cases"), it would probably be of little consequence which principle was actually applied to resolve them.[41] The problem is, however, that the principles – at least according to the only express statements made by the Supreme Court on the subject to date – do not seem to stretch equally far. The scope of the Norwegian principle seems both actually and potentially more limited for several reasons, two of which are as follows.

First, one can infer from the Norwegian Supreme Court's decisions in *Finanger I* and certain other cases, that the EU (and EEA) duty is viewed as one related solely to interpretative outcomes, and not as to any procedures or methods used in reaching them.[42] Indeed, the very application in certain cases of a *national* principle of presumption to seek to resolve conflicts between Norwegian and EEA law in itself indicates an innate predisposition for viewing the EU/EEA principle as one exclusively related to the result to be reached in a case, and not as impacting on the process(es) used in reaching it.

Support for such a view could naturally be drawn from certain earlier lines of the ECJ's case-law, and various statements made by the EFTA Court, which pay heed to the "interpretative methods recognized by national law".[43] Yet it is not the application of a national principle of presumption in itself which seems problematic in this regard, but rather the issue of whether – and if so, how – untouched by EEA law requirements it may remain in its application. Case-law of the ECJ clearly shows that the EU principle of consistent interpretation not only entails a duty of results, but may also impact on the national methods applied in order to reach them. Following *Björnekulla*, for example, the duty of national courts to interpret national law as far as possible in the light of the wording and the purpose of a directive "applies notwithstanding any contrary

---

41 For an example of a completely unproblematic interpretation of Norwegian law in light of EEA obligations, see e.g. Rt-2004-1474 (*Volvo*), concerning an alleged conflict between a provision of the Norwegian Trademark Act and Art. 7 of the Trademark Directive, as in turn interpreted by the EFTA Court and ECJ.

42 A view seemingly also held by several EEA law experts in Norway; see e.g. H.H. Fredriksen, "EU/EØS-rett i norske domstoler", *Rapport no. 3, Europautredningen, Utvalget for utredning av Norges avtaler med EU* (2011), pp. 71–72, and Arnesen and Stenvik (n. 38), p. 80.

43 See e.g. Case 14/83, *Von Colson*, ECLI:EU:C:1984:153, and Case C-106/89, *Marleasing*, ECLI:EU:C:1990:395; and Case E-01/07, *Criminal proceedings against A*, para. 39; Case E-6/13, *Metacom*, para. 69; Case E-28/13, *Merrill Lynch*, para. 42; Case E-25/13, *Engilbertsson*, para. 159; and as put in slightly different terms in Case E-18/11, *Irish Bank*, para. 123 – "to do whatever lies within its competence".

interpretation which may arise from the *travaux préparatoires* for the national rule".[44] And as the ECJ recently clarified in *Ajos* and *Ognyanov*, the duty may entail the obligation for national courts to change established case-law, if it is based on an interpretation of national law that is incompatible with the objectives of a directive.[45]

In light of the fundamental principle of homogeneity, parallel principles and rules under EEA and EU law should generally be understood in the same manner, unless the differences between them are so great as to warrant divergent approaches.[46] It has been suggested that recent developments of the EU principle of consistent interpretation by the ECJ might perhaps have exposed differences of such magnitude as to warrant a different approach under EEA law.[47] In the opinion of the present author, the general signs from the EFTA Court do not appear to support such a conclusion. For example, in *Irish Bank*, the EFTA Court framed the principle of consistent interpretation directly against the backdrop of a statement reminding the authorities of the EFTA States that the objectives of establishing a dynamic and homogenous EEA could only be achieved if everyone enjoyed the same rights under both the EU and EFTA pillars of the EEA.[48] Further, in *Engilbertsson*, the EFTA Court referred specifically to the ECJ's decision in *Dominguez* in its reiteration of the EEA principle of consistent interpretation, once again indicating that the remit of the principles should indeed by considered the same under both EU and EEA law.[49] In *Dominguez* the ECJ went very far in instructing the French national court as to how national law might be interpreted so as to render an EU-conform interpretation possible – despite the national court's clear indication in its referral that it had reached the limits of what it regarded to be possible.[50] Finally, in *Merrill Lynch*, the EFTA Court followed up by stating that in cases where national courts are dealing with disputes concerning the interpretation of domestic law provisions

---

44 Case C-371/02, *Björnekulla*, ECLI:EU:C:2004:275, para. 13.

45 Case C-441/14, *Ajos*, ECLI:EU:C:2016:278, para. 33; with further ref. to Case C-456/98, *Centrosteel*, ECLI:EU:C:2000:402, para. 17; confirmed in Case C-554/14, *Ognyanov*, ECLI:EU:C:2016:835, para. 67.

46 See e.g. Case E-3/98, *Rainford-Towning* [1998] EFTA Ct. Rep. 207, para. 21; *Sveinbjørnsdottir*, para. 60.

47 See Fredriksen and Mathisen (n. 38), p. 382. As for their contention that decisions in cases such as *Björnekulla* and *Ajos* may be seen to contribute to blurring the lines between direct effect and consistent interpretation, I would disagree: the results will undoubtedly be the same (and this is obviously also the aim), yet the interpretative results effectively prescribed by the ECJ in these cases did not involve any substitutionary effect, and were clearly based on national law. Whether or not the decisions in question could be said to contribute to blurring the lines between primacy requirements and consistent interpretation, is naturally a different matter.

48 Case E-18/11, *Irish Bank*, para. 122.

49 Case E-25/13, *Engilbertsson* [2014] EFTA Ct. Rep. 524, para. 163; Case C-282/10, *Dominguez*, ECLI:EU:C:2012:33, paras. 26–31.

50 See further M. de Mol, "Dominguez: A Deafening Silence" (2012) 8 *EUConst* 280–303, at p. 285.

specifically enacted for the purpose of transposing EEA law, "the national court *must* presume that the EEA/EFTA State had the intention of fulfilling entirely the obligations from the EEA directive [or regulation] concerned".[51] Presumably, such a mandatory presumption may prove rebuttable in the (highly unlikely) event that the national legislator expressly stated that it had no intention of implementing the directive/regulation in question – which in itself would naturally constitute a clear breach of EEA law. Such would also be the case under EU law. The main point here is nevertheless inescapable: the guidance provided by the EFTA Court was clearly directed towards the method (i.e. requirement of presumptive legislative intent), and not simply the result to be reached.

Second, the application of the Norwegian principle of presumption will always be potentially more limited than the EU and EEA principles of consistent interpretation, as the former rests on an initially negative approach born from the principle of dualism. According to the EFTA Court, the general rule and starting point under EEA law is that all national authorities must (as far as possible) seek to achieve interpretations of national law which are consistent with their EEA obligations. This principle is firmly based on ideals of effectiveness, and builds on the self-evident principle of international law that national law cannot be invoked in order to justify non-compliance with international obligations. The starting point under Norwegian law is different. The general rule flows from the principle of dualism: since Norwegian and international law constitute separate legal systems, where conflicts arise between them, the former will be given precedence. As mentioned previously, this is also one of the reasons why Norway has not chosen to become party to the Vienna Convention on the Law of Treaties. According to the Norwegian Supreme Court, the national principle of presumption is therefore to be viewed as a mere exception to the general rule borne from dualism.[52] And where the Supreme Court in certain cases has found it impossible to reach results consistent with Norway's international (including EEA) obligations, the principle of dualism has invariably been relied upon as one of the reasons underlying its conclusion.[53]

---

51 Case E-28/13, *Merrill Lynch*, para. 41 (emphasis added) – thus reflecting the ECJ's express statements to the same effect in Case C-334/92, *Wagner Miret*, ECLI:EU:C:1993:945.

52 See e.g. the Norwegian Supreme Court's decision in Rt-1997-580 (*OFS*); and more explicitly in Rt-2007-234 (*Care Expenses*), para. 54: "I point out that Norway, in situations where Norwegian law and international law conflict, is generally based on the dualist principle, which implies that Norwegian law has precedence over international law. However, in order to avoid conflict, Norway practices to some extent the principle of presumption, in that Norwegian law is presumed to be in compliance with our international obligations." (author's own translation). To much the same effect, see e.g. the District Court's decision in TOSLO-2003-806 (*KLM*).

53 See e.g. the Supreme Court's decisions in *Finanger I* (n. 39), *Care Expenses* (n. 52) and *Legal Capacity of A* (n. 39); and the District Court in *KLM* (n. 52).

Although the initial starting point for Norwegian courts facing actual/potential conflicts between Norwegian and EEA law is therefore clearly negatively charged, this is not to say that the principle of dualism is by any means contestable *per se* in the light of EEA law. To the contrary, it seems perfectly in tune with the stated limitations of both the EEA Agreement (which was not to involve any transfer of legislative sovereignty), and the EEA principle of consistent interpretation (which requires national courts to do only what is possible in this regard). Yet to contend that national methods of interpretation or construction – including the principles of dualism and/or presumption – must not at the very least be adapted in the light of EEA law requirements, would be denying of both duty and reality. The dualist principle has already been whittled down by the Norwegian Parliament, through the introduction of so-called "sector-monism" in many fields.[54] The Supreme Court itself has also contributed to piercing the dualist veil more particularly with regards to EEA obligations, through its unabridged and unreserved acceptance and application of the unwritten EEA principle of state liability. In *Finanger II* – where Ms Finanger finally received compensation after suing the Norwegian State for inadequate implementation of the Motor Vehicle Insurance Directives – the Supreme Court stated that Section 1 of the Norwegian EEA Act was to be understood as providing for the incorporation of the principle of state liability as a principle inherent in the EEA Agreement itself, and hence as grounds for its direct application under Norwegian law.[55] The same reasoning must presumably apply to all unwritten EEA principles inherent in the EEA Agreement, including therefore the principle of consistent interpretation.[56] The weight to be attached to the traditional dualist argument and starting point when seeking to perform consistent interpretations in an EEA setting therefore seems questionable at best. Yet to admit so may perhaps also ultimately entail admittance that EEA law is indeed something different to all other public international obligations that Norway has taken upon itself – a point which the Norwegian Supreme Court has yet to unequivocally confirm.

To their credit, however, it would seem as though some of the *lower Norwegian courts* have adopted a more positively charged understanding of the relation between the principles of dualism and presumption, at least in certain cases where the latter has been expressly applied. In *Fokus Bank*, for example, the Court of Appeal defined and applied the principle of presumption without any reference to the limiting effects of dualism.[57] Much the same approach appears

---

54 See e.g. Section 2 of the Human Rights Act (*Lov 21 mai 1999 nr. 30 om styrking av menneskerettighetenes stilling i norsk rett*); Section 1–2 of the Civil Procedure Act (*Lov 17. juni 2005 nr. 90 om mekling og rettergang i sivile tvister*); and Section 4 of the Criminal Procedure Act (*Lov 22 mai 1981 nr. 25 om rettergangsmåten i straffesaker*).

55 Rt-2005-1365.

56 Of the same opinion, see Fredriksen and Mathisen (n. 38), p. 361.

57 RG-2005-1542.

to have been adopted by the Court of Appeal in the *Postal Delivery* case, where the principle of presumption again was set out (yet ultimately not applied, as the case was decided on other grounds), without any indication as to it being an exception to the dualist starting point.[58]

As stated earlier, while the principle of presumption has been expressly applied in certain cases, in many cases the Norwegian courts refer to no principle whatsoever. This is rather surprising in itself, since Norwegian courts are generally very conscientious in elaborating the reasons underlying their decisions, and identifying the methods applied in reaching them. Common to all of the cases where no method or principle is expressly referred to, is that EEA-consistent interpretations of Norwegian law seem both discernible and proved possible in the end.[59] It has been contended that some of these cases should be understood as illustrating a willingness on the part of Norwegian courts to adapt the principle of presumption beyond the indications made by the Supreme Court in *Finanger I*.[60] Given the lack of any clear explanation, however, the courts' decisions in such cases might just as easily be understood as examples of an evolution towards application of the EEA principle of consistent interpretation itself. Exactly which principle is applied probably does not matter so much to the parties involved in such cases – as long as individual rights flowing from EEA measures are given effect in the end. Yet clarity on this point may naturally also prove important from a more practical perspective, since determination of whether a national or EEA principle applies will also impact on the limits thereto, and not least the issue of who may ultimately decide the content thereof.[61]

On a different note: concerning the preferred order of sequence for application of the various tools available for ensuring the effectiveness of EEA law, it is important to remember that unlike under EU law, only two mechanisms exist for giving legal effects to incorrectly or unimplemented EEA rules: consistent interpretation and state liability.[62] Given the lack of direct effect under EEA law, the principle of consistent interpretation arguably becomes even more important: in situations where the plaintiff is not seeking compensation but rather enforcement of a specific right, such vindication would only be achievable by way of consistent interpretation – at least in the dualist EFTA States. In *Merrill Lynch*, the EFTA Court has therefore provided

58 LB-2013-113726.

59 See e.g. the decisions in *Volvo*, *Lifebuoy* and *Tripp Trapp* (n. 27).

60 Fredriksen (n. 42), p. 73.

61 This point will be discussed further at section 5 below.

62 As mentioned above, since membership in the EEA was not to entail any transfer of legislative sovereignty, there is no requirement of direct effect or primacy of EEA law as understood under EU law. Primacy of EEA law is essentially reserved to giving precedence to Norwegian legislative measures that serve to correctly implement EEA obligations over other conflicting Norwegian legislative measures (see Section 2 of the EEA Act).

some welcome guidance on the preferred sequence between the two: consistent interpretation must be attempted first, with state liability only coming into play if an interpretation in line with EEA law "may be impossible according to the interpretative methods recognized by national law".[63] Norwegian court practice seems in line with the EFTA Court's understanding, at least as far as can be implied from the two *Finanger* cases: since consistent interpretation was not possible in *Finanger I*, the Supreme Court strongly hinted that a subsequent claim for compensation on the basis of state liability would be the way to go.[64] Ms Finanger therefore brought a new case against the Norwegian State (*Finanger II*), which she won.[65]

4. UNDERSTANDING OF THE PRINCIPLE'S SCOPE AND CRITERIA FOR APPLICATION

The following section will look at practice concerning various matters connected to Norwegian courts' understanding and reception of the scope and criteria for application of the EEA principle of consistent interpretation, including application in vertical and horizontal cases, to what types of national law it applies, and possible duties of *ex officio* application.

4.1. VERTICAL/HORIZONTAL APPLICATION OF THE PRINCIPLE

While it can be inferred from several EFTA Court rulings that the EEA principle of consistent interpretation applies equally in cases involving vertical and horizontal party constellations,[66] the practice of the Norwegian courts seems far from uniform on this point. In cases where the Norwegian principle of presumption is expressly applied in an attempt to resolve potential conflicts

63 Case E-28/13, *Merrill Lynch*, paras. 40–45.

64 The fact that Ms Finanger was asking for money may naturally have affected the Supreme Court's ultimate decision to rule out a consistent interpretation in *Finanger I*. Whether the Court would prove willing to stretch itself further in seeking an EEA-conform interpretation in a situation where the plaintiff was not seeking monetary compensation but rather enforcement of a specific right would be interesting to see. It is nevertheless interesting to note that *Finanger II* was also a majority decision (9-4), and that two of the four judges presiding both *Finanger* cases in fact voted to rule out application of both consistent interpretation and state liability(!).

65 Rt-2005-1365.

66 For an example of a vertical case, see e.g. Case E-01/07, *Criminal proceedings against A*; For examples of horizontal cases, see e.g. Case E-28/13, *Merrill Lynch* and Case E-06/13, *Metacom*, which both involved claims raised by one private individual against another.

between international (including EEA) obligations and Norwegian law, the mere existence of a horizontal party constellation has on several occasions provided (at least partial) grounds for ruling out consistent interpretation.

The Supreme Court's decision in *Finanger I* once again set the tone in this regard. The case involved a dispute between two private parties – an insurance company and the victim of a traffic accident claiming personal injury compensation. Ruling out the possibility of an EEA-consistent interpretation of the relevant Norwegian law, the Supreme Court held as one of the grounds for its conclusion that the Norwegian principle of presumption would have less of an impact in a horizontal case than in a dispute between a private individual and the Norwegian State.[67] If that were indeed the case, then there would seem to be even fewer grounds for contending that the EU principle of consistent interpretation stretched no further than the Norwegian principle of presumption.

Viewed by itself, and with no small amount of charity, the Supreme Court's statement could potentially have been understood as a rather clumsy attempt to reflect certain parts of the ECJ's case-law, according to which consistent interpretations must not lead to the imposition of (at least certain types of) obligations on individuals.[68] Yet this is not an altogether convincing explanation. The issue as to whether or not (or which kind of) civil obligations may be imposed on individuals by way of consistent interpretation was far from resolved by the ECJ at the time of the Supreme Court's decision, and indeed remains somewhat unresolved to this very day.[69] The Supreme Court has in any event confirmed its stance in *Finanger I* in later case-law. In the *Care Expenses* case from 2007, two Norwegian municipalities (Nes and Kongsberg) were locked in a dispute as to which was financially responsible for covering the care expenses of a severely disabled person.[70] According to Section 10-3 of the Norwegian Social Services Act, "[s]hould a dispute arise ... the municipalities may require the County Governor to settle the dispute".[71] The case was therefore brought before the County Governor, who decided the issue in favour of Nes municipality.

67 Rt-2000-1811: "*Det er i denne vurderingen også av vesentlig betydning at §7 tredje ledd bokstav b regulerer rettsforholdet mellom private parter, hvor presumsjonsprinsippet som tidligere nevnt ikke har den samme gjennomslagskraft som f.eks. i et tilfelle der folkerettslige forpliktelser gir den enkelte borger vern mot inngrep fra det offentlige.*"

68 See e.g. Case C-168/95, *Arcaro*, ECLI:EU:C:1996:363, para. 42; Case C-321/05, *Kofoed*, ECLI:EU:C:2007:408, para. 45.

69 As so excellently explained by Advocate General Jacobs in Case C-456/98, *Centrosteel*, ECLI:EU:C:2000:137, the ECJ's statements in *Arcaro* could not be said to be reflective of the general understanding at that point in time. For an overview of more recent ECJ developments on this point, see e.g. P. Craig and G. de Búrca, *EU Law – Text, Cases, and Materials* (6th ed., Oxford University Press, 2015), pp. 214–16.

70 Rt-2007-234.

71 Author's own translation. *Lov 13. des 1991 nr. 81 om sosiale tjenester.*

Kongsberg subsequently brought a case against the Norwegian State before the ordinary courts requesting judicial review of the administrative decision, which it lost.[72] When Kongsberg still refused to pay Nes the monies owed, the dispute was again brought before the courts, eventually making its way to the Supreme Court.

The Supreme Court started out by saying that under Norwegian law viewed in isolation, the County Governor's decision could not be reviewed by the courts.[73] The Supreme Court then asked whether this stance needed to be modified in the light of a recent Recommendation issued by one of the Council of Europe's bodies concerning the interpretation of Art. 11 of the Charter of Local Self-Government.[74] Art. 11 of the Charter provided: "Local authorities shall have the right of recourse to a judicial remedy in order to secure free exercise of their powers and respect for such principles of local self-government as are enshrined in the constitution or domestic legislation." The Expert Group upon which the Recommendation was based had found that the "Norwegian legislation, as interpreted by the courts, cannot be regarded as being entirely in compliance with Article 11 of the Charter of Local Self-Government in that it does not give local authorities the right to a judicial remedy … against decisions taken by the state authorities …". It therefore recommended that Norwegian authorities should bring their legislation and judicial practice into compliance with the Charter on this point.[75]

The Supreme Court held that the principle of presumption could not apply in this case, and that Norwegian law must therefore be given precedence over the international obligations in question. With express reference to its ruling in *Finanger I*, one of the grounds provided for its decision was that "Our case does not concern a situation where the Convention … gives 'citizens protection against public interventions', and where the principle of presumption is presumed to have greater impact".[76] Since this was a horizontal case between two public parties, the principle of presumption was therefore deemed to have less of an impact than in cases involving treaty rules protecting Norwegian citizens from public measures.

Compared to the situation in *Finanger I*, the *Care Expenses* case admittedly involved a different type of horizontal situation (i.e. a dispute between two public parties). It also involved different treaty obligations altogether. The Supreme Court nevertheless chose to treat both situations in the same way, recognising the horizontal party constellations as partial grounds for ruling out

---

72 LB-2004-7390; HR-2004-1483-U.

73 Paras. 35–44.

74 Recommendation 203 (2006) on the compliance of Norwegian legislation with Article 11 of the European Charter of Local Self-Government.

75 Recommendation 203 (2006) ibid., paras. 2–3.

76 Para. 55 (author's own translation).

consistent interpretations in both cases. The relevance of the party constellation in a case involving two public entities seems all the more surprising, as it raises no issue concerning the imposition of obligations on individuals in the first place. The Court's findings in *Care Expenses* would therefore seem to lend further credence to the contention that the Norwegian principle of presumption may have a more limited impact in any type of horizontal dispute than required under either the EU or EEA principles of consistent interpretation.[77]

Other cases nevertheless reveal a slightly different attitude of the Norwegian courts, more in tune with the overall tenet of the EU and EEA principles. In the *Lifebuoy* case from 2006, the Supreme Court for example had little difficulty in arriving at an interpretation of Norwegian trademark legislation consistent with Norway's EEA obligations under the Trademark Directive, notwithstanding the fact that the case concerned a dispute between two private parties.[78] It is worth pointing out, however, that the end result, according to which the trademark registrations of both parties were deemed valid, did not therefore have the effect of imposing obligations on either party to the case.

Three other clear examples of "soft" horizontal cases, where consistent interpretations similarly led to the imposition of what could only be described as "mere adverse repercussions" and therefore rather uncontroversial in themselves, are *Stavanger Catering*, *Topshop* and *Tripp Trapp*.[79] It is interesting to note, however, that neither the principle of presumption nor the EEA principle of consistent interpretation were expressly applied or even mentioned by the courts in these cases. No mention was made of any previous case-law concerning the scope of the principles, either. It is therefore difficult to say whether Norwegian courts, by placing less emphasis on the party constellation in these cases, should be understood as thereby having adapted their understanding of the national principle of presumption, or whether the change in attitude

---

77 At first glance, Rt-2001-248 (*Olderdalen Ambulance*) might have been taken as an example of a horizontal case where an application of the Norwegian principle of presumption led to the imposition of a more weighty individual obligation (i.e. duty to compensate following inclusion of an unfair employment contract clause forbidding trade union membership). On closer inspection, however, it seems as though consideration of international law obligations (ILO Convention no. 98 1949) was merely used as a supplementary argument in the end, with the Supreme Court relying primarily on an interpretation in light of the Norwegian statute's overall purpose and aims and analogies drawn from other parts of the statute in reaching its conclusion.

78 Rt-2006-1473. Directive 89/104/EEC. The *Norwegian Dental Depot* case (Rt-2004-122) has also been referred to as an example of the Norwegian Supreme Court's willingness to perform an EEA-consistent interpretation in a case involving two private parties; see e.g. Fredriksen (n. 42), p. 73. However, given that the Supreme Court's statements on the issue were clearly obiter in that case, and had no bearing on the outcome of the case at hand or the rights of the individual parties involved, its relevance in this connection seems somewhat limited.

79 Rt-1997-1965 (Supreme Court); RG-2004-187 (Court of Appeal); RG-2005-597 (District Court).

has resulted from implied application of the EEA principle of consistent interpretation instead. While the result in these four cases was in any event clearly welcome, with practice ultimately pointing in both directions, we are still left with a rather unclear picture as to how Norwegian courts may choose to handle similar cases in the future – especially where the principle of presumption is expressly relied upon in an attempt to resolve the norm-conflict at issue.

Beyond the horizontal cases mentioned so far, the present author is only aware of one example of a case where Norwegian authorities sought an interpretation of national law consistent with Norway's EEA obligations in a manner which could be deemed directly detrimental to the interests of a private party involved in the case (i.e. so-called inverse vertical reliance). *Aluminium (State Aid Recovery)* concerned a claim for repayment by the Norwegian State against several companies which had received state aid subsequently deemed contrary to EEA law by both the ESA and the EFTA Court.[80] Two of the companies against whom repayment was sought challenged the Norwegian State's claim as out of time under Norwegian procedural law rules. The question facing the Norwegian courts was essentially from what point in time the three-year limitation period stipulated in Section 3 of the Norwegian Limitation Act should be deemed as having started – from the date when the ESA had reached its decision (in which case the claim was out of time), or from when the Norwegian authorities issued their decision implementing the ESA's decision (in which case the claim was in time). By ruling in favour of the Norwegian State in the case, the Supreme Court was effectively interpreting the Norwegian procedural rules in conformity with Norway's obligation under EEA law to reclaim the illegal state aid – notwithstanding a "certain tension" that such an interpretation exposed in relation to the relevant preparatory legislative works.[81] The Supreme Court's decision clearly led to the imposition of rather hefty financial obligations on the two companies involved. The ruling nevertheless seems arguably justifiable and in line with EEA (and EU) law in light of the ECJ's decision in *Kofoed*, as any other result would have led to the companies obtaining an unfair financial and competitive advantage.[82]

Finally, and perhaps somewhat surprisingly, there would seem to be very few examples of classic vertical application of the principle(s) in the case-law of the Norwegian courts. In *Legal Capacity of A*, which involved a dispute between a private individual and the Norwegian State, the Supreme Court ruled out consistent interpretation even though this would clearly have been to the benefit of the private party concerned.[83] Whether the impact of the national principle

80 Rt-2013-1665; Joined Cases E-5-7/04, *ESA v. Norway* [2005] EFTA Ct Rep 117.

81 Ibid. at para. 50 of the Supreme Court's judgment.

82 Case 321/05, *Kofoed*, ECLI:EU:C:2007:408, para. 45.

83 HR-2016-2591-A. See also the Court of Appeal's decision in RG-2005-1542 (*Fokus Bank*). Both of these cases are examined in further detail below.

of presumption will therefore indeed prove greater in vertical situations, as contended by the Supreme Court in *Finanger I* and *Care Expenses*, remains to be seen.

4.2. "ALL NATIONAL LAW"

As far as application of the EEA principle to national law is concerned, according to the EFTA Court, national courts are clearly under a duty to consider national law as a whole.[84] As shown in the following, however, the practice of the Norwegian courts concerning particularly its willingness to change established case-law and to disregard preparatory works in seeking to arrive at EEA-consistent results, and in dealing with measures which are not designated by the legislator as specific implementing measures, seems mixed at best.

4.2.1. The Obligation to Change Established Case-Law

As mentioned earlier, according to the ECJ in *Ajos* and *Ognyanov*, a national court cannot validly claim that it is impossible for it to interpret the national provision at issue in a manner that is consistent with EU law by mere reason of the fact that it has consistently interpreted that provision in a manner that is incompatible with EU law – in such cases, they are obliged to change their case-law.[85] Although the EFTA Court for its part has yet to say anything explicitly on this point, as mentioned above, the fundamental EEA principle of homogeneity leads to a clear presumption that the same must apply under EEA law.[86]

---

84 The EFTA Court has put the duty in many different ways, varying from a reference to "national law" (Case E-4/01, *Karlsson*, para. 29; Case E-1/07, *Criminal proceedings against A*, para. 39; Case E-25/13, *Engilbertsson*, para. 159), to "domestic law" (Case E-18/11, *Irish Bank*, para. 123), "the whole body of rules of national law" (Case E-18/11, *Irish Bank*, para. 124) and "the whole body of domestic law" (Case E-25/13, *Engilbertsson*, para. 163; Case E-28/13, *Merrill Lynch*, para. 43).

85 Case C-441/14, *Ajos*, ECLI:EU:C:2016:278, para. 33; Case C-554/14, *Ognyanov*, ECLI:EU:C:2016:835, para. 67: "it must be made clear that the requirement to interpret national law in conformity with EU law includes the obligation, on national courts, including those ruling as courts of last instance, to alter, where necessary, settled case-law if that case-law is based on an interpretation of national law that is incompatible with the objectives of [the EU measure in question]"; and Case C-614/14, *Ognyanov*, ECLI:EU:C:2016:514, para. 35.

86 As mentioned previously, in the opinion of the present author, the limits to homogeneity are not reached here. Furthermore, the very reference by the EFTA Court to the principle applying to "national law" and/or "the whole body of domestic law" should equally be said to include national methods of construction as developed by the courts. In cases where Norwegian courts choose to apply the national principle of presumption, they must in any event therefore pay due regard to their EEA obligations in doing so.

Certain decisions of Norwegian courts also undoubtedly show that prior case-law – including judgments of the Supreme Court – may well be susceptible to change by way of consistent interpretation. In the *Lifebuoy* case, the Norwegian Supreme Court changed its approach in earlier case-law under specific reference to more recent developments in EU and EEA law.[87] The case concerned the validity of various trademark registrations by two insurance companies (Vesta and Trygg-Hansa) containing depictions of lifebuoys. According to Section 14(1)(7) of the Norwegian Trademark Act 1961 (since repealed), a trademark may not be registered if "it is liable to be confused with a trademark which someone else has started to use before the applicant, and the applicant was aware of this use when he filed his application for registration".[88] One of the main issues in the case turned on the interpretation of the requirement for prior knowledge. Arguing in favour of a restrictive interpretation of the provision, Vesta claimed that mere knowledge of use could not be enough – according to various provisions of the Trademark Directive, as incorporated into the EEA Agreement in 1992, an element of "bad faith" was also required (i.e. that registration would be contrary to loyal, established business practices). Trygg-Hansa for its part argued that Section 14(1)(7) of the Trademark Act should be interpreted literally, meaning that mere knowledge of another's use of the trademark would suffice to render a given trademark registration invalid. In support of its claim, Trygg-Hansa relied directly on the Supreme Court's findings precisely to such effect in earlier case-law. In the *BUD* case from 1998, the Supreme Court had deemed the Budvar company's registration of the "BUD" beer trademark to be invalid as contrary to Section 14(1)(7), simply on the grounds that Budvar was aware of the fact that another company (Anheuser, the producer of Budweiser beer) had been using the same trademark several years prior to it.[89] Budvar had unsuccessfully argued on the basis of the preparatory works to the Norwegian Trademark Act of 1910,[90] as amended in 1961, that the provision could and should be interpreted restrictively, as requiring an additional element of disloyalty.

In *Lifebuoy*, the Supreme Court nevertheless adopted a restrictive interpretation of Section 14(1)(7), and deemed the trademark registrations valid. While stating that the result under Norwegian law alone would have been different,[91] the Court found that neither the preparatory works to the Trademark Act nor its earlier decision in the *BUD* case barred the way for a restrictive interpretation in line with EEA law requirements. Applying a strong presumption of parliamentary intent to legislate in accordance with

[87] Rt-2006-1473.

[88] *Lov 3 mars 1961 nr. 4 om varemerker.*

[89] Rt-1998-1809.

[90] *Kommisjonsinnstilling 1904*, pp. 27 and 53; and *Ot.prp.nr.6 (1908)*, p. 43.

[91] Para. 40.

EEA obligations, the Supreme Court lay great emphasis on an interpretation of Section 14(1)(7) in line with the Trademark Directive as interpreted by decisions of the Office for Harmonisation in the Internal Market (OHIM). The Court concluded by stating that EU practice had been decisive in reaching its decision.

While rightly lauded as an example of the Norwegian Supreme Court changing its own previous case-law in order to arrive at an EEA-consistent result,[92] it was undeniably a rather "soft" case. In *BUD*, the Supreme Court had explicitly opened for a restrictive interpretation of the provision in other "special situations" – thus potentially negating any direct conflict between the two rulings to begin with.[93] The very wording of Section 14(1)(7) also seemed pliable enough, and there was nothing in the preparatory works which immediately ruled out such an interpretation. Indeed, as the Supreme Court rightly pointed out, the relevant rules under both Norwegian and EEA law were all based on the same fundamental considerations.[94] And given the Supreme Court's ignorance as to any potential EEA dimension in the *BUD* case – a point which will be discussed further below – who is to say whether it might have reached the same conclusion in that case, if it had been aware of the EEA law aspects to begin with.

Norwegian courts have proven far more reluctant to change earlier case-law in certain "hard" cases. As seen in *Finanger I*, according to Section 7(3)(b) ALA, no personal injury compensation could be awarded if the injury occurred while the injured party had allowed him/herself to be driven in the vehicle knowing that the driver was under the influence of alcohol. The Supreme Court deemed the provision to be incompatible with the EEA Motor Vehicle Insurance Directives, yet found it impossible to interpret it in conformity with EEA law. This was so notwithstanding an exception in Section 7(3)(b) itself, which specifically allowed for compensation to be awarded "in so far as special reasons are in favour of this". While the text of the statute and the preparatory works were silent as to what such special reasons might be, the Norwegian Supreme Court had for many years consistently interpreted this term as relating purely to factual circumstances surrounding the act of driving itself.[95] The only thing preventing using this "exception to the exception" to arrive at an interpretation consistent with EEA law was therefore the Supreme Court's own understanding of the term, as set out in its prior case-law. Asked whether "special reasons" might also extend to

---

92 See e.g. Fredriksen (n. 42), p. 73; and Fredriksen and Mathisen (n. 38), p. 389.

93 Rt-1998-1809, p. 1814. The statements made by the court in the case were nevertheless somewhat conflicting: after emphasising the escape route and the "same considerations" underlying both the Norwegian and EEA trademark rules (paras. 44 and 57), the Court later says that its decision is "contrary to" its ruling in BUD (para. 62). Whether or not it might be more fitting to speak of a differentiation as opposed to an overruling of prior case-law is therefore difficult to say.

94 Para. 57.

95 Rt-1978-321, Rt-1986-543, and Rt-1994-1461.

the supervening entry into force of the EEA Agreement, and the existence of EEA rules unintentionally incorrectly implemented by the Norwegian legislator, the Supreme Court held that such a construction did not seem "natural" to it. Yet just because something feels unnatural, does not necessarily make it impossible. According to ECJ case-law at the time of judgment, it had long been the case that where a mere possibility exists for the national court to interpret national law in line with EU law in a given case, then that possibility crystallises into an obligation to do so. Although it is difficult to say whether the Supreme Court would have reached the same decision today in the light of *Ajos* and *Ognyanov*, its decision in *Finanger I* could hardly have been reconciled with the ECJ's prevailing case-law even at the time of judgment.

The same reluctance to change prior case-law is further traceable in other cases concerning (non-)application of the national principle of presumption in the light of other international obligations – such as in the *Care Expenses* case, where the manner in which the Norwegian courts had interpreted the Social Services Act for almost a century was relied on as an argument against performing a consistent interpretation.[96] Another (albeit less explicit) example is provided in the *Sør-Aurdal* case.[97] This case concerned a claim for compensation raised by two surviving family members following the loss of the family's financial provider, who had died in a car crash while driving under the influence of alcohol. The central issue was how much damages could be reduced in light of the driver's contributory negligence, as imputed to his surviving family. Following the Supreme Court's earlier decision in the similar *Sunndal* case from 1997, the amount of damages to be covered by the insurance company in such situations could be reduced by 50 per cent.[98] The surviving family argued that *Sunndal* should be overruled in light of subsequent legal developments, including the EU/EEA Motor Vehicle Insurance Directives. The insurance company claimed that since rules concerning the imputation of liability fell outside the scope of the Directives and hence EEA law altogether, that there was no conflict between EEA and Norwegian law, and that the precedent in *Sunndal* should therefore apply.

Overruling its earlier case-law, the Supreme Court held that damages could only be reduced by 20 per cent owing to the contributory negligence of the driver, thus applying only a partial imputation of the driver's liability to his surviving family. The Supreme Court based its decision on "subsequent legal developments in the field". It referred first to the relatively recent change in analogous rules concerning reductions of damages for surviving family members of *passengers* killed in car accidents (instigated by legislative amendments directly linked

---

96 References in para. 37 to Rt-1911-303; in para. 41 to RG-1977-373; and in para. 43 to Rt-2006-618.

97 Rt-2014-1192.

98 Rt-1997-149.

to the outcome in the *Finanger I* case); and, second, to the increased weight to be attached to social considerations in cases concerning imputations of liability. Concerning the potential EEA law issues, and whether the same result might be required under EEA law, the court simply concluded in one short sentence that "Given [our] view in the case, it is not necessary to go into the EEA law issues".[99]

The Supreme Court thereby effectively side-stepped the issue of whether the Norwegian tort law rules on imputations of liability for contributory negligence might be seen to undermine the obligation under the EEA Motor Vehicle Directives to provide insurance coverage for victims of road traffic accidents. It is certainly true that the Supreme Court may freely choose whether or not to go into particular submissions presented by either of the parties, where it believes that this would be superfluous to the result in any event.[100] One should nevertheless be cautious in taking this as an indication that the same practical result (i.e. overruling its previous decision in *Sunndal*) would have flowed from an application of the principle of consistent interpretation/national principle of presumption. The issue as to whether or not rules concerning imputations of liability would be deemed to fall within the remit of EEA law seems too open and unresolved to be certain about what the Supreme Court meant about it not being necessary to address the EEA law issues. Nevertheless, the Supreme Court's apparent reticence in dealing with the issue does provide us with one particular insight: that overruling past case-law under reference to obligations under international (including EEA) law – even where merely presented as a supplementary or reinforcing argument – is still probably conceived as problematic for some Norwegian judges to unreservedly accept.[101]

4.2.2. *Presumptions of Parliamentary Intent and Preparatory Legislative Works*

As discussed earlier, the EFTA Court has stated that in cases where national courts are dealing with disputes concerning the interpretation of national law specifically enacted for the purpose of transposing EEA law, "the national court *must* presume that the EEA/EFTA State had the intention of fulfilling entirely the obligations from the EEA directive [or regulation] concerned".[102]

---

99 Para. 57 (author's own translation).

100 Section 11-3 of the Norwegian Civil Procedure Act.

101 Mestad poses an interesting question in this regard as to whether the "internationalist" Norwegian Supreme Court justices (i.e. those who would appear more loyal to fulfilling Norway's international obligations than Norwegian law) may be in the minority – a question which he answers in the affirmative. O. Mestad, "Dissensens alvor", in T. Schei and T.M. Øie (eds.), *Lov, Sannhet, Rett: Norges Høyesterett 200 år* (Universitetsforlaget, 2015), pp. 222–54, at p. 249.

102 Emphasis added. Case E-28/13 *Merrill Lynch*, para. 41.

The general starting point for Norwegian courts seems largely in tune with the EFTA Court's understanding, resting on a domestic presumption of parliamentary intent to legislate in line with Norway's EEA/international obligations. The preparatory works to the Norwegian EEA Act nevertheless set out an important qualification in this regard:

> Slightly simplified, one could say that only if [Parliament] has clearly stated that a law is to be used in a certain way without regard to whether this is contrary to international obligations, or if the relevant provision of law would otherwise be left devoid of any content, will Norwegian courts feel forced to apply the law in violation of international law.[103]

The Norwegian Parliament's Foreign and Constitutional Committee noted further, and in slightly more nuanced terms, that:

> In case of doubt as to whether a new law may violate our EEA obligations, the legal assessment must assume that [Parliament] will provisionally take decisions in accordance with our international obligations. If the Parliament in a particular case expressly indicates that a new law is to be implemented even if it contravenes existing laws or regulations that implement EEA obligations, Norwegian courts will have to respect this, even if it violates our international obligations.[104]

The presumption may therefore be rebutted on the rare occasion that Parliament were to clearly state that it had no intention of implementing the EEA obligation in question. Consequently, if Parliament has expressly stipulated that Norwegian law is to apply, then Norwegian courts will be effectively prevented from interpreting Norwegian law in line with EEA/international law.

Such stipulations – if any – will usually be found in the preparatory works to the Norwegian legislation in question. Legal cultural tradition in Norway generally begs in favour of a statutory drafting method geared towards simplification and brevity of the language used in the final legislative text – i.e. the shorter, the better. Longer explanations as to how one arrived at the final statutory text in question are therefore commonly reserved to the preparatory works alone. These may include any reports, inquiries, debates, expert opinions, legislative proposals or the like produced by any and all that have taken part in the preparatory stages and/or adoption of a given Norwegian statute. Nygård argues that if a given statutory norm is viewed as the "conclusion" flowing from the preparatory works, the adoption of the "conclusion" as law by Parliament

103 Author's own translation. Ot.prp.nr.79 (1991–1992), *Om lov om gjennomføring i norsk rett av hoveddelen i Avtale om Det europeiske økonomiske samarbeidsområde (EØS)*, p. 4.

104 Author's own translation. Innst.O.nr.14 (1992–1993), *Innstilling fra utenriks- og konstitusjonskomiteen om lov om gjennomføring i norsk rett av hoveddelen i Avtale om Det europeiske økonomiske samarbeidsområde (EØS)*, p. 4.

may in turn be seen as having a contaminating effect on the preparatory works, transforming these into legal sources in their own right.[105] Of course, the weight to be attached to the preparatory works may well vary from one case to another – sometimes dependent on their clarity, and at other times dependent on the body which has prepared them. On the whole, however, *travaux préparatoires* play a very important role in Norwegian legal method, deeply ingrained in Norwegian legal thinking, and a legal source actively used by Norwegian courts in the interpretation of Norwegian statutes. In light of Norwegian judges' natural predisposition towards loyally following them, the idea of completely ignoring the *travaux préparatoires* to a Norwegian statute so as to reach an EEA-consistent interpretation of Norwegian law – as notably required following the ECJ's decision in *Björnekulla* – would most probably be considered nigh on anathema by most Norwegian jurists.[106]

One recent and extremely rare example of a situation where Parliament has expressly stated that Norwegian law is to be applied notwithstanding Norway's obligations under international law is provided in *Legal Capacity of A*.[107] The case concerned a challenge against a County Governor's decision based on Sections 20 and 22 of the Norwegian Guardianship Act of 2010 depriving a psychiatric patient (A) of her legal capacity in all financial matters, including her right to dispose of a relatively large sum of monies inherited from her parents.[108] One of the issues facing the courts was whether such a complete removal of legal capacity was in line with Norway's obligations under Art. 12 of the UN Convention on Rights of Persons with Disabilities of 2006, which it became party to in 2013.[109] According to this provision, persons with disabilities shall enjoy legal capacity on an equal basis with others in all aspects of life, and any measures relating to the exercise thereof must be proportionate and tailored to the person's circumstances. In the preparatory works to the Guardianship Act, the Ministry of Justice had assumed that Art. 12 would not prohibit national measures actually depriving an individual of legal capacity – either in whole, or in part.[110] Based on this understanding, Norwegian authorities submitted a declaration concerning the interpretation of Art. 12 following ratification of the Convention in 2013: "Norway further declares its understanding that the Convention allows for deprivation of legal capacity or assistance to exercise legal capacity and/or

---

105 N. Nygård, *Rettsgrunnlag og standpunkt* (2nd ed., Universitetsforlaget, 2004), pp. 195–99.

106 Case C-371/02, *Björnekulla*, ECLI:EU:C:2004:275, para. 13. Indeed, taken to its furthest extent, *Björnekulla* might even be understood as requiring Norwegian courts to disregard even the preparatory works to the EEA Act itself(!).

107 HR-2016-2591-A.

108 *Lov 26 mars 2010 nr. 9 om vergemål.*

109 The United Nations Convention on the Rights of Persons with Disabilities, *Treaty Series 2515* (2006):3.

110 Ot.prp.nr.110 (2008-2009) *Om lov om vergemål*, p. 61.

compulsion where such measures are necessary, as a last resort and subject to control mechanisms".[111]

According to the Committee on the Rights of Persons with Disabilities, however, the system provided by the Norwegian Guardianship Act did in fact contravene Art. 12:

> States parties' obligation to replace substitute decision-making regimes by supported decision-making requires both the abolition of substitute decision-making regimes and the development of supported decision-making alternatives. The development of supported decision-making systems in parallel with the maintenance of substitute decision-making regimes is not sufficient to comply with article 12 of the Convention.[112]

Both the District Court and Court of Appeal partially reversed the County Governor's decision, finding that the legal incapacitation could not apply to A's inheritance from her parents.[113] However, in a majority decision of the Supreme Court (3-2), these decisions were overruled. Finding in favour of the Norwegian State, and making direct reference to the preparatory statements of the EEA Act and its findings in *Finanger I*, the Supreme Court held that the clear and express statements in the preparatory works barred application of the principle of presumption in the case. Crucial for the majority view was the fact that

> there is no doubt what Parliament assumed when it passed the Guardianship Act. These assumptions have been repeated upon ratification of the Convention. In my view, in the present case, the courts must therefore apply the solution provided for in the [national] law even if this contravenes international law.[114]

While the legislature's signals in *Legal Capacity of A* seemed unambiguous enough, other cases show how also less clear indications from Parliament may be interpreted and relied upon by Norwegian courts to rebut the presumption in practice. As seen in *Finanger I*, while the wording of Section 7(3)(b) ALA opened for compensation to be awarded where there were "special reasons" for doing so, and the preparatory works were silent on how this term was to be understood, the Supreme Court still deemed it impossible to arrive at an EEA-consistent result by way of interpretation in the case. The fact that Parliament had chosen not to amend Section 7(3)(b) in the course of transposing the Motor Vehicle Directives was taken by the Supreme Court as a sufficiently clear indication of

---

111 Prop. 106 S (2001–2012) *Samtykke til ratifikasjon av FN-konvensjonen av 13. desember 2006 om rettighetene til mennesker med nedsatt funksjonsevne*, p. 15.

112 General Comment No. 1 (2014) GC-2014-1-CRPD, para. III (28).

113 District Court: TSUMO-2014-204148; Court of Appeal: LF-2015-92239 – LF-2015-9935 – LF-2015-183241.

114 Para. 63 (author's own translation).

parliamentary intent to uphold the national rule even in the face of conflicting EEA obligations, and as (partial) grounds therefore for ruling out an EEA-consistent interpretation.[115] This was so notwithstanding express statements in the preparatory works that the ALA was intended to implement the Directives, that Parliament's decision to leave Section 7(3)(b) unamended had been based on a mistaken understanding of the scope of the directives to begin with,[116] and the fact that preparatory work was already underway to change Section 7(3)(b) to bring it in line with EEA requirements at the time when the case was making its way through the Norwegian court system.[117]

The Supreme Court's findings in *Finanger I* on this point also seem to have had a radiating effect in certain other cases.[118] As discussed earlier, in *Care Expenses* the Supreme Court deemed a Council of Europe Expert Committee statement to the effect that Section 10-3 of the Norwegian Social Services Act was contrary to Art. 11 of the European Council Charter of Local Self-Government as irrelevant in ruling out certain County Governor decisions from judicial review.[119] The very wording of Section 10-3 did not expressly rule out the possibility of reviewing the decisions in question – to the contrary, it seemed perfectly open to such an understanding on its bare face. The Supreme Court nevertheless held as partial grounds for its decision that both previous (i.e. historical) and current versions of the law, as emphasised in the preparatory works thereto and as consistently interpreted by the Norwegian courts in practice over the years, generally ruled out the possibility for judicial review of County Governor's decisions in such cases. The Court further pointed to a failed attempt to amend the Act in 2004 to allow for review in other circumstances, thus (in its view) reinforcing Parliament's clear intent that the provision should remain unchanged. Allowing judicial review of the County Governor's decision would in reality mean setting aside a more than 100 year old provision of Norwegian law in its entirety, in spite of the fact that Parliament had recently indicated that it wished to keep the rule. Judicial review of decisions adopted pursuant to Section 10-3 was therefore limited exceptionally to cases involving e.g. abuse of power.

---

115 Rt-2000-1881, p. 1831.

116 In its preparatory works, the Ministry of Justice had mistakenly assumed that Section 7(3)(b), as rule connected to tort law rules, remained without the scope of EEA law altogether – this proved not to be the case. Otprp.nr.72 (1991–1992), pp. 76–77.

117 Ot.prp.nr.26 (1999–2000), *Om lov om endring i lov 18. juni 1965 nr. 4 om vegtrafikk og i enkelte andre lover*, p. 24. The law was in fact amended by Parliament following the outcome of the case.

118 The Supreme Court has confirmed that its statements in *Finanger I* concerning the remit of the principle of presumption give expression to general principles, which will also apply in other cases – even those involving other international (i.e. not EEA) obligations. See e.g. HR-2016-2591-A (*Legal Capacity of A*): "The Supreme Court has found this to be the case in Rt-2000-1811 (*Finanger I*), see particularly p. 1831. In my opinion, the statements made there give expression to general principles that must also be applicable in a case such as that with which we are presently concerned" (author's own translation).

119 Rt-2007-234.

Finally, in the *Lifebouy* case, also mentioned above, the Supreme Court expressly noted that the addition of a further limitation beyond mere knowledge (i.e. a disloyal action, contrary to established business practices), as required under EEA law, was not contrary to any stipulations set out in the preparatory works to the Norwegian Trademark Act – thus indicating that the result might well have been different in the event that the preparatory works had signalled otherwise.[120]

Notwithstanding the cases looked at so far, *Norsk Dental Depot* has sometimes been referred to as an example of the Supreme Court's willingness to disregard preparatory legislative works in order to arrive at an EEA-consistent interpretation of Norwegian law.[121] The Norwegian Product Liability Act (PLA) was based on and intended to transpose the Product Liability Directive.[122] Section 2-1 PLA copied Art. 6 of the Directive almost verbatim, providing for producers' strict liability to compensate for damage caused by defective products which, all circumstances taken into account, fail to provide the safety which a person is entitled to expect. In the preparatory works to the PLA, the Norwegian Ministry of Justice had mistakenly presumed that Art. 13 of the Directive opened for liability to be established on other grounds than those stipulated, where this would be more advantageous for the claimant – a common misunderstanding in several EU Member States, as it turned out. Section 1-1(2) PLA therefore provided: "This Act does not limit the right to claim compensation on other grounds." In its decision in *Medicina Asturiana* from 2002, however, the ECJ held that since the Directive was a full harmonisation measure, the grounds of product liability were limited to those provided for in the Directive.[123] In its decision, the Supreme Court stated:

> I mention here that the ECJ, in its decision dated 25 April 2002 (Case C-183/00), found that Article 13 of the Directive cannot be relied upon in support of the maintenance of national rules which provide better protection than the provisions of the Directive, when the national rules establish liability on the same basis as regulated by the Directive. *This implies that earlier Norwegian practice regarding unwritten [i.e. based in case-law and/or custom] strict liability cannot be invoked if liability according to this practice goes further than Article 6 of the Directive.* (emphasis added)[124]

---

120 Rt-2006-1473, para. 43.

121 Rt-2004-122. See e.g. F. Arnesen and A. Stenvik, *Internasjonalisering og juridisk metode – særlig om EØS-rettens betydning i norsk rett* (1st ed., Universitetsforlaget, 2009), p. 104; and Fredriksen (n. 42), p. 73.

122 *Lov 23 desember 1988 nr. 104 om produktansvar*; Council Directive 85/374/EEC of 25 July 1985 on the approximation of the laws, regulations and administrative provisions of the Member States concerning liability for defective products [1985] OJ L210/29.

123 Case C-183/00, *Medicina Asturiana*, ECLI:EU:C:2002:255.

124 Author's own translation: "*Jeg nevner her at EF-domstolen i dom av 25. april 2002 (sak C-183/00) har slått fast at direktivets artikkel 13 ikke kan påberopes til støtte for en opprettholdelse av nasjonale rettsregler som gir en bedre beskyttelse enn direktivets bestemmelser, når de nasjonale*

While this may at first glance seem to represent a poignant example of blatant disregard for the preparatory works (not to mention the relatively clear wording of Section 1-1(2) itself), the statement was clearly made *obiter*. It had no bearing on the final outcome, and imposed no duties on either party to the case. Indeed, both applicant and defendant appeared to agree with the general contention that the PLA, as understood in the light of the ECJ's interpretation of the Directive, exhaustively regulated the grounds for liability, and no other grounds of liability were in any event claimed in the case.

Furthermore, exactly how express or clear the conflict between the Directive and the preparatory works actually was, may be open to debate. Most commentators seem to have unanimously taken the court's statement as unequivocally establishing that unwritten (i.e. case-law or custom-based) strict liability could henceforth no longer be called upon as separate or supplementary grounds by claimants.[125] Yet the Court's statement may arguably be open to a slightly different understanding altogether. The plaintiff had argued that even though the PLA exhaustively regulated the grounds for liability, one should still be able to rely on national case-law and/or custom providing the basis for strict liability under Norwegian law *as a tool in interpreting Section 2-1 of the PLA*. Read as a direct (if perhaps somewhat clumsy) response to the claimant's submission, the Supreme Court's statement does not seem so controversial – indeed, the Supreme Court even appears to rely on in its own previous case-law to such effect in its decision.[126] Earlier Norwegian practice concerning unwritten strict liability may therefore apparently be invoked as a tool in interpreting Section 2-1 of the PLA, as long as this stays within the bounds of Art. 6 of the Directive. The fact that the Supreme Court's *obiter* statement in *Norsk Dental Depot* has not been referred to again or confirmed in subsequent case-law, and that the PLA remains unamended by Parliament, seems further telling in this regard.

Other (admittedly rather "soft") cases offer slightly more encouraging signs. In *Stavanger Catering*, the Supreme Court faced a potential conflict between the Norwegian Working Conditions Act and Directive 77/187 on Employee's Rights following Transfers of Undertakings.[127] The case essentially concerned the issue of whether workers could claim certain pension rights from their new employer following a company take-over. Since both the Directive (as interpreted

---

regler statuerer ansvar på samme grunnlag som reguleres i direktivet. Det innebærer at tidligere norsk praksis vedrørende ulovfestet objektivt ansvar ikke kan påberopes hvis ansvaret etter denne praksis går lenger enn etter direktivets artikkel 6."

125 A. Kjønstad, "Det nyeste rettskildematerialet om det ulovfestede objektive erstatningsansvaret" (2004) 10 *Lov og Rett* 579–605; Arnesen and Stenvik (n. 38) p. 106; Fredriksen (n. 42), p. 73.

126 See the Supreme Court's reference to Rt-1992-64 (*P-Pille*), in para. 38.

127 Council Directive 77/187/EEC of 14 February 1977 on the approximation of the laws of the Member States relating to the safeguarding of employees' rights in the event of transfers of undertakings, businesses or parts of businesses [1977] OJ L61/26.

by the EFTA Court at an earlier stage in the case)[128] and the wording of the implementing Norwegian provision in question pointed in one direction, the Supreme Court disregarded a potentially contrary understanding which might otherwise have been read out of the preparatory works to the Norwegian statute in order to arrive at an EEA consistent result. This was hardly a big ask, however, as the preparatory works themselves were not unequivocal, and contained several contradictory statements on the point.[129] And as pointed out by the Supreme Court, the statement which might have been relied upon in favour of a different result was in any event itself "somewhat unclear".[130]

The Supreme Court's decision in *Aluminium (State Aid Recovery)* might similarly be understood as an example of how to exploit the equivocal nature of legislative preparatory works in order to arrive at an EEA-consistent interpretation.[131] In this case the Supreme Court interpreted the three-year limitation period set out in Section 3 of the Norwegian Limitation Act in a manner which effectively led to conformity with Norway's EEA obligation to reclaim the illegal state aid at issue. The companies involved in the case had argued that deeming the limitation period as having started when the Norwegian authorities issued their decision implementing the ESA's decision, and not from the earlier date when the ESA itself had reached its decision, would be contrary to the underlying objectives of the Limitation Act as spelt out in the preparatory works thereto. According to these, the whole point of the limitation period starting to run from the date on which the creditor first had the right to demand performance was to prevent creditors (i.e. in this case the Norwegian State) from being able to determine when time starts running at their own discretion.[132] Notwithstanding a "certain tension" that its eventual interpretation raised in relation to the relevant preparatory legislative works, the Supreme Court said that this could not be decisive of the issue.[133] Given state authorities' general duty to decide cases without undue delay and the risk of breaching EEA obligations in the event that the state aid was not reclaimed, the underlying objectives of the provision (i.e. ensuring performance with as little delay as possible) would in any event still be maintained following its decision.[134]

One final example is provided by the Court of Appeal's decision in *Tripp Trapp*.[135] This case concerned the issue of whether the use requirement of

---

128 Case E-2/95, *Eilert Eidesund v. Stavanger Catering* [1996] EFTA Ct. Rep. 3.

129 Conflicting statements may indeed be found in Ot.prp.nr.71 (1991–1992), pp. 15 and 34.

130 A fact emphasised twice by the Court – on p. 1975, and again on p. 1976.

131 Rt-2013-1665.

132 Ot.prp.nr.38 (1977–1978), p. 52.

133 Ibid., paras. 49–50.

134 For a critical appraisal of the Supreme Court's decision, and of a different opinion, see M. Skag, "Foreldelsesfristens start for krav fremmet ved enkeltvedtak" 21 (2015) 1 *Tidsskrift for forretningsjus* 31–53.

135 RG-2004-187.

a trademark registered for "furniture, including chairs" was fulfilled by its use to market a single chair and a few accessories thereto. According to the wording of Art. 12 of the Trademark Directive, the use requirement was satisfied for any trademark "put to genuine use ... *in connection with the goods* ... in respect of which it is registered".[136] According to Section 25a of the Norwegian Trademark Act, which acted as implementing legislation for the Directive, the use requirement was described as covering trademarks "taken into use in this country *for the goods* they are registered for".[137] The wording of the Norwegian law therefore seemed to impose a stricter requirement than the Directive, and the preparatory works seemed silent on the issue. Applying a strong presumption of legislative intent to resolve the issue in favour of the Trademark Directive's more liberally worded requirement, the Court of Appeal held that "It has to be presumed that the legislator has not meant to introduce a stricter use requirement than that which follows from the Directive".[138]

Whether or not these three latter cases may be said to represent a clear shift in practice – with Norwegian courts prepared to apply a strong presumption of parliamentary intent to legislate in line with EEA obligations, and to ignore/exploit signals in preparatory legislative works in order to arrive at interpretations consistent with EEA law – seems difficult to say with any degree of certainty. The reluctance of the Supreme Court to opt for an EEA-friendly interpretation of preparatory works which do not explicitly state an intention not to transform international obligations in some of the decisions noted above, is in any event rather difficult to grasp when considering its approach in various cases involving the interpretation of national law alone.[139] In situations where the wording of a statute and its preparatory works point to different possible interpretative conclusions, the rule of thumb is naturally to follow the wording of the statute.[140] Such an assumption is clearly based on fundamental considerations bound to the rule of law itself: it is the statutory text itself – not the preparatory works – which are communicated directly to the public, and on which they can therefore be expected to rely. As discussed earlier, however, where interpretations consistent with international obligations are at issue, the preparatory works may "trump" even ambiguous wording of the national legislation to which they relate. A very clear example of this is provided in *Care Expenses*, where

[136] First Council Directive 89/104/EEC of 21 December 1988 to approximate the laws of the Member States relating to trademarks [1989] OJ L40/1.

[137] *Lov 3 mars 1961 nr. 4 om varemerker.*

[138] Author's own translation.

[139] A valid (and in the present author's opinion convincing) point also raised in the dissenting minority opinion in *Finanger I* – Rt-2000-1881, p. 1839.

[140] See T. Eckhoff, *Rettskildelære* (5th ed., Universitetsforlaget, 2001), with further reference to the Supreme Court's decisions in e.g. Rt-1961-212, and Rt-1997-285.

the wording of the statute did not expressly exclude the possibility of judicial review of County Governors' decisions, yet the Supreme Court viewed the preparatory works as determinative in ruling out a consistent interpretation.[141] There are even (albeit rare) instances where Norwegian courts – in situations not involving international obligations – have interpreted a statute in a manner which finds no resonance in either its wording or the preparatory works, effectively rewriting the statutory provisions on grounds of reasonableness, fairness or a general notion of justice.[142] Indeed, there would seem to be few boundaries as to what Norwegian courts may deem possible to achieve by way of interpretation where Norwegian law is viewed in isolation. The same may not be unequivocally said where international obligations are involved.

4.2.3. Presumptions of Parliamentary Intent and Non-Specific Implementing Measures

As discussed earlier, unlike under the EU Treaties, all EEA directives and regulations incorporated into the EEA Agreement must be implemented into Norwegian national law in order to have any effects.[143] The reason for this is quite simply because the EEA Agreement was not intended to involve a direct transfer of legislative authority. There is also no principle of direct effect or primacy in EEA law – at least not as understood under EU law. According to primacy rules under EEA law, only EEA rules which are implemented into national law take precedence over conflicting national law provisions.[144] Which begs the analogous question as to whether only national law specifically intended to implement EEA rules may be subject to the duty of consistent interpretation?

According to the EFTA Court, the answer is clearly no. In *Criminal proceedings against A*, the Court opined that the duty applies to "national law, and in particular legislative provisions specifically adopted to transpose EEA rules into national law".[145] And, it went a step further in *Merrill Lynch*, stating that in light of the obligation under Art. 7 EEA requiring implementation of EEA Directives and Regulations, "the national court must presume that the EEA/EFTA State had the intention of fulfilling entirely the obligations arising

141 Conversely, it is also possible to find examples of Norwegian courts going so far as to interpret Norwegian statutes exclusively on the basis an understanding drawn from the preparatory works alone – even at the expense of the very wording of the statute itself (see e.g. Rt-1995-1333). In these kind of situations, the courts seem prepared to give such preparatory works the same status as the text of the statutory norm to which they relate.

142 See Eckhoff (n. 139), pp. 88–91, who refers to several Supreme Court decisions: Rt-1916-648 (*Child Support I*); Rt-1921-406 (*Child Support II*); Rt-1979-1079 (*Insanity – Right of Appeal*).

143 According to Art. 7 EEA, Directives may be transformed, while Regulations must be incorporated.

144 Protocol 35 EEA.

145 Case E-01/07, *Criminal proceedings against A*, para. 37.

from the Directive concerned".[146] While a heightened duty to perform consistent interpretations based on presumptive legislative intent would therefore seem to apply concerning national rules specifically adopted with a view to implementing EEA rules, the duty to interpret in conformity with EEA law clearly does not stop here. The EFTA Court made clear in *Merrill Lynch* that although the principle "*chiefly* concerns domestic provisions to implement the [EEA directive or regulation] in question, the national court must consider *the whole body of domestic law*" in applying the principle.[147] In *Irish Bank*, it specifically stated that the principle also applies to national rules that fail to transpose EEA rules correctly into national law.[148] And fully in line with the ECJ's case-law concerning the EU principle of consistent interpretation, the EFTA Court has recently clarified that the corresponding duty under EEA law applies to national law both pre- and post-dating the directive or regulation concerned.[149] In light of the principle of sincere cooperation on which it is partially based, the duty to perform consistent interpretation therefore applies not only to provisions specifically adopted to transpose EEA rules, but to national law as a whole – including non-specific implementing measures, such as national law pre-dating the EEA measure in question.

As far as the practice of Norwegian courts is concerned, the Supreme Court's decision in *Finanger I*, which pre-dated the above-mentioned EFTA Court rulings, seemed to hint rather strongly at EEA measures having to be specifically implemented in order to trigger the duty. The more recent decision of the Court of Appeal in the *Tippinga* case nevertheless points in a different direction.[150] The case concerned a challenge by Norsk Tipping – a state-owned undertaking operating gaming machines in Norway – against a decision of the Norwegian Industrial Property Office denying registration of the "Tippinga" trademark for certain services. While the trademark was registrable for certain but not all of the services covered, the application was nevertheless refused in its entirety. Norsk Tipping argued that this contravened Art. 13 of the First Trademark Directive, which stated that "Where grounds for refusal of registration ... of a trademark exist in respect of only some of the goods or services for which that trademark has been applied for or registered, refusal of registration ... shall cover those goods or services only".[151] The Norwegian State argued that since the Trademark Directive had not been fully (i.e. correctly) implemented by the specific implementation measures

146 Case E-28/13, *Merrill Lynch*, para. 41.
147 Emphasis added. E-28/13, *Merrill Lynch*, para. 43.
148 Case E-18/11, *Irish Bank*, para. 126.
149 Case E-28/13, *Merrill Lynch*, para. 42.
150 LB-2009-99914 (*Tippinga*).
151 First Council Directive 89/104/EEC of 21 December 1988 to approximate the laws of the Member States relating to trademarks [1989] OJ L40/1.

passed by Parliament seeking to amend the Norwegian Trademark Act,[152] and owing to the dualist principle with respect to international (and therefore EEA) obligations, that no specific duties on partial registration as required by Art. 13 of the Directive could apply. The insinuation was clearly that since implementation was not correct, there was no relevant national law upon which to base an interpretation consistent with the Directive on.

The Court of Appeal dismissed the argument. In what has rightly been described as a textbook example of consistent interpretation,[153] the Court of Appeal pointed out that the wording of Section 19 of the Norwegian Trademark Act – which provided that if there were obstacles that prevent registration of a trademark, the Patent Office shall notify the applicant who shall be given a suitable time limit in which to respond and to make any necessary corrections – while not specifically requiring partial registration, nevertheless appeared to be open to such an understanding. The provision did not contain any rules which directly conflicted Art. 13 of the Directive, either. The Court therefore held that "as a result of the implementation of the Directive and the Trademark Act's own rules on notification in situations where there are obstacles to registration, it must be held that the Act does not prevent application of Art. 13 of the Trademark Directive". Notwithstanding the lack of any specific implementing measures, the Court of Appeal found it perfectly possible to interpret Norwegian law pre-dating the Directive consistently with it.

4.3. *EX OFFICIO* APPLICATION OF THE PRINCIPLE

It is quite possible that Norwegian courts, particularly in the early years of Norway's EEA membership, may have decided cases without either the judge(s) or the parties to the case noticing or raising EEA law issues relevant thereto – including issues of consistent interpretation. For example, as mentioned earlier, the courts seemed entirely unaware of the EEA law aspects in the *BUD* case from 1998.[154] The Supreme Court's oversight in that case does seem somewhat understandable, at least to a certain extent, since Norwegian lawyers and judges at that time were probably less well-versed in EEA law than would be expected today. It nevertheless raises the (at times rather vexed) question as to what duties Norwegian courts have to raise EEA law issues – including

152 *Lov 3 mars 1961 nr. 4 om varemerker.*

153 See Fredriksen (n. 42), p. 70.

154 Rt-1998-1809, section 4.2.1 above. Similarly, albeit not specifically in an EEA context, see Rt-2007-234 (*Care Expenses*), where the issue of consistent interpretation was not apparently raised before the District Court or the Court of Appeal (LB-2005-57484), but only by the Supreme Court.

potential application of the EEA principle of consistent interpretation – of their own motion?[155]

According to the EU principles of equivalence and effectiveness, if national courts may or must raise points of national law of their own motion in proceedings or in their decisions, they may or must do the same in cases where points of EU law are at issue.[156] In light of the demands of homogeneity, these principles clearly apply under EEA law,[157] and presumably entail much the same duties.[158] Whether or not Norwegian courts either may or must raise EEA law matters *ex officio* will therefore ultimately turn on the application of Norwegian procedural rules.

According to Section 11-2 of the Civil Procedure Act, the general rule is that courts may only rule on the claims that are made by the parties to the case, and must base their rulings on the material facts invoked. Section 11-3 nevertheless goes on to state that Norwegian courts shall apply any and all current national law falling within the scope of the claims and facts of the case of their own motion, even where the rules in question have not been raised by the parties during the proceedings. The same *ex officio* duty will therefore presumably also apply to any relevant EEA law falling within the claims and facts of a given case.

Matters are more complicated, however, where the issue of *ex officio* application relates to or is based on claims or material facts not relied upon by the parties in their submissions. Under Norwegian law, a general distinction is made between cases where the parties are deemed to have full discretion with regards to their claims and the facts relied upon, and cases where their discretion is limited. In the latter type of cases (typically concerning issues of legal capacity, the legal status of children, administrative decisions on coercive measures, etc.), the courts are only bound by the parties' claims to the extent that these are compatible with public policy. In civil cases where the parties enjoy full discretion, however, the courts are exclusively bound by the claims and facts presented by the parties. In practical terms, this means that in any case where the parties are deemed to have full discretion with regards to the

---

155 See generally A. Robberstad, "Norske dommeres plikt til å veilede om EØS-retten" (2002) 4 *Lov og Rett* 195–223 and H.H. Fredriksen, "Tvisteloven og EØS-avtalen" 121(2008)3 *Tidsskrift for Rettsvitenskap* 289–359.

156 Case C-72/95, *Kraaijeveld*, ECLI:EU:C:1996:404; Case C-126/97, *Eco Swiss*, ECLI:EU:C:1999:269; Joined Cases C-222–225/05, *Van der Weerd and others*, ECLI:EU:C:2007:318. Generally concerning the authority of national courts to consider EU law of their own motion, see e.g. Craig and de Búrca (n. 69) pp. 239–41.

157 See e.g. Case E-11/12 *Koch* [2013] EFTA Ct. Rep. 272, paras. 121–25; Case E-07/13 *Creditinfo Lánstraust* [2013] EFTA Ct. Rep. 970, para. 45.

158 With the proviso that such application would not be irreconcilable with the peculiarities of the EEA Agreement – see e.g. P. Hreinsson, "General Principles", in C. Baudenbacher (ed.), *The Handbook of EEA Law* (Springer, 2016), p. 376.

claims and facts raised, Norwegian courts may generally consider themselves as prohibited from raising EEA law issues of their own motion.

The duty to raise points of EEA law *ex officio* – and also to make directions during the pre-trial phase – would nevertheless appear to move beyond the boundaries of mere equivalence where consumer protection law is concerned. In *Océano Grupo*, the ECJ held that the national court must have the power to evaluate unfair contract terms of its own motion, even where the consumer was obliged (yet had not) raised the issue himself before the court.[159] Further in *Banco Español de Crédito*, the ECJ held that national rules which prevented national courts from examining unfair contract terms of their own motion without the consumer lodging an objection first, were precluded under EU law.[160] As the same presumably applies under EEA law, Norwegian courts should consider themselves correspondingly bound to raise and enforce EEA consumer protection rules of their own motion, in a manner arguably going beyond the trappings of the Civil Procedure Act.

5. LIMITS TO CONSISTENT INTERPRETATIONS IN THE PRACTICE OF THE NORWEGIAN COURTS

The analyses carried out in the sections above have already provided several indications of both potential and actual limits to the application of the principle of consistent interpretation by Norwegian courts. It has been seen, for example, how the dualist tradition, established precedent of the Supreme Court, the clear wording of national provisions and statements made in preparatory legislative works may indeed prove significant barriers to achieving EEA-consistent interpretative results in practice. Rather than simply reiterate these points, the following section will instead focus on a few more general issues and observations which may be drawn from the practice of the ECJ, the EFTA Court and Norwegian courts concerning the limits to consistent interpretations.

The first point concerns the very definition of the general limits themselves. The ECJ has consistently held that it is for the national courts to interpret and apply national law consistently with EU law "as far as possible", and that the principle of consistent interpretation does not extend so far as to require interpretations in breach of general principles of law.[161] The EFTA Court has mirrored the general approach of the ECJ, stating that the corresponding duty

---

159 Joined Cases C-240–244/98, *Océano Grupo*, ECLI:EU:C:2000:346.

160 Case C-618/10, *Banco Español de Crédito*, ECLI:EU:C:2012:349; as confirmed in e.g. Case C-49/14, *Finanmadrid EFC*, ECLI:EU:C:2016:98.

161 See e.g. Case C-106/89, *Marleasing*, ECLI:EU:C:1990:395, para. 8; Case C-240–248/98, *Océano Grupo*, ECLI:EU:C:2000:346, para. 30; Case C-80/86, *Kolpinghuis Nijmegen*, ECLI:EU:C:1987:431, para. 13.

under EEA law only applies "as far as possible",[162] and "requires the referring court to do whatever lies within its competence".[163] While the now standard "as far as possible" reference of course entails an apparent limitation in itself, attempting to pin down its more precise meaning has remained notoriously difficult.[164] Who determines how far national courts must stretch themselves, and who decides on what might be possible or not to achieve by way of interpretation – the European courts or the national courts?

Certain Norwegian academics have contended that the boundaries of the principle must fall to be determined under national law alone – i.e. as fashioned by national principles of construction and interpretation, and the role that courts play under the Norwegian legal system.[165] It is certainly true that in many cases the ECJ has seemed content to leave questions concerning the limits of the principle to be decided by the national courts themselves, at least where it appeared immediately apparent that one of the other mechanisms for ensuring effectiveness of EU law (i.e. direct effect and/or state liability) could in any event come to the rescue.[166] In other cases, however, the ECJ has been much more forceful in its guidance to the national courts, either requiring a particular interpretative outcome in the case,[167] or dismissing arguments made by the parties and/or referring courts to the effect that an EU-consistent interpretation of national law would not be possible.[168] Interestingly, it would seem as though the ECJ is more prepared to instruct (as opposed to

---

162 See e.g. Case E-1/07, *Criminal proceedings against A*, para. 39; Case E-15/12, *Wahl*, para. 54; Case E-6/13, *Metacom*, para. 69; Case E-28/13 *Merrill Lynch*, paras. 42 and 44.

163 Case E-18/11, *Irish Bank*, para. 124. Put in slightly different terms in Case E-25/13, *Engilbertsson*, para. 163: "it is for the referring court ... to do whatever lies within its jurisdiction".

164 A fact which may have served the ECJ rather well in seeking to ensure the effectiveness of EU law through application of the principle. After all, is anything really impossible for a national court to achieve by way of interpretation? Examples from Norwegian case-law concerning the interpretation of national law alone would seem to suggest not – see e.g. the example of Rt-1950-573 (*Torbjørnsen*), posited by Eckhoff (n. 139), p. 359, where a clear conflict between two Norwegian legal provisions of equal rank was resolved without reference to the classic priority doctrines (*lex superior, lex specialis, lex posterior*), but instead by way of a highly creative, restrictive interpretation of one of the provisions, which effectively reduced its scope of application to nothing.

165 Arnesen and Stenvik (n. 38), e.g. at p. 58.

166 See e.g. Case C-334/92, *Wagner Miret*, ECLI:EU:C:1993:945; Case C-111/97, *EvoBus*, ECLI:EU:C:1998:434.

167 See e.g. Case C-106/89, *Marleasing*, ECLI:EU:C:1990:395; Case C-306/12, *Spedition Welter*, ECLI:EU:C:2013:650. See further C.N.K. Franklin, "Limits to the Limits of the Principle of Consistent Interpretation? Commentary on the Court's Decision in *Spedition Welter*" 40 (2015) *E.L.Rev* 910–24, at pp. 920–23.

168 There are numerous examples which indicate that the ECJ will not always be sympathetic to such claims – see e.g. Case C-32/93, *Webb*, ECLI:EU:C:1994:300; Case C-404/06, *Quelle*, ECLI:EU:C:2008:231; Case C-282/10, *Dominguez*, ECLI:EU:C:2012:33; Case C-18/13, *Maks Pen*, ECLI:EU:C:2014:69; Case C-441/14, *Ajos*, ECLI:EU:C:2016:278.

merely suggest) in situations where consistent interpretation remains the only potential option for ensuring the effectiveness of the EU measure in question (i.e. because one or more of the criteria for direct effect and state liability could not be considered fulfilled).

Although the EFTA Court has indicated a willingness to encroach on national methods,[169] it has yet to go as far as the ECJ in effectively instructing national courts as to the results to be achieved by way of consistent interpretation in particular cases. Given that its Advisory Opinions are not formally binding on the national courts of the EFTA States, and considering the potential additional cost this might have on their already rather strained relationship, this is perhaps not very surprising. Similarly to the ECJ's approach in state liability cases, however, it is worth noting that the EFTA Court has not refrained from providing specific appraisals as to whether the criteria for state liability are in fact fulfilled in a given case – notwithstanding the fact that such matters should formally be left to the national referring courts to determine.[170] One should therefore perhaps not rule out the possibility of the EFTA Court providing more robust guidance in cases concerning consistent interpretations in the future.

The second issue, which is also connected to the question of who ultimately decides what is or is not possible, is whether it is general principles of EU/EEA or national law which may serve to limit application of the principle of consistent interpretations in practice? Of course, where a given principle relied upon by a national court to limit such application proves commensurate under EU/EEA and national law, the issue may be rather academic. Yet practice shows that this will not always be the case. The *Ajos* case provides a good illustration of how different understandings under national and EU law of the general principle of legal certainty and the *contra legem* limit might lead to different results in practice.[171] By clarifying (and effectively restricting) the extent of the *contra legem* limit in that case, the ECJ was thereby also clearly indicating that it is legal certainty as a general principle of EU law, and as defined as a matter of EU law, which may serve to limit the principle of consistent interpretation – not notions of legal certainty or *contra legem* interpretations as these might be understood under national law alone.

The EFTA Court for its part, while implicitly recognising the *contra legem* limit in certain cases, has not gone as far in explaining what this limit entails under EEA law.[172] Indeed, the EFTA Court has yet to go to the same extent as the ECJ in defining or elaborating on the range of general principles which might potentially limit application of the principle more generally. In fairness,

169 See section 3 above.

170 See Case E-04/01, *Karlsson*, para. 36.

171 This case is examined in more detail in the Synthesis (pp. 32 and 65–6), and Denmark (pp. 281–88).

172 Case E-18/11 *Irish Bank*, para. 125; Case E-28/13 *Merrill Lynch*, para. 45.

the accidents of litigation have seldom provided it with a good opportunity to do so. There is in any event therefore little guidance to be drawn from the EFTA Court's case-law as to which general principles may act as limitations to consistent interpretations under EEA law, and whether it is those developed indigenously under EU/EEA law or those existing under the national laws of the Member States.

As far as the practice of the Norwegian courts is concerned, one thing seems clear: where the national principle of presumption is applied, general principles of national law will determine its limits. As much may be drawn from the Supreme Court's decision in *Finanger I*: beyond the specific considerations connected to the principle of dualism, presumed legislative intent and preparatory works, both the majority and dissenting judgments also discussed the ramifications of the case in light of the national principles of legal certainty, predictability and legitimate expectations.[173]

As discussed earlier, however, in many cases it is simply not clear whether it was the EEA principle of consistent interpretation or the national principle of presumption which was applied by the courts. If the EEA principle has been, or were to be, applied directly in certain cases, then the limits to the principle must also presumably be regarded as determinable as a matter of EEA law – just as the limits to the principle of state liability are governed by EEA law, and the underlying EU law to which it is so closely related. Notwithstanding the fact that the Norwegian principle of presumption is *theoretically* capable of being adapted to meet the requirements of the EEA principle of consistent interpretation, given that EEA law seems to require more of national courts than under the principle of presumption *in practice* (if not also arguably in theory), this would in the present author's opinion also seem to be the most convincing solution for Norwegian courts to adopt for the future.

A third observation concerns how the general methodological approach of Norwegian courts in certain cases may also contribute to preventing consistent interpretations in practice. In *Finanger I*, for example, the Supreme Court started out by looking at the Norwegian law in isolation, and arrived at the conclusion that there was no right to compensation under Norwegian law alone. It then proceeded to address the issue as to what impact the EEA Directives might have in interpreting the Norwegian law concerned. Since there was a clear conflict between the Norwegian legal provision and the EEA Directives, the national principle of presumption was not applicable, thus rendering it "impossible" to arrive at an interpretation in conformity with EEA law. The same methodological approach was adopted in the *Care Expenses* case, where the Supreme Court first interpreted Section 10-3 of the Social Services Act exhaustively before seeking to view it in light of Norway's commitments under the European Charter

[173] Rt-2000-1811, pp. 1832, 1837 and 1840–41.

of Local Self-Governance – with the result that the national rule provided no room for arriving at an interpretation consistent with the Charter.[174]

The method adopted in cases such as these is innately negative, and clearly inducive to arriving at non-EEA-consistent results from the very outset. First, the meaning of Norwegian law is established; following which, a consistent interpretation will only be possible where national law proves ambiguous. Yet the process of interpretation may not be touched upon at all in this way, as the meaning of national law is already established before it is viewed in the light of EU/EEA law, thus in all likelihood rendering the latter an irrelevance. That is not to say that it will prove impossible to arrive at EEA-consistent results in every case where national law is interpreted in isolation first. As discussed earlier, in the *Lifebuoy* case the Supreme Court found it possible to interpret the Norwegian Trademark Act in line with the Trademark Directive, notwithstanding its initial conclusion that the result would have been different under Norwegian law alone.[175] There seems to be general agreement in academic circles, however, that the process would be much more positively framed if the meaning of the EEA rule was established first, before moving on to decipher whether national law is capable of bearing the same meaning.[176] Awareness of this fact may also be traceable in certain decisions. In the *Stavanger Catering* case, for example, the Supreme Court started out by interpreting EEA law first, before looking to view Norwegian law in the light thereof.[177] The same approach was adopted in *Tippinga*, where the Court of Appeal looked to interpret Art. 13 of the Trademark Directive before viewing Section 19 of the Norwegian Trademark Act in the light thereof – again, a consistent interpretation proved possible in the end.

Finally, it is worth looking at one particular case where a Norwegian court proved willing to stretch itself exceedingly far in seeking to uphold Norway's EEA obligations. The Court of Appeal's decision in the *Wullum Amcar* case provides an interesting (albeit contentious) example of a remarkably strained interpretation of Norwegian law in light of EEA law providing the basis for disapplication of another conflicting rule of national law in accordance with the EEA principle of primacy, thereby leading to an EEA-consistent result in the case.[178] The facts and law in the case were quite technical and complex, but essentially concerned judicial review of three administrative decisions turning down a car dealer's applications to have three trucks imported from certain EU countries authorised for use in Norway, due to weight restrictions imposed

174 Rt-2007-234.
175 See section 4.2.1 above.
176 Of the same opinion, see Arnesen and Stenvike (n. 38), pp. 71–74; Fredriksen and Mathisen (n. 38), pp. 391–92.
177 Rt-1997-1965, see section 4.2.2 above.
178 LF-2010-21736.

by national law. According to Section 10-1(3)(1) of the Norwegian Statutory Instrument on Motor Vehicles, the permitted trailer weight including brakes for motor vehicles with a permissible gross weight of up to 3.5 tons could not be higher than the permissible total weight of the motor vehicle itself.[179] The highest permissible combined weight for a truck weighing 3.5 tons and its trailer was therefore 7 tons. One of the central issues in the case was whether, in the light of EEA law, such vehicles could nevertheless be approved for use even where their combined weight exceeded 7 tons.

Section 10-1(3)(1) had for many years been entirely in line with the rules set out in the Weight Directive.[180] Following an amendment to the Directive in 2003,[181] however, the limit of 3.5 tons for the largest technically permissible towable mass no longer applied to vehicles with continuous (i.e. complete trailer) braking systems. This exception was clearly not reflected in – in fact, it directly contradicted – the wording of Section 10-1(3)(1). Since all three of the trucks had continuous braking systems, and had been approved in the exporting states for combined weights in excess of 7 tons, the Norwegian car dealer had therefore requested approval for a maximum combined weight exceeding 7 tons for each truck. Although this was initially refused by the Norwegian authorities under reference to Section 10-1(3)(1), by the time the case came before the Court of Appeal, both parties to the case – and the Court itself – seemed to agree that Norwegian law no longer reflected the requirements of the Directive.

The Court of Appeal's attempt to resolve this clear conflict between EEA and Norwegian law was nevertheless creative to say the least. The Court started out by saying that according to Section 10-1(1) of the Statutory Instrument, vehicles must be designed and submitted to the approval authority with a manufacturer's guarantee as to its total weight and for the maximum total weight of any trailer that it might tow. And in accordance with Section 10-1(2)(4), any maximum weights stated by the manufacturer in accordance with the terms of the Directive had to be considered as acceptable weight guarantees which the authorities must accept. In a short and rather cryptic passage, the Court of Appeal therefore held that:

> The Court of Appeal bases its decision on the parties' agreement that the [Statutory Instrument], viewed in conjunction with the Weight Directive (Directive 97/27/EC), must be understood and applied so that the vehicles in question can be registered

---

179 *Forskrift om tekniske krav og godkjenning av kjøretøy, deler og utstyr (kjøretøyforskriften).*

180 Directive 97/27/EC of the European Parliament and of the Council of 22 July 1997 relating to the masses and dimensions of certain categories of motor vehicles and their trailers [1997] OJ L233/1.

181 See Annex IV, point 2.1.1.c of Commission Directive 2003/19/EC of 21 March 2003 amending for the purposes of adapting to technical progress Directive 97/27/EC [2003] OJ L79/6.

> with higher weight than stated in [Section 10-1(3) of the Statutory Instrument]. This follows from the interpretation of [Section 10-1(2)(4) of the Statutory Instrument]. [Author's own translation.]

The Court of Appeal did not state whether it was applying the Norwegian principle of presumption or the EEA principle of consistent interpretation; nor did it make any mention of the EEA principle of primacy. One can nevertheless imply from the Court's ruling that Section 10-1(2)(4) was to be construed as an EEA-conform exception to the clear prohibition set out in Section 10-1(3)(1), presumably thereby providing a basis for disapplication of the latter in accordance with Section 2 of the EEA Act (i.e. the incorporated principle of EEA primacy). Yet exactly how a rule concerning what constitutes *an acceptable manufacturer's guarantee* as to the vehicle's permissible weight could be viewed as related to and exempting from a rule stipulating *actual maximum weight limits*, remains something of a mystery. While undoubtedly a strained construction of Norwegian law,[182] the case provides a good example of how far at least certain lower Norwegian courts and judges seem prepared to go in more recent years in making the seemingly "impossible" possible by way of interpretation in order to arrive at EEA-consistent results in a case.[183]

6. SUMMARY

As this contribution has shown, Norwegian courts have seemed to struggle in many cases to fully embrace the concept of consistent interpretation and all that it entails as a matter of EEA law. The EEA principle itself has never been expressly applied in practice to date. Where a specific principle is referred to, Norwegian courts have instead invoked the national principle of presumption. This principle appears to be applied to the same extent regardless of the international obligations at issue. It also seems more limited – in its practical application, if not also in theory – than the EU and EEA principles of consistent interpretation, and therefore not certain to lead to the same interpretative outcomes in all cases. Where the national principle of presumption has proven more easily rebuttable, in light of the demands of homogeneity, the EEA principle of consistent interpretation would appear to require national courts to do more. Application of the principle of presumption seems redundant in

182 Of the same opinion, see Fredriksen (n. 42), p. 71.

183 The present author would nevertheless disagree with arguments that the Court of Appeal thereby came close to giving the Directive direct effect in the case (see e.g. Fredriksen (n. 42), p. 71) – this case clearly had more to do with a misconstruction of the principles of consistent interpretation and primacy than anything else.

any event, in the present author's opinion, since Section 1 of the Norwegian EEA Act may be understood as incorporating all unwritten EEA principles, including the principle of consistent interpretation, into Norwegian law. Tensions in the relationship between the principle of presumption and the EEA principle of consistent interpretation may arguably also go some way in explaining why no principle is referred to by Norwegian courts and judges in certain cases.

Notwithstanding a few encouraging exceptions, particularly in the case-law of the lower courts, Norwegian courts generally seem to have adopted quite a narrow understanding of the scope of the principle, with a correspondingly expansive view as to the reach of its limits. In the absence of any guidance provided by the EFTA Court – which in any event would only be regarded as advisory – Norwegian courts continue to apply the principle of presumption in certain cases, thereby also viewing the limits as those defined under national law. Horizontal party constellations, preparatory legislative works and previous case-law of national courts may pose significant barriers to achieving EEA-consistent interpretations of Norwegian law in practice. There appear to be relatively few examples of Norwegian courts demonstrating a genuine willingness to look hard(er) for possible solutions which might lead to EEA-consistent interpretations – which is interesting, considering the creativity shown by the courts when faced with potential conflicts between national law alone. Observance of EEA law obligations and the individual rights they give rise to, and Parliament's general intent that such rights should be defended, do not appear to provide equally good reasons for doing the same where potential conflicts between national and EEA law are concerned.

CONSISTENT INTERPRETATION IN THE CASE-LAW OF THE ICELANDIC SUPREME COURT 1994–2016

Gunnar Thor PETURSSON and Omar Berg RUNARSSON*

* The views expressed in this contribution are those of the authors.

1. INTRODUCTION

The Court of Justice of the European Union (ECJ) has developed a number of key principles in order to secure effective and uniform application of EU law throughout the national legal orders of the EU. Primacy, direct effect and the principle of consistent interpretation are core principles in this context. The last of these principles to emerge was the *principle of consistent interpretation,*[1] established by the ECJ in the *Von Colson* case.[2] These principles are playing an increasingly important role both in the case-law of the ECJ and in national courts in Europe, when private parties are seeking to have their EU originating rights recognised at the national level. Recently the ECJ has summarised the principle as follows:

> The principle that national law must be interpreted in conformity with European Union law also requires national courts to do whatever lies within their jurisdiction, taking the whole body of domestic law into consideration and applying the interpretative methods recognised by domestic law, with a view to ensuring that the directive in question is fully effective and achieving an outcome consistent with the objective pursued by it.[3]

It is also clear from the ECJ's case-law that the principle should come as the first alternative in order to secure conforming interpretation and application of EU law – before the principle of direct effect, which should be explored if conforming interpretation is not possible.[4]

---

1 In academic literature the EU law principle of consistent interpretation has also been referred to as "harmonious interpretation", "indirect effects" and "conform interpretation", to name but a few.

2 Case 14/83, *Von Colson*, ECLI:EU:C:1984:153.

3 Case C-282/10, *Dominguez*, ECLI:EU:C:2012:33, para. 27. See e.g. also Case C-212/04, *Adeneler and Others*, ECLI:EU:C:2006:443, para. 111.

4 *Dominguez*, ibid., para. 32. In fact, it has been held that instead of the principle of direct effect, the principle of consistent interpretation is the main method of ensuring the effects of Directives in national courts – irrespective of correct, incorrect or no transposition at all. See G. Betlem, "The doctrine of consistent interpretation: Managing legal uncertainty" in J.M. Prinssen and A. Schrauwen (eds.), *Direct Effect – Rethinking a Classic of EC Legal Doctrine* (Europa Law Publishing, 2002), p. 81.

In European Economic Area (EEA) law,[5] the principle of direct effect is not recognised – in fact, its absence is explicitly confirmed by the European Free Trade Association (EFTA) Court.[6] Therefore, in the national legal orders of the EEA EFTA States,[7] individuals and economic operators are unable to rely *directly* on non-implemented EEA rules before national courts in the EFTA States (i.e. in Iceland and Norway – Lichtenstein follows a monist tradition). Additionally, while certain primacy obligations are secured through Protocol 35 of the EEA Agreement, this principle is less far-reaching in EEA law than in EU law (see further below). In this sense, it is logical to take the view that a parallel *principle of consistent interpretation*[8] – as established and developed in the case-law of the EFTA Court – must play an even greater role in EEA law than in EU law.

The main focus of this contribution is to analyse the outcome of an in-depth research into the case-law of the Icelandic Supreme Court, answering the questions *if* and *how* the principle of consistent interpretation is applied in the Icelandic legal order for the purpose of bringing national law into line with EEA law. As will be seen, consistent interpretation – as a method to grant *indirect effect* to EEA rules – is quite often invoked in legal proceedings in Iceland. Accordingly, the Icelandic Supreme Court in a number of cases has had to adjudicate on the *scope and limits* of its "interpretative competence", i.e. *how far* it can construe Icelandic law in conformity with EEA law.

2. THE SCOPE, MATERIAL AND METHODOLOGY OF THE CONTRIBUTION

As indicated above, the *main material* of this contribution is the case-law of the Supreme Court of Iceland, with a focus on cases where the court has been called upon to resolve legal issues concerning the interaction between national law and EEA law. The main reason for selecting the Supreme Court's case-law as the primary source is due to the fact that the Supreme Court is a court of last instance and has the final say over legal disputes.[9] As concerns the time period covered by this contribution, the case-law analysis covers the period from 1 January 1994

5 The concept of "EEA law" covers the Agreement on the European Economic Area, secondary legislation (i.e. mainly EEA relevant directives and regulations) and protocols and annexes.

6 Case E-04/01, *Karl K. Karlsson hf. v. The Icelandic State* [2002] EFTA Ct. Rep. 240, para. 28.

7 Iceland, Norway and Liechtenstein.

8 The EFTA Court has referred to the principle as "the principle of conform interpretation", e.g. in Case E-18/11, *Irish Bank Resolution Corporation Ltd v. Kaupthing hf.* [2012] EFTA Ct. Rep. 592, para. 124. In this contribution, the principle is referred to as "the principle of consistent interpretation".

9 Under the current situation, and as provided for in the Judiciary Act No. 15/1998, the general judicial system in Iceland is based on *two levels*, i.e. eight district courts and the Supreme

to 31 December 2016. The EEA Agreement was ratified and incorporated into Icelandic law on 1 January 1994 by Act No. 2/1993 on the European Economic Area ("the EEA Act").

The cases were mainly collected by using the Supreme Court's online search engine (<www.haestirettur.is>). Overall, approximately 220 cases were collected.[10] By applying certain criteria – i.e. excluding cases where the EEA Agreement was effectively not dealt with, for reasons unrelated to the principles of primacy, consistent interpretation or other related principles (mostly by reason of the EEA Agreement clearly not being applicable in the case, or because for procedural reasons the issues were never dealt with by the Supreme Court) – the total number of cases was reduced to 115.

For the purposes of analysing and compiling these 115 cases in an organised and systematic manner, the *Google docs questionnaire* program was used, which allowed information on the cases to be imported into an Excel document in order to get *statistical data* for better overview and comparison of the different parameters.[11] Statistical information and substantive analysis of the cases will be provided in the subsequent sections of the present contribution. In that way, the approach contains elements of both quantitative and qualitative legal analysis. In addition to the Supreme Court's case-law, the contribution will take into account the following sources: (i) the EFTA Court's case-law and, where appropriate, case-law of the ECJ,[12] (ii) the applicable legal framework, for example the EEA Agreement and various types of national legislation, and (iii) existing academic literature published by domestic and foreign scholars.

Court. However, on 26 May 2016, the Icelandic Parliament passed a bill on the establishment of a *third tier* in the judicial system. The third and *middle* tier – *Landsréttur* (Court of Appeal), is expected to commence its activities at the beginning of 2018.

10 When searching for cases with the aforesaid search engine, the authors firstly used certain wide-ranging keywords, such as *EES-samningurinn* (EEA Agreement); *EFTA-dómstóllinn* (EFTA Court); *ráðgefandi álit* (Advisory Opinion); *Evrópudómstóllinn* (European Court of Justice); *fjórfrelsi* (four freedoms); *tilskipanir* (directives); and *EES* (EEA). Secondly, searches were undertaken with a reference to specific statutory Acts and individual provisions thereof, especially the EEA Act and Act No. 21/1994 on Applications to the EFTA Court for an Advisory Opinion on the Interpretation of the EEA Agreement ("Advisory Opinion Act").

11 The Google docs questionnaire included e.g. the following parameters and questions: (1) how the Supreme Court was composed in each case; (2) whether an Advisory Opinion of the EFTA Court had previously been sought; (3) whether the Supreme Court referred to any legislative preparatory works in its judgment; (4) the nature of the legal relationship between the disputing parties (i.e. vertical or horizontal); (5) whether the Supreme Court applied, or refused to apply, consistent interpretation; (6) whether the EFTA Court had instructed the national court to apply consistent interpretation; (7) if the principles of direct effect and state liability played a part in the case; (8) what type of an interpretive method the Supreme Court applied; and (9) what type of EEA legislation was challenged in the cases, i.e. the EEA Agreement, Directive, Regulation, etc.

12 The case-law of the EFTA Court and of the ECJ was mainly found by using their online search engines, i.e. <http://www.eftacourt.int/cases> and http://curia.europa.eu/juris/recherche.jsf>.

3. THE GENERAL CONSTITUTIONAL FRAMEWORK AND STATUS OF EEA LAW IN ICELAND

3.1. INTRODUCTION

Before analysing the application of the principle of consistent interpretation as an EU and EEA law principle, it is important to draw attention to certain specific characteristics in the Icelandic legal system. These characteristics relate to and are based on the constitutional setting, the doctrinal application of principles of consistent interpretation, and the way by which Iceland has implemented its legal obligations under the EEA Agreement through statutory law, particularly as regards its primacy obligations (Protocol 35 to the EEA Agreement). This prologue provides an essential backdrop and clarity in order to better comprehend and understand this contribution and its conclusions.

3.2. TRANSFER OF STATE POWERS

First, it should be emphasised that there are no provisions in the Icelandic Constitution No. 33/1944 that directly provide for the transfer of sovereign State powers (legislative, administrative or judicial), not even in the context of intergovernmental international cooperation.[13]

Art. 2 of the Icelandic Constitution provides that the *Althingi* (Parliament) and the President of Iceland jointly exercise legislative power; the President and other governmental authorities exercise executive power; and judges exercise judicial power. Furthermore, in Art. 21 of the Constitution it is stipulated that it is the President who concludes treaties with other States. Unless approved by the *Althingi*, the President may not conclude such treaties if they entail renouncement of or servitude on Icelandic territory or territorial waters, or if they require changes to the State system.[14]

Notwithstanding this lack of direct constitutional provisions on such matters, it has been maintained that an unwritten principle of Icelandic constitutional law may allow for the transfer of state powers in limited circumstances.[15] Indeed, this unwritten principle seems for example to have been the basis of international cooperation that has allowed for foreign rules and judgments to be applied and recognised at the national level (e.g. the Lugano Convention), and

---

13 Such provisions are to be found for example in the Danish and the Norwegian constitutions (Art. 20 and Art. 115 respectively). There have been long and still ongoing discussions in Iceland on the need to amend the Constitution in this respect.

14 The role of the President is limited by the fact that his powers may only be executed by the responsible Minister and that the President is "not reliable" as an executive authority, cf. Arts. 11, 13 and 19 of the Constitution.

15 D.Þ. Björgvinsson, *EES-réttur og landsréttur* (Codex Publishing, 2006), p. 478.

other international agreements such as the European Convention on Human Rights (ECHR), the EEA Agreement and the Schengen Agreement.[16] On the eve of the Icelandic State becoming a contracting party to the EEA Agreement, an opinion of four experts in constitutional law was prepared at the request of the Minister for Foreign Affairs. In their view, the EEA Agreement did not entail a transfer of state powers in breach of the Constitution.[17] It was in the light of this opinion and the unwritten principle on the transfer of state powers that the EEA Agreement was signed and ratified, and finally incorporated as statutory law on 1 January 1994 by the EEA Act.

The main problem with defining the exact ambit of this unwritten principle is that its boundaries have mainly been defined by academics, although with the backing of the actions of the Icelandic State concerning ratification and incorporation of international agreements. Additionally, there is no full consensus among academics about the nature and scope of the unwritten principle.[18] To date, the Icelandic Supreme Court has not stated its views on the exact scope and nature of this unwritten principle. Due to procedural law requirements, it may prove difficult to subject the question to judicial review[19] – although the possibility should perhaps not be entirely ruled out (e.g. in the event that the EFTA Surveillance Authority (ESA) issues decisions fining Icelandic corporates for breaches of Arts. 53–54 EEA).

It has been maintained, however, that the Supreme Court has confirmed the constitutionality of the EEA Agreement through its first use of the Advisory Opinion procedure under the EEA Agreement, as introduced more specifically in the Agreement between the EFTA States on the establishment of a Surveillance Authority and a Court of Justice (Surveillance and Court Agreement – SCA)[20] – a procedure which will be further explained below.[21] Even if those assumptions may have certain merits, it could at any rate not be seen as answering this question once and for all. The dynamic nature of the EEA Agreement, both at the legal and judicial level, has to be taken into consideration. Irrespective of this fact, and as will be seen from the findings of this contribution, the EEA Agreement and the precedents from the EFTA Court and even the ECJ, have frequently been applied in the case-law of the Supreme Court, without once drawing the constitutionality of the EEA Agreement into question.

---

16 See also, B. Thorarensen, *Stjórnskipunarréttur – Undirstöður og handhafar ríkisvalds* (Codex Publishing, 2015), pp. 143–44.

17 Alþingistíðindi A 1992 (þskj. 30, document I), pp. 682–713.

18 Björgvinsson (n. 15) 478–79 and Thorarensen (n. 16), pp. 145.

19 For example in Supreme Court Case No. 270/1994 of 20 June 1994, *Björn S. Stefánsson v. The Minister for Foreign Affairs*.

20 Consolidated Version of the Agreement between the EFTA States on the establishment of a Surveillance Authority and a Court of Justice [1994] OJ L344/3.

21 S.M. Stefánsson, *Evrópusambandið og Evrópska efnahagssvæðið* (Bókaútgáfa Orators, 2000), p. 65.

3.3. MONISM/DUALISM AND THE PRINCIPLE OF CONSISTENT INTERPRETATION

In light of the above, it is perhaps not surprising that Iceland, similarly to the other Nordic countries, has traditionally been regarded as a legal regime that adheres to the *dualistic* (as opposed to *monistic*) theory in terms of the status of international law in the domestic legal order. This view has traditionally been upheld by Icelandic legal scholars.[22]

The status of the Icelandic legal system as being dualistic is not directly bound in law. This is not surprising, since international law is generally neutral as to how international law obligations should be adhered to in national legal systems.[23] However, in Art. 2 of Act No. 62/1994, which incorporated the ECHR into Icelandic law, it was explicitly stipulated that the judgments of the European Court of Human Rights (and other decisions of the ECHR institutions) were not binding in the domestic legal order. In *Criminal proceedings against A and Others*,[24] the Icelandic Supreme Court referred to this as exemplifying "the general principle of dualism" in the Icelandic legal order in relation to the rulings of the institutions of the ECHR.

In three rulings from the 1980s, the Supreme Court rejected the idea that provisions of the ECHR that had not been incorporated into Icelandic law could automatically alter or change statutory or constitutional provisions.[25] This view changed dramatically following the *Ægisson* and *Þorbjörn Gunnarsson* (summarised in section 6.3.5 below) cases.[26] In those cases, the Supreme Court gave provisions of the ECHR such weight in interpreting national law (both procedural laws and the Constitution) that it effectively meant that provisions of the ECHR were given priority over incompatible national (procedural law) provisions – even if the ECHR had not been incorporated as statutory law at

22 Ármann Snævarr, a former law professor at the University of Iceland, reflects the traditional view of the Icelandic national legal order, i.e. as dividing the Icelandic legal system into "international law, and national law" – therefore, adhering to traditional Nordic view of the domestic legal system. Á. Snævarr, *Almenn lögfræði* (1989), pp. 263–64. This view of Ármann Snævarr has been echoed in subsequent writings of several Icelandic legal scholars, see further D.Þ. Björgvinsson, "Staða dóma Mannréttindadómstóls Evrópu í íslenskum landsrétti", 10 (2014) 1 *Tímarit Lögréttu* 23, 26.

23 D.Þ. Björgvinsson, *The Intersection of International Law and Domestic Law: A Theoretical and Practical Analysis* (Edward Elgar Publishing, 2015), p. 93.

24 Supreme Court Case No. 371/2010 of 22 September 2010, *Criminal proceedings against A and Others*.

25 Supreme Court Case No. 77/1985 of 25 November 1985, *Criminal proceedings against Jón Kristinsson*; Supreme Court Case No. 273/1986 of 10 March 1987, *Criminal proceedings against Einar Sverrisson*; Supreme Court Case No. 239/1987 of 15 December 1988, *Sigurjón Ármann Sigurjónsson v. the Committee for Taxicab Supervision*.

26 Supreme Court Case No. 120/1989 of 9 January 1990, *Criminal proceedings against Guðmundur Breiðfjörð Ægisson*; Supreme Court Case No. 494/1991 of 6 February 1992, *Criminal proceedings against Þorbjörn Gunnarsson*.

that time. In that context, it has been maintained that such application of the principle of consistent interpretation (i.e. interpreting constitutional provisions in light of international human rights obligations) goes further than what is regarded as traditionally required by this principle in Nordic law (i.e. as only to be applicable to statutory laws).[27] The Icelandic Supreme Court has confirmed this approach in subsequent case-law.[28]

These cases are a clear example of the principle of consistent interpretation being accepted as a general principle of Icelandic constitutional law – in particular, and not least, where the cases involve fundamental human rights obligations. It is not surprising, however, that it has been maintained that these cases – and in particular *Þorbjörn Gunnarsson* – go beyond what may traditionally be held to fall within the effects of international law in dualist legal regimes.[29]

3.4. PROTOCOL 35 AND ART. 3 OF THE ICELANDIC EEA ACT

It is against the background provided for above that Iceland became a member of the EEA, ratifying the Agreement and incorporating its main text as statutory law through the EEA Act in 1994. In the light of Iceland's dualistic approach, international treaties such as the EEA Agreement could not automatically become a part of the national legal order.[30] Furthermore, Art. 7 EEA and Protocol 35 of the EEA Agreement reflect similar ideas.

First, Art. 7 EEA stipulates that EEA Acts that are or become parts of the EEA Agreement are to be made part of the internal legal order as follows: (a) an act corresponding to a European Economic Community (EEC) regulation shall as such be made part of the internal legal order of the Contracting Parties; (b) an act corresponding to an EEC directive shall leave to the authorities of the Contracting Parties the choice of form and method of implementation.

Second, Protocol 35 to the EEA Agreement provides that:

> Whereas this Agreement aims at achieving a homogeneous European Economic Area, based on common rules, without requiring any Contracting Party to transfer legislative powers to any institution of the European Economic Area; and Whereas this consequently will have to be achieved through national procedures; For cases of possible conflicts between implemented EEA rules and other statutory provisions,

---

27 Thorarensen (n. 16), p. 208.

28 In Supreme Court Case No. 103/1994 of 18 May 1995, *Criminal proceedings against Sveinn Eiríkur Sigfússon*, the Supreme Court referred to its ruling in the *Ægisson* case and a line of cases subsequent to that case, confirming that it had prior to the incorporation of the ECHR into Icelandic law stated that "Icelandic law should be interpreted, including the Constitution, in the best conformity with the Convention".

29 Björgvinsson (n. 22), p. 26.

30 S. Norberg *et al.*, *EEA Law: A Commentary on the EEA Agreement* (Fritzes, 1993), p. 202.

> the EFTA States undertake to introduce, if necessary, a statutory provision to the effect that EEA rules prevail in these cases.

Protocol 35 must be seen in the light of the different legal traditions of the contracting parties to the EEA Agreement – including dualistic legal regimes – and taking those into consideration.[31] Its main aim is to secure homogeneity in the EEA[32] and primacy of EEA rules over national legislation – similar to the effects on the EU side based on the primacy principle, yet without requiring a transfer of legislative powers.[33] As Sevón has highlighted, the words "implemented EEA rules" and "other statutory provisions" were there for the specific dual purpose of avoiding direct effect and avoiding conflict with constitutional provisions of the EFTA States.[34] It does not therefore go as far as the EU principles of direct effect and primacy – the latter, for example, being regarded as giving priority to EU rules even in the case of conflicting constitutional principles.[35]

The EFTA Court has built up a line of cases explaining Protocol 35. In its very first case, *Restamark*,[36] the EFTA Court held that:

> Protocol 35 EEA on the Implementation of EEA Rules stipulates that the EFTA States are under an obligation to ensure, if necessary by a separate statutory provision, that in cases of conflict between implemented EEA rules and other statutory provisions the implemented EEA rules prevail. It is inherent in the nature of such a provision that individuals and economic operators in cases of conflict between implemented EEA rules and national statutory provisions must be entitled to invoke and to claim at the national level any rights that could be derived from provisions of the EEA Agreement, as being or having been made part of the respective national legal order, *if they are unconditional and sufficiently precise.*[37]

In the *Hörður Einarsson* case,[38] the EFTA Court emphasised that Protocol 35 applies in the case of *implemented* national provisions, and held that:

> Where a provision of national law is incompatible with Article 14 EEA, and that Article *has been implemented* in national law, a situation has arisen which is

31 Ibid., p 206.
32 The EFTA Court has explained the "homogeneity" requirements of the EEA Agreement as to be found additionally in the 15th preamble, and Arts. 1 and 3 EEA. In this respect, see e.g. Case E-28/13, *Merrill Lynch* [2014] EFTA Ct. Rep. 970, para. 42.
33 Björgvinsson (n. 15), pp. 100–04.
34 L. Sevón, "Primacy and direct effects in the EEA. Some reflections" in *Festskrift til Ole Due* (Forlaget Thomson, 1994), pp. 350–51.
35 Case 106/77, *Simmenthal*, ECLI:EU:C:1978:49 and Case 11/70, *Internationale Handelsgesellschaft*, ECLI:EU:C:1970:114.
36 Case E-1/94, *Restamark* [1994–1995] EFTA Ct. Rep. 15.
37 Ibid., para. 77 (emphasis added).
38 Case E-01/01, *Hörður Einarsson v. The Icelandic State* [2002] EFTA Ct. Rep. 1.

> governed by the undertaking assumed by the EFTA States under Protocol 35 to the EEA Agreement, the premise of which is that the implemented EEA rule shall prevail.[39]

In the *Karlsson* case,[40] the EFTA Court further explained the nature and the limits of Protocol 35, and its relations with Art. 7 EEA, and held that:

> It follows from Article 7 EEA and Protocol 35 to the EEA Agreement that EEA law does not entail a transfer of legislative powers. Therefore, EEA law does *not* require that individuals and economic operators can rely directly on *unincorporated EEA rules* before national courts. At the same time, it is inherent in the general objective of the EEA Agreement of establishing a dynamic and homogeneous market, in the ensuing emphasis on the judicial defence and enforcement of the rights of individuals, as well as in the public international law principle of effectiveness, namely that national courts will consider any relevant element of EEA law, whether implemented or not, when *interpreting* national law.[41]

In the *Criminal proceedings against A* case,[42] the EFTA Court also emphasised similar points by stating that[43] "EEA law does not require that non-implemented EEA rules takes precedence over conflicting national rules, including national rules *which fail to transpose* the relevant EEA rules correctly into national law".

In more recent case-law, the EFTA Court has continued to underline the principle. In the *HOB-Vín* case, the EFTA Court maintained that the principle was "inherent in the nature of the EEA Agreement".[44] Also, in the *Jan Anfinn Wahl* case, the EFTA Court relied on Art. 3 EEA (which sets out the duty of sincere cooperation) in the context of requirements of EEA law to prevail over conflicting national law:[45]

> Moreover, Article 3 EEA requires the EEA States to take all measures necessary, regardless of the form and method of implementation, to ensure that a directive which has been implemented and satisfies the conditions set out above *prevails over conflicting national law* and to guarantee the application and effectiveness of the directive.[46]

Iceland's reaction to Protocol 35 was to adopt *a specific statutory provision*, Art. 3 of the EEA Act (the Act No. 2/1993), which stipulates that "Statutes and

---

39 Ibid., para. 55 (emphasis added).
40 *Karlsson* (n. 6).
41 Ibid., para. 28 (emphasis added).
42 Case E-01/07, *Criminal proceedings against A* [2007] EFTA Ct. Rep. 246.
43 Ibid., para. 40 (emphasis added). This would seem to suggest that materially the Icelandic Supreme Court's approach to Protocol 35 in the *Sveinbjörnsdóttir* case (see below) was correct.
44 Case E-2/12, *HOB-vín v. ÁTVR*, [2012] EFTA Ct. Rep. 1092, para. 122.
45 Case E-15/12, *Jan Anfinn Wahl v. The Icelandic State* [2013] EFTA Ct. Rep. 534.
46 Ibid., para. 54 (emphasis added).

regulations shall be interpreted, in so far as appropriate, in conformity with the EEA Agreement and the rules based thereon".[47]

In the explanatory notes that accompanied the legislation when it was proposed, Art. 3 of the EEA Act is introduced as a "rule of interpretation".[48] A reference is made to the ruling of the Supreme Court in the *Ægisson* case. On the basis of that ruling, it is assumed that in the case of conflict of national rules implementing international obligations and other "internal rules", the "internal rule" will be interpreted in conformity with the international obligations to the extent that this is possible. Furthermore, on the basis of Art. 3 of the EEA Act, national rules based on the EEA Agreement would normally be interpreted as *lex specialis* rules, and more recent rules (*lex posterior*) would not prevail unless the legislator had explicitly said so.

The explanatory notes also stipulated that the "Statues and regulations" referred to in Art. 3 of the EEA Act should be considered to apply to both national statues and regulations that are unrelated to the EEA Agreement, and those statues and regulations that have been introduced in order to comply with obligations under the Agreement. As for the wording "to the extent appropriate", the explanatory notes stipulate that this wording limits this rule of interpretation in two ways. First, it applies only to rules that may be in conflict with the EEA Agreement and, second, it must respect the limitations of the Icelandic Constitution, meaning that the *Althingi* may not be limited in its future legislative activities by this rule.

Looking at the explanatory notes, Art. 3 of the EEA Act would appear to contain two types of rule: a rule requiring conforming interpretation; and a rule requiring priority of EEA rules based on *lex specialis*. The latter is strictly speaking not a rule of interpretation as such, but a rule to solve conflicts between norms.[49] Notwithstanding this fact, the focus and wording of this rule, as a principle of interpretation – and the somewhat confusing message in terms of it being a rule to secure primacy – means that it will play a key role in this research.

The primacy effects are of course by no means to be read from the wording of the rule itself, since it does not explicitly state that implemented EEA rules should prevail when and if in conflict with national rules. In that sense, it falls short of implementing Protocol 35, even if the explanatory notes try to fill in the gaps. This has in fact been the view of most commentators, who have held that the implementing measures in Art. 3 fall short of implementing

---

47 In Icelandic: "*Skýra skal lög og reglur, að svo miklu leyti sem við á, til samræmis við EES-samninginn og þær reglur sem á honum byggja.*"

48 These are the standard "*travaux préparatoires*" that accompany law proposals, and are frequently referred to in legal proceedings, and often deemed to reflect "the will of the legislator". See further section 6.3.4.

49 Björgvinsson (n. 15), p. 130.

Protocol 35 correctly in the Icelandic legal order.[50] In light of this method of implementation, it was nevertheless clear that the Supreme Court's reactions to Art. 3 of the EEA Act would be important.

As seen from this, Art. 3 of the EEA Act – with its underlying constitutional limitations – is a core provision. The following sections will focus on how it has been applied by the Supreme Court, along with any other principles of interpretation, and also the interactions with the EFTA Court.

4. THE SUPREME COURT'S VIEW ON PROTOCOL 35 AND ARTICLE 3 OF THE EEA ACT

This section focuses solely on the Supreme Court's case-law concerning Protocol 35 and Art. 3 of the EEA Act. The aim is to explain *how* the Supreme Court has developed its views on and interpretation of Art. 3 of the EEA Act. It should be stressed that a thorough understanding of this unique statutory provision is essential in order to understand the role of the principle of consistent interpretation in the Icelandic legal order, at least in the context of EEA law.

4.1. THE SUPREME COURT'S INITIAL APPROACH

In its landmark ruling in the *Sveinbjörnsdóttir* case, dating back to 1998, the Icelandic Supreme Court for the very first time addressed the issue of whether the Icelandic State could be held liable for damages due to wrongful implementation of an EEA Act.[51] The case was decided subsequent to an Advisory Opinion of the EFTA Court.[52] Interestingly, the Supreme Court also made a reference to Art. 3 of the EEA Act – stating that there was a significant discrepancy between the Directive in question and the applicable national law (that had not been altered after the entry into force of the EEA Agreement).[53] Therefore, in the view of the Supreme Court, the national law could not

50 Björgvinsson (n. 15), p. 132; M. Einarsdóttir, "Forgangsáhrif réttilega innleiddra EES-reglna" 7 (2010) 1 *Tímarit Lögréttu* 25–36; Ó.J. Einarsson, "Bókun 35 og staða EES-samningsins í íslenskum rétti" 57 (2007) 4 *Tímarit lögfræðinga* 371, 383–84; S. Líndal and S. Magnússon, *Réttarkerfi Evrópusambandsins og Evrópska efnahagssvæðisins – Megindrættir* (Hið íslenska bókmenntafélag, 2011), pp. 175–76. Líndal and Magnússon argue, however, that it cannot be asserted that Art. 3 of the EEA Act entails an insufficient implementation of Protocol 35 EEA.

51 Supreme Court Case No. 236/1999 of 16 December 1999, *The Icelandic State v. Erla María Sveinbjörnsdóttir*.

52 Case E-09/97, *Erla María Sveinbjörnsdóttir v. Iceland* [1998] EFTA Ct. Rep. 95.

53 Council Directive 80/987/(EEC) of 20 October 1980 on the approximation of the laws of the Member States relating to the protection of employees in the event of the insolvency of their employer (as amended by Council Directive 87/164/EEC) [2003] OJ L283/23.

"be interpreted in conformity, based on the rule of interpretation found in Article 3 of the EEA Act".[54] Finally, the Court ruled that the principle of state liability in the case of wrongful implementation of EEA rules was indeed part of Icelandic law.

In *Hörður Einarsson*, the Supreme Court gave further explanation on how to interpret and apply Art. 3 of the EEA Act.[55] The case concerned the question to what extent Art. 14 of Act No. 50/1988 on Value Added Tax, which introduced a lower VAT rate for books written in the Icelandic language than for books written in other languages, was compatible with Art. 14 of the EEA Agreement, which prohibits discriminatory taxation on products. The Supreme Court ruled that the national VAT rules led to discriminatory taxation in breach of Art. 14(2) EEA. In solving the conflict between the national VAT rules and Art. 14(2) EEA, the latter of which had also been incorporated into statutory law, the Supreme Court first made a reference to Art. 3 of the EEA Act and the explanatory notes thereto, which in the view of the Supreme Court were clearly to be seen as intending to fulfil the obligation of the Contracting Parties under Protocol 35. The Court then explained how the conflict of the two rules should be resolved:

> [I]t must be considered that the second paragraph of Article 14 of the EEA Agreement, which prohibits imposing on the products of other Contracting Parties any internal taxation of such a nature as to afford indirect protection to other products, must be interpreted *as a special rule* on tax treatment on imports from other EEA States, which takes precedence over *the older* previously existing second paragraph of Article 14 of Act No. 50/1988 providing for lower VAT on books in Icelandic language than on other books. After the EEA Agreement was given legal effect by Act No. 2/1993 it was, therefore, not permitted to make a distinction between books in Icelandic and other languages when imposing VAT.[56]

By referring to Art. 3 of the EEA Act and the explanatory notes as being the basis for the *lex specialis* approach, it has been argued that the Supreme Court had thereby seemingly settled the issue of conflict of norms and Protocol 35 once and for all. However, and perhaps understandably, this method of the Supreme Court on the application of Art. 3 of the EEA Act has not escaped criticism – especially from the point of view that EEA rules cannot always be defined

---

54 It should be emphasised that strictly speaking Protocol 35 was not applicable since the Directive had not been correctly implemented. However, this may be used as an example of the limitation of Art. 3 of the EEA Act, and rules of interpretation (also in conformity) in *contra legem* situations. Björgvinsson has pointed out that the Supreme Court's reference to Article 3 of the EEA Act was perhaps a mistake; Björgvinsson (n. 15), p. 115.

55 Supreme Court Case No. 477/2002 of 16 May 2003, *The Icelandic State v. Hörður Einarsson*. This case is also, similarly to *Sveinbjörnsdóttir*, a case that had previously been referred to the EFTA Court for an Advisory Opinion.

56 Emphasis added. Authors' translation.

as *lex specialis* rules, such as, for example, where the rules are at different hierarchical levels.[57]

In this light, most commentators have – at least up until 2011 – argued that Art. 3 of the EEA Act, despite not being fully compliant with Protocol 35, would not be problematic as such, since the judiciary had shown willingness to stretch itself quite far in terms of interpreting national law in compliance with EEA rules.[58]

4.2. A SHIFT IN THE SUPREME COURT'S CASE-LAW?

In subsequent case-law, mostly in situations involving conflicts between implemented EEA rules and *posterior* statutory law, the Supreme Court seems to have abandoned the *lex specialis* approach adopted in *Hörður Einarsson* – and even refrained from making a reference to Protocol 35 and any type of primacy of EEA rules.

The shift started in two cases that both concerned the potential application of fundamental principles of the EEA Agreement concerning free movement. First was the *Tobacco Advertisement* case.[59] The defendant in the case argued that Art. 7(6) of Act No. 6/2002 on Tobacco Protection, which stated that tobacco products in stores must be placed in a manner not visible to customers, was contrary to the Icelandic Constitution, the ECHR and Arts. 11 and 36 of the EEA Agreement. The case was not referred to the EFTA Court for an Advisory Opinion. Before the District Court of Reykjavík, the defendant made a reference to Protocol 35 and Art. 3 of the EEA Act. Concerning the applicability of the EEA Agreement, the Reykjavík District Court stated the following:

> Even if it would be concluded that Article 7(6) of Law No. 6/2002 would be inconsistent with Articles 11 or 36 of the EEA Agreement, such a conclusion would not have the consequence of not applying Article 7(6) of Law No. 6/2002 which was adopted based on constitutional processes. Such a result could, however, form the basis for liability, as provided for *inter alia* in a judgment of the Supreme Court of 16 of December 1999 [*Sveinbjörnsdóttir*]. For this reason, the plaintiff's claims which are based upon the argument that the said provision of Law No. 6/2002 violates Article 11 and 36 of the EEA agreement, is rejected.[60]

---

57 Björgvinsson (n. 15), pp. 122–23.

58 For example Líndal and Magnússon (n. 50), p. 176 and D.S. Tynes, "Ys og þys út af engu? Hugleiðingar um bókun 35 við samninginn um Evrópska efnahagssvæðið", 55 (2002) 3 *Úlfljótur* 473, 494–95.

59 Supreme Court Case No. 220/2005 of 6 April 2006, *JT International S.A. and Others v. The Icelandic State.*

60 Authors' translation.

Furthermore, concerning the applicability and effects of Directive 98/34 in light of non-implemented technical rules which was invoked by the defendant,[61] the District Court stated the following:

> Within the EU, rules concerning legal effects of EC law have had a considerable impact on the relationship between national rules and EU rules. Similar legal effects do not apply under Icelandic laws, as may be seen from the [*Sveinbjörnsdóttir*] ruling of the Supreme Court of 16 December 1999, where it was established that the EEA Agreement did not entail transfer of legislative power.[62]

The Supreme Court concluded the matter by finding that certain parts of the Tobacco Act were contrary to the Constitution, while other parts were not. Concerning the EEA Agreement, the Supreme Court did not rely on Art. 3 of the EEA Act or Protocol 35 at all, but confirmed the District Court's ruling on the issue. The Court did not explain that issue in any detail, however, irrespective of the fact that the case contained a potential conflict between timely and correctly implemented EEA rules (Art. 11 and 13 EEA) and other statutory norms (the Tobacco Advertising Act).

The *Alcohol Advertising* case is also relevant here – a criminal case concerning an advertisement for alcohol in breach of the total prohibition of alcohol advertisements found in Art. 20 of the Alcohol Act No. 75/1998.[63] The case effectively concerned the question as to whether a request for an Advisory Opinion should be made to the EFTA Court, since the defendant alleged that the prohibition was in conflict with Protocol 47 of the EEA Agreement.[64] The District Court of Reykjavík ruled against making such a referral, based on the following arguments:

> Cases of the same nature as this case have previously been dealt with by courts. In those cases the question has concerned whether Article 20 of the Alcohol Act was compliant with provisions of the Constitution, *inter alia* those concerning freedom of expression, property rights, and the principle of equality. Similarly, this case is about interpretation of Article 20 of the Alcohol Act and as to whether it is compliant with the Constitution, since laws adopted on the basis of constitutional processes, will not be set aside on any other ground. The EFTA Court will not deal with that type of legal interpretation. Therefore, it is not relevant to request an Advisory Opinion in this case.[65]

---

61 Directive 98/34 of the European Parliament and of the Council of 22 June 1998 laying down a procedure for the provision of information in the field of technical standards and regulations [1998] OJ L204/37.

62 Authors' translation.

63 Supreme Court Case No. 274/2006 of 24 May 2006, *Criminal proceedings against X*.

64 However, also mentioning Art. 36 EEA in its argumentation, although, not in the suggested questions.

65 This approach was confirmed in Supreme Court Case No. 60/2008 of 25 February 2008, *Criminal proceedings against X*, in which the Supreme Court overturned an order of a district

The Supreme Court confirmed the ruling, without adding any arguments of its own on the issue. Therefore, in this case, which also concerns (at least in principle) a conflict between implemented EEA rules and other statutory norms, neither Protocol 35 nor Art. 3 of the EEA Act seemed to play any role at all. At least materially, these cases therefore seem to paint a picture where Protocol 35 and Art. 3 of the EEA Act, as interpreted in the *Hörður Einarsson* case, are not deemed relevant. Emphasis is placed instead on an approach of the *lex posterior* nature, meaning in essence that the EEA rules will not supersede more recent statutory laws (hierarchically equal). Of course, it may be maintained that the fact, at least in the *Tobacco Advertisement* case, that it was finally dealt with on the basis of constitutional provisions made the questions of prevalence of EEA rules less relevant. Yet in the *Alcohol Advertising* case, similar constitutional arguments made by the District Court were not as convincing.

These ideas seemed to continue to evolve in more recent cases. First, in the *Biðskýlið í Njarðvík* case, the scope and nature of Art. 3 of the EEA Act was directly addressed and clarified by the Supreme Court.[66] The case was in essence a case concerning product liability where a child had suffered injury by consuming candy. Iceland had implemented Directive 85/374/EEC through Act No. 25/1991 on product liability.[67] In the case, the injured party had sued the supplier and the importer. Apart from liability for the producer and the importer as laid down in the Directive, Art. 10 of Act No. 25/1991 stipulated that the supplier should be directly liable to the injured party and subsequent suppliers for damage caused by a product defect. This provision, which aimed at increasing consumer protection, was similar to a provision in the Danish Product Liability Act that had been held by the ECJ to go beyond the fully harmonising provisions of Directive 85/374/EEC in the *Skov and Bilka* case, and therefore precluded.[68]

The Supreme Court stated that despite it being established that the Court of Justice had concluded that the provisions of Danish law on product liability providing for objective liability of the supplier in the same manner as Act No. 25/1991 were incompatible with Directive 85/374/EEC, it had to be observed

---

court judge on seeking an Advisory Opinion of the EFTA Court. In its judgment, the Supreme Court referred to its previous finding in the *Alcohol Advertising* case and submitted that the EFTA Court would not deal with a question concerning the compatibility of Article 20 of the Alcohol Act in the light of the Constitution. Furthermore, the Supreme Court pointed out that the EFTA Court had already given an answer to the suggested questions in Case E-04/04, *Pedicel AV v. Social og helsedirektoratet* [2005] EFTA Ct. Rep. 1. Authors' translation.

66 Supreme Court Case No. 79/2010 of 9 December 2010, *Biðskýlið í Njarðvík ehf. and CU 2 ehf. v. Írena Rut Sigríðardóttur.*

67 Council Directive 85/374/EEC of 25 July 1985 on the approximation of the laws, regulations and administrative provisions of the Member States concerning liability for defective products [1985] OJ L210/29.

68 Case C-402/03, *Skov Æg v. Bilka*, ECLI:EU:C:2006:6.

that the Directive itself was not part of Icelandic law. Furthermore, the Court held that:

> [A]ccording to Article 3 of Act No. 2/1993 on the European Economic Area, Icelandic statutes and regulations shall be interpreted, in so far as appropriate, in accordance with the EEA Agreement and the rules laid down therein. This interpretation entails, that the wording of the Icelandic legislation, shall as far as possible, to contain a meaning that falls within its scope and is the closest to be equivalent to the common rules that should apply in the EEA. However, the interpretation cannot lead to the wording of the Icelandic legislation being disregarded.[69] Article 10 of Act No. 25/1991 on direct liability of the supplier to the injured party of damages caused by a defect in a product, is unequivocally worded and allows for no flexibility in altering that liability through interpretation on the basis of Article 3 of Act No. 2/1993.[70]

This case has become the model case for the Supreme Court, referred to in later cases in order to demonstrate the scope (and limitations) of Art. 3 of the EEA Act, and in particular that it cannot lead to *contra legem* interpretation.[71] However, it also seems to mark the end of any hopes of viewing Art. 3 of the EEA Act as a proper implementation of Protocol 35. In that sense it demonstrates the close links between primacy and consistent interpretation, an issue raised further below. Art. 10 of the Product Liability Act was a statutory norm going against the fully harmonising provisions of the Product Liability Directive, which had also been implemented as a statutory norm. This issue had clearly been ruled upon in the *Skov and Bilka* case, which the Supreme Court was fully aware of. However, instead of blowing life into Art. 3 of the EEA Act in terms of requiring for EEA rules to prevail in this situation of conflict, the Supreme Court emphasised that it had no choice but to apply this clear provision of Art. 10 of the Product Liability Act.

---

69 Páll Hreinsson, the current Icelandic judge at the EFTA Court, has quoted this part as being, on the face of it, in compliance with the principle of consistent interpretation in EEA law. P. Hreinsson, "Samræmd EES-túlkun" 64 (2014) (3) *Tímarit lögfræðinga* 273, 291. Authors' translation.

70 Interestingly the District Court had ruled that an Advisory Opinion from the EFTA Court should be sought, since the defendant *Bíðskýlið í Njarðvik* had *inter alia* highlighted the presence and relevance of the *Skov and Bilka* case and the potential EEA-related rules to be interpreted, but the Supreme Court had rejected that request in its ruling in Case No. 195/2008 of 29 April 2008, by referring to the existence of the *Skov and Bilka* case (where, in the view of that party, the Danish model law, had been declared EU law compliant!). Authors' translation.

71 The meaning of the term "*contra legem*" was, for example, explained by Advocate General Bot in Case C-441/14, *Rasmussen*, ECLI:EU:C:2015:776, para. 68: "The Latin expression 'contra legem' literally means 'against the law' and must be understood as being an interpretation that contradicts the very wording of the national provision at issue." Further discussions on the scope and limits of Art. 3 of the EEA Act can be found in Hreinsson (n. 69).

In the context of these doubts about the compliance of Art. 3 of the EEA Act with Protocol 35, the statements from the EFTA Court in the *Hörður Einarsson* case should be revisited. The EFTA Court held in that case that it was not for the EFTA Court to "rule on the interpretation of national legislation" in proceedings brought under Art. 34 of the SCA.[72] However, the EFTA Court further observed that:

> Protocol 35 to the EEA Agreement provides direction for the resolution of conflicts between rules of EEA law and rules of national law. In adopting that Protocol, the EFTA States have undertaken to introduce, if necessary, a statutory provision to the effect that *EEA rules prevail in cases of possible conflict* between implemented EEA rules and other statutory provisions. The Court understands that Section 3 of the Icelandic EEA Act has been enacted to fulfil that undertaking. In the present proceedings, the Court has heard argument by the Plaintiff raising doubt about the sufficiency of Section 3 in that respect. In keeping with what was stated in paragraph 48 above, consideration and interpretation of that provision *fall to the national court*.[73]

A further step in the same direction, as reflected in the *Biðskýlið í Njarðvík* case, was taken in the *Flugastraumur* case.[74] This was another case dealing with a request for an Advisory Opinion, on the basis of the Advisory Opinion Act (see further discussion below). In essence, the case concerned a finance lease agreement between two Icelandic companies – a private company (Flugastraumur) and a bank (Landsbankinn hf.). The lease agreement was indexed to foreign currencies (so-called "currency basket"), although the loan itself and payments were seemingly in the Icelandic króna. The fall of the Icelandic economy and currency in the autumn of 2008 resulted in these type of agreements more than doubling in króna value, causing individuals and companies with low or no income in foreign currencies to suffer heavily. In its prior ruling in the *Currency loan* case,[75] the Supreme Court had ruled that indexing loan agreements in the Icelandic króna with foreign currencies was illegal, based on its reading of the Icelandic Act No. 38/2001 on interest rates and price indexation.

In the proceedings before the Reykjavík District Court, Flugastraumur asked the District Court to refer several questions to the EFTA Court concerning several EEA Acts of secondary nature,[76] the fundamental free movement

---

72 *Hörður Einarsson* (n. 38), para. 48.

73 Ibid., para. 51 (emphasis added).

74 Supreme Court Case No. 10/2013 of 24 January 2013, *Landsbankinn hf. v. Flugastraumur ehf.*

75 Supreme Court Case No. 92/2010 of 16 June 2010, *Óskar Sindri Atlason v. SP Fjármögnun hf.*

76 The following three secondary acts: (1) Commission Regulation (EC) No. 1725/2003 of 29 September 2003 adopting certain international accounting standards in accordance with Regulation (EC) No. 1606/2002 of the European Parliament and of the Council [2003] OJ L261/1; (2) Directive 2006/48 (EC) of the European Parliament and of the Council of

provisions in Arts. 36 and 40 EEA, and the compatibility of Act No. 38/2001 on interest rates and price indexation with the provisions that the Supreme Court had based its ruling on in the *Currency loan* case. Furthermore, Flugastraumur asked for specific questions concerning Protocol 35 and Art. 3 of the EEA Act to be referred to the EFTA Court, specifically in the light of its concerns that the former had not been correctly implemented by the latter.

In short, the District Court rejected this request in its entirety, since the case was mainly about whether "certain provisions of Icelandic statutory laws were applicable to their contract, and to the extent how the precedents of the Supreme Court should be interpreted in solving the dispute". The Supreme Court – on appeal concerning the issue of whether to refer – also rejected the request for an Advisory Opinion, on the following grounds:

> According to paragraph 1 of Article 2 of Law No. 2/1993 the main part of the EEA Agreement has legal effect in Iceland. In Article 40 it is stated that within the framework of the provisions of this Agreement, there shall be no restrictions between the Contracting Parties on the movement of capital belonging to persons resident in EC Member States or EFTA States and no discrimination based on the nationality or on the place of residence of the parties or on the place where such capital is invested. Annex XII. contains the provisions necessary to implement this Article. In Article 3 of Law No 2/1993 it is provided that Icelandic statutes and regulations shall be interpreted, in so far as appropriate, in accordance with the EEA Agreement and the rules laid down therein.[77]

Thereafter, the Supreme Court cites the precedent from the *Biðskýlið í Njarðvík* case recalling that the meaning of Art. 3 of the EEA Act requires interpretation "as far as possible" in compliance with EEA rules, but that such a requirement could not go as far as obliging an interpretation *contra legem* of "Icelandic statutory laws". The Court then argued that on the basis of its interpretation of Arts. 12 and 13 of the Act No. 38/2001 on interest rates and price indexation in the *Currency loan* case, these rules contained a clear prohibition that could not be set aside through interpretation on the basis of Art. 3 of the EEA Act. This applied both for Art. 36 and Art. 40 EEA. There were therefore no reasons for requesting an Advisory Opinion in this case. As for the question of Protocol 35 and Art. 3 of the EEA Act, the Supreme Court referred to its previous conclusions on the applicability of Arts. 36 and 40 EEA, and stated that it could not see that the answers to the questions posed would have any independent meaning in the case "which is pursued between two legal persons, since the case will be resolved

---

14 June 2006 relating to the taking up and pursuit of the business of credit institutions [2006] OJ L177/1; (3) Council Directive 88/361 EEC of 24 June 1988 for the implementation of Article 67 of the Treaty [1988] OJ L178/5.

77 Authors' translation.

on the basis of Icelandic rules of laws". Finally, and interestingly, the Supreme Court made a reference to Art. 31 of the SCA. It emphasised the substance of that provision, which concerns the ESA's competence to initiate infringement proceedings and to bring an EFTA State before the EFTA Court in the event that the state does not comply with the Authority's views.[78]

The final important case in this line of case-law from the Supreme Court is *Gunnarsson*.[79] The case concerned Mr Gunnarsson and his spouse, who were domiciled in Denmark but subject to tax in Iceland. Mr Gunnarsson argued that the rules in the Icelandic Tax Code No. 90/2003 were in breach of Art. 28 EEA, Art. 1 of Directive 90/365 and Art. 7(1)(b) and (d) of Directive 2004/38, as they prevented him from pooling his tax credits with his (Icelandic) wife, which he could have done if domiciled in Iceland.[80] Mr Gunnarsson argued *inter alia* that in line with Protocol 35, as implemented by Art. 3 of the EEA Act, correctly implemented EEA rules should have priority over the Tax Code. Furthermore, Mr Gunnarsson emphasised that, on the basis of the explanatory notes to Art. 3 of the EEA Act, EEA rules should be regarded as *lex specialis* when conflicting with posterior national acts, and therefore that the EEA rules should take priority.

On appeal to the Supreme Court, and at that Court's own initiative, the case was referred to the EFTA Court for an Advisory Opinion. In its ruling, the EFTA Court emphasised the importance of consistent interpretation in the following way: "The Court notes that the provisions of Directive 90/365 and Directive 2004/38 form part of the EEA Agreement, and must, as far as possible, be given an interpretation that renders them consistent with the provisions of the EEA Agreement *and general principles of EEA law*".[81] Finally, the EFTA Court ruled that there was no need to rule on the applicability of Art. 28 EEA in the light of its main answer, which was that:

> It is not compatible with Article 1 of Directive 90/365/EEC and Article 7(1)(b) and (d) of Directive 2004/38/EC that an EEA State does not give spouses who have moved to another EEA State the option of pooling their personal tax credits in connection with the assessment of income tax, whereas they would be entitled to pool

78 Interestingly, the Authority's proceedings referred to above, were first initiated with a letter of formal notice on the 11 November 2011, to which Iceland did not submit any observations, as concerning compliance with Protocol 35 to the EEA Agreement. The Supreme Court's reference to Art. 31 SCA might indicate that the Court is suggesting that ESA's infringement proceedings should proceed to the next level.

79 Supreme Court Case No. 92/2013 of 14 October 2014, *The Icelandic State v. Atli Gunnarsson*.

80 Council Directive 95/365 (EEC) of 28 June 1990 on the right of residence for employees and self-employed persons who have cease their occupational activity [1990] OJ L180/28; Directive 2004/38/EC of the European Parliament and of the Council of 29 April 2004 on the right of citizens of the Union and their family members to move and reside freely within the territory of the Member States [2004] OJ L158/77.

81 Case E-26/13, *The Icelandic State v. Atli Gunnarsson* [2014] EFTA Ct. Rep. 254, para. 83 (emphasis added).

> their personal tax credits if they lived in the home state, in a situation where one of them receives a pension from the home state, and that pension constitutes all or nearly all of that person's income, while the other spouse has no income.[82]

The ruling of the Supreme Court was of a different nature. Just like the EFTA Court, the Supreme Court pointed out that direct taxation falls within the competence of the EFTA States, but that they would have to exercise that competence consistently with the EEA Agreement. However, the Supreme Court highlighted that in this light the EEA Agreement contained no specific, detailed rules on how spouses' pooling of taxes should be. The Supreme Court held that when implemented, the Directives had not altered the Tax Code (seemingly Art. 7 of the Directive 2004/38 was not implemented with specific new measures in this respect). Thereafter, the Court made a reference to Art. 3 of the EEA Act and the *Biðskýlið í Njarðvík* and *Flugastraumur* cases, explaining the limitations of this rule of interpretation – i.e. that it may not lead to situations where "explicitly worded provisions of Icelandic law are side-stepped". Thereafter, the Supreme Court noted the Advisory Opinion of the EFTA Court, and that the EFTA Court had ruled that the provisions of the Tax Code were contrary to the provisions of the Directive. The Supreme Court stated, however, that since the Directives had not altered the Tax Code when they were implemented, Art. 3 of the EEA Act could not on the basis of rules of interpretation be given the flexibility to neglect "clear and unconditional rules of the Tax Code, that had been adopted on the basis of constitutional processes, cf. the instructions in Art. 40 of the Constitution, which requires that no tax may be imposed, altered or withdrawn, unless with a clear basis in statutory law".[83]

Consequently, and on the basis of direct claims to this effect made by Mr Gunnarsson, the Supreme Court dealt with the question of *state liability*, which it based on its ruling in the *Sveinbjörnsdóttir* case. The Supreme Court recalled from that case that if it is not possible to keep national law in compliance with the EEA Agreement, the state may be held liable for losses caused. In the view of the Court, it was to be read from the EFTA Court's Advisory Opinion that Mr Gunnarsson had been granted certain rights, effective as of 1994, when the EEA Agreement – including Directive 90/365 – was incorporated. The rights in question under Directive 90/365 were maintained in Directive 2004/38. However, after a thorough assessment – where precedents from the EFTA Court and the ECJ in terms of assessing the condition of "serious breach" were considered "meagre" – the Supreme Court concluded that the breach of the

82 Ibid., para. 28 of the EFTA Court's judgment.

83 It should be highlighted that the District Court of Reykjavík "managed" to interpret the Tax Code in compliance with the Directives involved, but that was before the case had been referred to the EFTA Court for an Advisory Opinion, since that only happened post appeal, before the Supreme Court. Authors' translation.

state was not sufficiently serious. In this regard, the Court *inter alia* referred to the views of the ESA which had changed its opinion during the proceedings as compared to its previous letter of formal notice: it was not obvious that rules on direct taxations were to be affected by the said Directives. At any rate, the state had not breached EEA rules intentionally. This was seemingly a fair analysis, but the final outcome was that the rules of the Directive were not given any effect in the case at hand. Subsequently, the Icelandic tax code has been amended with the purpose of complying with the requirements of the Directive.

4.3. SUMMARY OF THE RECENT CASE-LAW OF THE SUPREME COURT ON PROTOCOL 35 AND ART. 3 OF THE EEA ACT

In the cases discussed above, it seems clear that while the Supreme Court has applied Art. 3 as a "mere" rule of interpretation, it has excluded the application of that provision as entailing any elements of priority for EEA rules – at least in situations of posterior statutory norms in conflict with EEA rules.[84]

Flugastraumur is certainly in the same vein as the *Biðskýlið í Njarðvík* case, seemingly excluding the possibility of any primacy effects for EEA rules which conflict with posterior Icelandic statutory norms. Posterior statutory norms are less clear in the *Gunnarsson* case, since the Supreme Court is arguing for lack of implementing measures, but effectively the Supreme Court is upholding its understanding of the purpose and limitation of Art. 3 of the EEA Act as a rule of interpretation, rejecting arguments of the applicant (Gunnarsson) for primacy effects through Protocol 35.

What is worrying with the *Flugastraumur* case, and potentially also the *Tobacco Advertisement* and *Alcohol Advertising* cases, is that these rulings mean in effect that the fundamental free movement principles forming the core of the EEA Agreement are neutralised, since they are not applied in situations of *posterior* (restrictive) statutory norms. Given the wide scope of the fundamental freedoms, it is more likely than not that at least the statutory norms in the *Flugastraumur* and *Tobacco Advertisement* cases would fall within the ambit of those rules as *restrictions*. However, since the fundamental freedoms are not

---

84 Furthermore, in Supreme Court Case No. 552/2013 of 28 October 2013, *Commerzbank AG v. Kaupþing hf.* and Case No. 120/2014 of 8 May 2014, *De Nederlandsche Bank N.V. v. LBI hf.*, the Supreme Court found that Article 99(2)(j) of Act No. 161/2002 on Financial Undertakings (which implemented Directive 2001/24 of the European Parliament and of the Council of 4 April 2001 on the reorganisation and winding up of credit institutions [2001] OJ L125/15) could not lead to the disregarding of the provision of Article 100 of Act. No. 21/1991 on Bankruptcy etc. This was noted by ESA in a letter of formal notice of 6 July 2016 in Case No. 77038, where the Authority concluded *inter alia* that by not applying Art. 99(2)(j) of Act No. 161/2002, the Icelandic Supreme Court had failed to give full effect to the principle, set out in Protocol 35, that in the event of a conflict between an implemented EEA rule and another statutory provision, the EEA rule must prevail.

regarded as applicable, the relevant question – of whether they would have been justified restrictions – is not answered at all. Given the circumstances in these cases, that would in fact most likely have been the situation. It is also noteworthy that this assessment is often undertaken at a pre-proceedings stage (i.e. when a request for an Advisory Opinion is being dealt with), thereby possibly excluding the applicability of EEA norms before a material ruling takes place.

The reluctance to implement and apply a primacy principle may have its constitutional explanations. However, the fact that the courts refrain from applying the fundamental principles of free movement in the cases of apparent restrictions to these, even where the restrictions stem from posterior statutory norms, is worrying. Given this reluctance, it is perhaps no coincidence that many of the cases where the EFTA Court has been forming the principle of consistent interpretation as a general principle of EEA law stem from Advisory Opinion requests from Iceland.[85]

Finally, it should be recalled that the Supreme Court has suggested two alternatives in the situations where Art. 3 of the EEA Act is not being applied due to posterior or clear and unconditional statutory norms, namely (a) infringement proceedings on the basis of Art. 31 of the SCA (*Flugastraumur*) and; (b) state liability, based on the Supreme Court's ruling in *Sveinbjörnsdóttir* (*Gunnarsson*). Both of these alternatives have certain merits, but also drawbacks. As to the infringement proceedings on the basis of Art. 31 of the SCA, it should be recalled that those type of proceedings are at the sole prerogative of the ESA, and no external party may require or control such proceedings.[86] Concerning the principle of state liability, it should be recalled that the conditions of liability are quite narrowly construed, as demonstrated in the *Gunnarsson* case.[87]

5. ICELANDIC COURTS AND THE ADVISORY OPINIONS OF THE EFTA COURT

As has been seen in several of the cases discussed so far, Art. 34 SCA permits national courts and tribunals in the EFTA States to request an *Advisory Opinion*

---

85 For example: *Karlsson* (n. 6), ibid.; *Merrill Lynch* (n. 32), para. 42; *Irish Bank* (n. 8), para. 124.

86 See e.g. Case 247/87, *Star Fruit*, ECLI:EU:C:1989:58 and the rulings of the EFTA Court in the cases E-02/13, *Bentzen Transport v. ESA* [2013] EFTA Ct. Rep. 802, paras. 40–41 and Case E-02/16, *Gerhard Spitzer v. ESA* [2016] EFTA Ct. Rep. 513, para. 22.

87 See also Tobias Lock "Is private enforcement of EU law through state liability a myth? An assessment 20 years after Francovich", 49 (2012) *Common Market Law Review* 1675–1702, where he demonstrated that only one-third of cases of this nature in the UK finally end up recognising state liability, and only one-quarter of cases in Germany. In Iceland, over a period of more than 22 years, state liability has only been acknowledged once – in the case of *Sveinbjörnsdóttir*.

of the EFTA Court on the interpretation of EEA law.[88] Under this system of judicial dialogue, which is in many ways similar to the preliminary ruling procedure found in Art. 267 TFEU the goal is to ensure, as far as possible, a homogenous interpretation of EEA law in the EFTA States.[89] This contribution briefly discusses how the procedure of Art. 34 SCA has been applied by Icelandic courts since 1994.

For the period 1 January 1994 to October 2017, Icelandic courts have made 36 requests for Advisory Opinions of the EFTA Court (whereas the total number of Advisory Opinion cases is 124).[90] It is noteworthy that during the last few years the number of requests from Icelandic courts has increased significantly – as is evident from the latest annual reports of the Court. It is somewhat difficult to explain the increased number of requests, but one factor is certainly the aftermath of the financial crisis that hit Iceland in the autumn of 2008. The crisis raised many complicated legal issues and much litigation, and national courts referred questions to the EFTA Court in several of the cases which ensued.[91]

These statistics on the number of Advisory Opinion requests from Icelandic courts must to some extent be viewed in the light of two critical aspects found in Icelandic legislation. First, under the Advisory Opinion Act and Act No. 120/2016 on Public Procurement, only the district courts, the Supreme Court, the Labour Court and the Complaint Committee for Public Procurement are permitted by law to refer questions to the EFTA Court. This arrangement is certainly narrower than the one provided for in Art. 34(2) SCA, where it is stated that a "court or tribunal" in an EFTA State can ask the EFTA Court for an Advisory Opinion. The EFTA Court has interpreted the term "court or tribunal" in a broad manner, the result being that it covers both national courts and administrative bodies in the EFTA States, given that certain criteria are met.[92] In Iceland, several administrative bodies have the potential to meet that criteria, but have so far made no requests, most likely due to lack of a national legal basis for doing so.[93]

---

88 Further information about Art. 34 SCA and the Advisory Opinions of the EFTA Court (i.e. concerning its similarities and especially differences in comparison to Article 267 TFEU) can for example be found in the *Handbook of EEA law*, C. Baudenbacher (ed.), "The EFTA Court: Structure and Tasks" (Springer, 2015) 139.

89 Consolidated Version of the Treaty on the Functioning of the European Union [2012] OJ C326/47.

90 According to statistics available on the EFTA Court's website: <http://www.eftacourt.int/fileadmin/user_upload/Files/AnnualReports/Statistics_EFTA_Court__as_of_October_2017__004_.pdf>.

91 E.g. Case E-17/11, *Aresbank* [2012] EFTA Ct. Rep. 916; *Merrill Lynch* (n. 32); and Joined Cases E-08/15 and E-09/15, *Financial Services Compensation Scheme Ltd. and De Nederlandsche Bank N.V. v. The Depositors' and Investors' Guarantee Fund (TIF)* [2015] EFTA Ct. Rep. 586.

92 E.g. Joined Cases E-3/13 and E-20/13, *Fred Olsen and Others v. the Norwegian State* [2014] EFTA Ct. Rep. 400, para. 59–60.

93 However, it has been argued that despite these limitations found in Icelandic legislation, administrative bodies can nevertheless refer questions to the EFTA Court where the relevant

Second, in accordance with Art. 1(3) of the Advisory Opinion Act, parties to a given case are provided with the chance to appeal an order made by a district court judge on seeking – or not seeking – an Advisory Opinion from the EFTA Court to the Supreme Court.[94] On the basis of this particular (and peculiar) setting, the Supreme Court may be called upon to evaluate the existence of an EEA element in the case and whether that element needs to be further clarified. It should be pointed out that in these cases the rule on interpretation in Art. 3 of the EEA Act is very much present, and may be one of the reasons upon which the Supreme Court finally bases its decision to refer the case to the EFTA Court.

During the period 1994 to 2016, the Supreme Court has been called upon to give judgment on the basis of Art. 1(3) of the Advisory Opinion Act in a total of 45 cases. The legal relationship in these cases varies, i.e. they are both of "vertical" (the state v. private party) and "horizontal" (private party v. private party) nature. What is interesting, is that in the vertical cases, the party who appeals an order of a district court judge *on seeking* an Advisory Opinion is usually the state (be it for example the prosecutor's office, or the State Attorney).[95] While on the other hand, it is normally private parties who appeal an order of a district court on *not seeking* an Advisory Opinion – even though private parties are well aware of the fact that obtaining an Opinion of the EFTA Court can be both costly and time-consuming.[96] Indeed, the state seemingly appeals almost every order in which a district court judge decides to send a request to Luxembourg.

---

criteria are fulfilled. See e.g. K.B. Björgvinsson, "Samvinna EFTA-dómstólsins og íslenskra dómstóla", 68 (2015) 1 *Úlfljótur* 73, 85, and Ó.B. Rúnarsson, "Hvers konar stofnunum er heimilt að biðja EFTA-dómstólinn um ráðgefandi álit?", 11 (2015) 1 *Tímarit Lögréttu* 266, 289.

94 Furthermore, on an appeal to the Supreme Court in such circumstance, the Court has in several cases amended questions submitted by the district court judge. In *Irish Bank* (n. 8) the EFTA Court reacted to this practice of the Supreme Court, paras. 53–70.

95 For example, the following cases: Supreme Court Case No. 132/1998 of 1 April 1998, *The Icelandic State and the Pharmaceutical Pricing Committee v. The Federation of Icelandic Trade*; Supreme Court Case No. 497/1999 of 13 January 2000, *The State Debt Management v. Fjárfestingarbanki atvinnulífsins hf.*; Supreme Court Case No. 276/2004 of 7 September 2004, *The Icelandic State v. Omega Farma ehf.*; Supreme Court Case No. 212/2005 of 7 June 2005, *The Icelandic State v. HOB-vín ehf.*; Supreme Court Case No. 60/2008 (n. 65); Supreme Court Case No. 132/2010 of 23 March 2010, *The Icelandic State v. Þór Kolbeinsson*; Supreme Court Case No. 38/2011 of 7 February 2011, *The Central Bank of Iceland v. Pálmi Sigmarsson*; Supreme Court Case No. 612/2011 of 8 December 2011, *The Icelandic State v. Vín Tríó ehf.*; Supreme Court Case No. 37/2012 of 24 January 2012, *The State Alcohol and Tobacco Company of Iceland (ÁTVR) v. HOB-vínum ehf.*; Supreme Court Case No. 220/2015 of 27 April 2015, *The Icelandic State v. Ferskar kjötvörur ehf.*

96 For example, the following cases: Supreme Court Case No. 274/2006 (n. 63); Supreme Court Case No. 669/2012 of 30 November 2012, *Criminal proceedings against X*; Supreme Court Case No. 677/2013 of 21 November 2013, *The Icelandic Nature Conversation Association and Others v. The Icelandic Road and Coastal Administration*; Supreme Court Case No. 429/2014 of 15 July 2014, *Criminal proceedings against X and Others*; Supreme Court Case No. 267/2014 of 29 April 2014, *Stapi Pension Fund v. The Icelandic State*; Supreme Court Case No. 119/2014 of 26 February 2014, *The Icelandic Nature Conversation Association and*

In the 45 cases where the Supreme Court has been called upon to give a judgment on the basis of Art. 1(3) of the Advisory Opinion Act, the following scenario emerges: (i) the Supreme Court confirmed an order of a district court on requesting an Advisory Opinion in 14 cases (31 per cent); (ii) the Supreme Court overturned an order of a district court on requesting an Advisory Opinion in 4 cases (9 per cent); (iii) the Supreme Court confirmed an order of a district court on not requesting an Advisory Opinion in 25 cases (56 per cent); (iv) the Supreme Court overturned an order of a district court on not requesting an Advisory Opinion in 2 cases (4 per cent).

As can be seen *inter alia* from these statistics, the Supreme Court has in 9 per cent of cases (4 cases) *overturned* an order of a district court judge on seeking an Advisory Opinion.[97] Even though this may be seen as a rather small percentage, it is nevertheless quite clear that this practice – and perhaps moreover the *mere existence* of the appeal system itself – may be viewed as incompatible with Art. 3 EEA and hinders the aim of Art. 34 SCA, i.e. establishing a direct judicial dialogue between the EFTA Court and courts *on all levels* in the EFTA States.[98]

On the basis of Art. 3 of the Advisory Opinion Act, the Supreme Court may on its own motion refer questions to the EFTA Court. The Supreme Court has requested an Advisory Opinion in 8 cases,[99] but also refused to do so in a number of other judgments.[100] One of the reasons given by the Supreme

---

Others v. The Icelandic Road and Coastal Administration; Supreme Court Case No. 39/2015 of 16 January 2015, *Criminal proceedings against X*; Supreme Court Case No. 291/2015 of 5 May 2015, *Criminal proceedings against X*; Supreme Court Case No. 784/2016 of 15 December 2016, *S and Others v. Silicor Materials Inc., the Icelandic State and Others*.

97 The following cases: Supreme Court Case No. 195/2008 (n. 70); Supreme Court Case No. 60/2008 (n. 65); Supreme Court Case No. 276/2004 (n. 95); Supreme Court Case No. 660/2010 of 18 February 2011, *Frjálsi fjárfestingarbankinn hf. v. Sveinn Óskar Sigurðsson and Samsidanith Chan*. In the following two cases, the Supreme Court overturned an order on not seeking an Advisory Opinion: Supreme Court Case No. 527/2014 of 18 August 2014, *Icelandair ehf. and Isavia ohf. v. the Competition Authority and Wow air ehf.*; Supreme Court Case No. 451/2012 of 27 August 2012, *Yngvi Harðarson v. Askar Capital hf.*

98 For example Case C-210/06, *Cartesio*, ECLI:EU:C:2008:723, where the ECJ was quite critical against a similar appeal system in Hungary. See also the views of S. Magnússon, "Málskot ákvarðana um að leita ráðgefandi álits EFTA-dómstólsins frá sjónarhóli EES-réttar", 62 (2009) 1 *Úlfljótur* 5, 18–19, who argues that the system of appeal is most likely in breach of EEA law.

99 Case E-5/98, *Fagtún ehf. v. Byggingarnefnd Borgarholtsskóla, the Government of Iceland, the City of Reykjavík and the Municipality of Mosfellsbær* [1999] EFTA Ct. Rep. 51; Case E-06/07, *HOB-vín ehf. v. Faxaflóahafnir sf.* [2008] EFTA Ct. Rep. 128; Case E-17/11, *Aresbank S.A. v. Landsbankinn hf., the Financial Supervisory Authority and Iceland* [2012] EFTA Ct. Rep. 916; *Jan Anfinn Wahl* (n. 45); Case E-22/13, *Íslandsbanki hf. v. Gunnar V. Engilbertsson* [2013] EFTA Ct. Rep. 826; *Gunnarsson* (n. 81); Case E-29/15, *Sorpa bs. v. The Competition Authority* [2016] EFTA Ct. Rep. 825; Case E-05/17, *Merck Sharp & Dohme Corp. v. The Icelandic Patent Office* (at the time of writing the case is still pending).

100 For instance in: Supreme Court Case No. 426/1998 of 6 May 1999, *Criminal proceedings against Gunnsteinsson and Others*; Supreme Court Case No. 812/2013 of 29 January 2013, *Sigurður Sigurðsson and Guðfríður Einarsdóttir v. Arion banki hf.*; Supreme Court Case No. 805/2013 of 10 February 2014, *Páll Böðvar Valgeirsson and Sigríður Jónsdóttir v. Arion banki hf.*

Court for not referring questions to the EFTA Court is that the case at hand will be "resolved solely on the basis of Icelandic law", or in criminal cases that "the criminal liability of the defendant will be determined in accordance with Icelandic law".[101]

Overall, it can be submitted that Icelandic courts are relatively willing to refer questions to the EFTA Court. However, the above-mentioned provisions in the Advisory Opinion Act are likely to undermine the goal of Art. 34 SCA. Indeed, it is hard to justify the need for the Supreme Court to review and even overturn a decision where a district court judge has come to the conclusion that an Advisory Opinion from the EFTA Court is needed for the purpose of reaching a decision in the case before him/her. Should the request be unnecessary or ill-founded, the EFTA Court itself can rule on the admissibility of the request.

6. SUBSTANTIVE ANALYSIS OF THE CASE-LAW AND MAIN STATISTICAL OUTCOME

The following section will endeavour to portray both the statistical outcome along with a more substantive analysis of the case-law. As mentioned in section 2, 115 cases were collected in total.[102] These 115 cases can roughly be divided into two main categories. The *first category* contains 55 cases where the Supreme Court has given an *úrskurð* (ruling) on the basis of the Advisory Opinion Act. Most of these cases – along with some statistics – were already discussed in section 5 above, and will therefore not be given any further consideration. The *second category* consists of 60 cases where the Supreme Court has given a judgment on a particular legal issue which does not fall under the first category of cases (some of these cases were discussed in section 4 above, e.g. *Biðskýlið í Njarðvík* and *Gunnarsson*). Naturally, these cases cover a broad range of legal issues. However, most of these cases concern the interplay between EEA law and Icelandic law – and most have a relevant connection to the principle of consistent interpretation. These 60 cases can be divided as follows with regard to their relevance on matters concerning consistent interpretation: (i) 46 cases where the Supreme Court has interpreted national law in accordance with EEA law; (ii) 10 cases where the Supreme Court has for certain reasons refused to interpret national law in conformity with EEA law; and (iii) 4 cases where the

[101] For example the following cases (which were brought before the Supreme Court under Art. 1(3) of the Advisory Opinion Act): *Flugastraumur* (n. 74) and Supreme Court Case No. 291/2015 (n. 96).

[102] In addition, the present authors also collected 18 cases which were of some importance, e.g. due to the fact that an Advisory Opinion of the EFTA Court had previously been sought, but the case, before the Supreme Court, was finally decided without any recourse to the principle of consistent interpretation. These 18 cases were therefore not included here.

Supreme Court has both agreed and refused to interpret national law in the light of EEA law. The following discussion will focus on some of the cases in more detail and provide further statistical analysis.

6.1. THE HORIZONTAL AND VERTICAL ANGLE ON THE RELATIONSHIP BETWEEN PARTIES

In cases which belong to the second category discussed above, the horizontal or vertical legal relationship between the disputing parties was as follows:

1. 46 cases where the Supreme Court *applied principles of conforming interpretation* (individual v. the state – 13 cases (28 per cent); company v. the state – 4 cases (9 per cent); company v. company – 20 cases (43 per cent); company v. individual – 9 cases (20 per cent)).
2. 10 cases where the Supreme Court *refused to interpret national law in conformity with EEA law* (individual v. the state – 3 cases (30 per cent); individual v. company – 2 cases (20 per cent); company v. company – 5 cases (50 per cent)).
3. 4 cases where the Supreme Court has *both has agreed and declined* to interpret national law in conformity with EEA law (company v. the state – 1 case (25 per cent); company v. individual – 2 cases (50 per cent); individual v. the state – 1 case (25 per cent)).

As these statistics show, the legal relationship varies – i.e. they are both of a horizontal and vertical nature. In at least one case, consistent interpretation was applied clearly to the benefit of the state vis-à-vis the individual (*vertical*).[103] This was the so-called *deCODE* case,[104] which concerned criminal procedures against a former employee of a subsidiary of the company deCODE Genetics, due to unauthorised copying of 29 files from the company's database. When interpreting the term "database" in the Icelandic Copyright Act, the Supreme Court emphasised that the protection of databases was there due to an amendment based on the Database Directive.[105] It was in fact the purpose of these provisions of the Copyright Act to implement this Directive. Therefore, according to the Supreme Court, in this criminal case, the preparatory works of the amending act and Art. 3 of the EEA Agreement (duty of sincere cooperation) should be considered.

---

[103] Hreinsson (n. 69) 278.

[104] Supreme Court Case No. 107/2007 of 18 October 2007, *Criminal proceedings against Jesus Vicente Sainz Maza.*

[105] Directive 96/9/EC of the European Parliament and of the Council of 11 March 1996 on the legal protection of databases [1996] OJ L77/20.

Furthermore, the Court highlighted that the definition of the term "database" was comparable to the one found in the Database Directive. In addition, the Supreme Court noted that the ECJ had interpreted the term broadly in its case-law (albeit without citing specific cases). Consequently, the Court concluded that the documents that had been copied fell within the definition. Finally, the Court also defined the term "substantial investment" which was a condition for criminal liability, and stated that "This interpretation is in compliance (or 'consistent with') with the understanding of Art. 7 of Directive 96/9/EC". Thus, the final outcome was that – owing to an interpretation of national law in light of the Database Directive (at least so some extent) – the employee was sentenced on the ground of unauthorised copying of a "database", which was the result of "substantial investment".

6.2. THE COMPOSITION OF THE SUPREME COURT

According to Art. 7(1) of the Judiciary Act No. 15/1998, the President of the Supreme Court may decide that three or five judges sit on the bench in each case. However, in exceptionally important cases, the President can decide that more than five judges handle a case (in such circumstances the usual rule is that seven judges take a place on the bench).[106] Accordingly, the number of judges in each case depends on its importance. Understandably, it is quite rare for the bench to be composed of seven judges.

According to the statistical data compiled for this contribution, the Supreme Court was composed as follows in the 60 cases that belong to the second category mentioned above:

1. 46 cases *where the principle of consistent interpretation played a role* (7 judges in 11 cases (24 per cent); 5 judges in 16 cases (35 per cent); 3 judges in 19 cases (41 per cent)).
2. 10 cases *where the Supreme Court refused to interpret national law in conformity with EEA law* (7 judges in 1 case (10 per cent); 5 judges in 3 cases (30 per cent); 3 judges in 6 cases (60 per cent)).
3. 4 cases where the Supreme Court both *refused and agreed to interpret national law in the light of EEA law* (5 judges in 4 cases (100 per cent)).

What is noteworthy, is that in 35 cases out of 60 cases (58 per cent), the Supreme Court is either sitting in chambers of five or seven judges, which normally is the exception rather than the rule. This fact seems to indicate that the level of importance in cases in which consistent interpretation has been dealt with

[106] Information on the Supreme Court's website: <http://www.haestirettur.is>.

in relation to EEA law is rather high. The 11 cases in which the Court was composed of seven judges are all fairly recent and touch on a more or less similar legal issue,[107] namely the interpretation of the term "deposit" in Art. 1(1) of Directive 94/19/EC on deposit guarantee schemes.[108] In all of these 11 cases, consistent interpretation was applied. One of these cases, *Aresbank*,[109] will be further discussed below. In another case, the *Arnarsson* case, where the Court was composed of seven judges, an application of consistent interpretation was refused.[110] The *Arnarsson* case will be further analysed in section 6.3.5 below.

6.3. THE APPLICATION OF THE PRINCIPLE OF CONSISTENT INTERPRETATION

The following section will provide more detailed analyses of the cases where the Supreme Court has applied the principle of consistent interpretation. Furthermore, the concept and conceptual basis of the principle of consistent interpretation will be analysed. Thereafter, the section will explain how the Supreme Court has reacted to the Advisory Opinions of the EFTA Court in cases where consistent interpretation was involved. In addition, the section contains a specific discussion on the role of *travaux préparatoires* under Icelandic law – i.e. the role of the preparatory work as a tool for legal interpretation, with a specific focus on the "will of the legislator" that has traditionally been significantly weighted in Nordic law when interpreting statutory norms. Finally, an overview of cases where the Supreme Court has – for several different reasons – refused to interpret domestic law in conformity with EEA law will be provided.

6.3.1. *General Remarks*

Before proceeding further, four general introductory remarks will be made. First, as regards the question of language, or discourse, on *how* the duty of interpreting national law in the light of EEA law is described in Icelandic, the terms "consistent" or "conforming" interpretation (*skýring/túlkun til samræmis* or *samræmd túlkun/skýring*) seem to be most accurate. This contribution has mainly used the term "consistent interpretation".

[107] The following nine Supreme Court cases, all rendered on 28 October 2011: Case No. 276/2011; Case No. 277/2011; Case No. 300/2011; Case No. 301/2011; Case No. 310/2011; Case No. 311/2011; Case No. 312/2011; Case No. 313/2011; and Case No. 314/2011. In addition, the two following cases: Supreme Court Case No. 169/2011 of 17 January 2013, *Aresbank S.A. v. Landsbankinn hf.* and Supreme Court Case No. 722/2012 of 22 March 2013, *BNAP S.A.R.L. v. Kaupþing hf.*

[108] Directive 94/19/EC of the European Parliament and of the Council of 30 May 1994 on deposit guarantee schemes [1994] OJ L135/5.

[109] Supreme Court Case No. 169/2011 *Aresbank* (n. 107).

[110] Supreme Court Case No. 129/2001 of 25 October 2001, *Arnarsson*.

Second, the 60 cases involving consistent interpretation do not in general seem to concern one policy area more than another. In recent years, however, quite a few cases have concerned financial services or, more particularly, cases that are related to the aftermath of the severe financial crisis that hit Iceland in the autumn of 2008.

Third, in a number of cases, the Supreme Court has in essence interpreted Icelandic statutory law diligently in compliance with EEA law, but without specific reference to any principle of consistent interpretation or Art. 3 of the EEA Act. The *deCODE* case, discussed above, is a good example of a situation where the Supreme Court has done so. As demonstrated below, there are a number of other cases of this nature, i.e. where the Court has clearly been interpreting national law "in conformity" with the EEA Agreement, but without referring to Art. 3 of the EEA Act or any principle(s) of consistent interpretation.

Fourth, it seems clear that the principle of consistent interpretation is not limited to EEA Acts of a secondary nature, even if the majority of the cases concern EEA directives. This is perhaps understandable, particularly given the background of Art. 3 of the EEA Act, which by its reference to interpretation "in conformity with the EEA Agreement and the rules based thereon" clearly concerns all EEA Acts. This also seems to be the understanding of the EFTA Court.[111]

Furthermore, in the 50 cases in which consistent interpretation has taken place, several of the cases do not mention the term at all. Therefore, this is a fairly wide category. This contribution has therefore designated an importance level for these cases (high – medium – low), of which 16 of them may be deemed of "high importance". These would be cases where the principle of consistent interpretation is clearly being applied. As discussed above and further analysed below, this would in particular be the case when Art. 3 of the EEA Act is being invoked and applied.

Finally, this contribution has examined to some extent what method of interpretation the Supreme Court applied in the 60 cases where consistent interpretation played a part. In Iceland, as in most other countries with similar legal systems, methods of interpretation are usually not bound by law, meaning that the interpretation and application of the law has generally been left to the judiciary (although courts when interpreting the law must respect general principles of law, etc.).[112] In the Supreme Court's case-law (i.e. the Court's case-law

---

111 For example *Criminal proceedings against A* (n. 42), para. 39.

112 As Björgvinsson has noted, Art. 3 of the EEA Act would be an exception from this practice as this statutory provision clearly obliges national courts to interpret national law in conformity with EEA law. See further D.Þ. Björgvinsson, *Lögskýringar* (JPV útgáfa, 2008), p. 35. Art. 3 of the EEA Act does not however refer to any particular methods of interpretation that should be taken into account for this purpose. Furthermore, and as discussed above, the Supreme Court has abandoned the *lex specialis* approach taken in *Hörður Einarsson*.

in general – not limited to the cases with which this contribution is concerned), the following methods of interpretation can for example be identified:[113] (i) literal interpretation, where the focus on the written text and ordinary language is deemed important; (ii) historical interpretation, which seeks out the original meaning of the legal norm; (iii) teleological interpretation, where a provision is interpreted in the light of its aim or spirit; and (iv) systematic interpretation, where a provision is interpreted with regard to its systematic context with other provisions within the same Act, or in the light of its place within the general scheme of the legislative system.

The interpretative methods involved in the 46 cases where consistent interpretation was applied are divided as follows: nine cases where a reference is made to Art. 3 of the EEA Act; one case where a reference is made to Art. 3 of the EEA Act and general Icelandic methods of statutory interpretation; one case where a reference is made to Art. 3 of the EEA Act and a case from the ECJ; one case where a reference is made to case-law of the EFTA Court, Art. 3 of the EEA Act, and general methods of statutory interpretation; 29 cases where a reference is made to general methods of statutory interpretation; one case where a reference is made to the case-law of the EFTA Court and the ECJ; two cases where a reference is made to case-law of the EFTA/EU Courts, in addition to general methods of statutory interpretation; and two cases where a reference is made to case-law of the ECJ in addition to general methods of statutory interpretation.

In the 10 cases where consistent interpretation has been rejected, the Supreme Court referred to Art. 3 of the EEA Act in seven cases; to the case-law of the EFTA Court and the Court of Justice in one case; and to general principles of Icelandic law in two cases. For the four cases where the Supreme Court has both rejected and applied consistent interpretation, the Court, for example, referred to Art. 3 of the EEA Act in three cases and in one case to general methods of statutory interpretation.

6.3.2. *Reactions to the Advisory Opinions of the EFTA Court on Consistent Interpretation*

Contrary to what may be read from some of the more recent decisions of the ECJ,[114] the EFTA Court has never directly required the Icelandic Supreme

113 For example Björgvinsson (n. 112), and R.R. Spanó, *Túlkun lagaákvæða* (Codex Publishing, 2007).

114 For example Case C-306/12, *Spedition Welter*, ECLI:EU:C:2013:650, para. 32, where the ECJ stated the following: "... in circumstances such as those in the case in the main proceedings, where national legislation reproduced word for word the provision of Article 21(2) of the directive, the referring court is required, taking the whole body of domestic law into consideration and applying the interpretative methods recognised by domestic law, to interpret national law in a way that is compatible with the interpretation

Court (or any Icelandic court, as far as the present authors are aware) to apply consistent interpretation in a specific way.[115] The messages from the EFTA Court are fairly clear, such as, for example, in the case of *Atli Gunnarsson*:

> The Court notes that the provisions of Directive 90/365 and Directive 2004/38 form part of the EEA Agreement, and must, *as far as possible*, be given an interpretation that renders them consistent with the provisions of the EEA Agreement *and general principles of EEA law*.[116]

The EFTA Court arguably went further in the case of *Engilbertsson*,[117] citing the *Dominguez* case of the Court of Justice:[118]

> In that regard, it is for the referring court to ascertain what the national rules applicable to the dispute before it are and to do whatever lies within its jurisdiction, *taking the whole body of domestic law into consideration and applying the interpretative methods recognised by domestic law, with a view to ensuring* that Article 6(1) of the Directive is fully effective and achieving an outcome consistent with the objective pursued by it.[119]

Nevertheless, neither of these cases may be read as requiring consistent interpretation beyond what would be normally possible and acceptable in the light of national procedural and constitutional requirements.

In fact, several of the above listed cases have had a fundamental impact on the Icelandic legal order, and the Supreme Court has followed suit in its rulings subsequent to the Advisory Opinions in important cases such as *Sveinbjörnsdóttir* and *Hörður Einarsson*.[120] The same is true in cases such as *Merrill Lynch* and *Aresbank* (discussed below), that have become model cases in numerous rulings of the Supreme Court. Similar results may be seen in the cases of *Jan Anfinn Wahl* (discussed further below), and even (albeit less firmly) in *Irish Bank*. However, as discussed above, in its (material) ruling in the case of *Atli Gunnarsson*,

---

given to the directive by the Court." See further C.N.K. Franklin, "Limits to the Limits of the Principle of Consistent Interpretation? Commentary on the Court's Decision in Spedition Welter" 40 (2015) 6 *European Law Review* 910–24.

115 In this respect it is of some importance to note that an Advisory Opinion of the EFTA Court is strictly speaking not binding upon the referring national court. However, due to the duty of sincere cooperation provided for in Art. 3 EEA and the goal of ensuring homogeneity, national courts in Iceland generally follow the Advisory Opinions of the EFTA Court.

116 *Gunnarsson* (n. 81), para. 83 (emphasis added).

117 Case E-25/13, *Gunnar V. Engilbertsson v. Íslandsbanki hf.* [2014] EFTA Ct. Rep. 524.

118 *Dominguez* (n. 3).

119 *Engilbertsson* (n. 117), para. 163 (emphasis added).

120 As mentioned in section 5 above, the total number of references to the EFTA Court for an Advisory Opinion from Icelandic courts between 1 January 1994 and October 2017 is 36 cases. Of these cases, at least 16 of them concerned consistent interpretation, e.g. *Sveinbjörnsdóttir, Hörður Einarsson, Merrill Lynch, Aresbank, Jan Anfinn Wahl, Þór Kolbeinsson* and *Gunnar V. Engilbertsson*.

the Supreme Court felt that the limits of consistent interpretation had been reached – despite the advice from the EFTA Court.

The same holds partially true for the ruling of the Supreme Court in the case of *Engilbertsson*.[121] In this case, the Supreme Court explicitly stated – with a reference to Art. 3 of the EEA Act, as interpreted in the *Biðskýlið í Njarðvík* case – that it could not interpret a clear, national statutory provision in compliance with Directive 87/102/EEC,[122] noting that the Directive was not legally binding in the case at hand.[123] It is interesting that the Supreme Court even refers to Art. 3 of the EEA Act in this context, i.e. as concerning a Directive that seemingly was not applicable in the case – but that may possibly be explained by the (complex) factual circumstances in this case.[124] Interestingly, however, when interpreting the national implementing measures of Directive 93/13/EEC concerning unfair contractual terms,[125] the Supreme Court claimed that it was interpreting those "in compliance with the Directive" that had been interpreted by the EFTA Court in its Advisory Opinion.

In relation to the above discussion on how the Supreme Court has reacted to the Advisory Opinions of the EFTA Court, the highly interesting case of *Þór Kolbeinsson* is of relevance.[126] The case concerned Mr Kolbeinsson, who argued that he had sustained damages as a result of a wrongful interpretation of EEA law by the Supreme Court of Iceland. In its Advisory Opinion, the EFTA Court found that:

> The issue of State liability for losses resulting from incorrect application of EEA law by national courts falls outside the scope of this question. The Court observes, however,

---

121 Supreme Court Case No. 160/2015 of 13 May 2015, *Gunnar V. Engilbertsson v. Íslandsbanki hf.*

122 Council Directive 87/102/EEC of 22 December 1986 for the approximation of the laws, regulations and administrative provisions of the Member States concerning consumer credit [1986] OJ L042/48.

123 Its applicability in the case was unclear, emphasised by the EFTA Court in *Engilbertsson* (n. 117), paras 55–56: "However, in the case at hand, having regard to the subject-matter of the dispute, it is unclear whether, and if so to what extent, Directive 87/102/EEC concerning consumer credit and/or its relationship with Directive 93/13/EEC requires an interpretation. Consequently, the Court will limit its answers to an analysis of the provisions of Directive 93/13/EEC and will not provide guidance on the interpretation of Directive 87/102/EEC. It is the task of the referring court to assess whether it considers that sufficient guidance is given by the Advisory Opinion or whether it appears to it that a further request to the Court is required."

124 The present authors are not aware of a case where national courts are asked to interpret a directive prior to expiry of the deadline for its implementation. In fact, the majority of directives incorporated into the EEA Agreement, will have to be implemented as soon as the EEA Joint Committee decision is adopted, given the long time it takes to incorporate new Acts into the EEA Agreement.

125 Council Directive 93/13/EEC of 5 April 1993 on unfair terms in consumer contracts [1993] OJ L95/29.

126 Case E-02/10, *Þór Kolbeinsson v. The Icelandic State* [2009–2010] EFTA Ct. Rep. 234.

> that if States are to incur liability under EEA law for such an infringement as alleged by the Plaintiff, the infringement would in any case have to be manifest in character, see for comparison Köbler, cited above ...[127]

Although the EFTA Court's answer is more of an *obiter dictum*, it makes clear that the EEA principle of state liability applies to an infringement of EEA law by a decision of a national court adjudicating at last instance. In a similar vein as the judgment of the ECJ in the *Köbler* case,[128] decisions of the highest courts of the EFTA States in which EEA law are interpreted and applied in an incorrect manner may therefore in principle lead to state liability.

Finally, Mr Kolbeinsson's application for damages was rejected by the Icelandic courts, mainly on the ground that under Icelandic procedural law it was not possible to re-examine a case already decided by the Supreme Court (i.e. *res judicata* effects of judgments).[129] In a Reasoned Opinion of 20 January 2016,[130] the ESA submitted that the Icelandic procedural rules on *res judicata* which hindered a successful application for damages due to a wrongful interpretation of EEA law by the Supreme Court, were contrary to EEA law (i.e. the Icelandic State had failed to fulfil its obligation arising from the general principle of state liability under the EEA Agreement).

6.3.3. *The Conceptual Basis and the General Scope of the Principle of Consistent Interpretation*

As stated above, the principle of consistent interpretation is very much present in the case-law of the Supreme Court. Furthermore, as discussed in section 4, the principle – and its limitations – have emerged through the Supreme Court's application of Art. 3 of the EEA Act in the cases of *Sveinbjörnsdóttir, Hörður Einarsson, Biðskýlið í Njarðvík, Flugastraumur* and *Atli Gunnarsson*. In principle, Art. 3 of the EEA Act, as interpreted by the Supreme Court in *Biðskýlið í Njarðvík*, has all the potential to be compliant with the EEA principle of consistent interpretation.[131]

---

127 Ibid., para. 77.

128 Case C-224/01, *Köbler*, ECLI:EU:C:2003:513.

129 In a similar vein, the Supreme Court in Case No. 604/2008 of 18 June 2009, *Pétur Þór Sigurðsson v. The Icelandic State* rejected a claim for damages for a violation of the ECHR on the ground that Article 116 of the Act on Civil Procedure precluded a claim for damages based on the liability of the state for an erroneous judgment of the Supreme Court, as the subject matter in the judgment in question had been finally decided and could thus not be subject to further revision. See further ESA's letter of formal notice to Iceland in Case No. 75004 of 17 June 2015 concerning state liability for breach of EEA law by a court adjudicating at last instance.

130 Reasoned Opinion of ESA of 20 January 2016 in Case No. 75004, decision no. 016/16/COL.

131 A similar view is taken by Hreinsson (n. 69), p. 291.

The Supreme Court has handed down a substantial number of judgments where it has directly or indirectly adhered to the principle of consistent interpretation. Examples of the *indirect* approach (as opposed to direct reference to the principle of consistent interpretation or Art. 3 of the EEA Act) would for example include the *de-CODE* case, discussed above. Another case of a similar nature, where the Court is clearly seeking a conforming interpretation, is the *Jan Anfinn Wahl* case.[132] In this case, where a Norwegian citizen was denied admission to Iceland due to his membership of the Hells Angels Motorcycle Club, the question arose as to how to define the concept of *ordre public*. After the Supreme Court had defined that concept, it stated that "Conventional definition of European law [arguably covering EU and EEA law] on the terms public policy and public security also lead to the same conclusion". The Court had held that Art. 27(1) of Directive 2004/38 "was the model" for the Icelandic rules involved.

Another good example of where the Supreme Court applies consistent interpretation without referring to either the principle of consistent interpretation or Art. 3 of the EEA Act is the *Kaupthing* case.[133] Here, the Supreme Court stated that the background and the purpose of Art. 9 of the 1st Company law Directive,[134] was "to be kept in mind when interpreting Act No. 2/1995 (Icelandic Company Law Act)".

However, the best example of this type of indirect consistent interpretation is the Supreme Court's ruling in the *Merrill Lynch* case.[135] In this case, the Supreme Court explicitly made a reference to and relied on the EFTA Court's interpretation of Art. 30 of Directive 2001/24 in Case E-28/13, yet without mentioning either the principle of consistent interpretation or Art. 3 of the EEA Act.[136] This precedent was subsequently followed in a number of cases by the Supreme Court.[137] Despite the fact that in *deCODE*, *Jan Anfinn Wahl*, *Kaupthing* and *Merrill Lynch* the Supreme Court construed national law in accordance with EEA/EU law without explicitly referring to the legal (or conceptual) basis for such interpretation, the effects are nevertheless similar.

---

132 Supreme Court Case No. 191/2012 of 17 October 2013, *Jan Anfinn Wahl v. The Icelandic State*.

133 Supreme Court Case No. 201/2011 of 10 June 2011, *Kaupthing Singer & Friedlander Limited v. Kaupþing banki hf.*

134 First Council Directive 68/151/EEC of 9 March 1968 on co-ordination of safeguards which, for the protection of the interest of members and others, are required by Member States of companies within the meaning of the second paragraph of Article 58 of the Treaty, with a view to making such safeguards equivalent throughout the Community [1968] OJ L65/8.

135 Supreme Court Case No. 250/2015 of 21 April 2015, *Kaupþing hf. v. Merrill Lynch International*.

136 Directive 2001/24 of 4 April 2001 (n. 84); *Merrill Lynch* (n. 32).

137 For example: Supreme Court Case No. 228/2015 of 17 April 2015, *Kaupþing hf. v. Merrill Lynch International and Cambridge Securities Inc.*; Supreme Court Case No. 251/2015 of 21 April 2015, *Kaupþing hf. v. Bank of America Merrill Lynch International Ltd.* Furthermore, the following two cases: Supreme Court Case No. 681/2015 of 12 November 2015, *Western Asset Management Company v. Kaupþing hf.*; and; Supreme Court Case No. 685/2015 of 16 November 2015, *BNP Paribas S.A. v. Kaupþing hf. and Brains Inc. Ltd.*

The clearest recent example of the *direct* approach, where a clear reference is made to Art. 3 of the EEA Act and the case-law of the EFTA Court, is the *Aresbank* case.[138] This case was referred to the EFTA Court for an Advisory Opinion (Case E-17/11),[139] and in its (material) ruling, the Supreme Court was called upon to interpret the term "deposit" as referred to in Directives 94/19 and 97/9,[140] on deposit insurance schemes.[141] The Court made a reference to the fact that the national norms at issue had been set to comply with Iceland's international law obligations under the EEA Agreement. Thereafter, the Court made a reference to Art. 3 of the EEA Act, and also in detail to the Advisory Opinion of the EFTA Court, and relied almost entirely on that Opinion in its reasoning. This case has also been used as a precedent in subsequent rulings, such as in *Eksportfinans*.[142]

A comparison should also be made between the Icelandic principle of consistent interpretation and the one that has been developed by the EFTA Court. In fact, the Supreme Court has not made a specific reference to the case-law of the EFTA Court or that of the Court of Justice laying down a specific EEA and EU law principle to this effect. Indeed, according to our case-law analysis the Supreme Court has not in a single case so far made a reference to the principle of consistent interpretation as developed by the EFTA Court. It is submitted that given the strong status of the principle, as a well-honed statutory norm under Art. 3 of the EEA Act – the very Act that incorporated the EEA Agreement into Icelandic law – the Supreme Court has found no reason to make such references.[143]

However, it is by no means excluded that the Supreme Court would possibly do so, for example embracing some of the more recent elements of the principle, as interpreted by the EFTA Court, which arguably go further than Art. 3 of the EEA Act – such as, for example, when required to "consider any relevant element

138 *Aresbank* (n. 107).

139 *Aresbank*, i.e. the Advisory Opinion (n. 91).

140 Directive 97/9/EC of the European Parliament and of the Council of 3 March 1997 on investor-compensation schemes [1997] OJ L84/22.

141 Which has rocked the foundations of Iceland's economy from many angles for several years following the crisis, and culminated in Case E-16/11, *Icesave* [2013] EFTA Ct. Rep. 4. See further, G.T. Petursson and A.S. Sigurbjörnsdóttir, "The outer reach of state obligations under deposit guarantee schemes: What can we learn from the Icesave case?" (2013) *European Policy Analysis*. The article can be found at <http://www.sieps.se/en/publications/2013/the-outer-reach-of-state-obligations-under-deposit-guarantee-schemes--what-can-we-learn-from-the-icesave-case-201318epa/>.

142 Supreme Court Case No. 555/2013 of 14 October 2013, *Glitnir hf. v. Eksportfinans ASA*.

143 Furthermore, when explaining the Supreme Court's complete lack of direct references to the EEA principle of consistent interpretation, it has to be kept in mind that the principle arrived much later on the scene than Art. 3 of the EEA Act. It was not until quite recently, or in 2013 in the *Irish Bank* case (n. 8), that the EFTA Court formally confirmed that consistent interpretation was to be seen as a *principle* of EEA law.

of EEA law, whether implemented or not" (*Karlsson*);[144] or with a reference to Art. 3 EEA to go "as far as possible" in its interpretation (*Criminal proceedings against A*);[145] and that obligations of consistent interpretation "arise on the day the respective legal act is made part of the EEA Agreement" (*Liechtensteinische Gesellschaft für Umweltschutz*).[146] Given the Supreme Court's view on consistent interpretation in situations of posterior statutory norms conflicting with older EEA norms, however, it may have some issues in seeking to adhere to the view of the EFTA Court in *Merrill Lynch*:

> Moreover, it is inherent in the objectives of the EEA Agreement, as well as in recital 15 in its preamble and Articles 1 and 3 EEA, that when a national court applies domestic law, *whether adopted before or after the directive*, it is bound to interpret national law within its competence in conformity with EEA law.[147]

In its (material) ruling in the *Merrill Lynch* case of 21 April 2015,[148] the Supreme Court ruled that it would only apply the Icelandic legislation that was finally amended (after ESA's intervention) to comply with the Directive in line with the interpretation of the EFTA Court, to facts of law arising subsequently to that amendment. That sounds like a rational approach in the given circumstances, and in light of principles of legal certainty and foreseeability. Note should also be taken of the ruling of the Supreme Court in *Akureyrarbær*,[149] where it interpreted *older* national law (Act No. 28/1991 on gender equality) in compliance with Directive 75/117/EEC (which came into force with the EEA Agreement in 1994).[150]

Finally, as concerning the method of or methodology in applying the principle of consistent interpretation, a general reference can be made to what has been stated above and also to section 4, where it was articulated how the principle of primacy or priority of EEA norms when in conflict with national norms has been effectively diminished in the case-law of the Supreme Court. That fact, coupled with the fact that the principle of direct effect is not a part of EEA law, makes the role and importance of consistent interpretation even greater.

---

144 *Karlsson* (n. 6).

145 *Criminal proceedings against A* (n. 42), para. 39.

146 Case E-03/15, *Liechtensteinische Gesellschaft für Umweltschutz v. Gemeinde Vaduz* [2015] EFTA Ct. Rep. 512, para. 74.

147 *Merrill Lynch*, i.e. the Advisory Opinion (n. 32), para. 42 (emphasis added).

148 *Merrill Lynch*, i.e. the Supreme Court's ruling (n. 135).

149 Supreme Court Case No. 11/2000 of 31 May 2000, *Akureyrarbær v. The Equal Right Complaints Committee*.

150 Council Directive 75/117/EEC of 10 February 1975 on the approximation of the laws of the Member States relating to the application of the principle of equal pay for men and women [1975] OJ L45/19.

6.3.4. *The Will of the Legislator and the Role of* Travaux Préparatoires

In the *Björnekulla*[151] case, the ECJ held that the duty of a national court to interpret domestic law in accordance with EU law applied notwithstanding any contrary interpretation which might arise from the legislative preparatory works regarding the national rule in question.[152] While this view taken by the ECJ may very well be accepted in relation to the Member States of the EU, which have undeniably transferred parts of their legislative powers to the EU, the same could hardly be said to apply to the EFTA States, due to the fact that the EEA Agreement did not entail any transfer of legislative powers as discussed earlier with reference to Art. 7 EEA and Protocol 35.[153]

As far as Iceland is concerned, it is generally accepted by judges and the legal community more generally, that legislative preparatory work can be useful and even prove necessary when interpreting legal provisions.[154] It has been maintained that judges seem to be quite willing to inspect explanatory notes and other relevant data in order to find out the so-called "intention" or "will" of the legislator.[155] Similarly, the Supreme Court has in its case-law quite frequently relied on legislative preparatory works when interpreting statutory norms.[156]

In this light the ruling in *Merrill Lynch* is worth recalling.[157] In this case, the Reykjavík District Court stated *inter alia* the following, which upon appeal was confirmed by the Supreme Court:

> In the view of this court it has to be taken into account, that it is generally recognised that a one-sided view of the governments of the EFTA States has no meaning when interpreting EEA law. Therefore, it is clear, that the legislators' understanding of EEA rules cannot be decisive when it comes to interpreting those rules. In such circumstances, it may, however, be verified whether the will of the legislator indicates a clear intention to violate EEA rules, if another understanding of EEA rules will be adopted on behalf of those institutions who have the final saying on the interpretation of the rules of the EEA Agreement.[158]

Thereafter, the District Court further explained that national rules should generally be interpreted in accordance with the EEA Agreement under Art. 3 of the Act No. 2/1993 and that national law should, however, only be interpreted in conflict with the EEA Agreement if the legislator's will to that effect was clear and unambiguous.

---

151 Case C-371/02, *Björnekulla Fruktindustrie AB v. Procordia Food AB*, ECLI:EU:C:2004:275.
152 Ibid., para. 13.
153 Hreinsson (n. 69), pp. 293–94.
154 Björgvinsson (n. 112), p. 49 and Snævarr (n. 22), p. 400.
155 Snævarr (n. 22), p. 400.
156 Ibid.
157 Supreme Court Case No. 231/2015 of 17 April 2015, *LBI hf. v. Merrill Lynch International.*
158 Authors' translation.

Accordingly, it is submitted that views in Icelandic legislative preparatory works may raise limits to the principle of consistent interpretation. However, this type of a scenario is perhaps of more theoretical nature – at any rate, such clear intentions to breach EEA law would have far-reaching consequences for the Icelandic State.

6.3.5. *The Limits to the Principle of Consistent Interpretation*

Although the EFTA Court has laid emphasis on the application of the principle of consistent interpretation by national courts in the EFTA States, it has still recognised that the principle – as a rule requiring interpretation – is subject to certain limitations. The approach taken by the EFTA Court is indeed natural, and in fact unavoidable. There are of course limitations as to how far a legal text can be construed, not to mention the vital issue of respecting the boundaries between the judiciary and the legislator under the principle of the separation of powers.[159] Thus, the EFTA Court has frequently stated in its case-law that national courts are bound to interpret domestic law "as far as possible" in accordance with EEA law.[160]

The EFTA Court has not explained, however, exactly what is meant by the expression "as far as possible". Nevertheless, having regard to the relevant case-law of the ECJ, for example the *Pupino* case,[161] it is submitted that the expression must mean that national law should not be interpreted *contra legem*. Thus, if a legal provision is written in a clear manner it will not be interpreted otherwise. Furthermore, as the ECJ stated for example in *Kolpinghuis Nijmegen*,[162] the application of the principle is limited by general principles of law, in particular the principles of legal certainty and non-retroactivity.[163] This final section will discuss several cases where the Supreme Court has refused to interpret domestic law in the light of EEA law with a reference to the limitations of the principle of consistent interpretation.

As can be seen from the previous discussion on cases such as *Biðskýlið í Njarðvík*, *Flugastraumur* and *Engilbertsson*, the Supreme Court has not considered itself able on the basis of Art. 3 of the EEA Act to interpret Icelandic law in conformity with EEA law if the wording of the former is unambiguous. Therefore, under the current situation, it seems settled case-law that Art. 3 of

159 In this respect, see for example the Opinion of Advocate General Bot in the *Rasmussen* case (n. 71), para. 68, where he stated that "The Court has acknowledged that *contra legem* interpretation represents a limit on the obligation of consistent interpretation, since it cannot require national courts to exercise their interpretative competence to such a point that they substitute for the legislative authority."

160 For example Case E-13/11, *Granville Establishment* [2012] EFTA Ct. Rep. 400, para. 52.

161 Case C-105/03, *Pupino*, ECLI:EU:C:2005:386, para. 47.

162 Case C-80/86, *Kolpinghuis Nijmegen*, ECLI:EU:C:1987:431.

163 Ibid., para. 13.

the EEA Act will not be applied in order to grant EEA rules indirect effect by means of *contra legem* interpretations of national law. This practice seems to be *prima facie* in full compliance with the "as far as possible" expression used by the EFTA Court.[164]

In this context it is interesting to compare the current application of Art. 3 of the EEA Act (i.e. no *contra legem* interpretation) and the Supreme Court's case-law in the 1990s on the ECHR. As far as the ECHR is concerned, the Supreme Court clearly indicated that it would be willing to use far-reaching methods of interpretation in order to bring national law in line with the obligations undertaken by the Icelandic State. That was the situation in *Þorbjörn Gunnarsson,*[165] in which the Supreme Court interpreted clear provisions of the then existing Act No. 74/1974 on Criminal Procedure in conformity with Art. 6(3)(e) ECHR.[166] The result was that the defendant in the case, who did not speak Icelandic, was granted free assistance from a court interpreter, even though Icelandic procedural rules clearly stated that if the defendant was found guilty (which the Supreme Court found him to be), he himself had to bear the litigation cost, including the cost of an interpreter.

It has been pointed out that the wording of the Icelandic and ECHR provisions were so far apart that it was difficult – if not impossible – to reach a conforming solution through interpretation.[167] Consequently, the Supreme Court could be seen as either (i) applying a *contra legem* interpretation to a domestic legal provision for the purpose of safeguarding international obligations under the ECHR, or (ii) for the same reason, applying Art. 6(3)(e) of the ECHR directly as a source of law which prevailed over the said provision of national law.[168] Whichever view is taken, the case certainly illustrates the Supreme Court's willingness to fulfil certain international commitments, in this situation the ECHR.

It can be questioned whether the Court's ruling in this case exemplifies some distinction in the way (or the willingness) the Supreme Court gives effect to the ECHR and EEA law. At least it is clear that under the current standard of *Biðskýlið í Njarðvík*, it is hard to imagine the Supreme Court interpreting national law in conformity with EEA law in a similarly far-reaching way. Why the Supreme Court seems to make a difference here on methods of interpretation of

164 Hreinsson (n. 69), p. 291.

165 Supreme Court Case No. 494/1991 (n. 26).

166 This provision of the ECHR provides that everyone charged with a criminal offence should have the right to free assistance of an interpreter if the person in question cannot understand or speak the language used in court.

167 Björgvinsson (n. 112), pp. 282–83.

168 Ibid. At this point in time the ECHR had not been made part of Icelandic statutory law, but that happened in 1994 when the ECHR was incorporated into Icelandic law by Act No. 62/1994. Its provisions can therefore be directly invoked in court proceedings as domestic legislation.

national law between the ECHR and EEA law is not clear, bearing in mind that both the ECHR and the EEA Agreement are established to give certain rights to individuals, even fundamental human rights.

However, the *Árnason* case allows for an interesting (and perhaps new) development when it comes to consistent interpretation of EEA law.[169] Four individuals, all being former employees of *Landsbanki Íslands hf.*, were prosecuted for having violated (*inter alia*) Art. 117 of Act No. 108/2007 on Securities Transaction, which prohibited market manipulation. Due to an incorrect implementation of Directive 2003/6/EC,[170] the Securities Transaction Act provided for an exemption clause (which laid down several grounds of justification of market manipulation) in a different manner than stipulated in the provisions of the Directive. In short, the difference was that the exception clause in the Securities Transaction Act was applicable in more limited circumstances than according to the Directive. Notwithstanding the clear wording of the Securities Transaction Act in this respect, the Supreme Court interpreted the exemption clause in the Securities Transaction Act as having the same meaning and scope as in the provisions of the Directive. Consequently, it seems like the Supreme Court in this criminal case applied an interpretation *contra legem* in order to ensure that the defendants could rely on rights granted to them in EEA law. Interestingly, the Supreme Court made no reference to Art. 3 of the EEA Act or any principle of consistent interpretation in reaching this conclusion (therefore using the indirect approach discussed above).[171]

A highly interesting case (yet of a different nature) is the controversial *Arnarsson* case, in which firmly established case-law in Iceland was challenged in the light of EEA law.[172] The plaintiff had suffered an injury in a car accident as a passenger with an intoxicated driver, and brought proceedings against an insurance company due its refusal to pay compensation. According to domestic case-law dating back to 1969, the Supreme Court had taken the view that passengers who knew, or must have known, that they had accepted a ride from an intoxicated driver, forfeited their right to any compensation. The plaintiff relied on the EFTA Court's Advisory Opinion in the Norwegian *Finanger* case,[173] and argued that the case-law of the Supreme Court was incompatible with the EEA Motor Vehicle Directives.[174] Further, that the Icelandic State, with

---

169 Supreme Court Case No. 842/2014 of 4 February 2016, *Criminal proceedings against Árnason and Others*.

170 Directive 2003/6/EC of the European Parliament and of the Council of 28 January 2003 on insider dealing and market manipulation (market abuse) [2003] OJ L96/16.

171 The ruling of the Supreme Court in *Árnason* was recently endorsed in Supreme Court Case No. 498/2015 of October 2016, *Criminal proceedings against Sigurðsson and Others*.

172 Supreme Court Case No. 129/2001 (n. 110). A discussion on this case can also be found in S. Magnússon, "Icelandic Courts" in C. Baudenbacher, *The Handbook of EEA Law* (n. 88), p. 285.

173 Case E-01/99, *Storebrand Skadeforsikring AS v. Veronika Finanger* [1999] EFTA Ct. Rep. 119.

174 Council Directive 72/166 EEC of 24 April 1972 on the approximation of the laws of the Member States relating to insurance against civil liability in respect of the use of motor

respect to Art. 3 of the EEA Act, had undertaken to construe all national law – including case-law – in conformity with EEA law.

The Supreme Court firstly reasoned that the Advisory Opinion in the Norwegian *Finanger* case was not directly applicable in the case, due to dissimilarities between the Icelandic law on Motor Vehicles Insurance and the Norwegian equivalent. Second, the Supreme Court stated that the Icelandic rules on liability and risk taking were not in conflict with the Motor Vehicle Insurance Directives (referring *inter alia* to the *Ferreira* case).[175] However, with a reference to national law,[176] the Supreme Court overruled its own stable and consistent case-law regarding liability for passengers of intoxicated drivers (the result being that the plaintiff received compensation), but without any reference to Art. 3 of the EEA Act, which had been invoked by the plaintiff.[177]

The *Arnarsson* case demonstrates an interesting situation where the origin of the national rule being challenged in the light of EEA law does not stem from the legislator, but has instead been established and developed solely by the courts. It is clear that in these circumstances the courts may be reluctant to apply the principle of consistent interpretation to overrule stable precedents. In this context, it is however interesting to note that the ECJ has stressed that "the requirement to interpret national law in conformity with EU law entails the obligation for national courts to change its established case-law, where necessary, if it is based on an interpretation of national law that is incompatible with the objectives of a directive".[178]

Apart from cases such as *Biðskýlið í Njarðvík* and *Flugastraumur*, the Supreme Court has also defined other limits of consistent interpretation in a more traditional manner, where general principles of law and fundamental rights prevent national law from being interpreted in accordance with EEA law. The following cases, two of which are in the area of criminal law, demonstrate this point.

In the *Baugur I* case,[179] X was prosecuted for having provided wrong information in a financial statement which made him subject to criminal

---

vehicles, and to the enforcement of the obligation to insure against such liability [1972] OJ L103/1; Second Council Directive 84/5/EEC of 30 December 1983 on the approximation of the laws of the Member States relating to insurance against civil liability in respect of the use of motor vehicles [1983] OJ L8/17; Third Council Directive 90/232/EEC of 14 May 1990 on the approximation of the laws of the Member States relating to insurance against civil liability in respect of the use of motor vehicles [1990] OJ L129/33.

175 Case C-348/98, *Mendes Feirreira*, ECLI:EU:C:2000:442.

176 For example the Icelandic Traffic Act No. 50/1987.

177 The District court, on the contrary, with a reference to the "obligations of international law, to interpret national law in compliance with EEA law" found that the old precedents of the Supreme Court had to be overruled.

178 Case C-441/14, *Rasmussen*, ECLI:EU:C:2016:278, para. 33. As confirmed e.g. in Case C-554/14, *Ognyanov*, ECLI:EU:C:2016:835.

179 Supreme Court Case No. 181/2006 of 25 January 2007, *Criminal proceedings against Jóhannesson and Others.*

liability under Art. 43 of Act No. 144/1994 on Financial Statements. The Supreme Court, being composed of five judges, stated the following:

> The aforesaid provision of Article 43 of Act No. 144/1994, which the defendant is accused of having violated, stated that the duty to specify in explanations with the financial statement the amount of certain loans. In interpreting the meaning of the last-mentioned word it is inevitable to take into account that in this case it is solely being relied on in order to determine whether the defendant can be found guilty of criminal conduct. Therefore this word will not be given a broader meaning than its wording implies regardless of whether the provision was intended another aim than that interpretation, as could for instance be concluded on the basis of the legislative preparatory works where it was stated that it was to be consistent with Article 43(1)(13) of the Directive of the Council of the European Union 78/660/EC.[180]

Hence, by applying the method of interpretation which was the most favourable to the defendant (literal interpretation instead of a broad interpretation), the Supreme Court concluded that it would not be possible to interpret the then applicable Art. 43(1) of Act No. 144/1994 in conformity with Art. 43(1)(13) of Directive 78/660/EEC,[181] despite the fact the *travaux préparatoires* stated that the Act in question was supposed to be consistent with the said Directive. The reason, according to the Supreme Court, is that by applying consistent interpretation in this case, would have established *an additional act of offence*, which was not stipulated in Art. 43(1) of Act No. 144/1994.[182]

Another interesting example is the *Truck Driver* case.[183] The defendant, a truck driver, was prosecuted for having driven his truck for over a period of seven days and therefore violated rules on the so-called "driving and resting time". According to the prosecution, this conduct of the driver was held to be subject to a criminal liability under Art. 1 of the then applicable Administrative Act No. 136/1995, along with Council Regulation (EEC) No. 3820/85, in conjunction with the then in force Art. 100 of the Icelandic Traffic Act No. 50/1987. The EEA Act in question, Regulation No. 3820/85, was implemented into Icelandic law with the aforesaid Administrative Act No. 136/1995. The last-mentioned Act was adopted on the basis of the Traffic Act No. 50/1987.

What was unusual in this case is that the offence, i.e. not respecting the "driving and resting time", was not described in either the Administrative Act

---

180 Authors' translation.

181 Fourth Council Directive 78/660/EEC of 25 July 1978 based on Article 54(3)(g) of the Treaty on the annual accounts of certain types of companies [1978] OJ L222/11.

182 Hreinsson (n. 69), pp. 296–97.

183 Supreme Court Case No. 251/2004 of 28 October 2004, *Criminal proceedings against X*. A discussion on this case can also be found in Hreinsson (n. 69), pp. 295–96, and M.E. Méndez Pinedo and Ó.Í. Hannesson, *The Authority of European Law: Exploring Primacy of EU Law and Effect of EEA Law from European and Iceland Perspectives* (Codex Publishing, 2012), pp. 191–92.

No. 136/1995 or in the Traffic Act No. 50/1989. Instead, the description of the offensive act was to be found only in the relevant EU/EEA regulation. Taking this into account, the Supreme Court stated *inter alia* the following: "Accordingly, there seems to be no clear legal ground for punishment in this case which could be deemed compatible with Article 69(1) of the Constitution. As such, the appealed judgment of the district court on finding the defendant not guilty shall be confirmed."[184] Thus, with a reference to Art. 69(1) of the Constitution,[185] the Supreme Court concluded that no criminal liability could be imposed on the defendant, due to the fact that the act of offence in question had not been stipulated in the Icelandic legislation. Finding the defendant guilty in this case would therefore have violated the said provision of the Constitution as well as arguably some fundamental principles of criminal law, such as *nullum crime sine lege* (*no crime without law*) and *nulla poena sine lege* (no penalty without law).

The *Stjörnugrís* case also shows how constitutional rights and the principle of legality can raise limits to the application and effectiveness of EEA law.[186] The case evolved around a dispute between *Stjörnugrís* (a private company) and the Icelandic State, as to whether the Minister of Environment was entitled to adopt a decision which made the company's construction plans of building a farmhouse for 8,000 pigs subject to an environmental impact assessment under Art. 6 of Act No. 63/1999 on Environmental Impact Assessment. In this context, the *travaux préparatoires* which accompanied Art. 6 of Act No. 63/1999 stated that this provision was meant to be consistent with the aim and purpose of Directive 85/337/EEC,[187] which, among other things stated that constructions which could have significant impact on the environment should not be authorised before an environmental impact assessment had been carried out.

In its ruling, the Supreme Court referred to Art. 72 (protection of property rights) and Art. 75 (the freedom to conduct economic activity) of the Constitution, and held that neither of these provisions could be made subject to restriction unless prescribed by law and required by public interest. In the Court's view, Arts. 72 and 75 of the Constitution did not permit the legislator to delegate to the executive branch an unlimited decision-making power. Thereafter, the Court stated:

> The legislation must provide for general principles according to which the scope and limitations of the necessary restrictions is laid down. This also applies to measures

[184] Authors' translation.

[185] Art. 69 of the Icelandic Constitution stipulates that "no one may be subjected to punishment unless found guilty of conduct that constituted a criminal offence according to the law at the time when it was committed, or is totally analogous to such conduct".

[186] Supreme Court Case No. 15/2000 of 14 April 2000, *Stjörnugrís hf. v. The Icelandic State*. For further discussion on this case, see e.g. Hannesson (n. 183), pp. 188–91.

[187] Council Directive 85/337/EEC of 27 June 1985 on the assessment of the effects of certain public and private projects on the environment [1985] OJ L175/40.

> designed to adapt Icelandic law to the obligations undertaken by the Icelandic State according to the Agreement on the EEA.[188]

The Court reasoned that since Art. 6 of Act No. 63/1999 did not lay down any principles or substantive criteria for the Minister to follow when deciding whether an environmental impact assessment should be performed, the Minister had in fact an *unlimited discretion*, which violated the aforesaid provisions of the Constitution. In the light of this wide delegation of power, and the lack of a clear, sufficient legal basis, the Supreme Court deemed the decision of the Minister to be unlawful. The *Stjórnugrís* case demonstrates how the principle of legality and constitutional provisions may limit the effects of EEA law.[189] However, the result of this ruling, i.e. to completely rule out any effect of EEA law in the case, has been subject to some criticism.[190]

Another case where constitutional provisions appear to limit the principle of consistent interpretation is the *Gunnarsson* case discussed above,[191] where the Supreme Court cited Art. 40 of the Constitution as one of the reasons why provisions of the Tax Code could not be interpreted in conformity with EEA rules (see section 4.2 above).

The EFTA Court explained the consequences of what happens when consistent interpretation is not possible in *Irish Bank*,[192] as confirmed in the *Merrill Lynch* case, where it held that:

> [It] may be impossible according to the interpretative methods recognised by national law. If this leads to a violation of EEA law, the EEA State concerned is obliged to provide compensation for loss and damage caused to individuals and economic operators, in accordance with the principle of State liability. This principle is an integral part of the EEA Agreement.[193]

This approach was endorsed by the Supreme Court in the *Gunnarsson* case (see above), where it analysed the conditions for state liability, even if the conditions (rightfully, it seems) in the end were not regarded as being fulfilled. In the *Franz-Josef* case, the EFTA Court stated that in cases where a conforming interpretation of national law is not possible, that matter may be brought before the Court under the enforcement procedure prescribed by Art. 31 SCA. This was of course seemingly also the view of the Supreme Court in the *Flugastraumur* case, discussed in section 4 above.

---

188 Authors' translation.

189 Hannesson (n. 183), pp. 186–92.

190 Scholars have pointed out that due to several reasons *Stjörnugrís* is a unique case and wide conclusions should therefore be drawn carefully. See further Hannesson (n. 183), p. 190.

191 *Gunnarsson* (n. 79).

192 *Irish Bank* (n. 8), para. 125.

193 *Merrill Lynch* (n. 32), para. 45.

7. CONCLUSIONS

The analysis in previous sections demonstrates that the principle of consistent interpretation is clearly recognised by the Icelandic Supreme Court. It is fairly frequently invoked and applied, even if not always in a direct manner. In fact, a number of cases of high importance have been detected, where the Supreme Court has clearly been applying a principle of consistent interpretation, without citing Art. 3 of the EEA Act, or such a principle of either national or international origin.

Art. 3 of the EEA Act is in fact an implementation of such a rule of interpretation, as it has been interpreted and applied by the Supreme Court. However, as was discussed in section 4, Protocol 35 EEA, which was meant to secure the priority of implemented EEA rules in case of conflicting national provisions, is not recognised as a binding principle by the Icelandic Supreme Court. Therefore, Art. 3 of the EEA Act remains "only" a principle of consistent interpretation, but not a provision securing priority of implemented EEA rules. This lacunae in Icelandic law remains to be filled by the legislature – which could be inspired for example by the Norwegian implementation of Protocol 35 EEA. That type of priority rule should be compliant with Icelandic constitutional law, since it does not require priority over constitutional principles, which makes sense since this is not required by Protocol 35. Irrespective of this, as demonstrated in the *Árnason* case,[194] the Supreme Court has showed that it is able to stretch rules of interpretation quite far all the same, at least in order to secure individual rights in criminal proceedings.

What was demonstrated through the detailed analysis of the case-law carried out, is that the Icelandic Supreme Court is applying the principle of consistent interpretation in quite an independent way. In many cases it makes a reference to Art. 3 of the EEA Act, but in some important cases it does not, even if clearly interpreting national law consistently with EEA law. Furthermore, the Supreme Court has never cited an EEA principle of consistent interpretation or the case-law of the EFTA Court laying down the nature and boundaries of the principle. That may have the natural explanation that Art. 3 of the EEA Act has been a binding statuary norm since 1994 – even before the EFTA Court had expressed itself as concerning the principle. At the same time, it has to be admitted that the principle as interpreted by the EFTA Court has the ability to be more far-reaching than Art. 3 of the EEA Act, even if that provision has all the potentials to be compliant with the principle as interpreted by the EFTA Court.

The analysis of the follow-up of Advisory Opinions of the EFTA Court has demonstrated that the Icelandic Supreme Court has relied on those opinions in many important cases, also using the principle of consistent interpretation.

---

194 *Árnason* (n. 169).

However, there are clear examples where the Supreme Court has not done so – despite clear suggestions from the EFTA Court – most often with a reference to the limits of the rule of consistent interpretation. In those situations, the Supreme Court has suggested, and even ruled, that the principle of state liability should be invoked, and also implicitly suggested that infringement proceedings on the basis of Art. 31 SCA could be relevant.

The role of the principle of consistent interpretation in EEA law is quite important, partly due to the fact that EEA law does not recognise the principle of direct effect. Furthermore, the shortcomings in implementing Protocol 35 EEA in Icelandic law make its role even more important. The EFTA Court is seemingly aware of the importance of the principle, not least in the Icelandic context, and has emphasised its role and scope in Advisory Opinions that have its origin in Icelandic courts. That judicial dialogue may continue to evolve, but currently the application of the principle of consistent interpretation by the Icelandic Supreme Court is generally within the boundaries of the principle as defined by the EFTA Court.

THE PRINCIPLE OF CONSISTENT INTERPRETATION IN SLOVENIA

Inconsistently Consistent or Consistently Inconsistent?

Saša ZAGORC and Mohor FAJDIGA

1. BACKGROUND INFORMATION AND THE INSTITUTIONAL SETTING

The Republic of Slovenia, a country with 2 million inhabitants bordering Austria, Italy, Hungary and Croatia, lies between the Alps and the Balkan region. Historically, Slovenian people were under a strong German influence for a long time (from the eighth to the twentieth century). After the First World War, when the Austro-Hungarian Empire fell apart, German influence made way for connections with Slavic people living in the Balkan region. After the Second World War, communist Yugoslavia played a double role on the international stage: on one hand, it was a communist dictatorship free from control of the USSR; on the other, it had opened itself gradually to the West and allowed some traces of private economic initiative. In 1991, Slovenia became the first country to gain independence from then already defunct Yugoslavia, where the war burst out in all its cruelty. Since then, Slovenia's main foreign policy goal has been to become a part of important international and regional organisations. It became a member of the Council of Europe in 1993 and a member of NATO and the European Union (EU) in 2004. Slovenia switched to the euro currency as the first of the new EU Member States in 2007. Internally, the adoption of the Constitution in 1991 was a major achievement; the National Assembly has amended the country's supreme act several times since then.

Art. 3(2) of the Constitution of the Republic of Slovenia (the Constitution) is the constitutional basis for the principle of separation of powers between legislative, executive and judicial branch. Not being a part of the latter, the Constitutional Court of the Republic of Slovenia (the Constitutional Court) is competent to hear complaints on violations of human rights and fundamental liberties as well as to decide on the constitutionality of general legal acts. Being the highest authority when it comes to interpretations of Constitution and the guardian of the Constitution, the Constitutional Court's power is not to be underestimated. According to Slovenian legal scholars, it is one of the strongest Constitutional Courts in Europe in terms of competences and the legal consequences of its decisions.[1] Furthermore, the Constitutional Court's role is not only judicial, but also (*de facto*, at least) political – a feature confirmed in the aftermath of several high stakes decisions (e.g. the *Municipality of Ankaran* case,[2]

---

1 S. Zagorc and S. Bardutzky, "The application of EU Law in Slovenia: Teething troubles of the blue-eyed boy" in A. Łazowski (ed.), *The Application of EU Law in the New Member States*. (TMC Asser Press, 2010), pp. 421–23.

2 *Decision U-I-114/11* of 9 June 2011 (Uradni list RS, št. 47/2011; OdlUS XIX, 23) (in English: <http://odlocitve.us-rs.si/en/odlocitev/AN03546>). The case is famous because the court established municipality with the decision, despite the clear constitutional wording that municipalities are established by law. For the purpose of this contribution, this would be a *contra constitutionem* interpretation.

and a case on electoral systems).[3] The Court's political role became even more important in the last few years when the economic crisis struck the Slovenian economy, unveiling an even deeper recession of moral values. The Government presented unpopular but necessary reforms. However, legal acts enacting necessary measures were contested by claims for referendums that were, at the time, an easily accessible tool to block the austerity policy.[4] The Constitutional Court backed the Government policy by not allowing them to take place. Referendum sagas at the Constitutional Court still occur, thereby confirming the Constitutional Court as an important player in shaping the legal and political future of Slovenia.

The national court system in Slovenia is composed of three types of courts. First, administrative courts are competent for resolving administrative disputes. Second, specialised courts decide on issues concerning labour law and social security law. Third, regular courts consist of civil and criminal divisions. Higher courts hear appeals from both specialised and regular courts. The Supreme Court, the highest judicial authority in Slovenia, is an appellate court in administrative cases and rules on extraordinary legal remedies lodged against decisions of regular or specialised courts.

As seen from this brief historical background, Slovenia is a transitional country in all respects: it represents a transition from German to Slavic, from the Alps to the Adriatic and from a communist to a capitalist system. These characteristics, as well as the fact that the Slovenian people were constantly under foreign authority, have played an important role in shaping the Slovenian people's mentality, which is more relevant than some might think when it comes down to uncritical application of EU law and its role in the Slovenian legal system.

In the pre-accession period, the Government and the legislator adopted an EU-friendly approach, as integration into the EU enjoyed broad support of the citizens. Both continually highlighted the importance of conformity with the EU law in order to negate any opposing arguments and to justify the accelerated passing of the so-called "European legislation". The atmosphere in the pre-accession period was well described by a picturesque alliteration – "the European approximation highway".[5] Besides the legislator and the Government, the Constitutional Court also played an important role in the approximation period. In 1997, the Constitutional Court reviewed the constitutionality of the provisions of Slovenia's Europe Agreement,[6] concerning

---

3 *Decision U-I-12/97* of 8 October 1998 (Uradni list RS, št. 82/98; OdlUS VII, 180) (in English: <http://odlocitve.us-rs.si/en/odlocitev/AN01654>).

4 The amendment of Art. 90 of the Constitution in 2013 has dramatically decreased the access to legislative referendum.

5 Zagorc and Bardutzky (n. 1), pp. 421–23.

6 Europe Agreement establishing an association between the European Communities and their Member States, acting within the framework of the European Union, on the one part, and the Republic of Slovenia, on the other part [1999] OJ L51/3.

the acquisition of real estate by foreigners.[7] The Constitutional Court ruled that the Agreement, which treated foreigners (EU nationals) and Slovenian citizens equally, was contrary to Art. 68(2) of the Constitution.[8] The only way to harmonise the Slovenian legal system with the Agreement was thus to amend the Constitution, which happened in 1997. According to Zagorc and Bardutzky, the Constitutional Court considered interpretation in the light of EU law as "an additional tool to give more elaborate reasoning" in the pre-accession period.[9] This implies a certain level of interpretation which conforms to EU law. However, the principle of consistent interpretation was not applied fully, since EU law and the principle of consistent interpretation were not yet binding in this period.[10]

In addition to the amendment of 1997, the Constitution needed to be adjusted once more before accession, owing to EU law requirements. The National Assembly, in the capacity of a constituent power, adopted the so-called "European Article" (Art. 3a) in 2003. Art. 3a(1) allowed the transferal of exercise of a part of sovereign rights to the EU institutions.[11]

This contribution will try to illuminate the meaning, interpretation and impact of Slovenian case-law, with only scarce case commentaries in the academic literature to rely on – indeed, to the extent that the latter exist at all.[12] Court decisions were accessed and compiled mainly through the official online portal,[13] where the majority of the relevant cases are freely available (i.e. decisions of the Administrative Court, High Courts, Supreme Court, and Constitutional Court). With the exception of the Administrative Court, no other first instance court decisions formed part of this research (due to the decisions not being reported, being very difficult to access or subject to individual access only). A manageable amount of court decisions allowed the latest case-law to be analysed extensively, with only repetitive cases omitted. Based on previous research endeavours, it was initially assumed that the focus of this contribution would be in the triangle Administrative-Supreme-Constitutional Court.

No less than 100 judgments, orders and decisions of Slovenian courts, relevant to a greater or lesser extent, delivered before the end of 2016, were screened. The exact number of relevant cases is nevertheless hard to establish. The number

---

7 *Opinion Rm-1/97* of 5 June 1997 (Uradni list RS, št. 40/97; OdlUS VI, 86).

8 Art. 68(2) of the Constitution: "Aliens may not acquire title to land except by inheritance, under the condition of reciprocity".

9 Zagorc and Bardutzky (n. 1), pp. 421–23.

10 *Decision U-I-233/03* of 24 March 2005 (Uradni list RS, št. 37/2005; OdlUS XIV, 15), from which it can be inferred that Council Directive 79/1072/EC was not considered to be binding. See also *Order Up-328/04, U-I-186/04* of 8 July 2004 (OdlUS XIII, 82).

11 The same applies for transfers of powers to defence alliances such as NATO.

12 There are several scientific contributions addressing the theoretical aspects of the principle of consistent interpretation, but mainly from the EU law perspective, e.g. R. Zagradišnik, "Načelo skladne razlage – dolžnost nacionalnih sodnikov" (2008) 4–6 *Pravnik* 241.

13 The case-law of the supreme and appellate courts is available online at <https://www.sodnapraksa.si>.

of cases does not reflect the situation on "judicial ground level" for several reasons. First of all, as mentioned above, judgments and decisions of courts at the first instance level, that decide the biggest number of cases related to the EU law, were not screened at all (except the Administrative Court). Second, even in cases where the interpretational tools of EU law might be applicable, lower instance courts may – according to the Court of Justice of the European Union (ECJ) standards, but not necessarily from the national legal system point of view – refrain from addressing this issue if parties have not raised the issue themselves.

2. THE PRINCIPLE OF PRIMACY OF EU LAW

From the point of view of the relationship between domestic and EU law, Art. 3a(3) is of paramount importance. It provides that "legal acts and decisions, adopted within international organisations, to which Slovenia has transferred the exercise of part of its sovereign rights, shall be applied in Slovenia in accordance with the legal regulation of these organizations". Art. 3a(3) created a legal basis for the application of EU law in Slovenia. However, the provision's wording is very abstract, and thus provides a broad scope for interpretation by judicial and other authorities, in particular the Constitutional Court. Testen compares Art. 3a with a "crack in the Constitution", because the legal regulation of the EU changes and its evolution is unpredictable.[14]

Ribičič proposes three complementary approaches in this regard: positive (active), neutral and negative (passive). The positive approach allows the review of constitutionality of EU law in exceptional cases. This approach is inferred from the interpretation of Art. 3a(3) in connection with Art. 3a(1), which allows the transfer of "exercise of part of its sovereign rights to international organizations which are based on respect of human rights and fundamental freedoms, democracy and the rule of law ...".[15] This interpretation is questionable, as one simply cannot claim that the EU is not based on the respect of human rights, democracy or rule of law due to a single decision which violates these cornerstones of the EU. On the other hand, the *travaux préparatoires* to Art. 3a show that there was intent to give the Constitutional Court the power to intervene in exceptional cases where human rights would be violated.[16] In the opinion of the present authors, at the moment, this is more a theoretical than a practical issue, since only continuous violations of human rights (or the rule of law) could justify the intervention of the Constitutional Court. According to Cerar, the intervention of the Constitutional Court is possible only if the EU as a whole

[14] F. Testen, "Tretji odstavek 3. a člena: res (pre)velika razpoka v ustavi?" (2003) 6–7 *Podjetje in delo* 1484.

[15] Art. 3a(1) of the Constitution.

[16] C. Ribičič, "Položaj slovenske ustave po vključitvi v EU" (2006) 29–30 *Pravna praksa* 32.

was not founded on human rights, democracy and rule of law.[17] However, it is an important issue as far as the moral superiority of the Constitutional Court,[18] and the confidence of the Slovenian nation,[19] are concerned. The Constitutional Court should in the authors' opinion leave the door open for a potential, albeit probably extremely rare situation, where it would give primacy to the provisions of the Constitution over EU law in order to protect the fundamental values of the Slovenian legal order.[20] The positive approach should be used as *ultima ratio* – after the Constitutional Court had presented its arguments in a request for a preliminary ruling before the ECJ, and in the case where the ECJ would not offer an interpretation of EU law compatible with the Constitution.

The neutral approach allows rulings on the compatibility of EU law and the Constitution, but where the Constitutional Court would not decide on which provision prevails. This approach was adopted in *Opinion Rm-1/97*, where the Constitutional Court declared Slovenia's Europe Agreement incompatible with the Constitution.

By applying the negative approach, the Constitutional Court would refrain from reviewing the constitutionality of EU law, and would abide by the *Von Colson* requirement to opt for the most pro-European interpretation.[21] In exceptional cases, the Constitutional Court would make use of the preliminary ruling procedure, believing that the ECJ would provide an interpretation of EU law compatible with the Constitution.[22] The negative approach has been adopted by the Constitutional Court in almost all decisions, which means that the Constitutional Court adopted an EU-friendly interpretation of the domestic law. The positive approach has never been used. However, this does not mean that the Constitutional Court is not competent to assess the constitutionality of

---

17 M. Cerar, "URS in PUE: Usklajevanje Ustave RS z Ustavo za Evropo?" (2005) 10–11 *Pravna praksa* 8.

18 Moral superiority can be deducted from the fact that the EU is not a member of the Council of Europe and is not formally bound by the European Convention on Human Rights, even though it is hard to claim that the ECJ does not attain the same level of protection of human rights as the European Court of Human Rights (ECtHR). See the recent case of the ECtHR *Avotinš v. Latvia*, 23 May 2016, appl. no. 17502/07, confirming the validity of the *Bosphorus* presumption, even after an opinion of the ECJ was delivered (*Opinion 2/13 of 18 December 2014 on the draft agreement providing for the accession of the European Union to the European Convention on Human Rights* ECLI:EU:C:2014:2454).

19 Let us not forget that transferral of superior judicial authority to the Court of Justice of the European Union (ECJ) is a delicate issue from the point of view of each nation's history and constitutional identity.

20 See C. Ribičič, "Uveljavljanje evropskih standardov v praksi slovenskega Ustavnega sodišča" (2004) 2 *Revus* 69, 75; B. Zalar, "Ustavnopravna presoja pred rednimi sodišči: primer prakse Upravnega sodišča" (2010) 1 *Pravosodni bilten* 171, 183.

21 Case 14/83, *Sabine von Colson and Elisabeth Kamann v. Land Nordrhein-Westfalen*, ECLI:EU:C:1984:153.

22 S. Nerad, "Recepcija prava Evropske unije v nacionalno ustavno pravo: Ustavno sodišče med pravom Evropske unije in Ustavo" in I. Kaučič (ed.), *Dvajset let Ustave Republike Slovenije: pomen ustavnosti in ustavna demokracija* (Pravna fakulteta UL, 2012), p. 379.

acts implementing EU law.[23] The Constitutional Court has waited for a long time to request a preliminary ruling, although it has already opined several times that it could do so.[24] The Constitutional Court filed the first, and so far only, request to the ECJ in 2014.[25]

So far, the Constitutional Court has always avoided conflict between the Constitution and EU law, despite the fact that it has already assessed the constitutionality of provisions implementing EU law. When an annulment procedure against an EU law is already under way before the ECJ, the Constitutional Court decides to stay the procedure.[26] This approach ensures loyal cooperation between the Constitutional Court and the ECJ. In *U-I-65/13*, the Constitutional Court stayed the procedure and waited for the ECJ to decide on the validity of a directive under EU law. After the annulment of the Directive, the conflict no longer existed, and the problem was solved. However, in *U-I-113/04*, the ECJ did not eliminate the provisions of the Directive which according to the complainants were contrary to the Constitution. By claiming the unconstitutionality of the implementing act, the complainants were actually claiming that the Directive was unconstitutional. The conflict between EU law and the Constitution was obvious. Therefore, the Constitutional Court was in a more difficult position. The Constitutional Court clearly adopted the negative approach in this case. It explained that the Constitution did not afford more rights than EU law in this specific case. Consequently, the conflict between EU law and the Constitution did not exist. The most striking proof of the negative approach is that the Constitutional Court did not assess the equality of protection of relevant rights under EU law and under the Constitution, but simply concluded in a short statement that the level of protection was equal.[27]

A more confident and less EU-subordinated approach was adopted in *U-I-37/10*, where the Constitutional Court annulled the Government's regulation implementing two directives due to the fact that according to Art. 120(2) of the Constitution, an act of the legislator was required in this matter. However, the Constitutional Court was aware of its obligation to ensure *effet utile* of EU law.[28] Therefore, it decided that the annulment would only apply after

---

23 *Order U-I-65/13-16* of 26 September 2013 (Uradni list RS, št. 54/2014; OdlUS XX, 27), para. 7; *Decision U-I-146/12* of 14 November 2013 (Uradni list RS, št. 107/2013; OdlUS XX, 10), para. 31.

24 M. Avbelj, "Slovensko ustavno pravo v odnosu do prava EU" in I. Kaučič (ed.), *Dvajset let Ustave Republike Slovenije: Pomen ustavnosti in ustavna demokracija* (Pravna fakulteta UL, 2012), pp. 341, 348.

25 *Order U-I-295/13-132* of 6 November 2014 (Uradni list RS, št. 82/2014).

26 *Order U-I-113/04-17* of 8 July 2004 (Uradni list RS, št. 83/2004); Order U-I-65/13-16 of 26 September 2013 (Uradni list RS, št. 54/2014; OdlUS XX, 27).

27 *Decision U-I-113/04-33* of 7 February 2007 (Uradni list RS, št. 16/2007; OdlUS XVI, 16), para. 17.

28 *Decision U-I-37/10* of 18 April 2013 (Uradni list RS, št. 39/2013), para. 24.

a one-year period. In this case, the Constitutional Court showed its determination to navigate between the demands of EU law and the Constitution. Despite the fact that annulment of the implementing regulation potentially endangered the *effet utile* of EU law,[29] the Constitutional Court acted as a guardian of the Constitution and annulled the unconstitutional implementing regulation.

The most striking feature of the Slovenian understanding of EU law is, at least *in abstracto*, a full embrace of the principle of primacy, which is "at the same time an internal constitutional principle with the binding effect of the Constitution".[30] Two relevant court cases indicate that such a "more Catholic than the Pope position" does not fully resonate with the actual constitutional paradigm. Firstly, the Constitutional Court's position that the "Basic Constitutional Charter is … as such a permanent and inexhaustible constitutional source of the statehood of the Republic of Slovenia",[31] was given full support in the context of international law and constitutional methodology.[32] Second, the message in *U-II-1/12* that *effet utile* of EU law is a specifically protected good through Art. 3a of the Constitution, which in any case has to be attributed significant weight, is rather mystifying.[33] It may highlight the relative value of the principle of primacy of EU law and does not shy away from a possible balancing test of constitutional and European values in the future.

There are two procedures which bring EU law considerations before the Constitutional Court: a constitutionality review of legal acts, and a constitutional complaint.[34] The latter, more relevant in practice, is an action where the Constitutional Court rules on violations of human rights caused by individual acts of national or local authorities, or bearers of public authority. This violation could be a result of the non-application or wrongful application of EU law. In such a situation, Art. 22 of the Constitution – which guarantees equal protection of rights – could be violated. The Constitutional Court stated for example in *Up-282/09* that an unexplained deviation from established case-law of the ECJ could result in a violation of Art. 22 of the Constitution.[35] Furthermore, if the authorities overlooked a Regulation that should be applied, this would also result in violation of Art. 22 of the Constitution. Further still,

---

29 If the legislator would not fulfil its duty to adopt an implementing act within a one-year period, the Slovenian legal system would not comply with EU law requirements.

30 *Decision U-I-146/12* of 14 November 2013 (Uradni list RS, št. 107/2013; OdlUS XX, 10), para. 32. See also *Decision U-I-155/11* of 18 December 2013 (Uradni list RS, št. 114/201; OdlUS XX, 12), para. 14; *Decision U-I-295/13* of 19 October 2016 (Uradni list RS, št. 82/2014 in Uradni list RS, št. 71/2016), para. 66.

31 *Opinion Rm-1/09* of 18 March 2010 (Uradni list RS, št. 25/2010; OdlUS XIX, 12).

32 Concurring with *Opinion Rm-1/09*, judge Zobec calibrates it as "a lasting commitment of the state to international law". Avbelj refers to it as an "epistemical core" (M. Avbelj, "Trajni in neusahljivi vir slovenske državnosti?" (2010) 45–46 *Dignitas* 140).

33 *Decision U-II-1/12* of 17 December 2012 (Uradni list RS, št. 102/2012; OdlUS XIX, 39).

34 See further Nerad (n. 22).

35 *Order Up-282/09* of 24 November 2009 (Uradni list RS, št. 103/2009; OdlUS XVIII, 94).

national courts are obliged to discuss all relevant arguments of the parties to a case. Failing to do so would be a violation of the said Article. This applies also when a party's arguments are based on EU law. And, in one final example, Art. 22 of the Constitution could be violated also if a national court failed to send the case for a preliminary ruling and did not explain why, or the explanation was insufficient.[36] For the sake of clarity, the duty to elaborate on parties' arguments does not absolve a national judge of the duty to follow the maxim *iura novit curia*, and to interpret national provisions in accordance with EU law requirements of its own motion, even though none of the parties to the case may have argued for a specific interpretation. This obligation stems from the national legal system, and a breach thereof may result in the annulment of the judgment on the ground of wrongful application of material law.

Human rights violations could also result from individual decisions which are based on EU law. This implies a conflict between EU law and a human right guaranteed by the Constitution. According to Nerad, there should be no doubt that in such situations, the Constitutional Court's primary mission is to protect human rights. On the other hand, he is aware of the fact that the Constitutional Court is bound to ensure the *effet utile* of EU law.[37] He proposes that in such cases the Constitutional Court should request a preliminary ruling, demanding an interpretation compatible with the Constitution. Consequently, the Constitutional Court would have the final say on the matter. This actually happened in 2014, when the Constitutional Court asked the ECJ for a preliminary ruling in a case where the Bank of Slovenia had erased subordinate bonds of major Slovenian banks on the basis of an EU Commission Communication[38] which prescribed this action as a condition for state aid to be compatible with EU law. This enabled the survival of the banks, but interfered with the rights of the owners of the subordinate bonds.[39]

3. JUDICIAL DIALOGUE WITH THE COURT OF JUSTICE OF THE EUROPEAN UNION

Judicial dialogue forms an essential part in the functioning of the EU's judicial system. Yet Slovenian courts were "EU resistant" enough not to refer a single case to the ECJ for a preliminary ruling until 2009, despite the country's

---

36 *Up-958/09, U-I-199/09* of 15 April 2010 (Uradni list RS, št. 37/2010).

37 Nerad (n. 22), p. 386.

38 Communication from the Commission on the application, from 1 August 2013, of state aid rules to support measures in favour of banks in the context of the financial crisis ("Banking Communication"), [2013] OJ C216/01.

39 *Order U-I-295/13* (n. 25); Case C-526/14 *Tadej Kotnik and Others v. Državni zbor Republike Slovenije* ECLI:EU:C:2016:570.

membership since May 2004. The reasons for such inactivity are deeply rooted in the judiciary by a very formalistic understanding of interpretation of national legislation, and inadequate knowledge of EU law.[40] This passiveness is probably also a consequence of inadequate counselling of the parties to a case.

In 2014, the Constitutional Court made a request to the ECJ for the first time. Altogether, Slovenian courts have made referrals in less than 20 court proceedings, a number that is comparatively in line with smaller "newcomer" EU Member States. In the following section, four cases that include questions of consistent interpretation where national court referred the case to the ECJ for a preliminary ruling are described.

In *Grilc*,[41] the Supreme Court had doubts about the interpretation of a national provision – Art. 42.j of the Compulsory Motor Third-Party Liability Insurance Act[42] – which transposed Art. 6 of the Fourth Motor Vehicle Insurance Directive.[43] Each party asserted a different interpretation of relevant national law on the relationship between pre-lawsuit claims for damages and the subsequent lawsuit. In addition, the lower courts provided completely different interpretations of national law in their judgments. The first instance court recognised the right to claim compensation from the national insurers bureau, while the High Court on appeal interpreted national law to the contrary, and in a way that only a pre-lawsuit (non-judiciable) compensation claim against that party would be allowed.

What is striking in this case is that its logic runs contrary to the normal course of application of consistent interpretation of national legislation with EU law. As the ECJ clearly indicated in its preliminary ruling, the answer to the question referred admitted of no reasonable doubt. The existence of a dispute between lower courts on the interpretation of national law on matters lying in the field of EU law does not necessitate a referral by the Supreme Court to the ECJ for a preliminary ruling.[44] Interestingly enough, the High Court wrongly applied the principle of consistent interpretation, and the Supreme Court unnecessarily asked for the help of the ECJ. Only the first instance court, it seems, properly understood the EU dimension of the case. In the aftermath, the Supreme Court

---

40 See extensive contributions of Slovenian authors (A. Galič, J. Zobec, J. Letnar Černič, B. Zalar and M. Avbelj) in M. Bobek (ed.), *Central European Judges under the European Influence. The Transformative Power of the EU Revisited* (Hart Publishing, 2015), pp. 99–124, 125–48, 149–162, 275–91.

41 Case C-541/11, *Jožef Grilc v. Slovensko zavarovalno združenje GIZ*, ECLI:EU:C:2013:19; *Order of the Supreme Court II Ips 412/2010* of 30 May 2013.

42 *Zakon o obveznih zavarovanjih v prometu* (ZOZP), Uradni list RS, št. 93/07 and subsequent.

43 Directive 2000/26/EC of the European Parliament and of the Council of 16 May 2000 on the approximation of the laws of the Member States relating to insurance against civil liability in respect of the use of motor vehicles and amending Council Directives 73/239/EEC and 88/357/EEC [2000] OJ L181/65.

44 Case C-160/14, *Ferreira da Silva*, ECLI:EU:C:2015:565, where the Court emphasised another condition, that the "concept frequently gives rise to difficulties of interpretation in the various Member States".

found that the High Court did not establish whether the pre-lawsuit claim for compensation was filed due to misapplication of the relevant material law provisions, and quashed its decision. As not all decisions of regular courts are published, the final resolution of this dispute is not known. It was not possible to deduce the result even from a similar case dealt with by the Supreme Court in 2015, where the above-mentioned preliminary ruling was invoked once again.[45]

In *Pelati*,[46] a well-known case which has been subject to many commentaries in academic circles, the Administrative Court's request for a preliminary ruling from the ECJ touched upon the principle of consistent interpretation. However, neither the Administrative Court nor the Supreme Court made actual use of the principle to resolve the case, even though the Supreme Court explicitly mentioned it in its reasoning.

In *Vnuk*,[47] a textbook case when it comes to consistent interpretation and preliminary rulings, the Supreme Court once again dealt with motor insurance rules. This time, the main issue concerned interpretation of the term "use of vehicle" in Art. 15 of the Compulsory Motor Third-Party Liability Insurance Act, which transposed Art. 3 of the First Motor Insurance Directive into the Slovenian legal system.[48] The plaintiff was climbing a ladder when a tractor accidently hit him while reversing and parking a trailer into a barn, causing serious injury. The question was whether such use of the tractor constituted "use of vehicle" which was covered by the obligatory insurance. If not, the plaintiff could not claim damages from the insurer based on compulsory insurance. The Supreme Court rightly emphasised that "use of vehicle" is to be interpreted in the spirit of the relevant Motor Insurance Directives. However, it concluded that the Directives did not determine which situations were covered by "use of vehicle", or prescribe which criterion was decisive for determination of "use of vehicle". Consequently, the Supreme Court referred the case to the ECJ for a preliminary ruling. The ECJ interpreted use of vehicle broadly as meaning any use consistent with the normal function of the vehicle. The Supreme Court therefore annulled the decisions of the first and second instance courts, which had relied on previously settled national case-law that defined the use of vehicle more narrowly, and decided that the claim for damages was well-founded. The Supreme Court's decision is very important, as it reversed its own settled jurisprudence regarding what use

---

45 *Order of the Supreme Court II Ips 46/2014* of 24 September 2015.

46 Case C-603/10, *Pelati d.o.o. v. Republika Slovenija*, ECLI:EU:C:2012:639; Judgment of the Administrative Court *U 2561/2008* of 19 November 2012; Judgment of the Supreme Court *X Ips 18/2013* of 19 September 2013.

47 See Case C-162/13, *Vnuk*, ECLI:EU:C:2014:2146 and *Judgment and Order of the Supreme Court II Ips 415/2011* of 20 October 2014. The new position was confirmed in a later case – *Judgment the Supreme Court II Ips 334/2015* of 25 February 2016.

48 Council Directive 72/166/EEC of 24 April 1972 on the approximation of the laws of Member States relating to insurance against civil liability in respect of the use of motor vehicles, and to the enforcement of the obligation to insure against such liability [1972] OJ L103/1.

of vehicles out of traffic was not covered by the compulsory insurance. This will be discussed in more detail further below.

The *Hotel Sava Rogaška* case refers to a completely different domain of law to the cases discussed above.[49] The applicant wanted to register a trademark for his natural mineral water, despite the fact that water from the same underground source had already been registered under trademark "D". The relevant national law (Art. 12(4) of the Rules on Natural Mineral Water, Spring Water and Table Water), and Art. 8(2) of the Natural Mineral Waters Directive,[50] allowed only one trademark for water from the same "spring". The Supreme Court asked the ECJ whether the water, which was pumped from two different boreholes, had the same "spring". The Administrative Court's decision suggested that the words "spring" and "source" were synonymous, and that they had the same legal consequences. The underground source is the relevant circumstance for determination of whether it is possible to register two different trademarks for water. If the underground source is the same, the answer is negative, according to the Administrative Court. However, the ECJ explained that water that has the same underground source as the water that has already been registered can be registered under different trademarks subject to two conditions. First, if the water is pumped in two different locations; second, if the water pumped in one location does not have the same characteristics from the point of view of Annex I to the Natural Mineral Waters Directive as the water pumped in the second location. The Supreme Court therefore decided to quash the Administrative Court's decision, as it was not based on the correct interpretation of the relevant provisions. This in turn meant that the relevant factual background of the case was not identified, since the Administrative Court did not examine whether the characteristics of the water pumped from one location were the same as the characteristics of the water pumped from the other location. The aftermath of the case is not known since it was referred back to the ministerial level where decisions are not made public. However, we can assume from a subsequent case that the applicant did not succeed in registering a second trademark.[51]

These are not the only referrals to the ECJ for preliminary rulings. Slovenian courts have decided to open a dialogue with the ECJ on 19 occasions.[52]

49 See Case C-207/14 *Hotel Sava Rogaška, turizem in storitve, d.o.o. v. Republika Slovenija* ECLI:EU:C:2015:414, and the Supreme Court's *Judgment and Order X Ips 479/2012* of 8 July 2015.

50 Directive 2009/54/EC of the European Parliament and of the Council of 18 June 2009 on the exploitation and marketing of natural mineral waters [2009] OJ L164/45.

51 The applicant tried to revoke the trademark approval which prevented him from registering the second trademark for the same underground source. See *Judgment of the Administrative Court IV U 158/2015* of 8 November 2017; *Order of the Supreme Court X Ips 17/2017* of 15 February 2017. The second trademark cannot be found in the register of trademarks.

52 ECJ, *Annual Report 2015: Judicial Activity* (European Union, 2016) See also: "Predhodna vprašanja" <www.pisrs.si/Pis.web/strokovniClanki;jsessionid=20HzK-mEjVsMRI5B3GzrHYa8>.

All of the cases are not described in this contribution, as some were not relevant or are still pending before the ECJ in this moment. From what has been witnessed so far, however, Slovenian courts are in principle positively inclined towards EU-friendly interpretations of national law. After taking the first step by making a request for a preliminary ruling,[53] the last two cases show a more profound understanding of the judicial dialogue between the courts.

4. CONCEPTUAL BASIS

The national courts use different terms for describing the principle of consistent interpretation. The most common one is "*načelo lojalne razlage*" ("the principle of loyal interpretation"). The term "*načelo skladne razlage*" ("the principle of consistent interpretation") has also been used, but – it appears – only once.[54] This is probably the consequence of the fact that the word "*skladen*" is very frequently used in legal language, and thus lacks sufficient distinctiveness. The word "principle" is sometimes substituted by "doctrine", to give "the doctrine of loyal interpretation". Courts use also an abbreviated version, where they omit the words "principle" and "doctrine", simply using "loyal interpretation". However, the courts do not always name the principle; they often simply explain that a provision of national law should be "interpreted in the light/spirit" of a provision of a directive, jurisprudence of the ECJ, etc. The term "obligation of consistent interpretation of domestic law with EU law" is rarely used.[55] The Supreme Court once even used terms "*euro skladna razlaga*" and "*euro konsistentna razlaga*",[56] which both mean "euro consistent interpretation" and are a little bit strange from the point of view of Slovenian language.[57] In this same case and in *Judgment II Ips 228/2013* the Supreme Court used another term: "*harmonizirajoča razlaga*" ("harmonising interpretation"), which is not the best term, in the present authors' opinion.

This document contains 18 preliminary rulings. However, for an unknown reason, the Constitutional Court's request for a preliminary ruling in *U-I-295/13* (n. 25) is not included.

53 Some Central and Eastern European countries faced the same problem after EU accession. See A. Sajó, "Learning co-operative constitutionalism the hard way: The Hungarian Constitutional Court shying away from EU supremacy" [2004] *Zeitschrift für staats- und europawissenschaften* 171; Z. Kühn, "The application of European law in the new Member States: Several (early) predictions" (2005) 6 *German Law Journal* 563, 574.

54 *Decision of the Constitutional Court U-I-155/11* of 18 December 2013 (n. 30), para. 30.

55 *Judgment of the Supreme Court X Ips 18/2013* of 19 September 2013; *Judgment and Order of the Administrative Court I U 543/2013* of 30 January 2014.

56 *Order of the Supreme Court II Ips 160/2013* of 23 April 2015.

57 From the point of view of respect of syntax of the Slovenian language, it would be more appropriate to use another term. Furthermore, the word "euro" should have at least been substituted by "*evro*", as the word root is "*evro-*" as "*evropska*" (European).

4.1. ORIGIN OF LEGAL GROUNDS FOR APPLICATION OF THE PRINCIPLE OF CONSISTENT INTERPRETATION

National courts often explain that the principle of consistent interpretation originates in the *principle of loyal cooperation* under Art. 4(3) TEU.[58] Sometimes, they explain that national law should be interpreted in the light of the EU law due to the principle of supremacy of EU law.[59] Formally, national courts see the obligation to perform consistent interpretations of national law as an individual obligation, not directly linked to any duty to apply other methods of interpretation. Substantially, many cases indicate that courts see the principle of consistent interpretation fit to be part of the teleological method of interpretation. For example, courts rely on explanations of the purpose of a specific provision in the recital of the Directive,[60] or more generally on the purpose of the Directive.[61] Many times courts refer to leading cases on the principle of consistent interpretation (e.g. the courts have cited the *Von Colson* case 16 times according to the online web portal).

The principle of consistent interpretation normally requires authorities to interpret national legislation in an extensive manner and not narrowly. For example, the Administrative Court interpreted the provision of the Court Fees Act on the exemption from the payment of court fees for foreigners widely, due to "a bad quality of normative transposition of provisions concerning exercise of the right to family life".[62] The Court did not hesitate to do so to the extent that the phrase "documents and activities defined in international agreements that are in force in Slovenia" was understood as also encompassing "secondary law of the EU on the right to family reunification", and that "refugee" fell under the term "foreigners".[63]

While there is a counterpart in the jurisprudence of the Constitutional Court,[64] that requires all public authorities to interpret national legislation in line with the Constitution as much as it is possible, the two principles should not be mixed.[65] Any substantial impact of the Constitution-friendly interpretation

---

58 *Judgment of the Supreme Court I Up 357/2011* of 1 September 2011, para. 11; *Judgment of the Supreme Court X Ips 18/2013* of 19 September 2013, para. 14; *Decision of the Constitutional Court U-I-146/12* of 14 November 2013 (Uradni list RS, št. 107/2013; OdlUS XX, 10), para. 33; *Judgment of the Supreme Court X Ips 67/2014* of 12 November 2015, para. 12; *Judgment of the Supreme Court X Ips 269/2014* of 3 March 2016, para. 13.

59 *Judgment of the Supreme Court III Ips 9/2012* of 28 January 2014, para.10.

60 *Decision of the Constitutional Court U-I-309/13, Up-981/13* of 14 January 2015 (Uradni list RS, št. 6/2015).

61 *Judgment of the Supreme Court I Up 357/2011* of 1 September 2011.

62 *Zakon o sodnih taksah*, Uradni list RS, št. 37/08 and subsequent.

63 *Judgment of the Administrative Court I U 1179/2015* of 31 August 2015.

64 See extensively M. Pavčnik, "Ustavnoskladna razlaga (zakona)" in M. Pavčnik (ed.), *(Ustavno) sodno odločanje* (GV Založba, 2013), pp. 65, 73–80.

65 See further S. Zagorc, "Odškodninska odgovornost za kršitev človekovih pravic" [2013] *Pravni letopis* 167.

on the EU-based principle of consistent interpretation of national legislation could be understood by the ECJ as a challenge to the *effet utile* of EU law.

Another interesting feature of the principle of consistent interpretation having an indirect impact can be seen in a case where the Constitutional Court assessed the constitutionality of a national provision which obviously did not infringe EU law. In this case, the Family Reunification Directive allowed national authorities to extend the scope of family members beyond that explicitly set up in the Directive.[66] The Slovenian National Assembly did not opt for the extension. A refugee who had unsuccessfully sought family reunification with her sister from Kenya challenged the constitutionality of the national legislation at issue for having unconstitutional legal lacunae. The Constitutional Court ruled in her favour by applying the constitutional right to family life very broadly, and in line with recitals 4, 8 and 10 of the Directive. In this case, the principle of consistent interpretation had a radiating effect on the Slovenian constitutional system beyond the scope directly required by EU law, as such legal construction is an expression of autonomous and spontaneous deliberation of national authorities. Thus, it might be unconstitutional not to interpret national legislation consistently with EU law even in situations where EU law allows Member States some political discretion. This means that the national principle of consistent interpretation might substantially overlap with the EU counterpart.

Before Slovenia became a Member State of the EU, the Constitutional Court had been referring to EU law to strengthen its argumentation. This approach did not stop after Slovenia's accession to the EU on 1 May 2004. In case *U-I-321/02*, less than a month after the accession, the Constitutional Court recognised the principle of consistent interpretation. However, it did not place any additional importance on it, as compared to its position prior to accession – it was used at the end of the Constitutional Court's reasoning as an additional argument. It seems that the Constitutional Court treated the principle as one of the methods of interpretation that should be taken into account.[67] First, it held that in addition to literal, also historical, logical and systematic interpretation led to a certain conclusion. In the next paragraph, it stated that: "After all, this interpretation is dictated also by the principle of loyal interpretation, according to which, the national law should be interpreted in the light of the Community law."[68]

---

66 Council Directive 2003/86/EC of 22 September 2003 on the right to family reunification [2003] OJ L251/12; *Decision U-I-309/13, Up-981/13* (n. 60).

67 Slovenian courts developed a hierarchy of methods of statutory interpretation, albeit with many nuances and specificities, in which the literal and teleological methods play the most exposed role. See M. Pavčnik, *Argumentacija v pravu* (2nd ed., Cankarjeva založba, 2004), p. 57.

68 Translated by the authors.

The additional argument approach has been commonly used up to this very day.[69] However, it is not the only approach. The Constitutional Court has developed a very "consistent interpretation-friendly" jurisprudence. First, in 2008, the Constitutional Court held:

> The courts must, from the moment of the Directive's entry into force, irrespective of whether the time limit for implementation has expired or not, when interpreting a national legal rule, interpret a national legal rule as much as possible in accordance with the purpose and wording of the Directive in order for the Directive to attain its desired goal. National legislation should be interpreted in the light of the EC law. This means that it must be interpreted in accordance with the purpose defined by the EC law (the principle of loyal interpretation). That is why the administrative authorities and courts ... have to interpret undefined legal terms in accordance with Geneva Convention on the Status of Refugees and the purpose of the Directive.[70]

The Constitutional Court adds an important footnote to the above translated reasoning:

> Loyal interpretation is one of the most challenging tasks of national authorities which must interpret a national legal rule differently than before on the basis of European legal act's purpose, which may not have been taken into account by the national legislator when elaborating the national legal rule ....[71]

This reasoning embraced at least four important aspects of the principle of consistent interpretation. First, the Constitutional Court decided that both courts as well as administrative authorities must apply the principle. It could be said that the Constitutional Court in a way accepted the *Costanzo* doctrine as developed by the ECJ,[72] and demands the administrative authorities to apply EU law. By requiring them to do so, EU law prevails over national legislation in cases of incompatibility. This is in a way contrary to the Slovenian legal tradition, where administrative authorities do not have the *exceptio illegalis* by which courts can ignore a provision of a by-law.[73] Second, the Constitutional Court clearly

---

69 See *Decision U-I-308/07-31, Up-1094/06-31* of 2 April 2009 (Uradni list RS, št. 31/2009; OdlUS XVIII, 14), paras. 16–18, where the Constitutional Court primarily made use of its own *Decision U-I-219/03* to explain the object of the impugned legislation. Then it stated that the same conclusion could be drawn from loyal interpretation of recital 17 of Directive 2006/43/EC.

70 *Decision Up-2012/08* of 5 March 2009 (Uradni list RS, št. 22/2009; OdlUS XVIII, 65) (translated by the authors).

71 Ibid (translated by the authors). See also R. Knez, "Narava prava Skupnosti – evropsko pravoznanstvo" in *Evropsko pravo: Zbirka gradiv šole Evropskega prava* (Založniška hiša Primath, 2004), pp. 55, 55–72.

72 Case C-103/88, *Fratelli Costanzo SpA v. Comune di Milano*, ECLI:EU:C:1989:256.

73 M. Avbelj, "Neposredni učinek direktiv in problemi v praksi" (2010) 12 *Pravna praksa* 17.

explained that the principle of consistent interpretation implies interpretation conforming to the purpose of the EU law, irrespective of the purpose of the national legislation as reflected in any *travaux préparatoires*. Third, following the *Mangold*-doctrine of the ECJ, the Constitutional Court decided that the principle of consistent interpretation must be applied 'from the moment of the Directive's entry into force', i.e. even prior to expiry of the deadline for implementation of a directive. Finally, consistent interpretation in line with EU law is at the very least on an equal footing with the principle of Slovenian law requiring interpretations in line with international law.

Furthermore, in *U-I-146/12*,[74] the Constitutional Court explained that "Because of Article 3a(3) of the Constitution, the fundamental principles [of EU law] defining the relation between internal law and Community law are at the same time internal constitutional law principles with binding force of the Constitution".[75] In the next paragraph, the Constitutional Court listed the fundamental principles, including the principle of consistent interpretation.[76] This means that violations of this principle are unconstitutional, as they are contrary to Art. 3a(3) of the Constitution. This jurisprudence put the principle of consistent interpretation onto a pedestal of internal constitutional law principles, which cannot be compared to its previous role as a mere additional interpretative tool.

Another issue is worth briefly shedding light upon in relation to Art. 3 of the Constitution and the additional argument approach. First, an excessive use of EU law references in judicial proceedings can be observed. Other stakeholders, for example attorneys representing parties to a case, could do more in this regard. Quality legal counselling is a very important factor in any analysis of courts' work. In the authors' opinion, a large portion of inconsistent consistent interpretation is a consequence of inadequate legal counselling. A low level of cognisance of EU law by attorneys can be seen throughout the case-law analysed. First, many EU law arguments are not adequately elaborated. Attorneys often see them as an additional argument worth trying, but not much more. For instance, demands for preliminary rulings are frequently not based on research of the ECJ's jurisprudence, and do not take into account the *CILFIT* criteria.[77] Second, EU law arguments are often inadequately presented before the Constitutional Court. According to the settled case-law of the Constitutional Court, the Constitution does not afford any legal basis for the Constitutional Court to assess conformity of national law with a directive or regulation. However, the cases where the applicants alleged incompatibility of national law with the directive kept coming to the Constitutional Court since 2009,

---

74 *Decision U-I-146/12* of 14 November 2013 (Uradni list RS, št. 107/2013; OdlUS XX, 10).

75 Ibid., para. 32 (explanation in square brackets added; translated by the authors.).

76 Ibid., para. 33.

77 Case 283/81, *CILFIT v. Ministry of Health*, ECLI:EU:C:1982:335.

i.e. five years after EU accession. As a result, there are numerous decisions where the Constitutional Court rejected the EU law argument due to a lack of competence.[78] In this respect, the present authors share Nerad's opinion that the right way to raise such an argument would be to say that the Art. 3a of the Constitution requires that national law provisions are in conformity with the relevant directive (according to *Decision U-I-146/12*, the principle of primacy is a constitutional principle). The national provision is thus declared contrary not to the directive, but to Art. 3a of the Constitution. The Constitutional Court is competent to hear such a claim.[79]

4.2. INVERSE RELIANCE ON THE PRINCIPLE OF CONSISTENT INTERPRETATION

While one of the goals of indirect effect of EU law is to provide an additional safety net for individuals, enabling them to rely on EU law,[80] Slovenian case-law does not provide any clear evidence that national or other public authorities could not invoke the principle of consistent interpretation to the detriment of the rights of individuals. With the full acceptance of the *effet utile* of EU law in Slovenia, such a conclusion seems reasonable; however, the review undertaken of Slovenian case-law did not provide any examples where the authorities have actually made use of it.

The closest example found was a decision of the Administrative Court, which was later challenged before the Supreme Court and the Constitutional Court.[81] Since the case is not available on the web portal, its contents had to be deciphered from the reasoning of two hierarchically higher courts. It appears that an asylum seeker wanted to rely on the literal and more beneficial definition of the term "persecution" in the then Asylum Act.[82] All of the courts involved nevertheless supported consistent interpretation of national law with the then Qualification Directive, despite the time limit for transposition of the latter not having yet expired.

In another judgment, the Administrative Court used the principle of consistent interpretation to strengthen the reasoning in the judgment to prohibit the advertisement of electronic cigarettes.[83] By doing this, the court

78 *Order U-I-188/04* of 8 September 2005; *Decision U-I-32/04* of 9 February 2006 (Uradni list RS, št. 21/2006; OdlUS XV, 10); *Order U-I-116/07* of 25 May 2007; *Decision U-I-238/07* of 2 April 2009 (Uradni list RS, št. 32/2009; OdlUS XVIII, 13); *Order U-I-44/05* of 11 September 2007.

79 Nerad (n. 22), pp. 389–90.

80 See e.g. *Judgment and order of the Administrative Court I U 1450/2010* of 3 November 2010; *Judgment of the Administrative Court I U 1333/2013* of 8 October 2013.

81 *Judgment U 713/2007* of 6 February 2008.

82 *Zakon o azilu* (Uradni list RS, št. 51/06).

83 *Judgment III U 389/2013* of 8 January 2015.

refuted the implication of the plaintiff that the only issue of this case was whether the prohibition of advertisement of electronic cigarettes contravenes constitutionally protected residual liberty.

4.3. (DIS)ORDER OF SEQUENCE

The ECJ prescribed the methodology for deciding whether to use the principle of consistent interpretation, direct effect or state liability in the case of *Dominguez*,[84] although the approach itself is not always followed. In that case, the Court established a clear order of sequence: first consistent interpretation, then direct effect and then state liability. Courts in Slovenia do not follow any "recipe" prescribed in advance by statute or case-law when they are deciding which order to follow. In each case, the national court elaborates by itself the reasoning as to why it has chosen to use one of these possibilities. This is not problematic if courts do their job as we expect from them. However, there are cases where courts have given priority to the principle of consistent interpretation, despite their interpretation of national law being at least strained/artificial – if not *contra legem*. From the point of view of uniform application of EU law, it would be desirable that the Constitutional Court would give clearer guidelines about the sequence of application of these three possibilities.

Still, there are some indicative decisions from the general courts. Two Supreme Court cases raised a question of order of sequence.[85] Both cases are similar, as they were connected with Council Directive 90/314/EEC of 13 June 1990 on package travel, package holidays and package tours,[86] and dealt with directly applicable provisions of the Directive which were not adequately implemented into the Slovenian legal order. In both cases it is not known whether the Supreme Court was aware of the order of sequence established by the ECJ in the case of *Dominguez*. The Supreme Court used the principle of consistent interpretation, without an adequate explanation as to why it did not opt for the direct effect in both cases. In *Order II Ips 160/2013*, it stated that:

> Taking into account the circumstance that our country did not implement the Directive in the above explained way, it is correct to choose the interpretation of national legislation in the light of unimplemented Directive through the prism of interpretation of the judgment of the ECJ ...[87]

---

84 Case C-282/10, *Maribel Dominguez v. Centre informatique du Centre Ouest Atlantique and Préfet de la région Centre*, ECLI:EU:C:2012:33.

85 *Order II Ips 160/2013* of 23 April 2015; *Judgment II Ips* 228/2013 of 30 July 2015.

86 Council Directive 90/314/EEC of 13 June 1990 on package travel, package holidays and package tours [1990] OJ L158/59.

87 Translated by the authors.

This explanation unintentionally suggests that if the Directive had been implemented, the Supreme Court could have opted for direct effect of the directive. This is simply not the case, since the national law would apply in such a situation. Despite this inconsistency in the explanation, the Supreme Court's decision to adopt consistent interpretation was justified. In *Judgment II Ips 228/2013*, the Supreme Court did not explain its rationale in applying consistent interpretation. As discussed further below, while consistent interpretation in *Order II Ips 160/2013* seems convincing,[88] the Supreme Court went too far and made use of a *contra legem* interpretation in that judgment.[89]

Likewise, in the *Pelati* case, the Supreme Court stated that in cases of incompatibility of national rules with the provisions of a directive, the principle of consistent interpretation should be used before a provision of the directive prevails over the national rule according to the *Simmenthal* doctrine.[90]

In *Judgment I U 488/2015*,[91] the Administrative Court adopted an inconsistent approach in defining the order of sequence. In its general observations where it explained the legal basis, the Administrative Court stated that when a directive cannot be applied directly because it does not provide unconditional and sufficiently precise provisions, relevant national provisions should be interpreted in the light of the directive. This general observation of the court suggests that the national courts should first verify if a directive could be directly applied. If that is not possible, courts should use the principle of consistent interpretation. However, in applying the above-described rule to the particular circumstances of the case, the Administrative Court did not mention the direct effect of the directive at all but made use of the principle of consistent interpretation.

In another judgment of the Administrative Court,[92] the court correctly stated that it was not bound to assess the direct effect of a provision of the Directive at issue, since consistent interpretation of national law in line with the Directive would suffice. Likewise, there was no need to assess the proportionality of the national measure on the basis of Art. 52(1) of the EU Charter of fundamental rights.

---

88 Slovenian legislation did not explicitly provide a possibility to claim damages for the loss of enjoyment of the holiday. Art. 179 (1) of Code of Obligations (*Obligacijski zakonik* (OZ) Uradni list RS, št. 97/07 and subsequent) provided a possibility to claim non-material damage in certain exhaustively listed types of damage. One of them was also degradation of personal right (*okrnitev osebnostne pravice*). The Supreme Court referred to the *Leitner* case (Case C-168/00, *Simone Leitner v. Tui Deutschland GmbH Co. Kg*, ECLI:EU:C:2002:163), where the ECJ interpreted Directive 90/314/EEC (ibid.) in a way that it demands that Member States enable consumers to claim damages for the loss of enjoyment of the holiday. In the light of this jurisprudence, the Supreme Court explained that the right of personal integrity, which was a personal right, was degraded.

89 See section 6 below.

90 Case C-106/77, *Amministrazione delle finanze dello Stato v. Simmenthal*, ECLI:EU:C:1978:49.

91 *Judgment of the Supreme Court I U 488/2015* of 5 May 2015.

92 *Judgment of the Administrative Court I U 1179/2015* of 31 August 2015.

It is commonly accepted – even though no case-law has been found – that state liability for breaches of EU law remains an *ultima ratio* measure for the restitution of the breach.[93]

5. GENERAL SCOPE OF APPLICATION

5.1. HORIZONTAL SITUATIONS

According to the case-law of the ECJ, the principle of consistent interpretation applies in both vertical and horizontal situations. Slovenian courts have had no difficulties in adhering to this rule. There are many decisions where courts have relied on the principle of consistent interpretation in horizontal situations.[94]

5.2. CONSISTENT INTERPRETATION WITH EU LAW SOURCES OTHER THAN DIRECTIVES

Slovenian courts do not have any second thoughts about performing interpretations consistent with sources of EU law other than directives. However, a large majority of cases refer to directives because normally regulations apply directly and there is no need to interpret national law in line with them. The same applies for many provisions of the founding EU Treaties, especially in the domain of fundamental economic liberties. Slovenian judges frequently cite the jurisprudence of the ECJ,[95] provisions of the EU Charter on Fundamental Rights,[96] and even EU soft law.[97] In addition, there are many examples of

93 See V. Trstenjak and M. Brkan, *Pravo EU – Ustavno, procesno in gospodarsko pravo EU* (GV Založba, 2012), p. 248.

94 There were many cases concerning protection of consumers where a consumer relied on the principle of consistent interpretation against a company. See *Order of the Supreme Court II Ips 160/2013* of 23 April 2015; *Order of the Supreme Court II Ips 228/2013* of 30 July 2015. Some cases referred to trademarks where a company demanded the annulment of a so-called "dormant trademark", see *Order of the Supreme Court III Ips 179/2007* of 26 October 2010; *Judgment of the Supreme Court III Ips 68/2010* of 16 May 2013; *Judgment of the Supreme Court III Ips 9/2012* of 28 January 2014. Some cases come from the field of labour law; see *Order of the Supreme Court VIII Ips 191/2010* of 22 November 2011; *Order of the Supreme Court VIII Ips 107/2011* of 20 November 2011; *Judgment of the Supreme Court VIII Ips 431/2008* of 9 November 2010.

95 Most of the cases included in this contribution cite the jurisprudence of the ECJ, on either substantive or procedural issues. See e.g. *Judgment of the Administrative Court I U 498/2013* of 25 September 2013 with references to the *Elgafaji* case of the ECJ (Case C-465/07, *Meki Elgafaji and Noor Elgafaji v. Staatssecretaris van Justitie*, ECLI:EU:C:2009:94).

96 For example *Judgment of the Administrative Court I U 498/2013* of 25 September 2013; *Judgment of the Administrative Court I U 1327/2013* of 29 January 2014.

97 In *Decision U-I-295/13* of 19 October 2016 / Uradni list RS, št. 71/2016), paras. 73–76, the Constitutional Court addressed the indirect impact of EU soft law – in particular the Banking

consistent interpretation combining several sources within and outside EU law at the same time (e.g. European Convention on Human Rights,[98] UN Convention on the Rights of the Child and Geneva Convention on the Status of Refugees).[99]

In Decision G 8/2010,[100] the Supreme Court invoked Council Regulation (EC) No. 1/2003.[101] The Regulation was not directly applicable, because it defined the procedural guarantees before the European Commission, and did not determine their scope at the national level. However, the Supreme Court used the principle of consistent interpretation as an additional interpretational tool to arrive at the conclusion that the procedure before the Office for Protection of the Competition should have been inter partes.

5.3. DUTY OF CONSISTENT INTERPRETATION BEFORE THE EXPIRY OF A DEADLINE FOR TRANSPOSITION OF THE DIRECTIVE

National authorities are bound by the duty of consistent interpretation even though the deadline for transposition of the directive has not yet expired. A similar duty can be found in public international law.[102] Slovenian courts do not hesitate to apply this rule.

Communication from the European Commission – on the interpretation of national law. In the *Judgment of the Administrative Court I U 1327/2013* of 29 January 2014, the court referred to the Opinion of Advocate General Poiares Maduro on the methods of interpretation of EU law (Case C-465/07, *Meki Elgafaji and Noor Elgafaji v. Staatssecretaris van Justitie*, ECLI:EU:C:2008:479). In *Order no. 018-004/2010 Republika Slovenija, Državni zbor* of 4 February 2010, the National Review Commission for Reviewing Public Procurement Award Procedures (*Državna revizijska komisija za revizijo postopkov javnih naročil* – NRC) invoked page 26 of the Guide to the Community rules on public works contracts (European Commission, *Guide to the Community rules on public works contracts* <https://www.publictendering.com/pdf/legislation/works_en.pdf>). See also *Order no. 018-402/2011 Mestna občina Kranj* of 11 January 2012, where the NRC uses three different sources of soft law to support its argumentation: Opinion of AG Mazák (Case C-480/06, *Commission v. Germany*, ECLI:EU:C:2009:102; EU Parliament's Report on New Developments in Public Procurement (2009/2175(INI)) and Commission Staff Working Paper concerning application of EU public procurement law to relations between contracting authorities (public-public cooperation) of 4 October 2011 (<https://ec.europa.eu/docsroom/documents/21190/attachments/1/translations/en/renditions/pdf>).

98 *Judgment and decision of the Administrative Court I U 531/2009* of 1 April 2009.

99 *Judgment of the Administrative Court I U 42/2012* of 15 February 2012.

100 *Decision G 8/2010* of 20 April 2010.

101 Council Regulation (EC) No 1/2003 of 16 December 2002 on the implementation of the rules on competition laid down in Arts. 81 and 82 of the Treaty [2002] OJ L1/1.

102 Art. 18 of the Vienna Convention on the Law of Treaties of 23 May 1969 entered into force on 27 January 1980, United Nations, *Treaty Series*, vol. 1155, p. 331.

For example, in *Judgment III U 389/2013*, the Administrative Court dealt with a case concerning advertisements for electronic cigarettes.[103] The company that advertised the electronic cigarettes argued that electronic cigarettes were not tobacco products, and that advertisements should therefore be allowed. The Administrative Court upheld the decision of the administrative authority. It based its decision on Art. 10(3) of Restriction of the Use of Tobacco Products Act, which prohibited the advertising of products which were not tobacco or tobacco products but whose appearance and purpose of use directly promoted consumption thereof.[104] The Administrative Court interpreted this provision loyally to the new Tobacco Products Directive,[105] which had already come into force, but whose deadline for implementation had not yet expired. The new Tobacco Directive treated electronic cigarettes in a similar way to normal cigarettes. This made it possible for the Administrative Court to conclude that advertising electronic cigarettes was prohibited, despite the fact that the national law did not explicitly prohibit advertisements of electronic cigarettes. It was also arguable under national law whether electronic cigarettes directly promoted consumption of tobacco and tobacco products – a reasonable argument raised by the company was that the aim of (advertising) electronic cigarettes was to dissuade consumers from using normal cigarettes, and thus did not promote consumption of tobacco and tobacco products.

What is disputed in academic circles is the extent to which the national authorities should abide by this rule. According to one reading of the ECJ jurisprudence, there should be no practical difference in application of the principle of consistent interpretation before and after the expiry of deadline for implementation once the directive entered into force. However, *Adeneler* suggests a different solution.[106] Slovenian judiciary seems to have adopted the more pro-European reading.

The Constitutional Court stated in its *Decision Up-2012/08*:[107]

> [T]he Courts must, from the moment of the Directive's entry into force, irrespective of whether the time limit for implementation has expired or not, when interpreting

---

103 *Judgment of the Administrative Court I U 1561/2011* and *I U 1562/2011* of 15 September 2011; *Judgment of the Supreme Court III U 389/2013* of 8 January 2015.

104 *Zakon o omejevanju uporabe tobačnih izdelkov* (ZOUTI), Uradni list RS, št. 93/07.

105 Directive 2014/40/EU of the European Parliament and of the Council of 3 April 2014 on the approximation of the laws, regulations and administrative provisions of the Member States concerning the manufacture, presentation and sale of tobacco and related products and repealing Directive 2001/37/EC [2014] OJ L127/1.

106 Cf. Case C-212/04, *Konstantinos Adeneler and Others v. Ellinikos Organismos Galaktos (ELOG)*, ECLI:EU:C:2006:443, para. 123: "[F]rom the date upon which a directive has entered into force, the courts of the Member States must refrain as far as possible from interpreting domestic law in a manner which might seriously compromise, after the period for transposition has expired, attainment of the objective pursued by that directive."

107 *Decision Up-2012/08* (n. 70).

> a national legal rule, interpret a national legal rule as much as possible in accordance with the purpose and wording of the Directive in order for the Directive to attain its desired goal.[108]

The Constitutional Court repeated this in *Decision U-I-155/11*,[109] where it interpreted national legal provisions consistently with provisions of the Procedural Directive.[110] Other national court decisions seem to follow the Constitutional Court's footsteps. In *Judgment I Up 357/2011*, the Supreme Court recognised that before expiry of a deadline for transposition, the state is not *stricto iure* bound by the content of the directive. Nevertheless, it stated that in such a case, it was necessary to interpret national law as much as possible in the light of the directive.

5.4. CONSISTENT INTERPRETATION OF NATIONAL LAW IN GENERAL

All of the national court decisions that have been examined for the purpose of this contribution refer to consistent interpretation of statutory Acts (legislation), as Slovenia is a civil law country with a system of well-established case-law, and not a precedent system. It is therefore hard to say whether there is a real example where established case-law was or needed to be interpreted in the light of the EU law. However, some decisions can be found where Slovenian courts used the principle of consistent interpretation to interpret the statute contrary to the established jurisprudence.

For example, in the previously mentioned *Vnuk* case, the Supreme Court decided that the term "use of vehicle" refers not only to the use of vehicles in traffic, but also to any use of vehicle consistent with the normal function of the vehicle in question. This meant a change in well-established national jurisprudence,[111] where the term "use of vehicles" had been narrowly interpreted to cover only use of vehicles in public traffic. The decision in *Vnuk* had a strong impact, and new cases confirmed the change in jurisprudence shortly after.[112]

---

108 Translated by the authors.

109 *Decision U-I-155/11* of 18 December 2013 (Uradni list RS, št. 114/2013; OdlUS XX, 12), para. 19.

110 Council Directive 2005/85/EC of 1 December 2005 on minimum standards on procedures in Member States for granting and withdrawing refugee status [2005] OJ L326/13.

111 This is line with the obligation for national courts to change its established case-law, where necessary, if it is based on an interpretation of national law that is incompatible with the objectives of a directive (Case C-456/98, *Centrosteel*, ECLI:EU:C:2000:402, para. 17).

112 See *Judgment of the High Court of Ljubljana II Cp 1752/2015* of 24 June 2015; *Judgment and Order of the High Labour and Social Court Pdp 621/2015* of 21 January 2016; *Judgment of the Supreme Court II Ips 334/2015* of 25 February 2016.

5.5. (IR)RELEVANCE OF NATIONAL *TRAVAUX PRÉPARATOIRES*

Preparatory legislative works (*travaux préparatoires*) are sometimes relied on by the national courts when interpreting legal provisions. They provide important pointers as to the reasons behind the adoption of a particular legislative solution, and what its purpose was. According to Pavčnik, when the courts are referring to *travaux préparatoires* they perform historical interpretations. In his view, it is important that courts do not rely solely on historical interpretation but use other types of interpretation, which as a whole lead to the correct interpretation.[113] Historical interpretation is thus only one of the methods of interpretation and does not have greater significance in comparison to other methods.

Similarly to other courts, the Constitutional Court has invoked *travaux préparatoires* in many decisions as an additional interpretative tool to strengthen its reasoning. In *Decision U-I-221/00*, the Constitutional Court used literal, systematic and historical interpretation to explain that there is no appeal against a decision of the Administrative Courts in asylum cases.[114] In *Decision U-I-346/02*, the Constitutional Court invoked literal, logical and historical interpretation in a case concerning possibilities for the legislator to restrict the right to vote.[115]

There are not many decisions where national *travaux préparatoires* and the purpose of a legal provision (as understood in the light thereof) came into conflict with interpretation in the light of EU law. In principle, interpretation loyal to EU law should prevail in such cases. This can be concluded from the Constitutional Court's *Decision Up-2012/08*,[116] where the Constitutional Court made an important footnote, whereby it dismantled any importance of historical interpretation and gave priority to the purpose of the EU law.

Despite this, the National Review Commission for Reviewing Public Procurement Award Procedures (*Državna revizijska komisija za revizijo postopkov javnih naročil* – the NRC), a body competent to verify the legality of conduct of contracting authorities in public procurement cases, has in certain cases placed emphasis on the *travaux préparatoires* at the expense of interpretation consistent with EU law. In one of its decisions, the NRC used the *travaux préparatoires* to interpret national provisions concerning the amendment of bids broadly.[117] The NRC stated that there were no "evident reasons" that would contradict the interpretation of national rules in the light of the *travaux préparatoires* to the Amendment of Public Procurement Act, which established a broader possibility to correct the bid. The NRC should have instead interpreted the national law

---

113 M. Pavčnik, *Teorija prava* (3rd ed., GV Založba, 2007) 503–08.
114 *Decision U-I-221/00* of 29 June 2000 (Uradni list RS, št. 66/2000; OdlUS IX, 258), para. 3.
115 *Decision U-I-346/02* of 24 October 2002 (Uradni list RS, št. 73/2003; OdlUS XII, 70), para. 11.
116 *Decision Up-2012/08* (n. 70).
117 *Order no. 018-260/2014* of 18 December 2014.

consistently with the EU Public Procurement rules, as interpreted by the ECJ, which demanded a restrictive approach when interpreting the possibility of amendment of the bids. As a result, the NRC allowed the correction of the bid even though it was contrary to the EU public procurement rules and the jurisprudence of the ECJ.

6. LIMITS TO THE PRINCIPLE OF CONSISTENT INTERPRETATION

Before looking at the limits to the principle of consistent interpretation, one should have an understanding of the forces and rationale behind the principle. From the perspective of EU law and policy, it is inherent that these limits are construed and understood narrowly in order to give as wide as possible effect to the validity, persuasiveness and efficiency of EU law. The principle of consistent interpretation as such is also a means of achieving *effet utile* of EU law. Overstretching its limits would therefore endanger the practical meaning, existence and legitimacy of the EU. To better understand the scope of the limitations, it is necessary to shed some light on the other side of the coin, i.e. how the scope of application of the principle is framed.

6.1. DUTY TO INTERPRET CONSISTENTLY "AS FAR AS POSSIBLE"

The principle of consistent interpretation demands national courts to interpret a national provision as far as possible in the light of provisions of EU law. This principle has been recognised by the Constitutional Court as a fundamental constitutional principle in *Decision U-I-146/12*.[118] As the case-law presented in this contribution implies, Slovenian courts sincerely pursue that national legislation remains within the ambit of EU law, particularly where national and EU law are not completely in line.

Nevertheless, it remains to be seen if Slovenian courts entirely embrace an obligation to seek the most EU-friendly interpretation of national legislation. It seems that the Supreme Court has recognised some limits to the principle of consistent interpretation in two judgments in the field of asylum law.[119] It stated in both cases that "the provisions of the International Protection Act that are

118 The Constitutional Court repeated this position in *Decision U-I-295/13* of 19 October 2016 (Uradni list RS, št. 82/2014 in Uradni list RS, št. 71/2016), para. 67.

119 *Judgment of the Supreme Court I Up 95/2014* of 2 April 2014; *Judgment of the Supreme Court I Up 99/2014* of 3 April 2014.

in conformity with EU law may not be interpreted wider than their wording [*i.e. literal meaning*]".[120] At the first glance, one may deduce from this that the court is satisfied with the literal meaning of national provisions if there is no doubt about their conformity with EU law. By doing so, the Court does not follow the best endeavours obligation to find the most EU-friendly interpretation of the national provision. If this is so, then the national courts are willing to accept that national principles of construction and interpretation may hinder the full effect of the EU principle of consistent interpretation. From the case under consideration, clear and unambiguous national provisions prevent courts from performing teleological interpretations, irrespective of the provisions' autonomous (national or EU-level) character. It is only possible to speculate as to whether the driving force behind the Court's wording would be the principle of separation of powers and/or the principle of legality. Yet the issue is not so straightforward, as it is not clear if the Court only wanted to distance itself from applying national provisions *contra legem*, despite the interpretation thereof having been more EU-friendly.

To sum it up, as only two almost identical cases which are semi-relevant have been identified by the present authors, it is clear that Slovenian courts have not yet made a doctrinal move in any direction.

There are some cases where the Administrative and Supreme Courts understand the obligation "as far as possible" in a positive fashion, and reinterpret national provisions to make them EU-compliant.[121] One case is very interesting, since the question of consistent interpretation intertwined with the issue of constitutionality, and because the deadline for transposition of the Directive had not yet expired. The Ministry of the Interior had deported a foreign national without giving him an opportunity to voluntarily return within a reasonable deadline. The Ministry relied on the fact that the then Aliens Act did not require a special return decision and for a deadline for voluntary return to be set.[122] The returnee sued the Ministry before the Administrative Court. In the meantime, the Constitutional Court had rendered the relevant provisions of the Aliens Act unconstitutional. Taking the Constitutional Court's decision into account and interpreting the Aliens Act in an EU-friendly way, the Administrative Court decided that the deportation violated the rights of freedom of movement and preventing deprivation of liberty of the returnee.

The Ministry appealed, and claimed again that it could not be bound to issue a special return decision. While agreeing with the Ministry on the irrelevance of the decision of the Constitutional Court for the result of the case at hand, the Supreme Court rejected the assertions by highlighting the goal of the

120 Authors' insertion. Translated by the authors.

121 *Judgment and Order of the Administrative Court I U 1477/2010* of 9 May 2011; *Judgment of the Supreme Court I Up 357/2011* of 1 September 2011.

122 *Zakon o tujcih* (ZTuj-1), Uradni list RS, št. 64/09.

Return Directive that, *inter alia*, the ending of illegal stay of third-country nationals should be carried out through a fair and transparent procedure.[123] The Supreme Court stated that the principle of consistent cooperation obliges authorities to "refrain from any measure, which could jeopardise the attainment of the Directive's objectives" (i.e. negative obligation of the duty of consistent cooperation). In addition, they need to interpret "national law as much as possible in the light of the Directive" even if they are faced with a situation that occurred before the expiry of the deadline for transposition of the Directive.[124]

6.2. LACK OF COMPETENCE AS A "PRETEXT" NOT TO ENGAGE INTO CONSISTENT INTERPRETATION

As explained above, the Constitution does not afford any legal basis for the Constitutional Court to assess conformity of a law with a directive or regulation. For this reason, the Constitutional Court rejects all claims if the applicant only claims that national law contravenes a Directive.[125] Despite the fact that the Art. 3a of the Constitution requires that national law provisions be in conformity with the relevant Directive, the Constitutional Court declares a lack of competence to address such claims. The legal situation changes if an applicant raises the unconstitutionality of a provision of a national law, which contravenes the directive. In such a case, the Constitutional Court is competent to hear the claim.[126] It may declare a national provision contrary to Art. 3a of the Constitution and not contrary to the directive.

6.3. SLIPPERY NATURE AND SCOPE OF *CONTRA LEGEM* INTERPRETATIONS IN PRACTICE

The ECJ forbade interpretations *contra legem*, but did not define this term as such; however, it made very strict conclusions on how national courts should react once they establish that national law contravenes EU law.[127] It has repeatedly stated in its jurisprudence that the principle of consistent interpretation

123 Directive 2008/115/EC of 16 December 2008 on common standards and procedures in Member States for returning illegally staying third-country nationals [2008] OJ L348/98.

124 *Judgment of the Supreme Court I Up 357/2011* of 1 September 2011 (translated by the authors).

125 *Order U-I-188/04* of 8 September 2005; *Decision U-I-32/04* of 9 February 2006; *Order U-I-116/07* of 25 May 2007; *Order U-I-44/05* of 11 September 2007; *Decision U-I-238/07* of 2 April 2009.

126 Nerad (n. 22), pp. 389–90.

127 Case C-441/14, *Ajos*, ECLI:EU:C:2016:278, in particular: "… an obligation to provide, within the limits of its jurisdiction, the legal protection which individuals derive from EU law and to ensure the full effectiveness of that law, disapplying if need be any provision of national legislation contrary to that principle".

"is limited by general principles of law, particularly those of legal certainty and non-retroactivity, and that obligation [to perform consistent interpretations] cannot serve as the basis for an interpretation of national law *contra legem*".[128] However, the ECJ demands that national courts must do "whatever lies within their jurisdiction" to give EU law full effect.[129] The *contra legem* limitation is thus at least partly determined by national law.

Slovenian rules on interpretation are firmly rooted in legal theory, which forms a strong basis for interpretation in the judges' daily work. According to Marijan Pavčnik, the preeminent scholar in Slovenia on matters concerning interpretation:

> [T]ext is a start-point and a language framework, in which the interpreter operates. The interpreter's task is to stay within the boundaries of the text and within the boundaries that the wording offers. If the interpreter does not comply with this, we cannot speak about interpretation [... but] about creation of legal rules, which is in the competence of the legislator ...[130]

Pavčnik states that the literal interpretation is "only the first step which defines a possible meaning of the legal rule. However, it is also a step which defines an outer boundary, which must not be crossed by the interpreter."[131]

He cites the example of *Decision Up-9/95*,[132] where the Constitutional Court stated that "The text of Article 20(3) of the Constitution cannot be interpreted in a way, that the term submitted indictment should be understood as final indictment, because that would not be an interpretation but another meaning not based on the text of the Constitution".[133]

The literal interpretation should always be "supplemented and verified" by other interpretations – namely logical, systematic, historical and teleological interpretation – that confirm "one of more possible meanings which is correct (legal meaning)".[134]

Unfortunately, Pavčnik does not define a *contra legem* interpretation explicitly. Therefore we can only understand what *contra legem* interpretation means in the Slovenian legal system by taking into account other scholars' opinions. Nerad uses the term *contra legem* quite often. He describes *contra legem* interpretation as a situation where "under pretext of interpretation, the provision is given contents not made possible by methods of interpretation".[135]

---

128 *Adeneler* (n. 106), para. 110.
129 Ibid., para. 111.
130 Pavčnik (n. 113), p. 483 (translated by the authors).
131 Ibid., p. 486 (translated by the authors).
132 *Decision of the Constitutional Court Up-9/95* of 28 February 1995 (OdlUS IV, 144).
133 Pavčnik (n. 113), p. 491 (translated by the authors).
134 Ibid., p. 487 (translated by the authors).
135 S. Nerad, *Interpretativne odločbe Ustavnega sodišča* (Založba Uradni list RS, 2007), p. 166 (translated by the authors).

It is important to note that Nerad has a broad understanding of "methods of interpretation". According to Nerad, this does not cover only Von Savigny's classical methods (literal, logical, historical, systematic and teleological),[136] but also analogy and *argumentum a contrario*. This can be seen from an article where he reacted to (in his opinion) incorrect commentaries on decisions of the Constitutional and Supreme Court. He stated that courts should not go beyond what is possible from the point of view of interpretation of law.[137] He also thinks that "giving a provision a meaning which is totally contrary to the text" is prohibited for the courts.[138]

The *contra legem* limitation should in the present authors' opinion be understood as defined by Nerad in the broader context of Pavčnik's works on interpretation. Even though Pavčnik does not afford a clear definition, his works have to be borne in mind by practitioners, as the Constitutional Court commonly cites them in theoretical parts of its reasoning and thus accords them importance and quality.[139] These citations implicitly support an assumption that Pavčnik's works on legal theory constitute a basis for court interpretation, in the practice of the Slovenian courts.

Given the lack of a definition in Pavčnik's works, use of the term *contra legem* is not unified. In addition to what the present authors believe is the best definition of the term, many other approaches have also been adopted. First, the courts use the term *contra legem* when they want to stress that a provision is so clear that no interpretation is allowed.[140]A more exact approach in such cases would be to simply refer to the unwritten rule of interpretation – *in claris non fit interpretatio*. However, this does not mean that the present authors consider such an approach to be wrong, but in their opinion it is not nuanced enough and is thus open to arbitrary use. Second, the term *contra legem* is used as a synonym for "unlawful" or "illegal".[141] There is no reason to use a Latin word in this respect, except the fact that it may sound nicer. Third, some lawyers use this term when they want to describe a situation where the Government adopts an act despite the existence of a provision of a statute that prohibits normative activity of the Government in that specific case.[142] Finally, an interesting opinion suggests that *contra legem* interpretations are interpretations of a provision of an act that violate the provision of another act.[143]

---

136 M. Pavčnik, *Argumentacija v pravu* (GV Založba, 2013), p. 110.

137 S. Nerad, "Pravna praznina in protiustavna pravna praznina" (2010) 29–30 *Pravna praksa* 6.

138 Nerad (n. 135), p. 162 (translated by the authors).

139 *Decision U-I-115/14, Up-218/14* of 21 January 2016 (Uradni list RS, št. 8/2016); *Decision Up-645/13* of 3 March 2016 (Uradni list RS, št. 24/2016); *Order U-I-186/15* of 7 April 2016.

140 *Order of the High Court Maribor I Ip 232/2014* of 23 May 2014; *Order of the High Court Maribor I Ip 920/2014* of 5 December 2014; *Judgment of the Supreme Court VIII Ips 131/2014* of 13 January 2015.

141 *Judgment of the High Court of Ljubljana I Cp 3993/2010* of 22 June 2011.

142 G. Virant, "Ustavna odločba doktrinarnega pomena" (1997) 8 *Pravna praksa* 2.

143 M. Fabjančič, "Nedorečeno in contra legem" (1996) 1 *Podjetje in delo* 50.

The actual words "*contra legem*" are not found very often in the jurisprudence of Slovenian courts, even if jurisprudence unconnected with EU law is taken into account. For instance, the Constitutional Court has not yet used this term. However, other expressions were used instead. In most cases, Slovenian judges do not explicitly refer to a specific term; they simply explain that a provision should be interpreted in a certain way.[144] It is therefore very hard to find relevant decisions.

Being a necessary component of every legal system, the prohibition of *contra legem* interpretations can be inferred from several provisions of the Constitution, and primarily from Art. 2 thereof. It protects the rule of law, and according to the well-established case-law of the Constitutional Court, includes legal certainty as a sub-principle. In the event that a national court or other authority were to perform a *contra legem* interpretation, it would amount to a violation of the said constitutional provision on the ground that it would have been impossible to predict such an interpretation in advance. Furthermore, Art. 2 should be read jointly with Arts. 125 and 120 of the Constitution, which provide that judges and other public authorities are bound by laws and the Constitution (principle of legality in the functioning of state authorities).

In addition, by applying the principle of the separation of powers in Art. 3(2) of the Constitution, courts are barred from interpretation beyond the meaning of a provision, where unsupported by classical methods of interpretation. Otherwise it would mean that the court was acting as a legislator. The legislator has the exclusive power to create new legal rules "out of thin air", to provide new rights and impose new obligations. In a case not connected with EU law, the High Court of Maribor held that a judge's interpretation of the legal text should not be *contra legem* (i.e. contrary to a clear legal text), on the basis of the separation of judicial and legislative power.[145] In another almost identical purely national case, the same court stated that by creating a legal rule which differed from a clear legal text, the first instance court had exceeded its judicial competence and violated the principle of the separation of powers.[146]

---

[144] In *Judgment II Ips 305/2009 of 24 June 2009*, the Supreme Court was confronted with a situation where the legislator intentionally did not regulate the possibility to award damages in cases where violation of the right of trial in a reasonable time had accrued before 2007. The *travaux préparatoires* of the relevant legal act suggested that this legal lacuna would be filled by jurisprudence. Contrary to the inferior courts, the Supreme Court stated that there was no legal basis to award damages in such cases. It added that the "decision, whether a revision of regulation which does not afford legal validity to such damages is needed, is in the hands of the legislator" (translated by the authors). Despite the fact that the term *contra legem* would have been appropriate, the Supreme Court did not use it in its short and concise explanation.

[145] *Order of the High Court Maribor I Ip 232/2014* of 23 May 2014.

[146] *Order of the High Court Maribor I Ip 920/2014* of 5 December 2014.

These two cases concerned the interpretation of Art. 197(1)-3 of the Claim Enforcement and Security Act.[147] The relevant question of interpretation at issue in these cases is firmly rooted in the Slovene language. It is therefore impossible to translate this in a way that would expose the main issue at stake. However, it may be possible to simplify this complex but important question. Some higher courts (e.g. the High Court of Maribor) advocate a text-related approach. By this approach, the relevant text is interpreted so that a one-year time limit only applies to one of the protected categories. Debts falling into other protected categories are protected, despite coming into existence more than one year before the issuing of a relevant decision in the claim enforcement procedure. Under the other approach (advocated by other higher courts, for example the High Court of Ljubljana),[148] the time limit of one year extends to all debts which fall into one of the protected categories. This approach seems to strike a fair balance between protection of vulnerable creditors and the mortgagee's right of property. The latter approach was later confirmed by the Constitutional Court in *Decision U-I-47/15*.[149] This renders the two above-mentioned decisions of the High Court of Maribor wrong, as it neither interpreted the relevant provision in the light of Constitution (according to the High Court of Maribor, the provision was clear and should not be interpreted), nor stopped the procedure and questioned the constitutionality of the provision before the Constitutional Court. However, the Constitutional Court did not say that the relevant provision should be interpreted according to the second approach. It did not want to exclude the unconstitutional interpretation from the Slovenian legal system by adopting a negative interpretive decision, either.[150] Nor did it give any guidance concerning *contra legem* interpretations. It simply decided to annul the provision to the extent that it covered the alimony debts that came into existence before the one-year period. In a way, this means that the High Court of Maribor was not entirely wrong. It could have adopted the first approach, but should have seen that the provision in itself was problematic from the point of view of the Constitution. The idea of not interpreting when a court finds that this would amount to a *contra legem* interpretation is not wrong, despite the fact that such an interpretation could be contrary to the Constitution. This is so because the principle of separation of powers, which is also a constitutional principle, prevents the judge from interpreting the provision *contra legem*. However, in such cases, judges should stop the procedure and question the constitutionality of the provision.

---

147 *Zakon o izvršbi in zavarovanju* (ZIZ), Uradni list RS, št. 3/07 – 93/07, 37/08 – ZST-1, 45/08 – ZArbit, 28/09, 51/10, 26/11, 17/13 – odl. US, 45/14 – odl. US, 53/14, 58/14 – odl. US, 54/15 in 76/15 – odl. US.

148 *Order I Ip 1405/2010* of 18 November 2010.

149 *Decision U-I-47/15* of 24 September 2010 (Uradni list RS, št. 76/2015).

150 Such a negative interpretative decision was adopted for example in the Constitutional Court's *Decision U-I-66/08* of 11 December 2008 (Uradni list RS, št. 121/2008; OdlUS XVII, 73).

In some cases, *contra legem* interpretations also violate Art. 22 of the Constitution, which guarantees equal protection of rights in any proceeding before a court. As this Article encompasses the prohibition of evident judicial arbitrariness, it is relevant to check if the interpretation of the law goes beyond classical methods of interpretation. The Constitutional Court reviews it by application of the Schumann formula, i.e. the interpretation of a provision is declared unconstitutional if, hypothetically, such an interpretation transposed into the legislative act would be contrary to the Constitution.[151] The court's interpretation has to be manifestly defunct to violate Art. 22 of the Constitution. Where established methods of interpretation are used by courts, the Constitution is respected.[152] However, in the case where a court would not use the established methods of interpretation, but would interpret the provision *contra legem*, this would amount to a violation of Art. 22 of the Constitution.[153]

6.4. RELIANCE ON GENERAL PRINCIPLES OF LAW TO LIMIT THE SCOPE OF APPLICATION OF CONSISTENT INTERPRETATION

The principle of consistent interpretation demands that national courts interpret domestic provisions as far as possible in the light of provisions of the directive. However, courts in Slovenia are not always aware of the impact that general principles of law might have on the application of consistent interpretation, in particular the accentuation of the principles of legal certainty and non-retroactivity in the *Kolpinghuis* case.[154] This assertion is based on quantitative and qualitative research and the present authors have not found a single decision of national courts where these general principles are invoked to prevent consistent interpretations.[155] What is more, some cases have been found in which it would be at least appropriate, if not obligatory, to reject application of the principle. Nevertheless, national courts performed *contra legem* interpretations in these cases; therefore, the argumentation, not the decisions themselves, is criticised. These cases will be dealt with below.

---

151 *Decision of the Constitutional Court Up-611/07* of 6 November 2008 (Uradni list RS, št. 111/2008; OdlUS XVII, 88), para. 4.

152 *Order of the Constitutional Court Up-280/00* of 18 September 2001, para. 10.

153 A. Galič, "22. člen" in M. Avbelj and L. Šturm (eds.), *Komentar Ustave Republike Slovenije – dopolnitev A* (FDEŠ, 2011), pp. 322–25.

154 Case 80/86, *Criminal proceedings against Kolpinghuis Nijmegen*, ECLI:EU:C:1987:431; cf. *Judgment and Order of the Administrative Court I U 38/2006* of 11 January 2006, where the court referred to the ECJ case in a general way: "[W]hereby the court has to take into account general principles of law, legitimate expectations and prohibition of retroactivity."

155 However, see *Judgment of the Administrative Court I U 1353/2011* of 28 July 2011, where the court raises the question of equivalence between the national and EU understanding of the principle of proportionality, but refrained from clarifying the issue as it was not necessary for the decision in the case.

6.5. ARTIFICIAL INTERPRETATIONS OF NATIONAL LAW FOR THE PURPOSE OF AVOIDING THE INTERPRETATIVE CONFLICT

In the present authors' opinion, the question is whether Slovenian courts make use of *contra legem* interpretations in cases of conflicting provisions of national law as frequently as in cases of conflicts between a national law provision and a provision of EU law. It has not been possible to provide a complete answer due to lack of data, and so an in-depth and complete research of the jurisprudence has not therefore been carried out in this respect. As this was not a primary aim of this contribution, it has been limited to examining several decisions of the Constitutional Court where conformity of two conflicting national law provisions has been assessed. These decisions could provide useful pointers on how the Constitutional Court could decide on limitations of the principle of consistent interpretation in the future. However, the authors are aware of the potential misgivings that such an analogous approach might give rise to, due to the particular nature of EU law and its primacy over national law.

According to the Constitutional Court, whenever there is a conflict between two national provisions of the same hierarchical rank (e.g. two statutory provisions), inconsistencies are to be primarily resolved through standard methods of interpretation. The Constitutional Court is, in principle, not competent to resolve this conflict. If the conflict cannot be resolved, then the question of violation of Art. 2 of the Constitution arises. In such cases, the Constitutional Court is competent to review whether this incompatibility violates the principle of legal certainty.[156] In *Order U-I-193/99*, the Claim Enforcement and Security Act provided that, under certain conditions,[157] the creditor could retrieve banking data on the debtor in order to enforce a claim. However, the Banking Act allowed the transmission of such data only to the competent court at its request or order.[158] The inconsistency was capable of being remedied with the use of the principle of *lex posterior derogat legi priori*. Consequently, the Constitutional Court dismissed the claim due to lack of competence.[159] However, in *Decision U-I-75/01*,[160] the Constitutional Court

156 *Order U-I-193/99* of 31 January 2002 (OdlUS XI, 16); *Order of the Constitutional Court U-I-70/04* of 15 February 2007 (Uradni list RS, št. 18/2007; OdlUS XVI, 17), para. 16. See also S. Nerad, "160. člen" in M. Avbelj and L. Šturm (eds.), *Komentar Ustave – dopolnitev A.* (FDEŠ, 2011), pp. 1414, 1418–19.

157 *Zakon o izvršbi in zavarovanju* (n. 147).

158 *Zakon o bančništvu* (ZBan), Uradni list RS, št. 7/99 and subsequent.

159 *Order of the Constitutional Court U-I-193/99* of 31 January 2002 (OdlUS XI, 16). See also the *Decision of the Constitutional Court U-I-278/07* of 22 October 2009 (Uradni list RS, št. 94/2009; OdlUS XVIII, 47), where the Constitutional Court applied the interpretational rule *lex specialis derogat legi generali* to resolve a conflict between two laws.

160 *Decision U-I-75/01* of 12 February 2004 (Uradni list RS, št. 19/2004; OdlUS XIII, 8).

found that incompatibility of two provisions of a municipality's statute violated Art. 2 of the Constitution, as it was impossible to provide an interpretation that would resolve the conflict. Similarly, the Constitutional Court has annulled conflicting provisions of national laws in other decisions.[161]

How to deal with situations of inconsistency between two national provisions of the same rank is clear under national law. If the inconsistency cannot be eliminated using standard methods of interpretation, Art. 2 of the Constitution provides a barrier that prevents *contra legem* interpretations of national law. On the other hand, when national law that implements a directive is in conflict with a directive, the situation is less clear. As already stated, not a single clear-cut decision where a national court would limit the principle of consistent interpretation has been identified. Therefore, any conclusion at this stage would be only an educated guess.

In the relationship between EU law and national law, courts of EU Member States are under a "dual obligation of loyalty",[162] by paying respect to provisions on national and European level. In general, it would be inconceivable that national courts would defer to the EU law standards at the expense of standards of national statutory interpretation, in particular if methodology of interpretation offers a satisfactory untangling of both. Yet, there are some indications that courts employ such a "unilateral" approach unintentionally, and get away with it. There is a thin line between a strained and a *contra legem* interpretation, and there is a danger that the analysis here might suffer from crossing it for being over-zealous in searching relevant case-law.

In *Judgment II Ips 228/2013*,[163] the Supreme Court decided on the question of a tourist agency's liability for damage caused to its customers by its subcontractor. Slovenian legislation provided a possibility of exculpation for the tourist agency if it proved that it acted as a diligent professional when choosing its subcontractor. However, an EU Directive imposed liability on the tourist agency, despite its diligent and faultless choice of a subcontractor.[164] The Supreme Court first acknowledged that the Directive was not fully transposed into national law. In the second step, the Supreme Court explained that the relevant provision of the Directive might have direct effect in situations such as the one at hand.

---

161 *Decision U-I-227/00* of 14 February 2002 (Uradni list RS, št. 23/2002; OdlUS XI, 23); *Decision U-I-8/00* of 10 May 2001 (Uradni list RS, št. 43/2001; OdlUS X, 84).

162 D. Leczykiewicz, "Melloni and the future of constitutional conflict in the EU" (*UK Constitutional Law Blog*, 22 May 2013) <https://ukconstitutionallaw.org/2013/05/22/dorota-leczykiewicz-melloni-and-the-future-of-constitutional-conflict-in-the-eu>. See also a broader discussion on *multiple obligations of loyalty* in S. Zagorc, "Evropska unija in Evropska konvencija o človekovih pravicah: Preplet varstva človekovih pravic" in M. Žgur, N. Kogovšek Šalamon and B. Koritnik (eds.), *Izzivi ustavnega prava v 21. stoletju/Liber Amicorum Ciril Ribičič* (Lex Localis, 2017), pp. 121–23.

163 *Judgment II Ips 228/2013* of 30 July 2015.

164 Council Directive 90/314/EEC (n. 86).

This statement is strange for two reasons:[165] First, the case addresses the application of the Directive in horizontal relationships, and the *Marshall* doctrine should prevail. Second, one cannot interpret national legislation in the light of EU law to explain that a provision of EU law is directly effective at the same time. As the relationship was horizontal, the Court continued its explanation with the principle of consistent interpretation. The Court concluded that relevant provisions of Slovenian legislation should be interpreted in the light of EU law to give a result which was compatible with the Directive. Accordingly, it interpreted national law in a way that the tourist agency was liable for damages caused by its subcontractor. Such interpretation not only goes beyond the wording of the national legislation,[166] but also leaves no doubt that the Court gave *de facto* direct effect to the provision of the Directive in a horizontal relationship, through its *contra legem* interpretation of national law. The court thereby unintentionally succeeded in shifting the burden of carrying the consequences of non-transposition of the Directive from the state to the tourist agency. The tourist agency might then further claim damages incurred by a breach of EU law by a Member State, in line with *Francovich*.

Well-established jurisprudence of the Supreme Court reveals another example of a *contra legem* interpretation, this time of domestic labour law. In *Order VIII Ips 191/2010*,[167] the Supreme Court dealt with a case concerning compensation for unused annual leave. Art. 164 of Employment Relationship Act provided that "[a]n agreement by which an employee and an employer would settle for a pecuniary compensation for unused annual leave except in the case of termination of employment, is null".[168] The Supreme Court carefully elaborated the doctrine of consistent interpretation by citing the relevant Directive and the jurisprudence of the ECJ.[169] However, use of the principle of consistent interpretation led the Supreme Court to the following result: An employee has a right to compensation for annual leave in the case of termination of employment when the employee objectively could not make use of the annual leave before

165 The Supreme Court stated: "Taking into account the euro-consistent or harmonizing interpretation of Slovenian legislation on the basis of a clear and unconditional provision of the Directive, which has been widely accepted in the jurisprudence of the CJEU and Member States' courts also in horizontal relations in cases of non-implementation or wrongful implementation of the Directive, a conclusion that said provisions of the Directive do not have a direct effect, is wrong." (translated by the authors).

166 Art. 892(2) of the Code of Obligations (*Obligacijski zakonik* (OZ) Uradni list RS, št. 97/07 and subsequent) provides that the organiser of a trip who entrusted transport, accommodation or other services to a third party is responsible for damage that was caused by the third party, unless he/she proves that he/she chose them as a diligent organiser of a trip.

167 *Order VIII Ips 191/2010* of 22 November 2011.

168 *Zakon o delovnih razmerjih* (ZDR) Uradni list RS, št. 42/2002 and subsequent (translated by the authors).

169 Directive 2003/88/EC of the European Parliament and of the Council of 4 November 2003 concerning certain aspects of the organisation of working time [2003] OJ L299/9.

the termination of the contract (even though there was no agreement between the employee and the employer). It is required that the employee could have not predicted the cause of impossibility of using the annual leave before the termination of employment.

If Art. 164 of Employment Relationship Act is compared with the result of the Supreme Court's (consistent) interpretation, it seems clear that there is no legal basis in national law for such an interpretation. National legislation prohibits agreements about pecuniary compensation for annual leave except in the case of termination of the employment; it does not say anything at all about a situation where such an agreement does not exist. The Supreme Court used the principle of consistent interpretation to fill the legal lacuna in the national legislation. Despite the fact that legal lacunae are an inherent part of every legal system and that courts may be called on to fill them by way of interpretation, they are nevertheless limited in fulfilment of this task. Some legal lacunae (like the one in the case at hand) are of such a nature that they can only be filled by the legislator. In the case at hand, the Supreme Court's goal was to create an *ex lege* right for every employee to claim compensation for unused annual leave in cases of termination of employment under certain conditions. The view of the present authors, the Supreme Court thus used a *contra legem* interpretation and acted as a legislator, since there were several (not one!) alternative methods by which the situation at hand could be addressed. The decision of the Court is indeed EU-friendly, but it contravenes the constitutional principle of the separation of powers. This interpretation was nevertheless later confirmed in a series of cases by the Supreme Court.[170] The decision has the same deficiencies as the above-mentioned *Judgment II Ips 228/2013* from the point of view of limits to the principle of consistent interpretation (i.e. shifting the economic burden of non-implementation of the directive from the state to private persons, giving *de facto* direct effect in a horizontal relationship).

7. CONCLUSIONS

As explained in this contribution, Slovenian courts are in principle very positively inclined towards EU-friendly interpretation of national law. However, it is hard to say if the courts follow a set interpretative methodology in these endeavours, i.e. do they first look to define the EU law in question, before attempting to interpret the relevant national law in conformity with it? Or, do they first interpret the national law in question, before seeing if it might be interpreted consistently with EU law obligations? The questions themselves are

---

170 *Order of the Supreme Court VIII Ips 107/2011* of 20 December 2011; *Judgment VIII Ips 218/2010* of 7 February 2012; *Order VIII Ips 300/2010* of 19 March 2012.

epistemologically challenging, but from the information gathered, judges engage in this intellectual process starting from either the national or EU law angle.

The start of a judicial dialogue between the Slovenian national courts and the ECJ is being witnessed. But firmer conclusions could only be drawn after a series of references to the ECJ. In addition, the Constitutional Court delivered a major substantial decision that completely lifted the veil from its doctrinarian understanding of the relationship between these courts, the Constitution and EU law. The concept of the core EU principles – such as primacy, direct effect and consistent interpretation – as Slovenian internal(ised) constitutional principles, logically follows from the very EU-subservient wording of Art. 3a(3) of the Constitution. To this end, the possibility that the Slovenian judiciary might relativise the relationship in future, and may change its course to develop a more tailored approach to the concept of national constitutional identity from Art. 4(2) TEU, should not be excluded.

Judges rarely engage in doctrinal and methodological analysis or argumentation while exercising EU law postulates in practice. In particular, this is not done in a manner that would divert, even modestly, from the general understanding of EU law as enshrined by the ECJ. The concept of national constitutional identity in relation to the principle of consistent interpretation has never been raised in any official judicial text. Although there may be examples where judges actually follow such a constitutional narrative by intentionally not submitting cases for a preliminary ruling – or worse, by not even being willing to engage with EU law argumentation – such an approach (that resembles the security through obscurity paradigm) should nevertheless be criticised for obvious reasons.

Despite their generally positive attitude, judges are in no position to rub their hands in satisfaction with the current state of the case-law. There are instances where at least some of them still apply the principle inconsistently. While the Constitutional Court has developed a well-established practice in line with the requirements of EU law, the regular courts quite often fail to match EU law standards with the procedural and substantive matters of the national legal system. This could be described as inconsistently consistent in the end, rather than consistently inconsistent, since the positive efforts by the judiciary are visible.

This contribution has delved predominantly into a careful analysis of Slovenian case-law in order to provide a diagnosis (state of the affairs) of the judicial system with a view to presenting both its positive aspects and unmasking any abnormalities therein. What remains to be done is to attempt to expose the underlying causes, grounds and invisible patterns of behaviour that result in a deficient application of the EU law, in particular where the sensitive exercise of the principle of consistent interpretation comes into play. As can be seen from the literature, whether owing to slack education at faculties of law, insufficient training of judges, emergence of the new constitutional system in Central and Eastern European states, a generational gap in judicial staff, a burden of judicial monthly norm, lack of appropriate legal aid, etc., in summary it is to be concluded that there is indeed still room for improvement.

One special aspect of judicial proceedings nevertheless appears profoundly troubling. From what could be deciphered from many individual cases, it would be hard to maintain that there is only one culprit for inconsistent application of, or lack of doctrine concerning, the principle of consistent interpretation. First of all, systemic deficiencies (in financing, training, etc.) that go beyond the individual efforts of a single judge surely block the accelerated nestling of EU law in Slovenian jurisprudence. Second, even the most skilful judge will not be able to rectify a failure on the part of the parties in introducing EU-related concepts, principles and argumentation in the case at hand. This indicates deep-rooted problems on the side of other practising lawyers (attorneys, public prosecutors, state attorneys, etc.). The data clearly shows that individual judges are an important building block for consistent interpretation in the light of EU law. In the opinion of the present authors, it is due to certain individuals in crimson and black judicial robes, rather than a systemic endeavour by the judiciary as a whole, that the Slovenian reflection in the mirror is made at least bearable. Some advanced judges are even involved in cross-European judicial dialogues and actively participate in European-wide research projects.

If one compares this contribution with research completed almost 10 years ago by Zagorc and Bardutzky on the general application of EU law, grim conclusions and warnings have been realised. The task of carrying out a proper dialogue between the national administration, Slovenian judges and the European judiciary is still taken too lightly. The trend of consistent application of the principle is nevertheless heading in a positive direction. It surely resembles the generally acknowledged gradualism in many fields of society (politics, economics and law) that Slovenia – rightly or wrongly – employed after achieving independence. Those who expected that the judiciary would instantly digest the elephant of EU law were either naïve or unrealistic.

EFFECTIVENESS AND APPLICATION OF EU AND EEA LAW IN POLISH COURTS

The Principle of Consistent Interpretation

Małgorzata CYNDECKA*

* This contribution takes into account the law up to April 2017. The author wishes to thank Agnieszka Bułat for her research assistance.

1. INTRODUCTION

In Polish legal literature, quite a few analyses of the application of the principle of consistent interpretation by Polish courts and by public administrative bodies can be found.[1] Those analyses concern the period both before and following Poland's accession to the European Union (EU) on 1 May 2004. Yet, there are several different reasons why the principle of consistent interpretation remains an attractive object of research and why legal scholars continue (and should continue) to discuss its application.

With the view of the role of the Constitutional Tribunal in the Polish court system, it is both essential and thought-provoking to follow the ongoing constitutional crisis.[2] As observed by a number of national and international observers, the crisis poses a serious threat to the rule of law, democracy and human rights protection.[3] The current government of the Law and Justice

1 In this respect, see S. Biernat and P. Wróbel, "Stosowanie prawa Wspólnoty Europejskiej w polskim sądownictwie administracyjnym" SP–E 2007, vol. IX; R. Zenc, "Prowspólnotowa wykładnia polskiego prawa administracyjnego" in C. Mik (ed.), *Wykładnia prawa Unii Europejskiej* (Toruń, 2008); P. Brzeziński, *Unijny obowiązek odmowy zastosowania przez sąd krajowy ustawy niezgodnej z dyrektywą Unii Europejskiej* (Warsaw, 2010); A. Sołtys, "Wykładnia 'contra legem' jako kryterium wyznaczania granicy obowiązku wykładni prawa krajowego zgodnie z prawem UE w polskim porządku prawnym" in S. Biernat and S. Dudzik (eds.), *Doświadczenia prawne pierwszych lat członkostwa Polski w Unii Europejskiej* (Warsaw, 2011), pp. 121–43; A. Wentkowska, "Interpretacja 'In dubio pro communitate' – dyrektywa wykładni propeuropejskiej w orzecznictiwe sądów polskich" in S. Biernat and S. Dudzik (eds.), *Doświadczenia prawne pierwszych lat członkostwa Polski w Unii Europejskiej* (Warsaw, 2011), 144–71; A. Sołtys, *Obowiązek wykładni prawa krajowego zgodnie z prawem unijnym jako instrument zapewniania efektywności prawa Unii Europejskiej* (LEX, 2015; no 272106).

2 See also section 2.3.

3 See, in this respect, M. Szuleka, M. Wolny and M. Szwed, "The Constitutional Crisis in Poland 2015–2016", Helsinki Foundation for Human Rights (legislation in force as of August 2016), <http://www.hfhr.pl/wp-content/uploads/2016/09/HFHR_The-constitutional-crisis-in-Poland-2015-2016.pdf> accessed 28.04.2017. Helsinki Foundation for Human Rights was founded in 1989 by the members of the Helsinki Committee in Poland. Its mission is to promote the development of a culture based on the respect of freedom and human rights in Poland and abroad. Since 2007 they have a consultative status within the United Nations

Party has been, at an impressive pace and with a stunning determination, implementing an ambitious and comprehensive plan of amending the rules governing the Polish court system on all its levels. As a result, the courts and judges have become dependent on the government, in particular, the minister of justice, and on the Parliament, where the governing party has a majority.

Thus far, the question of whether one may observe or expect any change in the Tribunal's practice with regard to the principle of consistent interpretation and, whether this could have any influence on the Polish courts, remains open. Yet, in light of the fact that the openly EU-sceptical government keeps proposing and implementing further amendments concerning the court system, one might have one more reason for following closely the development of the Polish jurisprudence with an "EU element".

2. BACKGROUND INFORMATION

The Republic of Poland has been a member of the EU since 1 May 2004, and a member of the Schengen area since 21 December 2007. Its total area of 312,679 km^2 makes Poland the ninth largest country in Europe. With a population of 38,005,614 (2015), which amounts to 7.5 per cent of the total EU population (2015), it has 51 seats in the European Parliament. In 2015, Poland's gross domestic product was EUR 427,737 billion. Poland has held the presidency of the Council of the EU once (July–December 2011).[4]

2.1. THE EMPIRICAL DATA

The empirical data on which this contribution is based are the rulings of the Constitutional Tribunal, the Supreme Court and the Supreme Administrative Court with focus on the Constitutional Tribunal's jurisprudence. This is due to the unique role of the Tribunal in clarifying the principle of consistent interpretation and its consequences on the manner in which the national law should be interpreted in cases having an "EU element". The relevant rulings were identified and accessed through the Tribunal and the Courts' databases

---

Economic and Social Council (ECOSOC). Helsinki Foundation for Human Rights is a member of Human Rights House Foundation created by non-governmental organisations from Norway, the United Kingdom, Belarus, Azerbaijan, Kenya and Uganda, among other countries. The HFHR is also a member of a Civic Solidarity Platform, see <http://www.hfhr.pl/en/foundation>.

4 Source: <http://europa.eu/about-eu/countries/member-countries/poland/index_en.htm> and Eurostat, accessed 28.04.2017.

that are available online.[5] As regards the relevant cases referred to the Court of Justice of the European Union (ECJ) for a preliminary ruling, these were identified and accessed through the ECJ's database.[6]

2.2. THE NATIONAL COURT SYSTEM AND ITS FUNCTIONING IN THE CONTEXT OF THE NATIONAL CONSTITUTIONAL ORDER

The structure of the Polish court system is regulated in the Polish Constitution, in particular in Chapter VIII, and in a number of statutes. As stipulated in Art. 173 of the current Constitution from 1997,[7] "The courts and tribunals shall constitute a separate power and shall be independent of other branches of power". Art. 175 provides that "The administration of justice in the Republic of Poland shall be implemented by the Supreme Court, the common courts, administrative courts and military courts" while "Extraordinary courts or summary procedures may be established only during a time of war".[8] As regards the tribunals, the Constitution speaks of the Constitutional Tribunal and the Tribunal of State. As the Constitution merely outlines the Polish court system, any detailed regulations are to be found in lower legal acts, i.e. the relevant statutes and implementing acts.

2.2.1. *Sąd Najwyższy (The Supreme Court)*

According to Art. 183 paras. 1 and 2 of the Constitution, "The Supreme Court shall exercise supervision over common and military courts regarding judgments", and it shall "perform other activities specified in the Constitution and statutes". The Supreme Court not only performs the role of a cassation court (i.e. an appellate court of the highest instance), but also determines the validity of parliamentary and presidential election and referenda on the

---

5 The Constitutional Tribunal: <http://ipo.trybunal.gov.pl/ipo/Szukaj?cid=1> accessed 28.04.2017; the Supreme Court: <http://www.sn.pl/orzecznictwo/SitePages/Baza_orzeczen.aspx> accessed 28.04.2017; the Supreme Administrative Court: <http://orzeczenia.nsa.gov.pl/cbo/query> accessed 28.04.2017.

6 <curia.euriopa.eu>.

7 The 1997 Constitution is available at <http://trybunal.gov.pl/o-trybunale/akty-normatywne/konstytucja-rzeczypospolitej-polskiej> accessed 28.04.2017. The translation on which this contribution relies is available at <http://trybunal.gov.pl/en/about-the-tribunal/legal-basis/the-constitution-of-the-republic-of-poland> accessed 28.04.2017, and is provided by Albert Pol, Bureau of Research, and Andrew Caldwell M.A., of the Middle Temple, Barrister; Consultant: Paul S. Rundquist, Fulbright Professor of Politics, Specialist in American Government at Congressional Research Service, Library of Congress.

8 There is a limited number of cases that can be heard before a military court, such as for example espionage. The special proceedings before such courts aim at the protection of state secrets.

national level. Furthermore, the Supreme Court also passes resolutions to clarify specific legal provisions and resolve disputable questions in specific cases. In case of serious doubts concerning the interpretation of law, which is relevant in a cassation case or in a case where the Supreme Court is deciding on some other legal remedy, the Supreme Court may decide upon such questions. Importantly, such resolutions are not applicable in general unless the Supreme Court decides that they shall amount to a principle of law. Still, the position and the authority of the Supreme Court often results in extending the relevance and the binding effect of those resolutions which are formally only binding in a specific case.

Neither the Supreme Court nor any other lower court has the competence to review the constitutionality of statutes as such. This competence is entirely reserved for the Constitutional Tribunal. The idea behind this limitation is to secure the legal power of the hierarchically highest acts in the legal system.

2.2.2. *The Common Courts*

According to Art. 176 para. 1 of the Constitution, court proceedings have at least two stages. The court's decision is to be verified in terms of its legality and accuracy of the interpretation of facts. As provided in Art. 177 of the Constitution, "The common courts shall implement the administration of justice concerning all matters save for those statutorily reserved to other courts", meaning here administrative and military courts and the Supreme Court.

The organisational structure and jurisdiction of the common courts is regulated by separate statutes. The common courts consist of: *sądy rejonowe* (regional courts), *sądy okręgowe* (circuit courts)[9] and *sądy apelacyjne* (appeal courts). They adjudicate in all types of cases including those concerning criminal law, civil law, family law, labour and social security law, but with the exception of cases that are reserved for other courts or any other authorities outside the judiciary system.

As regards the internal division of jurisdiction, one relies on the presumption of jurisdiction on regional courts. These courts are competent to handle cases in the first instance, except for cases that are reserved for circuit courts as their first instance. Their territorial jurisdiction usually covers an area of several municipalities. Circuit courts function both as a second instance court for cases where the first instance was a regional court and as the first instance court in cases of high gravity.[10] Their territorial jurisdiction covers an area of at least two regional courts. Appeal courts are usually the second instance court in cases

9 In some translations they are referred to as "district courts".

10 In criminal law it concerns serious crimes, in civil law it concerns cases where the value of claim exceeds PLN 75,000 (approx EUR 17,500).

where the first instance court was a circuit court. Their territorial jurisdiction covers an area of several circuit courts.

As regards the common courts in Poland, one should note the constitutional principle of participation by citizens in the system of justice. As stipulated in Art. 182 of the Constitution, statutes specify the scope of participation by the citizenry in the administration of justice. In practice, lay judges participate in some cases before the regional and circuit courts.

2.2.3. *Administrative Courts*

Likewise in common court cases, judicial proceedings before the administrative courts in Poland have two stages. The first instance court is the *voivodship* (provincial) *wojewódzki sąd administracyjny* (administrative court) and the second instance court is the *Naczelny Sąd Administracyjny* (Supreme Administrative Court). As provided in Art. 184 of the Constitution:

> The Chief Administrative Court and other administrative courts shall exercise, to the extent specified by statute, control over the performance of public administration. Such control shall also extend to judgments on the conformity to statute of resolutions of organs of local self-government and normative acts of territorial organs of government administration.

2.2.4. *The Tribunal of State*

There are two types of tribunals in Poland: *Trybunał Konstytucyjny* (the Constitutional Tribunal) and the *Trybunał Stanu* (Tribunal of State).[11] The Constitutional Tribunal is described in more detail in section 2.3. This is due to the importance of its rulings as to the question of the relationship between Polish and international/EU law, and consequently as to the application of the principle of consistent interpretation.

As regards the Tribunal of State, it rules on the constitutional liability of persons holding the highest offices in Poland. According to Art. 198 para. 1 of the Constitution:

> For violations of the Constitution or of a statute committed by them within their office or within its scope, the following persons shall be constitutionally accountable to the Tribunal of State: the President of the Republic, the Prime Minister and members of the Council of Ministers, the President of the National Bank of Poland, the President of the Supreme Chamber of Control, members of the National Council of Radio

11 The Tribunal of State was introduced by the Constitution of 17 March 1921 and continued to exist when the Constitution of 23 April 1935 was adopted. After the WWII, it was reintroduced into the Polish legal system by Law on the Tribunal of State of 26 March 1982 1982 (Ustawa z dnia 26 marca 1982 r. o Trybunale Stanu. (jednolity tekst: Dz.U.2002.101.925).

Broadcasting and Television, persons to whom the Prime Minister has granted powers of management over a ministry, and the Commander-in-Chief of the Armed Forces.

As provided in Art. 198 para. 2, deputies and senators are also constitutionally accountable to the Tribunal of State. Their accountability, however, is limited to a breach of the prohibition to perform any business activity involving any benefit derived from the property of the State Treasury or local self-government or to acquire such property.

The composition of the Tribunal of State is regulated by Art. 199 of the Constitution. As provided therein, it consists of a chairperson, that is the First President of the Supreme Court, two deputy chairpersons and 16 members chosen by the Sejm (Polish Parliament) for the current term of office of the Sejm from amongst those who are not deputies or senators. The deputy chairpersons of the Tribunal, and at least one half of the members of the Tribunal, shall possess the qualifications required to hold the office of judge. The members of the Tribunal of State, within the exercise of their office as judges of the Tribunal, shall be independent and subject only to the Constitution and statutes.

Importantly, any allegations and investigation may concern only an individual holding a high state office. The responsibility will always be on the individual. The process of initiating the procedure, as well as the procedure itself, are highly formalistic as they should correspond with the gravity of the illegal actions at stake. Nowadays, the Tribunal of State functions merely as a preventive measure. A referral to the Tribunal of State corresponds to the impeachment procedure in other states.

2.3. THE COMPETENCES AND POSITION OF THE CONSTITUTIONAL TRIBUNAL IN THE POLISH COURT SYSTEM

The idea establishing a constitutional judiciary was first expressed in Polish doctrine in the beginning of 1970s. It was not until the 1980s and the Solidarity movement, however, that it was possible to go beyond the discussion and take the required measures. The necessary constitutional amendment that provided for introducing the Constitutional Tribunal into the Polish legal system was adopted in March 1982. As the establishment of an independent judiciary had many opponents, the Constitutional Tribunal Act of 1985 imposed a number of limitations on the Tribunal's position and competences. Most importantly, the *Sejm* (Polish Parliament) was empowered to review the Tribunal's decisions on the constitutionality of statutes, and to overrule them with resolutions adopted by a 2/3 majority vote. In this way, the Communist Party attempted to preserve the so-called "unity of state authority".

The transformation of the political system in 1989 allowed for changes in the position of the Tribunal, but introducing them took a few years. Parliament was still empowered to overrule the Tribunal's decisions concerning the constitutionality of statutes, yet the Tribunal's position and importance was gradually reinforced as its jurisprudence expanded several constitutional clauses, such as the rule of law and the principle of equality. The Tribunal successfully eliminated gaps and uncertainties resulting from the lack of a modern constitution. The 1997 Constitution and the Constitutional Tribunal Act of 1 August 1997 were a true breakthrough as regards securing the position and competence of the Constitutional Tribunal.

The Tribunal is an independent constitutional organ of the State and an organ of judicial authority, and unique for several reasons. One of them is the distinction between the courts and the tribunals. The courts constitute the system of organs established to adjudicate in individual cases ("to implement the administration of justice"[12]). They are subordinated to the Supreme Court and the Supreme Administrative Court. The Constitutional Tribunal and the Tribunal of State constitute a separate branch of judicial power.[13]

The fundamental competence of the Constitutional Tribunal is the review of norms, i.e. adjudicating on hierarchical (vertical) conformity of normative acts of lower rank to legal norms of higher rank, and eliminating provisions adjudicated as unconstitutional from the system of law in force. The Polish system of norm review prioritises *a posteriori* review, which refers to such normative acts which are already enacted, are in force or are still in the *vacatio legis* period. Only exceptionally may the review of norms be of a preventive nature (i.e. review conducted *a priori*) and the only person entitled to initiate such review is the President.

Constitutional review may be either abstract or specific, and as stipulated in Art. 191 para. 1, judgments of the Constitutional Tribunal are of universally binding application and final.

The above-mentioned ongoing "constitutional crisis" in Poland has two aspects.[14] The first aspect concerns the elections of new judges of the Constitutional Tribunal. The second concerns successive acts adopted since November 2015 amending the Act on the Constitutional Tribunal. Those acts aim to paralyse the Tribunal's work by introducing a number of amendments.[15]

---

12 Art. 175 para. 1 of the Constitution of 02.04.1997.

13 See section 2.2.

14 For a comprehensive description of the ongoing crisis by an independent non-governmental institution, see Szuleka, Wolny and Szwed (n. 3).

15 For example, the Act on the Constitutional Tribunal of July 2016 introduced: consideration of cases in the sequence in which they were filed, unless the President of the Constitutional Tribunal decides otherwise; necessity to defer the hearing in a full bench in case of an absence of the Prosecutor General (the government decided to assign this office to the Minister of Justice);

Moreover, the said acts were adopted at an exceptionally rapid pace while disregarding the critical remarks concerning the constitutionality of the act made by, *inter alia*, experts from the Legislative Bureau, the Commissioner for Human Rights, National Council of the Judiciary of Poland and the First President of the Supreme Court.

The crisis was initiated by one of the intertemporal provisions of the Act on the Constitutional Tribunal of June 2015, which allowed the previous governing majority to choose five new judges of the Constitutional Tribunal.[16] In 2015, three judges ended their tenure during the Sejm's seventh term and two during the term of the new Sejm, which was elected in October 2015 and had its first session on 12 November 2015.

The gravity of the ongoing crisis results from the fact that it disrupted the balance between different branches of power. The executive power not only intends to verify Constitutional Tribunal's judgments, but also refuses to acknowledge and execute them.[17] The crisis also caused a deep polarisation of the views and opinions on the systemic role of the Constitutional Tribunal. In particular, the representatives of the governing party have intentionally and consistently undermined the role of the Tribunal as such, as well as the status[18] and reputation of its members.[19]

Yet, the independence of the Constitutional Tribunal is being defended by interventions by courts (with the Supreme Court[20] and the Supreme

---

necessity to defer deliberations on the judgment by up to six months in the case when an objection is raised as to the content of the judgment by at least four judges and necessity to suspend the proceedings for six months if the initiating document does not fulfil formal criteria.

16 For a detailed calendar of events, see Szuleka, Wolny and Szwed (n. 3), pp. 8–12.

17 While it is an obligation of the Prime Minister to publish the judgments of the Constitutional Tribunal, the current Prime Minister refuses to publish those judgment that do not support the line of her party.

18 For example, the Deputy Minister of Justice referred to the Tribunal's hearing concerning the constitutionality of the Act of December 2015 amending the Act on the Constitutional Tribunal as not binding by stating: "Tomorrow, this will not be a hearing of the Constitutional Tribunal, but a gathering of people who sit in the Tribunal at best. From the institutional point of view, tomorrow's events, if they take place, will be an absolute scandal … The judges of the Tribunal are free people. They can meet when they want to, they can order espresso and cookies, and they can meet. We are not able to use any coercive measures, but we appeal and we ask. Do not destroy the Polish state." 07.03.2016, Radio Zet, Gość Radia Zet: Patryk Jaki.

19 The representatives of the governing party, including the Minister of Justice, regularly claim that the ongoing crisis is a result of the "political ambitions" of the Tribunal's President Andrzej Rzepliński which are the greatest threat to the independence of the Tribunal, see Letter from the Minister of Justice Zbigniew Ziobro to the First Vice-President of the European Commission of 11 January 2016, available at: <https://twitter.com/ZiobroPL/status/686833269913026560> (in English, accessed on 14.06.2018) and at https://www.ms.gov.pl/Data/Files/_public/aktual/2016/list_otwarty_frans_timmermans.pdf (in Polish, accessed on 14.06.2018) accessed 28.04.2017.

20 The Supreme Court's resolution was not particularly popular amongst the representatives of the governing majority. The spokesperson of the Law and Justice parliamentary club,

Administrative Court as leaders), the legal community, units of local government, law faculties, higher education institutions, non-governmental organisations and thousands of citizens who have marched in demonstrations and signed petitions to the government. The Supreme Court declared that the judgments delivered by the Constitutional Tribunal were binding. The same approach was adopted by some city councils. Yet, one cannot exclude the risk of having two "parallel legal orders" as the public administration, being controlled by the government, will most probably follow the government's policy towards the Constitutional Tribunal.

The ongoing constitutional crisis is no longer merely an internal issue. It has drawn attention from the international community, which has expressed a number of concerns at the changes with respect to the Constitutional Tribunal. The Secretary General of the Council of Europe, Commissioner for Human Rights and the Venice Commission[21] have all emphasised the importance of the Tribunal as a fundamental element protecting the rule of law and a guarantee of the human rights protection system.[22] Moreover, in January 2016, the European Commission made an unprecedented decision to initiate the rule of law procedure against Poland. This three-stage procedure may eventually result in the Commission requesting the Council to employ one of the sanction mechanisms provided in the Treaty on European Union (TEU).

Thus far, the stance of the Polish government may be explained by quoting the Minister of Justice who responded to a letter sent by the First Vice-President of the European Commission, Frans Timmermans, and the Prime Minister who spoke during the debate in the European Parliament. The Minister stated that he first learned of the "unfounded allegations and unjustified conclusions" of the Vice-President from the media and only then from official correspondence. "For those reasons, I perceive your letter as an attempt to exert pressure on a democratically elected parliament and a government of a sovereign

---

Beata Mazurek, described the Supreme Court's resolution as adopted by "a bunch of buddies who protect the status quo of the former government". Szuleka, Wolny and Szwed (n. 3), 50.

21 See <http://www.venice.coe.int/webforms/documents/?country=23&year=all> accessed 28.04.2017.

22 Serious concerns were also expressed by, *inter alia*, Barack Obama (during the NATO summit in Warsaw), US Embassy in Warsaw, *Wystąpienie Prezydenta Obama po spotkaniu dwustronnym z prezydentem Dudą*, available at <https://pl.usembassy.gov/wp-content/uploads/sites/23/2016/07/remarks_polish.pdf> accessed 28.04.2017, the American Department of State U.S. Embassy and Consulat in Poland, *Oświadczenie Rzecznika Departamentu Stanu w sprawie Trybunału Konstytucyjnego*, available at <https://pl.usembassy.gov/pl/oswiadczenie-rzecznika-departamentu-stanu-w-sprawie-trybunalu-konstytucyjnego> accessed 28.04.2017, and the OHCHR Regional Office for Europe (UN human rights office seriously concerned about measures affecting the Constitutional Tribunal), available at <http://www.europe.ohchr.org/EN/NewsEvents/Pages/DisplayNews.aspx?NewsID=10056&LangID=E> accessed 28.04.2017.

Polish state."[23] In further parts of the letter, the Minister of Justice explains that actions undertaken had a rectifying character and aimed at restoring pluralism within the Constitutional Tribunal. The Minister of Justice also noted that it is the "political ambitions" of the Tribunal's President Andrzej Rzepliński which are the greatest threat for the independence of the Tribunal.[24]

Prime Minister Beata Szydło during the debate in the European Parliament on 19 January 2016 stated:

> I think that Poland does not deserve to undergo examination by the European Commission because human rights are not violated, nor is the rule of law ... We should deal with our Polish matters within our Polish boarders. Foreign assistance has not always worked well for us.[25]

2.4. THE RELATIONSHIP BETWEEN NATIONAL LAW AND INTERNATIONAL/EU LAW

The relationship between Polish law and international/EU law must be seen in light of the Constitution and the case-law of the Constitutional Tribunal. The application of international agreements in Poland is regulated by Art. 9, 87 para. 1, 91, 188 and 241 paras. 1 and 2[26] of the Constitution. Art. 9 is particularly relevant here, as it stipulates that "The Republic of Poland shall respect international law binding upon it." This is understood as imposing an obligation on national authorities to comply with binding international law when adopting, applying and interpreting national rules. According to Art. 87 para. 1, "The sources of universally binding law of the Republic of Poland shall be: the Constitution, statutes, ratified international agreements, and regulations." As provided in Art. 91 para. 1, "After promulgation thereof in the Journal of Laws of the Republic of Poland (Dziennik Ustaw), a ratified international agreement shall

---

23 Letter from the Minister of Justice Zbigniew Ziobro to the First Vice-President of the European Commission, available at <https://n-0-119.dcs.redcdn.pl/dcs/o2/tvn/web-content/m/p1/f/1bc0249a6412ef49b07fe6f62e6dc8de/7a736b0b-1574-4727-b62c-4a9425a7de1d.pdf> accessed 28.04.2017.

24 Szuleka, Wolny and Szwed (n. 3), pp. 42–43.

25 Ibid., p. 43.

26 Art. 241 of the Constitution provides as follows: "1. International agreements, previously ratified by the Republic of Poland upon the basis of constitutional provisions valid at the time of their ratification and promulgated in Dziennik Ustaw, shall be considered as agreements ratified with prior consent granted by statute, and shall be subject to the provisions of Art. 91 of the Constitution if their connection with the categories of matters mentioned in Art. 89, para 1 of the Constitution derives from the terms of an international agreement. 2. The Council of Ministers shall, within 2 years of the coming into force of the Constitution, present to the Sejm a list of international agreements containing provisions not in conformity to the Constitution".

constitute part of the domestic legal order and shall be applied directly, unless its application depends on the enactment of a statute." If the interpretation of national law does not lead to conformity with international law, Art. 91 para. 2 provides: that "An international agreement ratified upon prior consent granted by statute shall have precedence over statutes if such an agreement cannot be reconciled with the provisions of such statutes." Furthermore, "If an agreement, ratified by the Republic of Poland, establishing an international organization so provides, the laws established by it shall be applied directly and have precedence in the event of a conflict of laws."[27]

As regards the case-law of the Constitutional Tribunal, as stipulated in Art. 188 of the Constitution, the Constitutional Tribunal:

> shall adjudicate regarding the following matters: 1) the conformity of statutes and international agreements to the Constitution; 2) the conformity of a statute to ratified international agreements whose ratification required prior consent granted by statute; 3) the conformity of legal provisions issued by central State organs to the Constitution, ratified international agreements and statutes; 4) the conformity to the Constitution of the purposes or activities of political parties; 5) complaints concerning constitutional infringements, as specified in Article 79 paragraph 1.[28]

The fundamental problems of the relationship between the Constitution on the one hand, and EU law and the conditions of the Polish membership in the EU on the other, were addressed by the Constitutional Tribunal in its ruling *K 18/04* of 11 May 2005. In this case, the Tribunal ruled on the question of whether the EU Accession Treaty of 16 April 2003,[29] and the documents that were its integral part, were in conformity with the Constitution. Most importantly, the Tribunal considered the supremacy of the Constitution as a source of law (Art. 8 of the Constitution[30]) and the sovereignty of the Nation (as expressed in the Preamble to the Constitution), which were raised as arguments against Poland's accession to the EU. The Tribunal did not adhere to the point of view of the applicants. It confirmed that the Constitution was the supreme law of the Republic of Poland. At the same time, however, it recalled that "The Republic of Poland shall respect international law binding upon it".[31] Thus, the Constitution recognises that norms that have not been adopted by the national legislator may still be binding within the Polish territory.

---

27 Art. 91 para. 3 of the Constitution.

28 See also Art. 3 of the Constitutional Tribunal Act of 25.06.2015, published in *Dziennik Ustaw* (Journal of Laws of the Republic of Poland) on 30.07.2015, item 1064.

29 [2003] OJ L236/17.

30 Art. 8 of the Constitution provides as follows: "1. The Constitution shall be the supreme law of the Republic of Poland. 2. The provisions of the Constitution shall apply directly, unless the Constitution provides otherwise."

31 Art. 9 of the Constitution.

Importantly, due to the principle of consistent interpretation,[32] when interpreting the provisions of the Constitution, the Tribunal takes into account EU law to the extent the provisions concerned refer to the terminology, notions and principles that are recognised by EU law and in the manner in which they are interpreted by the ECJ.[33] The Tribunal is thus obliged to interpret national law in a manner that is in line with well-established EU law and the EU case-law.[34] Yet the principle of referring to EU law as an "inspiration" does not amount to its direct application, or adopting it as a direct and singular starting point in verifying the constitutionality of Polish legislation.[35] EU law may only clarify the Constitutional provision and render it more accurate or precise.[36]

According to the Constitutional Tribunal, the idea and model of European law created a situation in which there exist two autonomous legal orders. Their interaction cannot be fully described by the traditional formulas of monism and dualism. The relative autonomy of those two legal orders, which are based on their own principles of hierarchy, does not rule out the possibility of conflict between EU law and the Constitution. This would be the case if a conflict between a provision of EU law and the Constitution could not be removed by referring to an interpretation that would respect the relative autonomy of both legal orders. Such hypothetical situations could not be ruled out, even though they may be rather rare due to the fact that the EU and Poland share common universal values, such as truth and justice, and their European heritage. Conflicts between EU law and the Constitution cannot be solved by either recognising the supremacy of the EU law, considering the Constitutional provision not binding, replacing it by a provision of EU law or limiting the scope of the Constitution by the scope of EU law. In such a case, the Polish legislator would either have to amend the Constitution, suggest changes to the EU law in question, or decide to leave the EU altogether.

Importantly, the Tribunal stressed in the same ruling that the principle of interpreting domestic law in a manner "sympathetic to European law" had its limits. In no event could it lead to results contradicting the explicit wording of constitutional norms or an outcome irreconcilable with the minimum guarantee functions recognised by the Constitution. In particular, individual rights and freedoms indicated a minimum and unsurpassable threshold which could not be lowered or questioned as a result of the introduction of EU provisions.

---

32 The necessity of taking into account the principle of consistent interpretation results from Art. 9 of the Constitution that is cited above. See also A. Wasilkowski, "Prawo krajowe – prawo wspólnotowe – prawo międzynarodowe. Zagadnienia wstępne" in *Prawo międzynarodowe i wspólnotowe w wewnętrznym porządku prawnym* (Warsaw, 1997), p. 15.

33 See *K 2/02* of 28.01.2003 and *K 33/03* of 21.04.2004.

34 See *P 16/06* of 17.07.2007.

35 See *K 2/02* of 28.01.2003 and *K 33/03* of 21.04.2004.

36 See *Lp 4/08* of 16.07.2009.

The first actual conflict between EU law and the Constitution was subject to the Tribunal's ruling in case *P 1/05* of 27 April 2005.[37] The Tribunal ruled here on the conformity of Art. 607t §1 of the Penal Procedure Code,[38] which allowed for the surrender of Polish citizens subject to the European Arrest Warrant (EAW) to other EU Member States, with Art. 55 para. 1 of the Constitution, which provides that "The extradition of a Polish citizen shall be prohibited". The judgment was delivered in answer to a legal question lodged by the regional court in Gdansk. The question was formulated in connection with a case concerning the issuance, subject to a EAW, of a decision involving the surrender of a private individual (Maria D), in order to enable the conduct of proceedings against her in the Netherlands.

Until 1 May 2004, the Penal Procedure Code did not contain the concept of "extradition". The provision that was challenged had been amended by virtue of the Act of 18 March 2004 amending the Law on the Criminal Code, the Law on the Code of Penal Procedure and the Law on the Code of Petty Offences. The said Act sought to implement the Council's EAW Framework Decision (2002/584/JHA of 13 June 2002) into the national legal order.[39] Poland had not requested any transition periods or derogations concerning the area of Justice and Home Affairs. So once membership of the EU was obtained, Poland was automatically bound by primary and derivative EU law in this field, including the obligation to enact the EAW Framework Decision in question. The respective legislative measures were undertaken in advance, in order to allow their entry into force by 1 May 2004.

The legal question referred to the Tribunal raised a number of issues. As regards the principle of consistent interpretation, the regional court was sceptical about the thesis that interpreting the Constitution consistently with legal provisions introduced into the Polish legal system following Poland's accession to the EU should be done in a "friendly mode of interpretation". As it noted, such an interpretation of Art. 55 of the Constitution would lead to the narrowing of the scope of constitutional freedoms and personal rights of citizens. The constitutional legislator had vested the provisions of the Constitution referring to personal rights and liberties with a particularly high ranking, as indicated by the institution of the constitutional complaint.

In this respect, the referring regional court drew attention to the examples of Austria, Germany and the United Kingdom as EU Member States which had regulated the issue of extradition of their own citizens similarly to

---

37 For the English version of the ruling see <http://www.law.uj.edu.pl/~kpk/eaw/judicial_decisions/Poland_Constitutional_Court.pdf> accessed 21.04.2017.

38 *Kodeks postępowania karnego* (Code of Penal Procedure), Dziennik Ustaw No 89, Item 555 with amendments.

39 2002/584/JHA: Council Framework Decision of 13.6.2002 on the European arrest warrant and the surrender procedures between Member States – Statements made by certain Member States on the adoption of the Framework Decision [2002] OJ L190/1.

Art. 55 para. 1 of the Polish Constitution, and which in connection with the obligation to implement the EAW Framework Decision had adopted or initiated the similar changes in their national legal orders.

When answering the question of whether the principle of consistent interpretation applied to Art. 55 para. 1 of the Constitution, first, the Tribunal rejected the necessity of taking a stand in the (at that time ongoing) discussion of whether this obligation also applied in the sphere of police and judicial cooperation concerning criminal matters, i.e. the third EU pillar.

Second, the Tribunal recalled that the prohibition of extradition guaranteed the right of Polish citizens to have their criminal responsibility evaluated by Polish courts. As provided in Art. 31 para. 3 of the Constitution,

> Any limitation upon the exercise of constitutional freedoms and rights may be imposed only by statute, and only when necessary in a democratic State for the protection of its security or public order, or to protect the natural environment, health or public morals, or the freedoms and rights of other persons. Such limitations shall not violate the essence of freedoms and rights.

The Constitutional prohibition of extradition was thus absolute and the right of citizens that was derived from it could not be limited.

Third, the Tribunal noted that the obligation of consistent interpretation had its limits – and those had been indicated by the ECJ. Namely, whenever its consequences would consist of making the situation of individuals worse, and especially if it implied the introduction or aggravation of penal liability. In the present case, there was no doubt that the surrender of a person indicted on the basis of an EAW in order to conduct criminal proceedings against this person in connection with an act, which according to Polish law was not a crime, could lead to the aggravation of the situation of the indicted person.

In conclusion, the Tribunal found that Art. 607t §1 of the Penal Procedure Code was unconstitutional, thus eliminating any binding force of that provision. In the present case, however, the effect of the judgment was not tantamount to ensuring conformity of the legal status with the Constitution – neither was it sufficient for this purpose. Such an objective could only be achieved by legislative intervention. Nevertheless, taking into account Art. 9 of the Constitution (which states that the Republic of Poland shall observe international law binding it), and given the obligations implied by Poland's membership in the EU, it was necessary to change the law in such a manner so as to enable not only full implementation of the EAW Framework Decision, and also to ensure its conformity with the Constitution. Therefore, one could not rule out an amendment of Art. 55 para. 1 of the Constitution, so as to provide room for an exception from the prohibition of extradition of Polish citizens, thus allowing for their surrender on the basis of the EAW to other EU Member States. In the case of amendment of the Constitution, the bringing of national law into conformity with EU requirements would also require the reintroduction by the legislator of the statutory provisions concerning the EAW, which were eliminated from the legal order as a result of the Tribunal's judgment.

As a rule, the judgments of the Tribunal enter into force on the day of their announcement.[40] However, in light of the fact that Poland's obligation to implement the EAW Framework Decision had existed since its accession to the EU (i.e. from 1 May 2004), the Tribunal deemed it necessary to defer the legal effects of its ruling (i.e. of rendering Art. 607t §1 of the Penal Procedure Penal without legal force). Art. 190 para. 3 of the Constitution vests the Tribunal with the competence to determine a different term for the cancellation of binding force of a provision found to be incompatible with a higher ranked Act.[41] Such deferral implies that the given provision temporarily remains justiciable in spite of its inconsistency with an act placed hierarchically higher up in the system of sources of the law.

In the present case, the Tribunal was guided by the need to assure the protection of constitutional rights and liberties of individuals. According to the Tribunal, the prolongation of the application of Art. 607t §1 of the Penal Procedure Code could be justified constitutionally on several grounds. First, under reference to the constitutional obligation to observe international law; second, by virtue of the need to ensure security and public order, the assurance of which was enhanced by the surrender of indicted persons to other states so as to make them face trial; and, third, due to the fact that Poland and the other EU Member States were bound by a community of political systemic principles protecting the proper administration of justice and trial before independent courts of law. According to the Tribunal, the decision to defer was justified even where it served to deprive Polish citizens of the guarantees resulting from the prohibition of extradition within the scope necessary for the implementation of the EAW. Moreover, the Tribunal stressed the need to protect Poland's credibility in international relations, as a State respecting the fundamental international law principle of *pacta sunt servanda*.[42]

Therefore, the Tribunal deferred the legal effects of its ruling by 18 months, until 5 November 2006 (the maximum constitutionally admissible term). Art. 607t §1 of the Penal Procedure Code thus maintained its binding force during this time. The judgment determined the consequences for the future and could not provide the basis for questioning legally valid court verdicts

---

40 By publication in the Official Journal, in which the respective normative act was published, or – in the case when the respective act had not been published – in the Official Journal "*Monitor Polski*".

41 The limits are: maximum by 18 months in the case of a legislative act and 12 months in the case of other normative acts. No such limits on the discretion of the Tribunal exist in the situation when the verdict is the result of abstract control.

42 Art. 9 of the Constitution.

adopted at an earlier date. During the period of deferral, the Polish state could fulfil the obligation of implementing the Framework Decision. The Constitution was amended on 8 September 2006 and entered into force on 6 November.[43]

The deferral enabled the Polish courts to issue EAWs. If the said ruling had taken effect from the day of its publication, one could have expected courts of other Member States to encounter difficulties in respecting Polish EAWs. In this respect, one may recall the example of the German *Bundesverfassungsgericht* and its judgment of 18 July 2005 concerning a EAW issued by a Spanish court. As a result, the Polish court of appeal in Szczecin in *III Kop 24/05* of 22 July 2005, refused to surrender a Polish national to Germany on the basis of an EAW issued by a Bavarian court. In that particular case, the elementary prerequisite that Framework Decisions are complied with by all Member States, was not present.

2.5. REFERENCES FOR A PRELIMINARY RULING

Before providing any observations on cases concerning the principle of consistent interpretation that have been referred to the ECJ by Polish courts, one should note that the right (and in some cases obligation) to refer a case for a preliminary ruling has itself been challenged before the Constitutional Tribunal.

In *K 18/04* of 11 May 2005, one of the issues raised concerned the constitutionality of references for preliminary rulings. According to one of the arguments, the right (and in some cases obligation) under what is now Art. 267 of the Treaty on the Functioning of the European Union (TFEU) led to an unacceptable subordination of Polish courts to the ECJ. Yet, as the Tribunal ruled, the principle according to which judges of the courts and the Tribunal were subject to the norms of the Constitution (Art. 178 para. 1 and Art. 195 para. 1), also encompassed the duty to apply EU law that was binding upon Poland. This was a consequence of the ratification of international agreements concluded with the Member States of the Communities and the EU, which constituted a part of international law binding upon Poland.[44] The ECJ's competence to declare a binding interpretation of Community law, particularly via the procedure for delivering preliminary rulings, was an element of these agreements. The referral of a question regarding the validity or content of EU law to the appropriate EU institution by a Polish court or tribunal, did not conflict with Art. 174 of the Constitution, pursuant to which "The courts and tribunals shall pronounce judgments in the name of the Republic of Poland".

---

43 *Ustawa z dnia 08.09.2006 r. o zmianie Konstytucji Rzeczypospolitej Polskiej, Dziennik Ustaw* No 200, Item 1471.

44 Art. 9 of the Constitution.

As the Tribunal recalled, Art. 188 of the Constitution determined the Tribunal's competences and scope of jurisdiction. The application of Art. 267 TFEU does not threaten or narrow those competences. If the Tribunal decided to request a preliminary ruling, the Tribunal would undertake this within the framework for exercising its adjudicative competences (Art. 188 of the Constitution), and only where, in accordance with the Constitution, the Tribunal ought to apply Community law.[45]

In *KP 3/08* of 18 February 2008, the Constitutional Tribunal ruled on the conformity of an Act of 10 July 2008, authorising the President to submit a declaration on acceptance of the jurisdiction of the ECJ pursuant to Art. 35(2) TEU as regards the competence of every Polish court to request preliminary rulings, with Art. 45 para. 1 of the Constitution. In the President's opinion, enabling all Polish courts, including the courts of first instance, to request preliminary rulings pertaining to police and judicial cooperation in criminal matters, would be inconsistent with Art. 45 para. 1 of the Constitution, which guaranteed everyone the right to a hearing without "undue delay".

In this respect, the Tribunal first pointed out that the right to a hearing without "undue delay" was a procedural guarantee of special significance to the individual. However, the concept was difficult to define when contained in a norm of such great generality as the constitutional provision in question. The assessment as to whether a delay was justified or not could be carried out only in a given case, taking into account the character of the case (i.e. criminal, civil or administrative), the procedural provisions which are appropriate for its examination, the degree of difficulty (i.e. complexity) and the circumstances surrounding the case, including the behaviour of the parties to the proceedings.[46]

The requirement for court proceedings to be carried out "without undue delay" corresponded to the principle of procedural economy which had been conceived on the basis of particular procedural statutes. The prevailing academic view is that the requirement should be construed as an imperative, meant for the legislator, that the procedure for examining cases by courts should be structured in such a way that proceedings would be carried out efficiently and, if possible, swiftly. However this imperative could not justify overlooking the procedural guarantees contained not only in Art. 45 para. 1, but also in other provisions of the Constitution.[47] The Tribunal therefore emphasised that

45 For the English version of the ruling *K 18/04*, see <http://trybunal.gov.pl/fileadmin/content/omowienia/K_18_04_GB.pdf> accessed 28.04.2017.

46 In this respect, the Tribunal referred to Z. Czeszejko-Sochacki, *Prawo do sądu w świetle Konstytucji RP*, Państwo i Prawo 16, 1997, Vols. 11–12, p. 103.

47 In this respect, the Tribunal referred to P. Hofmański, "Prawo do sądu w ujęciu Konstytucji i ustaw oraz standardów prawa międzynarodowego" in *Wolności i prawa jednostki oraz ich gwarancje w praktyce* (Warsaw, 2006), p. 276.

Art. 45 para. 1 was infringed in the case of delay in proceedings where there were no sufficient grounds for such delay, or where those grounds could not be accepted from the point of view of effective judicial protection.

The Tribunal then turned to the specific constitutional problem in the case at hand, i.e. whether granting all Polish courts the competence to refer questions to the ECJ for a preliminary ruling concerning the validity and interpretation of measures relating to police and judicial cooperation in criminal matters could constitute the source of undue delay in breach of Art. 45 para. 1 of the Constitution. As the Tribunal noted, the determination of this issue depended on the determination of a more general issue, namely whether the application of a procedure (by the court hearing a given case) which was provided by law and which was aimed at eliminating doubts as to the validity or interpretation of law, as well as any discrepancies in jurisprudence, could be regarded as an undue delay.

The President's application indicated that there were various procedures available under Polish law that allowed the court adjudicating in a case, whose intention was to explain legal issues that raised interpretative doubts, to refer a question of law to a court (or an enlarged panel of that court) occupying the highest position in the judicial hierarchy. Despite the slightly different definition of the object of questions of law, their common aim was to eliminate serious doubts as to the interpretation of the law applied by courts. Importantly, the referral of questions to the Supreme Court, the Supreme Administrative Court or the Constitutional Tribunal by the adjudicating courts inevitably extended the proceedings that were pending before those courts. In the Tribunal's opinion, the preliminary ruling procedure under EU law should be assessed analogically to the procedures for referring questions to the Supreme Court, the Supreme Administrative Court or the Constitutional Tribunal.

As the Tribunal stressed, since Poland's accession to the EU, EU law had been part of the current legal system in Poland. By ratifying the Treaty of Accession, Poland accepted the separation of functions within the EU institutional framework EU institutions. What remained as an element of that separation was the jurisdiction of the ECJ to interpret EU law and to ensure uniformity in its interpretation. The questions referred for preliminary rulings facilitated proper rulings by national courts. As the Tribunal emphasised, avoiding irregularities before rulings became final was of special significance in the realm of criminal law, as making an erroneous judgment by a court often resulted in grievous consequences which were difficult to remedy. Therefore, commencing a procedure aimed at eliminating doubts as to the interpretation or validity of an EU legal act could not be regarded as a cause of delay which would be unjustified within the meaning of Art. 45 para. 1 of the Constitution.

Moreover, as the Tribunal recalled, the assessment of the preliminary ruling procedure in the context of excessive length of court proceedings had already been dealt with by the European Court of Human Rights. The Strasbourg Court has held that extending the duration of court proceedings due to the reference of a question for a preliminary ruling could not be regarded as excessive length of proceedings.[48] Thus, the period of waiting for a preliminary ruling on a given question could not be counted when specifying the duration of proceedings for which the State could be held responsible.

In conclusion, the President's declaration on acceptance of the jurisdiction of the ECJ was held to be consistent with the regulation that courts shall hear cases without undue delay, as stipulated in Art. 45 para. 1 of the Constitution.

The Constitutional Tribunal has only referred one case to the ECJ for a preliminary ruling. The request was lodged on 20 July 2015 and registered as Case C-390/15.[49] The proceedings before the Constitutional Tribunal were initiated by the Ombudsman who questioned the constitutionality of certain provisions of Law on value added tax of 11 March 2004[50] to the extent to which they excluded the application of reduced tax rates to books published in digital format and other electronic publications.

2.5.1. Cases Referred to the ECJ

According to the ECJ's database (<curia.euriopa.eu>), Polish courts have asked for a preliminary ruling in 97 cases. As of 6 May 2016, 73 of those were closed. The principle of consistent interpretation was referred to in the following cases:

2.5.1.1. Case C-414/07, *Magoora sp. z o.o. v. Dyrektor Izby Skarbowej w Krakowie*

Case C-414/07, *Magoora sp. z o.o. v. Dyrektor Izby Skarbowej w Krakowie*[51] concerned the interpretation of Art. 17(2) and (6) of the Sixth VAT Directive of 1977.[52] The reference was made in the course of proceedings between a company called Magoora and the Director of the Tax Chamber in Krakow before the provincial administrative court in Krakow. The dispute concerned the interpretation of the scope and application of national tax law on the right to deduct VAT on the purchase of fuel for a vehicle used by Magoora under

48 *Pafitis v. Greece*, 26 February 1998, appl. no. 20323/92, *Koua Poirezz v. France*, 30 September 2003, appl. no. 40892/98; See also W. Czapliński, "Pytanie prejudycjalne w świetle art. 6 EKPC" in C. Mik (ed.), *Pytanie prejudycjalne w orzecznictwie ETS* (Toruń, 2006), pp. 178–79.

49 ECLI:EU:C:2017:174.

50 *Dziennik Ustaw* No 177, item 1054 with amendments.

51 Case C-414/07, *Magoora sp. z o.o. v Dyrektor Izby Skarbowej w Krakowie*, ECLI:EU:C:2008:766.

52 Sixth Council Directive 77/388/EEC of 17 May 1977 on the harmonisation of the laws of the Member States relating to turnover taxes – common system of value added tax: uniform basis of assessment [1977] OJ L145/1.

a leasing contract, namely the possibility for Magoora to deduct the input tax on the purchase of fuel for a vehicle used for the activities of that company under a leasing contract.

The referring court asked essentially whether Art. 17(2) and (6) of the Sixth VAT Directive precluded a Member State from repealing in their entirety, from the date of entry into force of that Directive on its territory, national provisions concerning restrictions on the deduction of input tax on purchases of fuel for vehicles used for a taxable activity and replacing them with measures laying down new criteria, and whether it precluded that Member State from subsequently amending those criteria again so as to extend those restrictions. If the answer was affirmative, the referring court asked whether a taxable person was entitled to insist on the application of the national provisions in force before the date when the directive entered into force.[53]

As the ECJ ruled, in the case in the main proceedings, it was for the national court, which had sole jurisdiction to interpret its national law, to determine whether the amendments introduced when the Sixth Directive was transposed into Polish law by the Law on VAT had the effect of extending, with respect to the previous national provisions, the scope of the restrictions on the right to deduct input VAT on the purchase of fuel for vehicles intended for taxable activities.[54] It was for the national court to interpret domestic law, so far as possible, in the light of the wording and the purpose of the Sixth Directive with a view to achieving the results sought by the latter, favouring the interpretation of the national rules which is the most consistent with that purpose in order thereby to achieve an outcome compatible with the provisions of the Directive,[55] setting aside, if necessary, any contrary provision of national law.[56]

Following the judgment of the ECJ, the referring court annulled the decisions taken by the tax authorities.[57] Its judgment was subject to an appeal before the Supreme Administrative Court,[58] which annulled the judgment and referred it back to the same court. This was because the provincial administrative court wrongly concluded that the relevant Polish regulations were to be set aside in their entirety. In the new ruling, the court annulled the decisions of the tax authorities and obliged them to review the case while taking into account the findings of the ECJ and the Supreme Administrative Court.[59] This time the provincial administrative court correctly noted that the Polish VAT Act,

---

53 *Magoora* (n. 51), see para. 26.
54 Ibid., see paras. 42–44.
55 In this respect, the ECJ referred to Case C-212/04, *Adeneler and Others*, ECLI:EU:C:2006:443, para. 124.
56 In this respect, the ECJ referred to Case C-144/04, *Mangold*, ECLI:EU:C:2005:709, para. 77.
57 *I SA/Kr 176/09* of 30.04.2009.
58 *I FSK 1471/09* of 18.03.2011.
59 *I SA/Kr 975/11* of 10.10.2011.

which transposed the Sixth VAT Directive, was to be set aside only to the extent to which it expanded the scope of limiting the right to the exemption. The principle of consistent interpretation was thus followed.

2.5.1.2. Case C-40/15, *Aspiro*

In a reference for a preliminary ruling in Case C-40/15, *Aspiro*,[60] the Supreme Administrative Court sought to ascertain whether settlement of claims carried out on behalf of the insurer by a third party which had no contractual relationship with the insured person was to be exempted from VAT under Art. 135(1)(a) of the 2006 VAT Directive.[61] The principle of consistent interpretation was recalled by the Polish company Aspiro, which supplied services consisting in comprehensive settlement of insurance claims on behalf of an insurer. It acted in the name and on behalf of the insurer vis-à-vis the insured person.

Aspiro submitted that the dispute in the main proceedings raised an issue of interpretation of national law only and, consequently, did not concern EU law. The question referred was thus entirely irrelevant for the purposes of determining the dispute and should therefore be deemed inadmissible. Aspiro emphasised that even if Art. 43(13) of the Polish VAT Act added an exemption that was not provided for in Art. 135(1)(a) of the VAT Directive, the national authorities could not impose on a private person the stricter provisions of that Directive.

As the ECJ noted, in the context of the cooperation between the ECJ and the national courts provided for in Art. 267 TFEU, it was solely for the national court before which a dispute has been brought, and which had to assume responsibility for the subsequent judicial decision, to determine in the light of the particular circumstances of the case both the need for a preliminary ruling and the relevance of the questions which it submits to the Court. Consequently, where the question put by a national court concerned the interpretation of a provision of EU law, the ECJ was, in principle, bound to give a ruling. The ECJ could refuse to rule on a question referred for a preliminary ruling by a national court only where it was quite obvious that the interpretation of EU law that was sought had no relation to the actual facts of the main action or its purpose, where the problem was hypothetical, or where the Court did not have before it the factual or legal material necessary to give a useful answer to the questions submitted to it.

As the ECJ recalled, the referring court was bound, as far as possible, to interpret national law in the light of EU law.[62] Since the referring court queried

---

60 Case C-40/15, *Minister Finansów v. Aspiro*, ECLI:EU:C:2015:850.

61 Council Directive 2006/112/EC of 28 November 2006 on the common system of value added tax [2006] OJ L347/1.

62 In this respect, the ECJ referred to its judgment C-397/01 to C-403/01, *Pfeiffer and Others*, ECLI:EU:C:2004:584, para. 113.

the scope of a national provision, the benefit of which was relied on in the main proceedings and which transposed the VAT Directive, it was not obvious that the question referred to the ECJ as to the interpretation to be given to that Directive was irrelevant for the determination of that dispute. In conclusion, the reference for a preliminary ruling was admissible.

On 17 March 2016, the ECJ clarified that the settlement of claims carried out on behalf of the insurer by a third party which had no contractual relationship with the insured person did not fall under exemption from VAT under Art. 135(1)(a) of the 2006 VAT Directive. On 5 October 2016, the Supreme Administrative Court gave its final ruling. Therein, it referred to its judicial practice, according to which the principle of consistent interpretation should not be taken into account if it contradicted the result of the linguistic interpretation. This could lead to an unacceptable *contra legem* interpretation.[63]

As the Court recalled, it had ruled on a limitation of the principle of consistent interpretation with regard to the VAT Act in a judgment of 23 March 2009.[64] As it explained, the obligation to apply the said principle is not absolute, in particular, where the EU law is in the form of a directive. The use of the principle of consistent interpretation cannot impose obligations on a taxpayer if such obligations are not explicitly provided in the national law. As Aspiro was better off under the Polish Vat Act, which included the disputed tax exemption, and the undertaking insisted on relying on the Polish law, the Court decided to set aside the principle of consistent interpretation.

2.5.1.3. Case C-397/14, *Polkomtel sp. z o.o. v. Prezes Urzędu Komunikacji Elektronicznej*

Case C-397/14, *Polkomtel sp. z o.o. v. Prezes Urzędu Komunikacji Elektronicznej* concerned the interpretation of Art. 28 of the Universal Service Directive of 2002,[65] and Art. 5(1) and 8(3) of the 2002 Access Directive.[66] The reference was made in proceedings between Polkomtel and the President of the Office for Electronic Communications (UKE), and Orange Polska, concerning a decision taken by the President of the UKE in proceedings between these undertakings on

---

63 See *I FSK 797/16* of 05.10.2016. The Court referred to A. Łazowski, "Proeuropejska wykładnia prawa przez polskie sądy i organy administracji jako mechanizm dostosowania systemu prawnego do acquis communautaire" in E. Piontek (ed.), *Prawo polskie a prawo Unii Europejskiej* (Warsaw, 2003), p. 191.

64 *I FPS 6/08* of 23.03.2009.

65 Directive 2002/22/EC of the European Parliament and of the Council of 7 March 2002 on universal service and users' rights relating to electronic communications networks and services [2002] OJ L108/51.

66 Directive 2002/19/EC of the European Parliament and of the Council of 7 March 2002 on access to, and interconnection of, electronic communications networks and associated facilities [2002] OJ L108/7.

conditions of cooperation and pricing procedures for non-geographic number access services.

The principle of consistent interpretation was recalled in the first question referred by the national court. As the ECJ noted, the Supreme Court asked in essence whether Art. 28 of the 2002 Universal Service Directive had to be interpreted as meaning that a Member State could provide that an operator of a public electronic communications network had to ensure that all end-users were able to access its network in that State, not only the end-users of other Member States. The ECJ answered in the affirmative.[67]

On 9 June 2016, the Supreme Court ruled that the Polish courts were obliged to interpret the national law in a way that enabled the President of UKE to solve disputes between the telecommunications undertakings, so as to ensure that all end-users were able to access its network in that State and not only the end-users of other Member States.[68] The principle of consistent interpretation was thus followed.

2.5.1.4. Case C-3/14, *Prezes Urzędu Komunikacji Elektronicznej and Telefonia Dialog sp. z o.o. v. T-Mobile Polska SA*

Case C-3/14, *Prezes Urzędu Komunikacji Elektronicznej and Telefonia Dialog sp. z o.o. v. T-Mobile Polska SA*[69] concerned the interpretation of Arts. 6, 7(3) and 20 of the 2002 Framework Directive for electronic communications,[70] and Art. 28 of the 2002 Universal Service Directive.[71] The request was made by the Supreme Court in proceedings between the President of the Office of Electronic Communications (UKE) and Telefonia Dialog on the one hand, and T-Mobile Polska on the other, concerning a decision made by the President of the UKE in a dispute between those undertakings.

On 4 April 2000, Telefonia Dialog and T-Mobile Polska concluded an agreement stipulating the rules governing cooperation and payments in respect of access for users of T-Mobile Polska's network to "intelligent network" services provided via Telefonia Dialog's network. In 2006, Telefonia Dialog requested that T-Mobile Polska open negotiations with a view to concluding an amendment to the cooperation agreement. As those undertakings did not arrive at an

---

67 Case C-397/14, *Polkomtel sp. z o.o. v. Prezes Urzędu Komunikacji Elektronicznej*, ECLI:EU:C:2016:256.

68 *III SK 28/13* of 15.05.2014.

69 Case C-3/14, *Prezes Urzędu Komunikacji Elektronicznej and Telefonia Dialog sp. z o.o. v. T-Mobile Polska SA*, ECLI:EU:C:2015:232.

70 Directive 2002/21/EC of the European Parliament and of the Council of 7 March 2002 on a common regulatory framework for electronic communications networks and services [2002] OJ L108/33.

71 Directive 2002/22/EC of the European Parliament and of the Council of 7 March 2002 on universal service and users' rights relating to electronic communications networks and services [2002] OJ L108/51.

agreement, Telefonia Dialog requested the President of the UKE to set a time-limit for closing further negotiations. As the negotiations were not closed within the given time-limit, Telefonia Dialog requested the President of the UKE to take a decision in order to resolve the dispute concerned. By decision of 19 December 2008, taken on the basis of Arts. 28 and 79 of the Polish Telecommunications Act of 16 July 2004,[72] which had transposed Art. 5 of the 2002 Access Directive[73] and Art. 28 of the 2002 Universal Service Directive respectively, the President of the UKE resolved the dispute. T-Mobile Polska brought an action against that decision before the Warsaw Regional Court, which annulled the decision on the ground that the President of the UKE had not complied with the consolidation procedure laid down in Art. 18 of Telecommunications Act. The President of the UKE and Telefonia Dialog lodged an appeal before the Warsaw Court of Appeal, which was dismissed. The President of the UKE and Telefonia Dialog each then lodged an appeal on a point of law against that judgment before the Supreme Court. The Supreme Court stated that the dispute in the main proceedings related to whether the President of the UKE should have followed the procedure laid down in Art. 7(3) of the 2002 Framework Directive before taking a decision which altered the cooperation agreement.

The Supreme Court recalled the principle of consistent interpretation with regard to the third question it referred to the ECJ. The Court queried whether Art. 7(3) in conjunction with Arts. 6 and 20 of the 2002 Framework Directive, read in conjunction with Art. 288 TFEU and Art. 4(3) TEU, had to be interpreted as meaning that a national court was obliged to refrain from applying provisions of national law which require the national regulatory authority to conduct consolidation proceedings in every case where a measure taken by that authority could affect trade between Member States. As it observed, if the answer to the third question were in the affirmative, it would then be impossible, in the case in the main proceedings, to interpret Art. 18 of the Law of 16 July 2004 in a way which is consistent with EU law.

The ECJ established that first, Arts. 7(3) and 20 of the 2002 Framework Directive had to be interpreted as meaning that a national regulatory authority was required to implement the procedure laid down in the former of those provisions if, in resolving a dispute between undertakings providing electronic communications networks or services in a Member State, it intended to impose obligations designed to ensure access to non-geographic numbers in accordance with Art. 28 of the 2002 Universal Service Directive and those obligations could affect trade between Member States. Second, Art. 7(3) of the 2002 Framework

[72] The Law on telecommunication of 16 July 2004, *Dziennik Ustaw* No 171, item 1800.

[73] Directive 2002/19/EC of the European Parliament and of the Council of 7 March 2002 on access to, and interconnection of, electronic communications networks and associated facilities [2002] OJ L108/7.

Directive had to be interpreted as meaning that a measure adopted by a national regulatory authority in order to ensure that end-users have access to non-geographic numbers in accordance with Art. 28 of the 2002 Universal Service Directive affected trade between Member States, within the meaning of that provision, if it could have, other than in an insignificant manner, an influence, direct or indirect, actual or potential, on that trade, this being a matter for the referring court to determine.

Following the judgment of the ECJ of 16 April 2015, the Supreme Court delivered its judgment on 15 September 2015.[74] In this respect, it followed the principle of consistent interpretation and ruled that the President of the UKE was obliged to resolve the dispute at stake as that was required to comply with the EU law.

2.5.1.5. Case C-499/13, *Marian Macikowski v. Dyrektor Izby Skarbowej in Gdańsk*

In Case C-499/13, *Marian Macikowski v. Dyrektor Izby Skarbowej in Gdańsk*, the request for a preliminary ruling concerned the interpretation of the principles of proportionality and fiscal neutrality, and Arts. 9, 193, 199, 206, 250 and 252 of the 2006 VAT Directive.[75] The request was made in proceedings between Mr. Macikowski, a court enforcement officer, and the Director of the Tax Chamber in Gdańsk, concerning the failure to pay in due time the VAT payable in respect of the sale of immovable property effected through enforcement.

Mr Macikowski, at the request of a creditor, took enforcement action against Royal sp. z o.o., which was a taxable person for VAT purposes. Mr Macikowski seized and subsequently sold immovable property belonging to Royal by means of an auction. In March 2007, the court awarded ownership of the immovable property to Mr and Mrs Babinski at the highest bid price. The purchasers paid that price in full to the court. By order of 27 October 2008, Mr Macikowski drew up a draft plan for dividing that sum, in which he identified an amount of PLN 256 823.13 due in respect of VAT to be paid to the Tax Office in Chojnice. Following Mr Macikowski's request, the court transferred that amount to his account to enable him, as paying agent, to pay the VAT due on the transfer of ownership by auction of Royal's immovable property. Mr Macikowski consequently issued an invoice documenting the VAT on the sale and informed the tax authority of the payment of the tax on 2 September 2009.

Referring *inter alia* to Art. 18 of the Polish VAT Act in conjunction with Arts. 8 and 30(1), (3) and (4) of the Polish Tax Code, the Head of the Tax Office in Chojnice ruled that Mr Macikowski was liable, as the paying agent,

---

74 *III SK 62/12* of 15.09.2015.

75 Council Directive 2006/112/EC of 28 November 2006 on the common system of value added tax [2006] OJ L347/1.

for VAT of PLN 256 823.13 which had been collected but not paid in time in connection with the sale of Royal's immovable property. Since Mr Macikowski was taking enforcement action, in November 2007 he had been required to issue a VAT invoice documenting the sale of Royal's immoveable property on behalf of Royal for a gross amount of PLN 1 424 201, including tax of PLN 256 823.13, and to pay that tax into the account of the competent tax office by 25 December 2007.

By judgment of 10 October 2011, the Gdańsk Provincial Administrative Court dismissed the action brought by Mr Macikowski against the decision of the Director of the Tax Chamber in Gdańsk ruling on the tax liability of the paying agent for the failure to pay in time the VAT on the enforced sale of Royal's immovable property. Mr Macikowski appealed on a point of law against that judgment to the Supreme Administrative Court. In the grounds of appeal, Mr Macikowski referred to the principle of consistent interpretation, claiming that the judgment had made an erroneous interpretation of Art. 18 of the VAT Law by not taking account of the provisions of EU law on VAT, namely the provisions of the 2006 VAT Directive.

In answer to the questions referred for a preliminary ruling, the ECJ ruled that Arts. 9, 193 and 199(1)(g) of the 2006 VAT Directive had to be interpreted as not precluding a provision of national law which, within the context of a sale of immovable property effected through enforcement, imposed on a person – namely the court enforcement officer who made the sale – obligations to calculate, collect and pay the VAT on the proceeds of that transaction within the prescribed time-limits. As regards the principle of proportionality, it had to be interpreted as not precluding a provision of national law under which a court enforcement officer had to be liable with his entire assets for the amount of VAT due on the proceeds of the sale of immovable property effected through enforcement where he did not discharge his obligation to collect and pay that tax, provided that the court enforcement officer concerned actually had all legal means to discharge that obligation, which was for the referring court to determine. Finally, Arts. 206, 250 and 252 of the 2006 VAT Directive and the principle of fiscal neutrality had to be interpreted as not precluding a provision of national law under which the paying agent as referred to in that provision was required to calculate, collect and pay an amount of VAT on a sale of goods effected through enforcement without being able to deduct the amount of VAT paid as input tax from the beginning of the tax period to the date of the collection of that tax from the taxable person.

As regards the judgment given by the Supreme Administrative Court, it fully followed the answers given by the ECJ and confirmed the correctness of the decisions issued by the tax authorities.[76]

---

[76] *I FSK 678/15* of 27.10.2015.

2.5.2. *Settling Cases Out of Court: Mediation and Arbitration*

The history of mediation in Poland is rather short.[77] Mediation was first introduced in the following legal acts: in 1991 in the statute concerning collective labour disputes, in 1997 in the Criminal Procedure Code, in 2001 in the Act on Juvenile Delinquency Proceedings, in 2004 in the administrative judicial proceedings, and finally in 2005 in the Civil Procedure Code.[78] Mediation may be initiated by the court, prosecutor or any other authority holding the proceedings or by the parties themselves. The general idea behind mediation, as strongly emphasised in the legal literature, is that the courts and other public authorities should encourage the parties to use settlement mechanisms. The recently introduced reform of the Civil Procedure Code aptly illustrates this approach. One of the amendments obliges the court to encourage the parties to consider mediation. It also provides that the court may delegate the case for mediation more than once and at any stage of the proceedings. When the mediation agreement is signed by the parties and approved by the court, it can be performed immediately.

Unfortunately, as concluded in the report "Diagnosis of the use of mediation and the reasons for its lower than expected popularity",[79] the level of use of mediation in Poland is low at courts and at prosecutor's offices.[80] This concerns all areas of law.[81] The report identifies and analyses reasons for low popularity of mediation from the perspective of individual participants of the mediation process: judges, prosecutors, mediators, the legal community, other professional groups, parties to the dispute, society and entrepreneurs.[82] As established, the

---

77 For more information on mediation in Poland, see <http://mediacja.gov.pl/en> accessed 25.04.2017.

78 For a full overview of the legal acts that regulate mediation in civil, business, penal and family cases, see <http://mediacja.gov.pl/Akty-prawne-.html> accessed 25.04.2017.

79 The report was commissioned by the Crime Victims and Promotion of Mediation Division in the Department of International Cooperation and Human Rights of the Ministry of Justice within the framework of the project entitled: "Promoting alternative methods of dispute resolution". The Project was implemented within the framework of Operational Programme "Judicial capacity building and cooperation/Improvement of the efficiency of justice", co-financed under the Norwegian Financial Mechanism 2009–2014. The authors are: A. Rudolf, M. Cichowicz-Major, M. Matysiak, S. Pałka, W. Pieniążek and C. Przybył.

80 The report may be found in Polish <http://mediacja.gov.pl/files/doc/rk-mediacje-agrotec-02.09.pdf> and in English at <http://mediacja.gov.pl/files/doc/rk-mediacje-agrotec-16.09-en.pdf> accessed 25.04.2017.

81 The percentage of business law cases referred by circuit courts to mediation in 2014 constituted 0.25% of all court proceedings (regional courts – 2.1%), for family law – 0.17%, for civil law – only 0.023% (at regional courts – 0.68%), for labour law – 0.21%, and for criminal law – 0.16%. The percentage of cases referred to mediation in years 2011–2014 at all levels of prosecutor's offices exceeded slightly 0.1% of all cases. Yet, efficiency of use of mediation in those cases can be assessed as high – on the average, 7 out of 10 mediation proceedings were concluded by a conciliation agreement. See "Diagnosis of the use of mediation and the reasons for its lower than expected popularity", p. 5.

82 Those are separately examined in the report, which also provides recommendations for improving the popularity of mediation in Poland.

role and usefulness of mediation is undermined by all participants involved. As regards the judges, for example, one may mention "the fact that they believe firmly in their own conciliation capacities, as well as their schematic way of thinking and proceeding, which does not contribute to referral of cases to mediation. A way to eliminate this barrier is continuous education; however ... the activity of judges with regard to participation in mediation trainings is not sufficient".[83] Neither the advocates nor parties are interested in using mediation. The report provides, however, a number of recommendations that should increase the popularity of mediation among all interested parties in both the shorter and longer term.

In Poland, arbitration is institutionalised. There are specific courts that deal with commercial arbitration cases. Even though the arbitration courts were established as early as in the 1950s, their role became truly significant after 1989. At present, there are over 20 courts of this type. Polish arbitration rules are based on the Polish civil procedure and the UNCITRAL rules. The arbitration has to be initiated by a motion filed by the parties.

3. THE CONCEPTUAL BASIS FOR THE OBLIGATION TO PERFORM CONSISTENT INTERPRETATION

In Polish, a few terms may be used when referring to the principle of consistent interpretation. Those are *inter alia* "*wykładnia zgodna*" ("consistent interpretation"), "*wykładnia prounijna*" ("pro-Union interpretation"), "*wykładnia zgodna z prawem UE*" ("interpretation in conformity with EU law"), "*wykładnia przyjazna prawu unijnemu*" ("EU law friendly interpretation"). Some legal scholars also refer to it as "*dubio pro communitate*". After the Lisbon Treaty had entered into force, the term "*wykładnia prowspólnotowa*" ("pro-Community interpretation") was replaced by "*wykładnia prounijna*" ("pro-Union interpretation").[84]

As explained in the legal literature, in Poland the principle of consistent interpretation is viewed as being derived from both EU law and national law. As regards EU law, reference is made the principle of loyalty, now found in Art. 4(3) TEU, the Accession Treaty[85] and the principle of primacy of EU law.

---

83 "Diagnosis of the use of mediation and the reasons for its lower than expected popularity", p. 5. See also pp. 20–28.

84 The terms have been translated by the present author.

85 In particular, Art. 2 of the Accession Treaty ([2003] OJ L236/17) provides that "From the date of accession, the provisions of the original Treaties and the acts adopted by the institutions and the European Central Bank before accession shall be binding on the new Member States and shall apply in those States under the conditions laid down in those Treaties and in this Act".

As regards Polish law, Arts. 9 and 91 para. 1 of the Constitution are of relevance in this respect.[86]

The Polish courts apply the principle of consistent interpretation directly, as an EU obligation in its own right. Importantly, this obligation has forced the Polish courts to reconsider the manner in which they must apply the principles governing the interpretation of law. For the purposes of this contribution, it is necessary to note the distinction between the first degree principles of interpretation, i.e. linguistic, functional (teleological) and systemic, and the second degree principles of interpretation. The latter determine the manner in which the former should be applied, i.e. the order in which they should be used and, if necessary, which interpretation should take precedence over the others in the case of conflicting results. As a rule, linguistic interpretation takes precedence, while the functional and systemic interpretation have only a subsidiary character, i.e. they are applied only if the linguistic interpretation leads to a grossly unjust, irrational or absurd understanding of the provision in question.[87]

As a result of introducing the principle of consistent interpretation, the Polish courts must take into account the following. First, they may no longer limit themselves to the result obtained by applying the linguistic interpretation, even if that result is unambiguous and clear-cut. The courts must apply all principles of interpretation. Most importantly, however, it is prohibited to assume the precedence of the linguistic interpretation. As a consequence, a result obtained by applying the principles of functional and systemic interpretation in a situation where the result of the linguistic interpretation was unambiguous and clear-cut may not be qualified as interpretation *contra legem*.[88]

Second, among the results obtained by applying all first degree principles of interpretation, the court must choose the one which is conform most closely to the EU law. In other words, the model of subsidiarity is replaced by the model of completeness.

This is well illustrated in the Supreme Court's judgment *III SK 27/08* of 2010 in which the Court considered Art. 71 para 3 of the Telecommunications Act,[89] in light of the 2002 Universal Service Directive,[90] and the ECJ's decision in

---

86 According to Art. 9 of the Constitution: "The Republic of Poland shall respect international law binding upon it." Art. 91 para. 1 provides that "After promulgation thereof in the Journal of Laws of the Republic of Poland (Dziennik Ustaw), a ratified international agreement shall constitute part of the domestic legal order and shall be applied directly, unless its application depends on the enactment of a statute".

87 Compare J. Wroblewski, *Sądowe stosowanie prawa* (Warsaw, 1988), p. 120.

88 Sołtys (n. 1), p. 619.

89 *Dziennik Ustaw* No 171, Item 1800, with amendments.

90 Directive 2002/22/EC of the European Parliament and of the Council of 7 March 2002 on universal service and users' rights relating to electronic communications networks and services [2002] OJ L108/51.

C-438/04 *Mobistar*.[91] In spite of obtaining a clear-cut meaning of the said provision through its linguistic interpretation which would have been in conflict with the directive, the Supreme Court applied functional and systemic interpretation, which allowed for meeting the obligation of consistent interpretation.

The consequences of introducing the principle of consistent interpretation are thus rather serious. They affect the rules governing the interpretation of a legal text that are deeply rooted in the Polish practice of applying law.[92]

As a final remark, it should be noted that in spite of many examples of judgments in which the principle of consistent interpretation was successfully applied, the Polish legal literature presents different views on that principle.[93] Some legal scholars submit that the principle of consistent interpretation may not result in changing the meaning of a provision that raises no doubts as regards its interpretation[94] or in setting aside national regulations.[95]

3.1. THE IMPORTANCE OF THE PRE-ACCESSION PERIOD

For the purpose of discussing the principle of consistent interpretation, it is necessary to stress the importance of the jurisprudence of the Constitutional Tribunal before 1 May 2004. This is because in that period, the Tribunal lay the foundations of understanding and applying the principle of consistent interpretation.

As early as 1997, the Tribunal referred to interpreting national law in a manner "sympathetic to the process of European integration and cooperation between the states". In its ruling *K 15/97* of 29 September 1997,[96] the Tribunal ruled on a specific form of discrimination against female civil servants who were dismissed due to lower retirement age for women. The Community-friendly interpretation performed in this case was based on the EC-Poland Association Agreement.[97] A similar reasoning may be found in subsequent rulings such as *K 27/99, K 15/99, K 35/99, K 12/00, K 2/02, K 11/03.*

---

91 ECLI:EU:C:2006:463.

92 Sołtys (n. 1), pp. 291–93.

93 See ibid., pp. 287–312.

94 See S. Biernat, "Wykładnia prawa krajowego w zgodzie z prawem Wspolnoty Europejskiej" in C. Mik (ed.), *Implementacja prawa integracji europejskiej w krajowych porządkach prawnych* (Toruń, 1998), p. 133.

95 See C. Mik, "Wykładnia zgodna prawa krajowego z prawem Unii Europejskiej" in S. Wronkowska (ed.), *Polska kultura prawna a proces integracji europejskiej* (Krakow, 2005), p. 162.

96 *K 15/97* of 29.09.1997. See also *K 12/00* of 24.10.2000, *K 15/04* of 31.05.2004 and *K 33/03* of 21.04.2004.

97 Agreement establishing an association between the European Communities and their Member States, of the one part, and the Republic of Poland, of the other part – Protocol 1 on textile and clothing products – Protocol 2 on ECSC products – Protocol 3 on trade between Poland and the Community in processed agricultural products not covered by Annex II to

As the Constitutional Tribunal emphasised, during the pre-accession period, there was no formal obligation to apply the rules of interpretation that were based on *acquis communautaire*. Yet, one had to reinforce the direction of interpretation that would be most consistent with the solutions adopted in the Community law and its case-law.[98] In other words, the principle of consistent interpretation was an instrument to harmonise national law with the Community law. In this respect, the Tribunal relied on Art. 91 para. 1 of the Constitution, which refers to a "ratified international agreement", here the above-mentioned Agreement establishing an association between the European Communities and their Member States, of the one part, and the Republic of Poland, of the other part. Obviously, in spite of certain common features, the pre-accession Community or EU law friendly interpretation may not be considered equivalent to the principle of consistent interpretation. Unlike the former, the latter imposes an obligation on EU Member States, has different legal grounds and provides for the procedure for making references for a preliminary ruling.

One final remark on the pre-accession period concerns the ruling in *K 2/02* of 21 April 2004,[99] where the Constitutional Tribunal referred to the principle of interpreting national law in a manner sympathetic to European law, but *à rebours*, i.e. reverse discrimination, as the Tribunal formulated its observation. In that ruling, the Ombudsman questioned the constitutionality of certain provisions of the Bio-components and Liquid Bio-fuels Act of 2003,[100] which in his opinion constituted substantial restrictions on economic freedom or were unfavourable from the perspective of consumer protection. First, manufacturers were obliged to market in any given year the amount of bio-components specified in an EU Regulation issued yearly. Second, "normal" liquid fuels with bio-component additives could be sold through unmarked pumps. The obligation to sell from separate pumps, marked in such a manner so as to enable identification of the bio-component content, related only to bio-fuels in the strict sense. Third, the Act prescribed an administrative fiscal penalty for undertakings failing to market bio-components or marketing them in lower quantities than those prescribed by the Regulation.

The Ombudsman considered that obliging producers to market bio-components restricted freedom of economic activity in contravention of

---

the EEC Treaty – Protocol 4 concerning the definition of the concept of originating products and methods of administrative cooperation – Protocol 5 on specific provisions relating to trade between Poland, of the one part, and Spain and Portugal, of the other part – Protocol 6 on mutual assistance in customs matters – Final Act – Joint Declarations was signed on 16.12.1991 and entered into force on 01.02.1994.

98 See *K 2/02* of 28.01.2003.

99 For the English version of the ruling *K 33/033*, see <http://trybunal.gov.pl/fileadmin/content/omowienia/K_33_03_GB.pdf> accessed 25.04.2017.

100 Bio-components Used in Liquid Fuels and Liquid Bio-fuels Act of 02.10.2003, *Dziennik Ustaw* No. 199, item 1934.

Art. 22 of the Constitution.[101] Such a restriction was not justified on the basis of protecting an important public interest, and the conditions laid down in Art. 31 para. 3[102] of the Constitution (the principle of proportionality) were not fulfilled. As regards the obligation imposed on consumers to purchase fuels containing bio-components, in the absence of any choice, it was incompatible with the principle of consumer protection stemming from Art. 76 of the Constitution.[103] Consumers purchasing "normal" liquid fuel (i.e. non bio-fuels) were denied information as to their bio-component content and therefore did not possess basic knowledge about the product they were purchasing. This constituted a breach of the consumers' right to information regarding the subject matter of the transaction.

The Bio-components Act was considered in the context of the 2003 Directive on the promotion of the use of bio-fuels or other renewable fuels for transport.[104] In this respect, the Tribunal stressed that the primary purpose of that Directive was readily apparent from its title: it aimed to promote the use of bio-fuels in transport, rather than to enforce such usage. An analysis of the Directive's provisions also led to the conclusion that its implementation did not allow for the possibility to enact national provisions making the use of bio-fuels compulsory. It could not be assumed that alteration of the Directive's aim – from promotion to imposition of an obligation – constituted the "detailing" of the Directive within the internal legal order, falling within the scope of the State's freedom to choose the form and methods of implementation.[105] Such reasoning was, firstly, incompatible with the principles of implementation into the internal legal order of Directives and, secondly, contrary to the substance of the Directive itself, which clearly stated that internal State policy promoting the use of bio-fuels could not hinder the free movement of fuels.

As the Tribunal noted, the scope of the freedom enjoyed by the legislator in enacting regulations concerning restrictions on economic freedom, its delimitation and the interpretation of the notion of "important public reasons", as contained in Art. 22 of the Constitution, had to be assessed in the light

---

101 Art. 22 of the Constitution provides as follows: "Limitations upon the freedom of economic activity may be imposed only by means of statute and only for important public reasons."

102 Art. 31 para. 3 of the Constitution provides as follows: "Any limitation upon the exercise of constitutional freedoms and rights may by imposed only by statute, and only when necessary in a democratic state for the protection of its security or public order, or to protect the natural environment, health or public morals, or the freedoms and rights of other persons. Such limitations shall not violate the essence of freedoms and rights."

103 Art. 76 of the Constitution provides as follows: "Public authorities shall protect consumers, customers, hirers or lessees against activities threatening their health, privacy and safety, as well as against dishonest market practices. The scope of such protection shall be specified by statute".

104 Directive 2003/30/EC of the European Parliament and of the Council of 8 May 2003 on the promotion of the use of biofuels or other renewable fuels for transport [2003] OJ L123/42.

105 A similar argument, i.e. an obligation to introduce certain regulations that was allegedly imposed by EU law was (also unsuccessfully) used in, *inter alia, K 38/04* of 13.09.2005.

of Poland's participation in the European Common Market. This had particular consequences in relation to the constitutional assessment of reverse discrimination – enacting restrictions on economic freedom which applied only to nationals, since their application to other EU citizens was prohibited by Community law. No legislator in other Member States imposed obligations similar to those imposed by the Polish legislator. While discrimination against national entities was irrelevant in the light of Community law, it was the constitutional duty of national authorities to protect against such discrimination.

Having recognised the problem of a reverse discrimination, the Tribunal ruled that the notion of economic freedom should be interpreted in conformity with the EU law. That amounted to precluding the national legislator from imposing restrictions due to the "important public reasons" referred to in Art. 22 of the Constitution. Since it was impossible for the reviewed provisions to apply to fuels produced abroad and placed on the Polish market, by reason of the country of origin (a consequence of ex Arts. 28 and 30 EC), it was impossible to deem the obligations imposed thereby as consistent with the "important public reasons". In conclusion, the questioned provisions of the bio-components Act were deemed to be unconstitutional.

3.2. MEMBER STATE AUTHORITIES SEEKING TO RELY UPON THE PRINCIPLE OF CONSISTENT INTERPRETATION IN A CASE AGAINST AN INDIVIDUAL

A situation in which the Polish authorities sought to rely upon the principle of consistent interpretation to their benefit in cases against individuals was the interpretation and application of the VAT Act of 11 March 2004, with amendments.[106] In an online database comprising the judgments the Supreme Administrative Court and the provincial administrative courts,[107] the principle of consistent interpretation was relied upon by either the applicant or the authorities or both in 43 cases concerning VAT. The Supreme Administrative Court considered such a case for the first time in June 2008.[108]

A good example of such a case is the judgment *I FSK 1209/14*, which was handed down by the Supreme Administrative Court on 17 November 2015. Therein, the applicant sought an annulment of a ruling of the provincial

106 *Ustawa z dnia 11 marca 2004 r. o podatku od towarów i usług (t.j. z 2011 r. Dz. U. Nr 177, poz. 1054, z późn. zm.) oraz rozporządzenia wykonawcze.*

107 <http://orzeczenia.nsa.gov.pl> accessed 25.04.2017.

108 According to the information provided on the website <http://www.nsa.gov.pl/baza-orzeczen.php> accessed 25.04.2017, the database contains the judgments of the administrative courts dated from January 2004 onwards and some selected earlier judgments of the Supreme Administrative Court. The database has a strictly educational character. In particular, it not does not have a status of the official publication.

administrative court in Gdansk of 2 April 2014 by which the court upheld a decision issued by the Director of Tax Chamber in Gdansk of 4 July 2013. As explained in the decision, the applicant carried out an economic activity consisting of, among other things, wholesale supply of liquid fuels and fuel additives. The decision was taken on the basis of the evidence that was collected in the course of a tax audit concerning the reliability of the stated tax bases and the correctness of calculation and payment of tax on goods and services and excise tax for the period from January 2007 to September 2009.

As established by the tax authorities, the applicant had illegally reduced the tax due by the input tax charged on invoices for the sale of diesel, which were issued by P [...] H., a limited liability company. This was because the said invoices did not show the actual course of events. As concluded on the basis of the evidence, the company P [...] H. did not carry out any economic activity, but only pretended to conduct such activity by issuing illegal invoices. P [...] H was established by a Ukrainian citizen who used a stolen passport of a deceased Lithuanian citizen for the purpose of registering P [...] H in the Polish National Court Register. As a result, the Polish authorities issued an arrest warrant for the Ukrainian citizen. Moreover, the tax audit questioned the identity of the president of the company, the origins of the liquid fuels and fuel additives that the applicant allegedly bought from P [...] H, and the existence of such sale transactions.

In conclusion, the tax authorities established that the applicant was not entitled to deduct VAT as stipulated in Art. 86 of the Act of 11 March 2004 on the Goods and Services Tax as the invoices relating to the transactions in question referred to a non-existent trader. This interpretation was consistent with the Council Directive 2006/112/EC of 28 November 2006 on the common system of value added tax.[109] Moreover, the Director concluded that the applicant did not act with due diligence, which was expected from an entrepreneur. He did not attempt to verify the credibility of the company P [...] H and, as he admitted in the course of the tax audit, he had decided to cooperate with P [...] H mainly because of the competitive price of the purchased liquid fuels. Moreover, the applicant did not submit any contract or other document proving that he had entered an agreement with P [...] H.

According to the tax authorities, the relatively low price of fuel offered by P [...] H should have raised doubts about the legality of its origin. Therefore, the applicant did not act in good faith. As the tax authorities recalled, in the opinion of the ECJ, if the authorities can prove that the taxpayer knew or should have known that the purpose of transactions which gave rise to a deduction of tax was abuse of law – then the taxpayer loses the right to deduct the tax due by the amount resulting from the disputed transactions.

---

109 Council Directive 2006/112/EC of 28 November 2006 on the common system of value added tax [2006] OJ L347/1.

The provincial administrative court upheld the decision of the tax authorities. As regards the principle of consistent interpretation, the court added that in Case C-255/02, *Halifax plc, Leeds Permanent Development Services Ltd and County Wide Property Investments Ltd v. Commissioners of Customs & Excise*, the ECJ ruled that the Sixth VAT Directive of 1977[110] as amended by the 1995 Directive,[111] had to be interpreted as precluding any right of a taxable person to deduct input VAT where the transactions from which that right derived constituted an abusive practice. For it to be found that an abusive practice existed, it was necessary, first, that the transactions concerned, notwithstanding formal application of the conditions laid down by the relevant provisions of the Sixth VAT Directive of 1977 and of national legislation transposing it, resulted in the accrual of a tax advantage the grant of which would be contrary to the purpose of those provisions. Second, it had to be apparent from a number of objective factors that the essential aim of the transactions concerned was to obtain a tax advantage.[112]

As the Court added, in Joined Cases C-487/01 and C-7/02,[113] the ECJ stressed that the wording of the Sixth VAT Directive of 1977 demonstrated that the prevention of possible tax evasion, avoidance and abuse was an objective recognised and encouraged by this Directive. In Joined Cases C-439/04 and C-440/04, the ECJ ruled that where a recipient of a supply of goods was a taxable person who did not and could not know that the transaction concerned was connected with a fraud committed by the seller, he could not be denied the right to deduct the value added tax he had paid.[114] In Joined Cases C-80/11 and C-142/11, the ECJ ruled that only an entrepreneur who took every step which could reasonably be required of him to satisfy himself that the transaction which he was effecting did not result in his participation in tax evasion, was entitled to deduct VAT. In other words, a reasonable trader, depending on the circumstances of the case, who made enquiries about another trader from whom he intended to purchase goods or services in order to ascertain the latter's trustworthiness.[115]

When considering the complaint lodged following the ruling of the provincial administrative court, the Supreme Administrative Court adhered to the manner in which the Director and the provincial administrative court applied the

---

110 Sixth Council Directive 77/388/EEC of 17 May 1977 on the harmonisation of the laws of the Member States relating to turnover taxes – common system of value added tax: uniform basis of assessment [1977] OJ L145/1.

111 [1995] OJ L102/18.

112 Case C-255/02, *Halifax plc, Leeds Permanent Development Services Ltd and County Wide Property Investments Ltd v. Commissioners of Customs & Excise*, ECLI:EU:C:2006:121.

113 Joined Cases C-487/01 and C-7/02, *Gemeente Leusden and Holin Groep BV cs v. Staatssecretaris van Financiën*, ECLI:EU:C:2004:263.

114 Joined Cases C-439/04 and C-440/04, *Axel Kittel v. Belgian State and Belgium v. Recolta Recycling SPRL*, ECLI:EU:C:2006:446.

115 Joined Cases C-80/11 and C-142/11, *Mahagében Kft and Péter Dávid*, ECLI:EU:C:2012:373.

principle of consistent interpretation by relying on the Sixth VAT Directive of 1977 and the case-law of the ECJ. Moreover, the Supreme Administrative Court referred to the conclusions that the ECJ made in Case C-277/14. As the ECJ ruled, the provisions of the Sixth VAT Directive of 1977 had to be interpreted as precluding national legislation by which a taxable person was not allowed to deduct the value added tax due or paid in respect of goods that were delivered to him on the grounds that the invoice was issued by a trader which was to be regarded, in the light of the criteria provided by that legislation, as a non-existent trader, and that it was impossible to determine the identity of the actual supplier of the goods, except where it was established, on the basis of objective factors and without the taxable person being required to carry out checks which were not his responsibility, that that taxable person knew, or should have known, that that transaction was connected with VAT fraud, this being a matter for the referring court to determine.[116]

Another example of a case in which the authorities sought to rely on the principle of the consistent interpretation to their benefit is the judgment of the Supreme Administrative Court *I FSK 101/14* of 10 March 2015. Yet, as one of judges argued in her dissenting opinion, the principle of consistent interpretation was also used to rectify the State's error in implementing the 2006 VAT Directive.[117] Therefore, this case may be also discussed in the context of limits of consistent interpretation.

In *I FSK 101/14*, the Supreme Administrative Court adhered to the ruling of the provincial administrative court in Wrocław that confirmed the decision issued by the Director of Tax Chamber in Wrocław. The tax authorities established that company C illegally deducted VAT for intra-Community acquisition of goods. In October 2004, company C entered a lease agreement with company X, which had its headquarters in Germany, by which C rented a warehouse (free of charge) in which C (as a tenant) stored the goods it purchased. Those goods were subsequently sold to buyers from the EU and from outside the EU. Buyers were taxpayers registered in the country where the transport of goods ended. The goods were always dispatched from and delivered in Germany. In the analysed month, C made intra-Community acquisition of goods from C established in Germany and D C established in Switzerland who used a Belgian identification number. These purchases were documented with invoices in which C used a Polish identification number.

As explained by the tax authorities, under Art. 25 paras. 1 and 2 of the VAT Act of 11 March 2004,[118] intra-Community acquisition of goods was subject to taxation in Poland because the applicant used the Polish tax identification

---

116 Case C-277/14, *PPUH Stehcemp sp. j Florian Stefanek, Janina Stefanek, Jaroslaw Stefanek*, ECLI:EU:C:2015:719.

117 Council Directive 2006/112/EC of 28 November 2006 on the common system of value added tax [2006] OJ L347/1.

118 *Dziennik Ustaw* No 177, item 1054 with amendments.

number, i.e. the number of a country other than that from which the goods were dispatched or transported. At the same time, C did not prove that the acquisition was taxed in the territory of the dispatch or transport of goods, i.e. in Germany. As the purchase did not serve the subsequent sale on the Polish territory, C was not entitled to deduct input VAT related to the acquisition. The transactions did not fall within the definition of intra-Community acquisitions of goods.

The Supreme Administrative Court first confirmed that the goods had never entered Polish territory, which was not disputed by the applicant. Second, it addressed the main bone of contention, i.e. the possibility of applying the principle of consistent interpretation to the Polish VAT Act, which was disputed by the applicant. This was because the Polish provisions did not explicitly refer to the situation of using a tax identification number in the manner in which C had used it. Thus, the Polish VAT Act did not fully mirror the wording used in the relevant EU law.

The Supreme Administrative Court decided to recall and elaborate on the fundamental rules governing situations in which the Polish courts deal with EU law. It noted that the directives were binding on the Member States to which they were addressed, and that the Member States were obliged to implement them in a way that safeguarded the attainment of their objectives or results. The 2006 VAT Directive[119] should have thus been fully reflected in the Polish VAT Act. In a situation where a national provision raised doubts, the national court was obliged to interpret it in light of the wording and purpose of the directive in order to ensure the achievement of a specific result.[120] Furthermore, the Court mentioned the necessity of refusing the application of national provisions and the presumption that the Member State intended to fully implement a directive in question. Having stated that the consistent interpretation was to be made within the discretion of the court and as far as possible, however, it recalled that it did not apply if it would lead to a denial of national law or rejecting it, or to a *contra legem* interpretation.

In addition, the Court referred to Case C-409/04, where the ECJ ruled that intra-Community acquisition of goods was effected and exemption of the intra-Community supply of goods became applicable only when the right to dispose of the goods as owner had been transferred to the purchaser and the supplier established that those goods had been dispatched or transported to another Member State and that, as a result of that dispatch or that transport, they had physically left the territory of the Member State of supply.[121]

---

119 Council Directive 2006/112/EC of 28 November 2006 on the common system of value added tax [2006] OJ L347/1.

120 In this respect, the Supreme Administrative Court referred to Case 14/83, *Sabine von Colson and Elisabeth Kamann v. Land Nordrhein-Westfalen*, ECLI:EU:C:1984:153.

121 Case C-409/04, *The Queen v. Commissioners of Customs & Excise*, ECLI:EU:C:2007:548, para. 42.

When disputing the application of the principle of the consistent interpretation to the Polish VAT Act, the applicant argued that the Court should limit itself to the linguistic interpretation of the relevant provision. As mentioned, the relevant Polish provision did not literally implement the text of Directive. It was only after the VAT Act was amended on 1 April 2013 that the legislator added a new provision according to which the right to a VAT deduction did not exist in a case of an intra-Community acquisition of goods if those goods did not enter the territory of the Member State that issued the tax identification number.

Importantly, the Court rejected the applicant's argument according to which the 2013 amendment had a normative character. In this respect, the Court relied on an opinion provided by a tax law expert. This view was confirmed in the *Facet* case.[122] The principle of consistent interpretation was thus central to rejecting the arguments of the applicant.

In her dissenting opinion, one of the judges referred to Art. 2 of the Constitution, i.e. the principle that Poland is a democratic state ruled by law, and the well-established case-law of the ECJ, according to which the authorities could not rely on the direct effect of a directive or rectify the provisions that were implemented in an erroneously or imprecise manner by applying the principle of consistent interpretation if this would worsen the situation of a taxpayer. In this respect, the judge referred to Case C-8/81 *Ursula Becker*[123] and Case C-80/86 *Kolpinguis Nijmegen*.[124]

Another different, but rather interesting, example of a case in which the Polish authorities attempted to rely on the principle of consistent interpretation to their benefit is a reference for a preliminary ruling in Case C-465/11 *Forposta v. Poczta Polska SA*.[125] This reference related to the interpretation of point (d) of the first subparagraph of Art. 45(2) of the Public Sector Directive of 2004,[126] as read in conjunction with Arts. 53(3) and 54(4) of the Utilities Directive of 2004.[127] The reference concerned a decision of Poczta Polska to exclude Forposta and ABC Direct Contact from the procedure for the award of a contract, for which the Poczta Polska had issued a call for tender. Importantly, Poczta Polska (The Polish Post) is a company owned by the Polish Treasury.

---

122 Joined Cases C-536/08 and C-539/08, *Staatssecretaris van Financiën v. X oraz fiscale eenheid Facet BV/Facet Trading BV*, ECLI:EU:C:2010:217.

123 Case C-8/81, *Ursula Becker*, ECLI:EU:C:1982:7.

124 Case C-80/86, *Kolpinguis Nijmegen*, ECLI:EU:C:1987:431.

125 Case C-465/11, *Forposta SA, ABC Direct Contact sp. z o.o. v. Poczta Polska SA*, ECLI:EU:C:2012:801.

126 Directive 2004/18/EC of the European Parliament and of the Council of 31 March 2004 on the coordination of procedures for the award of public works contracts, public supply contracts and public service contracts [2004] OJ L134/114.

127 Directive 2004/17/EC of the European Parliament and of the Council of 31 March 2004 coordinating the procurement procedures of entities operating in the water, energy, transport and postal services sectors [2004] OJ L134/1.

In the proceedings before the ECJ, the Polish Government intended to rely on the principle of consistent interpretation when arguing against the admissibility of the reference for a preliminary ruling itself. It submitted *inter alia* that the reference aimed to determine whether national legislation at issue in the main proceedings was compatible with the provisions of the Public Sector Directive, and not to obtain an interpretation of EU law in order to give guidance to the subject matter of the dispute, which had to be decided on the basis of national law. As the ECJ established, however, the referring court did not request the ECJ to assess the compatibility of national legislation with EU law, or to interpret that national legislation. It merely requested the interpretation of EU public procurement rules for the purpose of assessing whether it was necessary to disapply Art. 24(1)(1a) of the Polish Public Procurement Act in the main proceedings. Second, the questions referred were relevant for resolving that dispute, since Poczta Polska cancelled the tendering process of the contract at issue on the grounds that the economic operators which had put forward the tenders chosen were subject to compulsory exclusion from the procedure under that national provision.

4. THE STATUS OF PREPARATORY LEGISLATIVE WORKS IN THE POLISH LEGAL SYSTEM

In the Polish legal system, the status of preparatory legislative works should be considered in light of the closed catalogue of sources of universally binding law and the principles governing the interpretation of legal texts.

As stipulated in Art. 87 of the Constitution: "The sources of universally binding law of the Republic of Poland shall be: the Constitution, statutes, ratified international agreements, and regulations. Enactments of local law issued by the operation of organs shall be a source of universally binding law of the Republic of Poland in the territory of the organ issuing such enactments." Therefore, neither a draft of a legal act, nor an official explanation of or justification for introducing a new regulation may be seen as sources of law. As an exception, a preamble may be mentioned, if there is one. This is the case with regards to the Constitution and international agreements. Ordinary statutes do not usually have a preamble, unless the Act in question is of a very high importance to the legal system.

As regards the principles governing the interpretation of legal texts, many different divisions and subdivisions of the interpretation rules have been developed by philosophers and law theoreticians over the last decades.[128] Yet, the role and content of the first degree principles (or methods) remain undisputed. Those are the linguistic, systemic and functional (theological) approaches.

[128] See e.g. Z. Ziembiński, Problemy podstawowe prawoznawstwa (Warsaw, 1980), pp. 244–307.

The linguistic method of interpretation is often recognised as the most substantial.[129] This means that one may recur to the systemic and functional methods of interpretation only if the linguistic method leads to a result that contradicts the idea of a rational legislator or the aim of the legal text.[130] The well-established jurisprudence relies on this order of using the methods of interpretation.[131]

The linguistic method of interpretation focuses on the meaning of the terms used in a legal act. The legal terms may be defined in the legal text. Where they are not defined, the decisive meaning should be a common meaning. Once such a meaning is established, it must be followed in the rest of the legal act. In this context, one could imagine providing such meaning in the relevant preparatory legislative works. This could provide more clarity and thus legal certainty. Yet, if the Polish legislator decides to include any explanation or definition of legal terms it uses in the legal text in question, such explanations or definitions are included at the beginning of the legal act. Still, this is not a common practice and concerns only very complex pieces of legislation.

The importance of the linguistic interpretation and the role of the preparatory legislative texts should be seen in the context of the key limits to the interpretation of a legal text. These are its linguistic interpretation, i.e. the meaning of the given legal text, and the will of the legislator. The latter is based on the legal text and, at the same time, it is independent from preparatory legislative works.[132]

As regards the systemic interpretation, it establishes the meaning of the legal norm by referring to its location or position in the legal act concerned and in the whole legal system.

According to the functional (teleological) method, for the purpose of interpreting a legal text one must take into account its aim and function. In other words, this aim should be achieved even if it is not explicit in the text. In this context, the preparatory legislative works could allow for defining the relevant aim of function of the legal act. In Poland, one may refer to preparatory works, but they cannot be treated as conclusive or decisive in interpreting the legal act.

Finally, one should mention historical interpretation, which is quite common in Poland. The idea behind this method of interpretation is to identify arguments in favour and against a given meaning of the legal text that are based on the differences that occurred between the former and the latter version or versions of the same legal act. The starting point is still linguistic interpretation. The historical interpretation is linked to another very popular concept of the "rational legislator", which implies that there always is a certain reasoning

---

[129] See e.g. T. Spyra, *Granice wykładni prawa* (Zakamycze, 2006), pp. 72–90.

[130] The Supreme Court: *II CKN 873/97* of 04.11.1998.

[131] The Supreme Court: *I CKN 1405/98* of 03.04.2001; the Constitutional Tribunal: *P 2/87* of 03.03.1987, U 19/97 of 25.05.1998 and *U 4/96* of 29.10.1996.

[132] Spyra (n. 129), pp. 34–25.

behind a change in the legislation, and that this reasoning may be reconstructed by monitoring such changes.[133]

In light of the fact that the linguistic method of interpretation is the leading one, the preparatory legislative works may only be treated as a subsidiary set of interpretation rules. Admittedly, the use of preparatory legislative works may simplify the process of interpretation or even be necessary in this respect, but it should never be conclusive.[134] As regards the use of preparatory legislative works in practice, while legal scholars may refer to them, the Polish courts are more likely to rely on the judgments or resolutions of other courts, including the ECJ, and the Constitutional Tribunal.

5. LIMITS TO THE PRINCIPLE OF CONSISTENT INTERPRETATION

As regards the limits of the principle of consistent interpretation, its application may not lead to narrowing of the scope of constitutional freedoms and personal rights of citizens as they are guaranteed by the Constitution. The constitutional legislator has vested the provisions of the Constitution referring to personal rights and liberties with particularly high ranking and they cannot be limited.[135] Moreover, when verifying the constitutionality of an Act, the Constitutional Tribunal may rely on the principle of consistent interpretation if the domestic law, as it was adopted before accession to the EU, does not explicitly differ in its approach to the relevant issue from the approach adopted in EU law; and if the existence of a few possible interpretations allows for choosing the one most closely conforming to EU law.[136] As illustrated in *P1/05*, which concerned the European Arrest Warrant, even if EU law imposes an obligation to implement certain mechanisms into the national law, this cannot result in such interpretation of the provisions of the Constitution, which would result in the limitation of civil rights and liberties.

Another limitation of the principle of consistent interpretation results from the limits concerning the competences conferred upon the EU. As the Constitutional Tribunal ruled,[137] this principle cannot lead to a situation in which the EU would have received new competences without observing the conditions stipulated in Art. 90 of the Constitution.[138]

---

133 T. Grzybowski, *Wpływ zmian prawa na jego wykładnię* (LEX, 2013, nr 182601).

134 Z. Tabor, *W poszukiwaniu intencji prawodawcy* (Warsaw, 2013), pp. 261–63.

135 See the judgment of the Constitutional Tribunal *K 18/04* of 11.05.2005.

136 See *K 2/02* of 28.01.2003 and *K 33/03* of 21.04.2004.

137 See *K 32/08* of 24.11.2010.

138 Art. 90 of the Constitution provides as follows: "1. The Republic of Poland may, by virtue of international agreements, delegate to an international organization or international institution the competence of organs of State authority in relation to certain matters.

An interesting issue that was raised in the context of the limits to the principle of consistent interpretation was the application of EU law *ex officio*. This question is relevant in light of procedural rules which limit the scope of adjudication by the Supreme Court and the Supreme Administrative Court in appeals. As the Supreme Court ruled in *II PK 17/06* of 18 December 2006, the Supreme Court does not consider an infringement of EU law if the party fails to identify it as a basis for an appeal, unless there is a need to make a reference to the ECJ for a preliminary ruling. EU law must also be taken into account if it is obvious that it regulates the same issue that is regulated by the national law whose infringement is the basis for the complaint and there is an obligation to apply the principle of consistent interpretation. In this particular case, the applicant referred to the relevant EU law in the proceedings before the regional court and the circuit court, but not in the appeal while such an appeal may be dealt with by the Supreme Court only within the limits of its foundations, that is, the points of law that had been raised by the applicant, in addition to the annulment of proceedings on which the Court adjudicates on its own motion.

In a judgment handed down a few months earlier, *III SZP 3/06* of 1 3 July 2006, the Supreme Court ruled that when interpreting national law, EU law had to be taken into account when it concerned the case at hand. In this respect, the Court referred to the ECJ's decision in *Océano*.[139] This approach has been supported in legal literature,[140] in particular, in the case of directives.[141] However, it is also possible to find examples of the opposite approach, such as in the judgment delivered by the Supreme Administrative Court in *II GSK 355/10* of 27 May 2010 where the Court considered itself to be limited by the contents of the appeal. This approach was, however, criticised in the legal literature.[142]

A case in which the limits to the principle of consistent interpretation resulted in dissenting opinions among the judges of the Supreme Administrative Court, namely *I FSK 101/14* of 10 March 2015, was already discussed in section 3.2.

---

2. A statute, granting consent for ratification of an international agreement referred to in para1, shall be passed by the Sejm by a two-thirds majority vote in the presence of at least half of the statutory number of Deputies, and by the Senate by a two-thirds majority vote in the presence of at least half of the statutory number of Senators. 3. Granting of consent for ratification of such agreement may also be passed by a nationwide referendum in accordance with the provisions of Article 125. 4. Any resolution in respect of the choice of procedure for granting consent to ratification shall be taken by the Sejm by an absolute majority vote taken in the presence of at least half of the statutory number of Deputies."

139 Joined Cases C-240/98 to C-244/98, *Océano*, ECLI:EU:C:2000:346.

140 See N. Połtorak, *Ochrona uprawnień chrona uprawnień wynikających z prawa Unii Europejskiej w postępowaniach krajowych* (Warsaw, 2010), pp. 354–55; M. Baran, *Stosowanie z urzędu prawa Unii Europejskiej przez sądy krajowe* (Warsaw, 2014), pp. 324–98.

141 Compare Połtorak (n. 140), pp. 353, 355.

142 See e.g. P. Brzeziński, *Glosa do wyroku NSA z dnia 27 maja 2010 r., II GSK 355/10*, EPS 2011/9/37–44, <http://www.lex.pl/eps-akt/-/akt/glosa-do-wyroku-nsa-z-dnia-27-maja-2010-r-ii-gsk-35510> accessed 17.04.2017.

In case *U 6/07* of 24 March 2009, the Constitutional Tribunal stressed that even "the most pro-EU interpretation" cannot result in changing the Constitutional requirement that any regulation may be issued only on the basis of a statute.[143] Indeed, Art. 92 para. 1 of the Constitution stipulates that:

> Regulations shall be issued on the basis of specific authorization contained in, and for the purpose of implementation of, statutes by the organs specified in the Constitution. The authorization shall specify the organ appropriate to issue a regulation and the scope of matters to be regulated as well as guidelines concerning the provisions of such act.

In case *U 6/07*, the regulation concerning financial aid to farmers had been issued on the basis of a Commission decision. Yet, neither "agreements with the European Commission", which were included in the governmental agriculture plan and confirmed by the Commission's decision, nor imprecise EU rules to which the government referred before the Tribunal could replace a statute.

When the Constitutional Tribunal gave its ruling in *U 6/07*, the relevant regulation was no longer in force as it had been introduced for a limited period of time. As a rule, however, the mere fact that a given provision is no longer in force does not suffice to consider it non-applicable as long as it may affect the process of establishing the consequences of events that took place when that provision was in force.[144] Still, in order to rule on such a provision, a need to protect the constitutional freedoms and personal rights of citizens must be identified. In *U 6/07* it was not the case. Thus, the Tribunal decided to discontinue the proceedings.

6. CONCLUSIONS

In Poland, the principle of consistent interpretation was already recognised and applied in the pre-accession period. The Constitutional Tribunal has both formulated it and clarified its mechanism in a number of judgments. The principle is widely accepted and the Polish courts apply it in most of the cases. As noted in the legal literature, the fact of confirming the supremacy of the Constitution has stressed the role of the principle of consistent interpretation in ruling out any potential conflicts between the Polish and EU legal order.[145]

---

143 The Tribunal also referred to S. Wronkowska, "Model rozporządzenia jako aktu wykonawczego do ustaw w świetle konstytucji i praktyki" in A. Szmyt (ed.), *Konstytucyjny system źródeł prawa w praktyce* (Warsaw, 2005), p. 77.

144 The Constitutional Tribunal, see, in particular, *SK 5/01* of 28.11.2001 and *P 4/99* of 31.01.2001.

145 Sołtys (n. 1), p. 724.

TOWARDS AN INTERNALISATION OF EU LAW IN CYPRUS

The Effectiveness and Application of EU Law by National Courts

Stéphanie LAULHÉ SHAELOU and Katerina KALAITZAKI

1. THE BIRTH OF THE CYPRIOT CONSTITUTIONAL LEGAL ORDER

The Republic of Cyprus is a relatively "young" Republic, since the small island only gained the status of an independent and sovereign state in 1960 after the Zurich and London Agreements. The Agreements, reached between Greece and Turkey, provided a plan for the establishment of an independent state. They comprised three treaties on the basis of which the Constitution of the newly created state was drafted. The three treaties were the Treaty of Guarantee,[1] the

[1] Treaty of Guarantee between the Republic of Cyprus and Greece, the United Kingdom and Turkey of 16 August 1960.

Treaty of Alliance[2] and the Treaty of Establishment,[3] which collectively provided, *inter alia*, for Greece, Turkey and the UK to guarantee the independence, territorial integrity and security of the Republic, the establishment of Greek and Turkish military contingents in Cyprus, and the preservation of two British sovereign base areas in Cyprus.[4]

The Treaty of Establishment is incorporated into the 1960 Cyprus Constitution. The Treaty of Guarantee and the Treaty of Alliance, which are annexed to the Constitution (Annexes I and II respectively), have been given constitutional force by virtue of Art. 181 of the Constitution. The Cyprus Constitution was described "as the centrepiece of an intricate network of international agreements and undertakings, delicately but inextricably interwoven with one another and with the Constitution itself".[5] Papasavvas gives five attributes to the 1960 Constitution, namely "imposed, rigid, complex, anti-democratic and dividing".[6] Following the withdrawal of the Turkish Cypriots from the institutions of the Republic shortly after its birth in 1964, the Cypriot government has continued acting on the basis of the "law of necessity".[7] It is within this framework that the Republic of Cyprus is an actor in international law.[8]

---

2 Treaty of Alliance between the Republic of Cyprus, Greece and Turkey of 16 August 1960.

3 Treaty of Establishment of the Republic of Cyprus between the UK, Greece, Turkey and Cyprus of 16 August 1960.

4 For a comprehensive analysis of the constitutional history of Cyprus, including since independence see e.g. A. Emilianides, *Cyprus Constitutional Law* (Wolters Kluwer, 2013), pp. 13–21. For an in-depth legal analysis of the Cypriot legal order in an EU context, see S. Laulhé Shaelou, *The EU and Cyprus: Principles and Strategies of Full Integration* (SEUR vol. 3, Martinus Nijhoff, 2010); see also C. Kombos, *The Impact of EU Law on Cypriot Public Law* (Sakkoulas, 2015). For a review of the constitutional structure of Cyprus, see C. Kombos and S. Laulhé Shaelou, "The Cypriot Constitution under the impact of EU law: An asymmetrical formation" in A. Albi (ed.), *National Constitutions in European and Global Governance: Democracy, Rights and the Rule of Law* (TMC Asser Press, 2017). For a detailed legal analysis of the SBAs in Cyprus, see S. Laulhé Shaelou, "The principle of territorial exclusion in the EU: SBAs in Cyprus – a special case of sui generis territories in the EU", in D. Kochenov (ed.), *EU Law of the Overseas: Outermost Regions, Associated Overseas Countries and Territories, Territories Sui Generis* (Kluwer Law International, 2011).

5 S.A. De Smith, *The New Commonwealth and its Constitutions* (Stevens, 1964), p. 285.

6 S.S. Papasavvas, *La Justice Constitutionnelle à Chypre* (Economica, 1998), p. 258, (translated by the authors).

7 In constitutional law, "necessity" justifies acts done or proceedings taken under legislation passed in violation of a constitutional provision due to the occurrence of "necessitous" circumstances. The doctrine of necessity justifies the enforcement of an otherwise invalid and unlawful law. See e.g. C. Kombos, *The Doctrine of Necessity in Constitutional Law* (Sakkoulas, 2015).

8 S. Laulhé Shaelou, "'Back to reality': the implications of EU membership in the constitutional legal order of Cyprus" in A. Lazowski (ed.) *Brave New World: Application of EU Law in the New Member States* (TMC Asser Press, 2010), pp. 471–84.

2. NATIONAL COMPLIANCE WITH INTERNATIONAL LAW AND CONSTITUTIONAL RULES ON INTERNATIONAL ORGANISATIONS

Cyprus is a hybrid system stemming both from civil law and common law traditions[9] and arguably drawing both from monism and dualism.[10] Treaties, conventions and international agreements need to be ratified by the relevant authorities of the Republic in accordance with Art. 169 of the Constitution, the latter remaining the supreme law of the Republic under Art. 179(1) of the Constitution.[11] The ratification of treaties in Cyprus,[12] and the transfer of powers to international organisations (IOs), need to be considered within the framework of the status of the Republic of Cyprus in public international law and, as already mentioned, the rigid nature of its Constitution, which influence Cyprus's membership in IOs.[13] The relationship the Republic maintains with IOs must also be examined in the light of the *de facto* division of its territory and in view of the several attempts (including those currently on-going) to find a solution to the Cyprus problem.[14]

The Council of Ministers has the power to conclude any international agreement by virtue of Arts. 50 and 54 of the Constitution. There is a difference between international agreements concluded with a foreign state or an IO falling under the scope of Art. 169(1) of the Constitution and relating to "commercial matters, economic co-operation and *motus vivendi*", which are merely concluded under a decision of the Council of Ministers, and any other international agreement falling under Art. 169(2) of the Constitution, which requires them to be "negotiated and signed under a decision of the Council of Ministers" but will "only be operative and binding on the Republic when approved by a law

9 See N. Hatzimihail, "Cyprus as a mixed legal system" (2013) 6(1) *Journal of Civil Law Studies* 37.

10 For a legal analysis from a monist perspective, see S. Laulhé Shaelou (n. 8), p. 474. For a legal analysis from a dualist perspective, see Emilianides (n. 4).

11 Cyprus Constitution available in the English language at <http://www.presidency.gov.cy/presidency/presidency.nsf/all/1003AEDD83EED9C7C225756F0023C6AD/$file/CY_Constitution.pdf>.

12 For a legal analysis of the reception of international legal agreements in the Cypriot national legal order, see Laulhé Shaelou, *The EU and Cyprus* (n. 4) 130–40.

13 It should be noted that almost from the date of its creation up to its accession to the EU (1961–2004), the Republic of Cyprus was a member of the non-aligned movement. Cyprus is also the only EU Member State who is not a member of NATO or of the Partnership for Peace Programme.

14 For a detailed review of the implications of the *de facto* division of the territory of the Republic of Cyprus on the application of EU law in Cyprus, see Laulhé Shaelou, *The EU and Cyprus* (n. 4).

made by the House of Representatives whereupon it shall be concluded". In accordance with Art. 169(3) of the Constitution, all such agreements have, "as from their publication in the official Gazette of the Republic, superior force to any municipal law on condition that such treaties, conventions and agreements are applied by the other party thereto". This Article of the Constitution, combined with Art. 179, appears to constitute the formal framework of hierarchical incorporation of international law into the Cypriot constitutional legal order.

In this respect, Emilianides argues that the Constitution has adopted a strictly dualist approach in regards to the relationship between national and international law, stating that:

> It is only through publication in the Official Gazette that the international law instrument may be invoked before the Cypriot courts and applied in the Cypriot legal order. The international law instrument has superior force over any ordinary domestic legislation, not in the sense of repealing any inconsistent domestic law, but in the sense of having superiority and precedence in its application. International law, once incorporated in the national legal order and published in the Official Gazette, is superior to any other municipal law, irrespective of whether such law is prior or subsequent to the international law instrument; an international law instrument may obviously not be impliedly repealed through the enactment of conflicting subsequent municipal legislation.[15]

Moreover, in the hierarchy of norms, the international law instruments are placed above any other municipal legislation, provided that they also comply with the condition of reciprocity laid down by Art. 169(3). The Supreme Court has ruled, however, that due to the nature of certain international treaties and conventions (i.e. multilateral), the condition of reciprocity does not always apply.[16] International law instruments do not prevail over the Constitution, as the supreme law of the Republic does not fall within the definition of municipal law under Art. 169(3) of the Constitution.

It lies beyond the scope of this chapter to discuss the precise monist/dualist views adopted in Cyprus with respect to the relationship between national and international law (as it could be argued that there is a substantial difference between international agreements concluded under Art. 169(1) and (2), which appears to trigger a different approach to the incorporation of the given international agreement into national law). It would therefore be just to argue that the relationship is predominantly dualist and partly monist, since Art. 169(1) only covers international treaties concerning "commercial matters, economic co-operation and *modus vivendi*", while Art. 169(2) covers all the other matters stemming from international treaties. It remains, however, that

---

15 Emilianides (n. 4), pp. 33–34.

16 *Malachtou v. Armefti and Another* [1987] 1 CLR 207.

respective arguments pointing towards a strictly/predominantly dualist/monist tradition in Cyprus have repercussions on the perception of the principle of supremacy of European Union (EU) law as an (autonomous) source of international law, and consequently on the extent of the duty of harmonious interpretation under EU law, both implicitly underlying the jurisprudence in Cyprus and lying at the core of this chapter. In particular, arguing along strict dualist lines can lead to the conclusion that EU law forms an integral part of and is subject in all instances to the constitutional framework through the triggering of Arts. 169 and 179 of the Constitution.[17] This view on the relationship between EU law and national law, to which the present authors do not entirely subscribe, does not seem be supported by other scholars in Cyprus either.[18]

The above-mentioned provisions of the constitutional framework of the Republic of Cyprus were already at the centre of legal debates prior to Cyprus joining the EU in 2004.[19] It was recognised fairly early on by the Cypriot courts, before EU accession, that Community law, based on international treaties, forms "a distinct legal system which is capable of creating directly effective rights for those subject to it", which must be regarded as "independent of national laws" and "superior to them".[20] To this end, and in preparation for Cyprus's EU accession, there were voices recommending amending the Constitution to "make space" for EU law supremacy,[21] pointing to the procedure to amend non-basic constitutional provisions such as Arts. 169 and 179, under Art. 182 of the Constitution,[22] despite the division of the island and through the application of

---

17 Emilianides (n. 4), p. 34 and 37, where he classifies EU (and EC) law as an "intra-constitutional effect" and that it is the "Constitution itself which provides for the facilitation of [EU] law within the Cypriot legal order and its specific primacy".

18 C. Kombos and A. Pantazi Lambrou, "Cyprus" in J. Laffranque (ed.), *The Protection of Fundamental Rights Post-Lisbon* (Reports of the XXV FIDE Congress Tallinn 2012, vol. 1, Tartu University Press, 2012), pp. 303–54, 309: "the hierarchical rule resulting from Art. 179 does not apply to EU law"; see also C. Lycourgos, 'Cyprus public law as affected by accession to the EU' in C. Kombos (ed.), *Studies in European Public Law* (Sakkoulas, 2010), p. 101. For a detailed analysis, see also Laulhé Shaelou (n. 8).

19 See Kombos and Laulhé Shaelou (n. 4).

20 *Eracleous v. Municipality of Limassol*, No 5793, judgment of the Supreme Court, 14 December 1993 (translated by the authors); see N. Emiliou in TMC Asser Instituut, *The Impact of EU Accession on the Legal Orders of New EU Member States and (Pre-)candidate Countries: Hopes and Fears* (TMCA Press, 2006), p. 305; see also F. Hoffmeister, *Legal Aspects of the Cyprus Problem. Annan Plan and EU Accession* (Martinus Nijhoff Publishers, 2006), p. 205.

21 The example of the Irish Constitution, whereby the principle of Community law supremacy is incorporated into the Constitution, was brought forward in G. Bermann *et al.*, 'Opinion: Implications of membership in the EU for a constitutional settlement in Cyprus' of 29 March 2001 in A. Markides (ed.), *Cyprus and EU Membership: Important Legal Documents* (PIO, 2002) para. 44 and was said to provide a good precedent for Cyprus, see Emiliou (n. 20), p. 306.

22 Under Art. 182, basic Articles of the Constitution cannot be amended, while a two third majority of both Greek Cypriot and Turkish Cypriot votes at the House of Representatives is necessary to amend the rest.

the law of necessity.[23] The express reference to European Community (EC) law supremacy should have been decided by the House of Representatives on the basis of Art. 182(2)–(3) of the Constitution, but the Attorney General's office issued an opinion confirming that no amendment to the Constitution was necessary prior to ratification of the Treaty of Accession. The House of Representatives therefore ratified the Treaty on the basis of Art. 169 of the Constitution,[24] just like any other international treaty, with the "hope" that if and when subject to judicial review,[25] a situation of "tacit acceptance" of the supremacy of Community law, or at least, of "non-conflict between the two sets of legal norms", would arise.[26] In other words, it was "hoped that the courts would enable the effective and efficient participation of the Republic in the EU by harmoniously construing the obligations arising from EU membership with national constitutional law".[27]

Instead, the Supreme Court of Cyprus sent the matter back to the legislature by upholding the supremacy of the Cypriot Constitution on the first occasion provided by the challenge of the constitutionality of the European arrest warrant under Cypriot law,[28] pointing to the need for a formal constitutional amendment.[29] The measure challenged in this case concerned obligations imposed upon Member States to comply with a Framework Decision in criminal justice based on the old Third Pillar (the surrender of one of its nationals to another Member State in response to a European arrest warrant).[30] There were already clear signals at the time that the interpretation of Community law applicable during the judicial review process at national level should also apply to measures falling under the Third Pillar, including the competence of

---

23 See A. Markides, "The constitutional impact of Cyprus' accession to the EU" (speech, 21 May 2001, Nicosia), p. 6 (on file with the authors); see also Emiliou (n. 20), p. 307; *Contra* K. Chrysostomides, "Issues under constitutional and international law in the path of Cyprus towards accession to the EU" (speech, 29–30 June 2001, Nicosia) 5 as quoted in Hoffmeister (n. 20), pp. 205 and 150.

24 Ratifying law No 35(III)/2003, *Official Gazette* No 3740, 25.07.2003.

25 The Cypriot courts clarified through their case-law that an international treaty, being inferior to the Constitution, is subject to judicial review to the extent that the constitutional provisions prevail in case of conflict and within the framework of Arts. 169(3) and 179(1) of the Constitution.

26 Laulhé Shaelou (n. 8), p. 475.

27 Kombos and Laulhé Shaelou (n. 4), sections 1.2.1–1.2.4.

28 Council Framework Decision 2002/584/JHA of 13 June 2002 on the European arrest warrant and the surrender procedures between Member States [2002] OJ L190/1.

29 *Attorney General of the Republic of Cyprus v. Costas Constantinou* [2005] 1 CLR 1356, [2007] 3 CMLR 42; see case note by A. Tsadiras (2007) 44 CML Rev 1515. In the present case, the Attorney General of the Republic had requested the delivery of Mr Constantinou to the UK authorities on the basis of a European Arrest Warrant issued against him.

30 For a recent and comprehensive legal analysis of the case, see Kombos and Laulhé Shaelou (n. 4).

the European Court of Justice (ECJ) to hear such references by virtue of (old) Art. 35 of the Treaty on European Union (TEU).[31] Nevertheless, Cyprus had not at the time submitted to the jurisdiction of the Court regarding acts of the EU institutions in the area of police cooperation in criminal matters. Any attempt at judicial dialogue between the Supreme Court of Cyprus and the ECJ was therefore prevented, on formal grounds at least, to the detriment of the uniform interpretation of EU law (as it stood at the time).[32]

Instead, the main legal issue was dealt with by the Supreme Court within the ambit of the constitutional legal order, despite acknowledging the case-law of the ECJ on the supremacy of EU law and irrespective of the pleas made by the Attorney General to grant the EU law instrument superior force to the Constitution.[33] The Cypriot House of Representatives, like in other Member States, had to enact a law adopting the Framework Decision,[34] which was subject to judicial review. Based on a narrow understanding of judicial dialogue and of the duty of harmonious interpretation (which remained subject to the national court being able to interpret national law in accordance with Framework Decisions), any dispute before the national courts arising from the transposing law was found by the Supreme Court to be unconstitutional, since at that time Art. 11 of the Constitution did not provide for the extradition of Cypriot nationals with a view to the execution of a European Arrest Warrant.[35] The Supreme Court concluded that no provision in the law promulgated by the House of Representatives could be interpreted "in such a way so as to prevail and to be applied as regards the nationals of the Republic".[36]

---

31 "[J]urisdiction [under Art 35 EU] would be deprived of most of its useful effect if individuals were not entitled to invoke framework decisions in order to obtain a conforming interpretation of national law before the courts of the member states", Case C-105/03, *Pupino*, ECLI:EU:C:2005:386, para. 38.

32 Laulhé Shaelou (n. 8), pp. 476–78.

33 See para. 21, *Constantinou*, which reads as follows: "Thus, the main issue concerning the present case that remains to be discussed is the submission put forward by the [AG], namely that the Act which incorporated the [EAW] into the legal system of our country ranks higher than the Constitution and, consequently, it must be applied" (translation from Westlaw UK); see Tsadiras' review of the Supreme Court's ruling (2007) 44 CML Rev 1515, 1524–26.

34 Law 133(1)/2004, *Official Gazette* No 3850, 30.04.2004.

35 See Laulhé Shaelou (n. 8), p. 476. For a review of similar decisions of constitutional courts in other Member States at the time, see other contributions in Lazowksi (n. 8). The review of this case-law illustrated a certain degree of reluctance at the time, including among some new Member States, to accept the supremacy of EC/EU law unconditionally, in particular when fundamental rights of a national nature and/or with a particular meaning in the national system were involved. Nevertheless, the legality of the European Arrest Warrant under EU law was confirmed by the ECJ, rejecting any idea of violation of human rights and of abuse of powers under (old) Art. 34 TEU (see Case C-303/05, *Advocatenvoor de Wereld VZW*, ECLI:EU:C:2007:261).

36 Para. 24, *Constantinou*.

This decision of the Supreme Court forced a formal legislative (re)action in Cyprus which had been deferred so far and led to the creation of positive law. Amendments to the Cyprus Constitution were finally tabled before and passed by the House of Representatives with the clear objective to remove the potential conflict between EC/EU law and the Constitution.[37] Art. 1A was therefore added, to the effect that the supremacy of EU law over the Constitution is *prima facie* established, providing that:

> [n]o provision of the Constitution shall be deemed to annul laws enacted, acts done or measures taken by the Republic which become necessary by reason of its obligations as a member state of the European Union, nor does it prevent Regulations, Directives or other acts or binding measures of a legislative character, adopted by the European Union or the European Communities or by their institutions or competent bodies thereof on the basis of the Treaties establishing the European Communities or the Treaty on European Union, from having legal effect in the Republic.[38]

In addition to Art. 11 of the Constitution, which needed to be amended and supplemented for the purpose of the European Arrest Warrant,[39] Arts. 140,[40] 169,[41] and 179[42] of the Constitution were also amended and/or supplemented in order to give *a priori* full effect to the new Art. 1A of the Constitution. The precise impact of Art. 1A nevertheless remained unclear. In particular, while Art. 179(1) was made subject to Art. 1A, it still provided that the Constitution "remains the supreme law of the Republic".[43] No direct reference to the supremacy of EC/EU law was made in the amendments, thereby avoiding addressing the very difficult question at the time of what legal order prevails over the Constitution, i.e. EC law or EU law. It was contended at the time that it should have been EU law. Cyprus (like Lithuania) would then have been considered at the forefront

---

37 Fifth Amendment to the Constitution Law 127(I)/2006, Official Gazette No 4090, 28.07.2006 available at <http://www.olc.gov.cy/olc/olc.nsf/all/EC240D2A9413ABBB4225793A00403484/$file/The%20Fifth%20Amendment%20of%20the%20Constitution%20Law%20of%202006.pdf?openelement>.

38 Translated by the authors.

39 Art. 11(2)(f) was replaced with a new subpara. (f). For a comprehensive and up-to-date review of the various constitutional amendments made in the context of the European Arrest Warrant, see Kombos and Laulhé Shaelou (n. 4).

40 For a comprehensive and up-to-date legal analysis of the amendments to Art. 140 of the Constitution and their constitutional importance, see Kombos and Laulhé Shaelou (n 4).

41 A new para. (4) was inserted, to the effect that the Republic of Cyprus commits to act upon all the provisions deriving from EC and EU law, including when they amend national law.

42 Express reference to Art. 1A was made in para. (1); para. (2) now refers to the obligations imposed on the Republic arising out of EU membership.

43 It is clear, however, from Art. 4 of Law 35(III)/2003 that the rights and obligations of the Republic arising out of the Treaty of Accession prevail against contrary national rules and regulations.

of European integration by recognising such supremacy even before the ECJ. Should it have been merely EC law, then the conflict between the European arrest warrant and the relevant provisions of the Constitution would have remained.[44] The option was taken at the time to deal with the supremacy issue in a rather indirect or reverse way, by providing that no provision of the Constitution could be an obstacle to Cyprus complying with its obligations as a Member State of the EU. Thus, without expressly providing so, Art. 1A set out the principle of supremacy of EC and EU law,[45] in advance of the forthcoming "depillarisation" of the Union construct,[46] by treating the Community and intergovernmental spheres "uniformly".[47] The broad scope of Art. 1A appeared justified (or not) also for reasons related to the difficulties associated with amending the Cyprus Constitution and in view of the doctrine of necessity.[48]

The legislative objective of removing the potential conflict between EC/EU law and the Constitution appeared to have been achieved. However, the relationship between EU law and national law is subject to continuous judicial scrutiny. With respect to this aspect, the somewhat burdensome legacy of the *Constantinou* ruling cannot be ignored. In the light of Art. 19(1) TEU and the case-law of the ECJ on the effectiveness of EU law, Cypriot courts, guided by the duty of harmonious interpretation, should normally evaluate on the merits of each case whether national law, including the Constitution as amended, provides an effective remedy, thus allowing for the full and correct implementation, application and enforcement of EU law and rights deriving there from in Cyprus. It appears that in Cyprus, however, the Supreme Court – through its decision in *Constantinou* – has placed EU law supremacy under the authority of the national legal order, as opposed to deriving it from the inherent nature of EU law as promoted by the Court of Justice. Following the 2005 constitutional amendments, the Cypriot legal order had nevertheless appeared potentially well-equipped to receive and accommodate the principle of the supremacy of EU law to its fullest extent. Ten years onwards, however, the nature or the validity of Art. 1A of the Constitution remains untested before the Supreme Court, which continues to focus on the national legal order and national principles equivalent to EU law principles, in a (rather broad and fluctuating) comparative perspective. A brief review of the court structure and legal tradition in Cyprus would assist in encapsulating court practice in Cyprus with respect to the principle of harmonious interpretation and appreciating the methodology of the present contribution.

---

44 Laulhé Shaelou (n. 8), p. 479.

45 C. Lycourgos, "Cyprus public law as affected by accession to the EU" in C. Kombos (ed.), *Studies in European Public Law* (Sakkoulas, 2010), p. 105.

46 Burgorgue-Larsen describes Art. 1A as a "véritable profession de foi juridique européenne" in 'Jurisprudence européenne comparée' [2006] 4 *Revue du Droit Public* 1099, 1121.

47 See Tsadiras (2007) 44 *CML Rev* 1515, 1527.

48 On these last two points, see Kombos and Laulhé Shaelou (n. 4), section 1.2.

3. COURT STRUCTURE AND LEGAL TRADITION IN CYPRUS

3.1. THE PRINCIPLE OF SEPARATION OF POWERS AND THE ROLE OF THE JUDICIARY

Another important characteristic of the Constitution is the principle of separation of powers as developed mainly in the case-law of the Supreme Court. The Constitution itself does not expressly set out such a principle, but its provisions clearly point to the separation of powers as the basic principle of the polity. Namely, Arts. 46–49 and 54 vest the executive power in the President of the Republic or the Council of Ministers; Art. 61 vests the legislative power in the House of Representatives; and Arts. 133–164 vest the judicial power in the Supreme Court (formerly Supreme Constitutional Court and High Court) and its subordinate courts.

The principle thus inherently set out by the Constitution, although appearing relatively strict, is not an absolute one. As such, the Council of Ministers may undertake preparatory legislative acts by drafting bills before they are introduced to the House of Representatives,[49] while the Minister of Finance can submit the budget.[50] Moreover, ministers are granted the right to make statements to, and to follow, the proceedings of the House of Representatives,[51] and the Council of Ministers is also vested with executive powers to issue subsidiary legislation[52] in certain circumstances.[53] The principle is deemed to have constitutional status: the Supreme Court has persistently ruled that if a law is contrary or inconsistent with the principle of separation of powers, it is rendered unconstitutional.[54] The full independence of the judiciary must also be emphasised. Finally, the principle of the separation of powers must also be interpreted in the light of the doctrine of necessity.[55]

Originally, the Supreme Court has exercised the first instance jurisdiction as a Supreme Constitutional Court. Pursuant to Art. 144 of the Constitution, the Supreme Court has exclusive jurisdiction to decide on the constitutionality of any law of the Republic and to resolve any power struggle between the Executive and the Legislature. Therefore, whenever such a question was raised

---

49 Art. 54(f) of the Constitution of Cyprus.

50 Art. 167 of the Constitution of Cyprus.

51 Art. 79(2) of the Constitution of Cyprus.

52 More specifically the Council of Ministers is granted the power to issue administrative regulations or orders in the form of secondary legislation.

53 Art. 54(g) of the Constitution of Cyprus.

54 See S. Laulhé Shaelou and K. Kalaitzaki, "Cyprus" in L. Burgorgue-Larsen (ed.), *The EU Charter of Fundamental Rights seized by the national judges/La Charte des Droits Fondamentaux de l'Union Européenne saisie par les judges en Europe* (Pedone, 2016); see also Emilianides (n. 4), pp. 55–57 for a detailed account of the principle.

55 For a detailed account, see Emilianides (n. 4), pp. 22–24.

before any court, the latter should have reserved the question for the decision of the Supreme Court and stayed further proceedings until its determination. However, the events of 1964 in Cyprus resulted in the introduction of Law 33/64 on the Administration of Justice (Miscellaneous Provisions), adopted by the House of Representatives in the absence of Turkish Cypriot members of Parliament, which created a new Supreme Court and merged the jurisdictions of the constitutionally provided Supreme Constitutional Court and the High Court.[56] As a result, Art. 144 was no longer applicable. Since 1964, any court in the Republic therefore has jurisdiction to hear questions on the constitutionality of laws without having to resort to the procedure provided for in Art. 144 of the Constitution, or having to refer the question to the Supreme (Constitutional) Court.[57] The Supreme Court only has exclusive jurisdiction in relation to the constitutionality of family law matters and also to decide on the constitutionality of laws in connection with which the President of the Republic exercises the right for referral granted to him under the Constitution.[58]

Within the above framework, the Supreme Court exercises its powers in three different jurisdictions. First, the Supreme Court exercises the second instance jurisdiction as a Court of Appeal. Namely, the Supreme Court hears all appeals on decisions of first instance courts, which exercise jurisdiction in civil and criminal matters. As a rule, appeals are heard by three judges. When exercising its appellate jurisdiction the Supreme Court may confirm, differentiate or set aside the contested decision or order the retrial of the case.[59] Second, the Supreme Court exercises the revisional jurisdiction (judicial review) under Art. 146 of the Constitution, over which it, until recently, had exclusive jurisdiction, namely to hear applications in relation to the review of the legality of acts, decisions and omissions of any body, authority or person exercising executive or administrative authority.[60]

A new amendment to the Constitution was introduced in July 2015,[61] which changed the structure of the Supreme Court by establishing Administrative Courts in Cyprus, allegedly in order to help the Supreme Court to alleviate its workload. The amendments transferred the first instance jurisdiction of the Supreme Court under Art. 146 of the Constitution exclusively to the newly established Administrative Court. The Administrative Court started operations in January 2016, and even if the impact of its case-law on the court structure in Cyprus remains to be seen, a few points should be made for the purpose of the present discussion. The Cypriot legislator not only removed the exclusive

56 Kombos and Pantazi Lambrou, "Cyprus" (n. 18), p. 308.
57 For a detailed account, see Emilianides (n. 4), pp. 39–44.
58 See generally Emilianides (n. 4), pp. 119–21.
59 <http://www.supremecourt.gov.cy/judicial/sc.nsf/DMLSCourt_gr/DMLSCourt_gr?OpenDocument>.
60 See generally Emilianides (n. 4), pp. 197–98.
61 Eighth Amendment of the Constitution 2015 (130(I)/2015).

competence of the Supreme Court in cases of administrative law at first instance, but also made the Supreme Court a Court of Appeal only on legal grounds.[62] The formation and operation of the new Court is therefore bound to entail significant changes in the award of administrative justice in Cyprus, which, according to the Constitution, was defined as an exclusive competence of the Supreme Constitutional Court. The Administrative Court will also be involved in the internalisation of EU law in Cyprus. Instead of a solution deriving from the separation of the Supreme Court into two courts as provided by the Constitution itself, the adoption of an amending law creating the new Administrative Court was preferred. This will in turn also potentially impact on the legal reasoning of the Supreme Court, which would be expected to gain in substance and depth. Most importantly, however, some doubts can be expressed as to the legitimacy of the Administrative Court itself, in particular concerning the availability of an effective judicial remedy in administrative matters in Cyprus, given that the review of the legality of a controlled act or omission by the administration, which is now to be undertaken by the Administrative Court, has thereby been severed from the review of the substance of the matter which remains under the jurisdiction of the Supreme Court.[63]

Following the withdrawal of the Turkish Cypriot community from the government, the doctrine of necessity has been the cornerstone of the legal order. According to this doctrine, exceptional departures from constitutional provisions can take place under specific terms and requirements, when compliance with such provisions is rendered impossible owing to the withdrawal of the Turkish Cypriot community. Despite this rather extraordinary constitutional setting, the protection of fundamental rights in Cyprus, which lies at the core of a long legal tradition, has remained largely unaffected.

3.2. LEGAL TRADITION IN CYPRUS: FOCUS ON THE PROTECTION OF FUNDAMENTAL RIGHTS

With respect to the methodology of this chapter, the focus on the protection of fundamental rights is justified since such protection involves the application of not only constitutional provisions *per se* but also of relevant international and European instruments, as enshrined *inter alia* in the national legal order, thereby triggering *prima facie* the exercise of harmonious interpretation by the courts. As previously indicated, the balancing exercise pertaining to the

62 Law on the Establishment and Operation of the Administrative Court 2015 (Law 131(I)/2015).

63 The Administrative Court will however get involved in the substance of the matter in asylum and tax cases, so as to release the Supreme Court's workload in these two areas. It is to be hoped that the list of areas where the Court will be involved in substance will grow in the near future. See Laulhé Shaelou and Kalaitzaki, "Cyprus" (n. 54).

protection of constitutional and/or fundamental rights under national law must initially be considered with respect to the application of the doctrine of necessity.[64] In *Alloupas v. National Bank of Greece*,[65] a majority of the Supreme Court of Cyprus held that constitutional rights may only be restricted on the *express* basis of the Constitution and by applying the "strictest possible" criteria of necessity (i.e. does a state of necessity exist?) and of proportionality (i.e. are such restrictions proportionate to the necessity?).[66] It is worth noting at this stage the constitutional significance of proportionality which, although not a general principle deriving directly from the Constitution,[67] has been granted constitutional status as an "unwritten principle of law" and referred to by the Supreme Court very early on in its jurisprudence as an essential criterion in the application of the doctrine of necessity.[68] The application of the principle of proportionality is therefore dependent on the particular circumstances of each specific case and constitutes the cornerstone of judicial control. If the Supreme Court initially interpreted proportionality broadly, starting with the *Ibrahim* case,[69] this was where the application of the doctrine of necessity did not concern the exercise of legislative powers by the executive, or the restriction of fundamental individual rights.[70] Thus, it appears that the protection of constitutionally safeguarded fundamental rights in Cyprus has remained largely outside of the scope of the doctrine of necessity, leaving ample room for the courts to protect them to the highest possible level, and to balance the protection of such rights with other considerations whenever this was necessary.[71]

Having clarified the relationship between the doctrine of necessity and constitutional and/or fundamental rights and confirmed that such rights can only be restricted on the basis of an express provision of the Constitution, it is

---

64 For this section of the Report, see also Kombos and Laulhé Shaelou (n. 4), sections 1.2 and 2.2.

65 *Alloupas v. National Bank of Greece* (1983) 1 CLR 55.

66 Emilianides (n. 4), p. 47.

67 The principle of proportionality is only expressly mentioned in the Constitution in Art. 24 with respect to individual contributions towards the public burdens.

68 In its landmark ruling *The A.-G. of the Republic v. Mustafa Ibrahim* [1964] CLR 195; see C. Kombos, *The Doctrine of Necessity in Constitutional Law* (Sakkoulas, 2015).

69 Emilianides (n. 4), pp. 42–44.

70 Ibid., p. 42.

71 The relationship of the doctrine of necessity with fundamental rights in Cyprus however occasionally comes to the forefront in the case-law of the European Court of Human Rights; see Application No. 49247/08, *Kazali and Others v. Cyprus*, 6 March 2012 for the right to property of Turkish Cypriots and Application No. 69949/01, *Aziz v. Cyprus*, 22 June 2004 for their right to vote. See e.g. N. Kyriakou, "National judges and supranational laws on the effective application of EC law and the ECHR: the case of Cyprus" (EUI, 2010) available at <http://papers.ssrn.com/sol3/papers.cfm?abstract_id=1623560>; see also more generally S. Laulhé Shaelou, 'Market freedoms, EU fundamental rights and public order: views from Cyprus' (2011) 30(1) *Yearbook of European Law* 298, 326–33.

then necessary to turn to the Constitution itself in order to assess the balancing of these rights, including in the context of EU/European law. It appears that it is the accumulation of several key characteristics of the Cypriot Constitution which gives the essence of constitutional and/or fundamental rights in Cyprus and their protection. First of all, the Constitution contains a detailed and extensive list of constitutionally safeguarded fundamental rights,[72] extending beyond the substantive provisions of the European Convention on Human Rights (ECHR) to a number of social and economic rights[73] (to be exercised "within the framework of public interest and common good")[74] and also occasionally beyond the scope of the protection afforded by the Convention.[75]

The reader should also be reminded at this stage of the supremacy of the Constitution in the Cypriot legal order, to the effect that the ECHR cannot take precedence over constitutional provisions. As a result, the ECHR has been said to enjoy limited constitutional status in the Cypriot legal order,[76] even if its *prima facie* "weaker" constitutional status appears to be mitigated by the fact that the Convention is *in effect* part of the Constitution.[77] The subordinate constitutional status of the ECHR is also mitigated by the willingness of the Supreme Court of Cyprus to apply the Convention in its case-law, at least when the protection afforded under the Constitution and the ECHR "coincides" (many provisions are identical) or "shares common elements",[78] perhaps also to the detriment of the direct relevance of EU law and of the EU Charter more specifically.[79] While EU law (all provisions) should take precedence over conflicting constitutional provisions as a result of Art. 1A of the Constitution, the use of EU law (and in

72 In Part II, under the title "Fundamental Rights and Liberties" (Arts. 6 to 35). See further e.g. C. Tornaritis, *The State Law of the Republic of Cyprus* (Cyprus Research Centre, 1982) (in Greek).

73 Social and economic rights include *inter alia* the right to decent existence and social security (Art. 9 of the Constitution), the right to work (Art. 25 of the Constitution), the right to enter into a contract (Art. 26 of the Constitution) or the right to strike (Art. 27 of the Constitution).

74 C. Tornaritis, "The Social and Economic Rights under the Law of the Republic of Cyprus" in Mélanges Bridel (Lausanne, 1968) 533–56, available at <http://www.kypros.org/Documents/Tornaritis/docs/social.html>.

75 As acknowledged in judgments of the Supreme Court of Cyprus such as *A-G v. Ibrahim* [1964] CLR 195, 225; *A-G v. Afamis* 1 RSCC 121, 125–26. The right to property as set out in Art. 23 of the Constitution would be such an example. It corresponds to Art. 1 Protocol 1 of the ECHR but is much more detailed and extensive, as this was confirmed again recently by the Supreme Court of Cyprus in Joined Cases No. 740/2011-587/2012, *Maria Koutselini-Ioannidou and Others v. The Republic*, 7 October 2014, in the context of the austerity measures taken in Cyprus to tackle the sovereign debt and financial crisis. See Kombos and Laulhé Shaelou (n. 4), section 2.2.

76 Emilianides (n. 4), p. 149; see also Kombos and Pantazi Lambrou, "Cyprus" (n. 19), p. 309.

77 Kombos and Pantazi Lambrou, "Cyprus" (n. 19), p. 309.

78 N. Kyriakou, *National Judges and Supranational Laws on the Effective Application of EC Law and the ECHR: The Case of Cyprus* (EUI, 2010), p. 4. See also Emilianides (n. 4) 149.

79 For an up-to-date legal appraisal of the application of the EU Charter in the national legal order, see Laulhé Shaelou and K. Kalaitzaki, "Cyprus" (n. 54).

particular the EU Charter) by the Supreme Court, even by way of interpretation, is far less developed than the (much older) use of the ECHR. This could be explained by looking at the overall practice of the supremacy of EU law by the courts in Cyprus, as instructed by the Supreme Court in the post-*Constantinou* era. As mentioned previously, despite the reference to Art. 1A in Art. 179 of the Constitution, and because the Constitution in Cyprus still provides expressly for its own supremacy, considerations of EU law and the exercise of judicial control arising as a result of the application of EU law appear *prima facie* to be encompassed within the fabric of the Constitution. This may be the subject of some academic debate in Cyprus, but in judicial and/or practical terms the overall approach of the Supreme Court can be described as inconsistent and as ignoring EU law on most occasions (or even the ECHR), to concentrate merely on the protection of fundamental rights in accordance with express constitutional or ordinary legal provisions.[80]

It is also worth noting that the protection of the rule of law has been said to be a "cardinal principle" of the Constitution.[81] This, combined with the supremacy (or rather primacy with the "non-dictatorial" nature) of the Constitution, means that any trial court not only has the power to declare unconstitutional a law which is contrary to the provisions safeguarding individual human rights as set out in the Constitution, but also that constitutionally safeguarded fundamental rights must be interpreted in favour of the individual rather than the state in case of doubt,[82] arguably as an expression of the duty of harmonious interpretation. Finally, it should be noted that the fundamental rights safeguarded under the Constitution are minimum rights. Rights may be further protected or new rights may be established through legislation, in which case these are not protected as constitutional rights but as ordinary rights.[83] This last point may have direct implications on the protection afforded to rights deriving from EU law and their implementation in the national legal order, depending on the judicial construct of the supremacy of EU law in the Cypriot legal order and on the extent of compliance with the duty of harmonious interpretation in this context.[84]

As a general rule, restrictions or limitations to constitutionally safeguarded fundamental rights, can only be contained in express provisions of the Constitution (Part II), by virtue of Art. 33(1) of the Constitution. Such restrictions or limitations may also be contained in legislation within the limits of the Constitution itself,[85] as introduced by the House of Representatives,

80 See also Kombos and Laulhé Shaelou (n. 4), section 2.2.

81 Emilianides (n. 4), p. 53; see also A. Loizou, *The Constitution of Cyprus* (2011) (in Greek).

82 *Fina (Cyprus) Ltd v. Republic* (1962) 3 RSCC 26; see Emilianides (n. 4), p. 146.

83 Emilianides (n. 4), p. 146.

84 See also Kombos and Laulhé Shaelou (n. 4), section 2.2.

85 See more recently *President of the Republic v. House of Representatives* (2000) 3 CLR 238 (in Greek); see also *President of the Republic v. House of Representatives (No. 2)* (1992) 3 CLR 165 (in Greek).

or "deemed to be part of Cypriot law under Art. 188 of the Constitution",[86] or deriving from EU law,[87] subject to the general principles of *inter alia* reasonableness and proportionality, encompassing also *a priori* an expression of the duty of harmonious interpretation. Art. 33(2) of the Constitution expressly provides that such restrictions or limitations must be interpreted strictly and cannot be applied "for any purpose other than those for which they have been prescribed". This provides a strict framework of necessity and/or proportionality to the restriction/limitation to constitutionally safeguarded fundamental rights, potentially leaving little room for the expression of the duty of harmonious interpretation under EU law, unless enshrined in the necessity/proportionality test itself. This provision must be read in conjunction with Art. 35 of the Constitution, which casts a vertical duty on the state and its various branches of government (within the limits of their respective competence) to ensure the efficient application of Part II of the Constitution *vis-à-vis* the beneficiaries of these fundamental rights.[88] In addition to the vertical direct effect of constitutionally safeguarded fundamental rights, including as protected under the ECHR and EU law, the Supreme Court of Cyprus provided in the same case for the horizontal effect of such rights.[89] In the subsequent case of *Yiallouros v. Nicolaou*,[90] the Supreme Court clearly provided for the horizontal direct effect of such provisions, thereby effectively extending the exercise of the right to compensation by persons whose constitutional fundamental rights have been infringed by interference by other private persons.[91] The vertical duty imposed on the State under Art. 35 of the Constitution, as well as the Supreme Court's finding in *Yiallouros v. Nicolaou*, effectively mean that the principle of harmonious interpretation should be relevant to all types of legal disputes.

In view of all of the above, the protection of constitutionally safeguarded fundamental rights in the Cypriot legal order has always been at the core of the case-law of the Cypriot courts, independently of the supremacy of EU law and of the application of the duty of harmonious interpretation within the meaning of EU law. As such, the protection of such rights, as well as their balancing with other considerations, can be said to amount to a "routine" exercise for Cypriot courts within the fabric of the Constitution, arguably encompassing harmonious interpretation in the necessity/proportionality test, to which EU law merely added one more – albeit fundamental – dimension, thereby increasing in theory

---

86 *Police v. Hondrou and Another* (1962) 3 RSCC 82.
87 See Emilianides (n. 4), p. 146.
88 *Police v. Georghiades* [1983] 2 CLR 33, 66; see Emilianides (n. 4), p. 147.
89 Ibid.
90 [2001] 1 CLR 558 (in Greek).
91 This ruling was said to be a landmark ruling, progressive even today and participating to the building of the European legal order; see Kombos and Pantazi Lambrou, "Cyprus" (n. 18), p. 337; see also Emilianides (n. 4), pp. 147–48. See also Kombos and Laulhé Shaelou (n. 4), sections 2.1 and 2.2.

the likelihood of fundamental issues arising. Drawing some general trends from this protection and balancing exercise can prove useful, both for the content and the methodology of this contribution,[92] as they outline the courts' overall approach to consistent interpretation. It usually involves a strict (but careful and delicate) construction of the restrictions/limitations to such rights on the basis of Arts. 33 and 35 of the Constitution, and/or in accordance with the case-law of the ECHR (in the case of collision between classic rights).[93] With respect to EU law, there could however appear to be potential areas of conflict, for instance given the attachment to social rights of the Cypriot Constitution,[94] and to free movement and economic rights under EU law. Moreover, in a wider framework, the courts have also tried to safeguard rights under directives through the effective application of the principle of consistent interpretation. An example of this would be the (unanimous) Opinion of the Supreme Court in relation to the latest law amending the basic law on the protection of beaches (Chapter 59 of the laws of Cyprus) and transposing Directive 2006/123/EC on services in the internal market into national law. The President of the Republic, through exercising his right of reference to the Supreme Court under Art. 140 of the Constitution,[95] returned the bill voted by the House of Representatives to the Supreme Court to examine its compatibility with the corresponding EU Directive. The arguments of the House of Representatives based on the general public interest as an exception to the selection process, including under Art. 12(3) of the Directive and Art. 25 of the Constitution, were rejected by the Court, on the basis that the principles of free competition and of impartiality, as set out in EU law and in the Directive more specifically, should prevail.

It is, however, suggested that the overall protection and balancing exercise currently taking place in the Cypriot legal order, whereby the Supreme Court "advances its own perception" in the event that the standard of protection granted under the ECHR is lower, usually in the absence of any meaningful consideration of the case-law of the ECJ, will have to change in the near future, so that EU law considerations are also brought to the core of the exercise.

---

92 For a detailed review of the collision between classic rights and/or socio-economic and cultural rights, including within these sub-categories of rights, see Kombos and Pantazi Lambrou, "Cyprus" (n. 18), pp. 338–46.

93 Ibid., p. 344.

94 In *Apostolides Georghios & Others v. the Republic of Cyprus through the Ministry of Labour and Social Insurance & Others* (1982) 3 CLR 928, the Supreme Court ruled that social rights are on an equal footing with political rights but that the economic situation and capacity of the country must be taken into account when assessing compliance of a measure with Art. 9 of the Constitution (right to decent existence and social security); see Kombos and Pantazi Lambrou, "Cyprus" (n 18), pp. 314–15.

95 Art. 140 of the Constitution was one of the provisions of the Constitution amended in 2006 to reflect the supremacy of EU law, to the effect that the right of reference now expressly includes the review by the Supreme Court of the compatibility of national law with EU law, in the form of the Services Directive in the present instance.

This could perhaps result in a lowering (or at least alteration) of the standard of protection offered to certain rights in the Cypriot Constitution,[96] but such rights should in any case remain remediable through protection afforded under EU law and the principle of harmonious interpretation. In the meantime, and until any conflict arises, with respect to social rights in particular, what could be said is that the test to be satisfied for the protection of social rights "within the framework of public interest and common good" can appear in effect to be even higher than for other constitutionally protected fundamental rights, away from EU law considerations.[97]

With respect to the lower courts, the direct influence of EU law post-EU accession, with respect in particular to the protection of fundamental freedoms and the principle of non-discrimination, is not always clearly visible in their case-law. Issues of concern relate *inter alia* to the right of entry and residence for same-sex partners and/or third-country national spouses of EU citizens, the free movement of workers, social assistance, detention or expulsion orders of EU nationals,[98] including in the context of the recent financial crisis.[99] Issues of a more elevated nature, based on the Constitution, are not usually raised in their EU context. Even when they are raised, they are not really addressed in such cases, as legal actions brought before the courts normally fall within the (narrow) ambit of the judicial control of administrative acts under Art. 146 of the Constitution. These actions constitute administrative recourses, which until very recently fell under the exclusive revisionary jurisdiction of the Supreme Court, strictly limited to the review of the legality of an administrative act, a decision or an omission, and thereby excluding any review of the case on its merits. However, a new Constitutional amendment was introduced in July 2015,[100] which changed the structure of the Supreme Court by establishing Administrative Courts in Cyprus in January 2016, allegedly in order to help the Supreme Court to decongest from the workload and award justice faster. The said Law amended paragraphs 1, 4, 5 and 6 of Art. 146 and added paragraphs 1A, 4(d) and 5A to Art. 146 of the Constitution, in order to transfer the first instance jurisdiction of the Supreme Court under Art. 146, to the newly established Administrative Court, to be exercised exclusively by the latter. The amending Constitutional Law was also a transposing measure for paragraphs 1, 2 and 4 of Art. 46 of

---

96 Kombos and Pantazi Lambrou, "Cyprus" (n. 18), p. 345.

97 This seems to be confirmed by the recent case-law of the Supreme Court of Cyprus related to austerity measures put in place in response to the sovereign debt crisis; see Kombos and Laulhé Shaelou (n. 4), section 2.2.

98 See in particular N. Trimikliniotis, *Cyprus National Report 2012–2013* (Network on free movement of workers, 2013) available at <http://works.bepress.com/nicos_trimikliniotis/41> for a review of recent domestic case-law related to these issues, pp. 121–40.

99 See eg N. Trimikliniotis, "Migration and freedom of movement of workers: EU law, crisis and the Cypriot States of exception" (2013) 2 *Laws* 440.

100 Law of the Eighth Amendment of the Constitution 2015 (130(I)2015).

Directive 2013/32/EU,[101] paragraph 1 of Art. 26 of Directive 2013/33/EU,[102] as well as paragraph 1 of Art. 27 of Regulation (EU) No. 604/2013.[103]

As a result, the protection and balancing exercise established within the fabric of the Constitution for the protection of constitutionally safeguarded fundamental rights, as based, for example, on the principle of harmonious interpretation, cannot be easily triggered in such administrative nature cases.[104] Some situations concerning, for example, the right of residence of a third-country national spouse of a Cypriot citizen, or the rights of Cypriot workers in Cyprus, have also been considered by the courts as internal situations, thereby giving little role to EU law and to fundamental rights protected as such under EU law, as well as potentially raising issues of reverse discrimination.[105] It has been suggested that the national courts appear "unwilling" to properly check on the immigration authorities, limiting their control to mere administrative grounds arising under Art. 146,[106] technical and procedural in nature and limited to a review of legality.[107] More generally, although this corresponds to a (strict and literal) reading of the Constitution based *inter alia* on the principle of the separation of powers, it could be said that courts appear to hide behind the limitations inherent to the judicial review of administrative acts under the Constitution, and rarely adopt a more holistic or teleological approach to the rights of Cypriot citizens and other EU citizens and their family members under EU law.[108] In a wider framework, it is undeniable that there have been some

---

101 Directive 2013/32/EU of the European Parliament and of the Council of 26 June 2013 on common procedures for granting and withdrawing international protection [2013] OJ L180/60.

102 Directive 2013/33/EU of the European Parliament and of the Council of 26 June 2013 laying down standards for the reception of applicants for international protection [2013] OJ L180/96.

103 Regulation (EU) No 604/2013 of the European Parliament and of the Council of 26 June 2013 establishing the criteria and mechanisms for determining the Member State responsible for examining an application for international protection lodged in one of the Member States by a third-country national or a stateless person [2013] OJ L180/31.

104 Most cases are brought on the basis of Law 7(I)/2007, as amended, which transposes the Citizenship Directive 38/2004 and the Aliens and Immigration Law, Chapter 105 of the laws of Cyprus, as amended by Law 8(I)/2007, and challenge administrative acts, decisions or omissions falling within the ambit of this legal framework.

105 See Trimikliniotis, *Cyprus National Report 2012–2013* (n. 98); see also N. Trimikliniotis, *Free Movement of Workers in Cyprus and the EU* (PRIO, Fundamental Rights in Cyprus Series 1/2010) 59.

106 See Trimikliniotis, *Cyprus National Report 2012–2013* (n. 98).

107 As of July 2015, the Supreme Court is expected to decide asylum cases on merits.

108 In limited instances, the Supreme Court has proceeded with the annulment of a detention/deportation decision, thereby opening the way for an EU citizen to claim compensation before the courts under Art. 146(6) of the Constitution; see Case No. 1726/2010, *Robert Harvey v. The Republic of Cyprus*, 17 January 2012 (in Greek). Compensation however occurs within the narrow framework of the judicial review of an administrative act, decision or omission under Art. 146, since the annulment of such an act or decision or the ordering of the performance of an omission under Art. 146(4) is a pre-requisite to seek compensation before the District court under Art. 146(6).

gradual adjustments in the protection and balancing of fundamental rights including free movement rights, in the framework of EU law and/or in favour of economic freedoms as arising mainly from directly applicable instruments of EU law and their implementation in Cyprus, thus in a narrow EU law setting encompassing some role, albeit not all its potential role, for the principle of harmonious interpretation.

4. THE DUTY OF HARMONIOUS INTERPRETATION IN CYPRIOT CASE-LAW

The remaining sections of this contribution will be devoted to the principle of harmonious interpretation *per se*, through a focus on specific case-law. The methodology to be followed in this second part of the contribution appears to unfold quite logically from the first part. Court decisions are the focus, given the principle of separation of powers, the strong independence of the judiciary and the tight control it exercises on administrative acts. Such court decisions are easily accessible via online databases (in Greek)[109] but it is not possible to effectively isolate all the decisions involving the principle of harmonious interpretation. The reason for this is that the application of the principle forms part of a long established legal tradition in the country, pre-dating EU accession, and is very often not explicitly referred to in the decisions. Given the wide scope of the principle as set out in the sections above, it would appear more efficient to focus on specific cases from the perspective of the relevance, analysis and/or the application of the principle of harmonious interpretation arising under EU law – whether express or not; successful or not; or correct or not – not only by the Supreme Court, but also by lower courts, as may be applicable. The court decisions set out in the following have been selected primarily as they have been previously the focus of academic literature and arguably give a fair account of the evolution of the principle as applied by the courts in Cyprus from EU accession until today, while at the same time usefully setting out the backbone of the application of EU law in Cyprus. In this respect, the relevance of preliminary references to such case-law is quite relative, since opportunities for judicial dialogue arising under Art. 267 of the Treaty on the Functioning of the European Union (TFEU) used to be limited and are now gradually developing.[110] As such, preliminary references are not

[109] <http://www.cylaw.org>. There is no consistent manner to refer to the principle of harmonious interpretation in Cypriot case-law, neither to the duty arising under EU law. The following expressions are usually used in the case-law of the courts: "*ενιαία ερμηνεία*", "*ομοιόμορφη ερμηνεία*" or "*καθήκον εξασφάλισης της ομοιόμορφης ερμηνείας*". There has been no explicit attempt to refine the principle in an EU context.

[110] For an up-to-date and detailed account of preliminary references in Cyprus in the first 10 years of Cyprus's EU membership, C. Lycourgos, *Preliminary reference to the Court of Justice of the European Union – Law and Practice in Cyprus Ten Years After Accession to the EU*

always representative of the overall application of EU law in Cyprus, including of the principle of harmonious interpretation itself.[111] Due to the non-systematic – yet increasing – use of the preliminary reference mechanism,[112] it is believed that the focused review of the use/compliance with the principle of harmonious interpretation by the Cypriot courts in its EU context may actually offer an adequate alternative and a more comprehensive overview of the application of EU law in Cyprus.

The courts in Cyprus had long recognised the principle of harmonious interpretation of national law in the light of international treaty provisions, at least as far as the treaties concerned show an intention of promoting the "values and the protection of human rights".[113] As explained in the sections above, EU membership does not seem to have changed this vision much, even if the principle came again to the forefront of the national court's jurisprudence upon EU accession, explicitly so in the field of immigration, and continues to be an important companion of the modern jurisprudence of the courts in Cyprus, including in the practice of preliminary references and in the application of the principle of proportionality.

4.1. CYPRUS'S EU ACCESSION: THE PRINCIPLE OF HARMONIOUS INTERPRETATION AS A "SUBSTITUTE" FOR PRELIMINARY REFERENCES

In *Nebojsa Micovic*, Judge Nicolaides ruled on the basis of the case-law of the Court of Justice[114] that a directive for which the deadline for implementation

(March 2014, unpublished study) (on file with the authors); see also C. Lycourgos, 'Building Intra-Judicial Dialogue: the relationship between the ECJ and Cypriot National Courts' (2016) 41 *EL Rev* 623–37.

111 Only a minority of preliminary references can be said to have involved directly the application of the principle of harmonious interpretation so far. On the other hand, there are many instances whereby a national court may have used the principle of harmonious interpretation to reject a request for a preliminary reference (see below).

112 According to the Annual Report of the Court of Justice of the European Union, by the end of 2014, Cyprus had submitted *seven* references for preliminary ruling. The first two were submitted in 2009. In 2013 three more references were submitted and another two in 2014; see Court of Justice of the European Union Annual Report 2014 (Luxembourg, 2015) 80. Out of the seven references for preliminary ruling submitted, four were submitted by the Supreme Court of Cyprus and three by other courts or tribunals. The number of references for preliminary ruling submitted by the Cypriot courts is one of the lowest in the EU (along with Malta). Despite the low number of preliminary references to the ECJ, there is nevertheless a growing number of cases, either before the Supreme Court or lower courts, where the possibility of a preliminary reference is invoked, usually following the request of one of the parties, but all too often not submitted to the ECJ by the national court, usually acting without sufficient justification for doing so. See also Kombos and Laulhé Shaelou (n. 4).

113 *Shipowners Union v. The Registrar of Trademarks* (1988) 3 CLR 457.

114 Specifically see: Judgment of 10 April 1984, Case 14/83, *Von Colson and Kamann v. Land Nordrhein-Westfalen*, ECLI:EU:C:1984:153; Judgment of 13 November 1995, Case C-106/89, *Marleasing v. La Comercial Internacional de Alimentación*, ECLI:EU:C:1990:395.

into national law had not yet passed was nevertheless capable of indirect effect in the national legal order.[115] As a result, the Director of the Migration Services in Cyprus was ordered to interpret the relevant provisions of national law with respect to the right of permanent residence in Cyprus of a citizen of the Former Republic of Yugoslavia "in the spirit" and "in accordance with the objective" of Directive 2003/109/EC.[116] In the joined cases of *Vera Joudine*,[117] the Supreme Court reiterated the approach of Judge Nicolaides to the principle of indirect effect and harmonious interpretation, by recalling the obligation of the Member States to take all measures necessary to achieve the result prescribed by the Directive during the period for transposition into national law.[118] Yet the Court found it "irrelevant" in these two cases, as the applicants did not to meet the "necessary criteria" to benefit indirectly from the provisions of Directive 2003/109/EC in national law. The applicants did not meet the criteria under Art. 4(1) of the Directive concerning legal and continuous residence within the territory of the Member State for five years immediately prior to the submission of the relevant application. The time calculation in this case started on 31 August 2005, when the disputed decrees were issued. It is important to note that at the time of the rulings, the deadline for the implementation of the Directive into national law had passed without the Republic of Cyprus taking appropriate measures to ensure its full implementation into Cypriot law.[119] However, the disputed administrative decisions of the Migration Department had been taken before the expiry of the implementation deadline. The parties were therefore not able to rely on direct effect of the Directive, or on a potential failure of the Republic of Cyprus to implement the said instrument of (then) Community law into national law.

In the *Motilla* case,[120] yet another decision of the Migration Department rejecting the acquisition of the long-term resident status for a third-country national was challenged before the Supreme Court of Cyprus, this time following the expiry of the implementation deadline of Directive 2003/109/EC into national law.[121] The Interior Minister's decision was based on

115 Supreme Court, Administrative Case No. 1012/2005, *Nebojsa Micovic v. the Republic* [2005] 4 CLR 890.

116 Of 25 November 2003 concerning the status of third-country nationals who are long-term residents [2004] OJ L16/44.

117 Supreme Court, Administrative Case No. 1632-3/2005, *Vera Joudine v. the Republic* [2006] 4 CLR 430.

118 Supreme Court, Administrative Appeal No. 55/06, *Vera Joudine v. the Republic* [2006] 3 CLR 500.

119 Directive 2003/109/EC as well as Directive 38/2004/EC *inter alia* were implemented belatedly into Cypriot law in early 2007 in Laws 8(I)/2007 and 7(I)/2007 respectively (*Official Gazette* No 4110, 09.02.2007).

120 Supreme Court (full bench), Administrative Case No. 673/2006, *Cresencia Cabotaje Motilla v. the Republic* [2008] 3 CLR 29.

121 Law No 8(I)/2007 transposes Directive 2003/109/EC and amends the Aliens and Immigration Law Cap 105 of the laws of Cyprus as a result. This law was enacted in February 2007, whereas

Art. 18Z(2) of the Aliens and Immigration Chapter 105 of the laws of Cyprus (as amended), on the ground that the applicant's successive residence permits were "limited as to their duration" and that the applicant was therefore excluded from the scope of the law. The applicant applied to the Supreme Court to set aside the said decision. The Court proceeded to review the case in accordance with the Directive and with the Cypriot implementing legislation, by first attempting to interpret the disputed provisions under EU law (i.e. the Directive), before moving on to interpret the transposing national law in the light thereof. This method adopted by the Court – i.e. examining whether an interpretation in light of EU law is possible before interpreting national law – is usually more geared towards achieving consistent interpretation in practice, than before.

The central issue concerned the way that Art. 18Z(2)(c) of the implementing legislation transposed Art. 3(2)(e) of the Directive and whether this transposition affected the essence of the Directive. The provision of the implementing legislation excluded applicants whose residence permits had been limited "in time", whereas the Directive merely excluded "formal" limitation, arguably relating to the nature of the status or the sector of employment of the person concerned. In a majority decision (9–4), the Supreme Court rejected the challenge on the grounds that the fixed-term duration of the applicant's visas fell within the exceptions of Art. 18Z(2), and that the addition of the phrase "as to its duration" did not detract from the Directive's effectiveness. The Court also ruled that the fixed-term nature of the residence visas granted to the applicant could not create a reasonable expectation "that the person has put down root in the country", as per Recital 6 of the Directive's Preamble.[122]

In the dissenting judgment in the same case, however, it was argued that the phrase at issue fundamentally transformed the essence of the exception provided for in Art. 3(2)(e) of the Directive. The dissenting judges recalled the ECJ's decision in *Ratti*, establishing the principle that a Member State cannot rely on its own wrongdoing to frustrate the rights of individuals under a directive which it has failed to implement.[123] Pursuant to Art. 4(1) of the Directive, Member States should grant long-term resident status to third-country nationals when they have been residing "*legally* and *continuously*" within their territory for five years immediately prior to the submission of the relevant application, with no

the deadline for the implementation of the Directive ended in January 2006. The applicant was a female migrant who lived and worked lawfully as a housemaid in Cyprus for six years and applied to the Interior Minister as soon as the deadline for transposition expired.

122 See N. Trimikliniotis, *Cyprus Report 2007* (Network on the free movement of workers within the EU, 2009), pp. 31–32; see also C. Demetriou and N. Trimikliniotis, *Cyprus Update of the Data Collection Report on Ethnic and Racial Discrimination* (RAXEN National Data Collection Report 2007 – Cyprus, February 2008), pp. 16–22.

123 Case 148/78, *Pubblico Ministerio v. Tullio Ratti*, ECLI:EU:C:1979:110.

further conditions being imposed regarding the issue, nature or duration of the residence permit. While recognising the exclusive competence of the ECJ to interpret the Directive as an instrument of EU law, the judges interpreted the notion of "formal limitation" set out in Art. 3(2)(e) of the Directive as having a specific meaning common to the immigration policy of all Member States, as formulated in particular at a conference of experts held in Brussels on 7–8 July 2005. They recalled the recommendations of the Summit that the implementation of the Directive does not require the issue of a residence permit, but the mere legality of the residence; and that any formal limitation on residence permits should remain an exception to be interpreted strictly (*ejusdem generis*) and in line with the examples provided in Art. 3(2)(e) of the Directive (i.e. seasonal workers, volunteers, posted workers, etc.). As a result, the mere fact that the residence permit is limited in time but renewable does not make it fall under the exceptions set out in the Directive, which are the only ones which by their nature can constitute "formal limitations". Based on the above and on the principle of legitimate expectation, the dissenting judges found the drafting of the specific provision in the implementing law not only incorrect, but also in violation of the substantive meaning of the Directive, hence leading to improper implementation.

It does not clearly appear from this case to what extent the Court considered the direct effect of the Directive and/or the liability of the Republic of Cyprus arising out of the late/improper transposition of the Directive into national law in order to reach its decision. The Court appears to have merely applied the Directive indirectly, in order to interpret the implementing legislation which – albeit in existence at the time of the ruling – was enacted subsequently to the application made by the plaintiff. She could not therefore rely on provisions of national law when enforcing her rights initially, but only on rights deriving from Directive 2003/109/EC directly and/or indirectly. The fundamental disagreement between the majority and the dissenters in the Supreme Court did not appear to prompt any discussion as to the possibility of making a reference to the ECJ under (then) Art. 234 EC so as to clarify the meaning of the relevant provision of the Directive. While the interpretation of a Directive in the national legal order is left at the discretion of the national courts which are subject to a duty of harmonious interpretation,[124] the exercise of this discretion by the national courts also involves the possibility of making preliminary references to the ECJ regarding the interpretation of provision(s) of EU law, including directives deemed of relevance to the national proceedings at stake. This becomes an obligation for a court of last instance, as in the present case. For matters falling under (then) Title IV of Part Three of the EC Treaty on visa, asylum, immigration and other policies related to free movement of persons, however,

[124] Case C-212/04, *Konstantinos Adeneler et al. v. Ellinikos Organismos Galaktos (ELOG)*, ECLI:EU:C:2006:443, para. 116.

(former) Art. 68 EC provided that a reference could be brought by the final court or tribunal, at its own discretion. The Supreme Court did not refer to these provisions of the EU Treaties. The Court did not find it necessary either to refer questions of interpretation to the ECJ, despite the uncertainty surrounding the provisions of EU law at stake.

The decision of the Supreme Court to reject the recourse for administrative review in the *Motilla* case was eventually explained by the geographical location, the small size and the limited population of Cyprus as underlying features of its immigration policy. As noted by Trimikliniotis, the vast majority of migrant workers are, "as a matter of policy", issued with fixed-term visas in Cyprus.[125] This decision had therefore the effect of intentionally restricting in law and/or in fact the right to long-term residence provided by Directive 2003/109/EC, arguably in breach of EU law and of the principle/duty of harmonious interpretation,[126] as concluded in the dissenting judgment of the case as well. This approach was subsequently upheld by the Supreme Court in the *Rawuttar* case,[127] where Judge Erotokritou referred to the judgment reached by the Full Chamber of the Supreme Court in the *Motilla* case as a precedent where the relevant provisions of EU law had already been examined.[128]

The facts in the *Rawuttar* case are similar to the facts in the *Motilla* case, but for one important point: the applicant's entitlement to lawful residence had expired before the end of the deadline provided for the transposition of Directive 109/2003/EC into national law. The status of the applicant during the period running from the expiry of her work permit/right of residence up to the expiry of the deadline for implementation of the Directive (at which point in time no transposing legislation had been enacted) was therefore at stake in this case, given the new legal environment created by the Directive. In this respect, the applicant's lawyer requested the judge to exercise his discretion to refer to the ECJ as it was a clear case of interpretation of (then) Community law. Referring to Art. 8 of the Court's Guidance on References by National Courts for Preliminary Rulings, Judge Erotokritou expressly noted that for matters falling under Title IV Part III of the (then) EC Treaty, the right to

---

125 N. Trimikliniotis, *Cyprus Report 2007* (Network on the free movement of workers within the EU, 2009), p. 32.

126 Points of interpretation of Art. 3(2)(e) of Directive 2003/109/EC subsequently reached the ECJ, who confirmed that "the concept of 'residence permit [which] has been formally limited' does not include a fixed-period residence permit, granted to a specific group of persons, the validity of which may be extended indefinitely without however offering any prospect of a residence permit of indefinite duration where such a formal limitation does not prevent the long-term residence of the third-country national in the Member State concerned, that being a matter for the referring court to ascertain", see Case C-502/10, *Staatssecretaris van Justitiev v. Mangat Singh*, ECLI:EU:C:2012:636, para. 56.

127 Supreme Court, *Shahajan Mohamed Rawuttar v. The Republic*, Administrative Case No. 742/06, 24 September 2008.

128 See S. Laulhé Shaelou (n. 8), pp. 480–84.

refer to the ECJ was limited to final courts of law, at their own discretion. He concluded that the court did not satisfy the requirements set out in (old) Art. 68 EC in the present case, as it was not acting as a court of last instance. He then proceeded with the judicial review of the decision, based on the principle of harmonious interpretation of national law in the light of (then) Community law. It was held that given the unlawfulness of her residence for a period of 11 days between the expiry of her residence permit and the expiry of the deadline for implementation of the Directive into national law, the applicant fell outside the scope of the Directive.[129] The judge then added that even if the applicant had had a lawful right of residence upon the expiry of the deadline for implementation of the Directive into national law, her application would have been subject to the precedent created by the Supreme Court in the *Motilla* case (with no possibility to refer to the ECJ as a first instance administrative court), and she would therefore also have fallen outside the scope of the Directive as transposed into Cypriot law.[130] The decision of the Supreme Court acting at first instance, including the issue of non-referral to the ECJ, was subsequently appealed before the Supreme Court.[131] On the basis of Art. 267 TFEU, post-Treaty of Lisbon, it held that the Court acting at first instance was not under an obligation to refer questions of interpretation to the ECJ and that the rejection of the application was not based on matters related to the interpretation of the Directive at stake.

The above case-law is obviously based on a narrow (even probably erroneous, as far as the Supreme Court acting as a final instance jurisdiction is concerned) understanding of the practice of preliminary references, complemented by an equally strict perception of the duty of harmonious interpretation as limited primarily to the interpretation of EU secondary legislation in specific instances. A few years into EU membership, it is interesting to note the increasingly strong correlation developing in the case-law of the courts in Cyprus between preliminary references and the principle of harmonious interpretation.

4.2. THE PRINCIPLE OF HARMONIOUS INTERPRETATION AS A "COMPANION" TO PRELIMINARY REFERENCES AND PROPORTIONALITY

As already explained above, a handful of judgments from national courts in Cyprus in recent years pertaining to preliminary references can be correlated

---

129 Judge Erotokritou referred to other recourses in administrative control where similar decisions were reached by the Supreme Court, as a first instance administrative court, and therefore with no possibility to refer to the ECJ in this context.

130 See S. Laulhé Shaelou (n. 8), pp. 493–94.

131 Supreme Court, Administrative Appeal No. 159/2008, *Shahajan Mohamed Rawuttar v. The Republic* [2011] 3 CLR 508.

directly to (a strict approach of) the principle of harmonious interpretation. Either because the relevant court sought guidance from the ECJ on matters of interpretation of EU law, or on the contrary ruled against requesting such guidance from the Luxembourg Court, again based on the principle of harmonious interpretation.[132] Beyond this immediate correlation between harmonious interpretation and preliminary references, the principle has recently also been used explicitly, and in the context of the sovereign debt and financial crisis more implicitly, as a source of inspiration in the name of effective judicial protection, embodied in the principle of proportionality.

In *Alpha Bank Cyprus Ltd*,[133] the Supreme Court found that the case was dependent on the interpretation of the Regulation (EC) No. 1393/2007 on the Service in Member States of Judicial and Extrajudicial documents in Civil and Commercial matters, and therefore referred three questions to the ECJ. This ruling was preceded by a first ruling in the case, where the Supreme Court had held that all issues pertaining to the service of the documents at stake could be remedied under national law.[134] This meant that the only legal issue pending in the case pertained to the interpretation of the EU law instrument, which was seen by the Court as having implications on the "implementation of EU law in all the territory of the Union" and which was subsequently referred to the ECJ. This case represented an early attempt to interpret national law in the light of EU law by preference of relying on the preliminary reference mechanism, in order to preserve the principle of consistent interpretation.

In the case of *Thomas Kaoulla and Eleni Kaoulla*,[135] a preliminary reference was requested in relation to the interpretation of the EU Charter. The applicants requested *inter alia* to submit a question regarding the equality in tax schemes of refugee and non-refugee citizens of the Republic of Cyprus. This request for a preliminary reference was part of the grounds for appeal, challenging the decision of the first instance court. The Supreme Court indicated that the appellant could not invoke issues before the appeal court that had not been invoked or disputed before the lower court. Therefore, since no issues of violations of rights stemming from EU Law (including the Charter) were raised in the first instance decision, they could not be raised for the first time at the appeal stage. The Supreme Court concluded that for the reasons stated, a possible preliminary reference would just be an "academic exercise" and that this is not the purpose of a preliminary

---

132 There are more such examples, both from the Supreme Court and lower courts.

133 Supreme Court, Joined Civil Appeals E23/2013-29/2013, [2013] 1 CLR 1935; Case C-519/13, *Alpha Bank Cyprus*, ECLI:EU:C:2015:603.

134 Supreme Court, *Cypra Ltd v. The Republic*, Administrative Appeal 78/2009, 5 June 2013. See Lycourgos, *Preliminary reference to the Court of Justice of the European Union* (n. 110), p. 28.

135 Supreme Court, *Thomas Kaoulla and Eleni Kaoulla v. The Republic, through the Attorney General*, Civil Appeal No. 77/2012, 13 February 2013.

reference. Proceeding to interpret the provisions of the Charter itself, the Court added further that:

> in any case, the notions of Art. 20 and 21 of the Charter are largely identical with the corresponding notions of the Constitution [of Cyprus], which have been fully clarified by the Cypriot case-law and therefore there would be no reason for a preliminary reference, even if the issue could be raised on appeal.[136]

Unlike the above examples which arguably entail a narrow understanding of the scope of the duty of harmonious interpretation on the national courts, the principle and the duty deriving there from appear to have inspired directly or indirectly certain other (more EU acquainted) judges, both at the lower courts and the Supreme Court. Judge Pantazi Lambrou in the *Constantinos Oikonomou* case[137] referred to the duty of harmonious interpretation imposed on national courts with respect to the interpretation of national law, irrespective of whether the issue at stake is a cross-border dispute falling within the scope of EU law and whether direct effect can be triggered or not. The case concerned a dispute between two individuals, where the claimant was requesting damages for breach of a motor vehicle purchase contract. Specifically, Judge Pantazi stated that when applying provisions of national transposing laws – in this case-law 7(I)/2000 – the Court is bound to interpret it when possible, in the light of the wording and purpose of the applicable Directive (1999/44/EC on certain aspects of the sale of consumer goods and associated guarantees), in order to achieve an outcome consistent with the objective pursued. If the national law was not interpreted in the light of the Directive's wording, it would possibly affect the rights of the claimant in obtaining the benefit of the disputed guarantee, since the status of the defendants as "sellers" was contested. The Court cited relevant case-law of the ECJ to illustrate the argument and follow it in practice.[138]

Judge Erotokritou, in his landmark dissenting judgment in *Myrto Christodoulou* dealing with the bail-in measures taken by the Cypriot authorities and affecting thousands of depositors in Cyprus during the financial crisis,

---

136 Ibid, (translated by the authors).

137 District Court of Nicosia, Civil Case No. 1449/2009, 29 June 2015.

138 Case C-497/13, *Froukje Faber v. Autobedrijf Hazet Ochten BV*, ECLI:EU:C:2015:357, para. 33: It must be pointed out at the outset that the dispute in the main proceedings is between two individuals. It is true that in such an action neither of the parties may rely on the direct effect of Directive 1999/44. However, it is also settled case-law that a national court, when hearing a case exclusively between individuals, is required when applying the provisions of domestic law to consider the whole body of rules of national law, and to interpret them, so far as possible, in the light of the wording and purpose of the applicable directive in order to achieve an outcome consistent with the objective pursued by that directive (see, *inter alia*, judgment in Case C-565/12, *Crédit Lyonnais*, ECLI:EU:C:2014:190, para. 54 and the case-law cited).

developed a test of proportionality and reasonableness, encompassing EU law instruments with special reference to the EU Charter and to the free movement of capital.[139] He added that such a "compatibility test" could be undertaken by a national court directly applying EU law, including general principles, and referring questions of interpretation or of validity to the ECJ in the event of uncertainty. He recalled that judicial dialogue is available to all national courts, including the lower civil courts, provided that the measures at stake do not escape the scope of review by being classified as "acts of government", which is for the Supreme Court under its exclusive administrative revisional jurisdiction to determine. In the latter cases, the full essence of the test is thereby effectively restricted to application by the Supreme Court. Judge Erotokritou warned against political decisions being taken overnight under extreme pressure (including at the EU level), allegedly in the interest of the state, escaping the test and undermining the rule of law and the principle of legality common to both the national and the supranational legal orders. He then concluded that the compatibility test includes a review of the balance between the public interest and the restrictions on individual rights within the framework of the Constitution and of the EU Treaties, which can only be undertaken by the Supreme Court within its exclusive administrative revisional jurisdiction, and which must be maintained at all times, including during crisis time. Despite being a dissenting judgment, this arguably constitutes a powerful plea to all national courts to not only interpret national law in the light of EU law by fully embracing the core principles and values of EU law, but also to make use of the judicial dialogue route in every possible instance, including in times of crisis. With respect to the specific legal dispute, it should be noted that numerous civil actions are still pending before the District Courts in Cyprus, while the door to the Supreme Court through an administrative recourse remains closed after the *Myrto Christoudolou* case.[140]

In conclusion, in general terms the EU principle of consistent interpretation seems to have impacted the Cypriot method of statutory interpretation towards an internalisation of EU law in Cyprus. However, as explained above, the overall approach of the Cypriot Supreme Court can be described as inconsistent and as sometimes ignoring EU law (and even the ECHR),[141] when it comes to applying provisions of fundamental rights focusing on the protection of fundamental rights within the framework of the Cypriot Constitution. Moreover, it would appear that the Cypriot courts had initially been more willing in the past to achieve harmonious interpretations where conflicts arose between Cypriot and

139 *Myrto Christodoulou et al* [2013] 3 CLR 427 (dissenting judgment).

140 See also S. Laulhé Shaelou and P. Athanassiou, "Cyprus Report", in G. Bàndi *et al.* (eds.), *European Banking Union* (Congress Proceedings, vol. 1, Wolters Kluwer, 2016), pp. 294–96.

141 Interview with Dr. Demetrios Hadjihambis, former President of the Supreme Court of Cyprus (June 2013–July 2014) and judge at the Supreme Court (1999–2013), 9 January 2015.

ECHR law, than between Cypriot and EU law. A notorious example is the case of *Constantinou*, discussed above, where the Court had relied on the *contra legem* limitation to avoid achieving conformity with EU law in practice. In particular, the judges would use the principle of consistent interpretation to apply EU law only where no conflict arose with the national law. However, the Courts have moved a long way since the *Constantinou* case, especially after the amendment of Art. 1A of the Constitution, which grants legal and judicial supremacy to EU law. The Courts are now even trying to apply and interpret EU law when there is no such formal requirement.[142]

---

[142] See e.g. District Court, Case No. 4602/14, *Institute of Archbishop Makarios III and others v. CBC, Bank of Cyprus Plc, Resolution Authority, Attorney General of the Republic, Antri Antoniades (in her capacity as special administrator of Laiki) and Cyprus Popular Bank Public Co. Ltd*, 26 August 2014, where Judge Annie Pantazi Lambrou made multiple references to the EU Directive on Bank Resolution and Recovery as soon as it was published in the Official Journal of the EU and well before its implementation into national law, relying on the principle of indirect effect as developed in the case-law of the ECJ, paras. 14–15.

INDEX

ABOUT THE EDITOR

Christian N.K. Franklin (LLB Manchester, LLM Stockholm) is Professor of Law at the University of Bergen, specialising in EU and EEA law. He is Joint Manager of the University of Bergen Law Faculty's Research Group for Competition and Market Law, an Associate of the Bergen Centre for Competition Law and Economics (BECCLE), and has previously worked at the University of Oslo and the University of Stockholm. He is a barrister and member of Gray's Inn, and a board member of the Norwegian Association for European Law. His research interests cover a wide range of EU and EEA topics, including external relations, internal market regulation, and institutional and constitutional issues.

www.ingramcontent.com/pod-product-compliance
Ingram Content Group UK Ltd.
Pitfield, Milton Keynes, MK11 3LW, UK
UKHW051846100926
8556IPUK00005B/472

9 781780 68